MATERIAL PRECEDENT

The Typology of Modern Tectonics

GAIL PETER BORDEN

WILEY

John Wiley & Sons, Inc.

Published by John Wiley & Sons, Inc., Hoboken, New Jersey

Published simultaneously in Canada

For general information about our other products and services, please contact our Customer Care Department within the United States at (800) 762-2974, outside the United States at (317) 572-3993 or fax (317) 572-4002.

Wiley also publishes its books in a variety of electronic formats. Some content that appears in print may not be available in electronic books. For more information about Wiley products, visit our web site at www.wiley.com.

Library of Congress Cataloging-in-Publication Data:
Borden, Gail Peter.
     Material Precedent / Gail Peter Borden.
        p. cm.
     Includes index.
     ISBN 978-0-470-47729-8 (cloth)
        1. Building materials. 2. Architecture--Technological innovations. I. Title.
     TA403.B67   2010
     721'.044--dc22
     2009043685

Printed in the United States of America
10 9 8 7 6 5 4 3 2 1

CONTENTS

Each material has its specific characteristics in which we must understand it if we want to use it. In other words, no design is possible until the materials with which you design are completely understood.   - Mies van der Rohe

PREFACE

Material is the beginning and the end of architecture. It is the tangible that executes the intangible. It is the means of implementation and the means of expression. Materials are the palette from which architecture is made. The use of materials and the associated technologies of construction determine the form and articulation of buildings. The available material resources and the craft of their joinery define the history of architecture.

This analytical catalog unpacks the tectonics of architectural form through comparative diagramming of architectural precedents. These precedents document how architecture has been conceived of conceptually and physically. The material aspect is emphasized to illustrate the associated formal and spatial ramifications of the physical construction. As a catalog of thought and methodology, it presents material as the matter of architecture – that which makes the form, the space, the performance, and ultimately the experience that is architecture.

Focusing on material as the premise of design exploration, this book identifies and graphically illustrates how material and modern tectonics have defined the formal and conceptual premise for the making of architecture. As a collection consisting primarily of twentieth century buildings emerging from the modernist sensibilities, the diagrams illustrate contemporary formal and spatial repercussions emerging from the physicality of material manipulation.

The catalog tracks the conventions and concepts behind modern building science and material applications. The diagrammatic dissection of their application reveals the design influence of material, processes of fabrication, and the role of construction in architecture. The revelations of this diagrammatic comparative methodology allow for a material mastery through a catalog that illustrates material techniques and material use as expressions of architectural thought. Providing a horizontal and vertical graphic matrix with analytically cross-referenced historical, material, tectonic, and typological illustration, this book articulates the traditions and trends of material as the defining premise in the making of architecture.

Architecture and Materials

Architecture and material are intrinsically intertwined. The material matter from which built form is made serves as the medium with which architects work. The understanding of the technical components is matched by the sensorial effects. The balance between these elements creates the vocabulary for understanding and wielding material.

Materials have long remained subservient to issues of form, structure, sustainability, and geometry. Typically discussed only in technical terms of construction, material has not been at the core of conceptual architectural discourse.

The making of architecture is guided by a material's manufacturing process and construction techniques. These systems establish specific boundaries with the freedom to operate within their systems. Design is not simply ingenuity of form but rather a collaboration of poetry and rational systems. It is the balance of these two that produces architecture.

Material has tactility and an intrinsic nature. Its visual and emotional characteristics carry an interpretation. Its use, whether honest and integral, or applied, establishes an aura and a narrative. The aura comes from an emotive and experiential association, whereas the narrative tells the story of its history, fabrication, and application. Putting materials to their best use involves an appreciation of their innate sensory qualities as well as their technical potential. This must be at the root of architectural design.

Contemporary Material History

The history of architecture is the history of material application and invention. The use of new materials and the reinterpretation of existing materials have been at the root of architectural evolution. The formal and spatial developments in architecture incurred through material exploration have yet to be fully documented. The role of material precedent, though essential to architectural education, design, and practice, has been overlooked and talked around. The potential of this catalog of material precedent, not simply from a technical vantage point but also as an effectual design catalog of use, provides the opportunity to trend materiality and its relationship to architecture.

Prior to the Industrial Revolution, material was limited by the distance of transport [indigenous, locally found building supplies] and the technology of local craft [the traditions of making passed down through cultural generations]. These limitations provided a continuity of materiality to form and effect based upon the vernacular architecture. Wood was developed locally, bricks were fired out of soil found within the area, and stone was taken from local quarries. The connection between the material for making and the act of making was distinctly attached to place and region. The Industrial Revolution brought about great change. Infrastructures for movement, combined with large populations and the emergence of new technologies such as steel and concrete, shifted the palette available to the designer. The architect was suddenly presented with a selection of materials from which to choose. Considering cost, structure, form, and effect, materials were selected to ensure the ability to build relative to design intentions. Material limitation and abilities soon became expressive mechanisms bringing the influence of material to center stage in the design process. Suddenly aesthetics and form making were intertwined with material ability. The way skin to structure and frame to enclosure were handled was suddenly a provocative result of design intention and execution, all relative to the materials selected. With performance and technology as the only limitation, the expression of design came through the application, expression, and detailing of materiality. The role of architecture is no longer one of tradition or form, but one that is truly dependent upon material and its interrelation with all these other issues of architecture.

The advent of technology has also brought enormous advances in material processes. The invention of new materials and the updating of traditional materials through new methods of fabrication, installation, and application have all led to an expansion of material capability and opportunity. Glass, steel, plastic, and concrete can take on any form; wood technologies allow engineered lumber to accumulate smaller members into any shape and span; wood chips and sawdust are conglomerated to recycled sheet materials such as oriented strand board (OSB) and medium density fiberboard (MDF); and even masonry has found new formal and technical applications. The emergence of digital fabrication processes has similarly allowed a shift in methods of production and fabrication. Anything can be cut with ease and precision. Materials can be bent, rolled, and cast with infinite flexibility. The diversity of options grows logarithmically each day.

Material Presence of Making

At the root of these issues of choice, however, are the intentions that aid in selecting any material or process and deciding how such a selection can effectually and formally be deployed to aid in the design implementation. How a material is used and perceived is at the root of a material's application and design. This book provides an indexical examination of the historical choices made by the world's leading architects, illustrating the comparative methodologies, historical trends, and conceptual underpinnings of the interrelationship of architecture and materiality. Its pages unpack great works of architecture, explicating the material conceptual organization as well as comparatively positioning their use to the cultural, technical, and personal design influences of each architect's life, site, and design opportunity. The comparative nature of the book allows for the trends and sensibilities intrinsic to a material and provides a catalog of how to think about and compose with a material.

Material is the medium of architecture. It is a physical expression of context and culture. Its intrinsic qualities and limitations determine the approach to design and form. It has the ability to define architecture. With specific dimension, weight, and technical qualities, a material directs a design process. As the foundational premise of making, material influences all else. These precedents illustrate how a vernacular material and building construction influence design. Examining the influence of form, cost, methods of construction, fabrication of product, installation of materials, structural and aesthetic performance, ecological and sustainable impact, and spatial/light/visual/perceptual impact, these projects provide an analytical process for the implementation of the potential of a material. The projects emerge from a sensibility founded in material celebration. They work within the guidelines of a material's performance, modularity, structural capabilities, formal presence, and emotive power to produce an architecture that is of a material. As case studies, they represent a material methodology founded in architecture of material influence.

Organization
Material Precedent is organized into three parts.

The first section catalogs in a comparative grid forty-eight projects: eight each in wood, masonry, concrete, metal, glass, and plastic. A tab format is used on the right-hand side of the page described by the principal material. The grid has seven columns entitled, from left to right, from documentation [illustrating the building in four base drawings of plan, section, elevation, and axonometric], form [displaying the relation of material to form], proximity [addressing the interrelationships of materials], skin + surface [the articulation of material surface], structure [the material influence and articulation on the primary structural system], module [the role of material dimension], and detail [a closer scaling of the specific connections and detailed material design applications]. The matrix provides a comparative array of material application in a single spread. The rows are laterally organized with plan, section, elevation, and axonometric. An attempt has been made to keep scales consistent within each precedent, though at times, for clarity, a magnification of scale is necessary. In each of these instances, a graphic scale is included.

The second section reiterates the primary diagrams in greater detail. Larger in scale and superimposed on ghosted backgrounds of the detailed building, these drawings translate each column of diagrams into a four-square page providing a more detailed reading of each building. Set across several spreads, this section allows for a display of the specificity per project as opposed to the first section's comparative nature within a project.

The third and final section is a comparative matrix of one topical diagramming component across the diverse projects, yet still categorized within one material. Mapping the same material issue across diverse architectural precedents, the comparative array allows for an understanding of relative usage of material. The comparative application of material type to across building precedents allows for a depiction of the evolution of a specific material's application. These genealogies illustrate the technical, cultural, and conceptual underpinnings of material use.

ACKNOWLEDGMENTS

This book is possible because of generous support from:
The University of Southern California Arts and Humanities Grant Program
The University of Southern California Undergraduate Research Scholars Program

A special thanks goes to my research assistants:
Gregory Creech, Alexandre Salice with contributions from TJ Tutay, Hua Li, Jun Liang, Enoch Chow, Joyce Tsai, Wili-Mirel Luca, Jeffrey Kuruvilla

I would first and foremost like to thank the architects who are included in this book. Their work inspired the content and all efforts have been made to identify and represent their work as accurately as possible.

A special thanks to Roger Clark and Michael Pause for their work with precedent, and Roger for his magnanimous friendship.

I would also like to thank several people for their support throughout my career: Professors Lars Lerup, John Casbarian, Michael Bell, William Cannady, Yung-Ho Chang, Fares el Dada, Elizabeth Gamard, David Gutherie, Dave Hickey, Carlos Jimenez, Danny Samuels, Mark Wamble, and Gordon Wittenberg from my time at Rice; Renzo, Bernard and Paul from my time in Piano's Office; Professors Rafael Moneo, Mack Scogin, Jorge Silvetti, Scott Cohen, Ron Witte and Nader Tehrani from Harvard's GSD; North Carolina colleagues Patrick Rand (for nurturing my material teachings), Bryan Bell, Robert Burns, Louis Cherry, Jeremy Ficca, Frank Harmon, Kenneth Hobgood, Jeffrey Lee, Dennis Stallings, Vinny Petrarca, and Charles Holden; and from USC Dean Ma, Kim Coleman, Diane Ghirardo, Charles Lagreco, Amy Murphy, Doug Noble, Victor Regnier, Roger Sherwood, Marc Schiller, Jim Steele, for welcoming me into your community; as well as Brian Andrews and Michael Meredith for setting a high standard. I thank my mother, father, and sister for making me who I am and I would most importantly like to thank my greatest supporters, my wife Brooke, for her constant support and belief in me and my work, and my children Frieda Dorothy, and Gail Calvin, who give me the greatest hope for tomorrow.

| | DOCUMENTATION | | | FORM | | | PROXIMITY | | | SKIN + SURFACE | |

SECTION MARKER

PRIMARY DOCUMENTARY PLAN

DETAIL MARKER

ELEVATION MARKER

SCALE

PLAN — 25'

MATERIAL FUNCTION diagrams in plan the relationship between material use and the formal and technical associations requiring its functional application.

MATERIAL FUNCTION

MATERIAL APPLICATION diagrams in plan the deployment of material and the associated perceptual, formal, and functional readings.

MATERIAL APPLICATION

MATERIAL ENCLOSURE [PERIMETER] diagrams in plan the relationship of the outer plane of enclosure [skin] to the spatial, formal, and structural organization.

MATERIAL ENCLOSURE [PERIMETER]

PRIMARY DOCUMENTARY SECTION

DETAIL MARKER

SECTION

MATERIAL GEOMETRY diagrams the sectional geometric implications of material on form.

MATERIAL GEOMETRY

MATERIAL TO GROUND diagrams the sectional relationship by which a building meets the ground, engages landscape, and addresses the material point of connection with the site.

MATERIAL TO GROUND

MATERIAL ENCLOSURE [EDGE] diagrams in section the relationship of the outer plane of enclosure [skin] to the spatial, formal, and structural organization.

MATERIAL ENCLOSURE [EDGE]

PRIMARY DOCUMENTARY ELEVATION

DETAIL MARKER

ELEVATION

MATERIAL ORDER diagrams in elevation the hierarchy, sequence, and organizational methods of material on the architectural form.

MATERIAL ORDER

PRIMARY / SECONDARY diagrams the elevational relationship of the primary building material to the secondary building material, focusing on the formal, functional and practical interrelationship of this material application.

PRIMARY/SECONDARY

MATERIAL TEXTURE diagrams the elevational legibility of the material texture, color, and surface.

MATERIAL TEXTURE

DOCUMENTARY AXONOMETRIC

DETAIL MARKER

AXONOMETRIC

MATERIAL MASSING diagrams in axonometric the overall legibility of the material to the superstructural form, presence, and mass of the architectural form.

MATERIAL MASSING

MATERIAL TO PROGRAM diagrams in axonometric the overall relationship of material usage to the primary programmatic and functional usages.

MATERIAL TO PROGRAM

MATERIAL PERCEPTION diagrams in axonometric the primary reading of material experience.

MATERIAL PERCEPTION

| STRUCTURE | | MODULE | | DETAIL | |

STRUCTURAL MATERIAL [BAY/MODULE] diagrams in plan the structural module of the building. Focusing on the influence of the structural material, it illustrates the engineered structural response of material relative to performative need.

STRUCTURAL MATERIAL [BAY/MODULE]

MATERIAL MODULE diagrams in plan the relationships of the manufacturing module intrinsic to a material to the space, form, and dimensions.

MATERIAL MODULE

MATERIAL CORNER diagrams in plan the articulation of the primary material at the corner. These diagrams illustrate the detail of the legibility of a material changing direction in space and articulate the intended legibility of the building's tectonic and formal expression.

MATERIAL CORNER

STRUCTURAL MATERIAL [BAY/MODULE] diagrams the sectional implications of the structural module. Focusing on the influence of the structural material, it illustrates the engineered structural response of material relative to performative need.

STRUCTURAL MATERIAL SYSTEM

MATERIAL MODULE diagrams in section the relationships of the manufacturing module intrinsic to a material to the space, form, and dimensions.

MATERIAL MODULE

MATERIAL SPACE diagrams the sectional implications of material joints [connections] and their articulation of spatial legibility.

MATERIAL SPACE

STRUCTURAL MATERIAL LEGIBILITY diagrams the elevational reading of the structural material. Focusing on the influence of the structural material, it illustrates the interrelation of the engineered structural response of material and performative need to the form and composition.

STRUCTURAL MATERIAL LEGIBILITY

MATERIAL MODULE diagrams the elevational implications of the relationships of the manufacturing module intrinsic to a material to the space, form, and dimensions.

MATERIAL MODULE

MATERIAL APERTURE diagrams the elevational articulation of material at an opening, giving a localized reading of larger tectonic, formal, and spatial intentions.

MATERIAL APERTURE

STRUCTURAL MATERIAL [LINE/POINT] diagrams in axonometric the primary geometric and formal response of the structural material/system.

STRUCTURAL MATERIAL [LINE/POINT]

MATERIAL GEOMETRY diagrams in axonometric the three-dimensional relationships of the manufacturing module intrinsic to a material to the space, form, and dimensions.

MATERIAL GEOMETRY

MATERIAL CONNECTION diagrams in axonometric how materials meet, join, and connect on a localized level while giving a reading of larger tectonic, formal, and spatial intentions.

MATERIAL CONNECTION

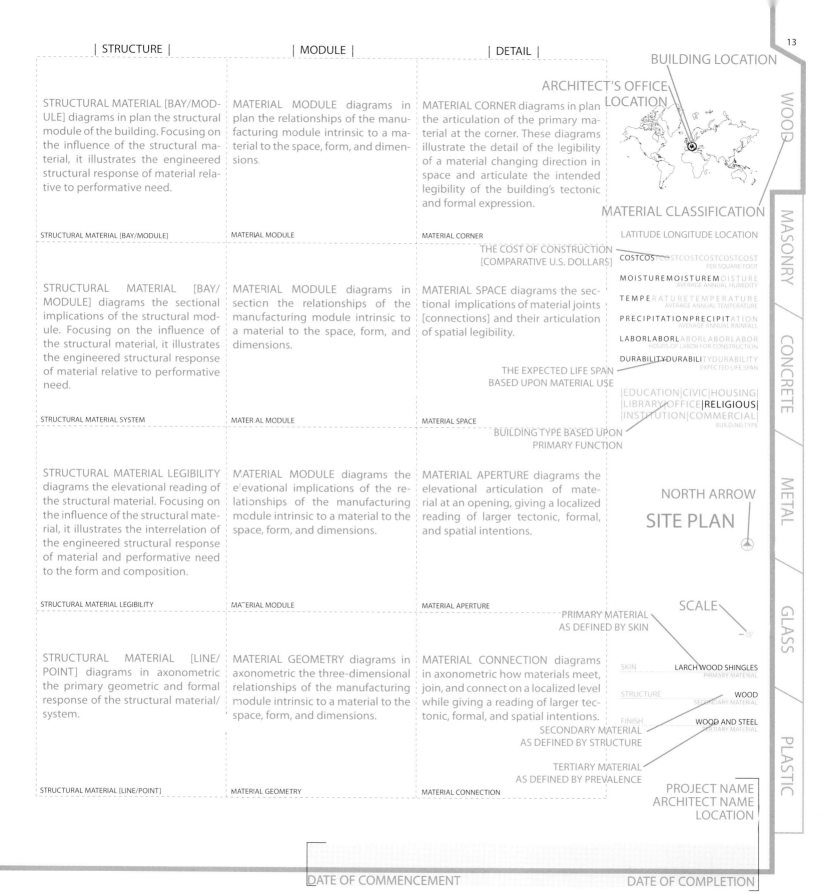

BUILDING LOCATION

ARCHITECT'S OFFICE LOCATION

WOOD

MATERIAL CLASSIFICATION

LATITUDE LONGITUDE LOCATION

MASONRY

THE COST OF CONSTRUCTION [COMPARATIVE U.S. DOLLARS]

COSTCOSTCOSTCOSTCOSTCOSTCOST
PER SQUARE FOOT

MOISTUREMOISTUREMOISTURE
AVERAGE ANNUAL HUMIDITY

TEMPERATURETEMPERATURE
AVERAGE ANNUAL TEMPERATURE

PRECIPITATIONPRECIPITATION
AVERAGE ANNUAL RAINFALL

LABORLABORLABORLABORLABOR
HOURS OF LABOR FOR CONSTRUCTION

DURABILITYDURABILITYDURABILITY
EXPECTED LIFE SPAN

THE EXPECTED LIFE SPAN
BASED UPON MATERIAL USE

CONCRETE

EDUCATION	CIVIC	HOUSING
LIBRARY	OFFICE	RELIGIOUS
INSTITUTION	COMMERCIAL
BUILDING TYPE

BUILDING TYPE BASED UPON
PRIMARY FUNCTION

NORTH ARROW

SITE PLAN

METAL

SCALE

GLASS

PRIMARY MATERIAL
AS DEFINED BY SKIN

SKIN   LARCH WOOD SHINGLES
PRIMARY MATERIAL

STRUCTURE   WOOD
SECONDARY MATERIAL

FINISH   WOOD AND STEEL
TERTIARY MATERIAL

SECONDARY MATERIAL
AS DEFINED BY STRUCTURE

TERTIARY MATERIAL
AS DEFINED BY PREVALENCE

PLASTIC

PROJECT NAME
ARCHITECT NAME
LOCATION

PRECEDENTS

The use of architectural precedent provides a historical and typological cross section of case studies in material application. Through the comparative dissection of their conceptualization, organization, material selection, material use, and material articulation, trends emerge. Their diagramming clearly reveals their position in architectural theory, the approach to material use, available technological capability, and the historical environment [both cultural and architectural]. The aggregation of these in classified material chapters allows for the revelation of subtrends of the evolution of a material usage across the twentieth century. The broad array of comparative diagramming illustrates the interrelationships within a project and the sequential evolutionary approach to space and material from case study to case study.

| DOCUMENTATION | | FORM | | PROXIMITY | | SKIN + SURFACE |

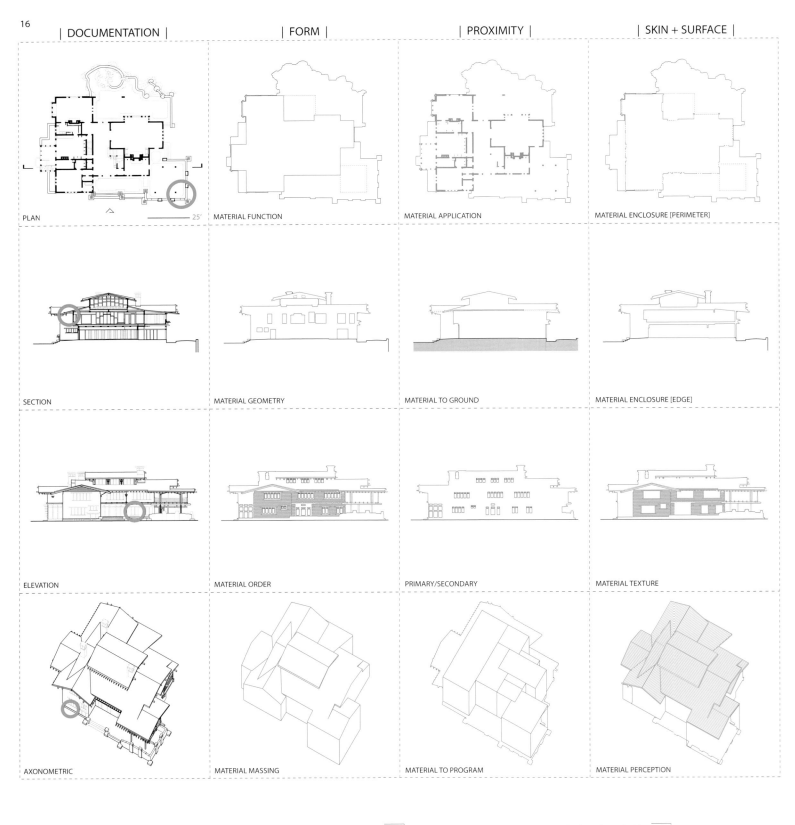

PLAN

MATERIAL FUNCTION

MATERIAL APPLICATION

MATERIAL ENCLOSURE [PERIMETER]

SECTION

MATERIAL GEOMETRY

MATERIAL TO GROUND

MATERIAL ENCLOSURE [EDGE]

ELEVATION

MATERIAL ORDER

PRIMARY/SECONDARY

MATERIAL TEXTURE

AXONOMETRIC

MATERIAL MASSING

MATERIAL TO PROGRAM

MATERIAL PERCEPTION

25′

1894
Charles Sumner Greene and
Henry Mather Greene establish
Greene and Greene

Rolls-Royce Company founded by
Charles Rolls and Frederick Royce

1904

Josef Hoffmann designs the Palais Stoclet

1905

| STRUCTURE | | MODULE | | DETAIL |

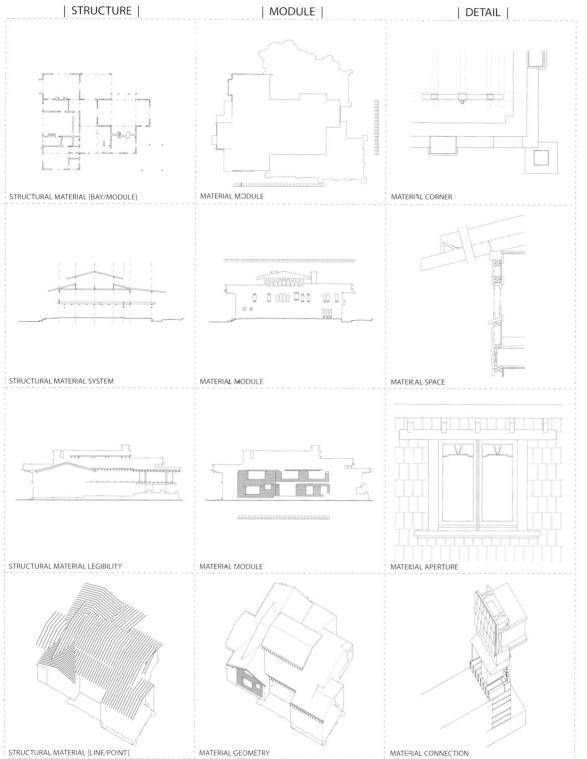

STRUCTURAL MATERIAL [BAY/MODULE]

MATERIAL MODULE

MATERIAL CORNER

STRUCTURAL MATERIAL SYSTEM

MATERIAL MODULE

MATERIAL SPACE

STRUCTURAL MATERIAL LEGIBILITY

MATERIAL MODULE

MATERIAL APERTURE

STRUCTURAL MATERIAL [LINE/POINT]

MATERIAL GEOMETRY

MATERIAL CONNECTION

34° 9' 6" N 118° 9' 39" W

COSTCOSTCOSTCOSTCOSTCOSTCOST
PER SQUARE FOOT

MOISTUREMOISTUREMOISTURE
AVERAGE ANNUAL HUMIDITY

TEMPERATURETEMPERATURE
AVERAGE ANNUAL TEMPERATURE

PRECIPITATIONPRECIPITATION
AVERAGE ANNUAL RAINFALL

LABORLABORLABORLABORLABOR
HOURS OF LABOR FOR CONSTRUCTION

DURABILITYDURABILITYDURABILITY
EXPECTED LIFE SPAN

|EDUCATION|CIVIC|HOUSING|
LIBRARY|OFFICE|RELIGIOUS|
|INSTITUTION|COMMERCIAL|
BUILDING TYPE

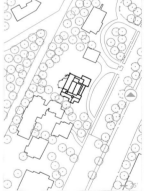

SKIN   WOOD SHINGLES
PRIMARY MATERIAL

STRUCTURE   WOOD
SECONDARY MATERIAL

FINISH   TEAK, MAPLE, OAK, MAHOGANY
AND PORT ORFORD CEDAR
TERTIARY MATERIAL

GAMBLE HOUSE
GREENE AND GREENE
PASADENA, CALIFORNIA

The San Francisco earthquake
and fire left 503 dead and
$350 million in damages

1906

Deutscher Werkbund, an organization to raise
the quality of German manufactures,
is established in Munich, Germany

1907

1908

1909

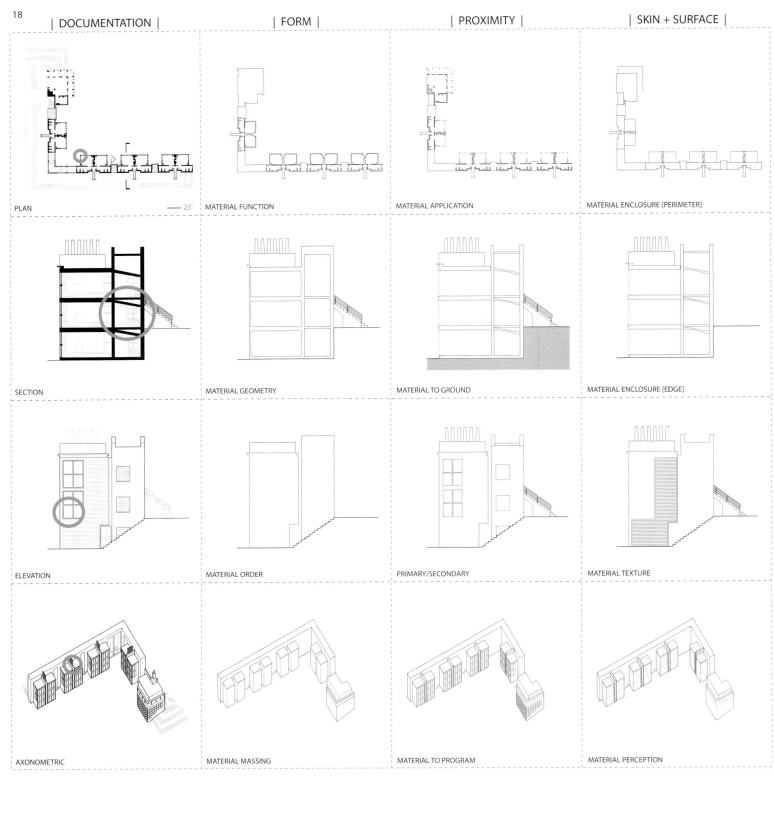

PLAN   — 25'

MATERIAL FUNCTION

MATERIAL APPLICATION

MATERIAL ENCLOSURE [PERIMETER]

SECTION

MATERIAL GEOMETRY

MATERIAL TO GROUND

MATERIAL ENCLOSURE [EDGE]

ELEVATION

MATERIAL ORDER

PRIMARY/SECONDARY

MATERIAL TEXTURE

AXONOMETRIC

MATERIAL MASSING

MATERIAL TO PROGRAM

MATERIAL PERCEPTION

Alvar Aalto dies

1976

1977

Menefee receives B.A. from Carnegie Mellon

Charles Jencks publishes
Post-Modern Architecture

1978

IBM presents the first laser printer-copier

1979

| STRUCTURE | | MODULE | | DETAIL |

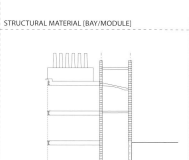

STRUCTURAL MATERIAL [BAY/MODULE]

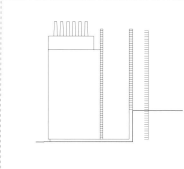

MATERIAL MODULE

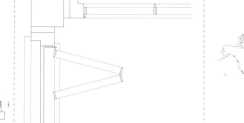

MATERIAL CORNER

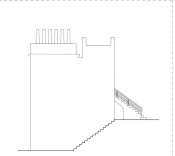

STRUCTURAL MATERIAL SYSTEM

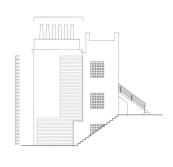

MATERIAL MODULE

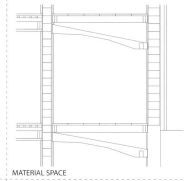

MATERIAL SPACE

STRUCTURAL MATERIAL LEGIBILITY

MATERIAL MODULE

MATERIAL APERTURE

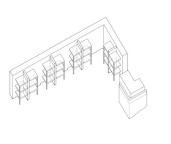

STRUCTURAL MATERIAL [LINE/POINT]

MATERIAL GEOMETRY

MATERIAL CONNECTION

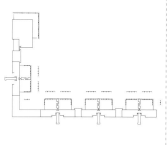

32° 53′ 58″ N 80° 7′ 55″ W

COSTCOSTCOSTCOSTCOSTCOSTCOST
PER SQUARE FOOT

MOISTUREMOISTUREMOISTURE
AVERAGE ANNUAL HUMIDITY

TEMPERATURETEMPERATURE
AVERAGE ANNUAL TEMPERATURE

PRECIPITATIONPRECIPITATION
AVERAGE ANNUAL RAINFALL

LABORLABORLABORLABORLABOR
HOURS OF LABOR FOR CONSTRUCTION

DURABILITYDURABILITYDURABILITY
EXPECTED LIFE SPAN

EDUCATION	CIVIC	HOUSING
LIBRARY	OFFICE	RELIGIOUS
INSTITUTION	COMMERCIAL
BUILDING TYPE

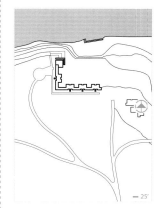

— 25′

| SKIN | CHARLESTON GREEN PAINTED WOOD |
| | PRIMARY MATERIAL |

| STRUCTURE | "SLAVE COAT" STUCCO |
| | SECONDARY MATERIAL |

| FINISH | WOOD, CONCRETE, GLASS AND GLASS BLOCK |
| | TERTIARY MATERIAL |

MIDDLETON INN
CLARK AND MENEFEE
CHARLESTON, SOUTH CAROLINA

1981

1985
Clark and Menefee Architects formed

1986

| | DOCUMENTATION | | | FORM | | | PROXIMITY | | | SKIN + SURFACE | |

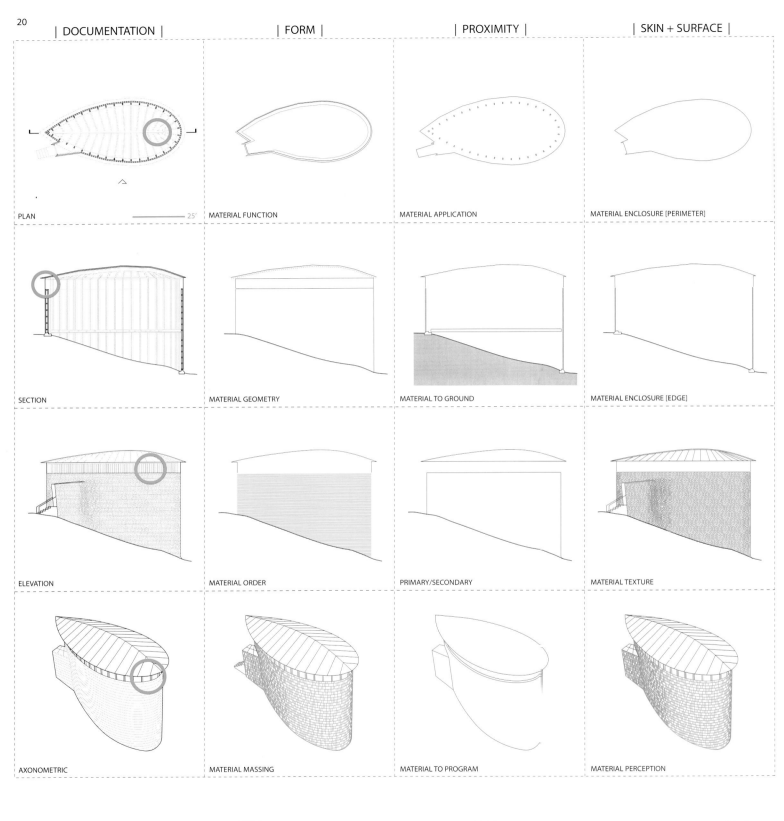

PLAN   25'

MATERIAL FUNCTION

MATERIAL APPLICATION

MATERIAL ENCLOSURE [PERIMETER]

SECTION

MATERIAL GEOMETRY

MATERIAL TO GROUND

MATERIAL ENCLOSURE [EDGE]

ELEVATION

MATERIAL ORDER

PRIMARY/SECONDARY

MATERIAL TEXTURE

AXONOMETRIC

MATERIAL MASSING

MATERIAL TO PROGRAM

MATERIAL PERCEPTION

Charles Jencks publishes
Post-Modern Architecture.

The second oil crisis

Kevin Roche, U.S.,
wins the Pritzker Prize.

1968

Zumthor becomes architect for the
Department for the Preservation of
Monuments of the Canton of Graubünden

1978

1980

1982

| STRUCTURE | | MODULE | | DETAIL |

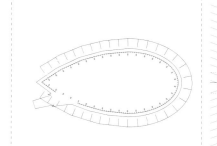

STRUCTURAL MATERIAL [BAY/MODULE]

MATERIAL MODULE

MATERIAL CORNER

46° 44′ 5″ N 8° 56′ 21″ E

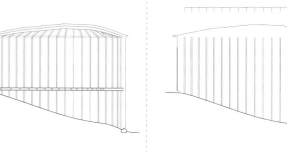

STRUCTURAL MATERIAL SYSTEM

MATERIAL MODULE

MATERIAL SPACE

COSTCOSTCOSTCOSTCOSTCOSTCOST
PER SQUARE FOOT

MOISTUREMOISTUREMOISTURE
AVERAGE ANNUAL HUMIDITY

TEMPERATURETEMPERATURE
AVERAGE ANNUAL TEMPERATURE

PRECIPITATIONPRECIPITATION
AVERAGE ANNUAL RAINFALL

LABORLABORLABORLABORLABOR
HOURS OF LABOR FOR CONSTRUCTION

DURABILITYDURABILITYDURABILITY
EXPECTED LIFE SPAN

EDUCATION	CIVIC	HOUSING
LIBRARY	OFFICE	RELIGIOUS
INSTITUTION	COMMERCIAL
BUILDING TYPE

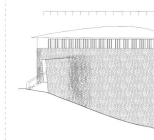

STRUCTURAL MATERIAL LEGIBILITY

MATERIAL MODULE

MATERIAL APERTURE

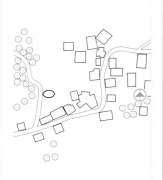

— 50′

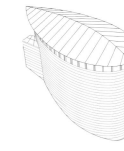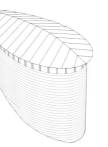

STRUCTURAL MATERIAL [LINE/POINT]

MATERIAL GEOMETRY

MATERIAL CONNECTION

SKIN   LARCH WOOD SHINGLES
PRIMARY MATERIAL

STRUCTURE   WOOD
SECONDARY MATERIAL

FINISH   WOOD AND STEEL
TERTIARY MATERIAL

CHAPEL OF ST. BENEDICT
PETER ZUMTHOR
SUMVITG
SWITZERLAND

Apple introduces the
Macintosh SE home computer designed by
Hartmut Esslinger and Frogdesign

1984

1985

1987

Zumthor receives the Auszeichnung guter Bauten im Kanton Graubünden award in Switzerland

1988

| DOCUMENTATION | | FORM | | PROXIMITY | | SKIN + SURFACE | |

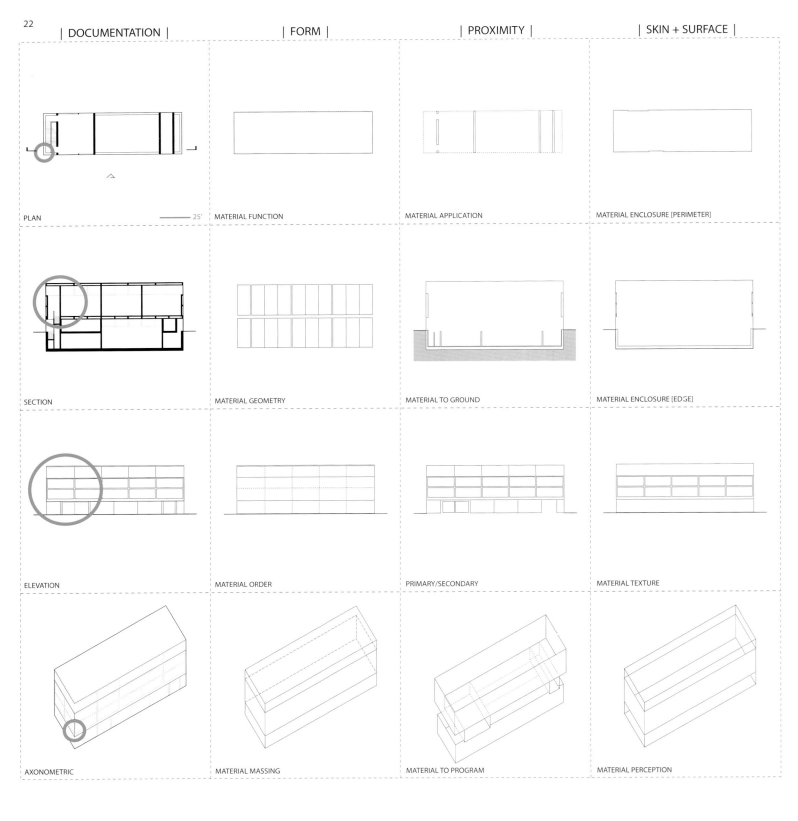

PLAN — 25′

MATERIAL FUNCTION

MATERIAL APPLICATION

MATERIAL ENCLOSURE [PERIMETER]

SECTION

MATERIAL GEOMETRY

MATERIAL TO GROUND

MATERIAL ENCLOSURE [EDGE]

ELEVATION

MATERIAL ORDER

PRIMARY/SECONDARY

MATERIAL TEXTURE

AXONOMETRIC

MATERIAL MASSING

MATERIAL TO PROGRAM

MATERIAL PERCEPTION

Ray Tomlinson, a programmer at Bolt Beranek & Newman, invents e-mail

Chrysler designers invent the minivan

Michael Graves designs the "Singing Bird" teakettle for Alessi

1978

1981

1983

1985

Jacques Herzog and Pierre de Meuron found Herzog & de Meuron Architekten

| STRUCTURE | | MODULE | | DETAIL |

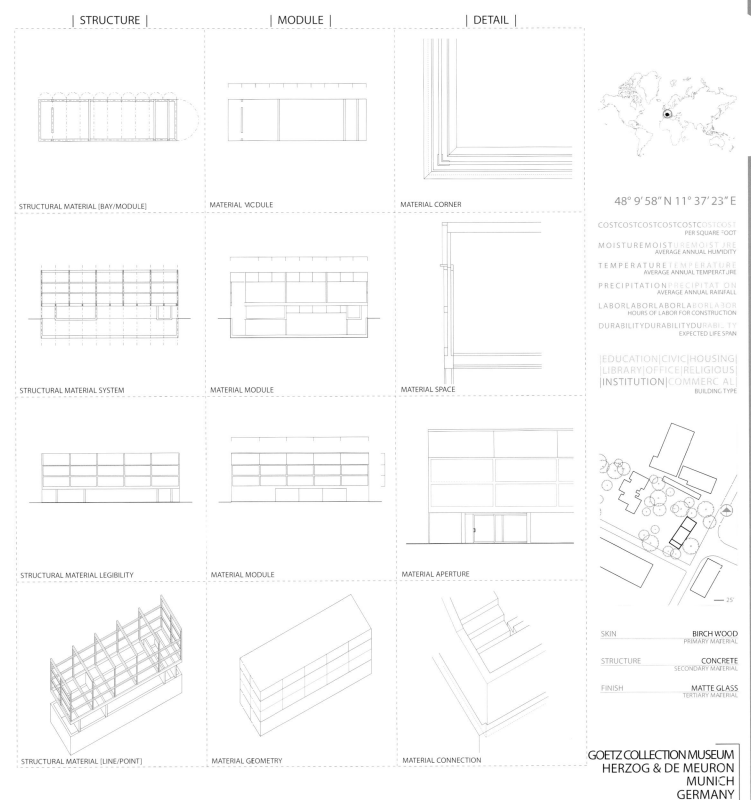

STRUCTURAL MATERIAL [BAY/MODULE]

MATERIAL MODULE

MATERIAL CORNER

STRUCTURAL MATERIAL SYSTEM

MATERIAL MODULE

MATERIAL SPACE

STRUCTURAL MATERIAL LEGIBILITY

MATERIAL MODULE

MATERIAL APERTURE

STRUCTURAL MATERIAL [LINE/POINT]

MATERIAL GEOMETRY

MATERIAL CONNECTION

WOOD

MASONRY

CONCRETE

METAL

GLASS

PLASTIC

48° 9′ 58″ N 11° 37′ 23″ E

COSTCOSTCOSTCOSTCOSTCOSTCOST
PER SQUARE FOOT

MOISTUREMOISTUREMOISTURE
AVERAGE ANNUAL HUMIDITY

TEMPERATURETEMPERATURE
AVERAGE ANNUAL TEMPERATURE

PRECIPITATIONPRECIPITATION
AVERAGE ANNUAL RAINFALL

LABORLABORLABORLABORLABOR
HOURS OF LABOR FOR CONSTRUCTION

DURABILITYDURABILITYDURABILITY
EXPECTED LIFE SPAN

EDUCATION	CIVIC	HOUSING
LIBRARY	OFFICE	RELIGIOUS
INSTITUTION	COMMERCIAL
BUILDING TYPE

— 25′

SKIN   BIRCH WOOD
PRIMARY MATERIAL

STRUCTURE   CONCRETE
SECONDARY MATERIAL

FINISH   MATTE GLASS
TERTIARY MATERIAL

GOETZ COLLECTION MUSEUM
HERZOG & DE MEURON
MUNICH
GERMANY

1987
Herzog & de Meuron receive Architecture Award
from Akademie der Künste in Berlin

1989

1991
Herzog & de Meuron become professors
at Tulane University, New Orleans

1992

| | DOCUMENTATION | | | FORM | | | PROXIMITY | | | SKIN + SURFACE | |

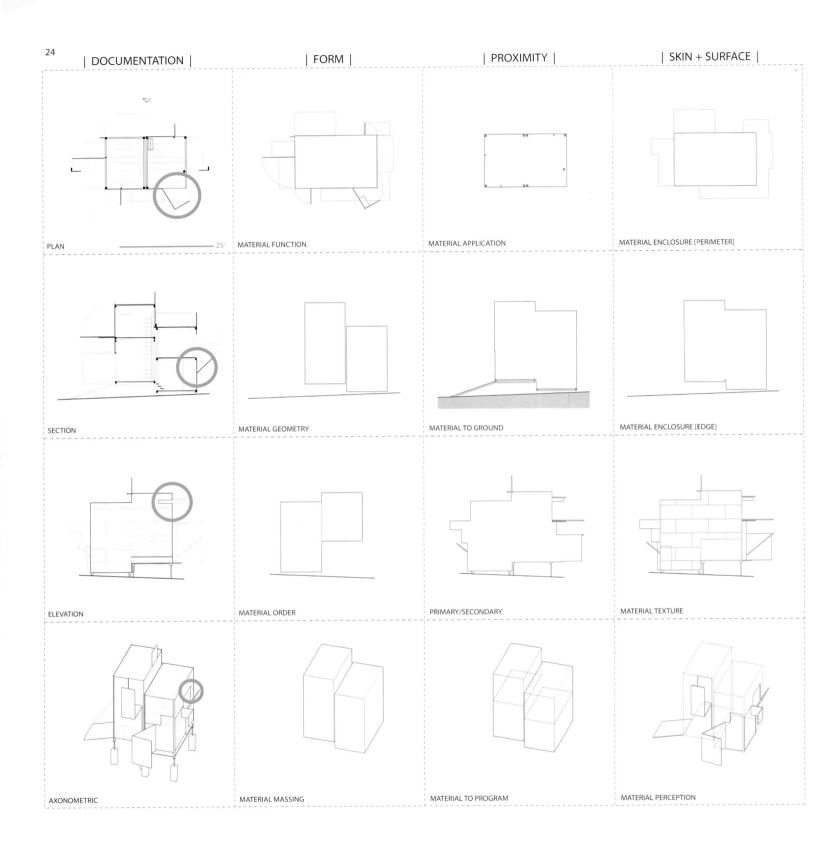

PLAN ————————— 25'

MATERIAL FUNCTION

MATERIAL APPLICATION

MATERIAL ENCLOSURE [PERIMETER]

SECTION

MATERIAL GEOMETRY

MATERIAL TO GROUND

MATERIAL ENCLOSURE [EDGE]

ELEVATION

MATERIAL ORDER

PRIMARY/SECONDARY

MATERIAL TEXTURE

AXONOMETRIC

MATERIAL MASSING

MATERIAL TO PROGRAM

MATERIAL PERCEPTION

Robert Venturi, U.S.,
wins the Pritzker Prize

1991

Frank Gehry designs his
"Gehry Hat Trick Chair," the "Cross Check Armchair"
and the "Face-Off Table" furniture for Knoll

1992

| STRUCTURE | | MODULE | | DETAIL |

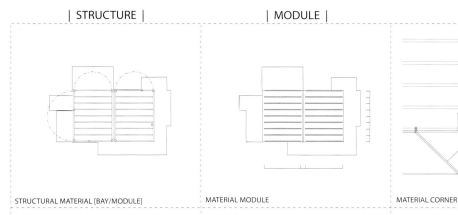

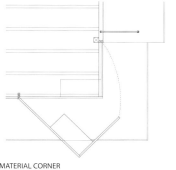

STRUCTURAL MATERIAL [BAY/MODULE]

MATERIAL MODULE

MATERIAL CORNER

47° 49′ 52″ N 13° 23′ 35″ E

COSTCOSTCOSTCOSTCOSTCOSTCOST
PER SQUARE FOOT

MOISTUREMOISTUREMOISTURE
AVERAGE ANNUAL HUMIDITY

TEMPERATURETEMPERATURE
AVERAGE ANNUAL TEMPERATURE

PRECIPITATIONPRECIPITATION
AVERAGE ANNUAL RAINFALL

LABORLABORLABORLABORLABOR
HOURS OF LABOR FOR CONSTRUCTION

DURABILITYDURABILITYDURABILITY
EXPECTED LIFE SPAN

EDUCATION	CIVIC	HOUSING
LIBRARY	OFFICE	RELIGIOUS
INSTITUTION	COMMERCIAL
BUILDING TYPE

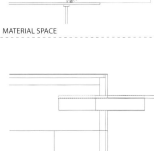

STRUCTURAL MATERIAL SYSTEM

MATERIAL MODULE

MATERIAL SPACE

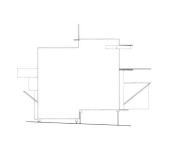

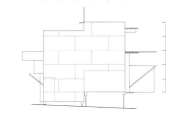

STRUCTURAL MATERIAL LEGIBILITY

MATERIAL MODULE

MATERIAL APERTURE

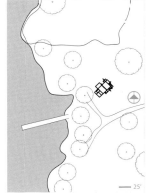

— 25′

SKIN   ENAMELED MARINE PLYWOOD
PRIMARY MATERIAL

STRUCTURE   WOOD
SECONDARY MATERIAL

FINISH   ENAMELED MARINE PLYWOOD
TERTIARY MATERIAL

STRUCTURAL MATERIAL [LINE/POINT]

MATERIAL GEOMETRY

MATERIAL CONNECTION

GUCKLHUPF
HANS PETER WÖRNDL
MONDSEE
AUSTRIA

Intel begins shipping the Pentium chip,
which operates twice as fast as the best
previous Intel chip for personal computers

1993

1993-7   1993-9

| DOCUMENTATION | | FORM | | PROXIMITY | | SKIN + SURFACE |

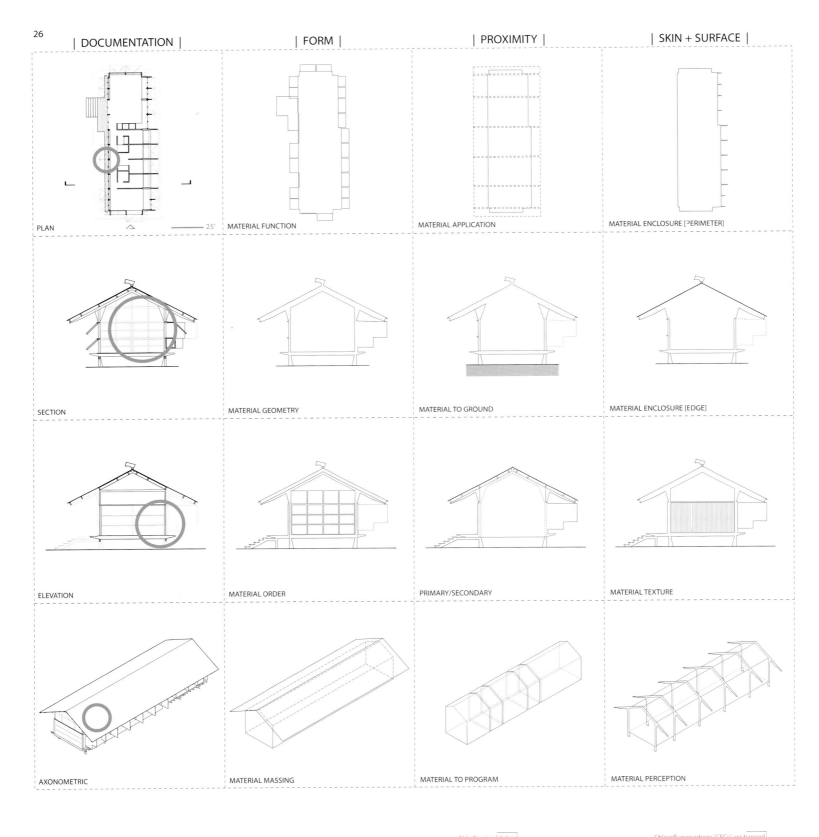

PLAN — 25'

MATERIAL FUNCTION

MATERIAL APPLICATION

MATERIAL ENCLOSURE [PERIMETER]

SECTION

MATERIAL GEOMETRY

MATERIAL TO GROUND

MATERIAL ENCLOSURE [EDGE]

ELEVATION

MATERIAL ORDER

PRIMARY/SECONDARY

MATERIAL TEXTURE

AXONOMETRIC

MATERIAL MASSING

MATERIAL TO PROGRAM

MATERIAL PERCEPTION

Aldo Rossi publishes
Architecture of the Town

Chlorofluorocarbons [CFCs] are banned

1956-1961

1984

1985

1987

Murcutt studies architecture at University of New South Wales

Murcutt completes
Magney House, Bingle Point

| STRUCTURE | | MODULE | | DETAIL |

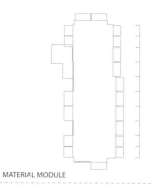

STRUCTURAL MATERIAL [BAY/MODULE]

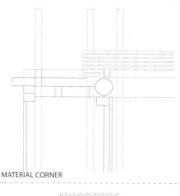

MATERIAL MODULE

MATERIAL CORNER

12° 29' 49" S 136° 46' 37" E

COSTCOSTCOSTCOST COSTCOST COST
PER SQUARE FOOT

MOISTUREMOISTUREMOISTURE
AVERAGE ANNUAL HUMIDITY

TEMPERATURETEMPERATURE
AVERAGE ANNUAL TEMPERATURE

PRECIPITATIONPRECIPITATION
AVERAGE ANNUAL RAINFALL

LABORLABORLABORLABORLABOR
HOURS OF LABOR FOR CONSTRUCTION

DURABILITYDURABILITYDURABILITY
EXPECTED LIFE SPAN

EDUCATION	CIVIC	HOUSING
LIBRARY	OFFICE	RELIGIOUS
INSTITUTION	COMMERCIAL
BUILDING TYPE

STRUCTURAL MATERIAL SYSTEM

MATERIAL MODULE

MATERIAL SPACE

STRUCTURAL MATERIAL LEGIBILITY

MATERIAL MODULE

MATERIAL APERTURE

SKIN   PLYWOOD WALLS AND
        TALLOW-WOOD SHUTTERS
        PRIMARY MATERIAL

STRUCTURE   PREFABRICATED
            STEEL TRUSSES
            SECONDARY MATERIAL

FINISH   CORRUGATED IRON ROOFING
         TERTIARY MATERIAL

STRUCTURAL MATERIAL [LINE/POINT]

MATERIAL GEOMETRY

MATERIAL CONNECTION

MARIKA-ALDERTON HOUSE
GLENN MURCUTT
NORTHERN TERRITORY
AUSTRALIA

Frank O. Gehry receives the Pritzer Prize

1989

1991

1992
Murcutt receives the Alvar Aalto Medal

1994

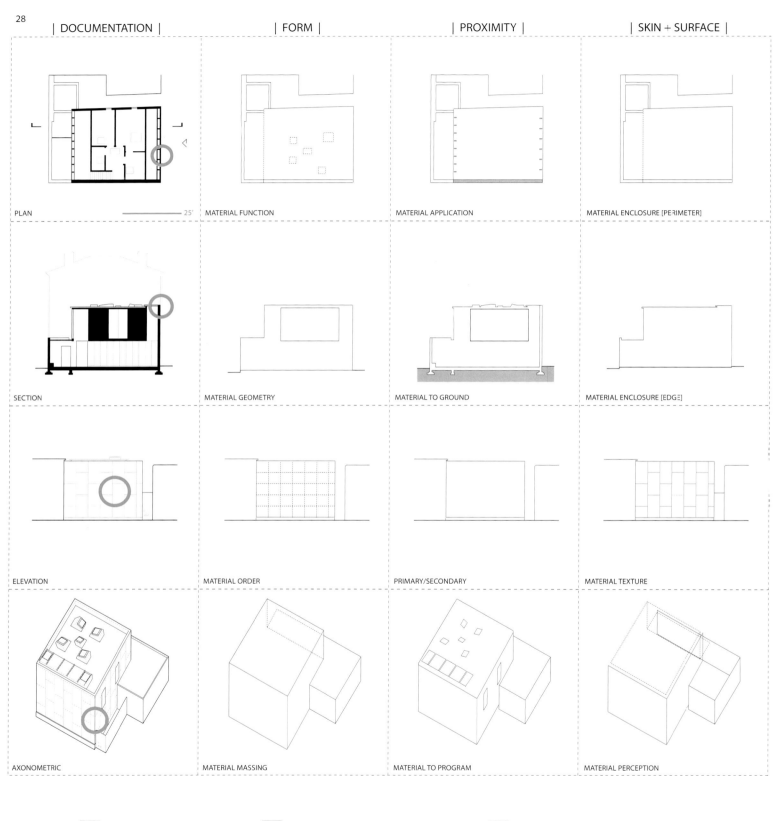

| DOCUMENTATION | FORM | PROXIMITY | SKIN + SURFACE |

PLAN ———————— 25'

MATERIAL FUNCTION

MATERIAL APPLICATION

MATERIAL ENCLOSURE [PERIMETER]

SECTION

MATERIAL GEOMETRY

MATERIAL TO GROUND

MATERIAL ENCLOSURE [EDGE]

ELEVATION

MATERIAL ORDER

PRIMARY/SECONDARY

MATERIAL TEXTURE

AXONOMETRIC

MATERIAL MASSING

MATERIAL TO PROGRAM

MATERIAL PERCEPTION

The B-2 stealth bomber is
introduced by the United States

1988

The start of the second
"Organic Design" period begins

1990

Expo '92, Seville: Nicholas Grimshaw
designs the British pavilion

1992

1993
Adjaye graduates from Royal College of Art.
Wins the RIBA First Prize Bronze Medal
in the same year

| STRUCTURE | | MODULE | | DETAIL | |

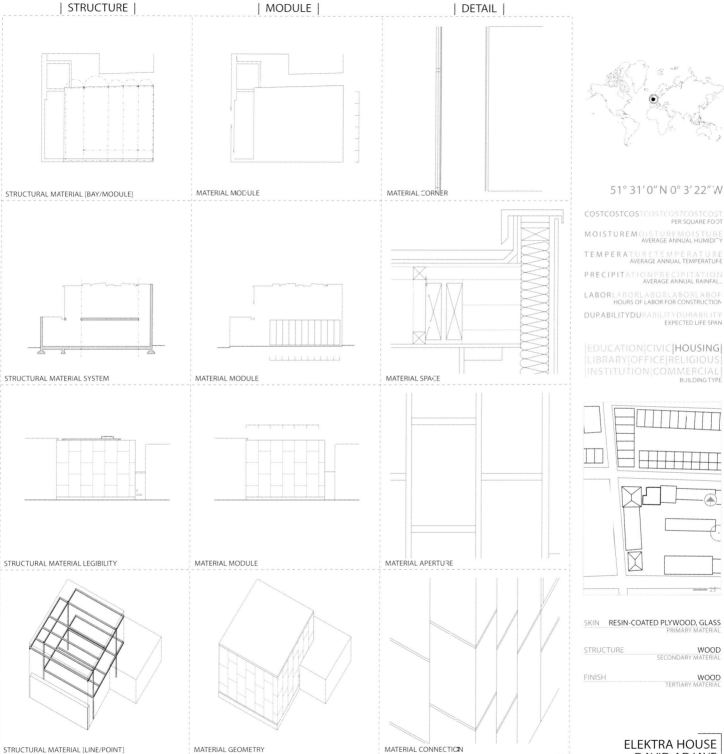

STRUCTURAL MATERIAL [BAY/MODULE]

MATERIAL MODULE

MATERIAL CORNER

STRUCTURAL MATERIAL SYSTEM

MATERIAL MODULE

MATERIAL SPACE

STRUCTURAL MATERIAL LEGIBILITY

MATERIAL MODULE

MATERIAL APERTURE

STRUCTURAL MATERIAL [LINE/POINT]

MATERIAL GEOMETRY

MATERIAL CONNECTION

WOOD

MASONRY

CONCRETE

METAL

GLASS

PLASTIC

51° 31' 0" N 0° 3' 22" W

COSTCOSTCOSTCOSTCOSTCOSTCOST
PER SQUARE FOOT

MOISTUREMOISTUREMOISTURE
AVERAGE ANNUAL HUMIDITY

TEMPERATURETEMPERATURE
AVERAGE ANNUAL TEMPERATURE

PRECIPITATIONPRECIPITATION
AVERAGE ANNUAL RAINFALL

LABORLABORLABORLABORLABOR
HOURS OF LABOR FOR CONSTRUCTION

DURABILITYDURABILITYDURABILITY
EXPECTED LIFE SPAN

EDUCATION	CIVIC	HOUSING
LIBRARY	OFFICE	RELIGIOUS
INSTITUTION	COMMERCIAL
BUILDING TYPE

SKIN RESIN-COATED PLYWOOD, GLASS
PRIMARY MATERIAL

STRUCTURE   WOOD
SECONDARY MATERIAL

FINISH   WOOD
TERTIARY MATERIAL

ELEKTRA HOUSE
DAVID ADJAYE
LONDON
UNITED KINGDOM

1994
Adjaye starts Adjaye Architects

Dr. Brent Townshend
invents the 56k Modem

1996

1998

2000

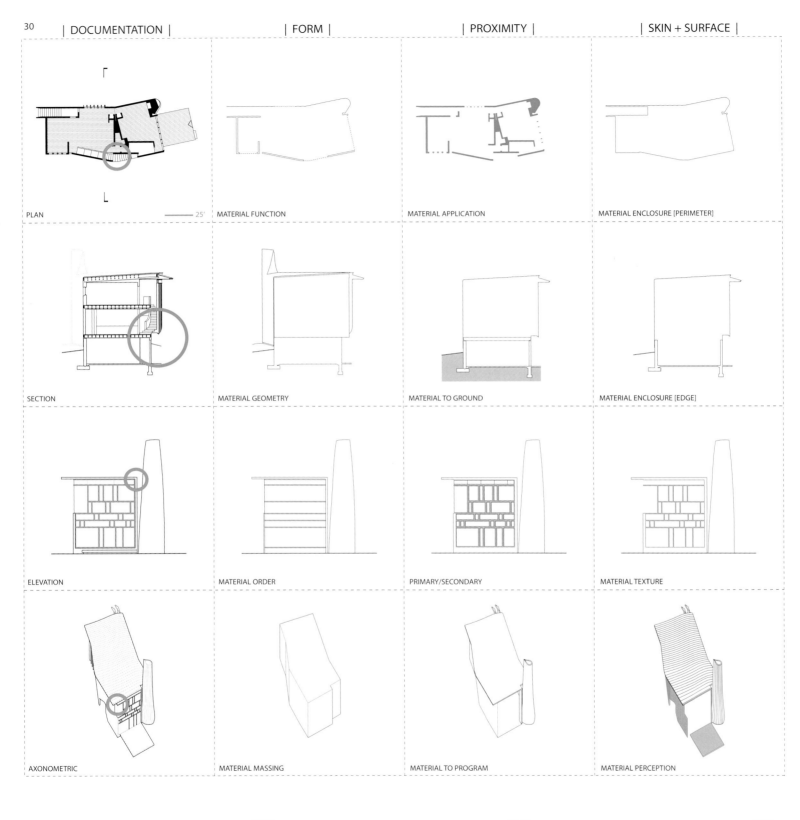

PLAN   25'

MATERIAL FUNCTION

MATERIAL APPLICATION

MATERIAL ENCLOSURE [PERIMETER]

SECTION

MATERIAL GEOMETRY

MATERIAL TO GROUND

MATERIAL ENCLOSURE [EDGE]

ELEVATION

MATERIAL ORDER

PRIMARY/SECONDARY

MATERIAL TEXTURE

AXONOMETRIC

MATERIAL MASSING

MATERIAL TO PROGRAM

MATERIAL PERCEPTION

Frank Gehry designs his "Gehry Hat
Trick Chair," the "Cross Check Armchair"
and the "Face-Off table" furniture for Knoll

Studio 1, Studio 2, Studio 3,
by Syd Mead, is published

Rafael Moneo, Spain,
wins the Pritzker Prize

1992   1994   1996

| STRUCTURE | | MODULE | | DETAIL |

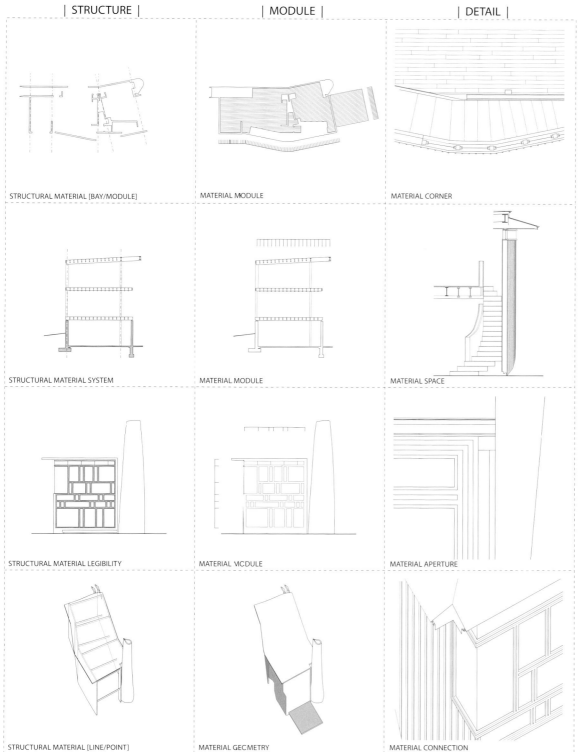

STRUCTURAL MATERIAL [BAY/MODULE]

MATERIAL MODULE

MATERIAL CORNER

STRUCTURAL MATERIAL SYSTEM

MATERIAL MODULE

MATERIAL SPACE

STRUCTURAL MATERIAL LEGIBILITY

MATERIAL MODULE

MATERIAL APERTURE

STRUCTURAL MATERIAL [LINE/POINT]

MATERIAL GEOMETRY

MATERIAL CONNECTION

MASONRY / CONCRETE / METAL / GLASS / PLASTIC

UNDISCLOSED

COSTCOSTCOSTCOSTCOSTCOSTCOST
PER SQUARE FOOT

MOISTUREMOISTUREMOISTURE
AVERAGE ANNUAL HUMIDITY

TEMPERATURETEMPERATURE
AVERAGE ANNUAL TEMPERATURE

PRECIPITATIONPRECIPITATION
AVERAGE ANNUAL RAINFALL

LABORLABORLABORLABORLABOR
HOURS OF LABOR FOR CONSTRUCTION

DURABILITYDURABILITYDURABILITY
EXPECTED LIFE SPAN

EDUCATION	CIVIC	HOUSING
LIBRARY	OFFICE	RELIGIOUS
INSTITUTION	COMMERCIAL
BUILDING TYPE

— 25'

SKIN   WOOD, RUBBER AND GLASS
PRIMARY MATERIAL

STRUCTURE   WOOD
SECONDARY MATERIAL

FINISH   WOOD
TERTIARY MATERIAL

NEW ENGLAND HOUSE
OFFICE dA
BOSTON, MASSACHUSETTS

| DOCUMENTATION | | FORM | | | PROXIMITY | | | SKIN + SURFACE |

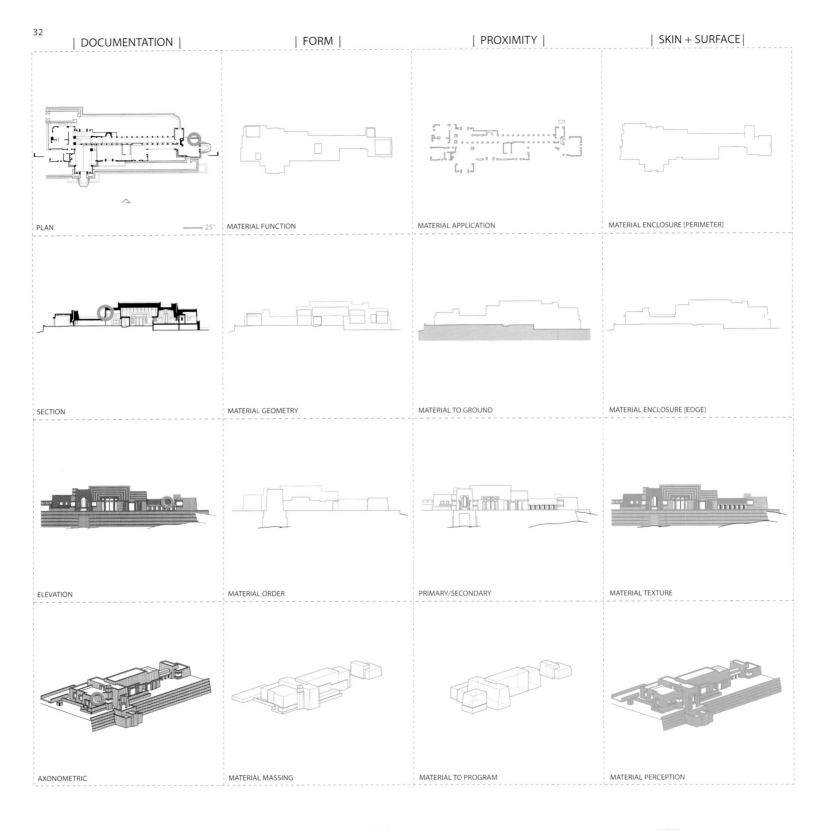

PLAN   25'   MATERIAL FUNCTION   MATERIAL APPLICATION   MATERIAL ENCLOSURE [PERIMETER]

SECTION   MATERIAL GEOMETRY   MATERIAL TO GROUND   MATERIAL ENCLOSURE [EDGE]

ELEVATION   MATERIAL ORDER   PRIMARY/SECONDARY   MATERIAL TEXTURE

AXONOMETRIC   MATERIAL MASSING   MATERIAL TO PROGRAM   MATERIAL PERCEPTION

The San Francisco World's Fair held

In Russia, the October Revolution spawned
an artistic movement called "Constructivism."

1890

Wright works for Louis Sullivan   1915   1917

| STRUCTURE | | MODULE | | DETAIL |

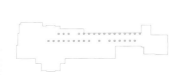

STRUCTURAL MATERIAL [BAY/MODULE]

MATERIAL MODULE

MATERIAL CORNER

34° 6′ 58″ N 118° 17′ 34″ W

COSTCOSTCOSTCOSTCOSTCOSTCOST
PER SQUARE FOOT

MOISTUREMOISTUREMOISTURE
AVERAGE ANNUAL HUMIDITY

TEMPERATURETEMPERATURE
AVERAGE ANNUAL TEMPERATURE

PRECIPITATIONPRECIPITATION
AVERAGE ANNUAL RAINFALL

LABORLABORLABORLABORLABOR
HOURS OF LABOR FOR CONSTRUCTION

DURABILITYDURABILITYDURABILITY
EXPECTED LIFE SPAN

EDUCATION	CIVIC	HOUSING
LIBRARY	OFFICE	RELIGIOUS
INSTITUTION	COMMERCIAL
BUILDING TYPE

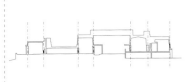

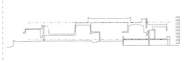

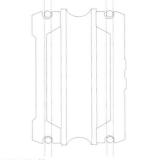

STRUCTURAL MATERIAL SYSTEM

MATERIAL MODULE

MATERIAL SPACE

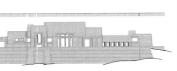

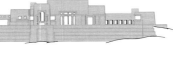

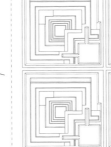

STRUCTURAL MATERIAL LEGIBILITY

MATERIAL MODULE

MATERIAL APERTURE

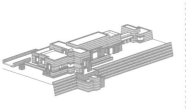

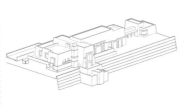

STRUCTURAL MATERIAL [LINE/POINT]

MATERIAL GEOMETRY

MATERIAL CONNECTION

SKIN   CONCRETE TEXTILE BLOCK
PRIMARY MATERIAL

STRUCTURE   CONCRETE TEXTILE BLOCK
SECONDARY MATERIAL

FINISH   CONCRETE TEXTILE BLOCK
TERTIARY MATERIAL

ENNIS-BROWN HOUSE
FRANK LLOYD WRIGHT
LOS ANGELES, CALIFORNIA

WOOD

MASONRY

CONCRETE

METAL

GLASS

PLASTIC

1919
Wright designs Hollyhock House in Los Angeles, California

Mondrian paints
"Composition in Red, Yellow, and Blue."

1921

1923

1924

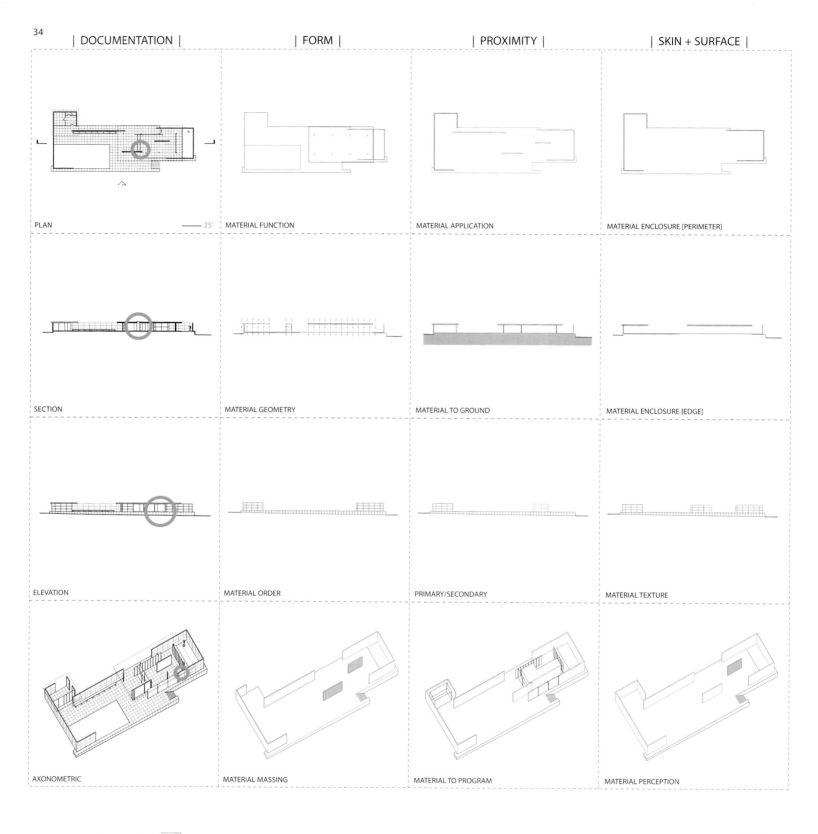

DOCUMENTATION	FORM	PROXIMITY	SKIN + SURFACE
PLAN —— 25'	MATERIAL FUNCTION	MATERIAL APPLICATION	MATERIAL ENCLOSURE [PERIMETER]
SECTION	MATERIAL GEOMETRY	MATERIAL TO GROUND	MATERIAL ENCLOSURE [EDGE]
ELEVATION	MATERIAL ORDER	PRIMARY/SECONDARY	MATERIAL TEXTURE
AXONOMETRIC	MATERIAL MASSING	MATERIAL TO PROGRAM	MATERIAL PERCEPTION

Bauhaus ("builder's house") is
established by Walter Gropius

1919

1921

Mies proposes faceted al–glass Friedrichstraße skyscraper

Le Corbusier writes and publishes
Vers une Architecture

1923

| STRUCTURE | | MODULE | | DETAIL |

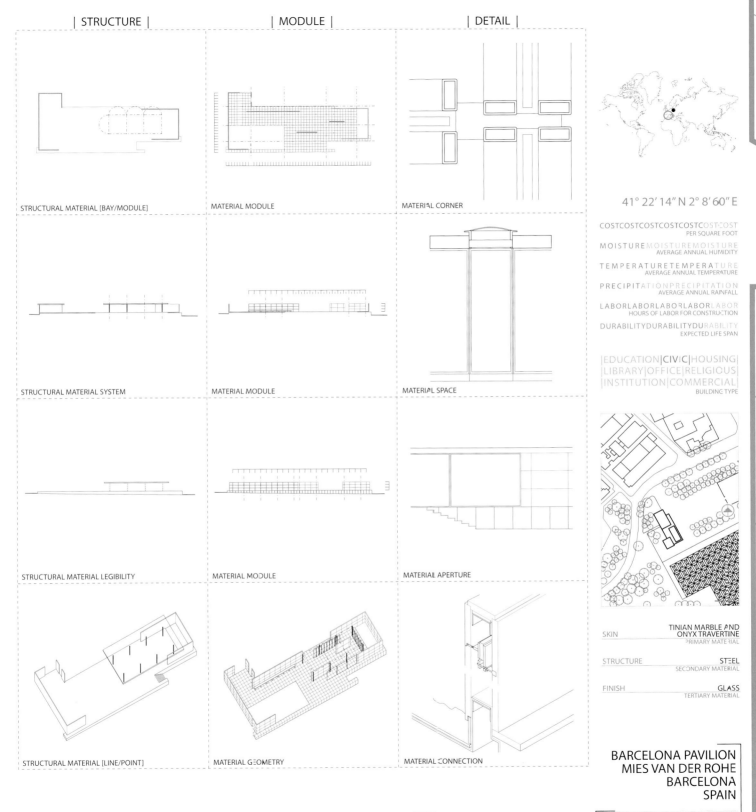

STRUCTURAL MATERIAL [BAY/MODULE]

MATERIAL MODULE

MATERIAL CORNER

STRUCTURAL MATERIAL SYSTEM

MATERIAL MODULE

MATERIAL SPACE

STRUCTURAL MATERIAL LEGIBILITY

MATERIAL MODULE

MATERIAL APERTURE

STRUCTURAL MATERIAL [LINE/POINT]

MATERIAL GEOMETRY

MATERIAL CONNECTION

MASONRY

41° 22' 14" N 2° 8' 60" E

COSTCOSTCOSTCOSTCOSTCOSTCOST
PER SQUARE FOOT

MOISTUREMOISTUREMOISTURE
AVERAGE ANNUAL HUMIDITY

TEMPERATURETEMPERATURE
AVERAGE ANNUAL TEMPERATURE

PRECIPITATIONPRECIPITATION
AVERAGE ANNUAL RAINFALL

LABORLABORLABORLABORLABOR
HOURS OF LABOR FOR CONSTRUCTION

DURABILITYDURABILITYDURABILITY
EXPECTED LIFE SPAN

EDUCATION	CIVIC	HOUSING
LIBRARY	OFFICE	RELIGIOUS
INSTITUTION	COMMERCIAL
BUILDING TYPE

CONCRETE

METAL

GLASS

SKIN	TINIAN MARBLE AND ONYX TRAVERTINE
	PRIMARY MATERIAL
STRUCTURE	STEEL
	SECONDARY MATERIAL
FINISH	GLASS
	TERTIARY MATERIAL

PLASTIC

**BARCELONA PAVILION
MIES VAN DER ROHE
BARCELONA
SPAIN**

Le Corbusier and Pierre Jeanneret
develop the "Plan Voisin" for Paris

1925

Pez candy is introduced as a
breath freshener for smokers

1927

1927
Mies designs his "Armchair"

1928   1929

| DOCUMENTATION | | FORM | | PROXIMITY | | SKIN + SURFACE |

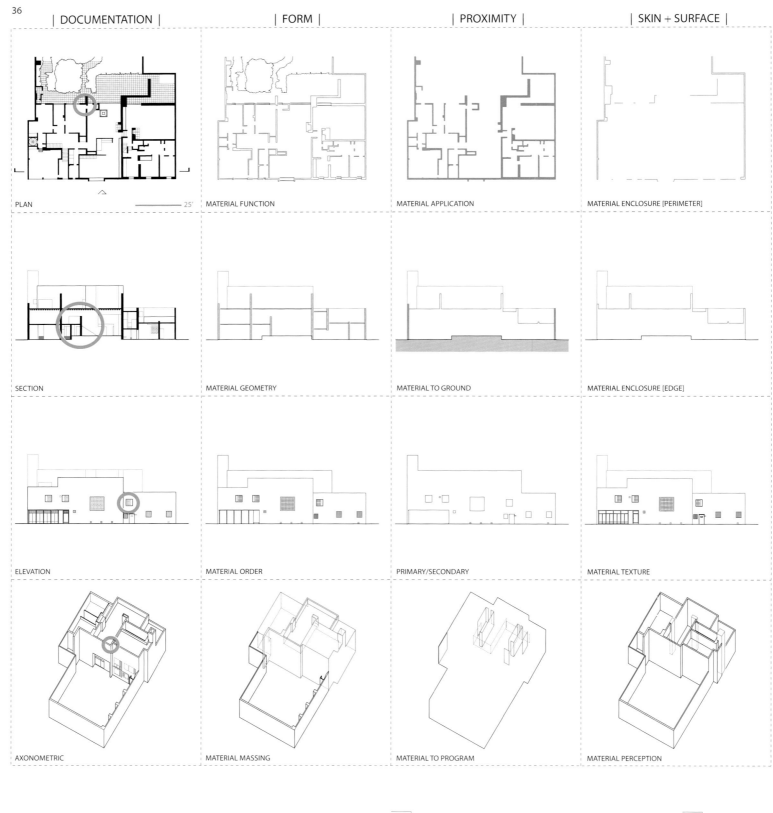

PLAN   25'   MATERIAL FUNCTION   MATERIAL APPLICATION   MATERIAL ENCLOSURE [PERIMETER]

SECTION   MATERIAL GEOMETRY   MATERIAL TO GROUND   MATERIAL ENCLOSURE [EDGE]

ELEVATION   MATERIAL ORDER   PRIMARY/SECONDARY   MATERIAL TEXTURE

AXONOMETRIC   MATERIAL MASSING   MATERIAL TO PROGRAM   MATERIAL PERCEPTION

Britain and France declare war on Germany

The "Manhattan Project," of
intensive atomic research, begins

1935

Barragan moves to Mexico City

1939

1941

| STRUCTURE | | MODULE | | DETAIL |

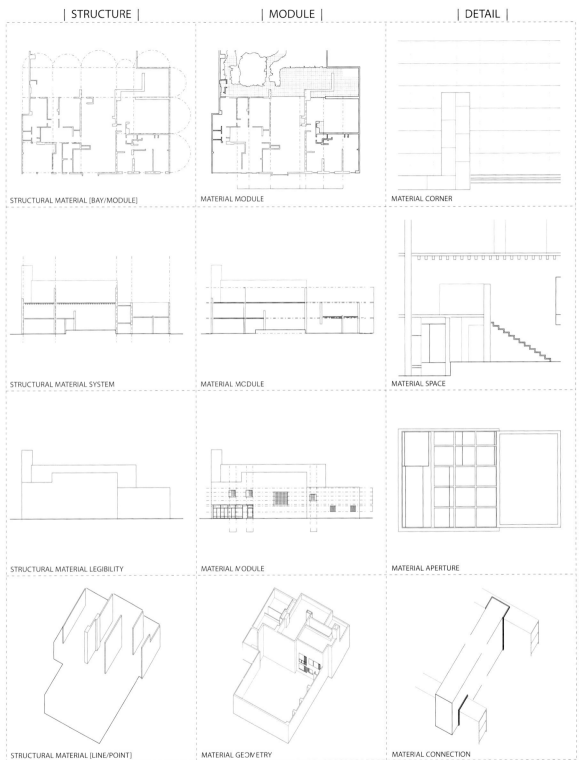

STRUCTURAL MATERIAL [BAY/MODULE]

MATERIAL MODULE

MATERIAL CORNER

STRUCTURAL MATERIAL SYSTEM

MATERIAL MODULE

MATERIAL SPACE

STRUCTURAL MATERIAL LEGIBILITY

MATERIAL MODULE

MATERIAL APERTURE

STRUCTURAL MATERIAL [LINE/POINT]

MATERIAL GEOMETRY

MATERIAL CONNECTION

WOOD
MASONRY
CONCRETE
METAL
GLASS
PLASTIC

19° 24' 40" N 99° 11' 33" W

COSTCOSTCOSTCOST COSTCOSTCOST
PER SQUARE FOOT

MOISTUREMOISTUREMOISTURE
AVERAGE ANNUAL HUMIDITY

TEMPERATURETEMPERATURE
AVERAGE ANNUAL TEMPERATURE

PRECIPITATIONPRECIPITATION
AVERAGE ANNUAL RAINFALL

LABORLABORLABORLABORLABOR
HOURS OF LABOR FOR CONSTRUCTION

DURABILITYDURABILITYDURABILITY
EXPECTED LIFE SPAN

EDUCATION	CIVIC	HOUSING
LIBRARY	OFFICE	RELIGIOUS
INSTITUTION	COMMERCIAL
BUILDING TYPE

SKIN   PLASTERED ADOBE MASONRY
PRIMARY MATERIAL

STRUCTURE   MASONRY AND CONCRETE
SECONDARY MATERIAL

FINISH   WOOD, GLASS AND CANVAS
TERTIARY MATERIAL

CASA BARRAGAN
LUIS BARRAGAN
MEXICO CITY
MEXICO

Le Corbusier publishes
Urbanisme des CIAM, la Charte d'Athenes

1943

1945
Barragan plans a new development in El Pedregal

1947   1948

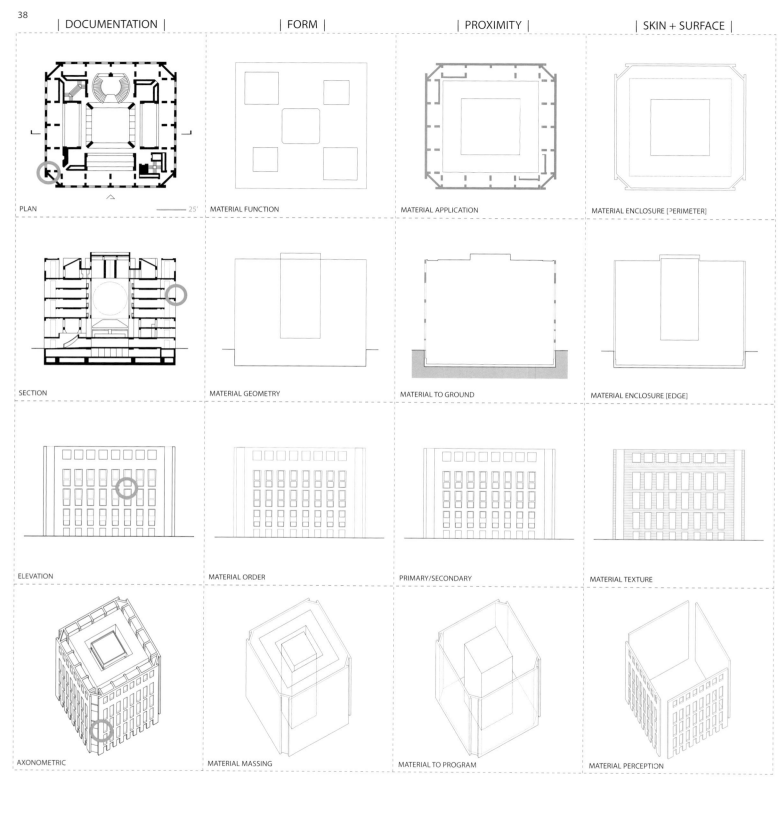

DOCUMENTATION	FORM	PROXIMITY	SKIN + SURFACE
PLAN	MATERIAL FUNCTION	MATERIAL APPLICATION	MATERIAL ENCLOSURE [PERIMETER]
SECTION	MATERIAL GEOMETRY	MATERIAL TO GROUND	MATERIAL ENCLOSURE [EDGE]
ELEVATION	MATERIAL ORDER	PRIMARY/SECONDARY	MATERIAL TEXTURE
AXONOMETRIC	MATERIAL MASSING	MATERIAL TO PROGRAM	MATERIAL PERCEPTION

25'

1950
Kahn serves as Resident Architect
at the American Academy in Rome

Alvar Aalto, Helsinki,
wins the AIA Gold Medal

1963

Le Corbusier dies

1965

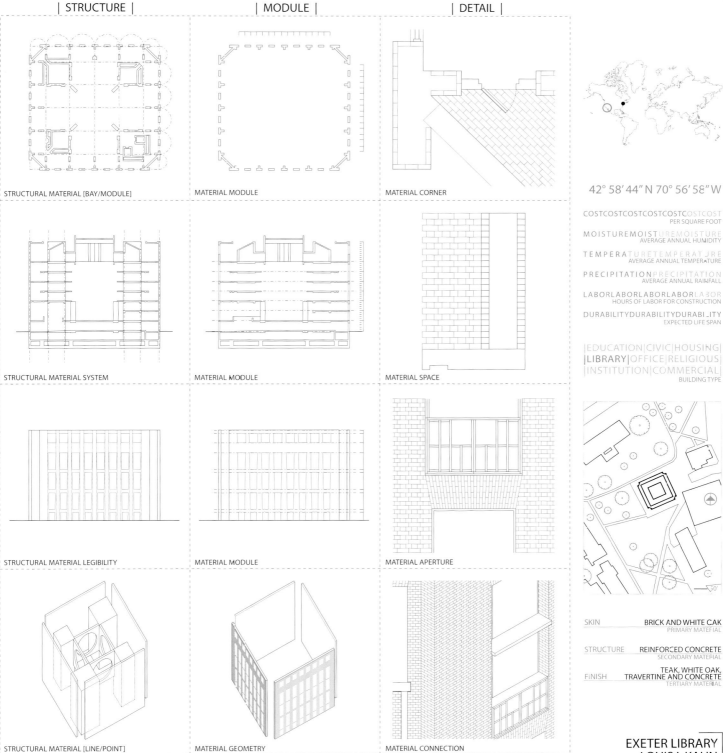

STRUCTURE	MODULE	DETAIL
STRUCTURAL MATERIAL [BAY/MODULE]	MATERIAL MODULE	MATERIAL CORNER
STRUCTURAL MATERIAL SYSTEM	MATERIAL MODULE	MATERIAL SPACE
STRUCTURAL MATERIAL LEGIBILITY	MATERIAL MODULE	MATERIAL APERTURE
STRUCTURAL MATERIAL [LINE/POINT]	MATERIAL GEOMETRY	MATERIAL CONNECTION

WOOD

MASONRY

CONCRETE

METAL

GLASS

PLASTIC

42° 58' 44" N 70° 56' 58" W

COSTCOSTCOSTCOSTCOSTCOSTCOST
PER SQUARE FOOT

MOISTUREMOISTUREMOISTURE
AVERAGE ANNUAL HUMIDITY

TEMPERATURETEMPERATURE
AVERAGE ANNUAL TEMPERATURE

PRECIPITATIONPRECIPITATION
AVERAGE ANNUAL RAINFALL

LABORLABORLABORLABORLABOR
HOURS OF LABOR FOR CONSTRUCTION

DURABILITYDURABILITYDURABILITY
EXPECTED LIFE SPAN

EDUCATION	CIVIC	HOUSING
LIBRARY	OFFICE	RELIGIOUS
INSTITUTION	COMMERCIAL
BUILDING TYPE

SKIN	BRICK AND WHITE OAK
	PRIMARY MATERIAL
STRUCTURE	REINFORCED CONCRETE
	SECONDARY MATERIAL
FINISH	TEAK, WHITE OAK, TRAVERTINE AND CONCRETE
	TERTIARY MATERIAL

EXETER LIBRARY
LOUIS I. KAHN
EXETER, NEW HAMPSHIRE

1966
Salk Institute in La Jolla, California, is completed

1967

1972

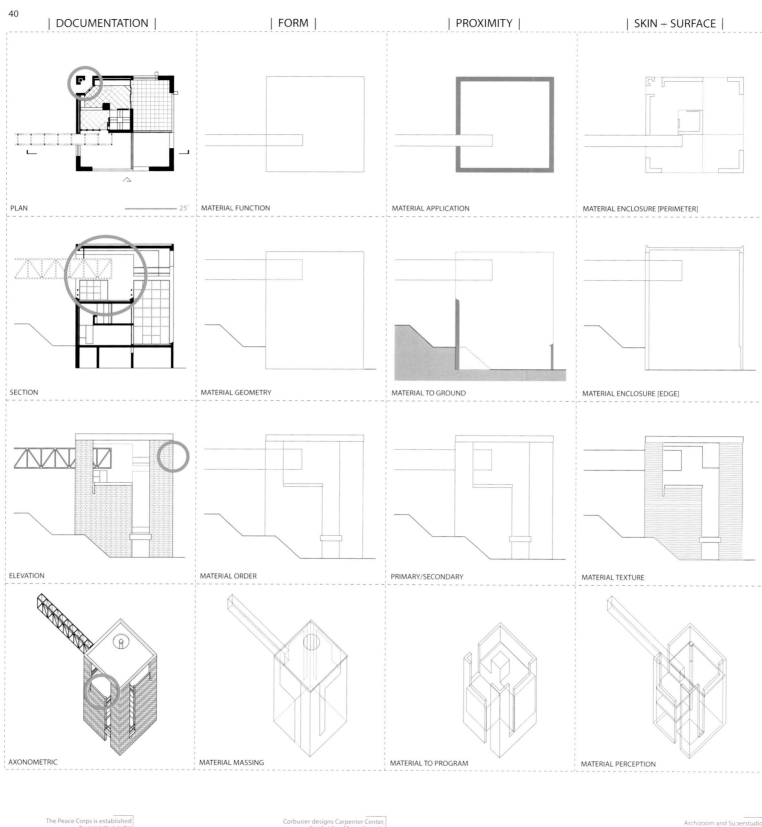

| | DOCUMENTATION | | | FORM | | | PROXIMITY | | | SKIN – SURFACE | |

PLAN   25'

MATERIAL FUNCTION

MATERIAL APPLICATION

MATERIAL ENCLOSURE [PERIMETER]

SECTION

MATERIAL GEOMETRY

MATERIAL TO GROUND

MATERIAL ENCLOSURE [EDGE]

ELEVATION

MATERIAL ORDER

PRIMARY/SECONDARY

MATERIAL TEXTURE

AXONOMETRIC

MATERIAL MASSING

MATERIAL TO PROGRAM

MATERIAL PERCEPTION

The Peace Corps is established
by executive order

Corbusier designs Carpenter Center,
Cambridge, Massachusetts

Archizoom and Superstudio
founded in Italy

1964

1965

1961

1963

Botta enrolls in Instituto
Universitario di Architettura, Venice

Botta works for Le Corbusier

1966

| STRUCTURE | | MODULE | | DETAIL |

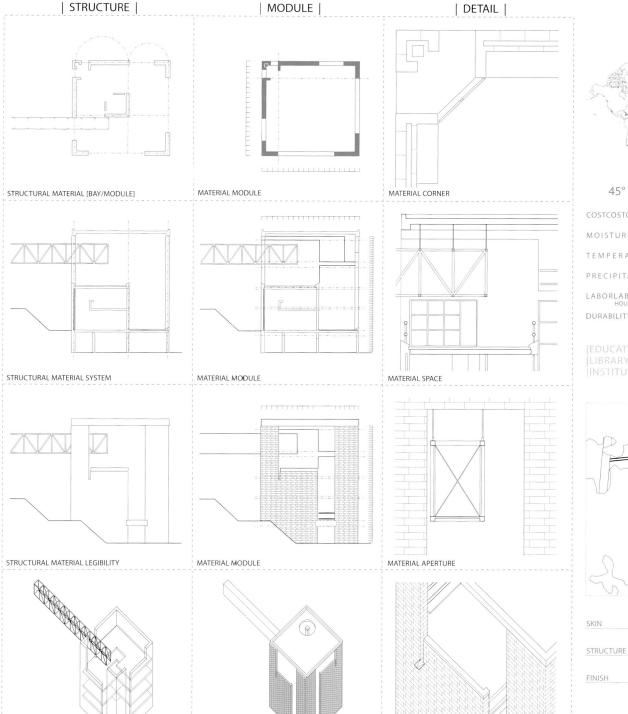

STRUCTURAL MATERIAL [BAY/MODULE]

MATERIAL MODULE

MATERIAL CORNER

STRUCTURAL MATERIAL SYSTEM

MATERIAL MODULE

MATERIAL SPACE

STRUCTURAL MATERIAL LEGIBILITY

MATERIAL MODULE

MATERIAL APERTURE

STRUCTURAL MATERIAL [LINE/POINT]

MATERIAL GEOMETRY

MATERIAL CONNECTION

WOOD

MASONRY

CONCRETE

METAL

GLASS

PLASTIC

45° 55' 2" N 8° 58' 10" E

COSTCOSTCOSTCOSTCOST COSTCOST
PER SQUARE FOOT

MOISTUREMOISTUREMOISTURE
AVERAGE ANNUAL HUMIDITY

TEMPERATURE TEMPERATURE
AVERAGE ANNUAL TEMPERATURE

PRECIPITATIONPRECIPITATION
AVERAGE ANNUAL RAINFALL

LABORLABORLABORLABORLABOR
HOURS OF LABOR FOR CONSTRUCTION

DURABILITYDURABILITYDURABILITY
EXPECTED LIFE SPAN

EDUCATION	CIVIC	HOUSING
LIBRARY	OFFICE	RELIGIOUS
INSTITUTION	COMMERCIAL
BUILDING TYPE

SKIN	CONCRETE BLOCK
	PRIMARY MATERIAL
STRUCTURE	LOAD-BEARING CONCRETE MASONRY
	SECONDARY MATERIAL
FINISH	STEEL AND GLASS
	TERTIARY MATERIAL

HOUSE AT RIVA SAN VITALE
MARIO BOTTA
TICINO
SWITZERLAND

Martin Luther King and
Robert Francis Kennedy assassinated

1968

1970
Botta opens own practice in Lugano

1971

1973

| | DOCUMENTATION | | | FORM | | | PROXIMITY | | | SKIN + SURFACE | |

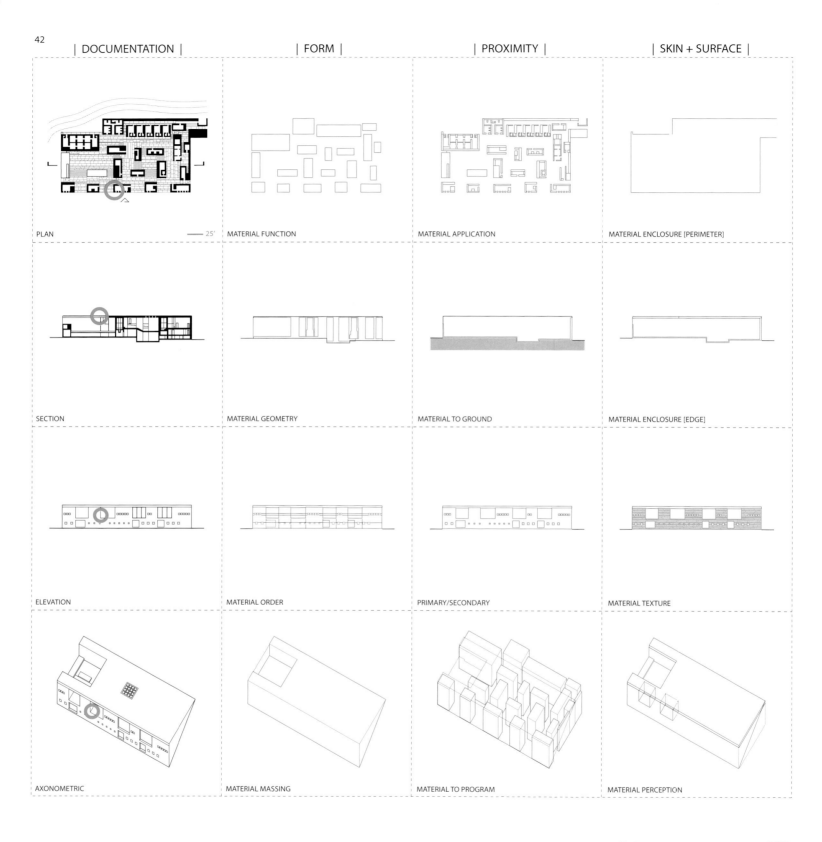

PLAN   — 25'

MATERIAL FUNCTION

MATERIAL APPLICATION

MATERIAL ENCLOSURE [PERIMETER]

SECTION

MATERIAL GEOMETRY

MATERIAL TO GROUND

MATERIAL ENCLOSURE [EDGE]

ELEVATION

MATERIAL ORDER

PRIMARY/SECONDARY

MATERIAL TEXTURE

AXONOMETRIC

MATERIAL MASSING

MATERIAL TO PROGRAM

MATERIAL PERCEPTION

Software writer Tim Berners-Lee
writes the program for the World Wide Web

The Soviet Union dissolves;
the seventy-four-year Communist reign ends

1979

1988

1990

1991

Zumthor founds Architekturbüro Peter Zumthor

Chapel of St. Benedict in Graubünden, Switzerland, is completed

| STRUCTURE | | MODULE | | DETAIL |

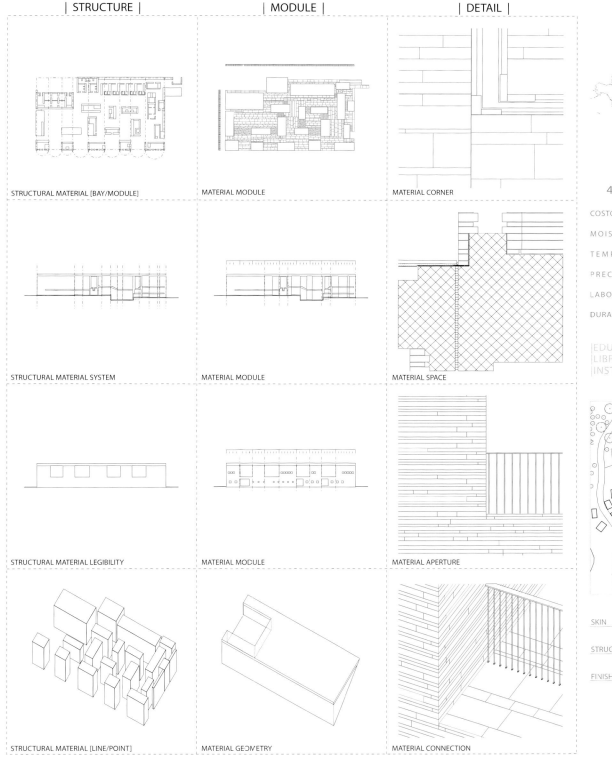

STRUCTURAL MATERIAL [BAY/MODULE]

MATERIAL MODULE

MATERIAL CORNER

STRUCTURAL MATERIAL SYSTEM

MATERIAL MODULE

MATERIAL SPACE

STRUCTURAL MATERIAL LEGIBILITY

MATERIAL MODULE

MATERIAL APERTURE

STRUCTURAL MATERIAL [LINE/POINT]

MATERIAL GEOMETRY

MATERIAL CONNECTION

WOOD

MASONRY

CONCRETE

METAL

GLASS

PLASTIC

46° 37' 18" N 9° 10' 52" E

COSTCOSTCOSTCOSTCOST COSTCOST
PER SQUARE FOOT

MOISTUREMOISTUREMOIST JRE
AVERAGE ANNUAL HUMIDITY

TEMPERATURETEMPERATURE
AVERAGE ANNUAL TEMPERATURE

PRECIPITATIONPRECIPITATION
AVERAGE ANNUAL RAINFALL

LABORLABORLABORLABORLABOR
HOURS OF LABOR FOR CONSTRUCTION

DURABILITYDURABILITYDURABILITY
EXPECTED LIFE SPAN

EDUCATION	CIVIC	HOUSING
LIBRARY	OFFICE	RELIGIOUS
INSTITUTION	COMMERCIAL
BUILDING TYPE

SKIN	VALS GNEISS
	PRIMARY MATERIAL
STRUCTURE	REINFORCED CONCRETE
	SECONDARY MATERIAL
FINISH	VALS GNEISS
	TERTIARY MATERIAL

THERMAL BATHS
PETER ZUMTHOR
VALS
SWITZERLAND

Alvaro Siza, Portugal,
wins the Pritzker Prize

1992

1993

1994
Zumthor elected to the Akademie der Künste in Berlin

1996

44

| | DOCUMENTATION | | | FORM | | | PROXIMITY | | | SKIN + SURFACE | |

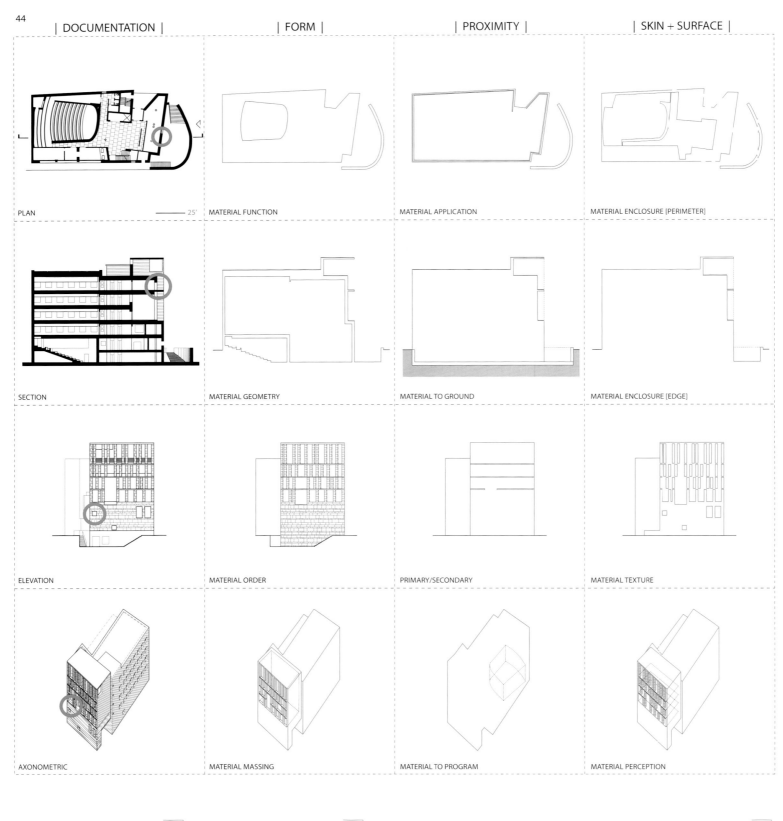

PLAN ————— 25'

SECTION

ELEVATION

AXONOMETRIC

MATERIAL FUNCTION

MATERIAL GEOMETRY

MATERIAL ORDER

MATERIAL MASSING

MATERIAL APPLICATION

MATERIAL TO GROUND

PRIMARY/SECONDARY

MATERIAL TO PROGRAM

MATERIAL ENCLOSURE [PERIMETER]

MATERIAL ENCLOSURE [EDGE]

MATERIAL TEXTURE

MATERIAL PERCEPTION

Chariots of Fire is awarded
Best Picture for the Academy Awards

1981

Internet, a global on-line network, is initiated

1983

1985
Moneo becomes architecture chairman at Harvard's GSD

McDonalds
opens in Moscow

1988

| STRUCTURE | | MODULE | | DETAIL |

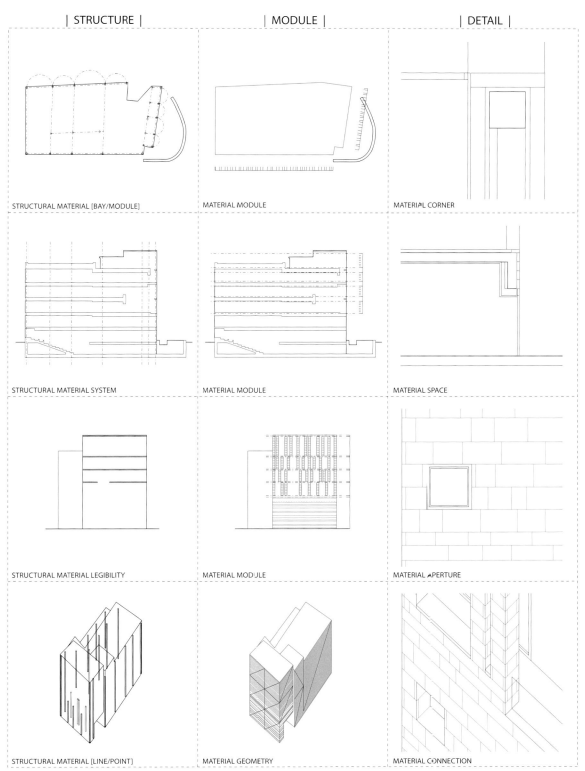

STRUCTURAL MATERIAL [BAY/MODULE]

MATERIAL MODULE

MATERIAL CORNER

STRUCTURAL MATERIAL SYSTEM

MATERIAL MODULE

MATERIAL SPACE

STRUCTURAL MATERIAL LEGIBILITY

MATERIAL MODULE

MATERIAL APERTURE

STRUCTURAL MATERIAL [LINE/POINT]

MATERIAL GEOMETRY

MATERIAL CONNECTION

WOOD

MASONRY

CONCRETE

METAL

GLASS

PLASTIC

37° 59' 2" N 1° 7' 48" W

COSTCOSTCOSTCOST COSTCOSTCOST
PER SQUARE FOOT

MOISTUREMOISTUREMOISTURE
AVERAGE ANNUAL HUMIDITY

TEMPERATURETEMPERATURE
AVERAGE ANNUAL TEMPERATURE

PRECIPITATIONPRECIPITATION
AVERAGE ANNUAL RAINFALL

LABORLABORLABORLABORLABOR
HOURS OF LABOR FOR CONSTRUCTION

DURABILITYDURABILITYDURABILITY
EXPECTED LIFE SPAN

EDUCATION	CIVIC	HOUSING
LIBRARY	OFFICE	RELIGIOUS
INSTITUTION	COMMERCIAL
BUILDING TYPE

SKIN	LUMAQUELA SANDSTONE MASONRY
	PRIMARY MATERIAL
STRUCTURE	CONCRETE PILLARS AND SLABS
	SECONDARY MATERIAL
FINISH	WOOD PANELLING
	TERTIARY MATERIAL

MURCIA TOWN HALL
RAFAEL MONEO
MURCIA
SPAIN

The reunification of
East and West Germany

1990

1991

1992
Moneo completes Miro Foundation, Barcelona

1996
Moneo receives Pritzker Prize

1998

| DOCUMENTATION | | FORM | | PROXIMITY | | SKIN + SURFACE |

PLAN   — 25'

MATERIAL FUNCTION

MATERIAL APPLICATION

MATERIAL ENCLOSURE [PERIMETER]

SECTION

MATERIAL GEOMETRY

MATERIAL TO GROUND

MATERIAL ENCLOSUFE [EDGE]

ELEVATION

MATERIAL ORDER

PRIMARY/SECONDARY

MATERIAL TEXTURE

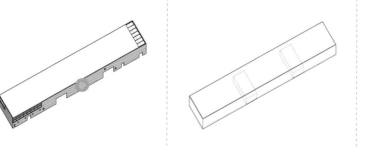

AXONOMETRIC

MATERIAL MASSING

MATERIAL TO PROGRAM

MATERIAL PERCEPTION

Six Memos For the Next Millenium,
by Italo Calvino, published

The Eurotunnel, also known as the Chunnel,
connecting England and France beneath
the English Channel, is officially opened

1978

Herzog & de Meuron Architekten is founded

1993

1994

| STRUCTURE | | MODULE | | DETAIL | |

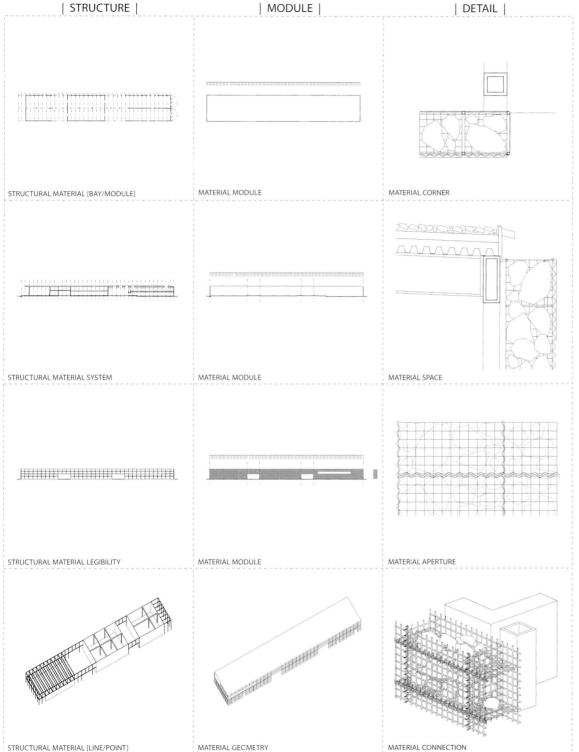

STRUCTURAL MATERIAL [BAY/MODULE]

MATERIAL MODULE

MATERIAL CORNER

STRUCTURAL MATERIAL SYSTEM

MATERIAL MODULE

MATERIAL SPACE

STRUCTURAL MATERIAL LEGIBILITY

MATERIAL MODULE

MATERIAL APERTURE

STRUCTURAL MATERIAL [LINE/POINT]

MATERIAL GECMETRY

MATERIAL CONNECTION

WOOD

MASONRY

CONCRETE

METAL

GLASS

PLASTIC

38° 24' 18" N 122° 22' 26' W

COSTCOSTCOSTCOST COSTCOSTCOST
PER SQUARE FOOT

MOISTUREMOISTUREMOISTURE
AVERAGE ANNUAL HUMIDITY

TEMPERATURETEMPERATURE
AVERAGE ANNUAL TEMPERATURE

PRECIPITATIONPRECIPITATION
AVERAGE ANNUAL RAINFALL

LABORLABORLABORLABORLABOR
HOURS OF LABOR FOR CONSTRUCTION

DURABILITYDURABILITYDURABILITY
EXPECTED LIFE SPAN

EDUCATION	CIVIC	HOUSING
LIBRARY	OFFICE	RELIGIOUS
INSTITUTION	COMMERCIAL
BUILDING TYPE

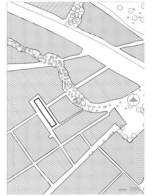

SKIN — GABION CLADDING ON STEEL TUBE FRAME
PRIMARY MATERIAL

STRUCTURE — STEEL AND REINFORCED CAST-IN-PLACE CONCRETE
SECONDARY MATERIAL

FINISH — STEEL AND GLASS
TERTIARY MATERIAL

DOMINUS WINERY
HERZOG & DE MEURON
YOUNTVILLE, CALIFORNIA

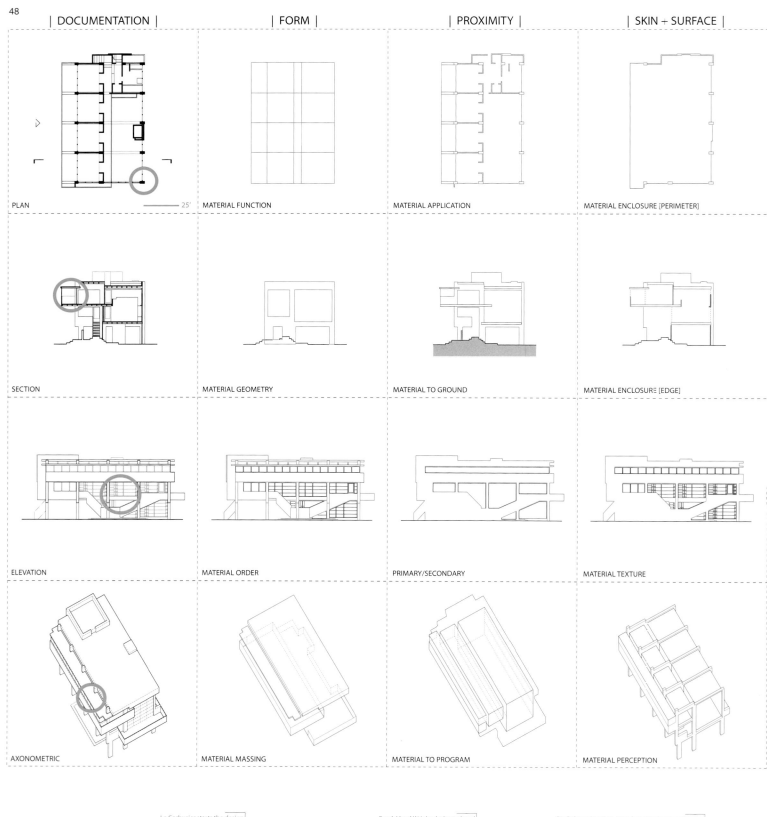

	DOCUMENTATION			FORM			PROXIMITY			SKIN + SURFACE	
PLAN — 25'	MATERIAL FUNCTION	MATERIAL APPLICATION	MATERIAL ENCLOSURE [PERIMETER]
SECTION	MATERIAL GEOMETRY	MATERIAL TO GROUND	MATERIAL ENCLOSURE [EDGE]
ELEVATION	MATERIAL ORDER	PRIMARY/SECONDARY	MATERIAL TEXTURE
AXONOMETRIC	MATERIAL MASSING	MATERIAL TO PROGRAM	MATERIAL PERCEPTION

1912

Schindler meets lifelong friend and rival
Richard Neutra at Vienna Polytechnic University

Le Corbusier starts the design
project for Domino house

1914

Frank Lloyd Wright designs glazed
porcelain china for the Imperial Hotel

1916

Daylight saving time introduced in the United States

1918

| STRUCTURE | | MODULE | | DETAIL |

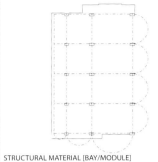

STRUCTURAL MATERIAL [BAY/MODULE]

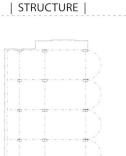

MATERIAL MODULE

MATERIAL CORNER

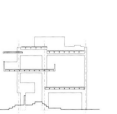

STRUCTURAL MATERIAL SYSTEM

MATERIAL MODULE

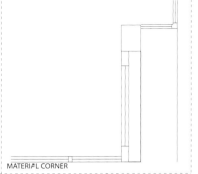

MATERIAL SPACE

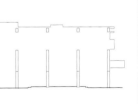

STRUCTURAL MATERIAL LEGIBILITY

MATERIAL MODULE

MATERIAL APERTURE

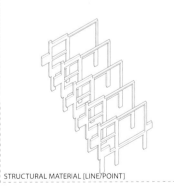

STRUCTURAL MATERIAL [LINE/POINT]

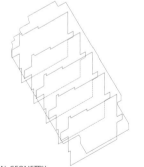

MATERIAL GEOMETRY

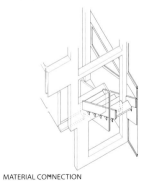

MATERIAL CONNECTION

33° 36′ 21″ N 117° 55′ 4″ W

COSTCOSTCOSTCOST COSTCOSTCOST
PER SQUARE FOOT

MOISTUREMOISTUREMOISTURE
AVERAGE ANNUAL HUMIDITY

TEMPERATURETEMPERATURE
AVERAGE ANNUAL TEMPERATURE

PRECIPITATIONPRECIPITATION
AVERAGE ANNUAL RAINFALL

LABORLABORLABORLABORLABOR
HOURS OF LABOR FOR CONSTRUCTION

DURABILITYDURABILITYDURABILITY
EXPECTED LIFE SPAN

EDUCATION	CIVIC	HOUSING
LIBRARY	OFFICE	RELIGIOUS
INSTITUTION	COMMERCIAL
BUILDING TYPE

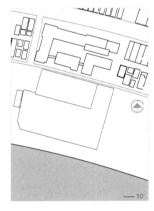

SKIN   CAST-IN-PLACE CONCRETE
                      PRIMARY MATERIAL

STRUCTURE CAST-IN-PLACE CONCRETE
                      SECONDARY MATERIAL

FINISH   GLASS
                      TERTIARY MATERIAL

LOVELL BEACH HOUSE
R.M. SCHINDLER
ORANGE COUNTY, CALIFORNIA

1920
Wright summons Schindler to Los Angeles
to work on the Barnsdall House

1922

1922
Schindler completes Schindler House, West Hollywood, CA

1926

| DOCUMENTATION | | FORM | | PROXIMITY | | SKIN + SURFACE |

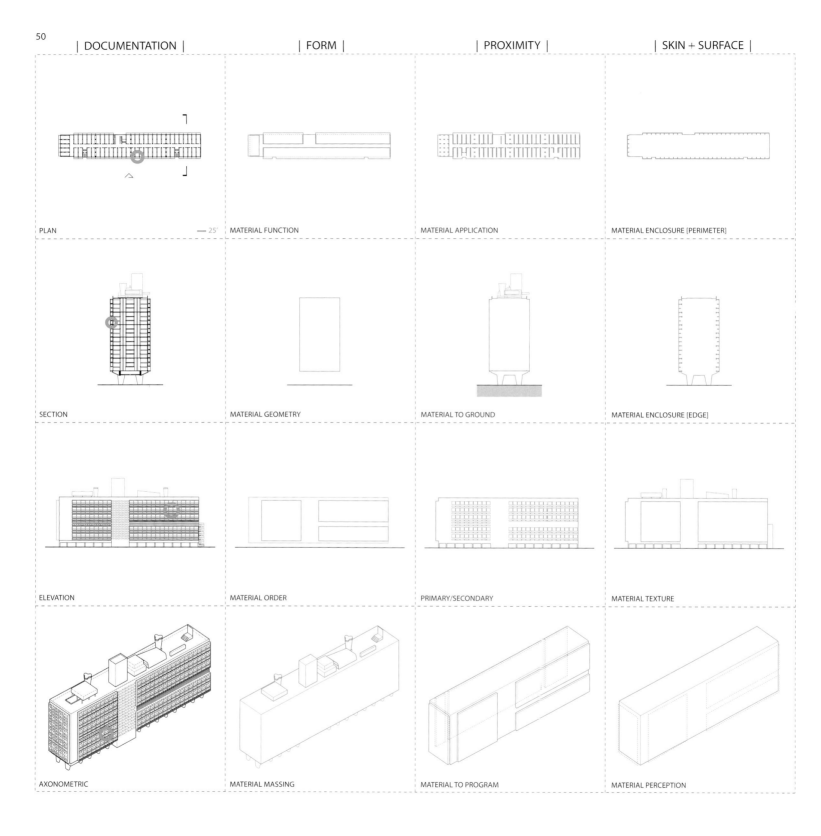

PLAN — 25'	MATERIAL FUNCTION	MATERIAL APPLICATION	MATERIAL ENCLOSURE [PERIMETER]
SECTION	MATERIAL GEOMETRY	MATERIAL TO GROUND	MATERIAL ENCLOSURE [EDGE]
ELEVATION	MATERIAL ORDER	PRIMARY/SECONDARY	MATERIAL TEXTURE
AXONOMETRIC	MATERIAL MASSING	MATERIAL TO PROGRAM	MATERIAL PERCEPTION

1928

Villa Savoye in Poissy-sur-Seine, France, is completed

Peter Carl Goldmark invents and demonstrates the first successful color television system

1940

Ayn Rand's *The Fountainhead* is published

1943

| STRUCTURE | | MODULE | | DETAIL |

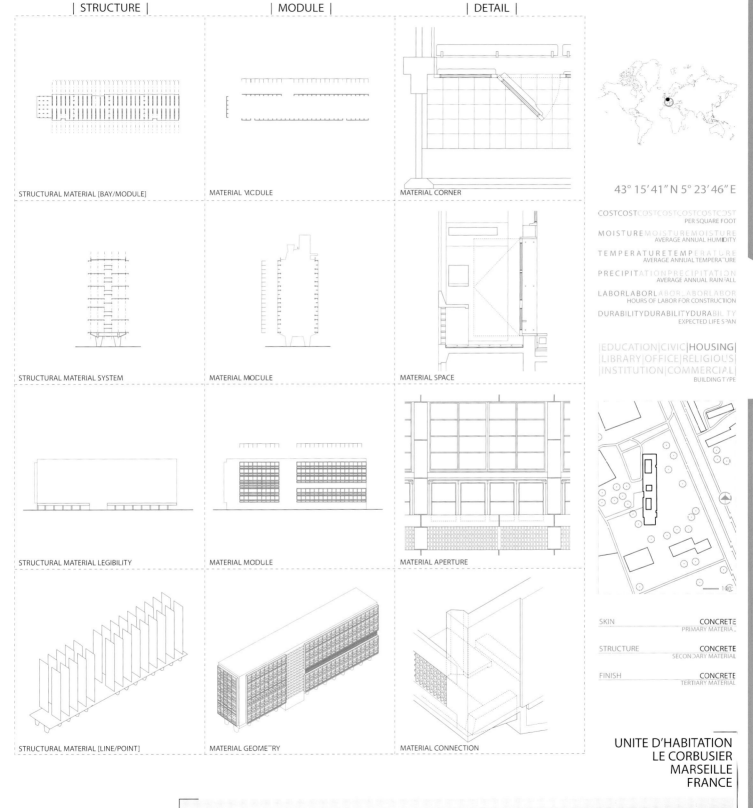

STRUCTURAL MATERIAL [BAY/MODULE]

MATERIAL MODULE

MATERIAL CORNER

STRUCTURAL MATERIAL SYSTEM

MATERIAL MODULE

MATERIAL SPACE

STRUCTURAL MATERIAL LEGIBILITY

MATERIAL MODULE

MATERIAL APERTURE

STRUCTURAL MATERIAL [LINE/POINT]

MATERIAL GEOMETRY

MATERIAL CONNECTION

WOOD

MASONRY

CONCRETE

METAL

GLASS

PLASTIC

43° 15' 41" N 5° 23' 46" E

COSTCOST COSTCOSTCOSTCOSTCOST
PER SQUARE FOOT

MOISTURE MOISTUREMOISTURE
AVERAGE ANNUAL HUMIDITY

TEMPERATURETEMPERATURE
AVERAGE ANNUAL TEMPERATURE

PRECIPITATION PRECIPITATION
AVERAGE ANNUAL RAINFALL

LABORLABORLABOR LABORLABOR
HOURS OF LABOR FOR CONSTRUCTION

DURABILITYDURABILITYDURABILITY
EXPECTED LIFE SPAN

EDUCATION	CIVIC	HOUSING
LIBRARY	OFFICE	RELIGIOUS
INSTITUTION	COMMERCIAL
BUILDING TYPE

SKIN   **CONCRETE**
PRIMARY MATERIAL

STRUCTURE   **CONCRETE**
SECONDARY MATERIAL

FINISH   **CONCRETE**
TERTIARY MATERIAL

UNITE D'HABITATION
LE CORBUSIER
MARSEILLE
FRANCE

1946

1948
Corbusier publishes *Le Modulor* (The Modulor)

1952

| DOCUMENTATION | | FORM | | PROXIMITY | | SKIN + SURFACE |

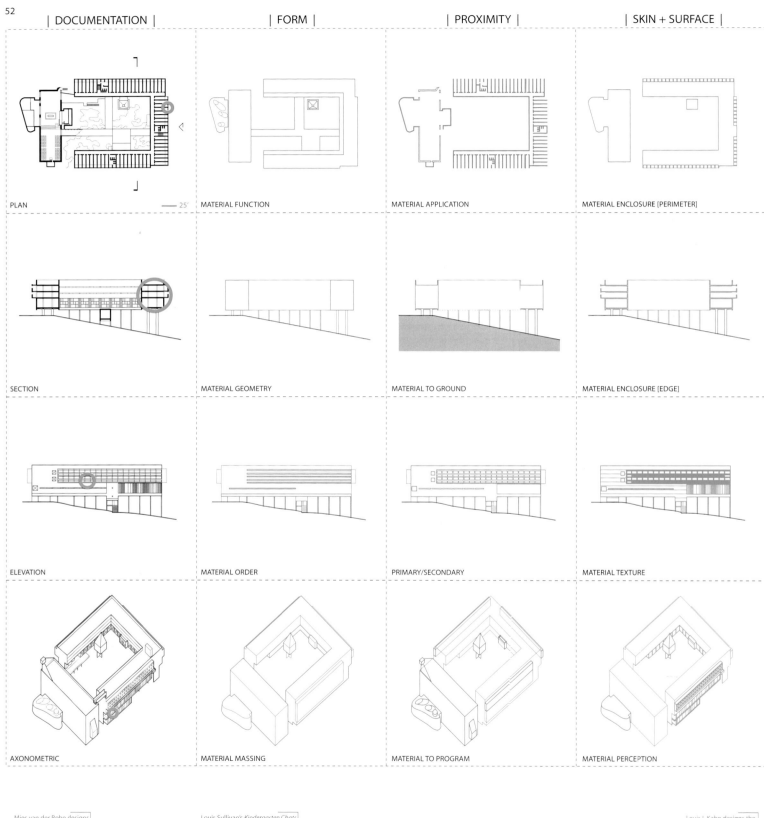

PLAN ———— 25'

MATERIAL FUNCTION

MATERIAL APPLICATION

MATERIAL ENCLOSURE [PERIMETER]

SECTION

MATERIAL GEOMETRY

MATERIAL TO GROUND

MATERIAL ENCLOSURE [EDGE]

ELEVATION

MATERIAL ORDER

PRIMARY/SECONDARY

MATERIAL TEXTURE

AXONOMETRIC

MATERIAL MASSING

MATERIAL TO PROGRAM

MATERIAL PERCEPTION

Mies van der Rohe designs
the Alumni Memorial Hall, IIT

Louis Sullivan's *Kindergarten Chats*
reedited and published

1950

Louis I. Kahn designs the
Yale University Art Gallery, New Haven

1946

1948

Le Corbusier designs
Notre Dame du Haut, Ronchamp

1952

| STRUCTURE | | MODULE | | DETAIL |

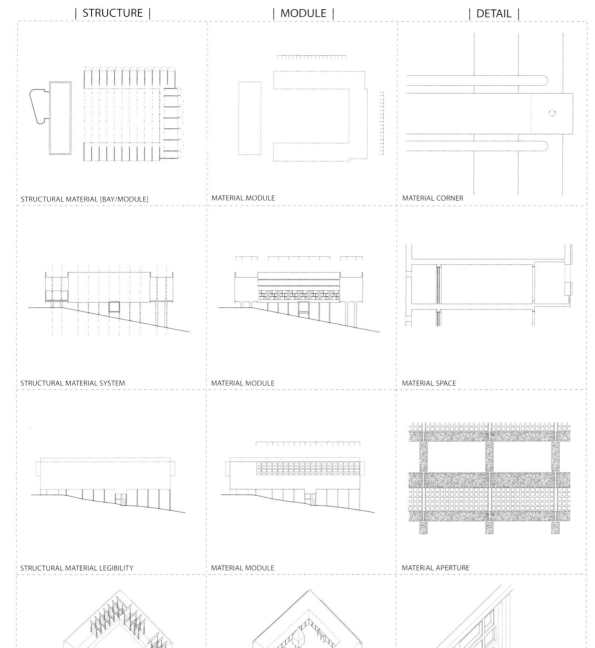

STRUCTURAL MATERIAL [BAY/MODULE]

MATERIAL MODULE

MATERIAL CORNER

STRUCTURAL MATERIAL SYSTEM

MATERIAL MODULE

MATERIAL SPACE

STRUCTURAL MATERIAL LEGIBILITY

MATERIAL MODULE

MATERIAL APERTURE

STRUCTURAL MATERIAL [LINE/POINT]

MATERIAL GEOMETRY

MATERIAL CONNECTION

WOOD

MASONRY

CONCRETE

METAL

GLASS

PLASTIC

45° 49' 10" N 4° 37' 22" E

COSTCOSTCOSTCOSTCOST COSTCOST
PER SQUARE FOOT

MOISTUREMOISTUREMOISTURE
AVERAGE ANNUAL HUMIDITY

TEMPERATURETEMPERATURE
AVERAGE ANNUAL TEMPERATURE

PRECIPITATIONPRECIPITATION
AVERAGE ANNUAL RAINFALL

LABORLABORLABORLABORLAEOR
HOURS OF LABOR FOR CONSTRUCTION

DURABILITYDURABILITYDURABILITY
EXPECTED LIFE SPAN

EDUCATION	CIVIC	HOUSING
LIBRARY	OFFICE	RELIGIOUS
INSTITUTION	COMMERCIAL
BUILDING TYPE

SKIN	CONCRETE
	PRIMARY MATERIAL
STRUCTURE	CONCRETE
	SECONDARY MATERIAL
FINISH	GLASS
	TERTIARY MATERIAL

CONVENT DE LA TOURETTE
LE CORBUSIER
EVEUX-SUR-ARBRESLE
FRANCE

Charles and Ray Eames design their
"Eames Sofa Compact" for Herman Miller

1954

1956

1960

54

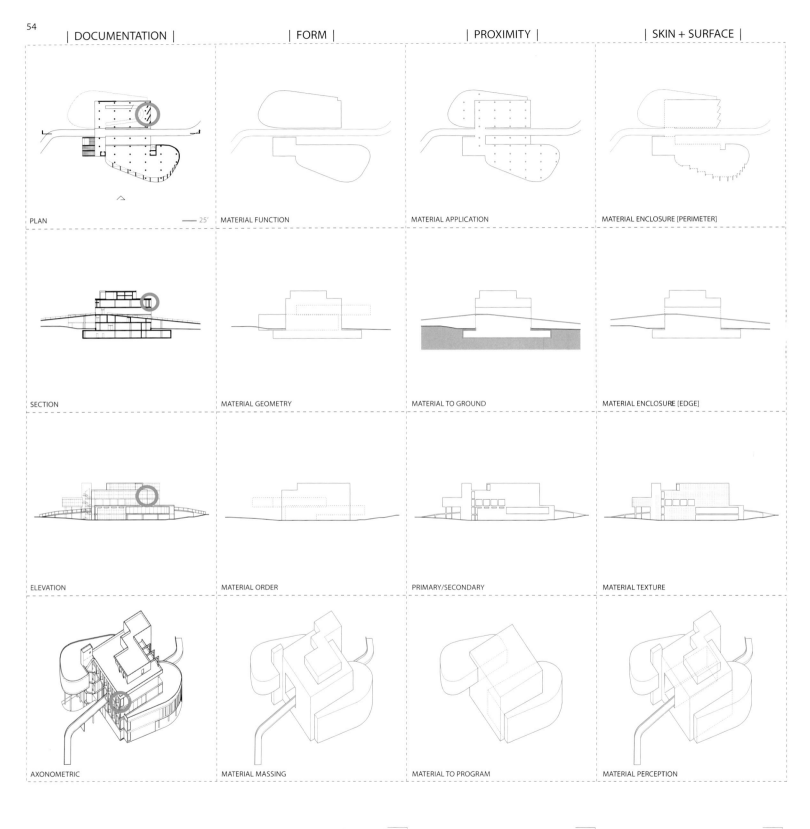

PLAN — 25'   MATERIAL FUNCTION   MATERIAL APPLICATION   MATERIAL ENCLOSURE [PERIMETER]

SECTION   MATERIAL GEOMETRY   MATERIAL TO GROUND   MATERIAL ENCLOSURE [EDGE]

ELEVATION   MATERIAL ORDER   PRIMARY/SECONDARY   MATERIAL TEXTURE

AXONOMETRIC   MATERIAL MASSING   MATERIAL TO PROGRAM   MATERIAL PERCEPTION

The "Space Age" begins   Poul Henningsen designs the "Artichoke" lamp   Walter Gropius wins the AIA Gold Medal

1955
Corbusier publishes *Le Modulor 2 (The Modulor 2)*   1957   1958   1959

| STRUCTURE | | MODULE | | DETAIL |

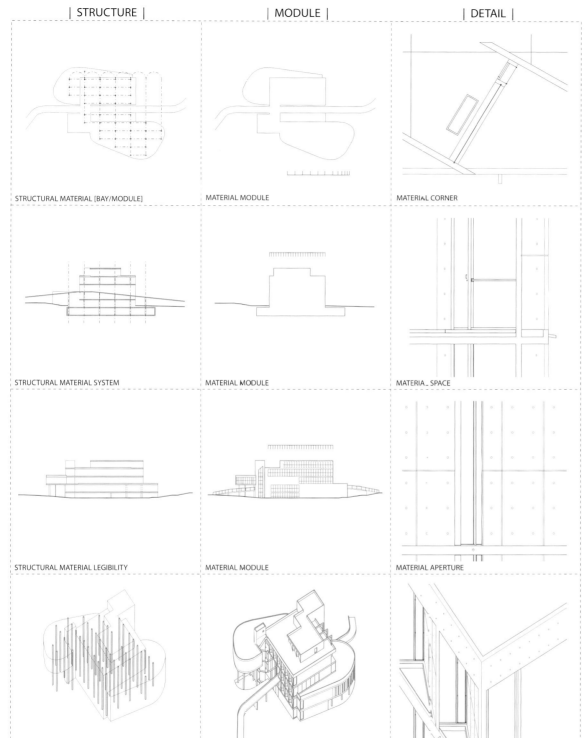

STRUCTURAL MATERIAL [BAY/MODULE]

MATERIAL MODULE

MATERIAL CORNER

STRUCTURAL MATERIAL SYSTEM

MATERIAL MODULE

MATERIAL SPACE

STRUCTURAL MATERIAL LEGIBILITY

MATERIAL MODULE

MATERIAL APERTURE

STRUCTURAL MATERIAL [LINE/POINT]

MATERIAL GEOMETRY

MATERIAL CONNECTION

WOOD
MASONRY
CONCRETE
METAL
GLASS
PLASTIC

42° 22' 25" N 71° 6' 52" W

COSTCOSTCOSTCOST COSTCOSTCOST
PER SQUARE FOOT

MOISTUREMOISTURE MOISTURE
AVERAGE ANNUAL HUMIDITY

TEMPERA URE TEMPERATURE
AVERAGE ANNUAL TEMPERATURE

PRECIPITATIONPRECIPITATION
AVERAGE ANNUAL RAINFALL

LABORLABORLABORLA BORLABOR
HOURS OF LABOR FOR CONSTRUCTION

DURABILITYDURABILITYDURABILITY
EXPECTED LIFE SPAN

EDUCATION	CIVIC	HOUSING
LIBRARY	OFFICE	RELIGIOUS
INSTITUTION	COMMERCIAL
BUILDING TYPE

SKIN   CAST-IN-PLACE CONCRETE
PRIMARY MATERIAL

STRUCTURE   REINFORCED CONCRETE
SECONDARY MATERIAL

FINISH   CAST-IN-PLACE CONCRETE
TERTIARY MATERIAL

CARPENTER CENTER
LE CORBUSIER
CAMBRIDGE, MASSACHUSETTS

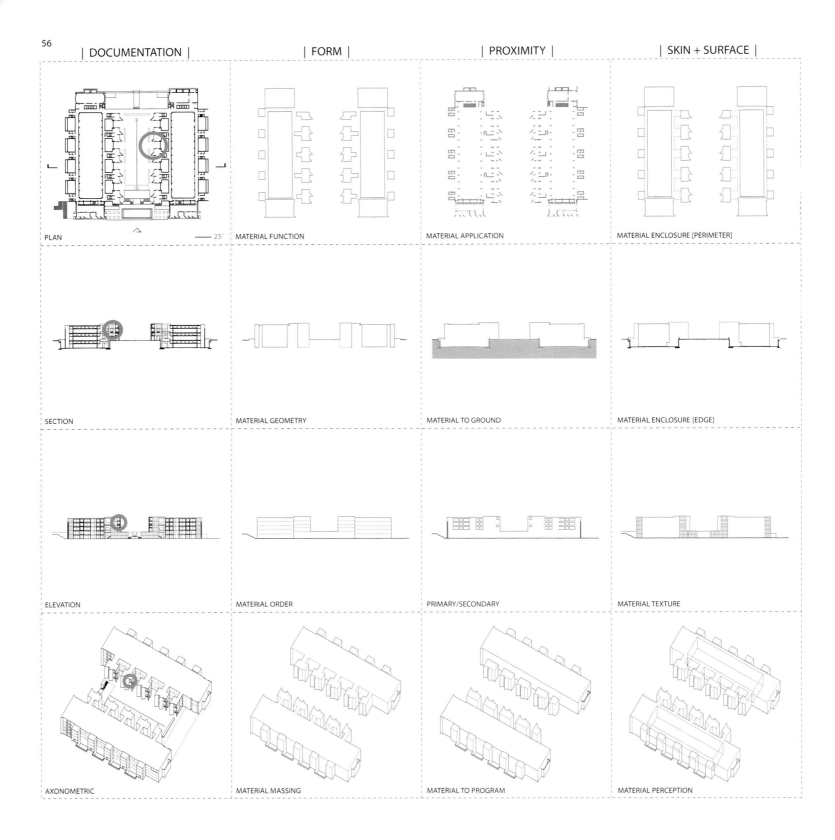

| DOCUMENTATION | | FORM | | PROXIMITY | | SKIN + SURFACE |

PLAN — 25'

MATERIAL FUNCTION

MATERIAL APPLICATION

MATERIAL ENCLOSURE [PERIMETER]

SECTION

MATERIAL GEOMETRY

MATERIAL TO GROUND

MATERIAL ENCLOSURE [EDGE]

ELEVATION

MATERIAL ORDER

PRIMARY/SECONDARY

MATERIAL TEXTURE

AXONOMETRIC

MATERIAL MASSING

MATERIAL TO PROGRAM

MATERIAL PERCEPTION

The start of the "Pop" design
period (1958-1972)

1947-1957
Kahn serves as design critic and professor
of architecture at Yale School of Architecture

1957
Kahn serves as professor of architecture
at the School of Design at the University of Pennsylvania

1958

| STRUCTURE | | MODULE | | DETAIL |

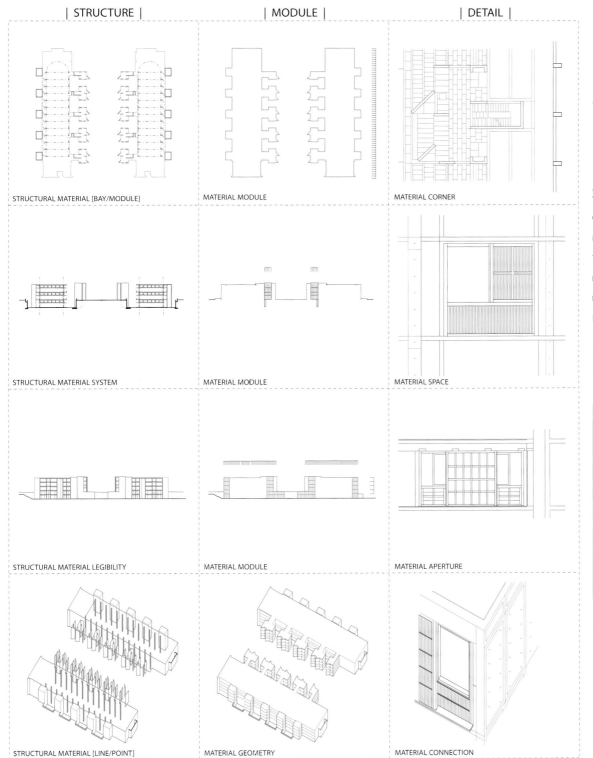

STRUCTURAL MATERIAL [BAY/MODULE]

MATERIAL MODULE

MATERIAL CORNER

STRUCTURAL MATERIAL SYSTEM

MATERIAL MODULE

MATERIAL SPACE

STRUCTURAL MATERIAL LEGIBILITY

MATERIAL MODULE

MATERIAL APERTURE

STRUCTURAL MATERIAL [LINE/POINT]

MATERIAL GEOMETRY

MATERIAL CONNECTION

32° 53' 14" N 117° 14' 46" W

COSTCOSTCOSTCOSTCOSTCOSTCOST
PER SQUARE FOOT

MOISTUREMOISTUREMOISTURE
AVERAGE ANNUAL HUMIDITY

TEMPERATURETEMPERATURE
AVERAGE ANNUAL TEMPERATURE

PRECIPITATIONPRECIPITATION
AVERAGE ANNUAL RAINFALL

LABORLABORLABORLABORLABOR
HOURS OF LABOR FOR CONSTRUCTION

DURABILITYDURABILITYDURABILITY
EXPECTED LIFE SPAN

EDUCATION	CIVIC	HOUSING
LIBRARY	OFFICE	RELIGIOUS
INSTITUTION	COMMERCIAL
BUILDING TYPE

SKIN — CONCRETE AND TEAK
PRIMARY MATERIAL

STRUCTURE — REINFORCED CONCRETE AND VIERENDEEL TRUSS
SECONDARY MATERIAL

FINISH — WOOD AND CONCRETE
TERTIARY MATERIAL

**SALK INSTITUTE OF
BIOLOGICAL SCIENCES
LOUIS I. KAHN
LA JOLLA, CALIFORNIA**

WOOD / MASONRY / CONCRETE / METAL / GLASS / PLASTIC

1959

1966

| DOCUMENTATION | | FORM | | PROXIMITY | | SKIN + SURFACE |

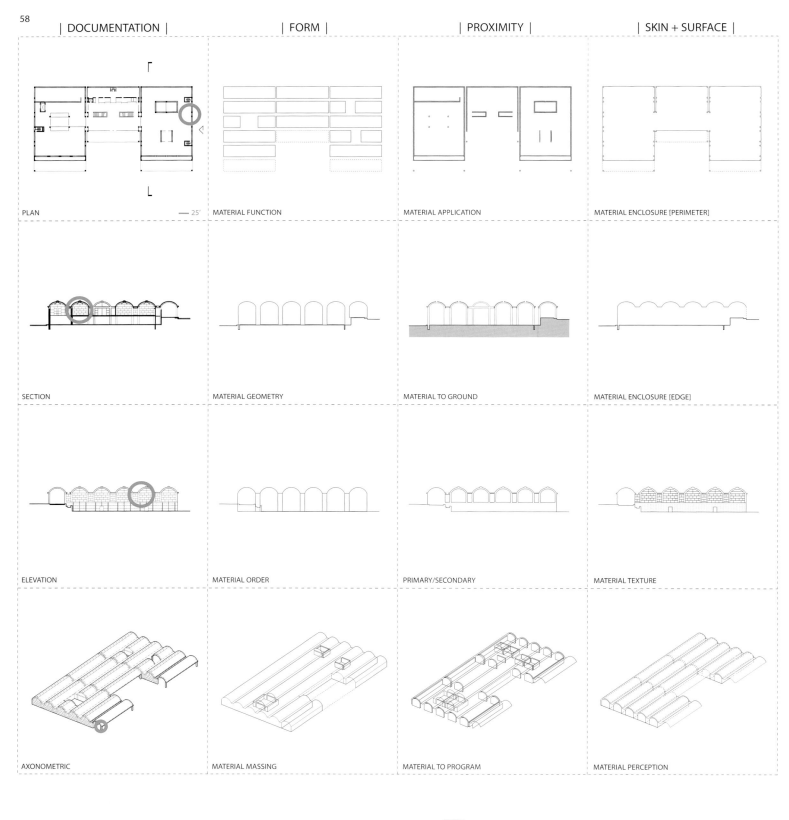

PLAN —— 25'	MATERIAL FUNCTION	MATERIAL APPLICATION	MATERIAL ENCLOSURE [PERIMETER]
SECTION	MATERIAL GEOMETRY	MATERIAL TO GROUND	MATERIAL ENCLOSURE [EDGE]
ELEVATION	MATERIAL ORDER	PRIMARY/SECONDARY	MATERIAL TEXTURE
AXONOMETRIC	MATERIAL MASSING	MATERIAL TO PROGRAM	MATERIAL PERCEPTION

1962
Construction for National Assembly in Dhaka, Bangladesh, begins

Pier Luigi Nervi, Rome,
wins the AIA Gold Medal
1964

1965
Salk Institute in La Jolla, California, is completed

STRUCTURE		MODULE		DETAIL

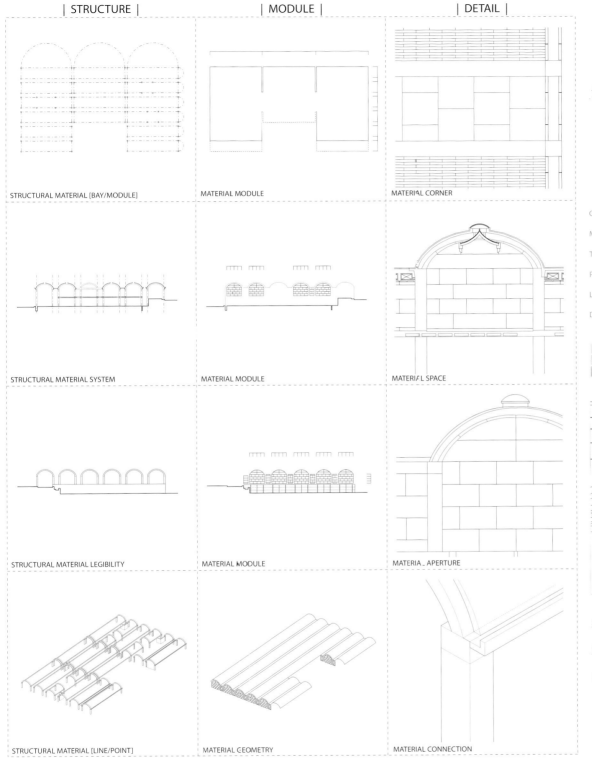

STRUCTURAL MATERIAL [BAY/MODULE]

MATERIAL MODULE

MATERIAL CORNER

STRUCTURAL MATERIAL SYSTEM

MATERIAL MODULE

MATERIAL SPACE

STRUCTURAL MATERIAL LEGIBILITY

MATERIAL MODULE

MATERIAL APERTURE

STRUCTURAL MATERIAL [LINE/POINT]

MATERIAL GEOMETRY

MATERIAL CONNECTION

WOOD

MASONRY

CONCRETE

METAL

GLASS

PLASTIC

32° 44′ 55″ N 97° 21′ 54″ W

COSTCOSTCOSTCOSTCOSTCOSTCOST
PER SQUARE FOOT

MOISTUREMOISTUREMOISTURE
AVERAGE ANNUAL HUMIDITY

TEMPERATURETEMPERATURE
AVERAGE ANNUAL TEMPERATURE

PRECIPITATIONPRECIPITATION
AVERAGE ANNUAL RAINFALL

LABORLABORLABORLABORLABOR
HOURS OF LABOR FOR CONSTRUCTION

DURABILITYDURABILITYDURABILITY
EXPECTED LIFE SPAN

|EDUCATION|CIVIC|HOUSING
|LIBRARY|OFFICE|RELIGIOUS
|INSTITUTION|COMMERCIAL|
BUILDING TYPE

SKIN   CONCRETE
PRIMARY MATERIAL

STRUCTURE   REINFORCED CONCRETE
SECONDARY MATERIAL

FINISH   WOOD, CONCRETE AND GLASS
TERTIARY MATERIAL

KIMBELL ART MUSEUM
LOUIS I. KAHN
FORT WORTH, TEXAS

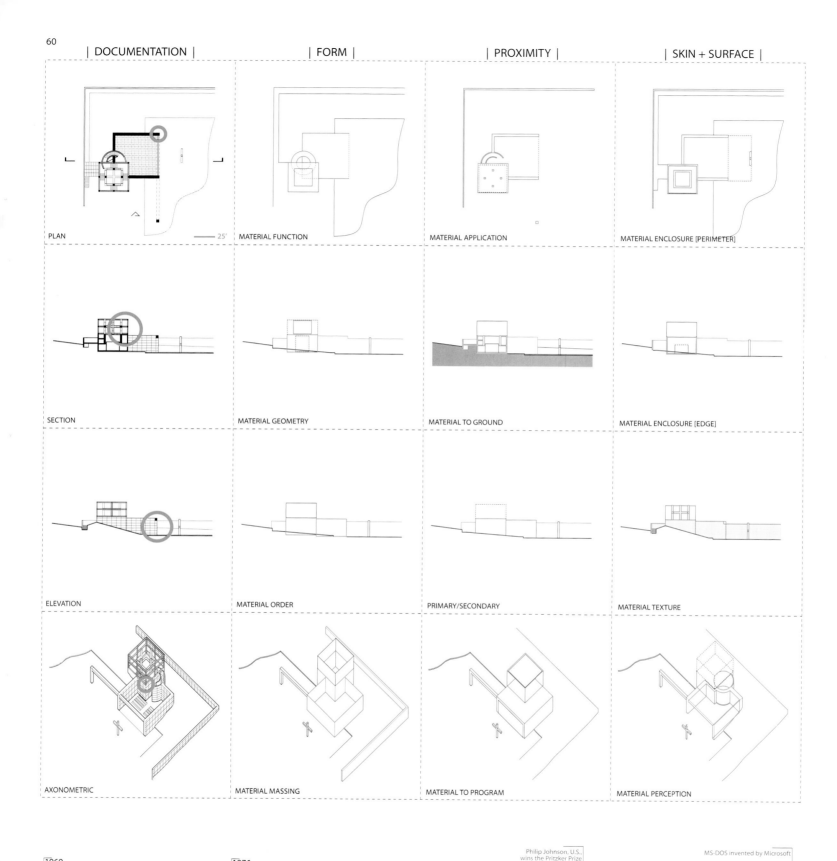

| DOCUMENTATION | | FORM | | PROXIMITY | | SKIN + SURFACE | |

PLAN — 25'

MATERIAL FUNCTION

MATERIAL APPLICATION

MATERIAL ENCLOSURE [PERIMETER]

SECTION

MATERIAL GEOMETRY

MATERIAL TO GROUND

MATERIAL ENCLOSURE [EDGE]

ELEVATION

MATERIAL ORDER

PRIMARY/SECONDARY

MATERIAL TEXTURE

AXONOMETRIC

MATERIAL MASSING

MATERIAL TO PROGRAM

MATERIAL PERCEPTION

1969
Ando establishes Tadao Ando Architects & Associates

1976
Ando completes Azuma House

Philip Johnson, U.S., wins the Pritzker Prize

1979

MS-DOS invented by Microsoft

1981

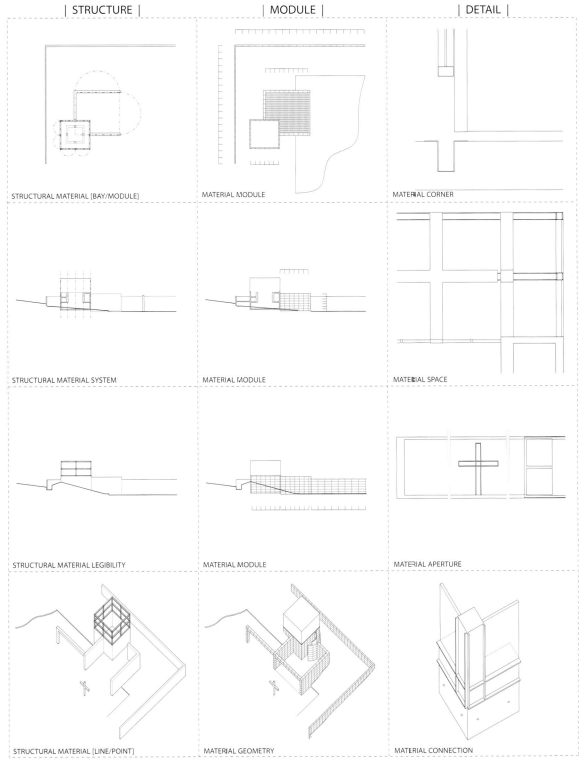

STRUCTURE	MODULE	DETAIL
STRUCTURAL MATERIAL [BAY/MODULE]	MATERIAL MODULE	MATERIAL CORNER
STRUCTURAL MATERIAL SYSTEM	MATERIAL MODULE	MATERIAL SPACE
STRUCTURAL MATERIAL LEGIBILITY	MATERIAL MODULE	MATERIAL APERTURE
STRUCTURAL MATERIAL [LINE/POINT]	MATERIAL GEOMETRY	MATERIAL CONNECTION

43° 3' 43" N 142° 37' 34" E

COSTCOSTCOSTCOSTCOSTCOSTCOST
PER SQUARE FOOT

MOISTUREMOISTUREMOISTURE
AVERAGE ANNUAL HUMIDITY

TEMPERATURETEMPERATURE
AVERAGE ANNUAL TEMPERATURE

PRECIPITATIONPRECIPITATION
AVERAGE ANNUAL RAINFALL

LABORLABORLABORLABORLABOR
HOURS OF LABOR FOR CONSTRUCTION

DURABILITYDURABILITYDURABILITY
EXPECTED LIFE SPAN

EDUCATION	CIVIC	HOUSING
LIBRARY	OFFICE	RELIGIOUS
INSTITUTION	COMMERCIAL
BUILDING TYPE

SKIN	CAST-IN-PLACE CONCRETE
	PRIMARY MATERIAL
STRUCTURE	CAST-IN-PLACE CONCRETE
	SECONDARY MATERIAL
FINISH	GLASS
	TERTIARY MATERIAL

CHURCH ON THE WATER
TADAO ANDO
HOKKAIDO
JAPAN

61

WOOD
MASONRY
CONCRETE
METAL
GLASS
PLASTIC

I.M. Pei, U.S., wins the Pritzker Prize

1983

1985

1985
Ando receives Alvar Aalto Medal

1988

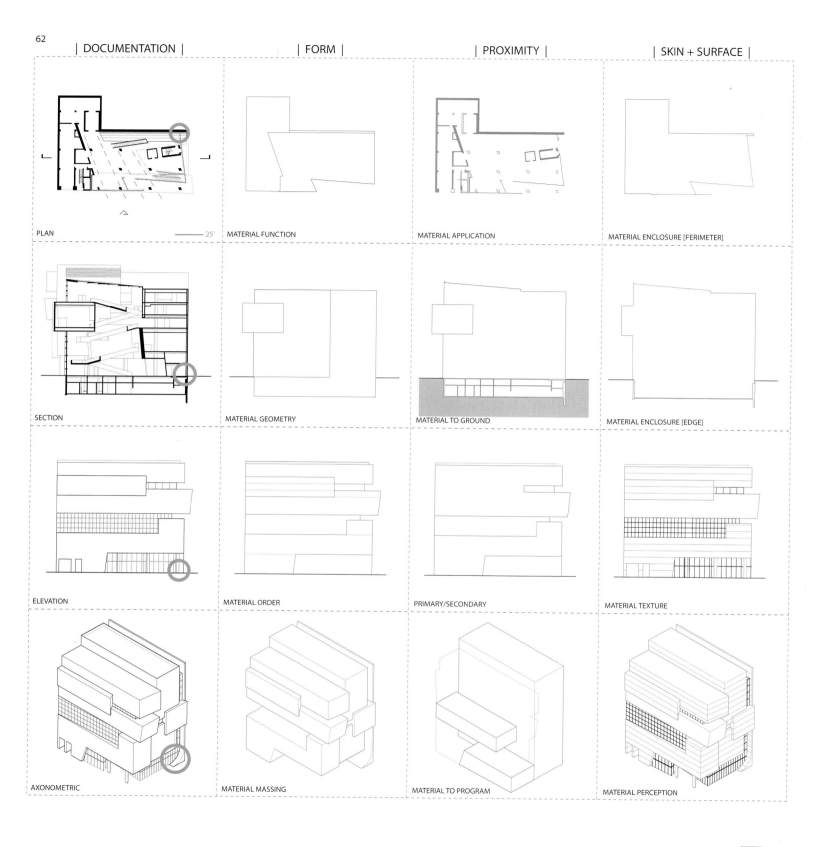

DOCUMENTATION	FORM	PROXIMITY	SKIN + SURFACE
PLAN	MATERIAL FUNCTION	MATERIAL APPLICATION	MATERIAL ENCLOSURE [FERIMETER]
SECTION	MATERIAL GEOMETRY	MATERIAL TO GROUND	MATERIAL ENCLOSURE [EDGE]
ELEVATION	MATERIAL ORDER	PRIMARY/SECONDARY	MATERIAL TEXTURE
AXONOMETRIC	MATERIAL MASSING	MATERIAL TO PROGRAM	MATERIAL PERCEPTION

25'

1977
Hadid becomes partner at Office for Metropolitan Architecture (OMA)

1980
Hadid establishes Zaha Hadid Architects

Sverre Fehn, Norway, wins the Pritzker Prize
1997

| STRUCTURE | | MODULE | | DETAIL |

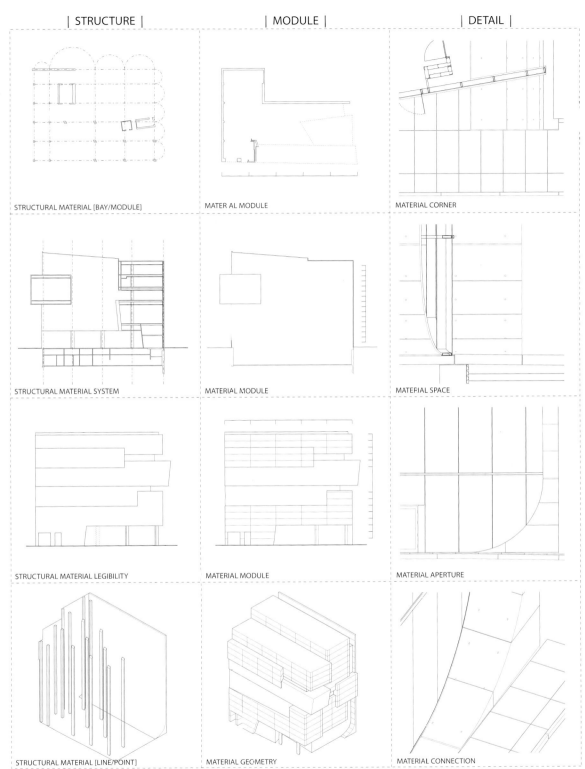

STRUCTURAL MATERIAL [BAY/MODULE]

MATERIAL MODULE

MATERIAL CORNER

STRUCTURAL MATERIAL SYSTEM

MATERIAL MODULE

MATERIAL SPACE

STRUCTURAL MATERIAL LEGIBILITY

MATERIAL MODULE

MATERIAL APERTURE

STRUCTURAL MATERIAL [LINE/POINT]

MATERIAL GEOMETRY

MATERIAL CONNECTION

WOOD
MASONRY
CONCRETE
METAL
GLASS
PLASTIC

39° 6' 11" N 84° 30' 44" W

COSTCOSTCOSTCOSTCOSTCOSTCOST
PER SQUARE FOOT

MOISTUREMOISTUREMOISTURE
AVERAGE ANNUAL HUMIDITY

TEMPERATURETEMPERATURE
AVERAGE ANNUAL TEMPERATURE

PRECIPITATIONPRECIPITATION
AVERAGE ANNUAL RAINFALL

LABORLABORLABORLABORLABOR
HOURS OF LABOR FOR CONSTRUCTION

DURABILITYDURABILITYDURABILITY
EXPECTED LIFE SPAN

EDUCATION	CIVIC	HOUSING
LIBRARY	OFFICE	RELIGIOUS
INSTITUTION	COMMERCIAL
BUILDING TYPE

SKIN	CONCRETE, GLASS AND ALUMINUM
	PRIMARY MATERIAL
STRUCTURE	REINFORCED CONCRETE
	SECONDARY MATERIAL
FINISH	CONCRETE, GLASS AND ALUMINUM
	TERTIARY MATERIAL

ROSENTHAL CENTER
FOR CONTEMPORARY ART
ZAHA HADID
CINCINNATI, OHIO

Euro, the new European currency, is introduced

1999

Rem Koolhaas, the Netherlands, wins the Pritzker Prize

2000

2001

2001
Hadid receives special mention for Equerre d'argent Prize

2003

| | DOCUMENTATION | | | FORM | | | PROXIMITY | | | SKIN + SURFACE | |

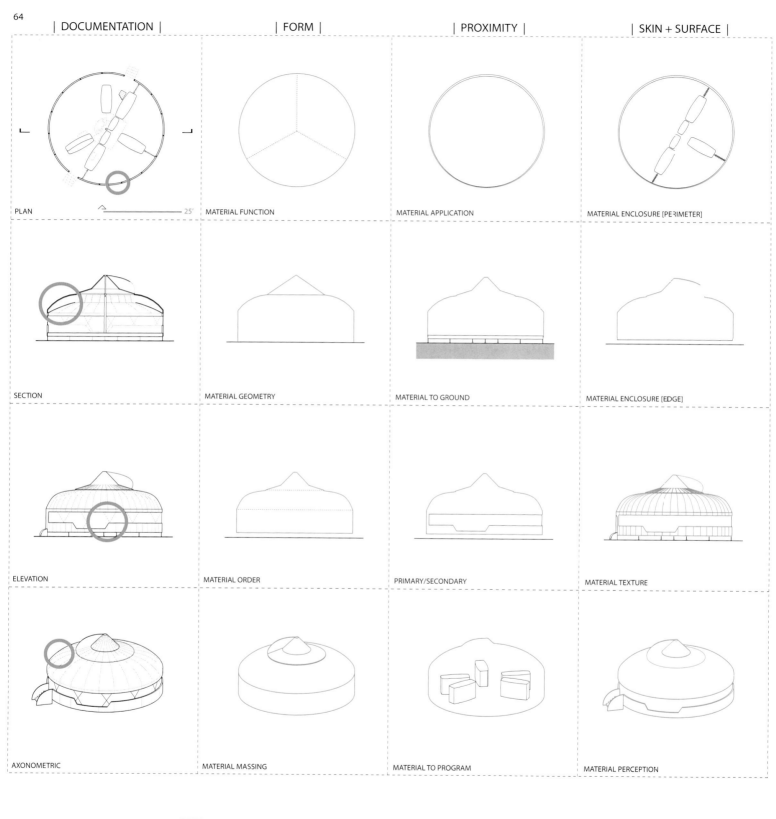

PLAN 25'	MATERIAL FUNCTION	MATERIAL APPLICATION	MATERIAL ENCLOSURE [PERIMETER]
SECTION	MATERIAL GEOMETRY	MATERIAL TO GROUND	MATERIAL ENCLOSURE [EDGE]
ELEVATION	MATERIAL ORDER	PRIMARY/SECONDARY	MATERIAL TEXTURE
AXONOMETRIC	MATERIAL MASSING	MATERIAL TO PROGRAM	MATERIAL PERCEPTION

The "Atomic Age" begins

1942

Le Corbusier publishes
Urbanisme des CIAM, la Charte d'Athenes

1943

D-Day: the Allies land
in Normandy on June 6

1944

| STRUCTURE | | MODULE | | DETAIL |

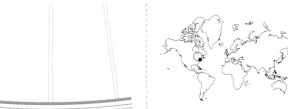

42° 18' 13" N 83° 14' 3" W

STRUCTURAL MATERIAL [BAY/MODULE]

MATERIAL MODULE

MATERIAL CORNER

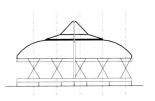

STRUCTURAL MATERIAL SYSTEM

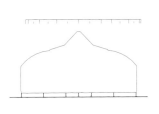

MATERIAL MODULE

MATERIAL SPACE

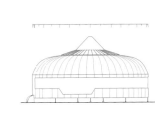

STRUCTURAL MATERIAL LEGIBILITY

MATERIAL MODULE

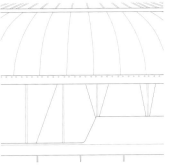

MATERIAL APERTURE

STRUCTURAL MATERIAL [LINE/POINT]

MATERIAL GEOMETRY

MATERIAL CONNECTION

COSTCOSTCOSTCOSTCOSTCOSTCOST
PER SQUARE FOOT

MOISTUREMOISTUREMOISTURE
AVERAGE ANNUAL HUMIDITY

TEMPERATURETEMPERATURE
AVERAGE ANNUAL TEMPERATURE

PRECIPITATIONPRECIPITATION
AVERAGE ANNUAL RAINFALL

LABORLABORLABORLABORLABOR
HOURS OF LABOR FOR CONSTRUCTION

DURABILITYDURABILITYDURABILITY
EXPECTED LIFE SPAN

EDUCATION	CIVIC	HOUSING
LIBRARY	OFFICE	RELIGIOUS
INSTITUTION	COMMERCIAL
BUILDING TYPE

SKIN	ALUMINUM
	PRIMARY MATERIAL
STRUCTURE	STEEL AND ALUMINUM
	SECONDARY MATERIAL
FINISH	ALUMINUM AND PLASTIC
	TERTIARY MATERIAL

**WICHITA HOUSE
BUCKMINSTER FULLER
DEARBORN, MICHIGAN**

METAL

WOOD / MASONRY / CONCRETE

GLASS / PLASTIC

Beginning of the Cold War: Rivalry between
the United States and the Soviet Union feeds the space
race and a high-stakes nuclear arms buildup

1945

1946   1946-5

| | DOCUMENTATION | | | FORM | | | PROXIMITY | | | SKIN + SURFACE | |

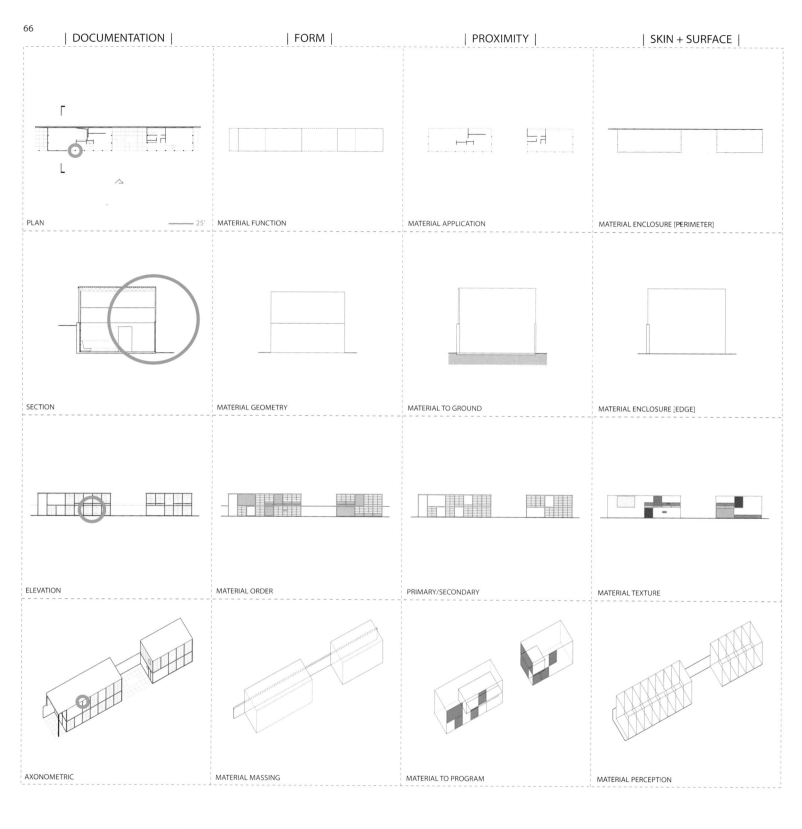

PLAN — 25'

MATERIAL FUNCTION

MATERIAL APPLICATION

MATERIAL ENCLOSURE [PERIMETER]

SECTION

MATERIAL GEOMETRY

MATERIAL TO GROUND

MATERIAL ENCLOSURE [EDGE]

ELEVATION

MATERIAL ORDER

PRIMARY/SECONDARY

MATERIAL TEXTURE

AXONOMETRIC

MATERIAL MASSING

MATERIAL TO PROGRAM

MATERIAL PERCEPTION

Frank Lloyd Wright designs
Johnson's Wax Administration Building

1936

1938

Charles Eames enrolls at Cranbrook Academy of Art

The start of commercial television
in the United States

1940

1941

Ray Kaiser and Charles Eames marry

| STRUCTURE | | MODULE | | DETAIL |

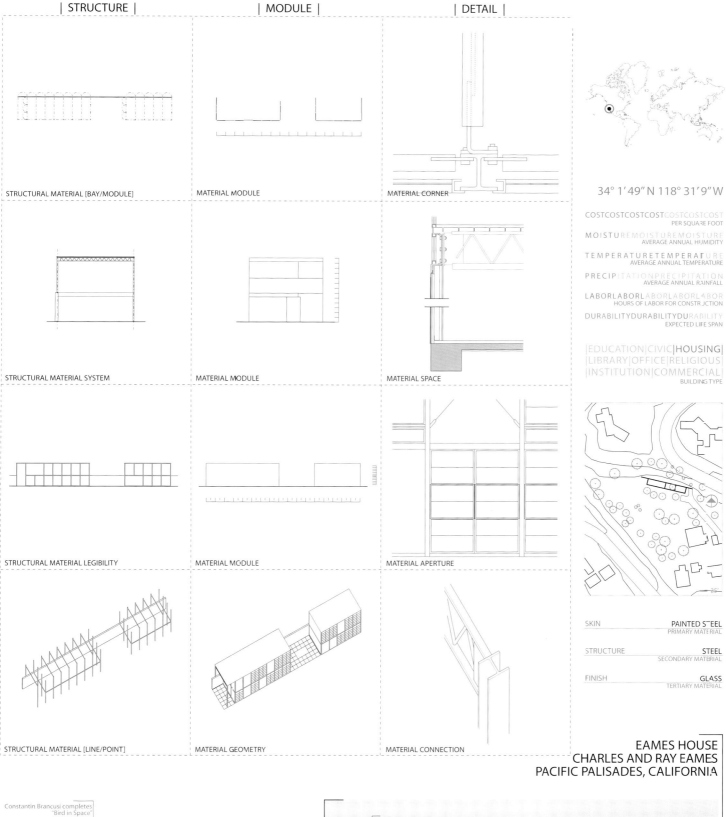

STRUCTURAL MATERIAL [BAY/MODULE]

MATERIAL MODULE

MATERIAL CORNER

STRUCTURAL MATERIAL SYSTEM

MATERIAL MODULE

MATERIAL SPACE

STRUCTURAL MATERIAL LEGIBILITY

MATERIAL MODULE

MATERIAL APERTURE

STRUCTURAL MATERIAL [LINE/POINT]

MATERIAL GEOMETRY

MATERIAL CONNECTION

WOOD

MASONRY

CONCRETE

METAL

GLASS

PLASTIC

34° 1′ 49″ N 118° 31′ 9″ W

COSTCOSTCOSTCOSTCOSTCOSTCOST
PER SQUARE FOOT

MOISTUREMOISTUREMOISTURE
AVERAGE ANNUAL HUMIDITY

TEMPERATURETEMPERATURE
AVERAGE ANNUAL TEMPERATURE

PRECIPITATIONPRECIPITATION
AVERAGE ANNUAL RAINFALL

LABORLABORLABORLABORLABOR
HOURS OF LABOR FOR CONSTRUCTION

DURABILITYDURABILITYDURABILITY
EXPECTED LIFE SPAN

EDUCATION	CIVIC	HOUSING
LIBRARY	OFFICE	RELIGIOUS
INSTITUTION	COMMERCIAL
BUILDING TYPE

SKIN — PAINTED STEEL
PRIMARY MATERIAL

STRUCTURE — STEEL
SECONDARY MATERIAL

FINISH — GLASS
TERTIARY MATERIAL

EAMES HOUSE
CHARLES AND RAY EAMES
PACIFIC PALISADES, CALIFORNIA

Constantin Brancusi completes
"Bird in Space"

1943

1945

1945

Eames Lounge Chair Wood [LCW] produced

1949

| DOCUMENTATION | | FORM | | PROXIMITY | | SKIN + SURFACE |

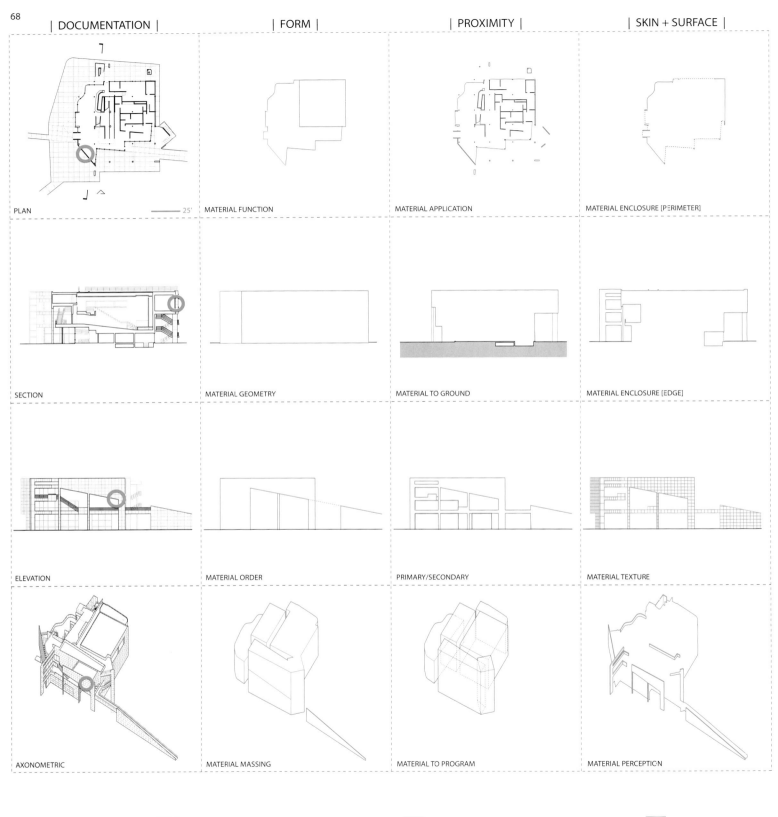

PLAN   25'

MATERIAL FUNCTION

MATERIAL APPLICATION

MATERIAL ENCLOSURE [PERIMETER]

SECTION

MATERIAL GEOMETRY

MATERIAL TO GROUND

MATERIAL ENCLOSURE [EDGE]

ELEVATION

MATERIAL ORDER

PRIMARY/SECONDARY

MATERIAL TEXTURE

AXONOMETRIC

MATERIAL MASSING

MATERIAL TO PROGRAM

MATERIAL PERCEPTION

R. Buckminster Fuller is awarded the
Gold Medal by the Royal Institute of British Architects

A Bauhaus retrospective is held in Paris

Louis I. Kahn, Philadelphia,
wins the AIA Gold Medal

1968   1969   1971

| STRUCTURE | | MODULE | | DETAIL |

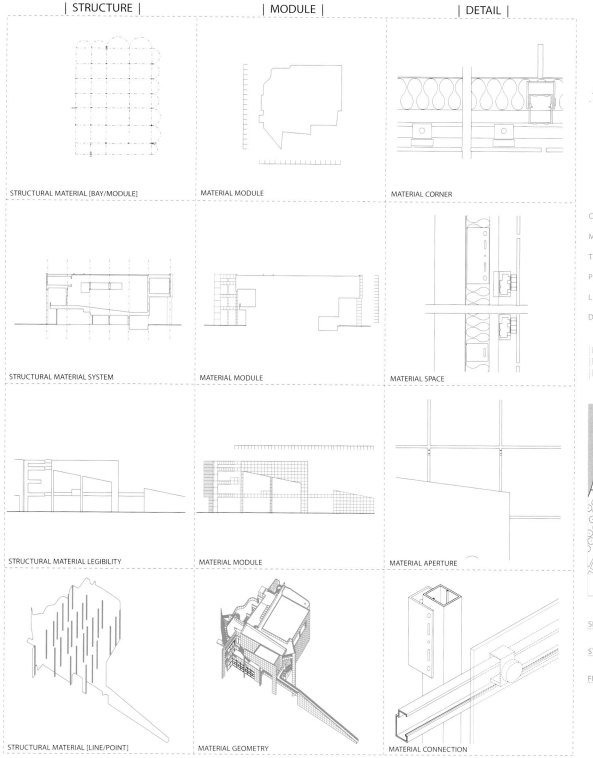

STRUCTURAL MATERIAL [BAY/MODULE]

MATERIAL MODULE

MATERIAL CORNER

STRUCTURAL MATERIAL SYSTEM

MATERIAL MODULE

MATERIAL SPACE

STRUCTURAL MATERIAL LEGIBILITY

MATERIAL MODULE

MATERIAL APERTURE

STRUCTURAL MATERIAL [LINE/POINT]

MATERIAL GEOMETRY

MATERIAL CONNECTION

38° 7' 55" N 87° 56' 19" W

COSTCOSTCOSTCOSTCOSTCOSTCOST
PER SQUARE FOOT

MOISTUREMOISTUREMOISTURE
AVERAGE ANNUAL HUMIDITY

TEMPERATURETEMPERATURE
AVERAGE ANNUAL TEMPERATURE

PRECIPITATIONPRECIPITATION
AVERAGE ANNUAL RAINFALL

LABORLABORLABORLABORLABOR
HOURS OF LABOR FOR CONSTRUCTION

DURABILITYDURABILITYDURABILITY
EXPECTED LIFE SPAN

EDUCATION	CIVIC	HOUSING
LIBRARY	OFFICE	RELIGIOUS
INSTITUTION	COMMERCIAL
BUILDING TYPE

SKIN	PORCELAIN-ENAMELED CLADDING AND GLASS
	PRIMARY MATERIAL
STRUCTURE	REINFORCED CONCRETE AND STEEL
	SECONDARY MATERIAL
FINISH	CONCRETE, WOOD AND ALUMINUM
	TERTIARY MATERIAL

THE ATHENEUM
RICHARD MEIER
NEW HARMONY, INDIANA

WOOD

MASONRY

CONCRETE

METAL

GLASS

PLASTIC

1973
Douglas House, Harbor Springs,
Michigan, is completed

1975

1979

| DOCUMENTATION | | FORM | | PROXIMITY | | SKIN + SURFACE |

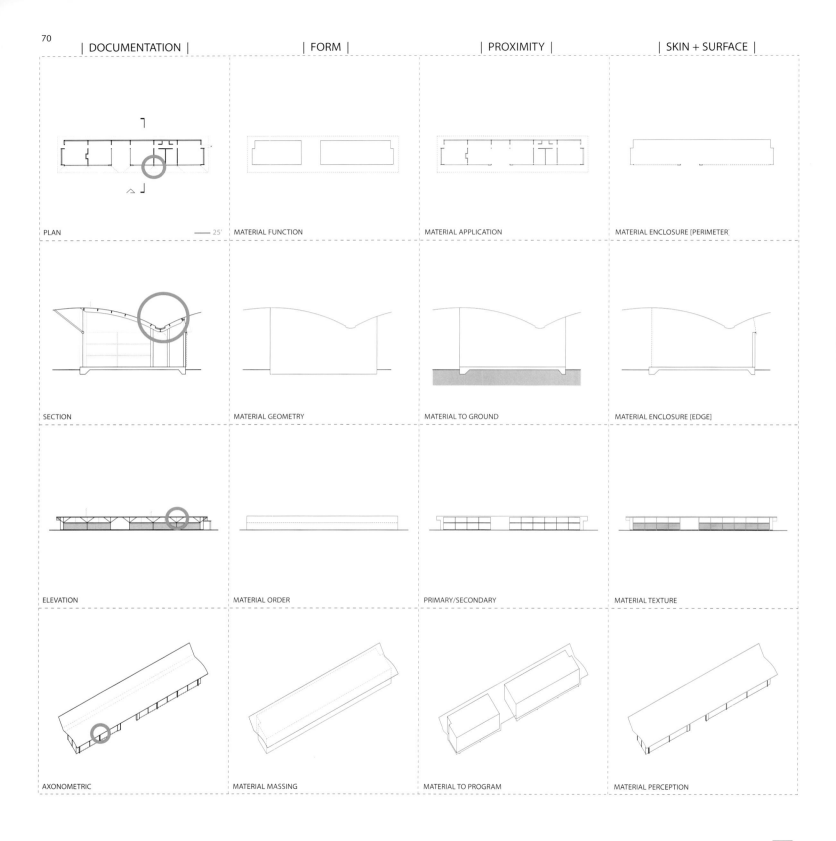

PLAN — 25'

MATERIAL FUNCTION

MATERIAL APPLICATION

MATERIAL ENCLOSURE [PERIMETER]

SECTION

MATERIAL GEOMETRY

MATERIAL TO GROUND

MATERIAL ENCLOSURE [EDGE]

ELEVATION

MATERIAL ORDER

PRIMARY/SECONDARY

MATERIAL TEXTURE

AXONOMETRIC

MATERIAL MASSING

MATERIAL TO PROGRAM

MATERIAL PERCEPTION

Philip Johnson wins the AIA Gold Medal

1956 -1961

Murcutt studies architecture at University of New South Wales

1976

Berowra Waters nn begins construction

1978

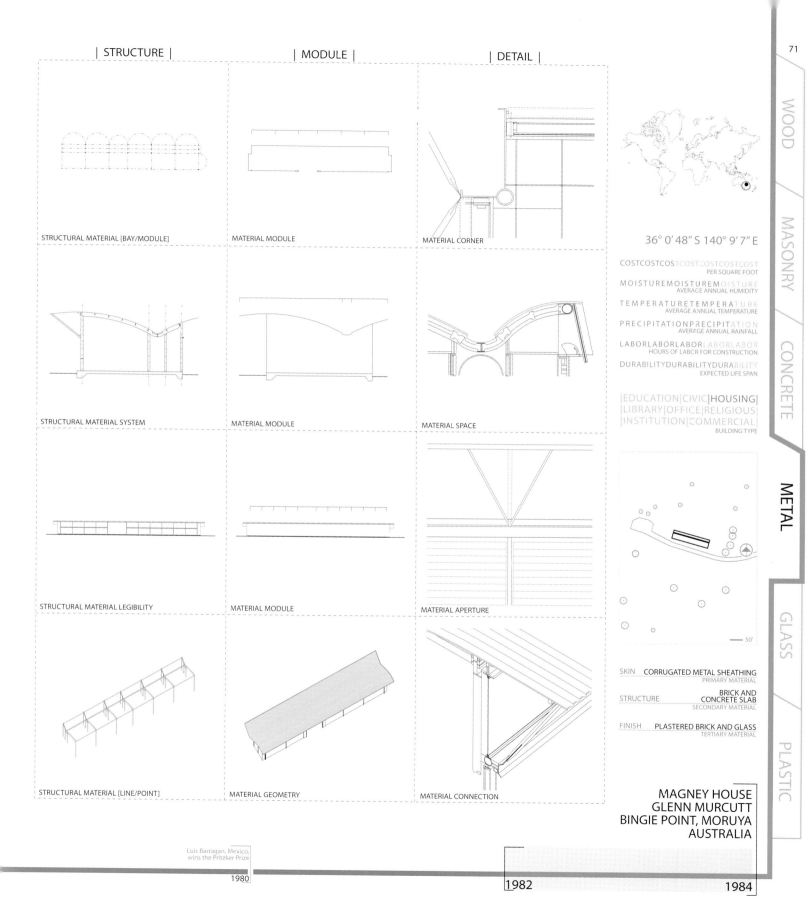

| STRUCTURE | | MODULE | | DETAIL |

STRUCTURAL MATERIAL [BAY/MODULE]

MATERIAL MODULE

MATERIAL CORNER

STRUCTURAL MATERIAL SYSTEM

MATERIAL MODULE

MATERIAL SPACE

STRUCTURAL MATERIAL LEGIBILITY

MATERIAL MODULE

MATERIAL APERTURE

STRUCTURAL MATERIAL [LINE/POINT]

MATERIAL GEOMETRY

MATERIAL CONNECTION

WOOD
MASONRY
CONCRETE
METAL
GLASS
PLASTIC

36° 0′ 48″ S 140° 9′ 7″ E

COSTCOSTCOSTCOST COSTCOSTCOST
PER SQUARE FOOT

MOISTUREMOISTUREMOISTURE
AVERAGE ANNUAL HUMIDITY

TEMPERATURETEMPERATURE
AVERAGE ANNUAL TEMPERATURE

PRECIPITATIONPRECIPITATION
AVERAGE ANNUAL RAINFALL

LABORLABORLABORLABORLABOR
HOURS OF LABOR FOR CONSTRUCTION

DURABILITYDURABILITYDURABILITY
EXPECTED LIFE SPAN

EDUCATION	CIVIC	HOUSING
LIBRARY	OFFICE	RELIGIOUS
INSTITUTION	COMMERCIAL
BUILDING TYPE

— 50′

SKIN   CORRUGATED METAL SHEATHING
PRIMARY MATERIAL

STRUCTURE   BRICK AND CONCRETE SLAB
SECONDARY MATERIAL

FINISH   PLASTERED BRICK AND GLASS
TERTIARY MATERIAL

MAGNEY HOUSE
GLENN MURCUTT
BINGIE POINT, MORUYA
AUSTRALIA

Luis Barragan, Mexico,
wins the Pritzker Prize

1980

1982

1984

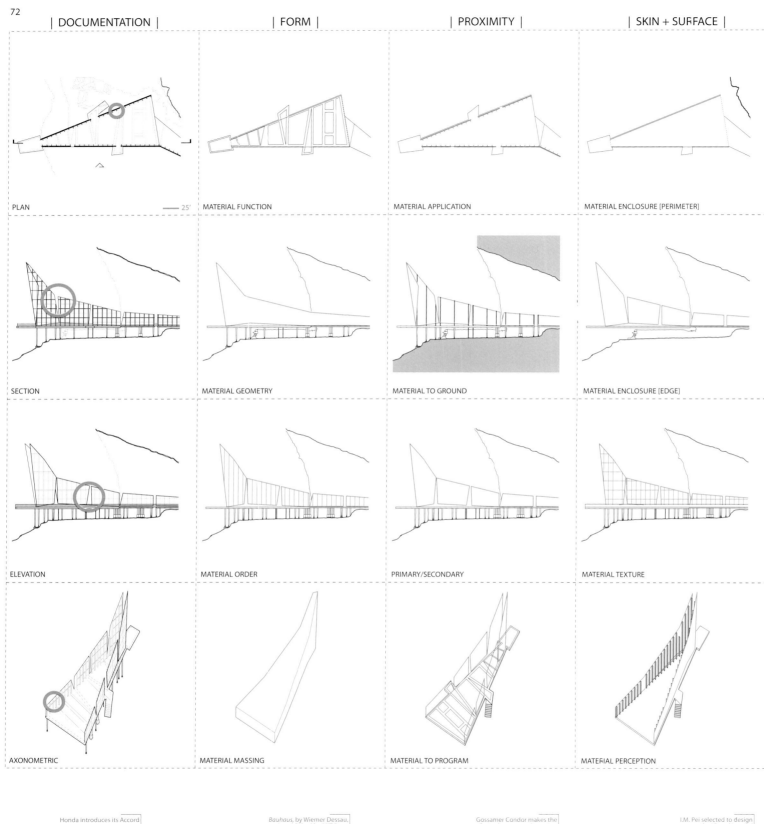

DOCUMENTATION	FORM	PROXIMITY	SKIN + SURFACE
PLAN — 25'	MATERIAL FUNCTION	MATERIAL APPLICATION	MATERIAL ENCLOSURE [PERIMETER]
SECTION	MATERIAL GEOMETRY	MATERIAL TO GROUND	MATERIAL ENCLOSURE [EDGE]
ELEVATION	MATERIAL ORDER	PRIMARY/SECONDARY	MATERIAL TEXTURE
AXONOMETRIC	MATERIAL MASSING	MATERIAL TO PROGRAM	MATERIAL PERCEPTION

Honda introduces its Accord

Bauhaus, by Wiemer Dessau, is published by MIT Press

Gossamer Condor makes the first solar-powered crossing of the English Channel

I.M. Pei selected to design the "Grand Louvre"

1976   1978   1981   1984

| STRUCTURE | | MODULE | | DETAIL |

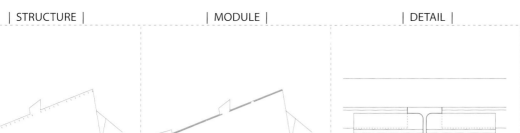

STRUCTURAL MATERIAL [BAY/MODULE]

MATERIAL MODULE

MATERIAL CORNER

42° 49' 10" N 1° 35' 39" E

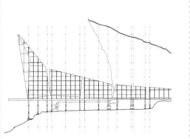

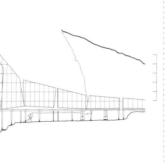

STRUCTURAL MATERIAL SYSTEM

MATERIAL MODULE

MATERIAL SPACE

COSTCOSTCOSTCOST COSTCOSTCOST
PER SQUARE FOOT

MOISTU REMOISTUREMO STURE
AVERAGE ANNUAL HUMIDITY

TEMPE RATURE TEMPERATURE
AVERAGE ANNUAL TEMPERATURE

PRECIPITATIONPRECI PITATION
AVERAGE ANNUAL RAINFALL

LABORLABOR LABORLABORLABOR
HOURS OF LABOR FOR CONSTRUCTION

DURABILITYDURABILITYDURABILITY
EXPECTED LIFE SPAN

EDUCATION	CIVIC	HOUSING
LIBRARY	OFFICE	RELIGIOUS
INSTITUTION	COMMERCIAL
BUILDING TYPE

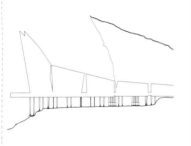

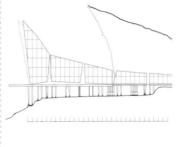

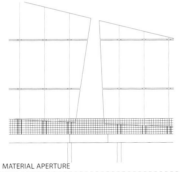

STRUCTURAL MATERIAL LEGIBILITY

MATERIAL MODULE

MATERIAL APERTURE

METAL

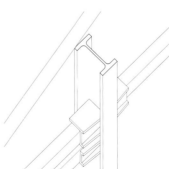

STRUCTURAL MATERIAL [LINE/POINT]

MATERIAL GEOMETRY

MATERIAL CONNECTION

— 100'

SKIN — CORTEN STEEL
PRIMARY MATERIAL

STRUCTURE — CORTEN STEEL
SECONDARY MATERIAL

FINISH — CORTEN STEEL
TERTIARY MATERIAL

WOOD
MASONRY
CONCRETE
METAL
GLASS
PLASTIC

NIAUX CAVE
MASSIMILIANO FUKSAS
ARIEGE
FRANCE

Mir Soviet space station
launched without crew

1986

1988

1989
Fuksas establishes architecture practice in Paris

1993

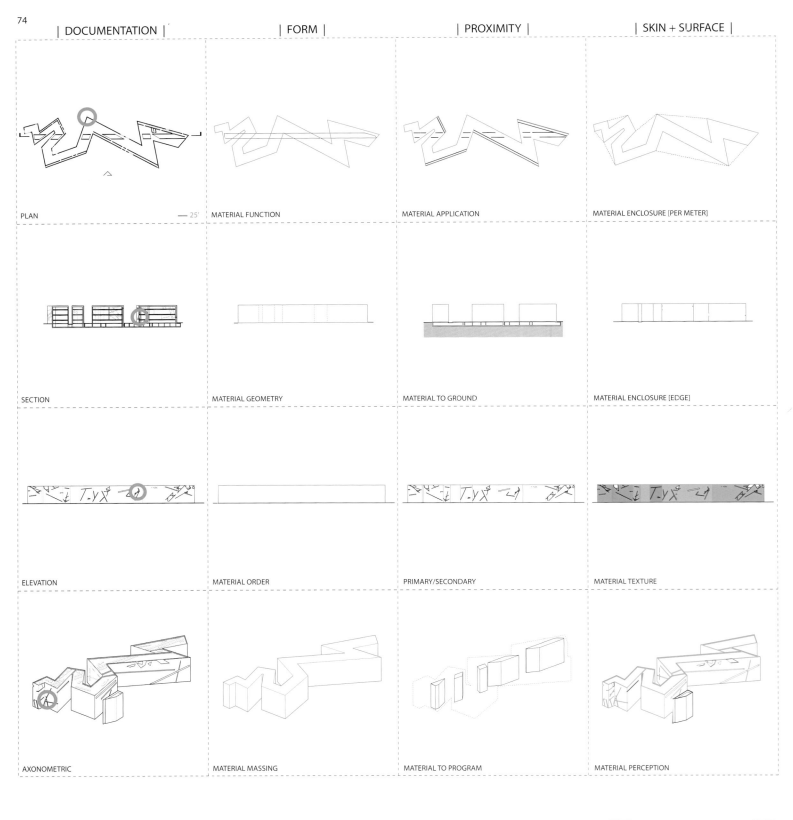

| DOCUMENTATION | | FORM | | PROXIMITY | | SKIN + SURFACE |

PLAN — 25′ MATERIAL FUNCTION MATERIAL APPLICATION MATERIAL ENCLOSURE [PER METER]

SECTION MATERIAL GEOMETRY MATERIAL TO GROUND MATERIAL ENCLOSURE [EDGE]

ELEVATION MATERIAL ORDER PRIMARY/SECONDARY MATERIAL TEXTURE

AXONOMETRIC MATERIAL MASSING MATERIAL TO PROGRAM MATERIAL PERCEPTION

1970
Libeskind receives architectural degree
from Cooper Union for the Advancement of Science and Art

Richard Meier, U.S.,
wins the Pritzker Prize

1984

Richard Rogers designs the
Lloyds Building in London

1986

There is global recognition that
the ozone layer is being depleted

1988

| STRUCTURE | | MODULE | | DETAIL |

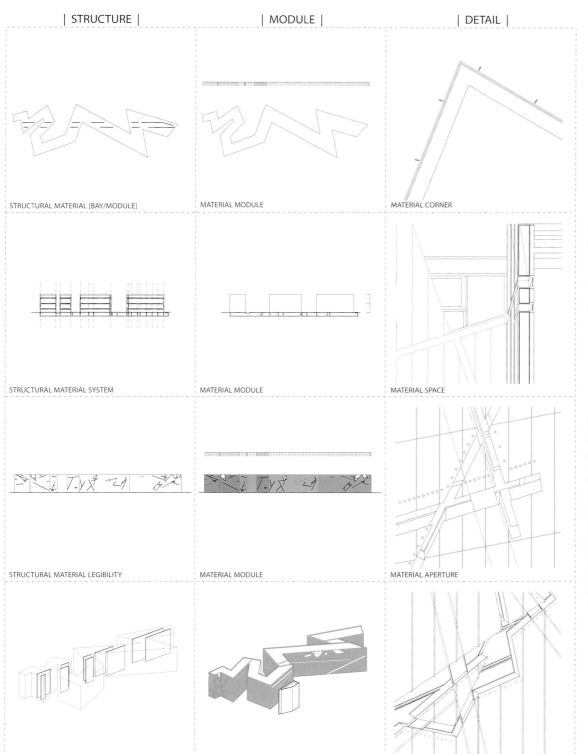

STRUCTURAL MATERIAL [BAY/MODULE]

MATERIAL MODULE

MATERIAL CORNER

STRUCTURAL MATERIAL SYSTEM

MATERIAL MODULE

MATERIAL SPACE

STRUCTURAL MATERIAL LEGIBILITY

MATERIAL MODULE

MATERIAL APERTURE

STRUCTURAL MATERIAL [LINE/POINT]

MATERIAL GEOMETRY

MATERIAL CONNECTION

WOOD
MASONRY
CONCRETE
METAL
GLASS
PLASTIC

52° 30' 6" S 13° 23' 43" E

COSTCOSTCOSTCOSTCOSTCOSTCOST
PER SQUARE FOOT

MOISTUREMOISTUREMOISTURE
AVERAGE ANNUAL HUMIDITY

TEMPERATURETEMPERATURE
AVERAGE ANNUAL TEMPERATURE

PRECIPITATIONPRECIPITATION
AVERAGE ANNUAL RAINFALL

LABORLABORLABORLABORLABOR
HOURS OF LABOR FOR CONSTRUCTION

DURABILITYDURABILITYDURABILITY
EXPECTED LIFE SPAN

EDUCATION	CIVIC	HOUSING
LIBRARY	OFFICE	RELIGIOUS
INSTITUTION	COMMERCIAL
BUILDING TYPE

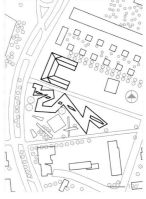

SKIN   ZINC
PRIMARY MATERIAL

STRUCTURE   REINFORCED CONCRETE
SECONDARY MATERIAL

FINISH   CONCRETE AND GLASS
TERTIARY MATERIAL

JEWISH MUSEUM
DANIEL LIBESKIND
BERLIN
GERMANY

Aldo Rossi, Italy,
wins the Pritzker Prize

1990

1992

1996

Libeskind is elected to to the American Academy of Arts and Letters

1999

| DOCUMENTATION | | FORM | | PROXIMITY | | SKIN + SURFACE |

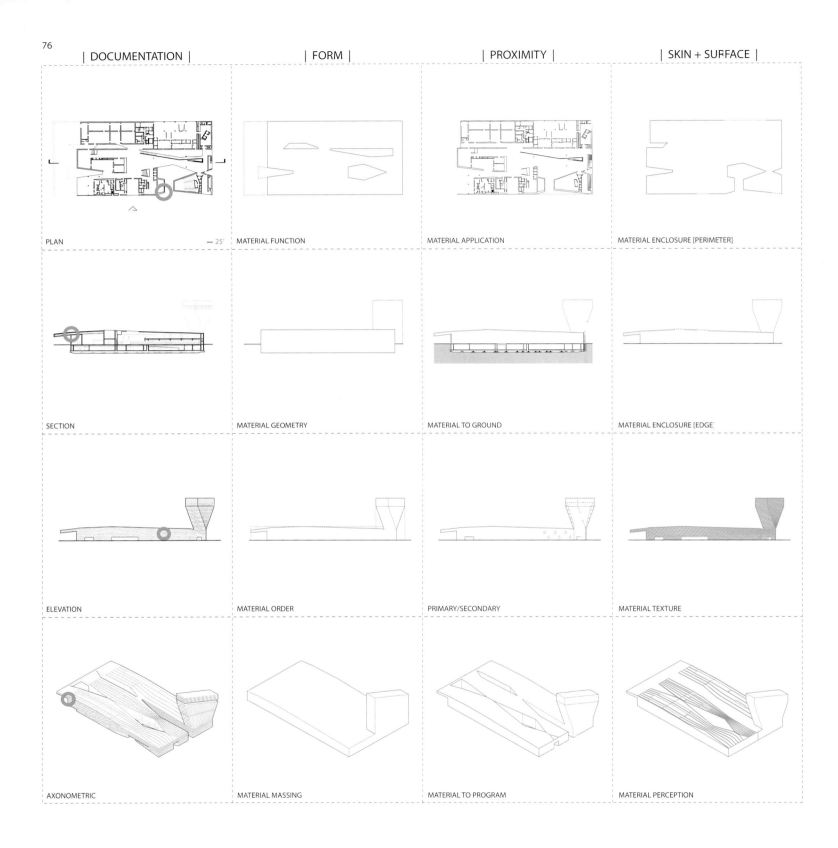

PLAN — 25'

MATERIAL FUNCTION

MATERIAL APPLICATION

MATERIAL ENCLOSURE [PERIMETER]

SECTION

MATERIAL GEOMETRY

MATERIAL TO GROUND

MATERIAL ENCLOSURE [EDGE]

ELEVATION

MATERIAL ORDER

PRIMARY/SECONDARY

MATERIAL TEXTURE

AXONOMETRIC

MATERIAL MASSING

MATERIAL TO PROGRAM

MATERIAL PERCEPTION

The Guggenheim Museum in Bilbao, Spain, designed by Gehry, inaugurated

Sir Norman Foster, U.K., wins the Pritzker Prize

1978

Jacques Herzog and Pierre de Meuron found Herzog & de Meuron Architekten

1997

1999

| STRUCTURE | | MODULE | | DETAIL |

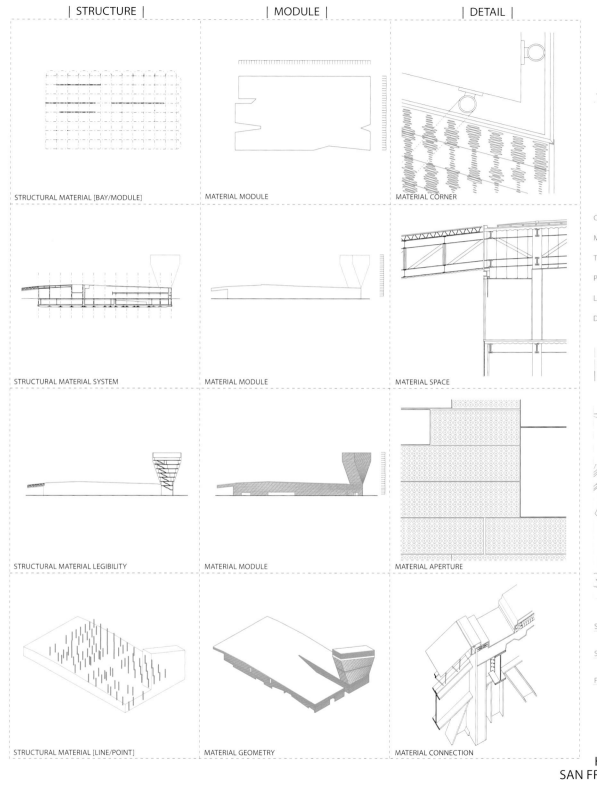

STRUCTURAL MATERIAL [BAY/MODULE]

MATERIAL MODULE

MATERIAL CORNER

STRUCTURAL MATERIAL SYSTEM

MATERIAL MODULE

MATERIAL SPACE

STRUCTURAL MATERIAL LEGIBILITY

MATERIAL MODULE

MATERIAL APERTURE

STRUCTURAL MATERIAL [LINE/POINT]

MATERIAL GEOMETRY

MATERIAL CONNECTION

37° 46′ 17″ N 122° 28′ 7″ W

COSTCOSTCOSTCOSTCOSTCOSTCOST
PER SQUARE FOOT

MOISTUREMOISTUREMOISTURE
AVERAGE ANNUAL HUMIDITY

TEMPERATURETEMPERATURE
AVERAGE ANNUAL TEMPERATURE

PRECIPITATIONPRECIPITATION
AVERAGE ANNUAL RAINFALL

LABORLABORLABORLABORLABOR
HOURS OF LABOR FOR CONSTRUCTION

DURABILITYDURABILITYDURABILITY
EXPECTED LIFE SPAN

EDUCATION	CIVIC	HOUSING
LIBRARY	OFFICE	RELIGIOUS
INSTITUTION	COMMERCIAL
BUILDING TYPE

SKIN	PERFORATED COPPER
	PRIMARY MATERIAL
STRUCTURE	REINFORCED CONCRETE
	SECONDARY MATERIAL
FINISH	CONCRETE, YORKSHIRE LIMESTONE AND GLASS
	TERTIARY MATERIAL

DE YOUNG MUSEUM
HERZOG & DE MEURON
SAN FRANCISCO, CALIFORNIA

WOOD
MASONRY
CONCRETE
METAL
GLASS
PLASTIC

2001
Herzog & De Meuron, Switzerland,
wins Pritzker Prize

2002

2003
Herzog & De Meuron wins Stirling Prize

2005

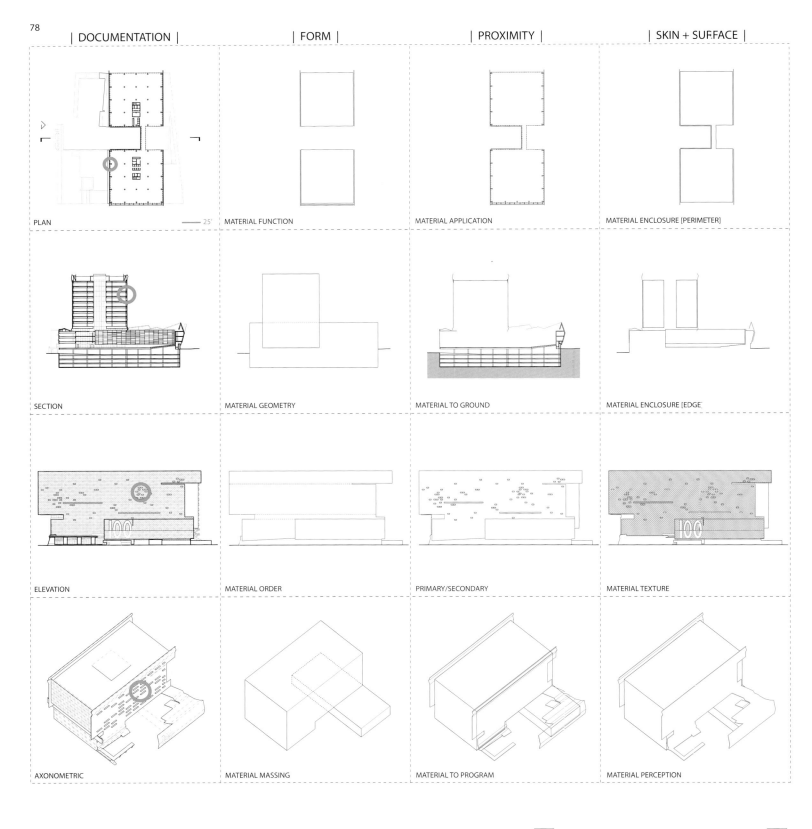

	DOCUMENTATION			FORM			PROXIMITY			SKIN + SURFACE	
PLAN	MATERIAL FUNCTION	MATERIAL APPLICATION	MATERIAL ENCLOSURE [PERIMETER]
SECTION	MATERIAL GEOMETRY	MATERIAL TO GROUND	MATERIAL ENCLOSURE [EDGE]
ELEVATION	MATERIAL ORDER	PRIMARY/SECONDARY	MATERIAL TEXTURE
AXONOMETRIC	MATERIAL MASSING	MATERIAL TO PROGRAM	MATERIAL PERCEPTION

25'

Dr. Brent Townshend invents the 56k Modem

Maya Lin designs and produces her furniture
"Stone Collection" for Knoll's 60th anniversary

1972
Thom Mayne and Michael Rotondi
founds Morphosis

1987
Mayne is awarded the Rome Prize Fellowship
of the American Academy in Rome, Italy

1996

1998

| STRUCTURE | | MODULE | | DETAIL |

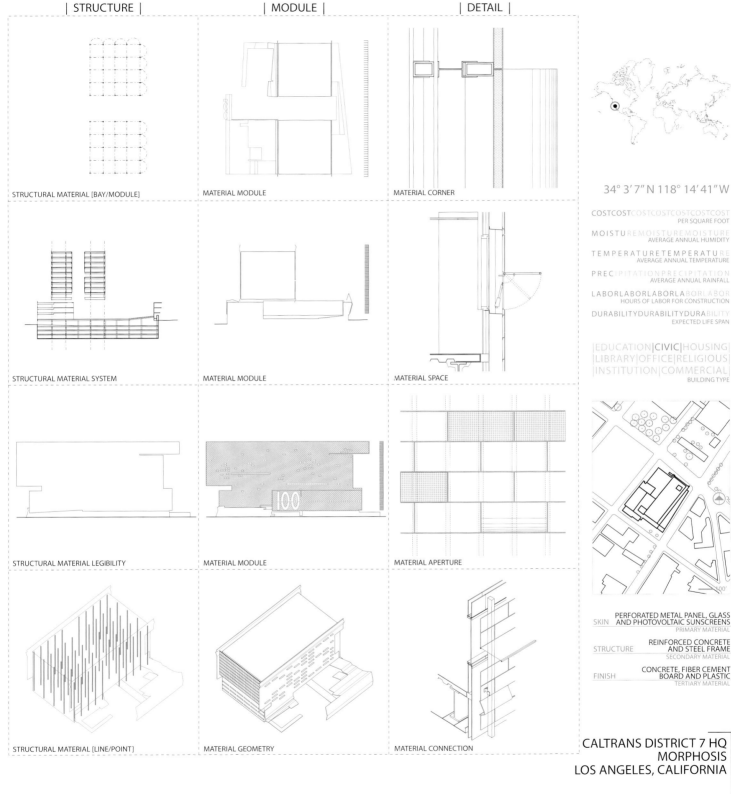

STRUCTURAL MATERIAL [BAY/MODULE]

MATERIAL MODULE

MATERIAL CORNER

STRUCTURAL MATERIAL SYSTEM

MATERIAL MODULE

MATERIAL SPACE

STRUCTURAL MATERIAL LEGIBILITY

MATERIAL MODULE

MATERIAL APERTURE

STRUCTURAL MATERIAL [LINE/POINT]

MATERIAL GEOMETRY

MATERIAL CONNECTION

WOOD

MASONRY

CONCRETE

METAL

GLASS

PLASTIC

34° 3′ 7″ N 118° 14′ 41″ W

COSTCOSTCOSTCOSTCOSTCOSTCOST
PER SQUARE FOOT

MOISTUREMOISTUREMOISTURE
AVERAGE ANNUAL HUMIDITY

TEMPERATURETEMPERATURE
AVERAGE ANNUAL TEMPERATURE

PRECIPITATIONPRECIPITATION
AVERAGE ANNUAL RAINFALL

LABORLABORLABORLABORLABOR
HOURS OF LABOR FOR CONSTRUCTION

DURABILITYDURABILITYDURABILITY
EXPECTED LIFE SPAN

EDUCATION	CIVIC	HOUSING
LIBRARY	OFFICE	RELIGIOUS
INSTITUTION	COMMERCIAL
BUILDING TYPE

SKIN — PERFORATED METAL PANEL, GLASS AND PHOTOVOLTAIC SUNSCREENS
PRIMARY MATERIAL

STRUCTURE — REINFORCED CONCRETE AND STEEL FRAME
SECONDARY MATERIAL

FINISH — CONCRETE, FIBER CEMENT BOARD AND PLASTIC
TERTIARY MATERIAL

CALTRANS DISTRICT 7 HQ
MORPHOSIS
LOS ANGELES, CALIFORNIA

| | DOCUMENTATION | | | FORM | | | PROXIMITY | | | SKIN + SURFACE | |

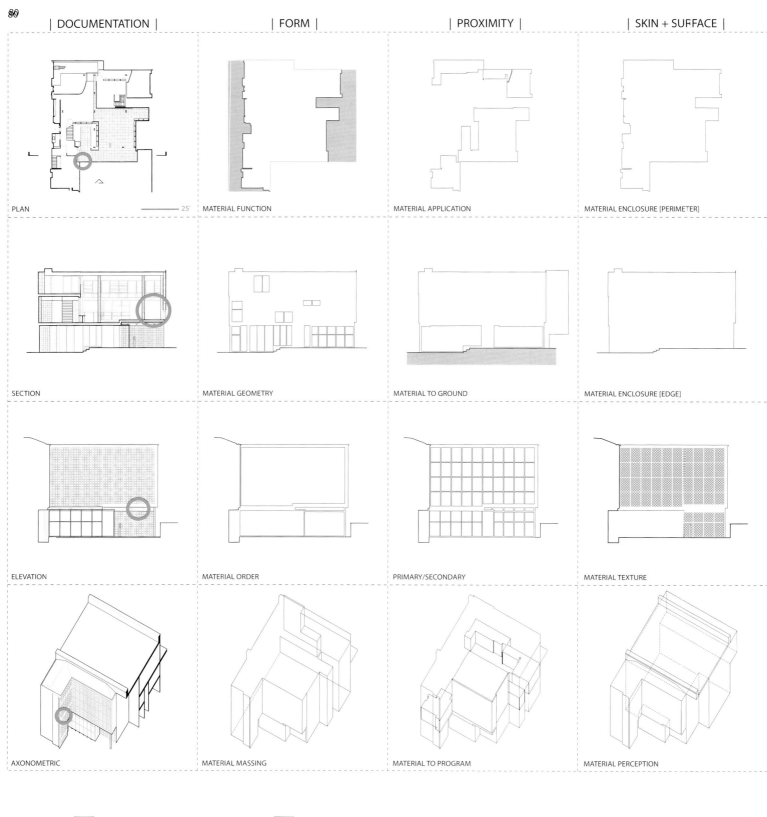

PLAN   — 25′

MATERIAL FUNCTION

MATERIAL APPLICATION

MATERIAL ENCLOSURE [PERIMETER]

SECTION

MATERIAL GEOMETRY

MATERIAL TO GROUND

MATERIAL ENCLOSURE [EDGE]

ELEVATION

MATERIAL ORDER

PRIMARY/SECONDARY

MATERIAL TEXTURE

AXONOMETRIC

MATERIAL MASSING

MATERIAL TO PROGRAM

MATERIAL PERCEPTION

Frank Lloyd Wright designs
the Robie House, Oak Park, IL

1909

The first Futurist Exhibition
is held in Paris

1912

1914-1919

Chareau conscripted for military service
in the First World War

The Chinese Communist Party is created

1921

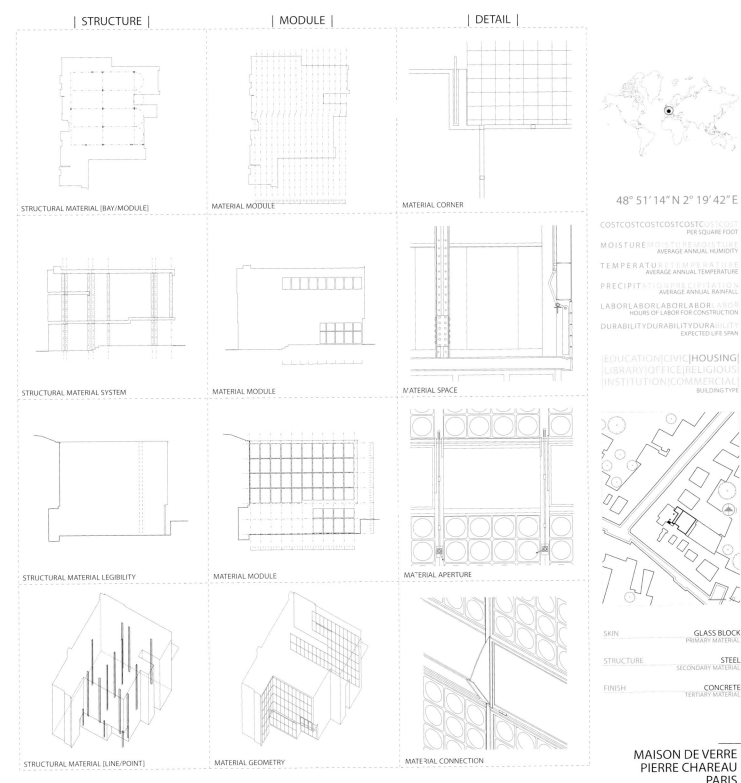

| STRUCTURE | | MODULE | | DETAIL |

STRUCTURAL MATERIAL [BAY/MODULE]

MATERIAL MODULE

MATERIAL CORNER

STRUCTURAL MATERIAL SYSTEM

MATERIAL MODULE

MATERIAL SPACE

STRUCTURAL MATERIAL LEGIBILITY

MATERIAL MODULE

MATERIAL APERTURE

STRUCTURAL MATERIAL [LINE/POINT]

MATERIAL GEOMETRY

MATERIAL CONNECTION

WOOD

MASONRY

CONCRETE

METAL

GLASS

PLASTIC

48° 51′ 14″ N 2° 19′ 42″ E

COSTCOSTCOSTCOSTCOSTCOSTCOST
PER SQUARE FOOT

MOISTUREMOISTUREMOISTURE
AVERAGE ANNUAL HUMIDITY

TEMPERATURETEMPERATURE
AVERAGE ANNUAL TEMPERATURE

PRECIPITATIONPRECIPITATION
AVERAGE ANNUAL RAINFALL

LABORLABORLABORLABORLABOR
HOURS OF LABOR FOR CONSTRUCTION

DURABILITYDURABILITYDURABILITY
EXPECTED LIFE SPAN

EDUCATION	CIVIC	HOUSING
LIBRARY	OFFICE	RELIGIOUS
INSTITUTION	COMMERCIAL
BUILDING TYPE

SKIN | GLASS BLOCK
PRIMARY MATERIAL

STRUCTURE | STEEL
SECONDARY MATERIAL

FINISH | CONCRETE
TERTIARY MATERIAL

MAISON DE VERRE
PIERRE CHAREAU
PARIS
FRANCE

Barker and Skinner invent Plexiglas

1924

1925

1928

Chareau becomes a joint founder of the CIAM

1932

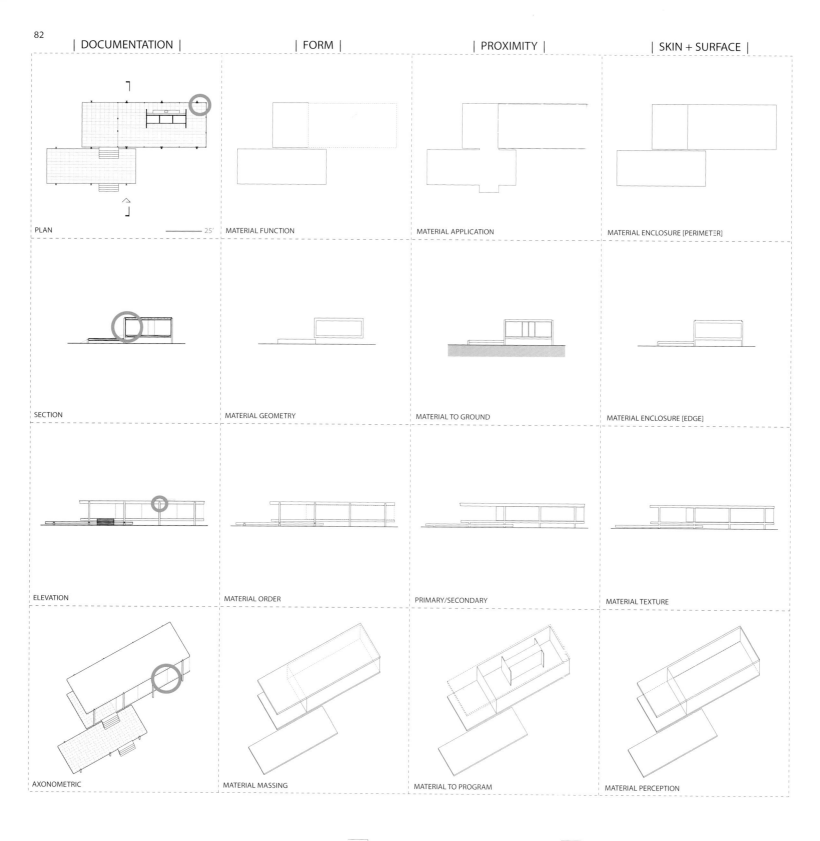

DOCUMENTATION		FORM		PROXIMITY		SKIN + SURFACE

PLAN — 25'

MATERIAL FUNCTION

MATERIAL APPLICATION

MATERIAL ENCLOSURE [PERIMETER]

SECTION

MATERIAL GEOMETRY

MATERIAL TO GROUND

MATERIAL ENCLOSURE [EDGE]

ELEVATION

MATERIAL ORDER

PRIMARY/SECONDARY

MATERIAL TEXTURE

AXONOMETRIC

MATERIAL MASSING

MATERIAL TO PROGRAM

MATERIAL PERCEPTION

Opening of the first VW factory, in Germany

J. M. Richards writes and publishes
An Introduction to Modern Architecture

Le Corbusier writes and publishes
La Maison des homes

1928
Mies designs Barcelona Pavilion for the
International Exposition in Barcelona, Spain

1938

1940

1942

| STRUCTURE | | MODULE | | DETAIL |

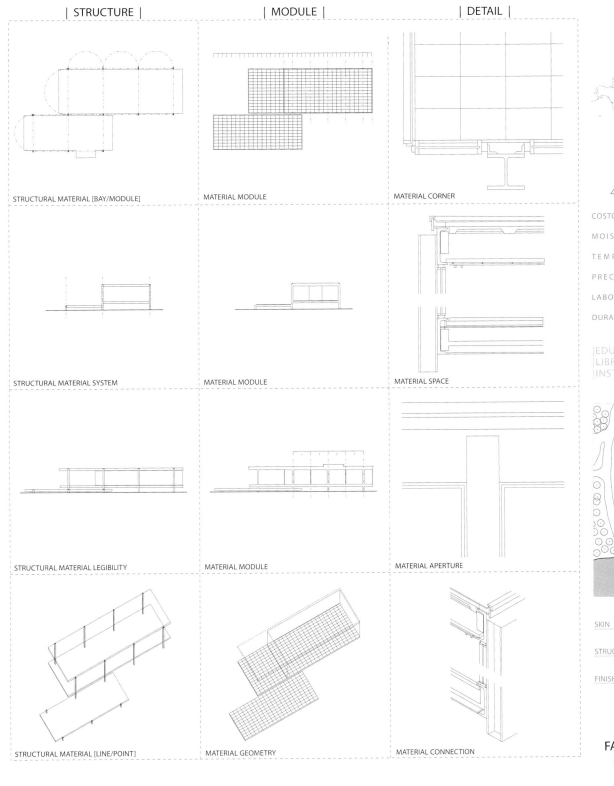

STRUCTURAL MATERIAL [BAY/MODULE]

MATERIAL MODULE

MATERIAL CORNER

STRUCTURAL MATERIAL SYSTEM

MATERIAL MODULE

MATERIAL SPACE

STRUCTURAL MATERIAL LEGIBILITY

MATERIAL MODULE

MATERIAL APERTURE

STRUCTURAL MATERIAL [LINE/POINT]

MATERIAL GEOMETRY

MATERIAL CONNECTION

WOOD / MASONRY / CONCRETE / METAL / GLASS / PLASTIC

41° 38' 7" N 88° 32' 9" W

COSTCOSTCOSTCOSTCOSTCOSTCOST
PER SQUARE FOOT

MOISTUREMOISTUREMOISTURE
AVERAGE ANNUAL HUMIDITY

TEMPERATURETEMPERATURE
AVERAGE ANNUAL TEMPERATURE

PRECIPITATIONPRECIPITATION
AVERAGE ANNUAL RAINFALL

LABORLABORLABORLABORLABOR
HOURS OF LABOR FOR CONSTRUCTION

DURABILITYDURABILITYDURABILITY
EXPECTED LIFE SPAN

EDUCATION	CIVIC	HOUSING
LIBRARY	OFFICE	RELIGIOUS
INSTITUTION	COMMERCIAL
BUILDING TYPE

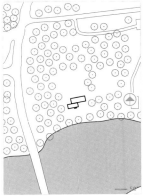

| SKIN | GLASS |
| | PRIMARY MATERIAL |

| STRUCTURE | STEEL |
| | SECONDARY MATERIAL |

| FINISH | WOOD |
| | TERTIARY MATERIAL |

FARNSWORTH HOUSE
MIES VAN DER ROHE
PLANO, ILLINOIS

1944
Mies becomes American citizen

1946

1950

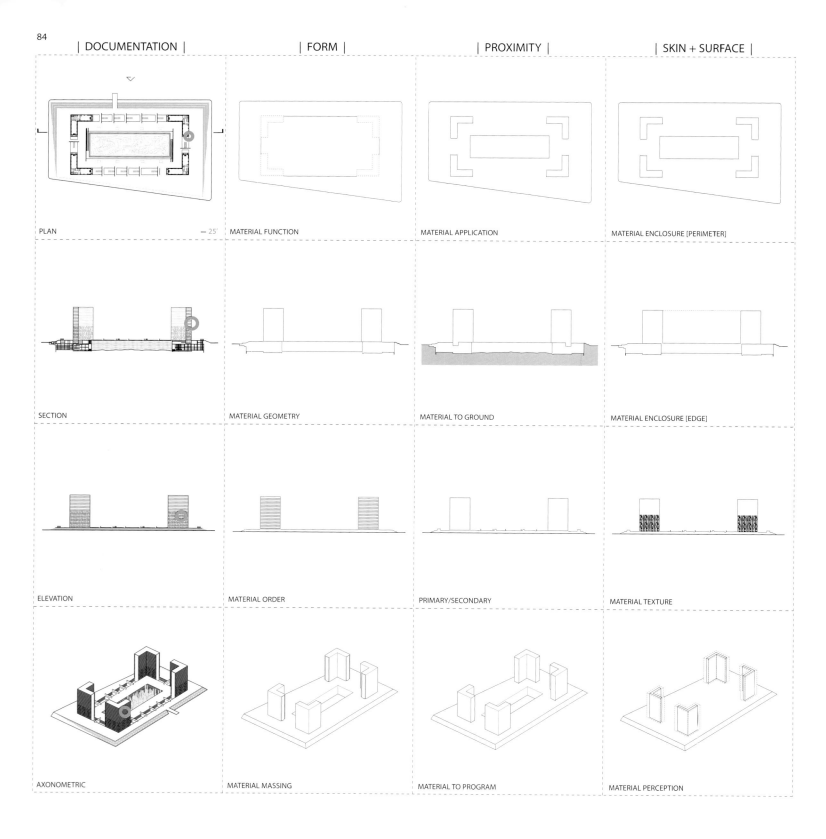

	DOCUMENTATION			FORM			PROXIMITY			SKIN + SURFACE	

PLAN — 25'

MATERIAL FUNCTION

MATERIAL APPLICATION

MATERIAL ENCLOSURE [PERIMETER]

SECTION

MATERIAL GEOMETRY

MATERIAL TO GROUND

MATERIAL ENCLOSURE [EDGE]

ELEVATION

MATERIAL ORDER

PRIMARY/SECONDARY

MATERIAL TEXTURE

AXONOMETRIC

MATERIAL MASSING

MATERIAL TO PROGRAM

MATERIAL PERCEPTION

Internet, a global on-line network, initiated

Gottfried Boehm, Germany,
wins the Pritzker Prize

1978
Perrault receives architecture degree

1980
Perrault receives postgraduate degree in history
at the Ecole des Hautes Etudes in social sciences

1981
Perrault opens his Paris office.
Dominique Perrault Architecte

1983

1986

| STRUCTURE | | MODULE | | DETAIL |

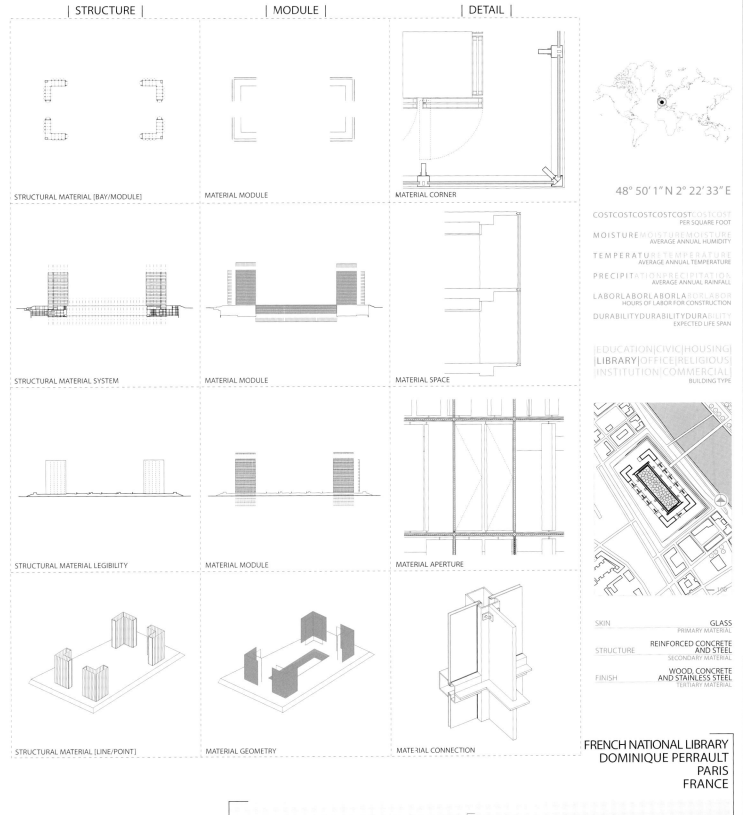

STRUCTURAL MATERIAL [BAY/MODULE]

MATERIAL MODULE

MATERIAL CORNER

STRUCTURAL MATERIAL SYSTEM

MATERIAL MODULE

MATERIAL SPACE

STRUCTURAL MATERIAL LEGIBILITY

MATERIAL MODULE

MATERIAL APERTURE

STRUCTURAL MATERIAL [LINE/POINT]

MATERIAL GEOMETRY

MATERIAL CONNECTION

WOOD

MASONRY

CONCRETE

METAL

GLASS

PLASTIC

48° 50′ 1″ N 2° 22′ 33″ E

COSTCOSTCOSTCOSTCOSTCOSTCOST
PER SQUARE FOOT

MOISTUREMOISTUREMOISTURE
AVERAGE ANNUAL HUMIDITY

TEMPERATURETEMPERATURE
AVERAGE ANNUAL TEMPERATURE

PRECIPITATIONPRECIPITATION
AVERAGE ANNUAL RAINFALL

LABORLABORLABORLABORLABOR
HOURS OF LABOR FOR CONSTRUCTION

DURABILITYDURABILITYDURABILITY
EXPECTED LIFE SPAN

EDUCATION	CIVIC	HOUSING
LIBRARY	OFFICE	RELIGIOUS
INSTITUTION	COMMERCIAL
BUILDING TYPE

SKIN	GLASS
	PRIMARY MATERIAL
STRUCTURE	REINFORCED CONCRETE AND STEEL
	SECONDARY MATERIAL
FINISH	WOOD, CONCRETE AND STAINLESS STEEL
	TERTIARY MATERIAL

FRENCH NATIONAL LIBRARY
DOMINIQUE PERRAULT
PARIS
FRANCE

1989

1992
Perrault wins the international competition for the
Olympic velodrome and swimming pool in Berlin

1995

| DOCUMENTATION | | FORM | | PROXIMITY | | SKIN + SURFACE |

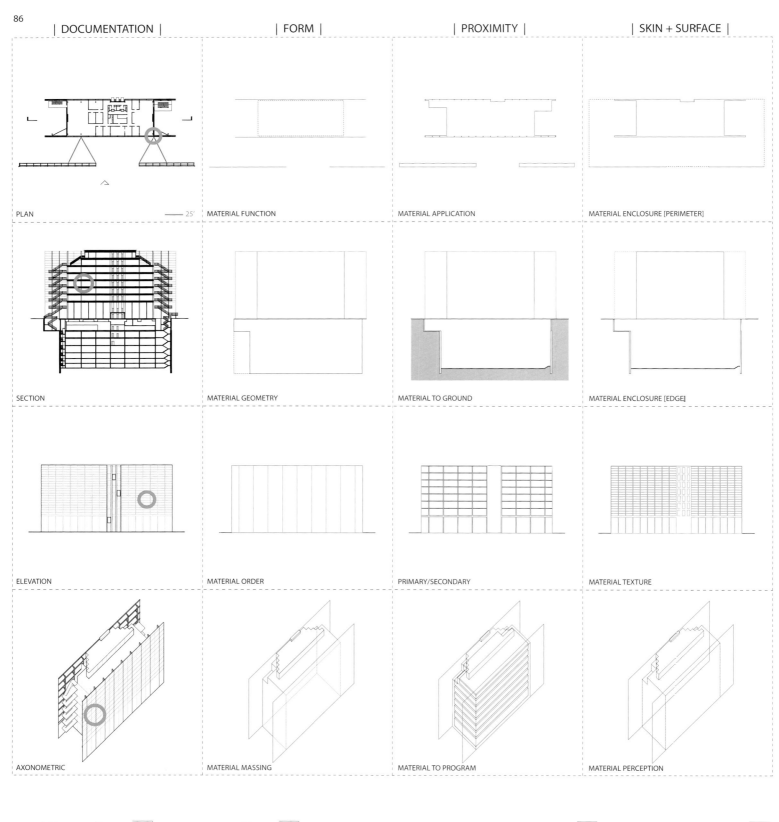

| PLAN — 25' | MATERIAL FUNCTION | MATERIAL APPLICATION | MATERIAL ENCLOSURE [PERIMETER] |

| SECTION | MATERIAL GEOMETRY | MATERIAL TO GROUND | MATERIAL ENCLOSURE [EDGE] |

| ELEVATION | MATERIAL ORDER | PRIMARY/SECONDARY | MATERIAL TEXTURE |

| AXONOMETRIC | MATERIAL MASSING | MATERIAL TO PROGRAM | MATERIAL PERCEPTION |

U.S. Department of Energy established

Philip Johnson, U.S., wins the Pritzker Prize

1981

Philippe Starck designs Costes Chair

British scientists discover that a hole in the ozone layer develops over Antarctica each winter

1977   1979   Nouvel wins competition for   1982   1985
                                      L'Institut du Monde Arabe

| STRUCTURE | | MODULE | | DETAIL |

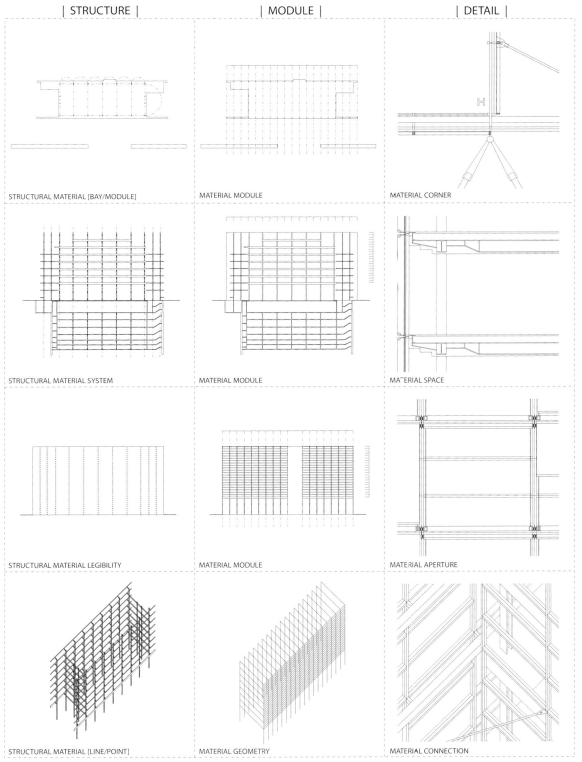

STRUCTURAL MATERIAL [BAY/MODULE]

MATERIAL MODULE

MATERIAL CORNER

STRUCTURAL MATERIAL SYSTEM

MATERIAL MODULE

MATERIAL SPACE

STRUCTURAL MATERIAL LEGIBILITY

MATERIAL MODULE

MATERIAL APERTURE

STRUCTURAL MATERIAL [LINE/POINT]

MATERIAL GEOMETRY

MATERIAL CONNECTION

WOOD
MASONRY
CONCRETE
METAL
GLASS
PLASTIC

48° 50' 14" N 2° 19' 55" E

COSTCOSTCOSTCOSTCOSTCOSTCOST
PER SQUARE FOOT

MOISTUREMOISTUREMOISTURE
AVERAGE ANNUAL HUMIDITY

TEMPERATURETEMPERATURE
AVERAGE ANNUAL TEMPERATURE

PRECIPITATIONPRECIPITATION
AVERAGE ANNUAL RAINFALL

LABORLABORLABORLABORLABOR
HOURS OF LABOR FOR CONSTRUCTION

DURABILITYDURABILITYDURABILITY
EXPECTED LIFE SPAN

EDUCATION	CIVIC	HOUSING
LIBRARY	OFFICE	RELIGIOUS
INSTITUTION	COMMERCIAL
BUILDING TYPE

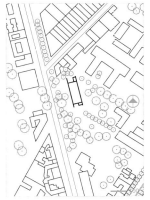

SKIN	GLASS
	PRIMARY MATERIAL
STRUCTURE	STEEL
	SECONDARY MATERIAL
FINISH	VARIOUS METALS
	TERTIARY MATERIAL

CARTIER FOUNDATION
JEAN NOUVEL
PARIS
FRANCE

1987
Nouvel completes L'Institut du Monde Arabe, Paris

1991

1993
Nouvel made honorary fellow of the AIA

1995

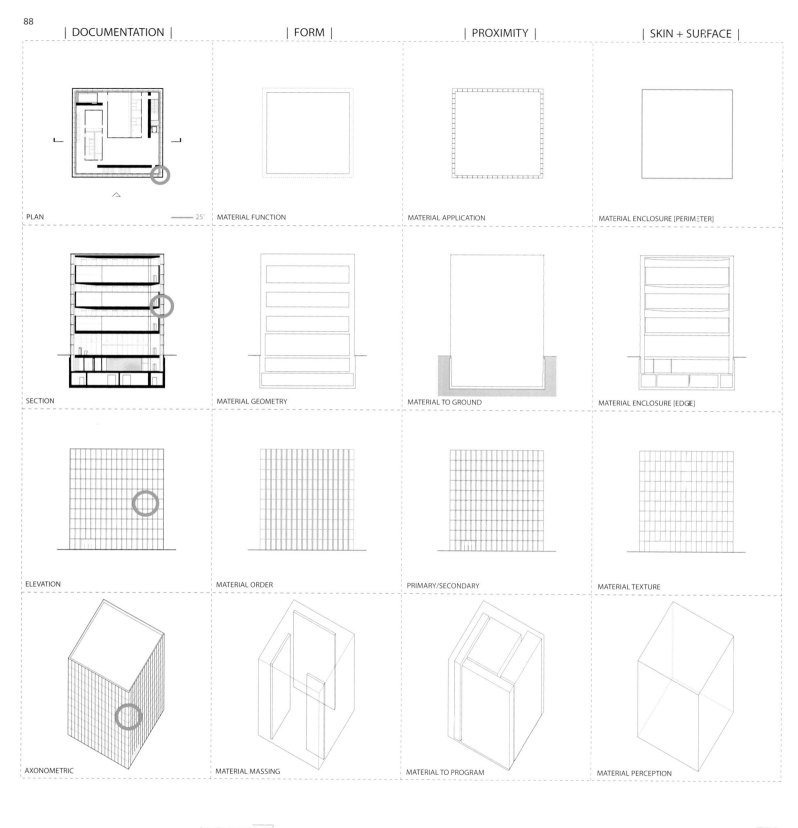

| | DOCUMENTATION | | FORM | | PROXIMITY | | SKIN + SURFACE |

PLAN ———— 25'   MATERIAL FUNCTION   MATERIAL APPLICATION   MATERIAL ENCLOSURE [PERIMETER]

SECTION   MATERIAL GEOMETRY   MATERIAL TO GROUND   MATERIAL ENCLOSURE [EDGE]

ELEVATION   MATERIAL ORDER   PRIMARY/SECONDARY   MATERIAL TEXTURE

AXONOMETRIC   MATERIAL MASSING   MATERIAL TO PROGRAM   MATERIAL PERCEPTION

1979
Zumthor founds Architekturbüro Peter Zumthor

Peter Greenaway releases
The Belly of an Architect
1986

1988
Chapel of St. Benedict in
Graubünden, Switzerland, is completed

1989
Zumthor receives the Heinrich Tessenow Medal,
Technische Universität Hannover, Germany

The reunification of
East and West Germany
1990

| STRUCTURE | | MODULE | | DETAIL |

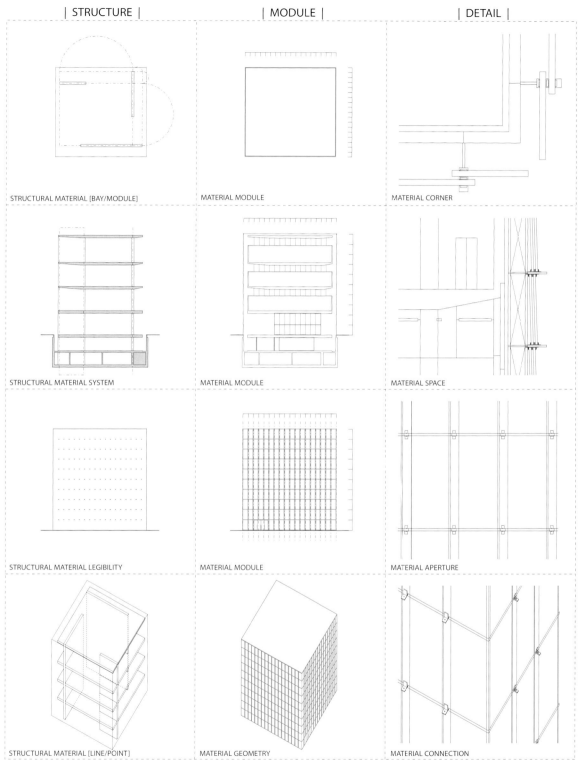

STRUCTURAL MATERIAL [BAY/MODULE]

MATERIAL MODULE

MATERIAL CORNER

STRUCTURAL MATERIAL SYSTEM

MATERIAL MODULE

MATERIAL SPACE

STRUCTURAL MATERIAL LEGIBILITY

MATERIAL MODULE

MATERIAL APERTURE

STRUCTURAL MATERIAL [LINE/POINT]

MATERIAL GEOMETRY

MATERIAL CONNECTION

WOOD

MASONRY

CONCRETE

METAL

GLASS

PLASTIC

47° 30′ 17″ N 9° 44′ 51″ E

COSTCOSTCOSTCOSTCOST COSTCOST
PER SQUARE FOOT

MOISTUREMOISTUREMOISTURE
AVERAGE ANNUAL HUMIDITY

TEMPERATURETEMPERATURE
AVERAGE ANNUAL TEMPERATURE

PRECIPITATIONPRECIPITATION
AVERAGE ANNUAL RAINFALL

LABORLABORLABORLABORLABOR
HOURS OF LABOR FOR CONSTRUCTION

DURABILITYDURABILITYDURABILITY
EXPECTED LIFE SPAN

|EDUCATION|CIVIC|HOUSING|
LIBRARY|OFFICE|RELIGIOUS|
|INSTITUTION|COMMERCIAL|
BUILDING TYPE

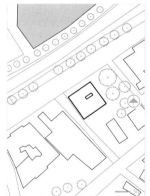

SKIN   ETCHED GLASS SHINGLES
PRIMARY MATERIAL

STRUCTURE   REINFORCED CONCRETE
SECONDARY MATERIAL

FINISH   CONCRETE AND GLASS
TERTIARY MATERIAL

KUNSTHAUS BREGENZ
PETER ZUMTHOR
BREGENZ
AUSTRIA

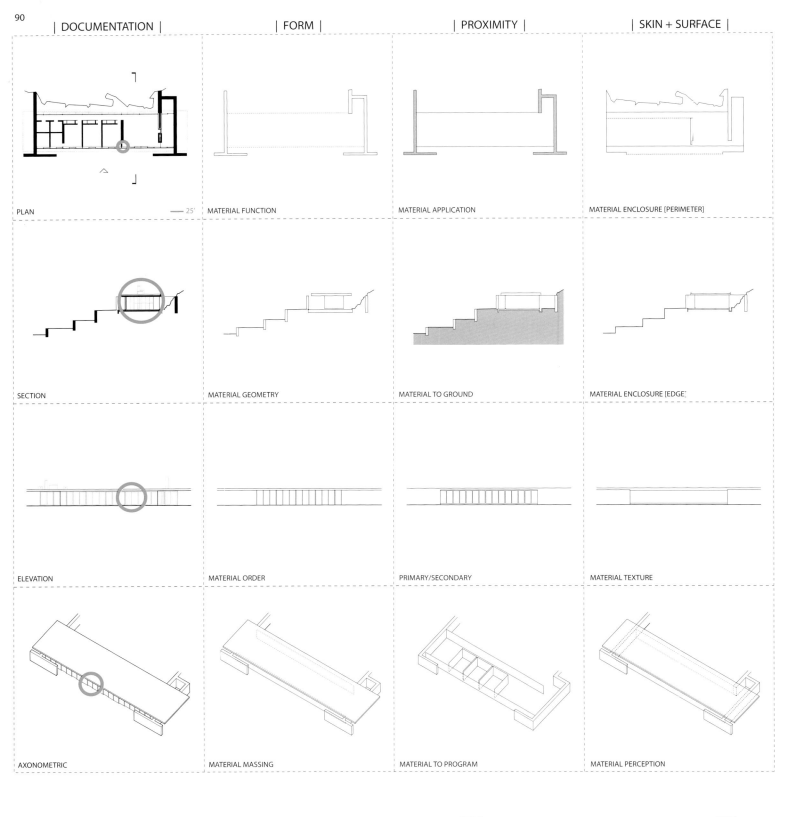

| | DOCUMENTATION | | | FORM | | | PROXIMITY | | | SKIN + SURFACE | |

PLAN — 25'   MATERIAL FUNCTION   MATERIAL APPLICATION   MATERIAL ENCLOSURE [PERIMETER]

SECTION   MATERIAL GEOMETRY   MATERIAL TO GROUND   MATERIAL ENCLOSURE [EDGE]

ELEVATION   MATERIAL ORDER   PRIMARY/SECONDARY   MATERIAL TEXTURE

AXONOMETRIC   MATERIAL MASSING   MATERIAL TO PROGRAM   MATERIAL PERCEPTION

1974
Souto de Moura works with Álvaro Siza Vieira

1981
Souto de Moura becomes
Assistant Professor at University of Porto

I. M. Pei selected to design
the "Grand Louvre."

1984

Design in Context, by Penny Sparke,
published by Quarto Publishing

1987

| STRUCTURE | | MODULE | | DETAIL |

STRUCTURAL MATERIAL [BAY/MODULE]

MATERIAL MODULE

MATERIAL CORNER

41° 51′ 7″ N 8° 50′ 44″ W

COSTCOSTCOSTCOST COSTCOSTCOST
PER SQUARE FOOT

MOISTUREMOISTUREMOISTURE
AVERAGE ANNUAL HUMIDITY

TEMPERATURETEMPERATURE
AVERAGE ANNUAL TEMPERATURE

PRECIPITATIONPRECIPITATION
AVERAGE ANNUAL RAINFALL

LABORLABORLABORLABORLABOR
HOURS OF LABOR FOR CONSTRUCTION

DURABILITYDURABILITYDURABILITY
EXPECTED LIFE SPAN

EDUCATION	CIVIC	HOUSING
LIBRARY	OFFICE	RELIGIOUS
INSTITUTION	COMMERCIAL
BUILDING TYPE

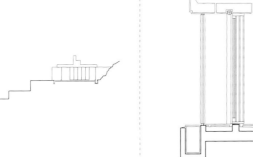

STRUCTURAL MATERIAL SYSTEM

MATERIAL MODULE

MATERIAL SPACE

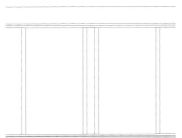

STRUCTURAL MATERIAL LEGIBILITY

MATERIAL MODULE

MATERIAL APERTURE

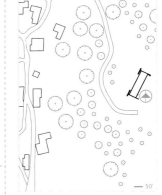

— 50′

SKIN   GLASS
PRIMARY MATERIAL

STRUCTURE   REINFORCED CONCRETE
SECONDARY MATERIAL

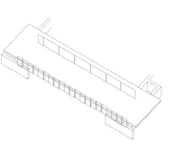

STRUCTURAL MATERIAL [LINE/POINT]

MATERIAL GEOMETRY

MATERIAL CONNECTION

FINISH   WOOD AND STONE
TERTIARY MATERIAL

HOUSE AT MOLEDO
EDUARDO SOUTO DE MOURA
CAMINHA
PORTUGAL

Aldo Rossi, Italy,
wins the Pritzker Prize

1990

1991

1998

| DOCUMENTATION | | FORM | | PROXIMITY | | SKIN + SURFACE |

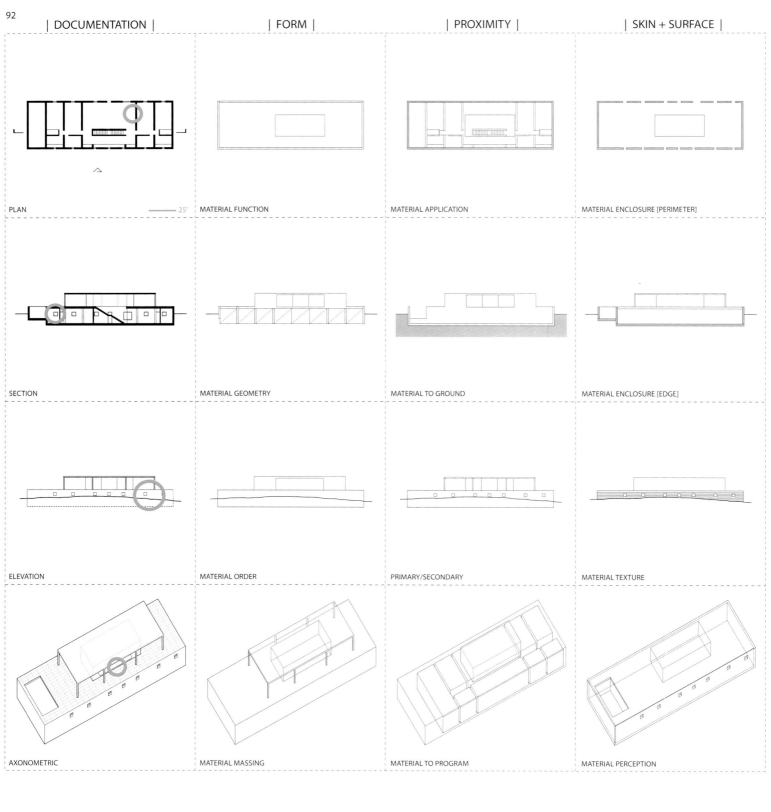

PLAN   25'   MATERIAL FUNCTION   MATERIAL APPLICATION   MATERIAL ENCLOSURE [PERIMETER]

SECTION   MATERIAL GEOMETRY   MATERIAL TO GROUND   MATERIAL ENCLOSURE [EDGE]

ELEVATION   MATERIAL ORDER   PRIMARY/SECONDARY   MATERIAL TEXTURE

AXONOMETRIC   MATERIAL MASSING   MATERIAL TO PROGRAM   MATERIAL PERCEPTION

Precedents in Architecture,
by Roger H. Clark and Michael Pause,
published by Van Nostrand Reinhold

The start of the "Biodesign Movement."

Robert Venturi, U.S.,
wins the Pritzker Prize

Wired magazine introduced

1985

1987

Campo Baeza appointed Director of
the Department of Design at ETSAM

1989

1991

1993

| STRUCTURE | | MODULE | | DETAIL |

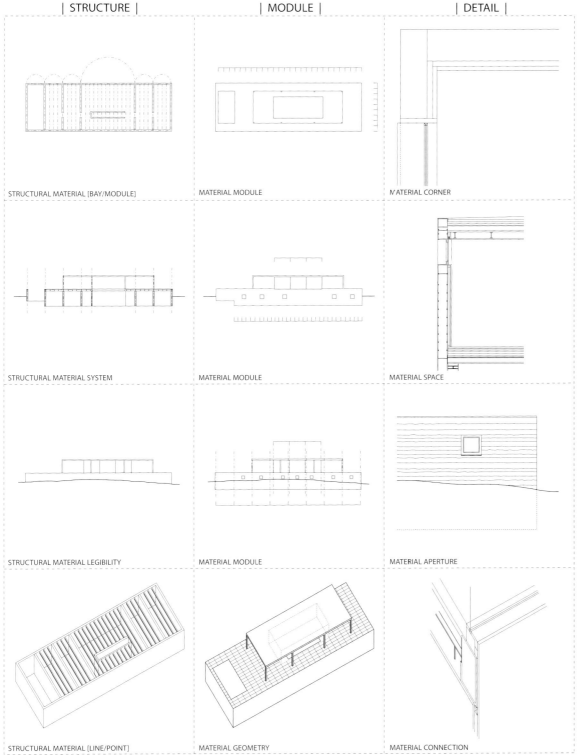

STRUCTURAL MATERIAL [BAY/MODULE]

MATERIAL MODULE

MATERIAL CORNER

STRUCTURAL MATERIAL SYSTEM

MATERIAL MODULE

MATERIAL SPACE

STRUCTURAL MATERIAL LEGIBILITY

MATERIAL MODULE

MATERIAL APERTURE

STRUCTURAL MATERIAL [LINE/POINT]

MATERIAL GEOMETRY

MATERIAL CONNECTION

WOOD / MASONRY / CONCRETE / METAL / GLASS / PLASTIC

40° 20' 55" N 4° 7' 6" W

COSTCOSTCOSTCOSTCOSTCOSTCOST
PER SQUARE FOOT

MOISTUREMOISTUREMOISTURE
AVERAGE ANNUAL HUMIDITY

TEMPERATURETEMPERATURE
AVERAGE ANNUAL TEMPERATURE

PRECIPITATIONPRECIPITATION
AVERAGE ANNUAL RAINFALL

LABORLABORLABORLABORLABOR
HOURS OF LABOR FOR CONSTRUCTION

DURABILITYDURABILITYDURABILITY
EXPECTED LIFE SPAN

EDUCATION	CIVIC	HOUSING
LIBRARY	OFFICE	RELIGIOUS
INSTITUTION	COMMERCIAL
BUILDING TYPE

SKIN	GLASS
	PRIMARY MATERIAL

STRUCTURE	CONCRETE AND STEEL
	SECONDARY MATERIAL

FINISH	WOOD FLOORING
	TERTIARY MATERIAL

DE BLAS HOUSE
ALBERTO CAMPO BAEZA
MADRID
SPAIN

1996
Campo Baeza becomes Visiting Professor
at the Virginia Polytechnic Institute

1997

1999
Campo Baeza teaches at the University of Pennsylvania

2001

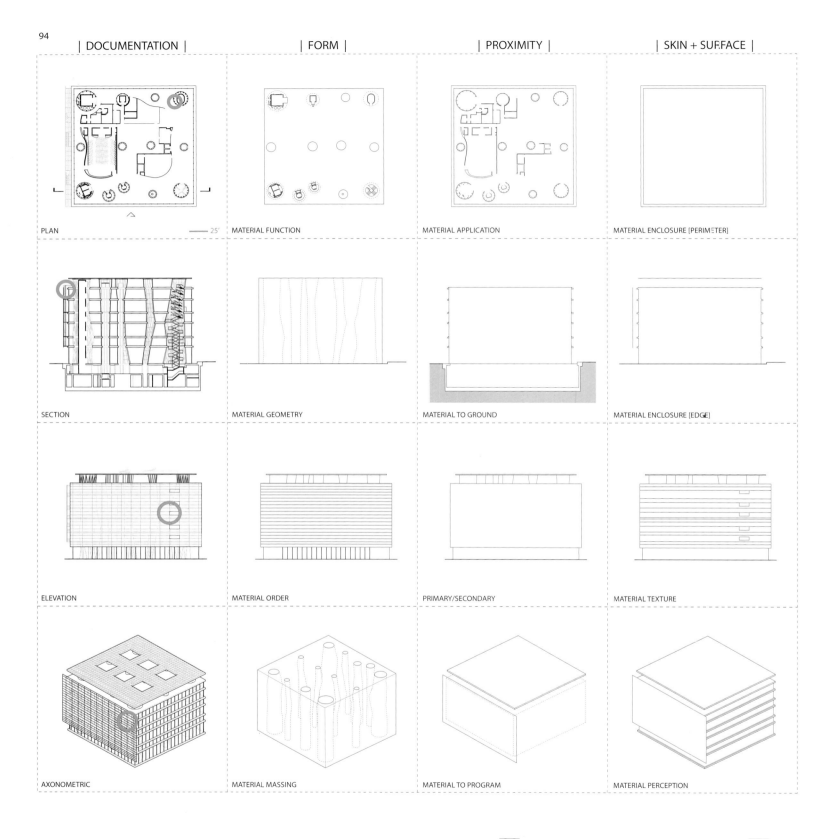

| DOCUMENTATION | FORM | PROXIMITY | SKIN + SURFACE |

PLAN ——— 25'

MATERIAL FUNCTION

MATERIAL APPLICATION

MATERIAL ENCLOSURE [PERIMETER]

SECTION

MATERIAL GEOMETRY

MATERIAL TO GROUND

MATERIAL ENCLOSURE [EDGE]

ELEVATION

MATERIAL ORDER

PRIMARY/SECONDARY

MATERIAL TEXTURE

AXONOMETRIC

MATERIAL MASSING

MATERIAL TO PROGRAM

MATERIAL PERCEPTION

The Soviet Union dissolves, the
seventy-four-year Communist reign ends

Fumihiko Maki, Japan,
wins the Pritzker Prize

1971

Toyo Ito starts Urbot ("Urban Robot"),
predecessor to Toyo Ito & Associates, Architects

1991

1993

| STRUCTURE | | MODULE | | DETAIL |

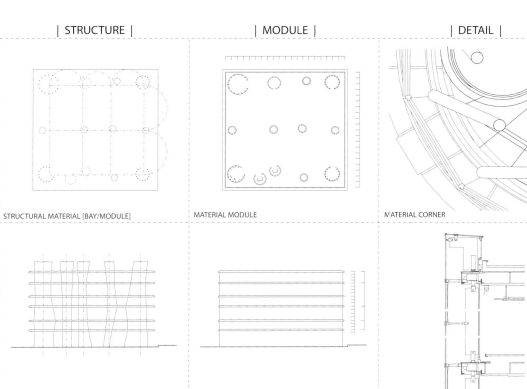

STRUCTURAL MATERIAL [BAY/MODULE]

MATERIAL MODULE

MATERIAL CORNER

STRUCTURAL MATERIAL SYSTEM

MATERIAL MODULE

MATERIAL SPACE

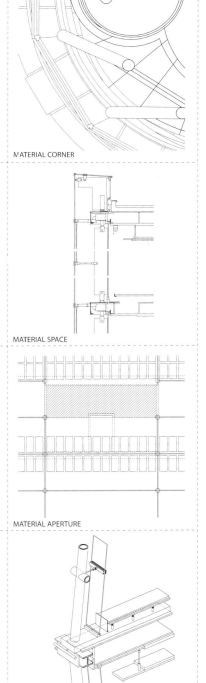

STRUCTURAL MATERIAL LEGIBILITY

MATERIAL MODULE

MATERIAL APERTURE

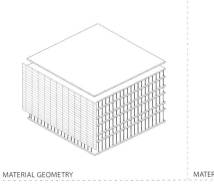

STRUCTURAL MATERIAL [LINE/POINT]

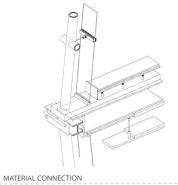

MATERIAL GEOMETRY

MATERIAL CONNECTION

WOOD
MASONRY
CONCRETE
METAL
GLASS
PLASTIC

38° 15′ 56″ N 140° 51′ 56″ E

COSTCOSTCOSTCOST COSTCOSTCOST
PER SQUARE FOOT

MOISTUREMOISTUREMOISTURE
AVERAGE ANNUAL HUMIDITY

TEMPERATURETEMPERATURE
AVERAGE ANNUAL TEMPERATURE

PRECIPITATIONPRECIPITATION
AVERAGE ANNUAL RAINFALL

LABORLABORLABORLABORLABOR
HOURS OF LABOR FOR CONSTRUCTION

DURABILITYDURABILITYDURABILITY
EXPECTED LIFE SPAN

EDUCATION	CIVIC	HOUSING
LIBRARY	OFFICE	RELIGIOUS
INSTITUTION	COMMERCIAL
BUILDING TYPE

SKIN	GLASS
	PRIMARY MATERIAL
STRUCTURE	STEEL TUBE SHAFT, CONCRETE, HONEY-COMB METAL SLABS
	SECONDARY MATERIAL
FINISH	CONCRETE, GLASS, MARBLE AND PLASTIC
	TERTIARY MATERIAL

SENDAI MEDIATHEQUE
TOYO ITO
SENDAI-SHI
JAPAN

Tadao Ando, Japan, wins the Pritzker Prize

1995

1997

1998
Ito receives the Education Minister's Art Encouragement Prize in Japan

2001

| | DOCUMENTATION | | | FORM | | | PROXIMITY | | | SKIN + SURFACE | |

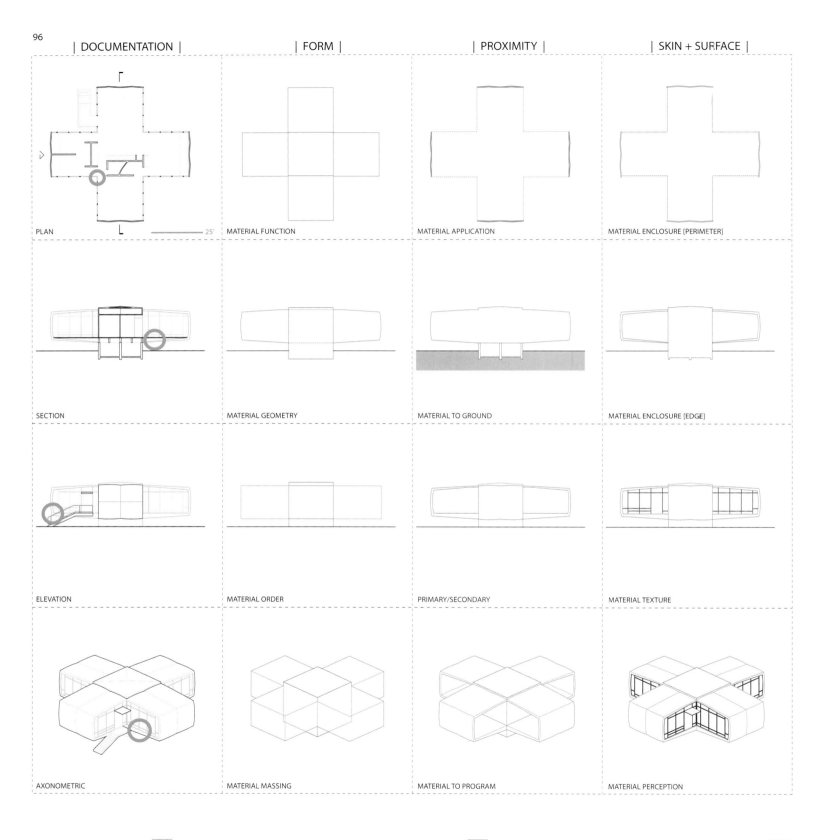

PLAN   MATERIAL FUNCTION   MATERIAL APPLICATION   MATERIAL ENCLOSURE [PERIMETER]

SECTION   MATERIAL GEOMETRY   MATERIAL TO GROUND   MATERIAL ENCLOSURE [EDGE]

ELEVATION   MATERIAL ORDER   PRIMARY/SECONDARY   MATERIAL TEXTURE

AXONOMETRIC   MATERIAL MASSING   MATERIAL TO PROGRAM   MATERIAL PERCEPTION

Automatic Binding Bricks
are now called Lego Bricks

1953

The U.S. tests a 15-megaton
hydrogen bomb at Bikini Atoll, in the Pacific Ocean

1954

The Vietnam War begins

1955

| STRUCTURE | | MODULE | | DETAIL |

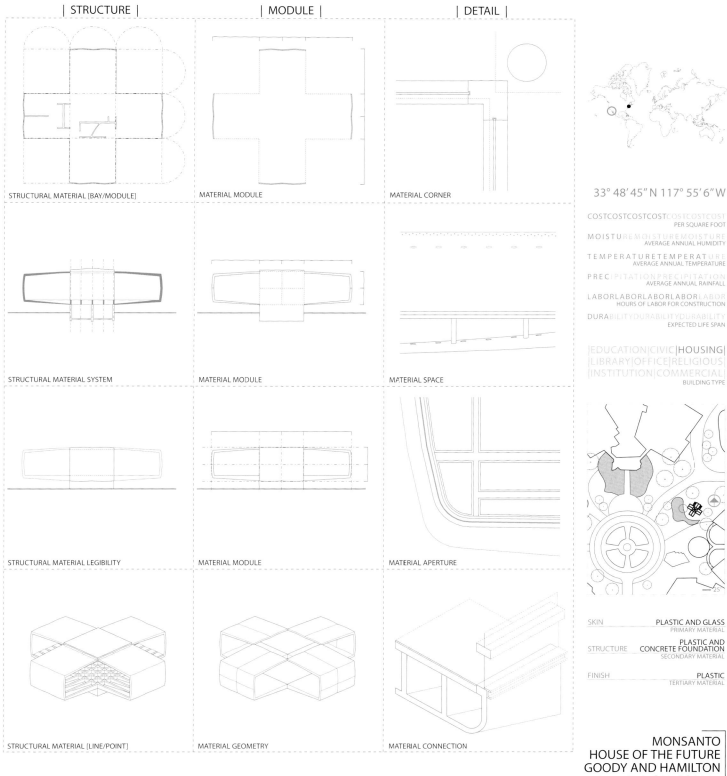

STRUCTURAL MATERIAL [BAY/MODULE]

MATERIAL MODULE

MATERIAL CORNER

STRUCTURAL MATERIAL SYSTEM

MATERIAL MODULE

MATERIAL SPACE

STRUCTURAL MATERIAL LEGIBILITY

MATERIAL MODULE

MATERIAL APERTURE

STRUCTURAL MATERIAL [LINE/POINT]

MATERIAL GEOMETRY

MATERIAL CONNECTION

WOOD

MASONRY

CONCRETE

METAL

GLASS

PLASTIC

33° 48' 45" N 117° 55' 6" W

COSTCOSTCOSTCOST COSTCOSTCOST
PER SQUARE FOOT

MOISTUREMOISTUREMOISTURE
AVERAGE ANNUAL HUMIDITY

TEMPERATURETEMPERATURE
AVERAGE ANNUAL TEMPERATURE

PRECIPITATIONPRECIPITATION
AVERAGE ANNUAL RAINFALL

LABORLABORLABORLABORLABOR
HOURS OF LABOR FOR CONSTRUCTION

DURABILITYDURABILITYDURABILITY
EXPECTED LIFE SPAN

EDUCATION	CIVIC	HOUSING
LIBRARY	OFFICE	RELIGIOUS
INSTITUTION	COMMERCIAL
BUILDING TYPE

SKIN	PLASTIC AND GLASS
	PRIMARY MATERIAL
STRUCTURE	PLASTIC AND CONCRETE FOUNDATION
	SECONDARY MATERIAL
FINISH	PLASTIC
	TERTIARY MATERIAL

MONSANTO
HOUSE OF THE FUTURE
GOODY AND HAMILTON
ANAHEIM, CALIFORNIA

| | DOCUMENTATION | | | FORM | | | PROXIMITY | | | SKIN + SURFACE | |

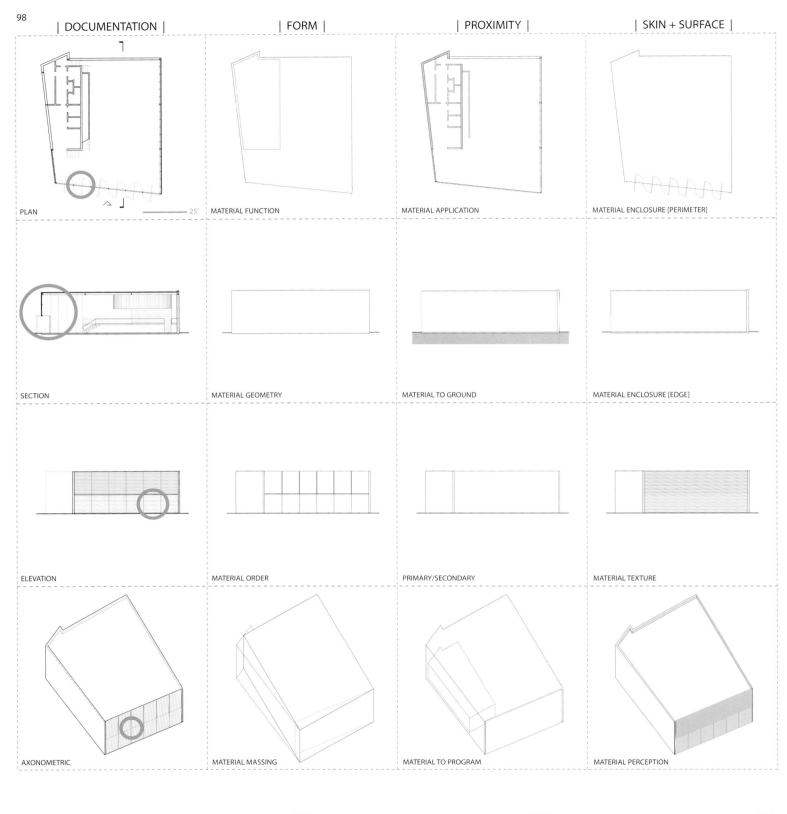

PLAN	MATERIAL FUNCTION	MATERIAL APPLICATION	MATERIAL ENCLOSURE [PERIMETER]
SECTION	MATERIAL GEOMETRY	MATERIAL TO GROUND	MATERIAL ENCLOSURE [EDGE]
ELEVATION	MATERIAL ORDER	PRIMARY/SECONDARY	MATERIAL TEXTURE
AXONOMETRIC	MATERIAL MASSING	MATERIAL TO PROGRAM	MATERIAL PERCEPTION

25'

Frank O. Gehry, U.S., wins the Pritzer Prize

Robert Venturi, U.S., wins the Pritzker Prize

Intel begins shipping the Pentium chip, which operates twice as fast as the best previous Intel chip for personal computers

1984

Inaki Abalos and Juan Herreros found Abalos & Herreros

1989

1991

1993

| STRUCTURE | | MODULE | | DETAIL |

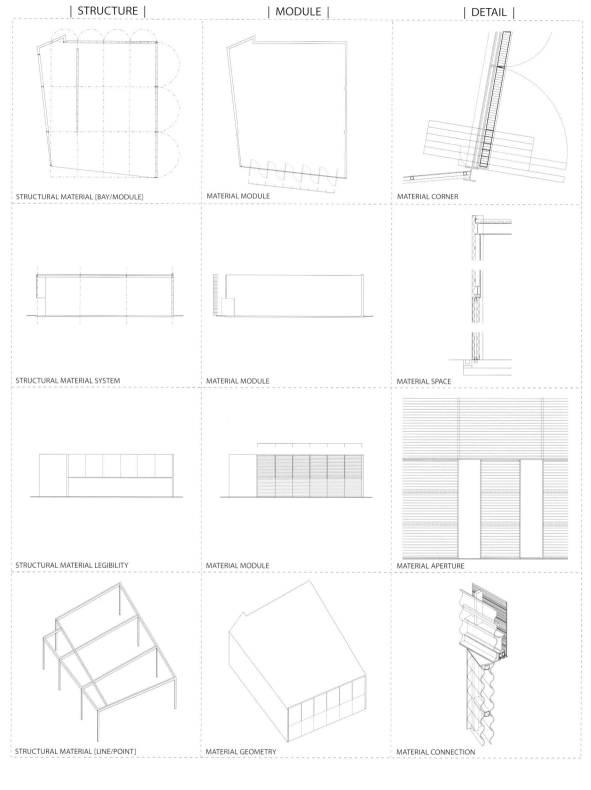

STRUCTURAL MATERIAL [BAY/MODULE]

MATERIAL MODULE

MATERIAL CORNER

STRUCTURAL MATERIAL SYSTEM

MATERIAL MODULE

MATERIAL SPACE

STRUCTURAL MATERIAL LEGIBILITY

MATERIAL MODULE

MATERIAL APERTURE

STRUCTURAL MATERIAL [LINE/POINT]

MATERIAL GEOMETRY

MATERIAL CONNECTION

40° 33' 38" N 4° 0' 60" W

COSTCOST COST COST COST COST COST
PER SQUARE FOOT

MOISTURE MOISTURE MOISTURE
AVERAGE ANNUAL HUMIDITY

TEMPERATURE TEMPERATURE
AVERAGE ANNUAL TEMPERATURE

PRECIPITATION PRECIPITATION
AVERAGE ANNUAL RAINFALL

LABOR LABOR LABOR LABOR LABOR
HOURS OF LABOR FOR CONSTRUCTION

DURABILITY DURABILITY DURABILITY
EXPECTED LIFE SPAN

EDUCATION	CIVIC	HOUSING
LIBRARY	OFFICE	RELIGIOUS
INSTITUTION	COMMERCIAL
BUILDING TYPE

| SKIN | CORRUGATED POLYCARBONATE |
| | PRIMARY MATERIAL |

| STRUCTURE | STEEL |
| | SECONDARY MATERIAL |

| FINISH | WOVEN PLANT, WOOD |
| | TERTIARY MATERIAL |

COLMENAREJO
MUNICIPAL HALL
ABALOS & HERREROS
COLMENAREJO, SPAIN

DVD (Digital Versatile Disc or
Digital Video Disc) invented

1995

1997

1999

| DOCUMENTATION | | FORM | | PROXIMITY | | SKIN + SURFACE |

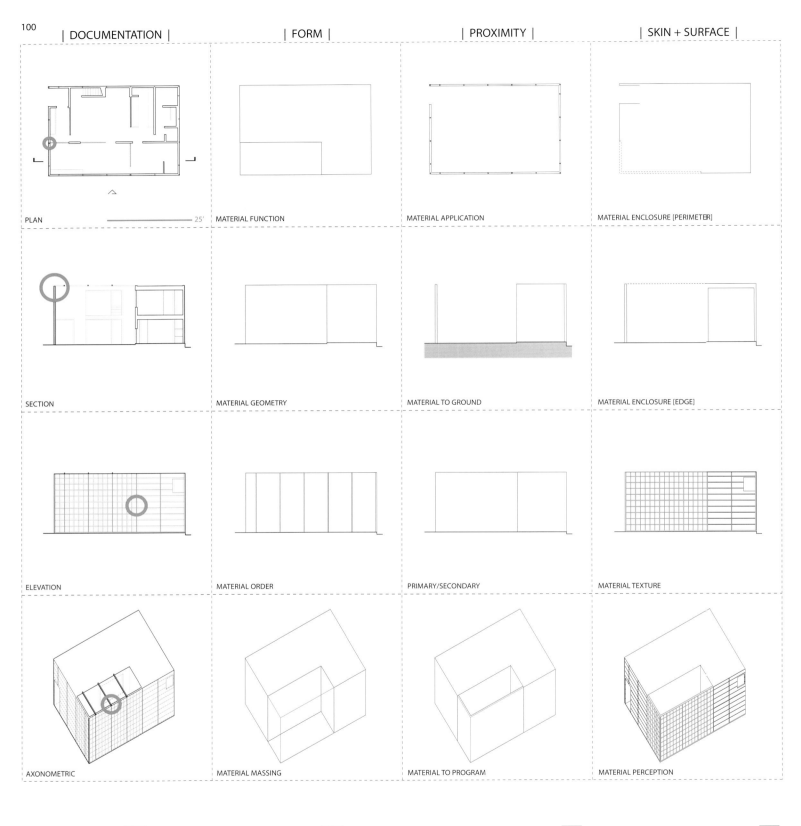

PLAN   25'   MATERIAL FUNCTION   MATERIAL APPLICATION   MATERIAL ENCLOSURE [PERIMETER]

SECTION   MATERIAL GEOMETRY   MATERIAL TO GROUND   MATERIAL ENCLOSURE [EDGE]

ELEVATION   MATERIAL ORDER   PRIMARY/SECONDARY   MATERIAL TEXTURE

AXONOMETRIC   MATERIAL MASSING   MATERIAL TO PROGRAM   MATERIAL PERCEPTION

Kenzo Tange, Japan, wins the Pritzker Prize

First portable computers with color
liquid crystal displays (LCDs) announced

The term "universal design" is introduced by
Ron Mace, FAIA, to describe special design concerns

Fumihiko Maki, Japan, wins the Pritzker Prize

1987   1989   1991   1993

| STRUCTURE | | MODULE | | DETAIL |

STRUCTURAL MATERIAL [BAY/MODULE]

MATERIAL MODULE

MATERIAL CORNER

UNDISCLOSED

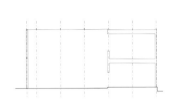

STRUCTURAL MATERIAL SYSTEM

MATERIAL MODULE

MATERIAL SPACE

COSTCOSTCOSTCOSTCOSTCOSTCOST
PER SQUARE FOOT

MOISTUREMOISTUREMOISTURE
AVERAGE ANNUAL HUMIDITY

TEMPERATURETEMPERATURE
AVERAGE ANNUAL TEMPERATURE

PRECIPITATIONPRECIPITATION
AVERAGE ANNUAL RAINFALL

LABORLABORLABORLABORLABOR
HOURS OF LABOR FOR CONSTRUCTION

DURABILITYDURABILITYDURABILITY
EXPECTED LIFE SPAN

EDUCATION	CIVIC	HOUSING
LIBRARY	OFFICE	RELIGIOUS
INSTITUTION	COMMERCIAL
BUILDING TYPE

STRUCTURAL MATERIAL LEGIBILITY

MATERIAL MODULE

MATERIAL APERTURE

STRUCTURAL MATERIAL [LINE/POINT]

MATERIAL GEOMETRY

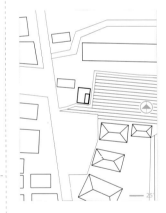

MATERIAL CONNECTION

SKIN — CORRUGATED POLYCARBONATE AND CORRUGATED GALVARIUM
PRIMARY MATERIAL

STRUCTURE — REINFORCED CONCRETE
SECONDARY MATERIAL

FINISH — WOOD AND CONCRETE
TERTIARY MATERIAL

HOUSE IN IMAZATO
KATSUYASU KISHIGAMI
IMAZATO
JAPAN

Tadao Ando, Japan, wins the Pritzker Prize

| | DOCUMENTATION | | | FORM | | | PROXIMITY | | | SKIN + SURFACE | |

PLAN   ~ 25'

MATERIAL FUNCTION

MATERIAL APPLICATION

MATERIAL ENCLOSURE [PERIMETER]

SECTION

MATERIAL GEOMETRY

MATERIAL TO GROUND

MATERIAL ENCLOSURE [EDGE]

ELEVATION

MATERIAL ORDER

PRIMARY/SECONDARY

MATERIAL TEXTURE

AXONOMETRIC

MATERIAL MASSING

MATERIAL TO PROGRAM

MATERIAL PERCEPTION

1976
Rogers establishes Richard Rogers Partnership

French and English Channel Tunnel workers
meet under the English Channel
1990

1991
Rogers is knighted

Lotus staff designs racing bicycles
for the Olympic games
1992

| STRUCTURE | | MODULE | | DETAIL |

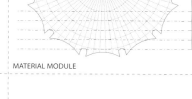

STRUCTURAL MATERIAL [BAY/MODULE]

MATERIAL MODULE

MATERIAL CORNER

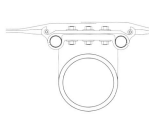

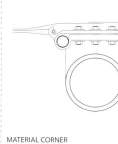

51° 30' 10" N 0° 0' 11" E

COSTCOSTCOSTCOSTCOSTCOSTCOST
PER SQUARE FOOT

MOISTUREMOISTUREMOISTURE
AVERAGE ANNUAL HUMIDITY

TEMPERATURETEMPERATURE
AVERAGE ANNUAL TEMPERATURE

PRECIPITATIONPRECIPITATION
AVERAGE ANNUAL RAINFALL

LABORLABORLABORLABORLABOR
HOURS OF LABOR FOR CONSTRUCTION

DURABILITYDURABILITYDURABILITY
EXPECTED LIFE SPAN

EDUCATION	CIVIC	HOUSING
LIBRARY	OFFICE	RELIGIOUS
INSTITUTION	COMMERCIAL
BUILDING TYPE

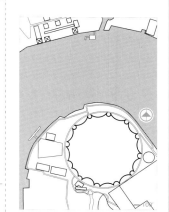

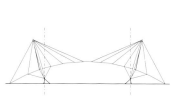
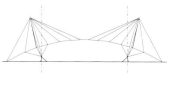

STRUCTURAL MATERIAL SYSTEM

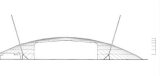
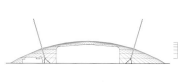
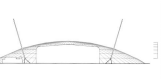

MATERIAL MODULE

MATERIAL SPACE

SKIN   PTFE-COATED GLASS FIBER FABRIC
PRIMARY MATERIAL

STRUCTURE   STEEL FRAME
SECONDARY MATERIAL

FINISH   CONCRETE
TERTIARY MATERIAL

STRUCTURAL MATERIAL LEGIBILITY

MATERIAL MODULE

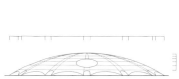
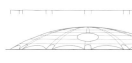

MATERIAL APERTURE

STRUCTURAL MATERIAL [LINE/POINT]

MATERIAL GEOMETRY

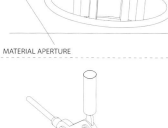

MATERIAL CONNECTION

MILLENNIUM DOME
RICHARD ROGERS
LONDON
UNITED KINGDOM

Sir Norman Foster, London,
wins the AIA Gold Medal

1994

1996
Site for the Millennium Dome is selected

1998   1999

| | DOCUMENTATION | | | FORM | | | PROXIMITY | | | SKIN + SURFACE | |

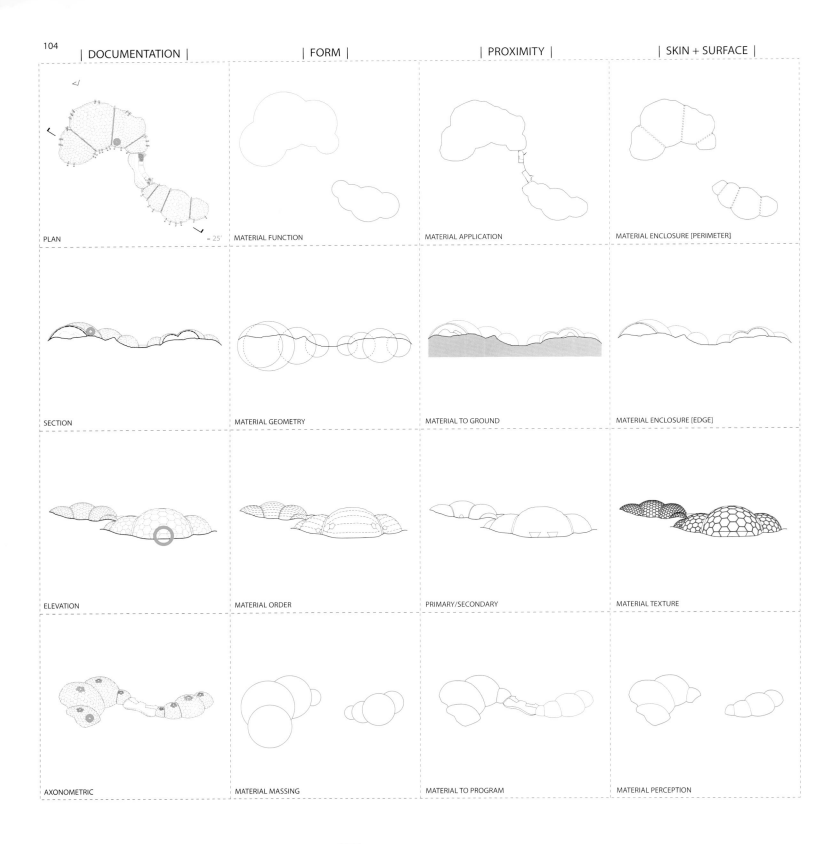

PLAN

≈ 25'

MATERIAL FUNCTION

MATERIAL APPLICATION

MATERIAL ENCLOSURE [PERIMETER]

SECTION

MATERIAL GEOMETRY

MATERIAL TO GROUND

MATERIAL ENCLOSURE [EDGE]

ELEVATION

MATERIAL ORDER

PRIMARY/SECONDARY

MATERIAL TEXTURE

AXONOMETRIC

MATERIAL MASSING

MATERIAL TO PROGRAM

MATERIAL PERCEPTION

The First Persian Gulf War begins

1980
Grimshaw founds Nicholas Grimshaw & Partners

1991

1993
Grimshaw is appointed a Commanders of
the Order of the British Empire (CBE)

| STRUCTURE | | MODULE | | DETAIL |

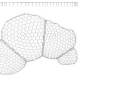
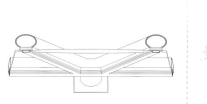

STRUCTURAL MATERIAL [BAY/MODULE]

MATERIAL MODULE

MATERIAL CORNER

STRUCTURAL MATERIAL SYSTEM

MATERIAL MODULE

MATERIAL SPACE

STRUCTURAL MATERIAL LEGIBILITY

MATERIAL MODULE

MATERIAL APERTURE

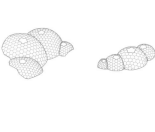
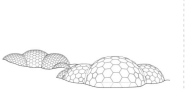

STRUCTURAL MATERIAL [LINE/POINT]

MATERIAL GEOMETRY

MATERIAL CONNECTION

50° 21' 40" N 4° 44' 34" W

COSTCOSTCOSTCOSTCOSTCOSTCOST
PER SQUARE FOOT

MOISTUREMOISTUREMOISTURE
AVERAGE ANNUAL HUMIDITY

TEMPERATURETEMPERATURE
AVERAGE ANNUAL TEMPERATURE

PRECIPITATIONPRECIPITATION
AVERAGE ANNUAL RAINFALL

LABORLABORLABORLABORLABOR
HOURS OF LABOR FOR CONSTRUCTION

DURABILITYDURABILITYDURABILITY
EXPECTED LIFE SPAN

EDUCATION	CIVIC	HOUSING
LIBRARY	OFFICE	RELIGIOUS
INSTITUTION	COMMERCIAL
BUILDING TYPE

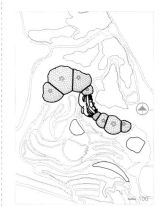

— 100

SKIN	**ETFE**
	PRIMARY MATERIAL
STRUCTURE	**GEODESIC STEEL STRUCTURE**
	SECONDARY MATERIAL
FINISH	**CONCRETE**
	TERTIARY MATERIAL

EDEN PROJECT
NICHOLAS GRIMSHAW
CORNWALL
UNITED KINGDOM

WOOD / MASONRY / CONCRETE / METAL / GLASS

PLASTIC

Cesar Pelli, New Haven, wins the AIA Gold Medal

Sverre Fehn, Norway, wins the Pritzker Prize

1995

1997

1999

2001

| DOCUMENTATION | FORM | PROXIMITY | SKIN + SURFACE |

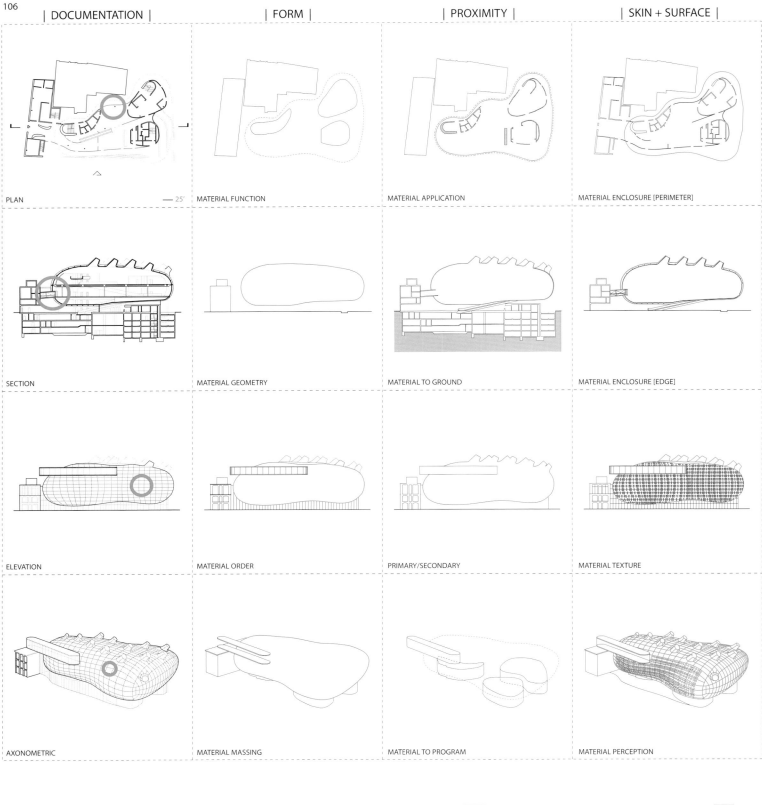

PLAN — 25'	MATERIAL FUNCTION	MATERIAL APPLICATION	MATERIAL ENCLOSURE [PERIMETER]
SECTION	MATERIAL GEOMETRY	MATERIAL TO GROUND	MATERIAL ENCLOSURE [EDGE]
ELEVATION	MATERIAL ORDER	PRIMARY/SECONDARY	MATERIAL TEXTURE
AXONOMETRIC	MATERIAL MASSING	MATERIAL TO PROGRAM	MATERIAL PERCEPTION

Fujitsu begins to market a
256-megabit memory chip

A lamb is cloned
from a cell in an adult ewe

Sir Norman Foster, U.K.,
wins the Pritzker Prize

1990

Cook becomes Professor at the Bartlett School of Architecture   1993

1996

1999

| STRUCTURE | | MODULE | | DETAIL |

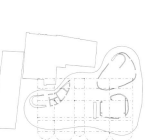

STRUCTURAL MATERIAL [BAY/MODULE]

MATERIAL MODULE

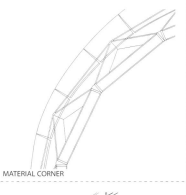

MATERIAL CORNER

STRUCTURAL MATERIAL SYSTEM

MATERIAL MODULE

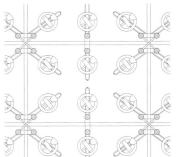

MATERIAL SPACE

STRUCTURAL MATERIAL LEGIBILITY

MATERIAL MODULE

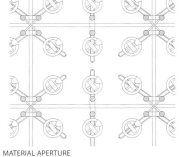

MATERIAL APERTURE

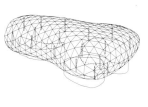

STRUCTURAL MATERIAL [LINE/POINT]

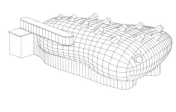

MATERIAL GEOMETRY

MATERIAL CONNECTION

48° 51' 14" N 2° 19' 42" E

COSTCOSTCOSTCOSTCOSTCOSTCOST
PER SQUARE FOOT

MOISTUREMOISTUREMOISTURE
AVERAGE ANNUAL HUMIDITY

TEMPERATURETEMPERATURE
AVERAGE ANNUAL TEMPERATURE

PRECIPITATIONPRECIPITATION
AVERAGE ANNUAL RAINFALL

LABORLABORLABOR LABORLABOR
HOURS OF LABOR FOR CONSTRUCTION

DURABILITYDURABILITYDURABILITY
EXPECTED LIFE SPAN

EDUCATION	CIVIC	HOUSING
LIBRARY	OFFICE	RELIGIOUS
INSTITUTION	COMMERCIAL
BUILDING TYPE

SKIN	TRANSLUCENT WARM BLUE ACRYLIC PLASTIC
	PRIMARY MATERIAL
STRUCTURE	STEEL AND REINFORCED CONCRETE
	SECONDARY MATERIAL
FINISH	GLASS, WHITE PLASTER AND METAL MESH
	TERTIARY MATERIAL

WOOD / MASONRY / CONCRETE / METAL / GLASS

PLASTIC

KUNSTHAUS GRAZ
COOK AND FOURNIER
GRAZ
AUSTRIA

The human genome sequence completed, providing a road map to 90 percent of the genes on every chromosome

2000

2002

2001

Archigram receives the Gold Medal of the Royal Institute of British Architects

2003

| DOCUMENTATION | | FORM | | PROXIMITY | | SKIN + SURFACE |

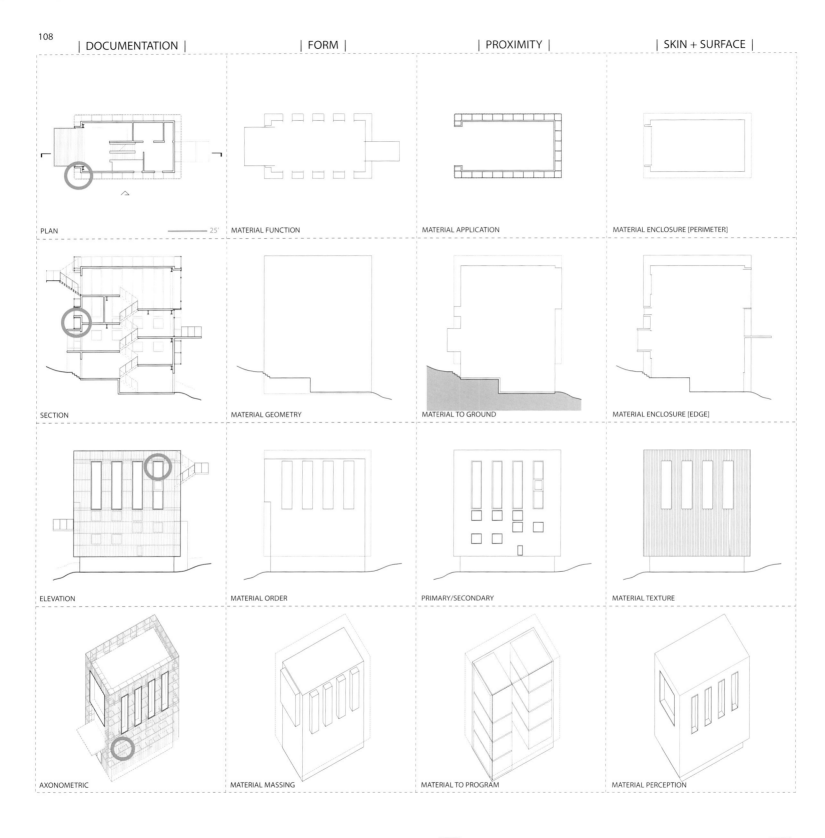

PLAN   25'   MATERIAL FUNCTION   MATERIAL APPLICATION   MATERIAL ENCLOSURE [PERIMETER]

SECTION   MATERIAL GEOMETRY   MATERIAL TO GROUND   MATERIAL ENCLOSURE [EDGE]

ELEVATION   MATERIAL ORDER   PRIMARY/SECONDARY   MATERIAL TEXTURE

AXONOMETRIC   MATERIAL MASSING   MATERIAL TO PROGRAM   MATERIAL PERCEPTION

Sir Norman Foster, U.K.,
wins the Pritzker Prize

Apple Computer introduces the iPod MP3 player

1984

Mark Anderson and Peter Anderson found
Anderson & Anderson Architecture

1999

2001

| STRUCTURE | | MODULE | | DETAIL |

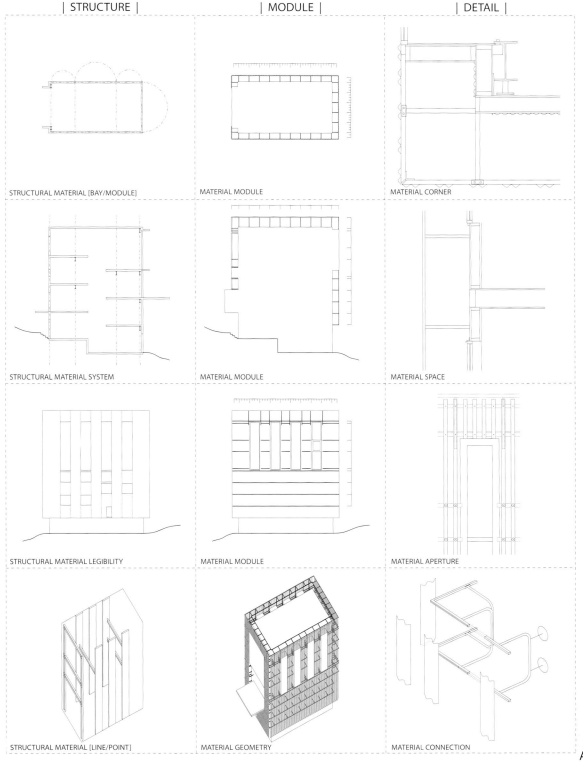

STRUCTURAL MATERIAL [BAY/MODULE]

MATERIAL MODULE

MATERIAL CORNER

STRUCTURAL MATERIAL SYSTEM

MATERIAL MODULE

MATERIAL SPACE

STRUCTURAL MATERIAL LEGIBILITY

MATERIAL MODULE

MATERIAL APERTURE

STRUCTURAL MATERIAL [LINE/POINT]

MATERIAL GEOMETRY

MATERIAL CONNECTION

45° 5' 18" N 85° 40' 2" W

COSTCOSTCOSTCOST COSTCOSTCOST
PER SQUARE FOOT

MOISTUREMOISTUREMOISTURE
AVERAGE ANNUAL HUMIDITY

TEMPERATURETEMPERATURE
AVERAGE ANNUAL TEMPERATURE

PRECIPITATIONPRECIPITATION
AVERAGE ANNUAL RAINFALL

LABORLABORLABORLABORLABOR
HOURS OF LABOR FOR CONSTRUCTION

DURABILITYDURABILITYDURABILITY
EXPECTED LIFE SPAN

EDUCATION	CIVIC	HOUSING
LIBRARY	OFFICE	RELIGIOUS
INSTITUTION	COMMERCIAL
BUILDING TYPE

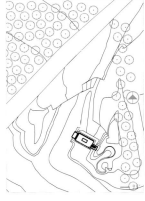

SKIN   COFRUGATED ACRYLIC
PRIMARY MATERIAL

STRUCTURE   STEEL FRAME
SECONDARY MATERIAL

                   STRUCTURAL
FINISH   INSULATED PANELS (SIP)
TERTIARY MATERIAL

WOOD
MASONRY
CONCRETE
METAL
GLASS
PLASTIC

CHAMELEON HOUSE
ANDERSON & ANDERSON
NORTHPORT, MICHIGAN

Toyota's hybrid car, the Prius, is marketed

2003   2005   2006

| | DOCUMENTATION | | | FORM | | | PROXIMITY | | | SKIN + SURFACE | |

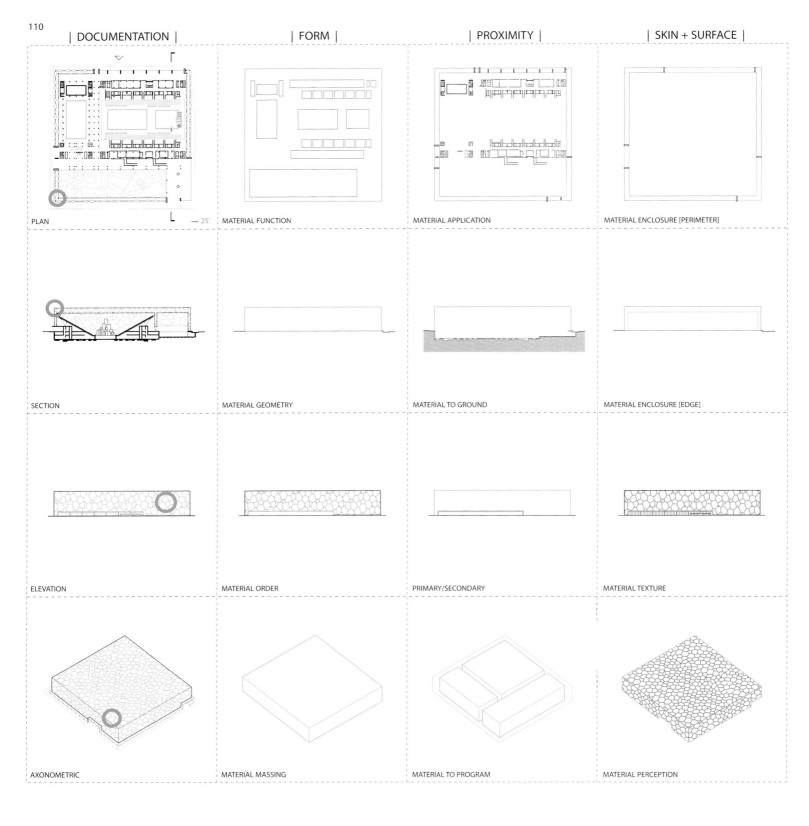

PLAN	MATERIAL FUNCTION	MATERIAL APPLICATION	MATERIAL ENCLOSURE [PERIMETER]
SECTION	MATERIAL GEOMETRY	MATERIAL TO GROUND	MATERIAL ENCLOSURE [EDGE]
ELEVATION	MATERIAL ORDER	PRIMARY/SECONDARY	MATERIAL TEXTURE
AXONOMETRIC	MATERIAL MASSING	MATERIAL TO PROGRAM	MATERIAL PERCEPTION

— 25'

1889
Peddle Thorp and Walker, predecessor of
PTW Architects, is founded

1997
PTW Architects designs
National Gallery of Australia Extension

Following Silicon Valley's lead,
80 percent of corporate America goes casual

1998

Airbus begins production of the first
super jumbo passenger jet, the A380

2000

| STRUCTURE | | MODULE | | DETAIL |

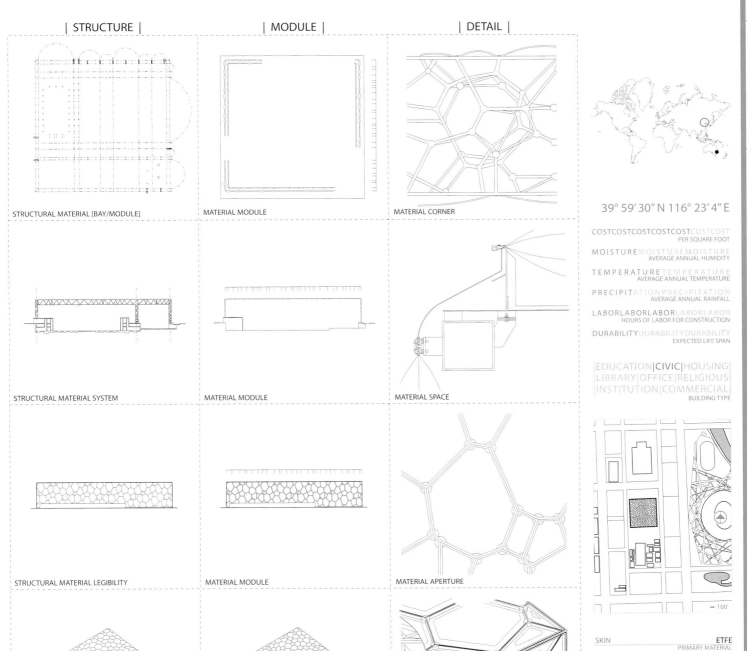

STRUCTURAL MATERIAL [BAY/MODULE]

MATERIAL MODULE

MATERIAL CORNER

STRUCTURAL MATERIAL SYSTEM

MATERIAL MODULE

MATERIAL SPACE

STRUCTURAL MATERIAL LEGIBILITY

MATERIAL MODULE

MATERIAL APERTURE

STRUCTURAL MATERIAL [LINE/POINT]

MATERIAL GEOMETRY

MATERIAL CONNECTION

WOOD

MASONRY

CONCRETE

METAL

GLASS

PLASTIC

39° 59' 30" N 116° 23' 4" E

COSTCOSTCOSTCOSTCOST COSTCOST
PER SQUARE FOOT

MOISTURE MOISTURE MOISTURE
AVERAGE ANNUAL HUMIDITY

TEMPERATURE TEMPERATURE TEMPERATURE
AVERAGE ANNUAL TEMPERATURE

PRECIPITATION PRECIPITATION
AVERAGE ANNUAL RAINFALL

LABOR LABOR LABOR LABOR LABOR
HOURS OF LABOR FOR CONSTRUCTION

DURABILITY DURABILITY DURABILITY
EXPECTED LIFE SPAN

EDUCATION	CIVIC	HOUSING
LIBRARY	OFFICE	RELIGIOUS
INSTITUTION	COMMERCIAL
BUILDING TYPE

— 100'

SKIN   ETFE
PRIMARY MATERIAL

STRUCTURE   STEEL SPACE FRAME
SECONDARY MATERIAL

                              GLASS AND
FINISH   POWDER-COATED ALUMINUM
TERTIARY MATERIAL

WATER CUBE
PTW ARCHITECTS
BEIJING
CHINA

Nano-tex LLC staff invents Nano-tex –
nanotechnology wearable fabrics

2002

2004

2007

DETAILED PRECEDENTS

A detailed examination of each project allows for a more in-depth and specific examination of the material precedent. Each diagram is superimposed on a detailed base drawing of the building. The juxtaposition allows for a specific catalog representing the interrelationship of the organizational concepts of material usage to the architectural application.

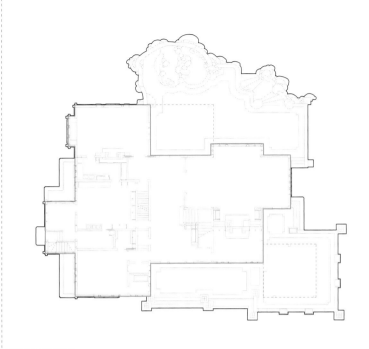

MATERIAL FUNCTION

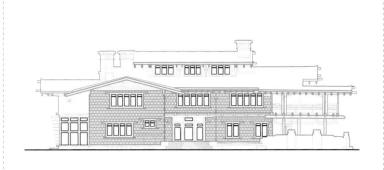

MATERIAL ORDER

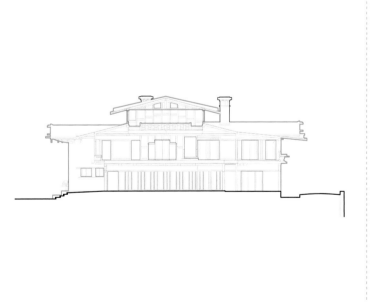

MATERIAL GEOMETRY

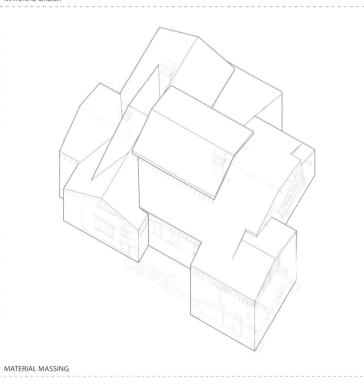

MATERIAL MASSING

WOOD SHINGLES

GAMBLE HOUSE
GREENE AND GREENE
PASADENA, CALIFORNIA

1909

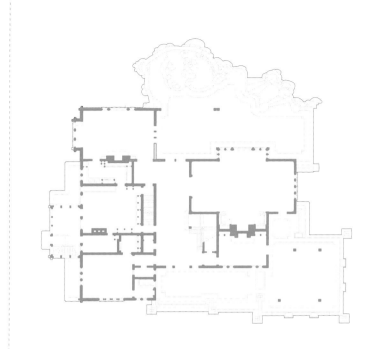

MATERIAL APPLICATION

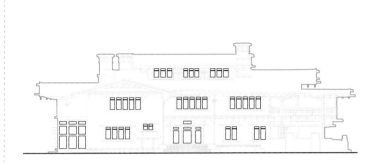

PRIMARY/SECONDARY

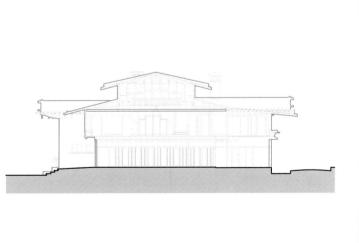

MATERIAL TO GROUND

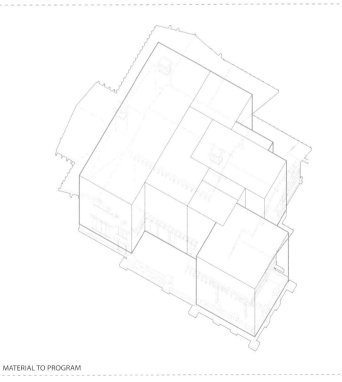

MATERIAL TO PROGRAM

WOOD SHINGLES

GAMBLE HOUSE
GREENE AND GREENE
PASADENA, CALIFORNIA

1909

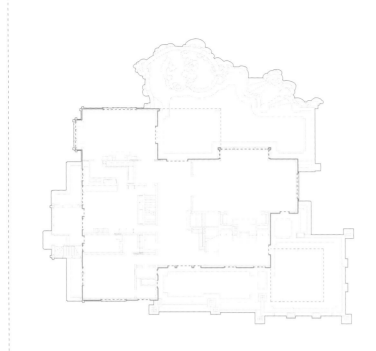

MATERIAL ENCLOSURE [PERIMETER]

MATERIAL ORDER

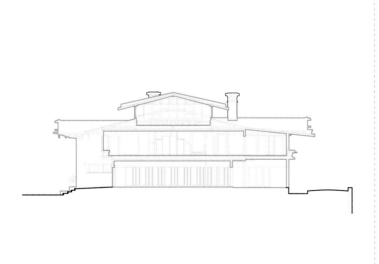

MATERIAL ENCLOSURE [EDGE]

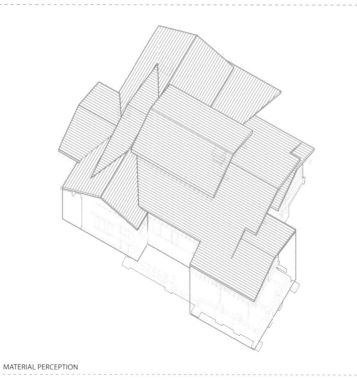

MATERIAL PERCEPTION

WOOD SHINGLES

GAMBLE HOUSE
GREENE AND GREENE
PASADENA, CALIFORNIA

1909

STRUCTURAL MATERIAL [BAY/MODULE]

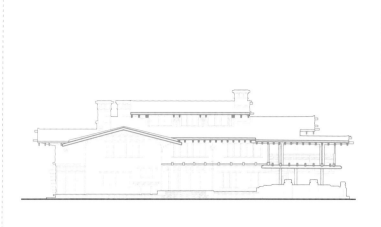

STRUCTURAL MATERIAL LEGIBILITY

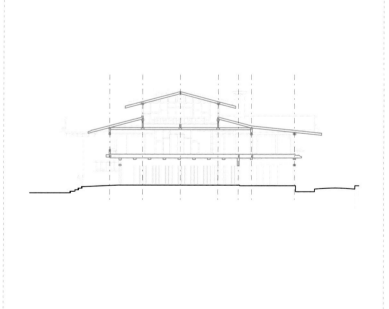

STRUCTURAL MATERIAL SYSTEM

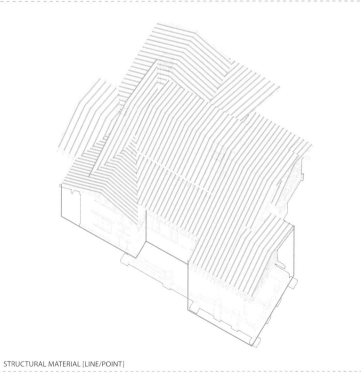

STRUCTURAL MATERIAL [LINE/POINT]

WOOD SHINGLES

GAMBLE HOUSE
GREENE AND GREENE
PASADENA, CALIFORNIA

1909

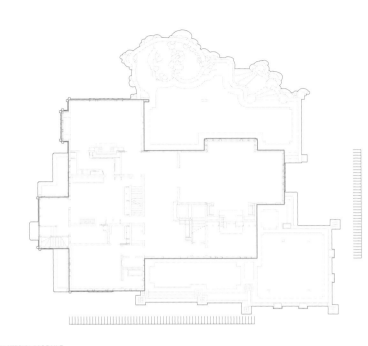

MATERIAL MODULE

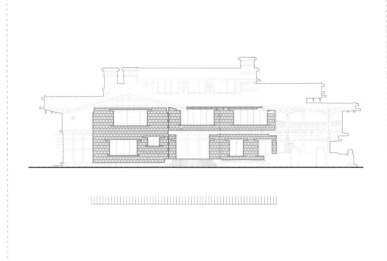

MATERIAL MODULE

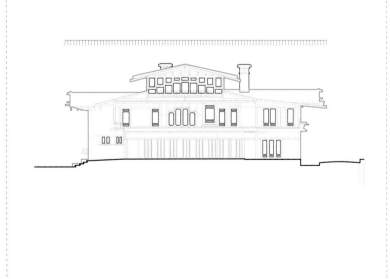

MATERIAL MODULE

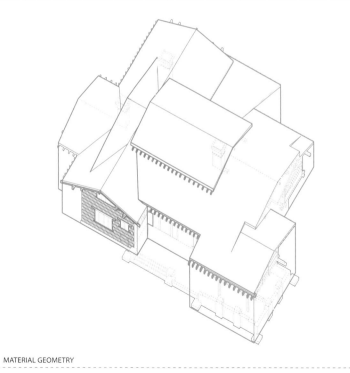

MATERIAL GEOMETRY

WOOD SHINGLES

GAMBLE HOUSE
GREENE AND GREENE
PASADENA, CALIFORNIA

1909

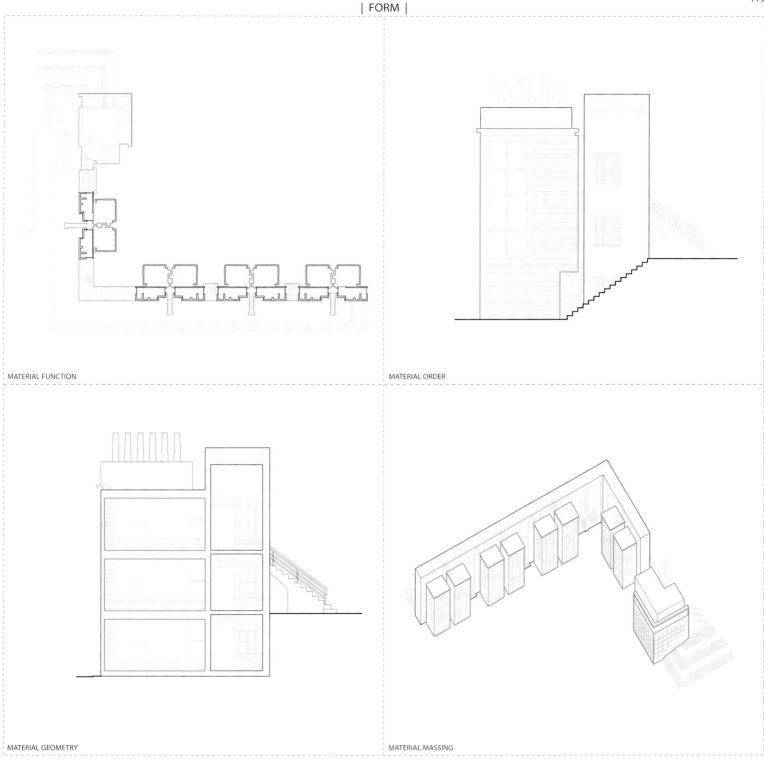

MATERIAL FUNCTION

MATERIAL ORDER

MATERIAL GEOMETRY

MATERIAL MASSING

CHARLESTON GREEN PAINTED WOOD

MIDDLETON INN
CLARK AND MENEFEE
CHARLESTON, SOUTH CAROLINA

1986

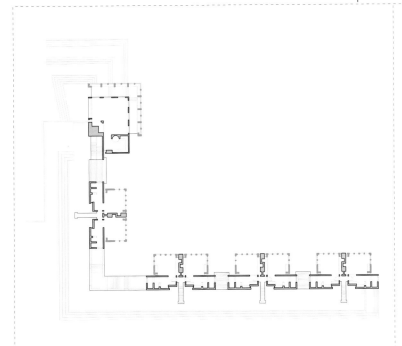

MATERIAL APPLICATION

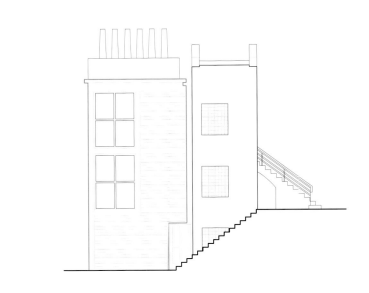

PRIMARY/SECONDARY

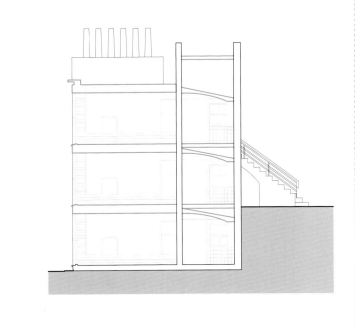

MATERIAL TO GROUND

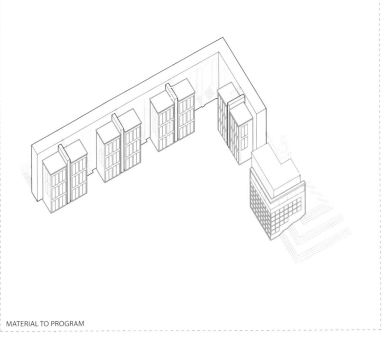

MATERIAL TO PROGRAM

CHARLESTON GREEN PAINTED WOOD

MIDDLETON INN
CLARK AND MENEFEE
CHARLESTON, SOUTH CAROLINA

1986

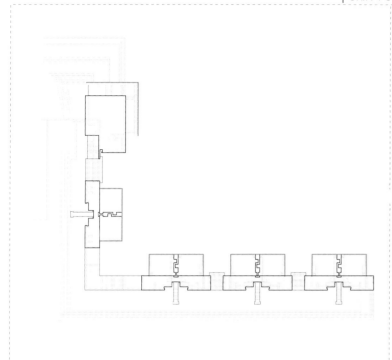

MATERIAL ENCLOSURE [PERIMETER]

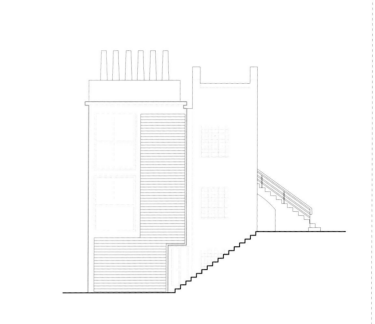

MATERIAL ORDER

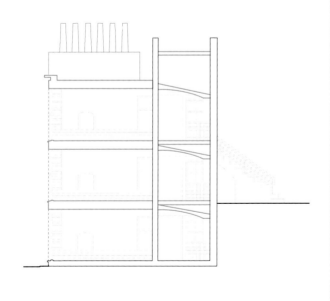

MATERIAL ENCLOSURE [EDGE]

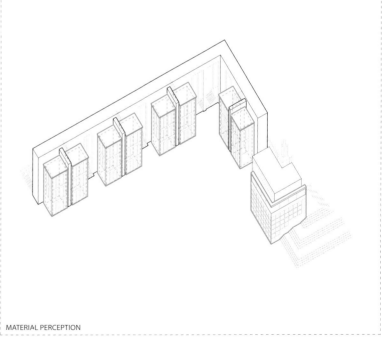

MATERIAL PERCEPTION

CHARLESTON GREEN PAINTED WOOD

MIDDLETON INN
CLARK AND MENEFEE
CHARLESTON, SOUTH CAROLINA

1986

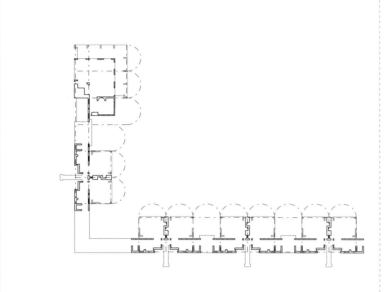

STRUCTURAL MATERIAL [BAY/MODULE]

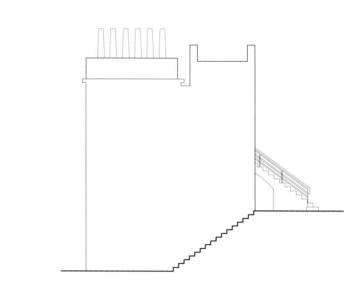

STRUCTURAL MATERIAL LEGIBILITY

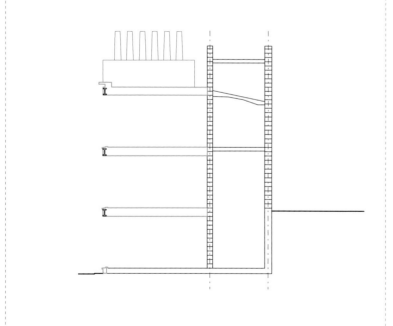

STRUCTURAL MATERIAL SYSTEM

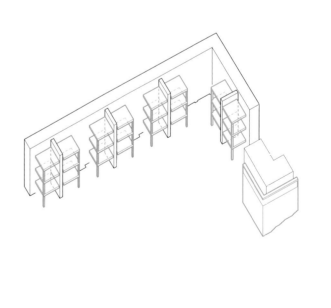

STRUCTURAL MATERIAL [LINE/POINT]

CHARLESTON GREEN PAINTED WOOD

MIDDLETON INN
CLARK AND MENEFEE
CHARLESTON, SOUTH CAROLINA

1986

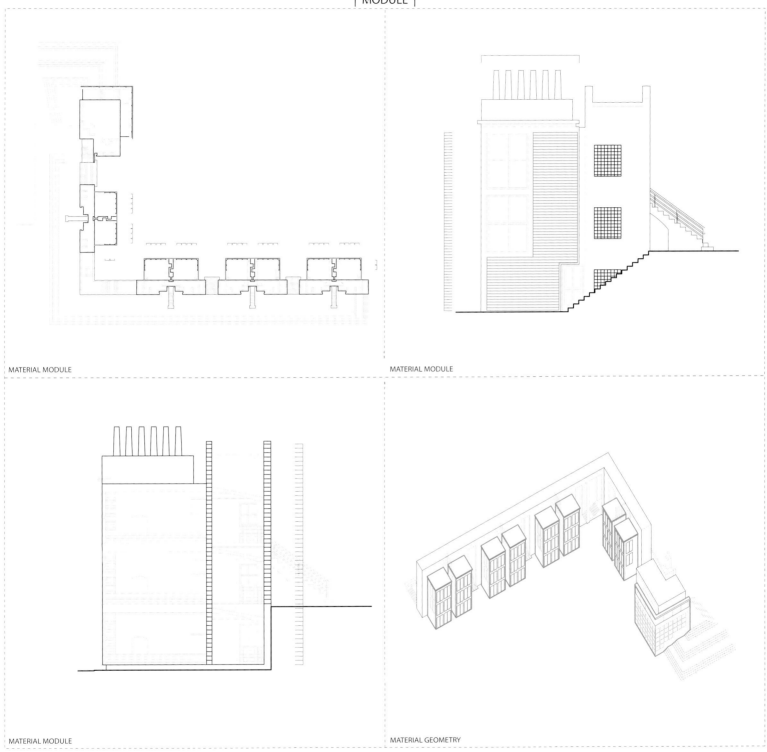

MATERIAL MODULE

MATERIAL MODULE

MATERIAL MODULE

MATERIAL GEOMETRY

CHARLESTON GREEN PAINTED WOOD

MIDDLETON INN
CLARK AND MENEFEE
CHARLESTON, SOUTH CAROLINA

1986

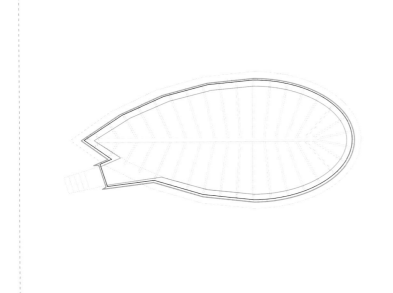

MATERIAL FUNCTION

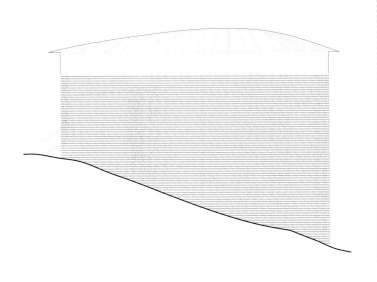

MATERIAL ORDER

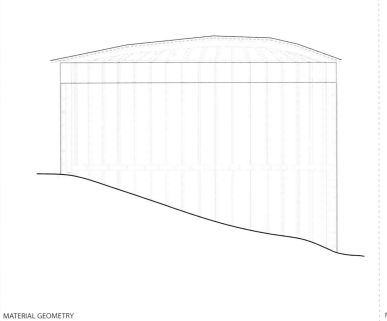

MATERIAL GEOMETRY

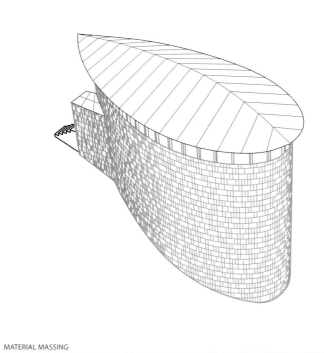

MATERIAL MASSING

LARCH WOOD SHINGLES

CHAPEL OF ST. BENEDICT
PETER ZUMTHOR
SUMVITG, SWITZERLAND

1988

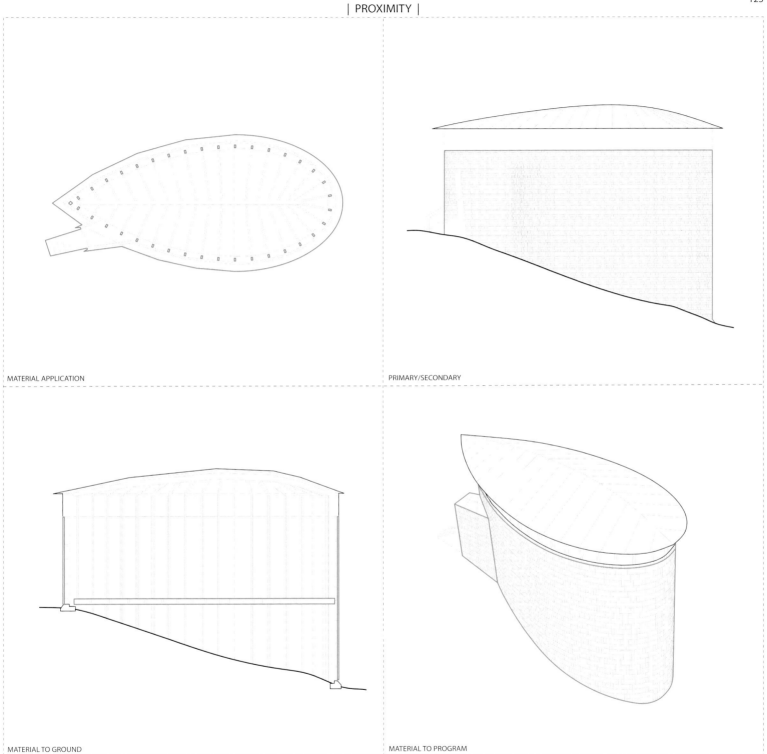

MATERIAL APPLICATION

PRIMARY/SECONDARY

MATERIAL TO GROUND

MATERIAL TO PROGRAM

LARCH WOOD SHINGLES

CHAPEL OF ST. BENEDICT
PETER ZUMTHOR
SUMVITG, SWITZERLAND

1988

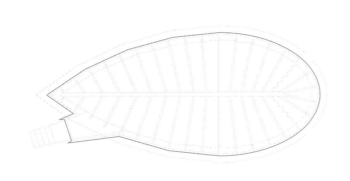

MATERIAL ENCLOSURE [PERIMETER]

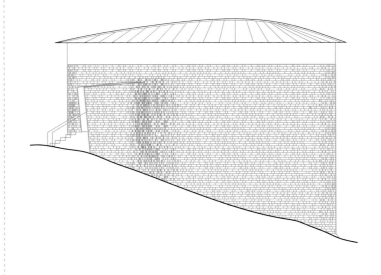

MATERIAL ORDER

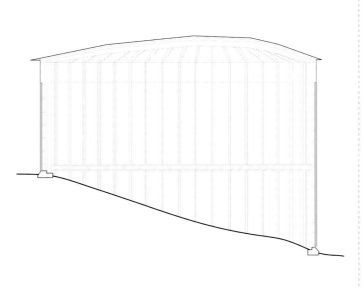

MATERIAL ENCLOSURE [EDGE]

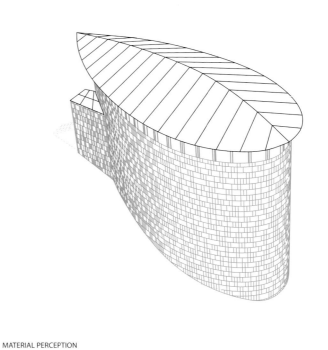

MATERIAL PERCEPTION

LARCH WOOD SHINGLES

CHAPEL OF ST. BENEDICT
PETER ZUMTHOR
SUMVITG, SWITZERLAND

1988

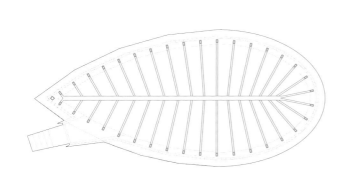

STRUCTURAL MATERIAL [BAY/MODULE]

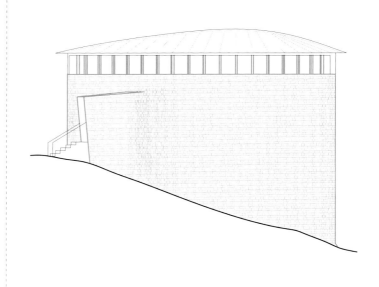

STRUCTURAL MATERIAL LEGIBILITY

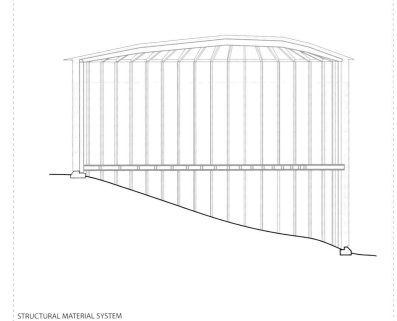

STRUCTURAL MATERIAL SYSTEM

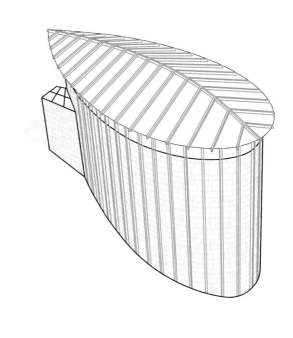

STRUCTURAL MATERIAL [LINE/POINT]

LARCH WOOD SHINGLES

CHAPEL OF ST. BENEDICT
PETER ZUMTHOR
SUMVITG, SWITZERLAND

1988

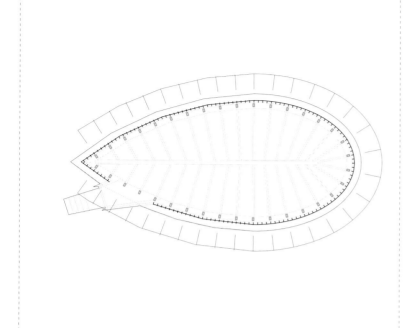

MATERIAL MODULE

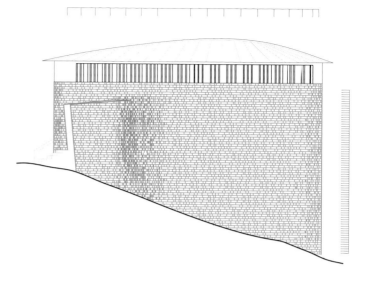

MATERIAL MODULE

MATERIAL MODULE

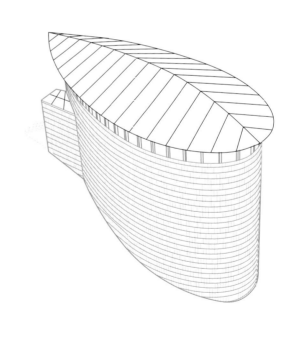

MATERIAL GEOMETRY

LARCH WOOD SHINGLES

CHAPEL OF ST. BENEDICT
PETER ZUMTHOR
SUMVITG, SWITZERLAND

1988

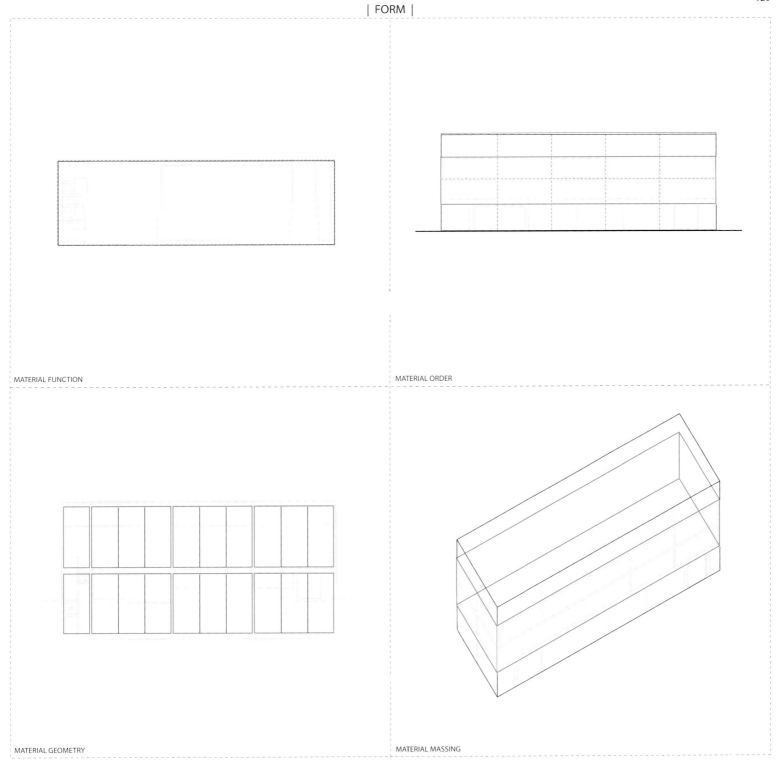

MATERIAL FUNCTION

MATERIAL ORDER

MATERIAL GEOMETRY

MATERIAL MASSING

BIRCH WOOD

GOETZ COLLECTION MUSEUM
HERZOG & DE MEURON
MUNICH, GERMANY

1992

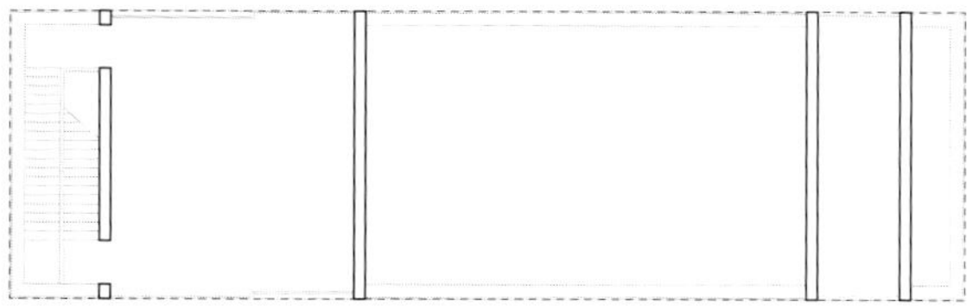

MATERIAL APPLICATION

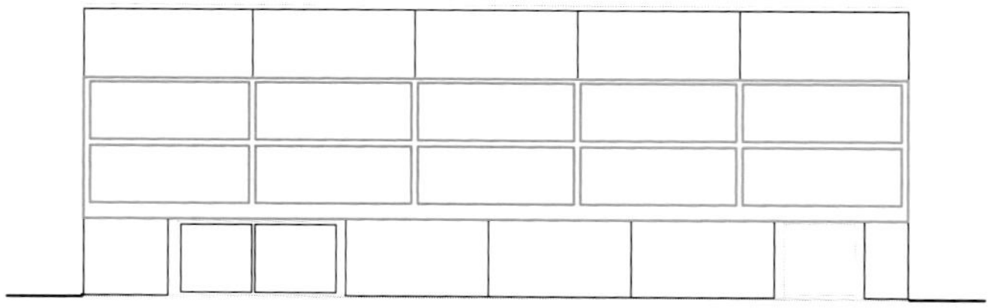

PRIMARY/SECONDARY

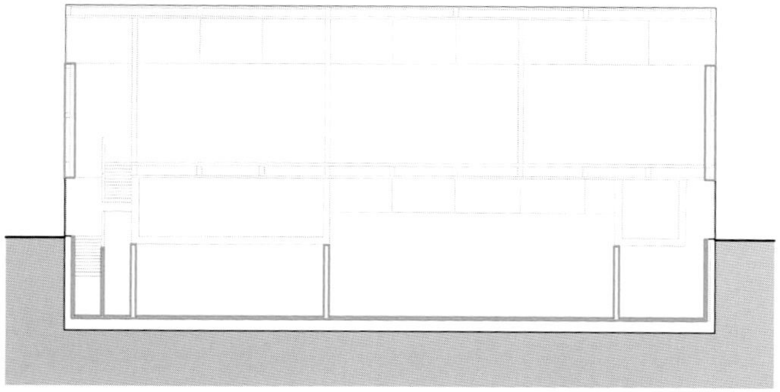

MATERIAL TO GROUND

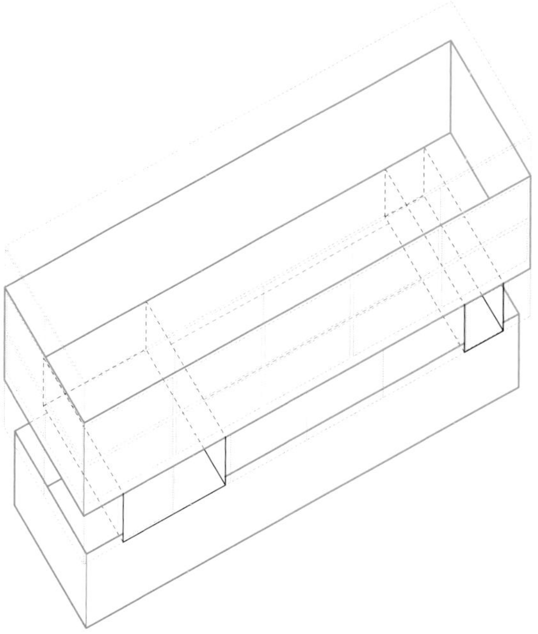

MATERIAL TO PROGRAM

BIRCH WOOD

GOETZ COLLECTION MUSEUM
HERZOG & DE MEURON
MUNICH, GERMANY

1992

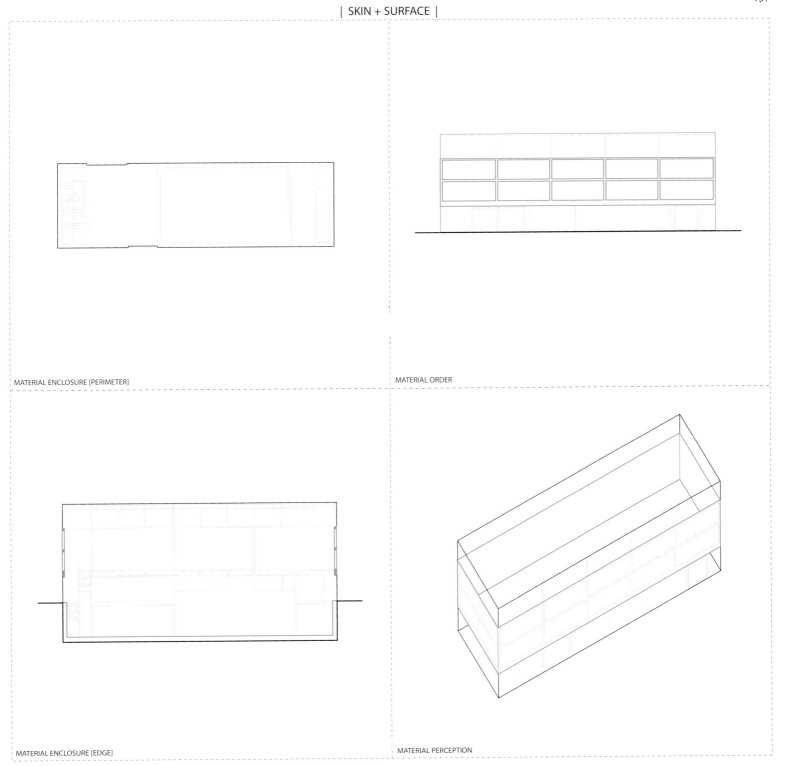

MATERIAL ENCLOSURE [PERIMETER]

MATERIAL ORDER

MATERIAL ENCLOSURE [EDGE]

MATERIAL PERCEPTION

BIRCH WOOD

GOETZ COLLECTION MUSEUM
HERZOG & DE MEURON
MUNICH, GERMANY

1992

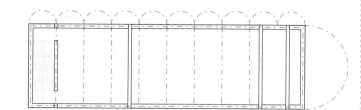

STRUCTURAL MATERIAL [BAY/MODULE]

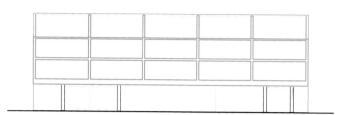

STRUCTURAL MATERIAL LEGIBILITY

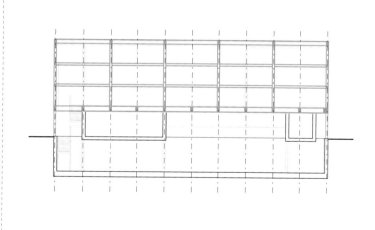

STRUCTURAL MATERIAL SYSTEM

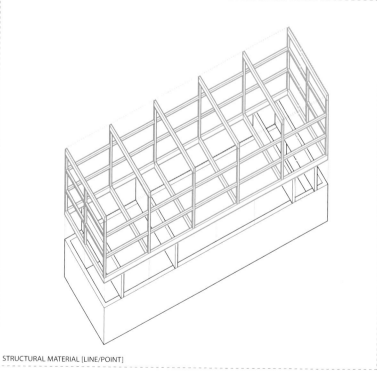

STRUCTURAL MATERIAL [LINE/POINT]

BIRCH WOOD

GOETZ COLLECTION MUSEUM
HERZOG & DE MEURON
MUNICH, GERMANY

1992

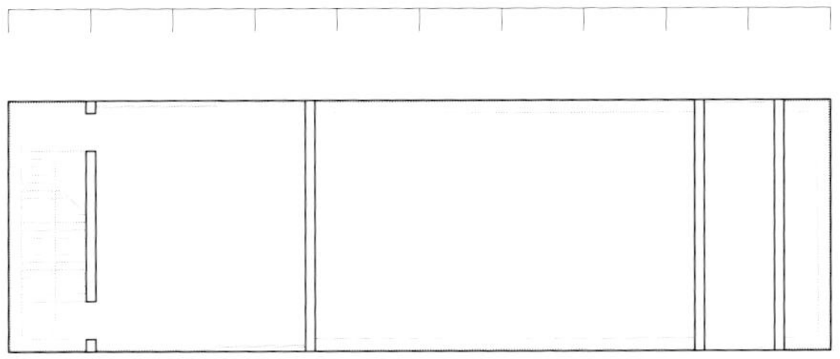

MATERIAL MODULE

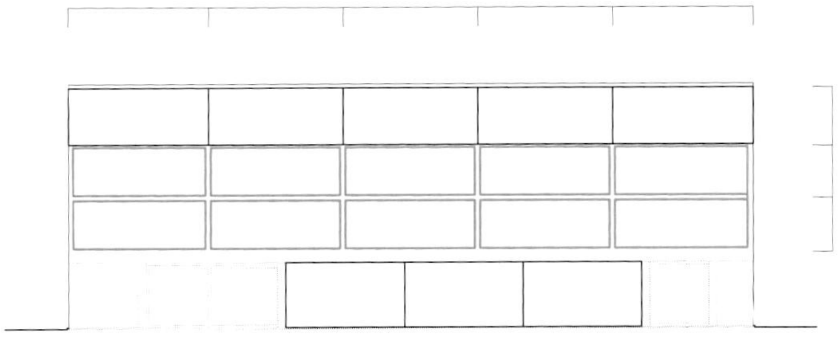

MATERIAL MODULE

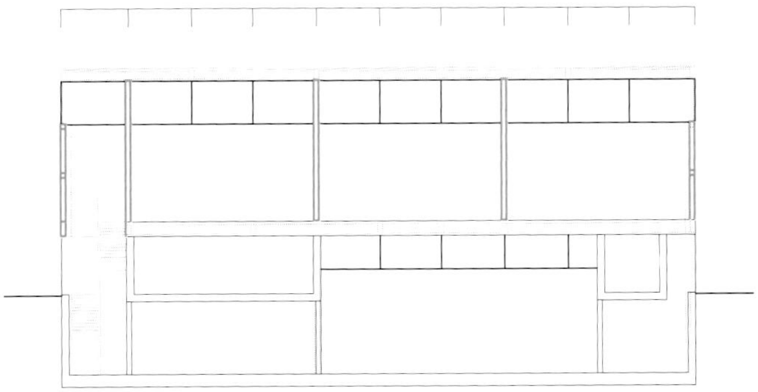

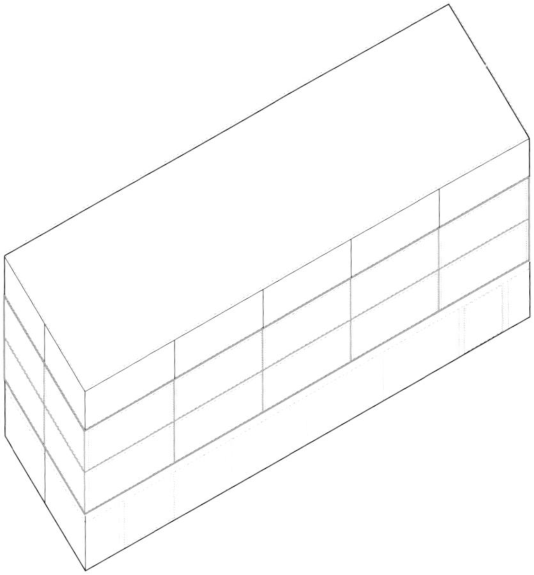

MATERIAL MODULE

MATERIAL GEOMETRY

BIRCH WOOD

GOETZ COLLECTION MUSEUM
HERZOG & DE MEURON
MUNICH, GERMANY

1992

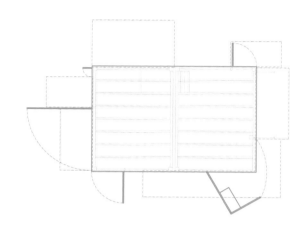

MATERIAL FUNCTION

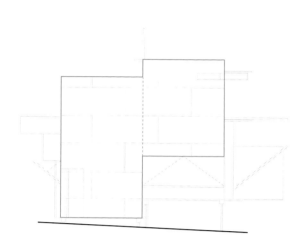

MATERIAL ORDER

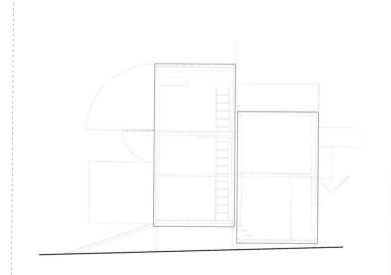

MATERIAL GEOMETRY

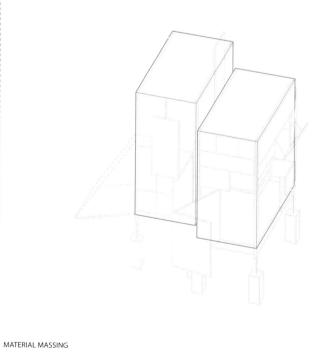

MATERIAL MASSING

ENAMELED MARINE PLYWOOD

GUCKLHUPF
HANS PETER WÖRNDL
MONDSEE, AUSTRIA

1993

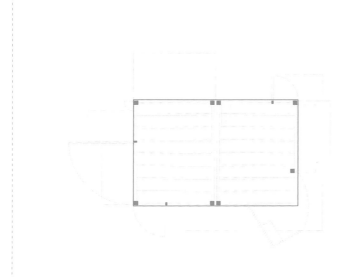

MATERIAL APPLICATION

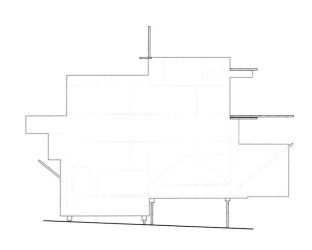

PRIMARY/SECONDARY

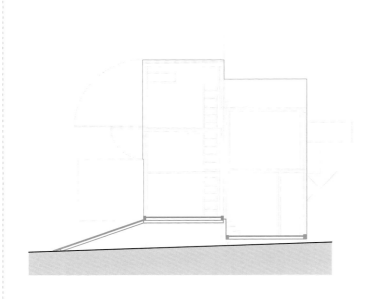

MATERIAL TO GROUND

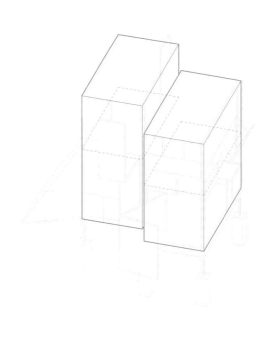

MATERIAL TO PROGRAM

ENAMELED MARINE PLYWOOD

GUCKLHUPF
HANS PETER WÖRNDL
MONDSEE, AUSTRIA

1993

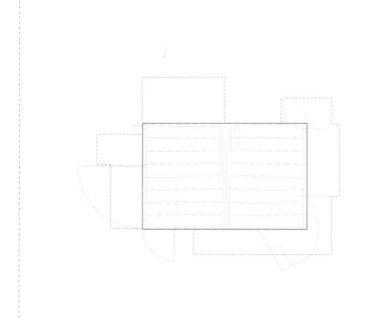

MATERIAL ENCLOSURE [PERIMETER]

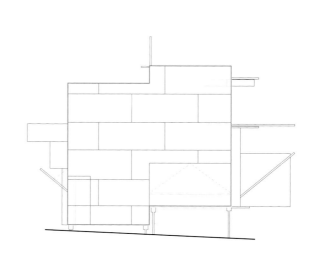

MATERIAL ORDER

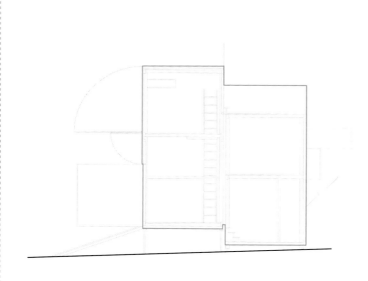

MATERIAL ENCLOSURE [EDGE]

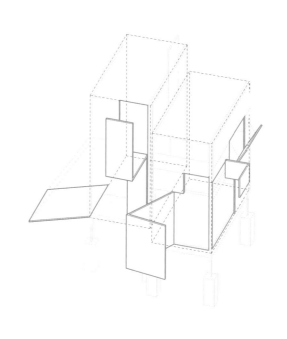

MATERIAL PERCEPTION

ENAMELED MARINE PLYWOOD

GUCKLHUPF
HANS PETER WÖRNDL
MONDSEE, AUSTRIA

1993

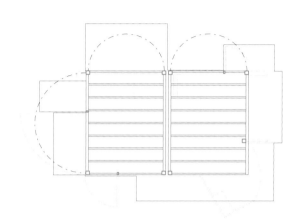

STRUCTURAL MATERIAL [BAY/MODULE]

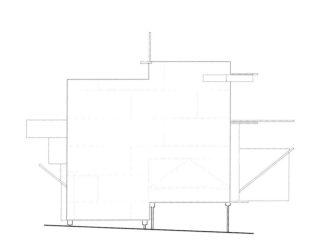

STRUCTURAL MATERIAL LEGIBILITY

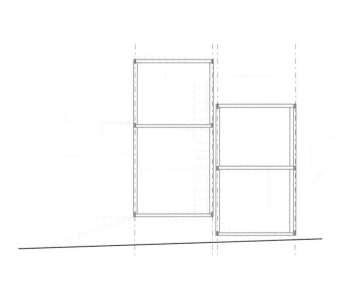

STRUCTURAL MATERIAL SYSTEM

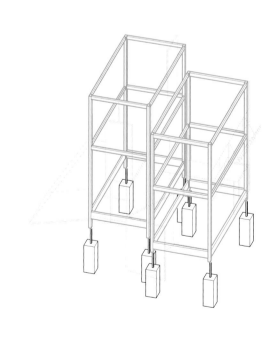

STRUCTURAL MATERIAL [LINE/POINT]

ENAMELED MARINE PLYWOOD

GUCKLHUPF
HANS PETER WÖRNDL
MONDSEE, AUSTRIA

1993

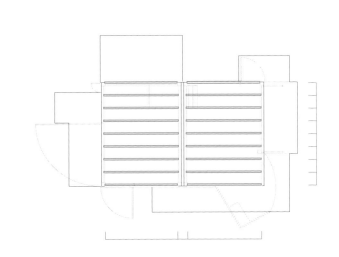

MATERIAL MODULE

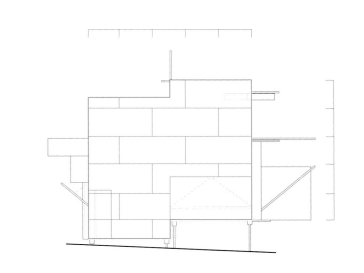

MATERIAL MODULE

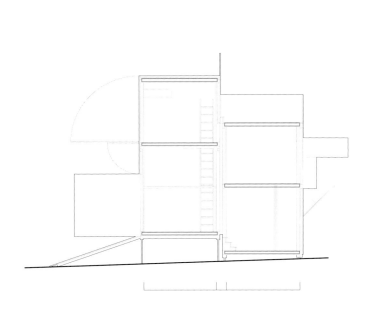

MATERIAL MODULE

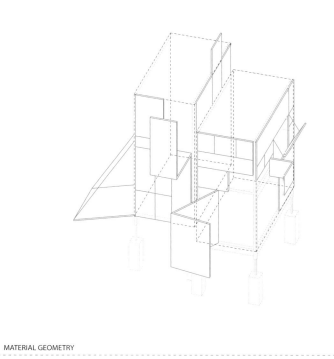

MATERIAL GEOMETRY

ENAMELED MARINE PLYWOOD

GUCKLHUPF
HANS PETER WÖRNDL
MONDSEE, AUSTRIA

1993

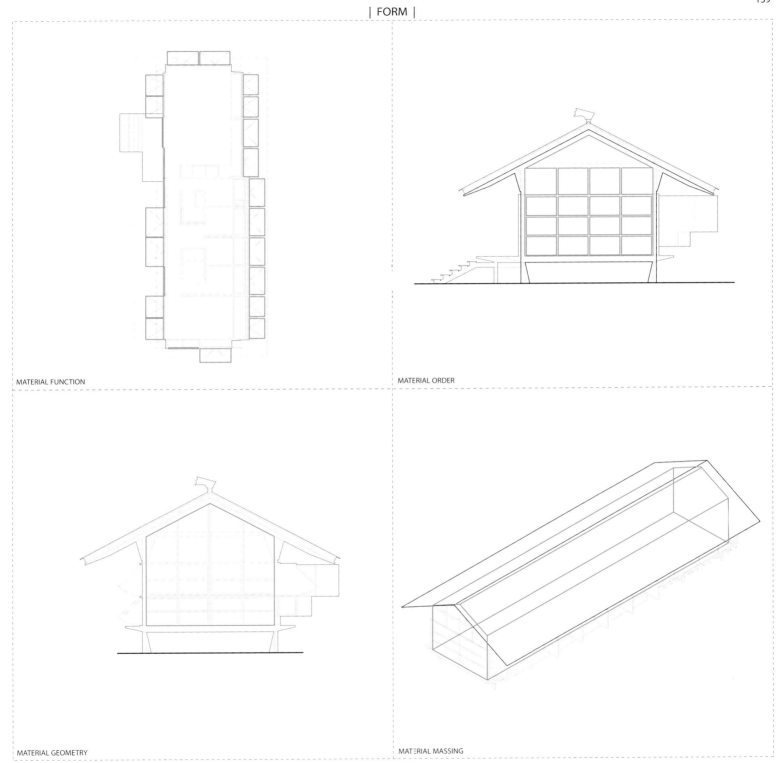

MATERIAL FUNCTION

MATERIAL ORDER

MATERIAL GEOMETRY

MATERIAL MASSING

PLYWOOD WALLS AND TALLOW-WOOD SHUTTERS

MARIKA-ALDERTON HOUSE
GLENN MURCUTT
NORTHERN TERRITORY, AUSTRALIA

1994

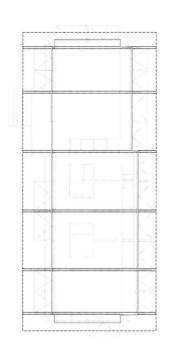

MATERIAL APPLICATION

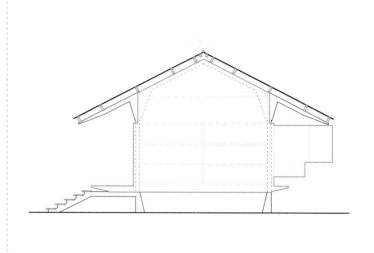

PRIMARY/SECONDARY

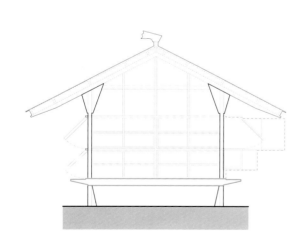

MATERIAL TO GROUND

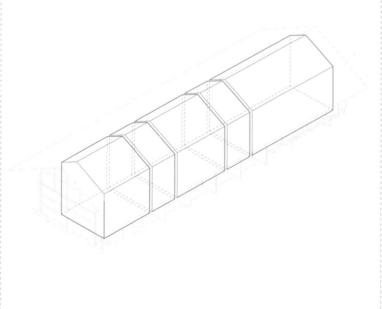

MATERIAL TO PROGRAM

PLYWOOD WALLS AND TALLOW-WOOD SHUTTERS

MARIKA-ALDERTON HOUSE
GLENN MURCUTT
NORTHERN TERRITORY, AUSTRALIA

1994

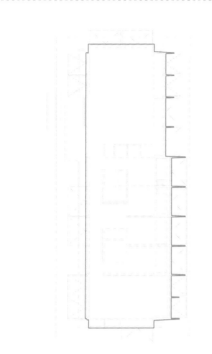

MATERIAL ENCLOSURE [PERIMETER]

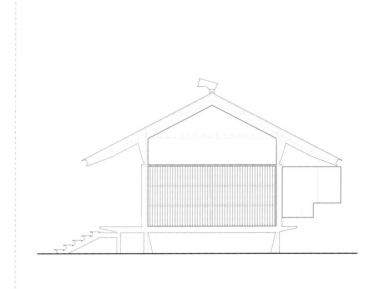

MATERIAL ORDER

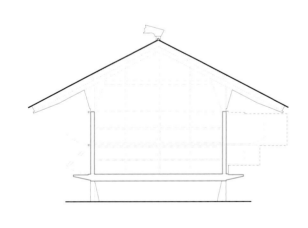

MATERIAL ENCLOSURE [EDGE]

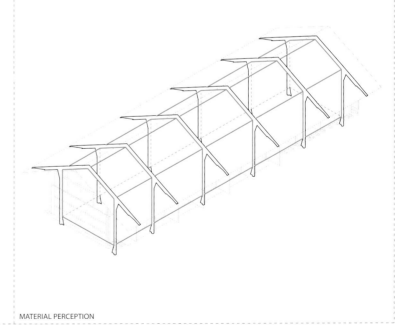

MATERIAL PERCEPTION

PLYWOOD WALLS AND TALLOW-WOOD SHUTTERS

MARIKA-ALDERTON HOUSE
GLENN MURCUTT
NORTHERN TERRITORY, AUSTRALIA

1994

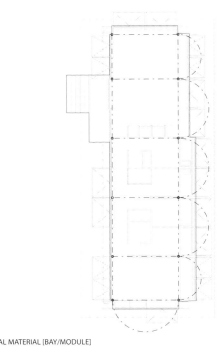

STRUCTURAL MATERIAL [BAY/MODULE]

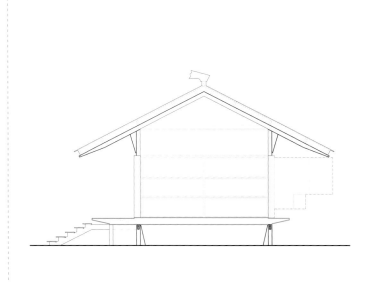

STRUCTURAL MATERIAL LEGIBILITY

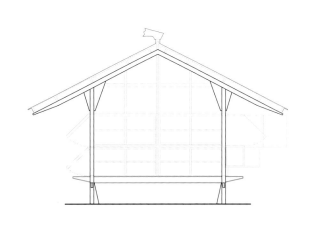

STRUCTURAL MATERIAL SYSTEM

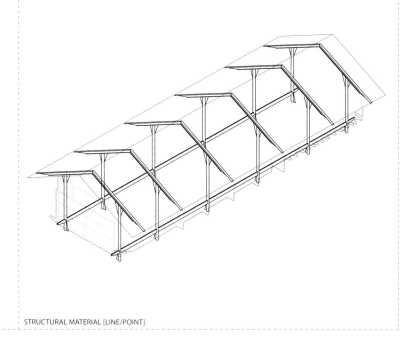

STRUCTURAL MATERIAL [LINE/POINT]

PLYWOOD WALLS AND TALLOW-WOOD SHUTTERS

MARIKA-ALDERTON HOUSE
GLENN MURCUTT
NORTHERN TERRITORY, AUSTRALIA

1994

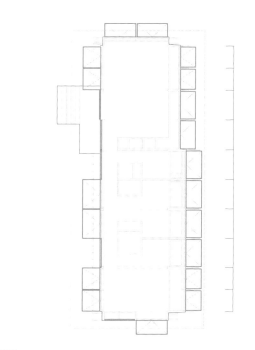

MATERIAL MODULE

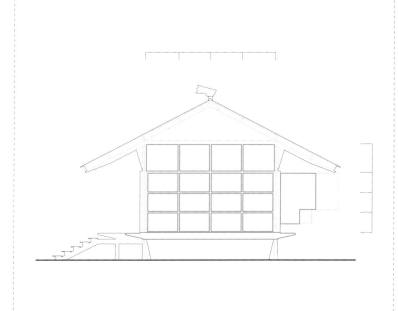

MATERIAL MODULE

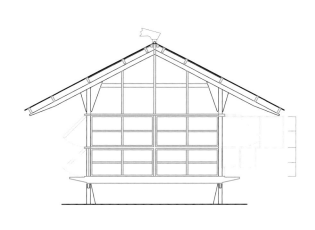

MATERIAL MODULE

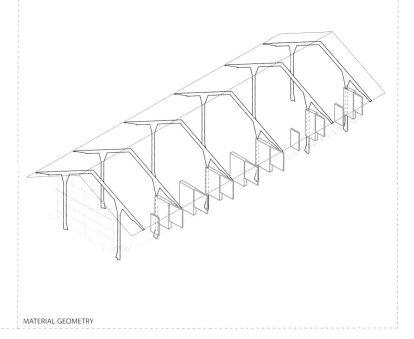

MATERIAL GEOMETRY

PLYWOOD WALLS AND TALLOW-WOOD SHUTTERS

MARIKA-ALDERTON HOUSE
GLENN MURCUTT
NORTHERN TERRITORY, AUSTRALIA

1994

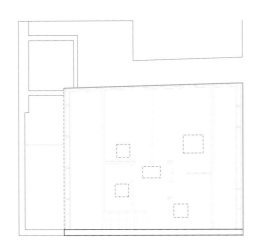

MATERIAL FUNCTION

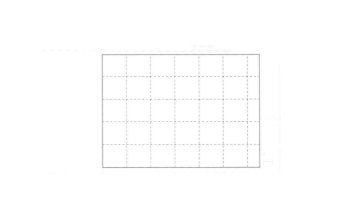

MATERIAL ORDER

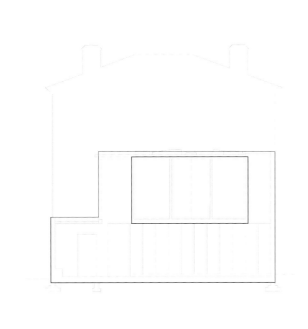

MATERIAL GEOMETRY

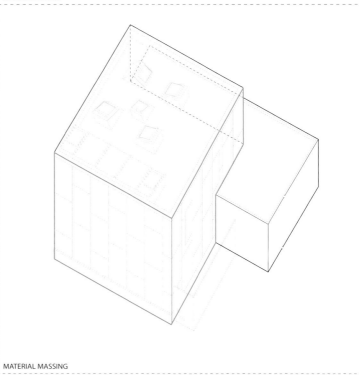

MATERIAL MASSING

RESIN-COATED PLYWOOD

ELEKTRA HOUSE
DAVID ADJAYE
LONDON, UNITED KINGDOM

2000

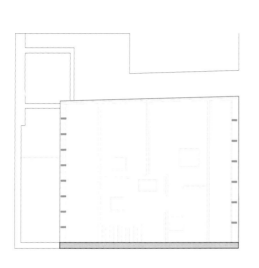

MATERIAL APPLICATION

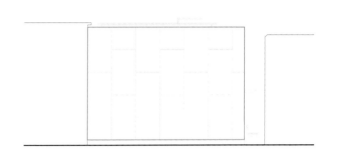

PRIMARY/SECONDARY

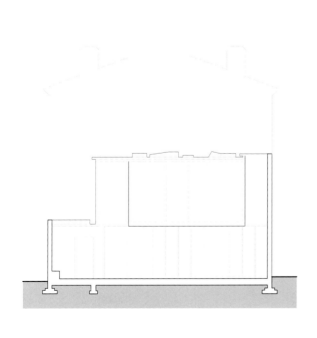

MATERIAL TO GROUND

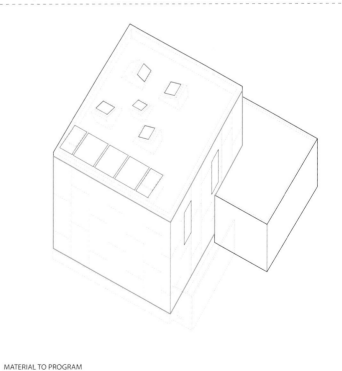

MATERIAL TO PROGRAM

RESIN-COATED PLYWOOD

ELEKTRA HOUSE
DAVID ADJAYE
LONDON, UNITED KINGDOM

2000

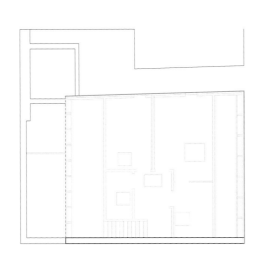

MATERIAL ENCLOSURE [PERIMETER]

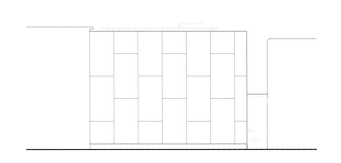

MATERIAL ORDER

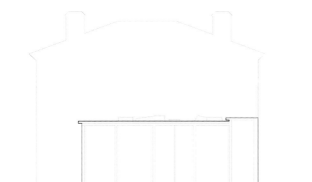

MATERIAL ENCLOSURE [EDGE]

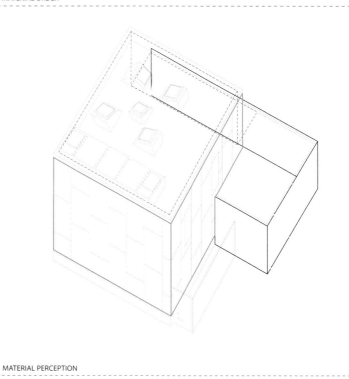

MATERIAL PERCEPTION

RESIN-COATED PLYWOOD

ELEKTRA HOUSE
DAVID ADJAYE
LONDON, UNITED KINGDOM

2000

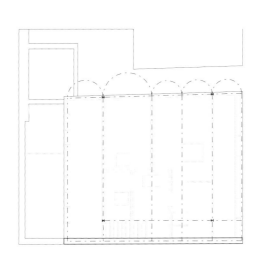

STRUCTURAL MATERIAL [BAY/MODULE]

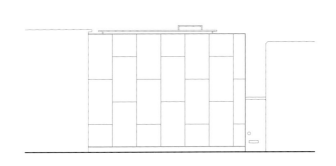

STRUCTURAL MATERIAL LEGIBILITY

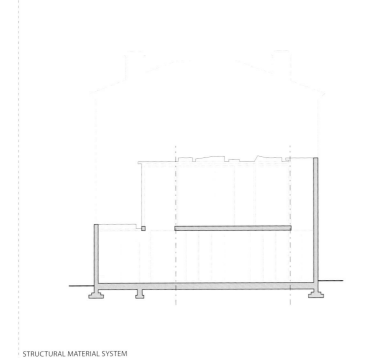

STRUCTURAL MATERIAL SYSTEM

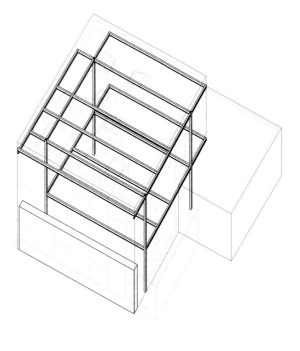

STRUCTURAL MATERIAL [LINE/POINT]

RESIN-COATED PLYWOOD

ELEKTRA HOUSE
DAVID ADJAYE
LONDON, UNITED KINGDOM

2000

| MODULE |

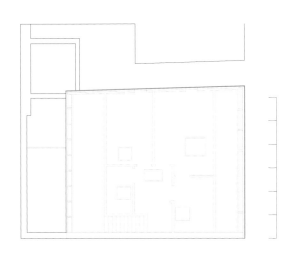

MATERIAL MODULE

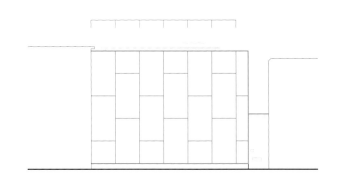

MATERIAL MODULE

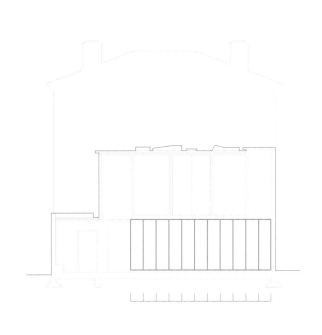

MATERIAL MODULE

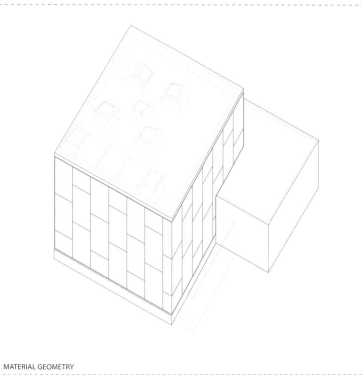

MATERIAL GEOMETRY

RESIN-COATED PLYWOOD

ELEKTRA HOUSE
DAVID ADJAYE
LONDON, UNITED KINGDOM

2000

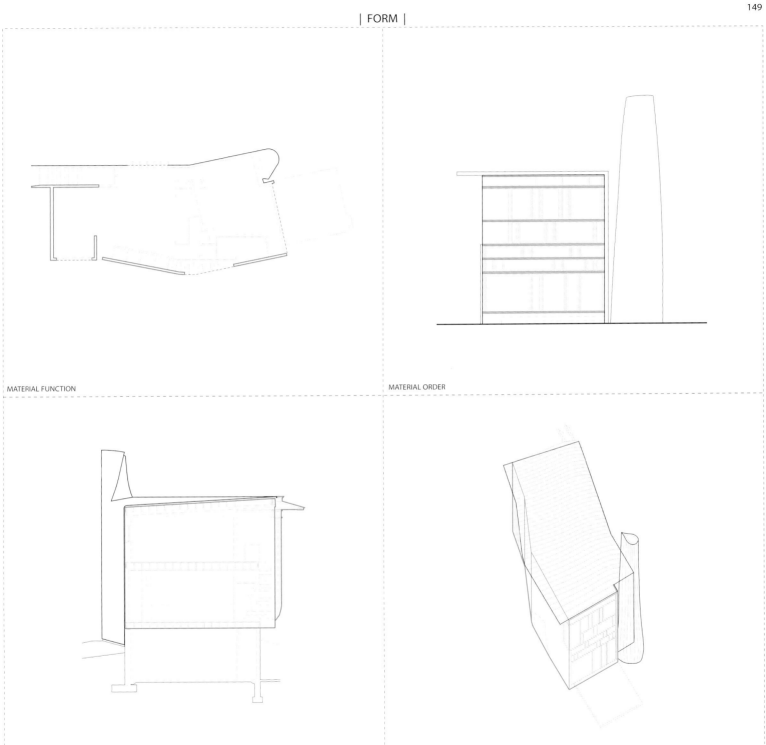

MATERIAL FUNCTION

MATERIAL ORDER

MATERIAL GEOMETRY

MATERIAL MASSING

CEDAR WOOD

NEW ENGLAND HOUSE
OFFICE dA
BOSTON, MASSACHUSETTS

2002

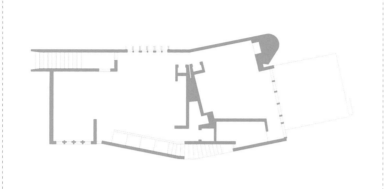

MATERIAL APPLICATION

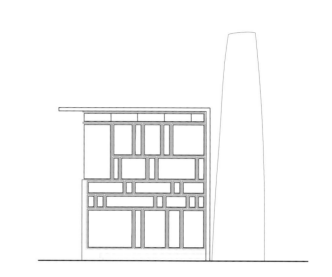

PRIMARY/SECONDARY

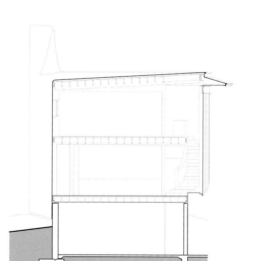

MATERIAL TO GROUND

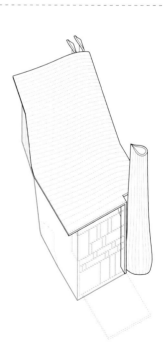

MATERIAL TO PROGRAM

CEDAR WOOD

NEW ENGLAND HOUSE
OFFICE dA
BOSTON, MASSACHUSETTS

2002

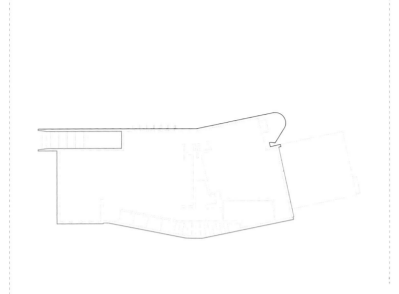

MATERIAL ENCLOSURE [PERIMETER]

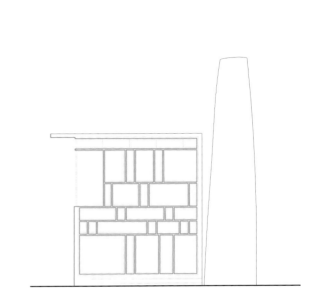

MATERIAL ORDER

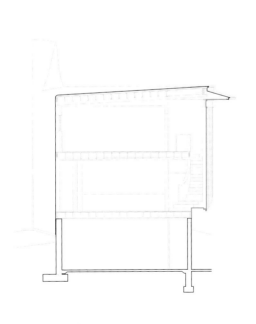

MATERIAL ENCLOSURE [EDGE]

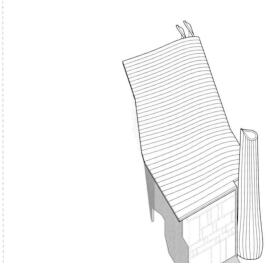

MATERIAL PERCEPTION

CEDAR WOOD

NEW ENGLAND HOUSE
OFFICE dA
BOSTON, MASSACHUSETTS

2002

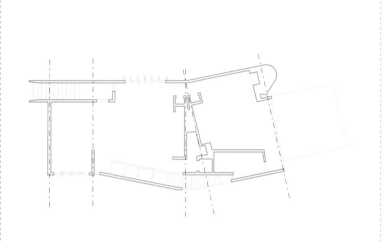

STRUCTURAL MATERIAL [BAY/MODULE]

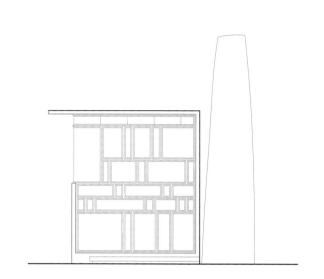

STRUCTURAL MATERIAL LEGIBILITY

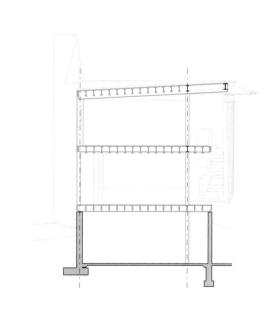

STRUCTURAL MATERIAL SYSTEM

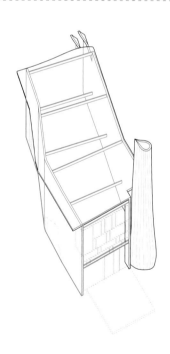

STRUCTURAL MATERIAL [LINE/POINT]

CEDAR WOOD

NEW ENGLAND HOUSE
OFFICE dA
BOSTON, MASSACHUSETTS

2002

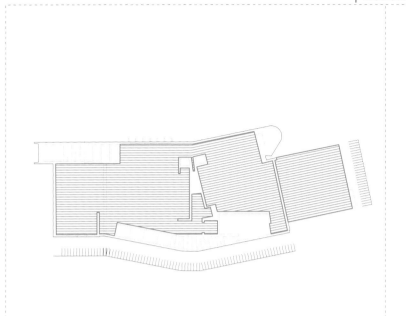

MATERIAL MODULE

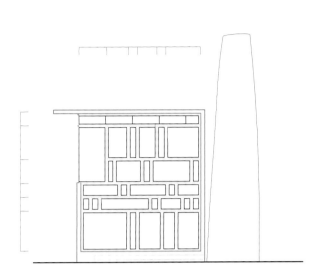

MATERIAL MODULE

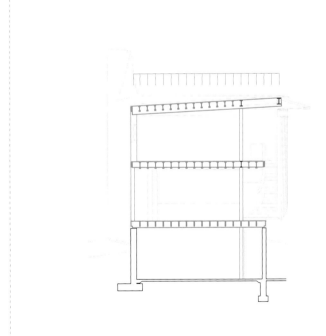

MATERIAL MODULE

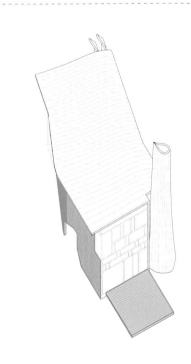

MATERIAL GEOMETRY

CEDAR WOOD

NEW ENGLAND HOUSE
OFFICE dA
BOSTON, MASSACHUSETTS

2002

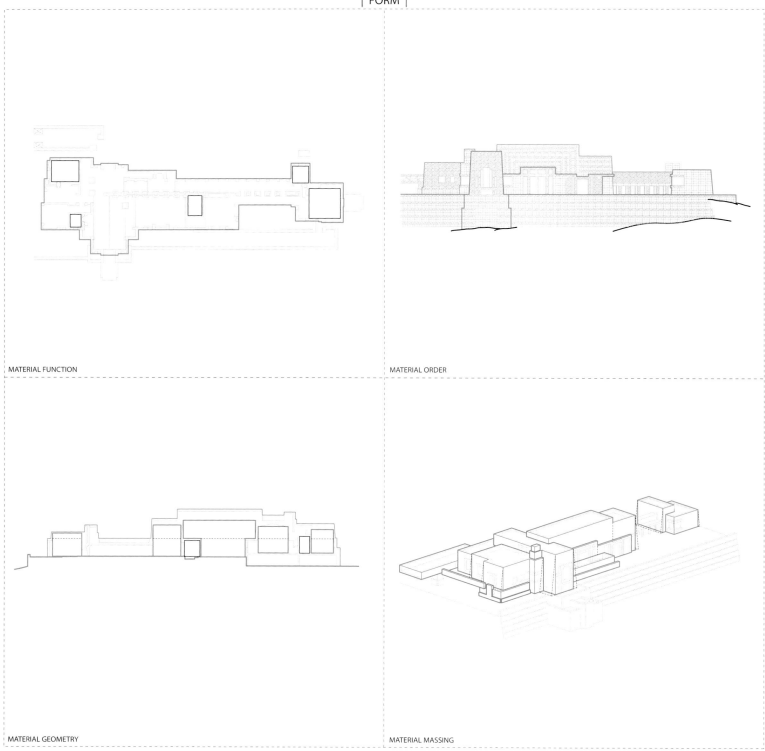

MATERIAL FUNCTION

MATERIAL ORDER

MATERIAL GEOMETRY

MATERIAL MASSING

CONCRETE TEXTILE BLOCK MASONRY

ENNIS-BROWN HOUSE
FRANK LLOYD WRIGHT
LOS ANGELES, CALIFORNIA

1924

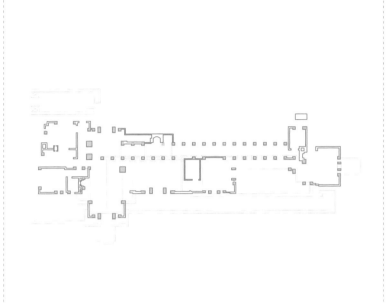

MATERIAL APPLICATION

PRIMARY/SECONDARY

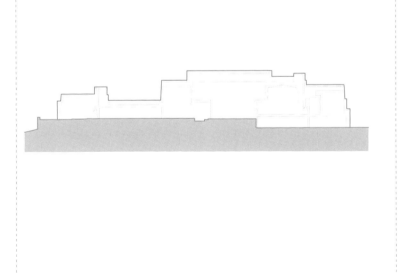

MATERIAL TO GROUND

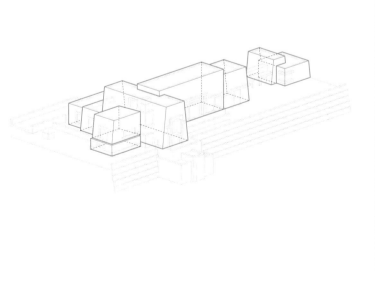

MATERIAL TO PROGRAM

CONCRETE TEXTILE BLOCK MASONRY

ENNIS-BROWN HOUSE
FRANK LLOYD WRIGHT
LOS ANGELES, CALIFORNIA

1924

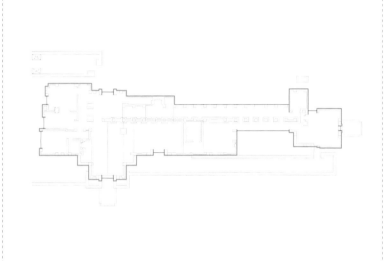

MATERIAL ENCLOSURE [PERIMETER]

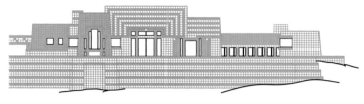

MATERIAL ORDER

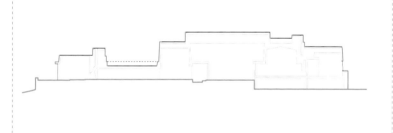

MATERIAL ENCLOSURE [EDGE]

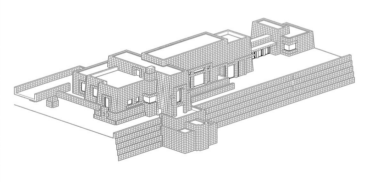

MATERIAL PERCEPTION

CONCRETE TEXTILE BLOCK MASONRY

ENNIS-BROWN HOUSE
FRANK LLOYD WRIGHT
LOS ANGELES, CALIFORNIA

1924

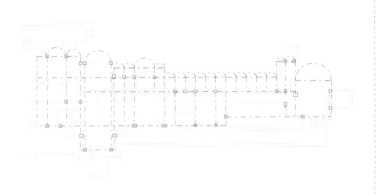

STRUCTURAL MATERIAL [BAY/MODULE]

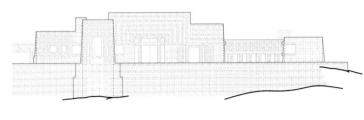

STRUCTURAL MATERIAL LEGIBILITY

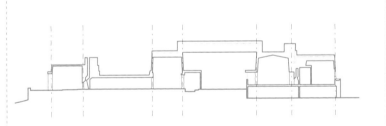

STRUCTURAL MATERIAL SYSTEM

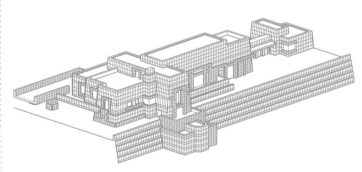

STRUCTURAL MATERIAL [LINE/POINT]

CONCRETE TEXTILE BLOCK MASONRY

ENNIS-BROWN HOUSE
FRANK LLOYD WRIGHT
LOS ANGELES, CALIFORNIA

1924

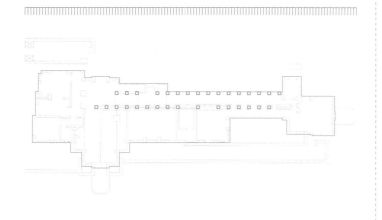

MATERIAL MODULE

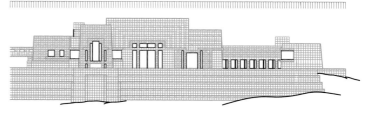

MATERIAL MODULE

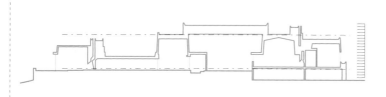

MATERIAL MODULE

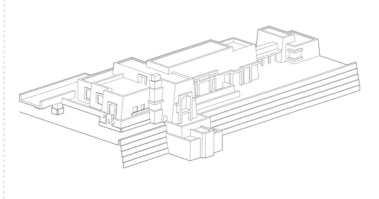

MATERIAL GEOMETRY

CONCRETE TEXTILE BLOCK MASONRY

ENNIS-BROWN HOUSE
FRANK LLOYD WRIGHT
LOS ANGELES, CALIFORNIA

1924

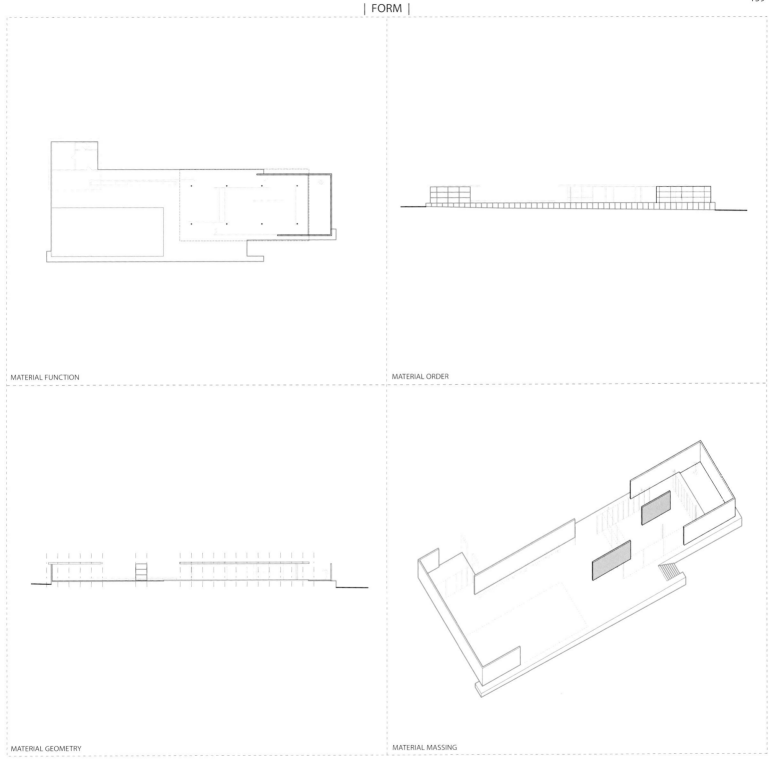

MATERIAL FUNCTION

MATERIAL ORDER

MATERIAL GEOMETRY

MATERIAL MASSING

TINIAN MARBLE AND ONYX TRAVERTINE MASONRY

BARCELONA PAVILION
MIES VAN DER ROHE
BARCELONA, SPAIN

1929

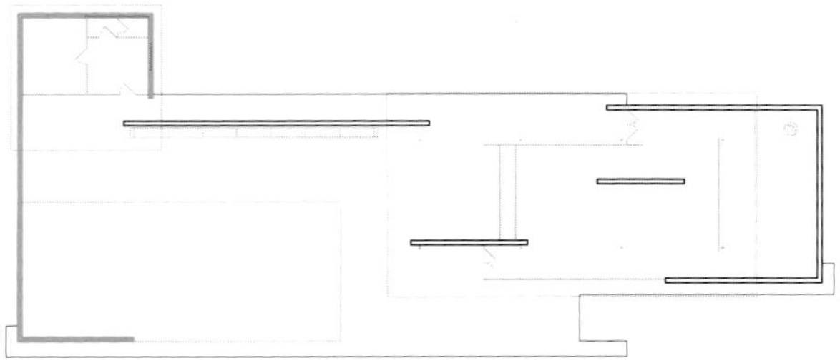

MATERIAL APPLICATION

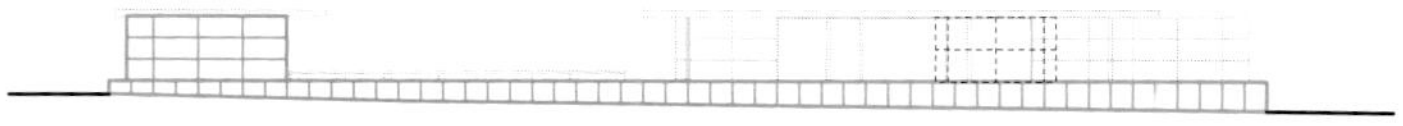

PRIMARY/SECONDARY

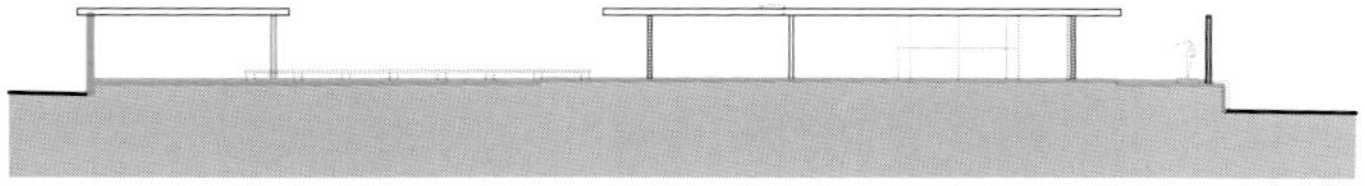

MATERIAL TO GROUND

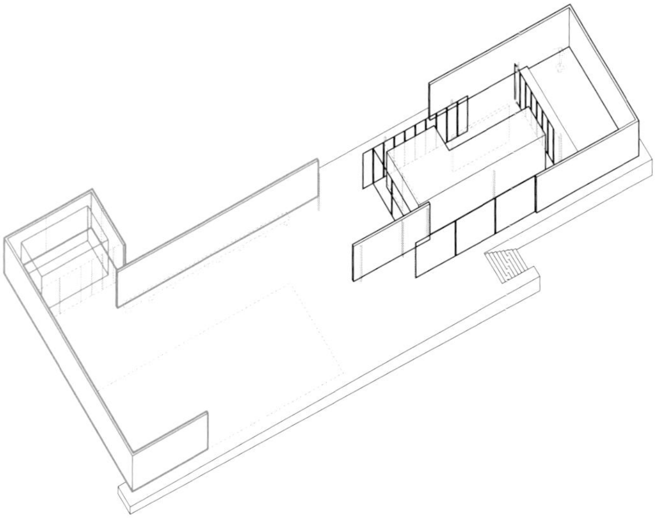

MATERIAL TO PROGRAM

TINIAN MARBLE AND ONYX TRAVERTINE MASONRY

BARCELONA PAVILION
MIES VAN DER ROHE
BARCELONA, SPAIN

1929

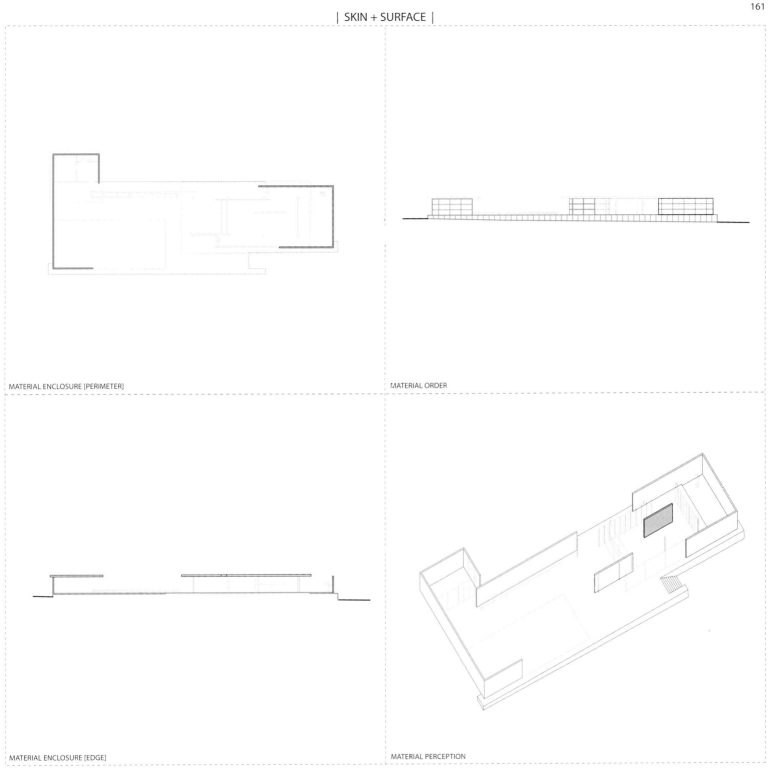

MATERIAL ENCLOSURE [PERIMETER]

MATERIAL ORDER

MATERIAL ENCLOSURE [EDGE]

MATERIAL PERCEPTION

TINIAN MARBLE AND ONYX TRAVERTINE MASONRY

BARCELONA PAVILION
MIES VAN DER ROHE
BARCELONA, SPAIN

1929

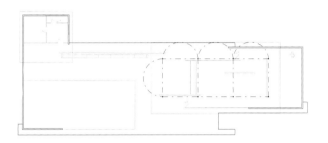

STRUCTURAL MATERIAL [BAY/MODULE]

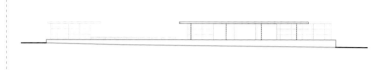

STRUCTURAL MATERIAL LEGIBILITY

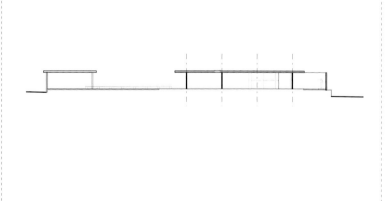

STRUCTURAL MATERIAL SYSTEM

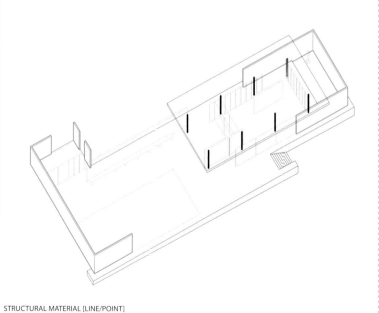

STRUCTURAL MATERIAL [LINE/POINT]

TINIAN MARBLE AND ONYX TRAVERTINE MASONRY

BARCELONA PAVILION
MIES VAN DER ROHE
BARCELONA, SPAIN

1929

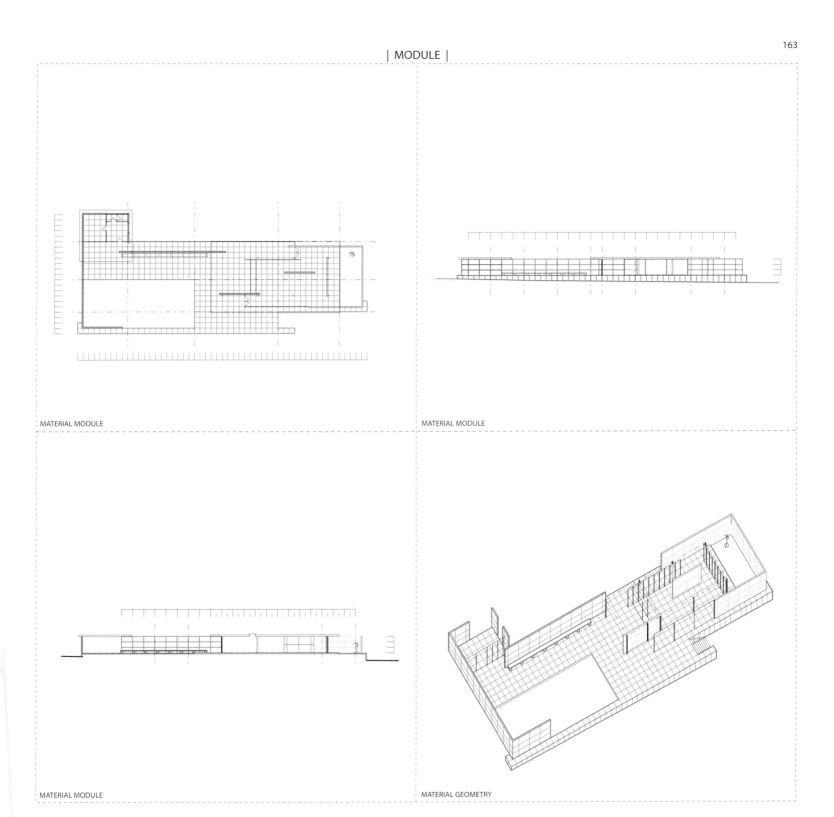

MATERIAL MODULE

MATERIAL MODULE

MATERIAL MODULE

MATERIAL GEOMETRY

TINIAN MARBLE AND ONYX TRAVERTINE MASONRY

BARCELONA PAVILION
MIES VAN DER ROHE
BARCELONA, SPAIN

1929

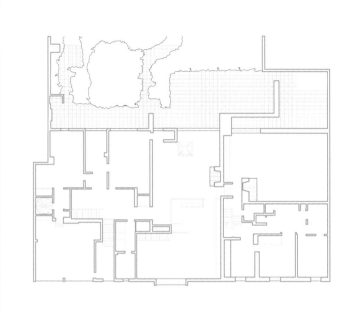

MATERIAL FUNCTION

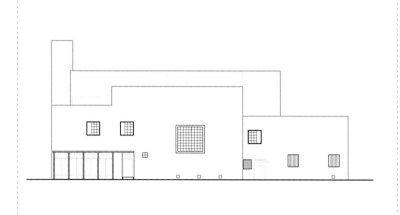

MATERIAL ORDER

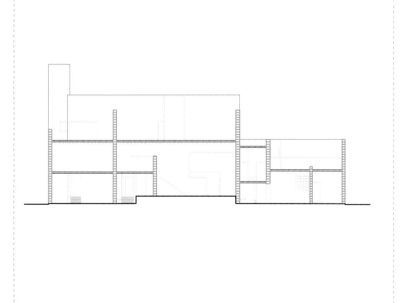

MATERIAL GEOMETRY

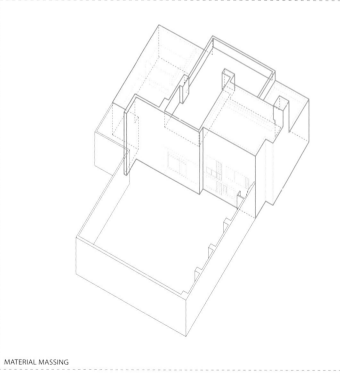

MATERIAL MASSING

PLASTERED ADOBE MASONRY

CASA BARRAGAN
LUIS BARRAGAN
MEXICO CITY, MEXICO

1948

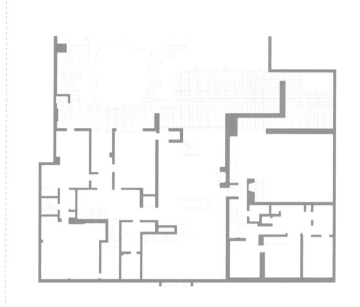

MATERIAL APPLICATION

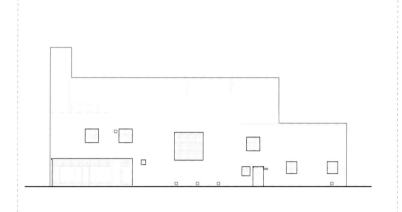

PRIMARY/SECONDARY

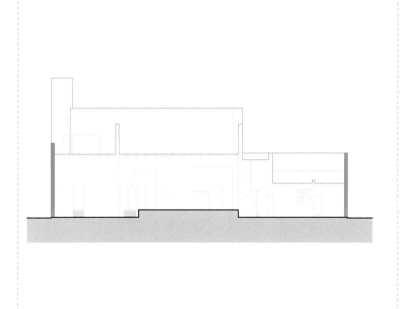

MATERIAL TO GROUND

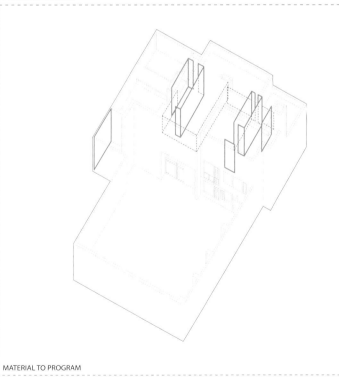

MATERIAL TO PROGRAM

PLASTERED ADOBE MASONRY

CASA BARRAGAN
LUIS BARRAGAN
MEXICO CITY, MEXICO

1948

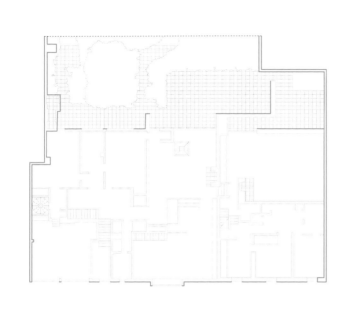

MATERIAL ENCLOSURE [PERIMETER]

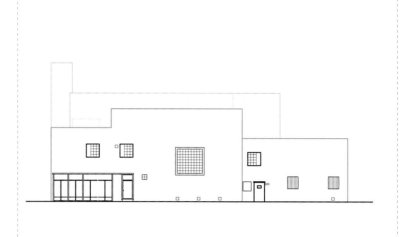

MATERIAL ORDER

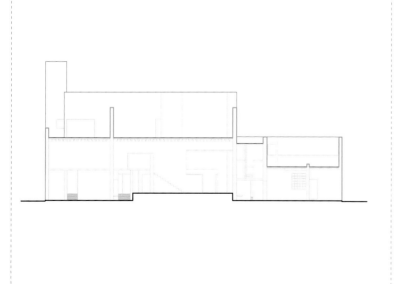

MATERIAL ENCLOSURE [EDGE]

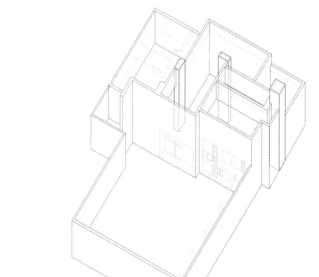

MATERIAL PERCEPTION

PLASTERED ADOBE MASONRY

CASA BARRAGAN
LUIS BARRAGAN
MEXICO CITY, MEXICO

1948

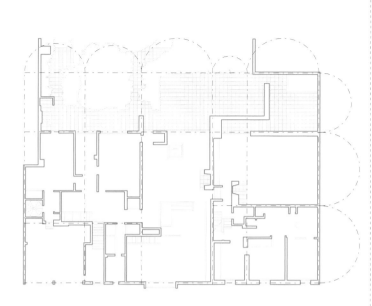

STRUCTURAL MATERIAL [BAY/MODULE]

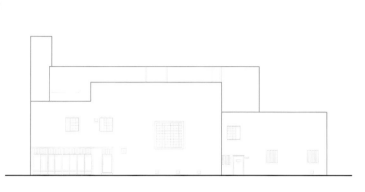

STRUCTURAL MATERIAL LEGIBILITY

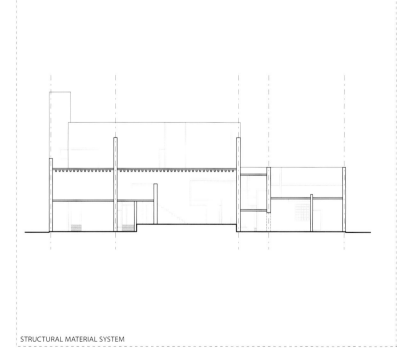

STRUCTURAL MATERIAL SYSTEM

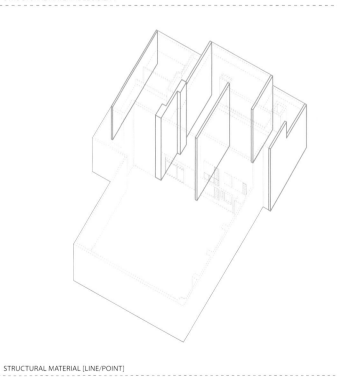

STRUCTURAL MATERIAL [LINE/POINT]

PLASTERED ADOBE MASONRY

CASA BARRAGAN
LUIS BARRAGAN
MEXICO CITY, MEXICO

1948

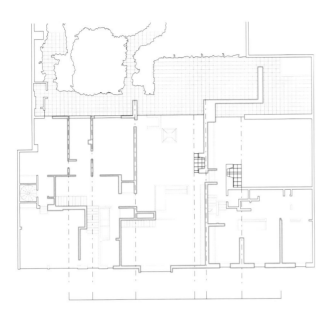

MATERIAL MODULE

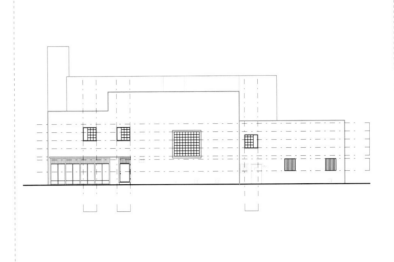

MATERIAL MODULE

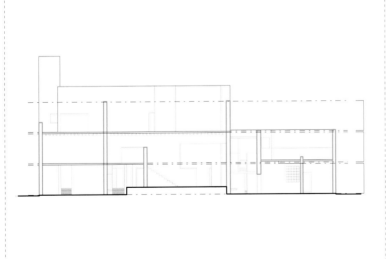

MATERIAL MODULE

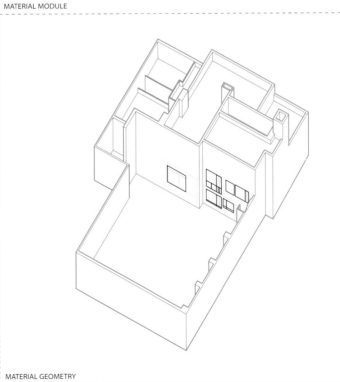

MATERIAL GEOMETRY

PLASTERED ADOBE MASONRY

CASA BARRAGAN
LUIS BARRAGAN
MEXICO CITY, MEXICO

1948

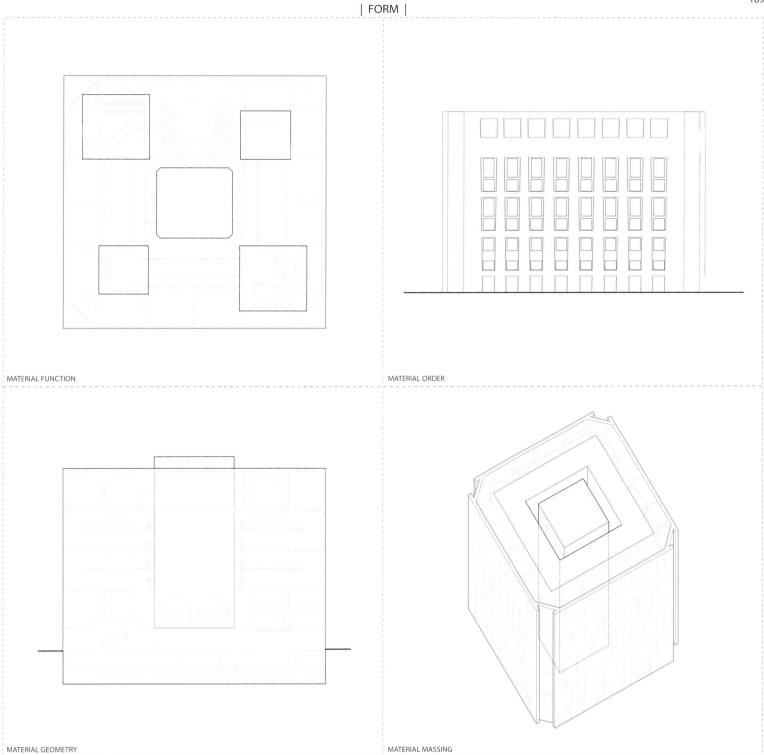

MATERIAL FUNCTION

MATERIAL ORDER

MATERIAL GEOMETRY

MATERIAL MASSING

CLAY BRICK MASONRY

EXETER LIBRARY
LOUIS I. KAHN
EXETER, NEW HAMPSHIRE

1972

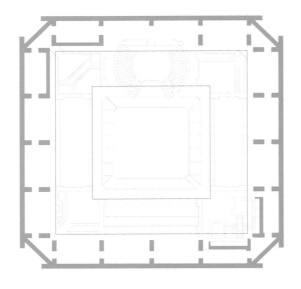

MATERIAL APPLICATION

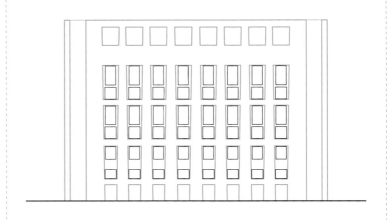

PRIMARY/SECONDARY

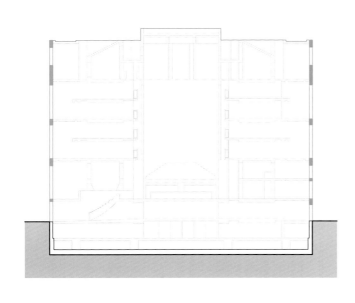

MATERIAL TO GROUND

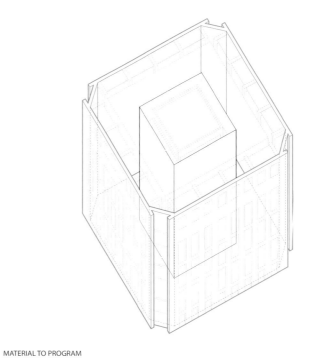

MATERIAL TO PROGRAM

CLAY BRICK MASONRY

EXETER LIBRARY
LOUIS I. KAHN
EXETER, NEW HAMPSHIRE

1972

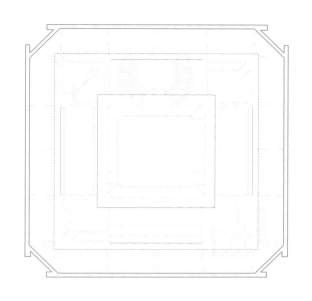

MATERIAL ENCLOSURE [PERIMETER]

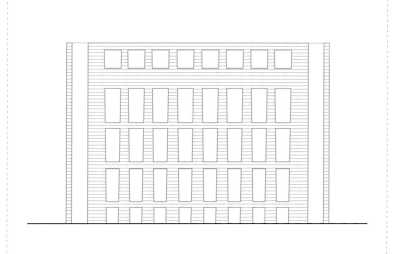

MATERIAL ORDER

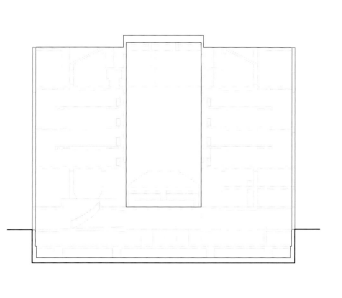

MATERIAL ENCLOSURE [EDGE]

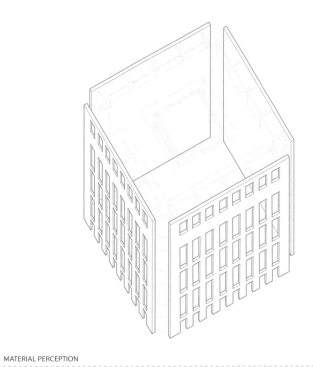

MATERIAL PERCEPTION

CLAY BRICK MASONRY

EXETER LIBRARY
LOUIS I. KAHN
EXETER, NEW HAMPSHIRE

1972

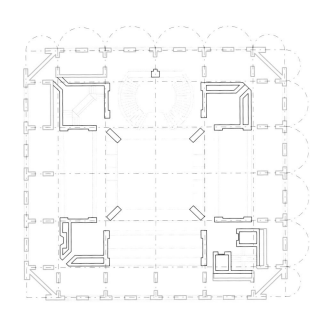

STRUCTURAL MATERIAL [BAY/MODULE]

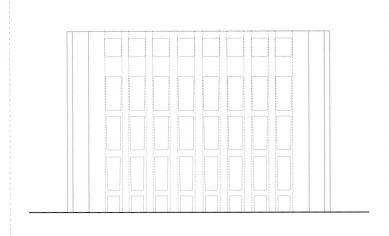

STRUCTURAL MATERIAL LEGIBILITY

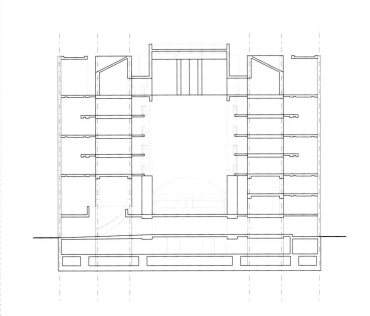

STRUCTURAL MATERIAL SYSTEM

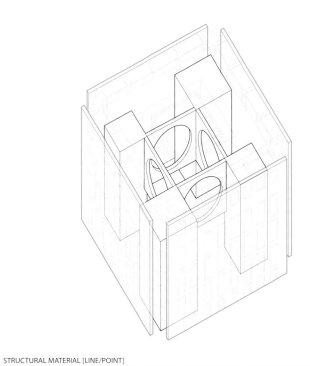

STRUCTURAL MATERIAL [LINE/POINT]

CLAY BRICK MASONRY

EXETER LIBRARY
LOUIS I. KAHN
EXETER, NEW HAMPSHIRE

1972

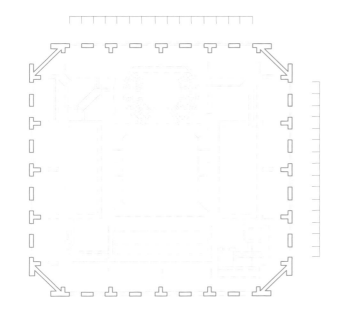

MATERIAL MODULE

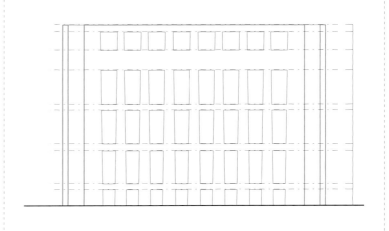

MATERIAL MODULE

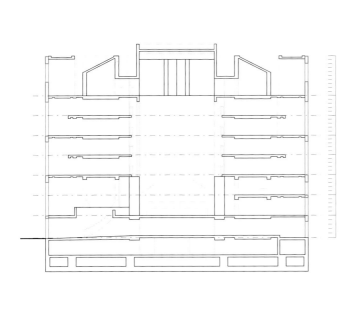

MATERIAL MODULE

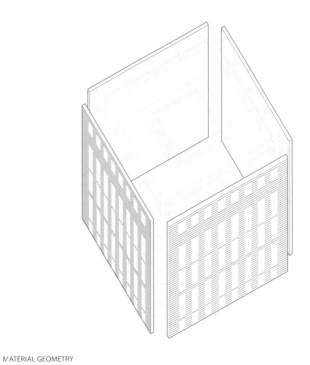

MATERIAL GEOMETRY

CLAY BRICK MASONRY

EXETER LIBRARY
LOUIS I. KAHN
EXETER, NEW HAMPSHIRE

1972

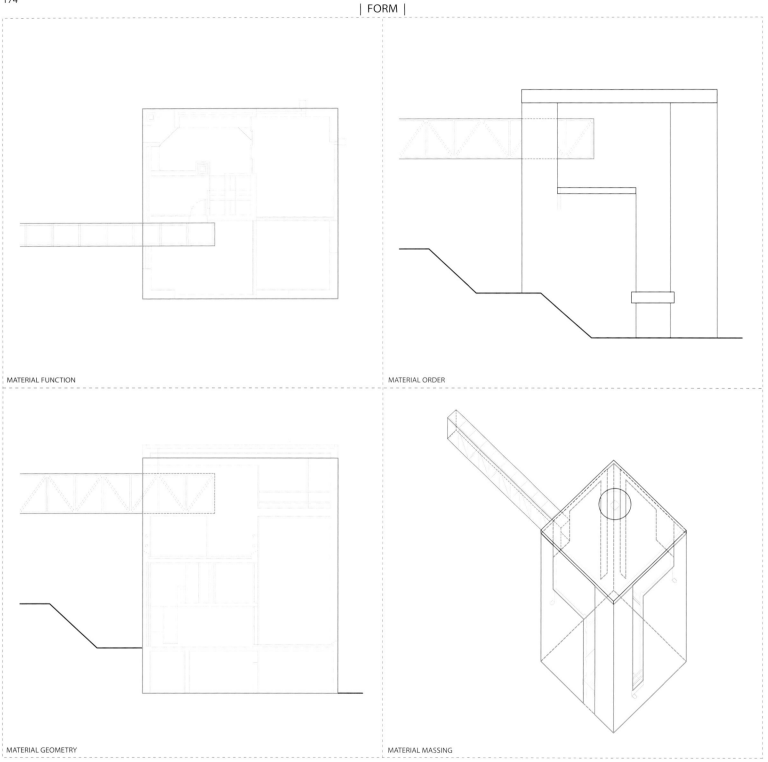

MATERIAL FUNCTION

MATERIAL ORDER

MATERIAL GEOMETRY

MATERIAL MASSING

CONCRETE BLOCK MASONRY

HOUSE AT RIVA SAN VITALE
MARIO BOTTA
TICINO, SWITZERLAND

1973

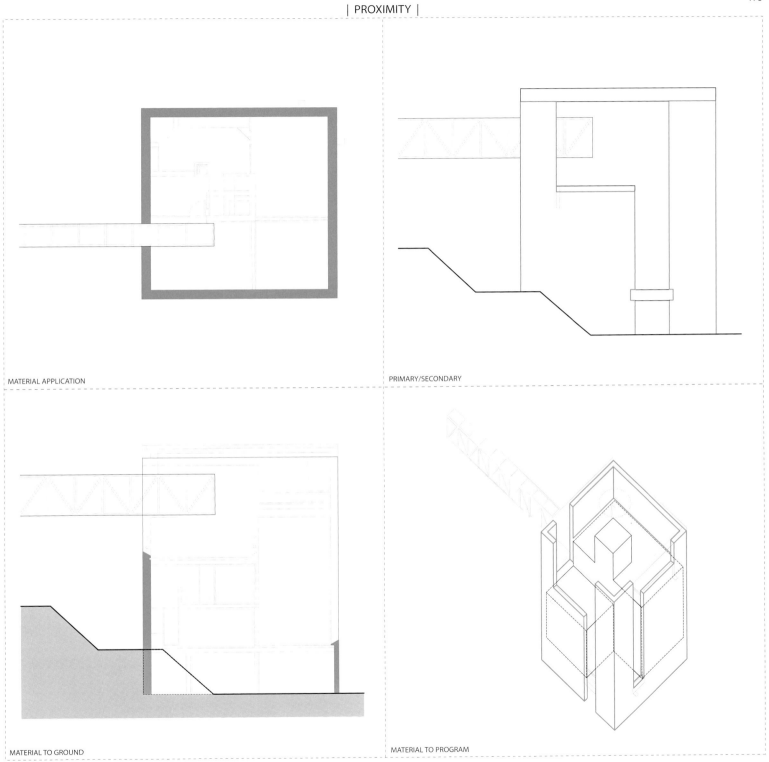

MATERIAL APPLICATION

PRIMARY/SECONDARY

MATERIAL TO GROUND

MATERIAL TO PROGRAM

CONCRETE BLOCK MASONRY

HOUSE AT RIVA SAN VITALE
MARIO BOTTA
TICINO, SWITZERLAND

1973

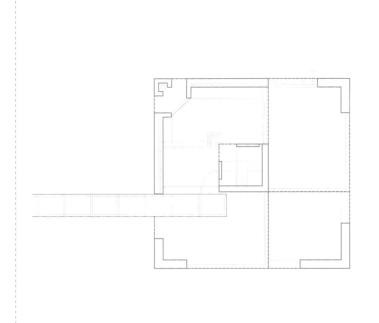

MATERIAL ENCLOSURE [PERIMETER]

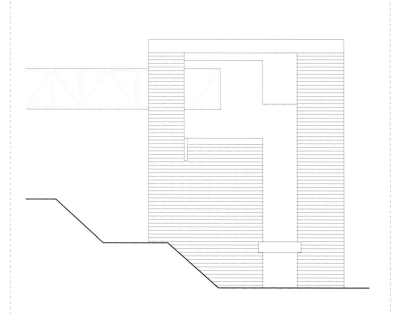

MATERIAL ORDER

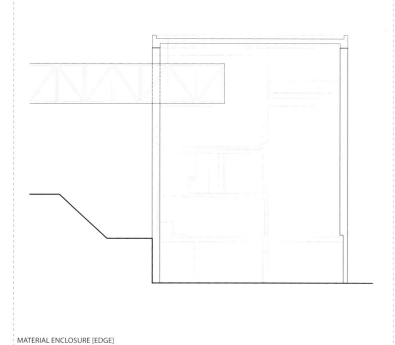

MATERIAL ENCLOSURE [EDGE]

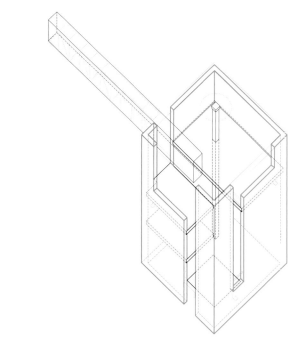

MATERIAL PERCEPTION

CONCRETE BLOCK MASONRY

HOUSE AT RIVA SAN VITALE
MARIO BOTTA
TICINO, SWITZERLAND

1973

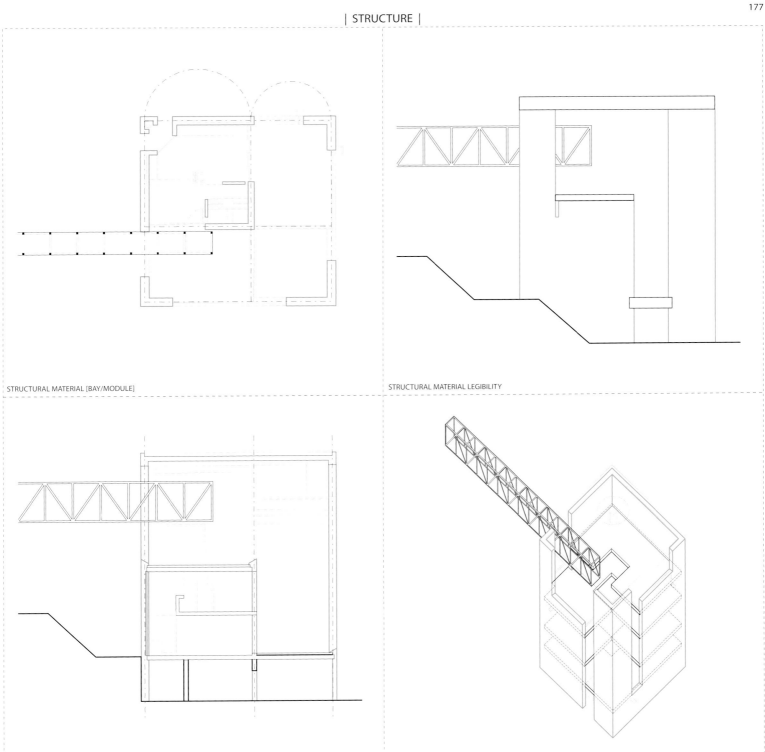

STRUCTURAL MATERIAL [BAY/MODULE]

STRUCTURAL MATERIAL LEGIBILITY

STRUCTURAL MATERIAL SYSTEM

STRUCTURAL MATERIAL [LINE/POINT]

CONCRETE BLOCK MASONRY

HOUSE AT RIVA SAN VITALE
MARIO BOTTA
TICINO, SWITZERLAND

1973

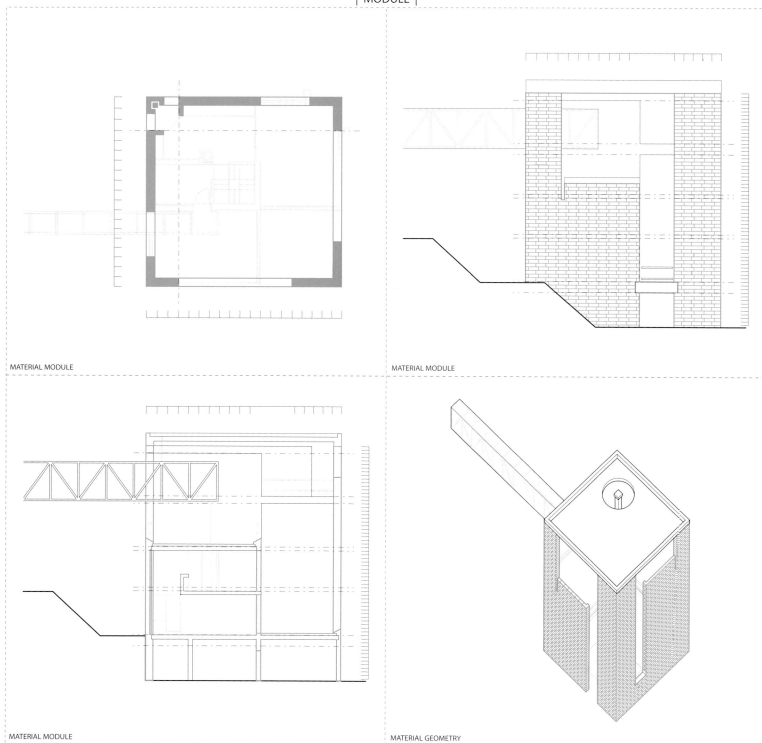

MATERIAL MODULE

MATERIAL MODULE

MATERIAL MODULE

MATERIAL GEOMETRY

CONCRETE BLOCK MASONRY

HOUSE AT RIVA SAN VITALE
MARIO BOTTA
TICINO, SWITZERLAND

1973

| FORM |

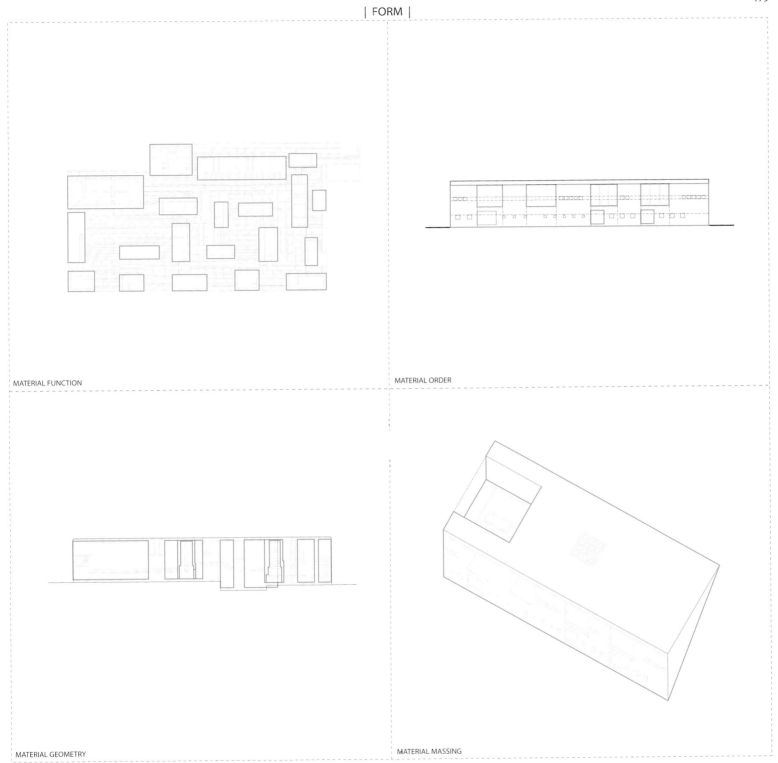

MATERIAL FUNCTION

MATERIAL ORDER

MATERIAL GEOMETRY

MATERIAL MASSING

VALS GNEISS STONE MASONRY

THERMAL BATHS
PETER ZUMTHOR
VALS, SWITZERLAND

1996

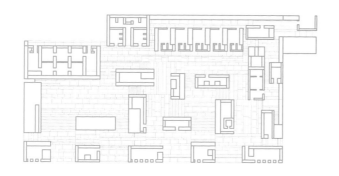

MATERIAL APPLICATION

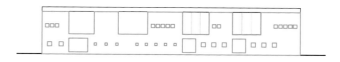

PRIMARY/SECONDARY

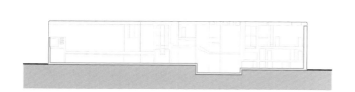

MATERIAL TO GROUND

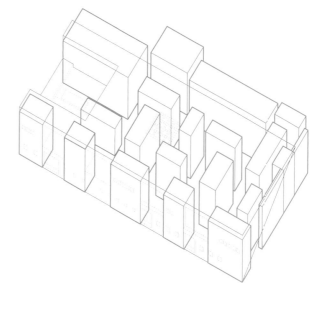

MATERIAL TO PROGRAM

VALS GNEISS STONE MASONRY

THERMAL BATHS
PETER ZUMTHOR
VALS, SWITZERLAND

1996

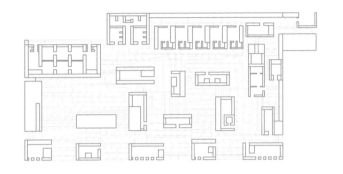

MATERIAL ENCLOSURE [PERIMETER]

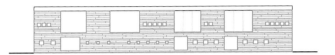

MATERIAL ORDER

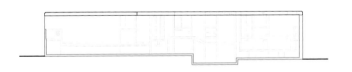

MATERIAL ENCLOSURE [EDGE]

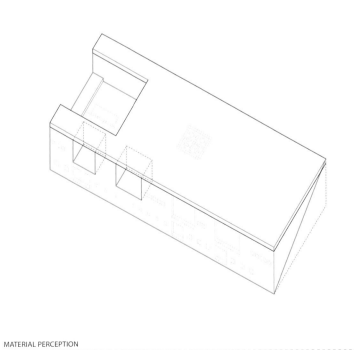

MATERIAL PERCEPTION

VALS GNEISS STONE MASONRY

THERMAL BATHS
PETER ZUMTHOR
VALS, SWITZERLAND

1996

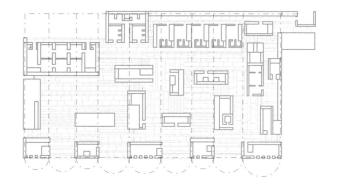

STRUCTURAL MATERIAL [BAY/MODULE]

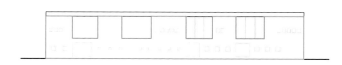

STRUCTURAL MATERIAL LEGIBILITY

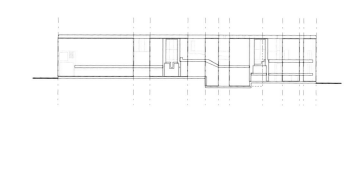

STRUCTURAL MATERIAL SYSTEM

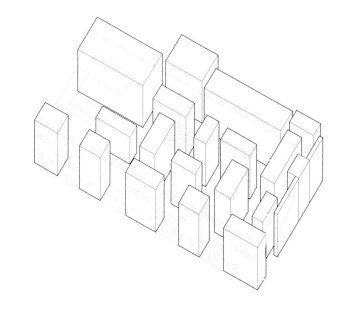

STRUCTURAL MATERIAL [LINE/POINT]

VALS GNEISS STONE MASONRY

THERMAL BATHS
PETER ZUMTHOR
VALS, SWITZERLAND

1996

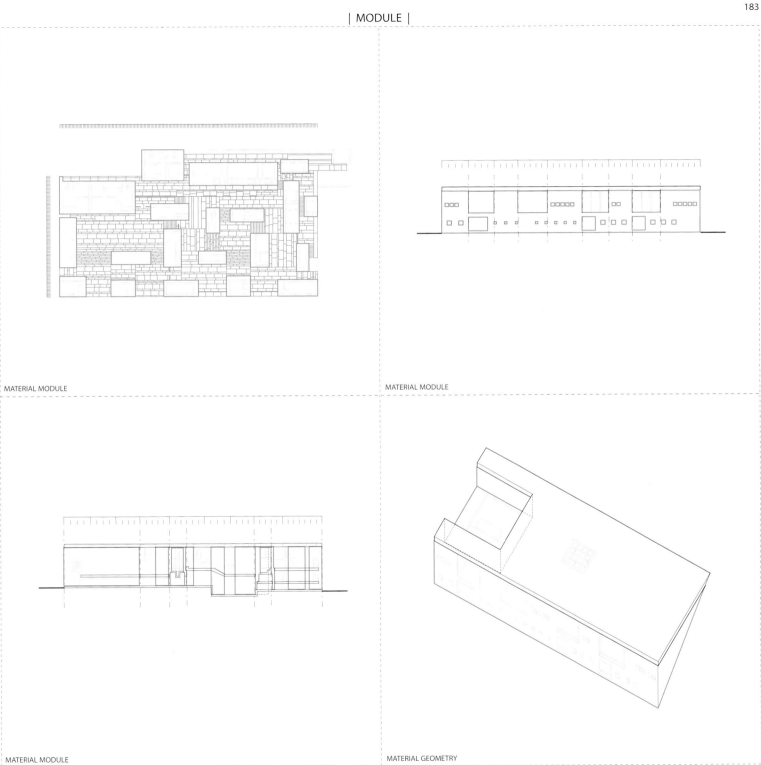

MATERIAL MODULE

MATERIAL MODULE

MATERIAL MODULE

MATERIAL GEOMETRY

VALS GNEISS STONE MASONRY

THERMAL BATHS
PETER ZUMTHOR
VALS, SWITZERLAND

1996

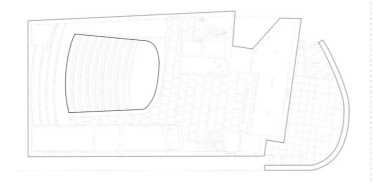

MATERIAL FUNCTION

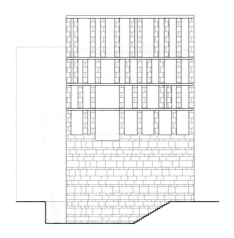

MATERIAL ORDER

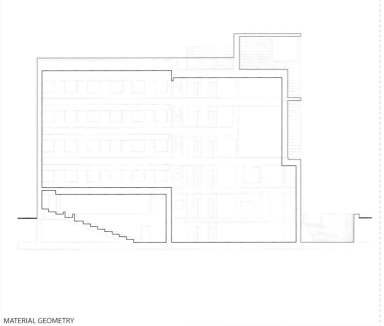

MATERIAL GEOMETRY

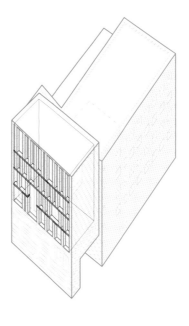

MATERIAL MASSING

LUMAQUELA SANDSTONE MASONRY

MURCIA TOWN HALL
RAFAEL MONEO
MURCIA, SPAIN

1998

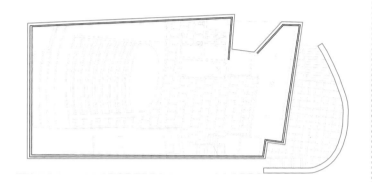

MATERIAL APPLICATION

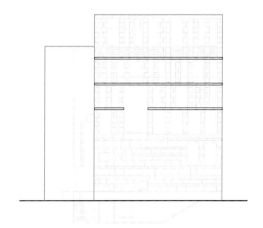

PRIMARY/SECONDARY

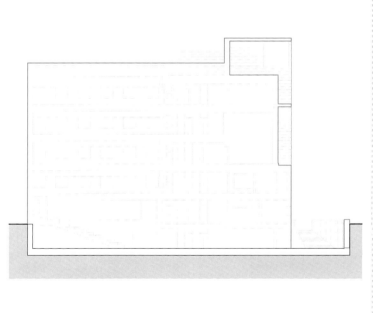

MATERIAL TO GROUND

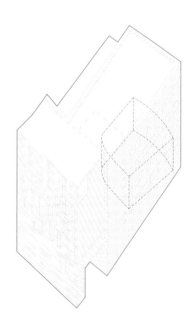

MATERIAL TO PROGRAM

LUMAQUELA SANDSTONE MASONRY

MURCIA TOWN HALL
RAFAEL MONEO
MURCIA, SPAIN

1998

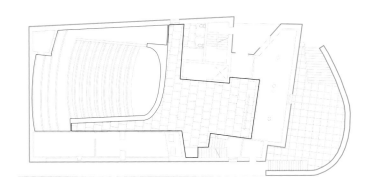

MATERIAL ENCLOSURE [PERIMETER]

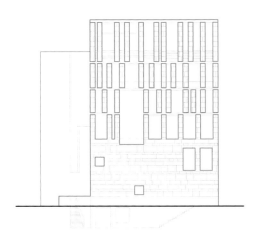

MATERIAL ORDER

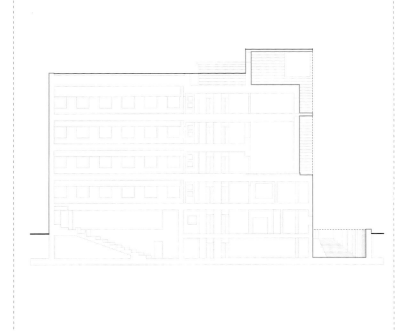

MATERIAL ENCLOSURE [EDGE]

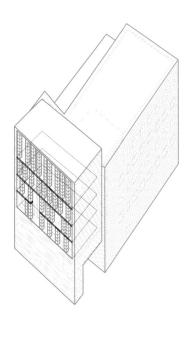

MATERIAL PERCEPTION

LUMAQUELA SANDSTONE MASONRY

MURCIA TOWN HALL
RAFAEL MONEO
MURCIA, SPAIN

1998

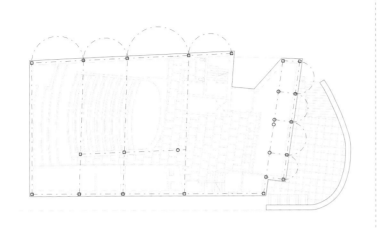

STRUCTURAL MATERIAL [BAY/MODULE]

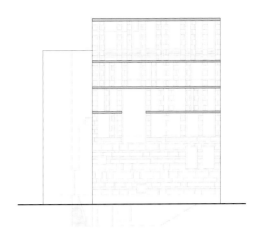

STRUCTURAL MATERIAL LEGIBILITY

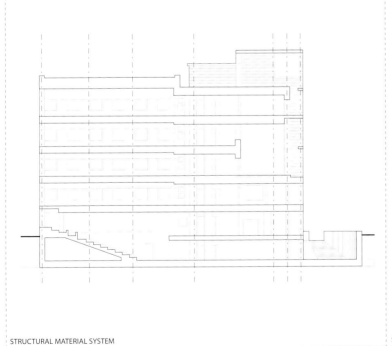

STRUCTURAL MATERIAL SYSTEM

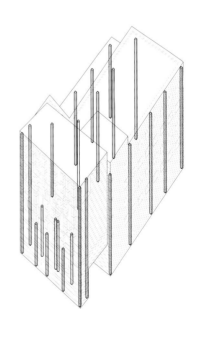

STRUCTURAL MATERIAL [LINE/POINT]

LUMAQUELA SANDSTONE MASONRY

MURCIA TOWN HALL
RAFAEL MONEO
MURCIA, SPAIN

1998

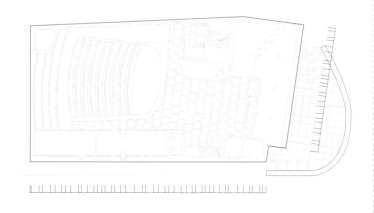

MATERIAL MODULE

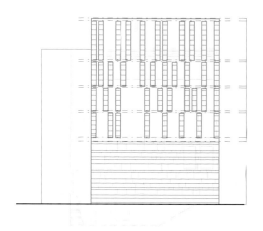

MATERIAL MODULE

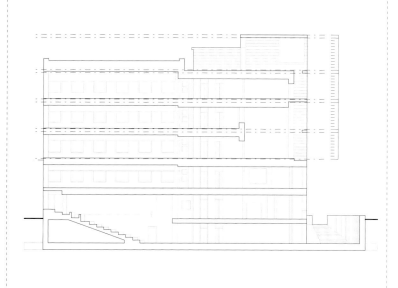

MATERIAL MODULE

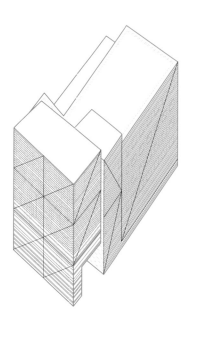

MATERIAL GEOMETRY

LUMAQUELA SANDSTONE MASONRY

MURCIA TOWN HALL
RAFAEL MONEO
MURCIA, SPAIN

1998

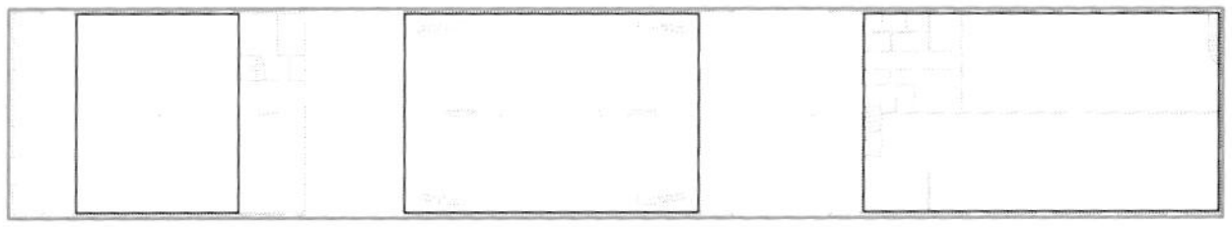

MATERIAL FUNCTION

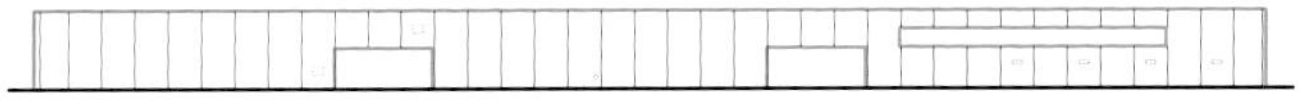

MATERIAL ORDER

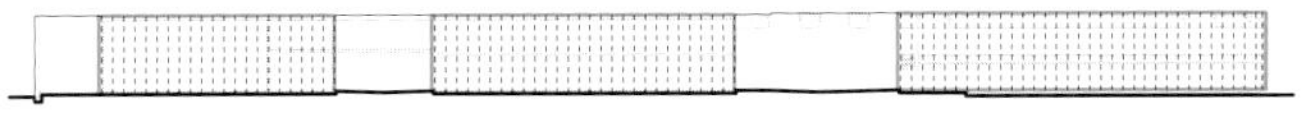

MATERIAL GEOMETRY

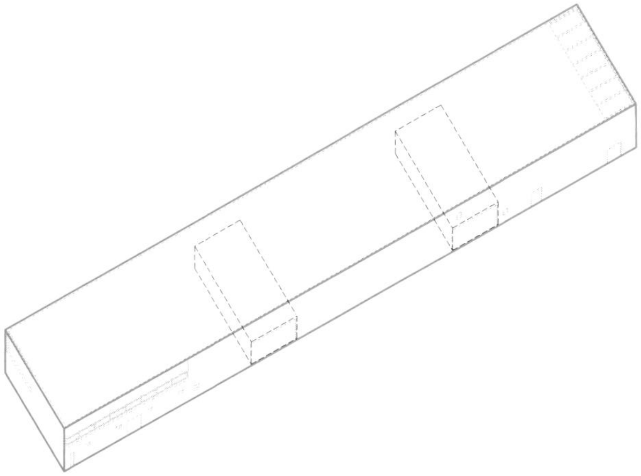

MATEFIAL MASSING

GABION STONE MASONRY CLADDING

DOMINUS WINERY
HERZOG & DE MEURON
YOUNTVILLE, CALIFORNIA

1998

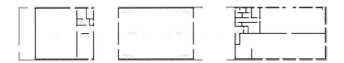

MATERIAL APPLICATION

PRIMARY/SECONDARY

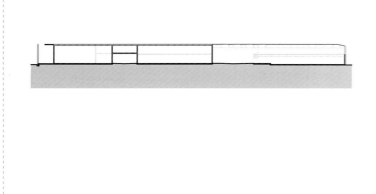

MATERIAL TO GROUND

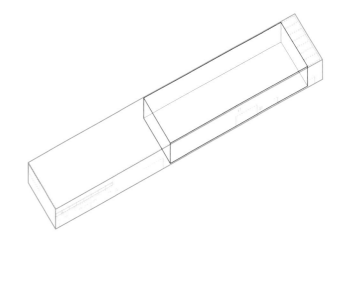

MATERIAL TO PROGRAM

GABION STONE MASONRY CLADDING

DOMINUS WINERY
HERZOG & DE MEURON
YOUNTVILLE, CALIFORNIA

1998

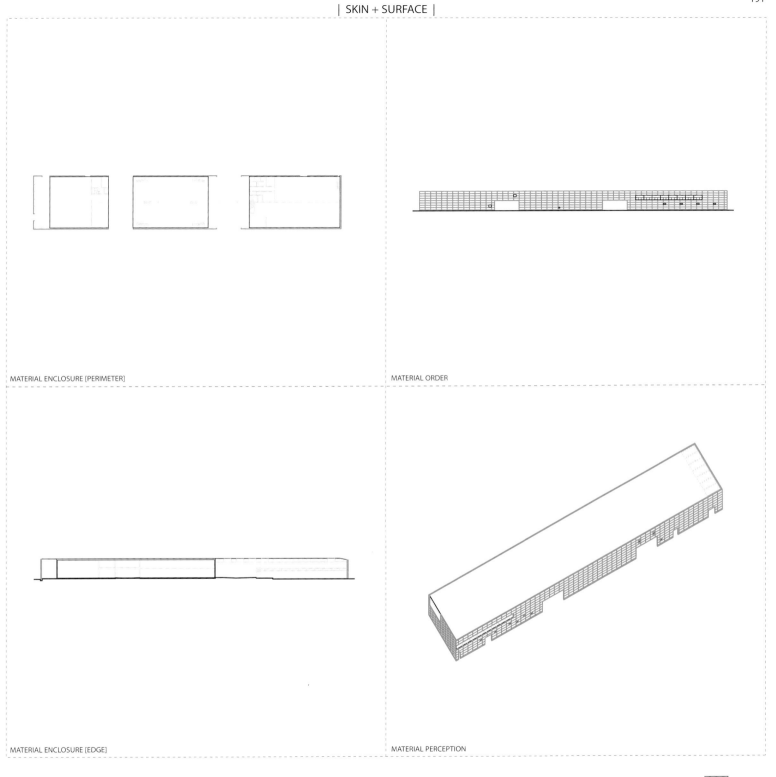

MATERIAL ENCLOSURE [PERIMETER]

MATERIAL ORDER

MATERIAL ENCLOSURE [EDGE]

MATERIAL PERCEPTION

GABION STONE MASONRY CLADDING

DOMINUS WINERY
HERZOG & DE MEURON
YOUNTVILLE, CALIFORNIA

1998

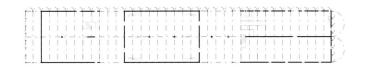

STRUCTURAL MATERIAL [BAY/MODULE]

STRUCTURAL MATERIAL LEGIBILITY

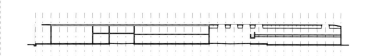

STRUCTURAL MATERIAL SYSTEM

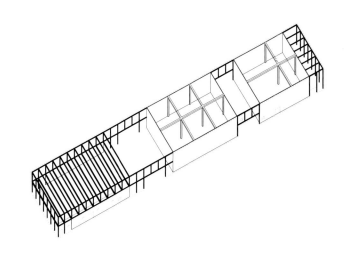

STRUCTURAL MATERIAL [LINE/POINT]

GABION STONE MASONRY CLADDING

DOMINUS WINERY
HERZOG & DE MEURON
YOUNTVILLE, CALIFORNIA

1998

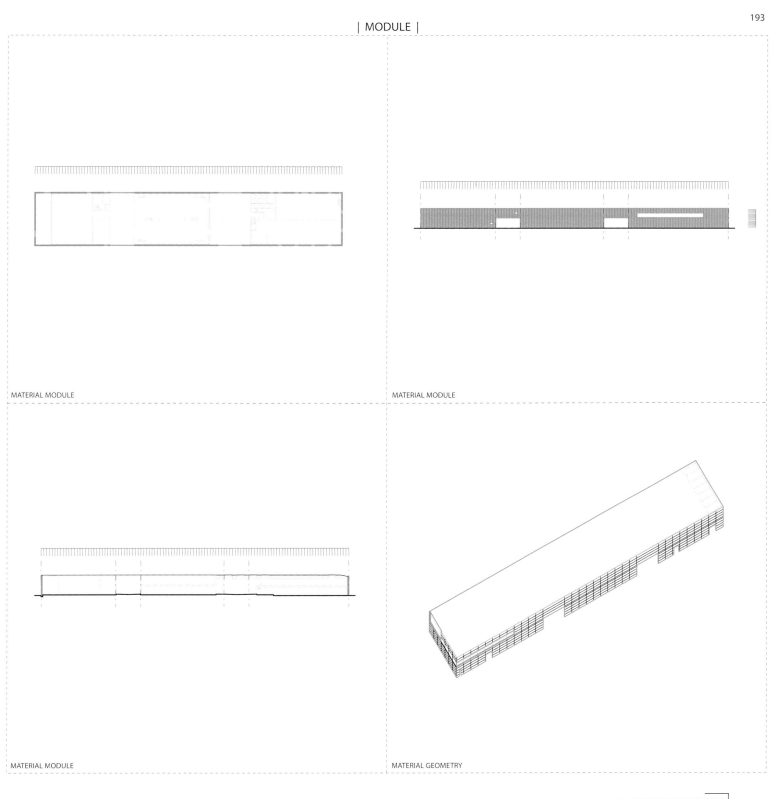

MATERIAL MODULE

MATERIAL MODULE

MATERIAL MODULE

MATERIAL GEOMETRY

GABION STONE MASONRY CLADDING

DOMINUS WINERY
HERZOG & DE MEURON
YOUNTVILLE, CALIFORNIA

1998

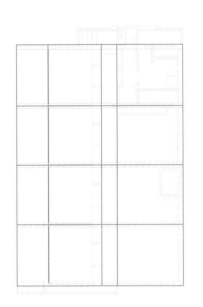

MATERIAL FUNCTION

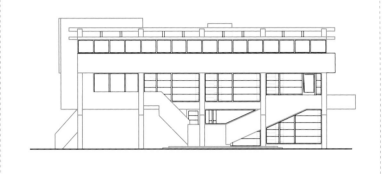

MATERIAL ORDER

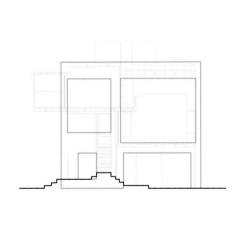

MATERIAL GEOMETRY

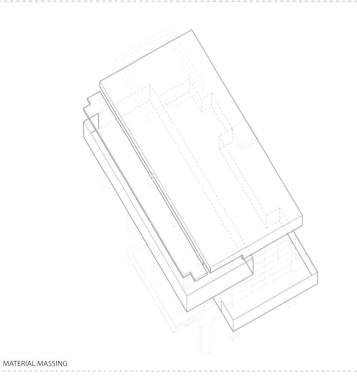

MATERIAL MASSING

CAST-IN-PLACE CONCRETE

LOVELL BEACH HOUSE
R.M. SCHINDLER
ORANGE COUNTY, CALIFORNIA

1926

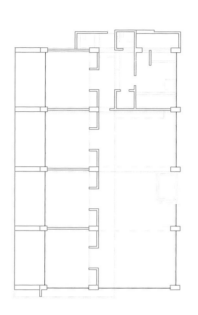

MATERIAL APPLICATION

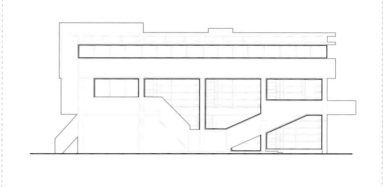

PRIMARY/SECONDARY

MATERIAL TO GROUND

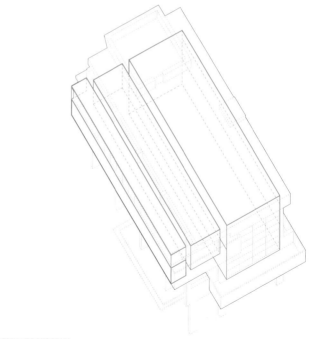

MATERIAL TO PROGRAM

CAST-IN-PLACE CONCRETE

LOVELL BEACH HOUSE
R.M. SCHINDLER
ORANGE COUNTY, CALIFORNIA

1926

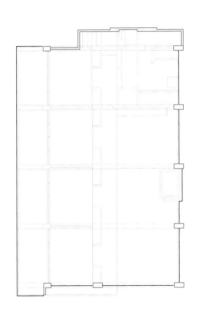

MATERIAL ENCLOSURE [PERIMETER]

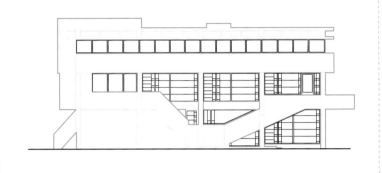

MATERIAL ORDER

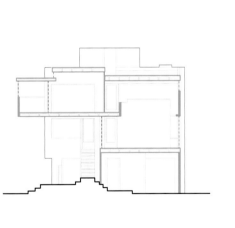

MATERIAL ENCLOSURE [EDGE]

MATERIAL PERCEPTION

CAST-IN-PLACE CONCRETE

LOVELL BEACH HOUSE
R.M. SCHINDLER
ORANGE COUNTY, CALIFORNIA

1926

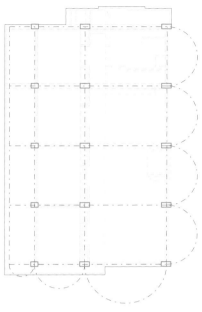

STRUCTURAL MATERIAL [BAY/MODULE]

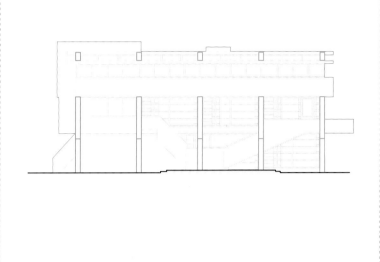

STRUCTURAL MATERIAL LEGIBILITY

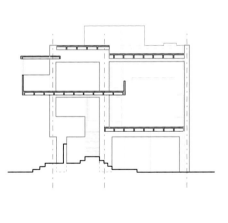

STRUCTURAL MATERIAL SYSTEM

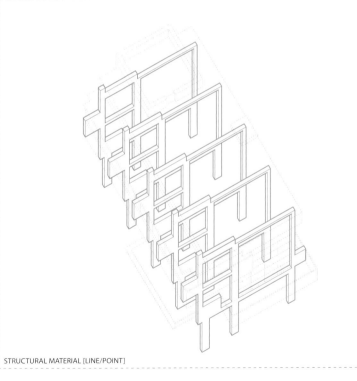

STRUCTURAL MATERIAL [LINE/POINT]

CAST-IN-PLACE CONCRETE

LOVELL BEACH HOUSE
R.M. SCHINDLER
ORANGE COUNTY, CALIFORNIA

1926

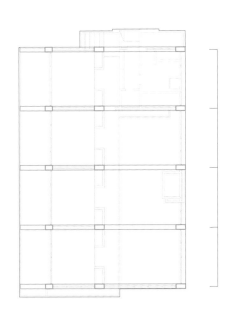

MATERIAL MODULE

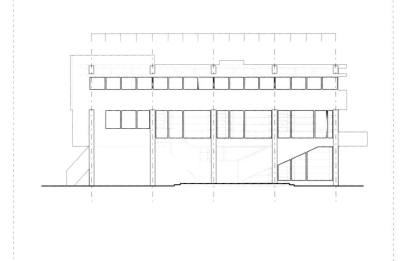

MATERIAL MODULE

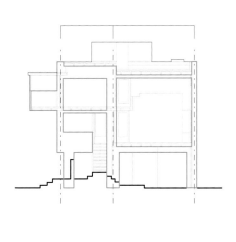

MATERIAL MODULE

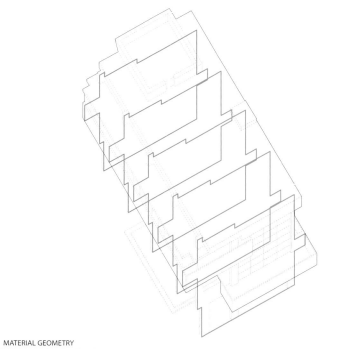

MATERIAL GEOMETRY

CAST-IN-PLACE CONCRETE

LOVELL BEACH HOUSE
R.M. SCHINDLER
ORANGE COUNTY, CALIFORNIA

1926

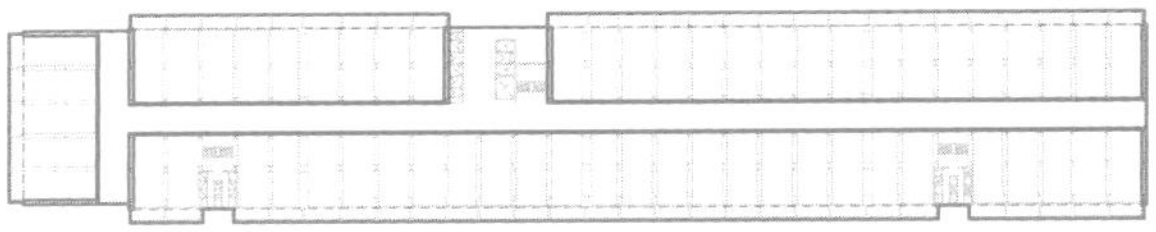

MATERIAL FUNCTION

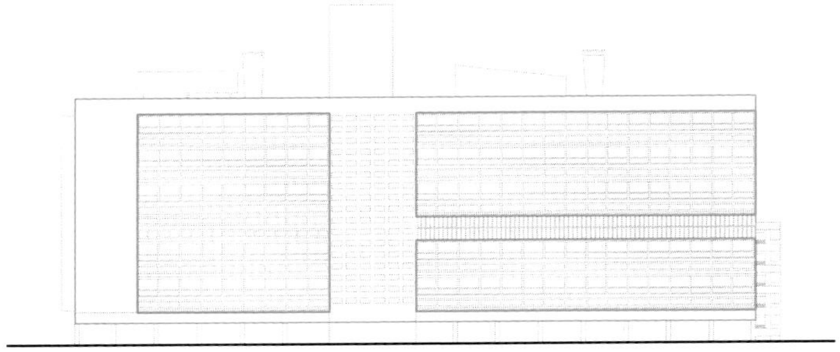

MATERIAL ORDER

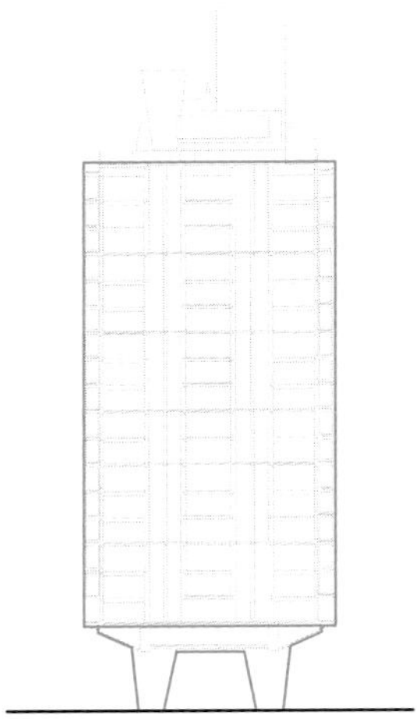

MATERIAL GEOMETRY

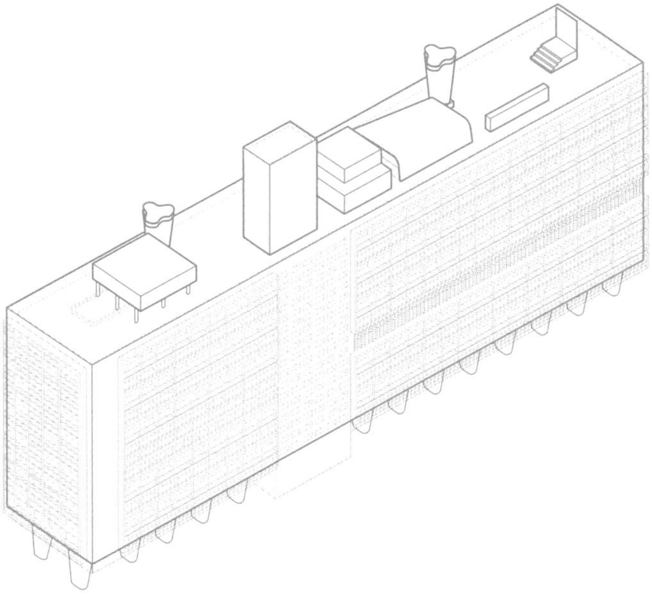

MATERIAL MASSING

CAST-IN-PLACE CONCRETE

UNITE D'HABITATION
LE CORBUSIER
MARSEILLE, FRANCE

1952

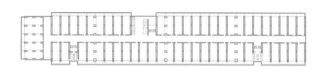

MATERIAL APPLICATION

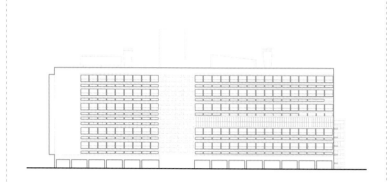

PRIMARY/SECONDARY

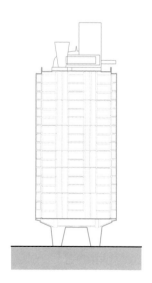

MATERIAL TO GROUND

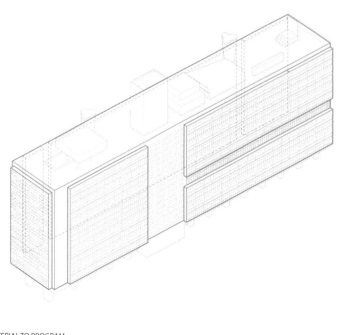

MATERIAL TO PROGRAM

CAST-IN-PLACE CONCRETE

UNITE D'HABITATION
LE CORBUSIER
MARSEILLE, FRANCE

1952

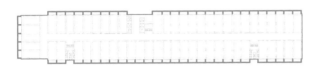

MATERIAL ENCLOSURE [PERIMETER]

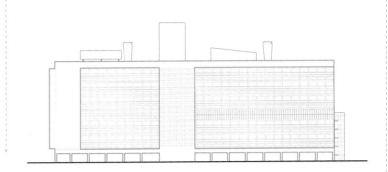

MATERIAL ORDER

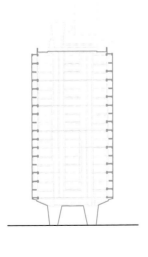

MATERIAL ENCLOSURE [EDGE]

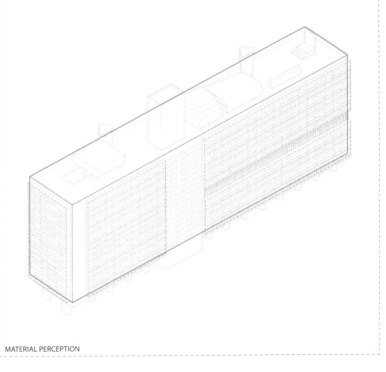

MATERIAL PERCEPTION

CAST-IN-PLACE CONCRETE

UNITE D'HABITATION
LE CORBUSIER
MARSEILLE, FRANCE

1952

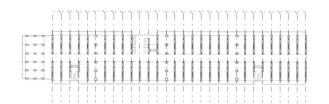

STRUCTURAL MATERIAL [BAY/MODULE]

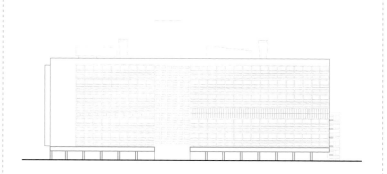

STRUCTURAL MATERIAL LEGIBILITY

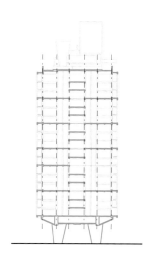

STRUCTURAL MATERIAL SYSTEM

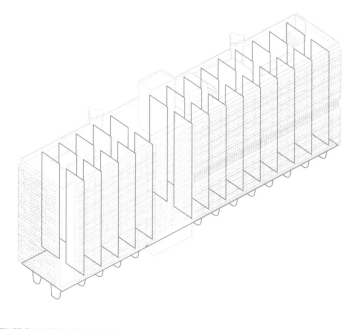

STRUCTURAL MATERIAL [LINE/POINT]

CAST-IN-PLACE CONCRETE

UNITE D'HABITATION
LE CORBUSIER
MARSEILLE, FRANCE

1952

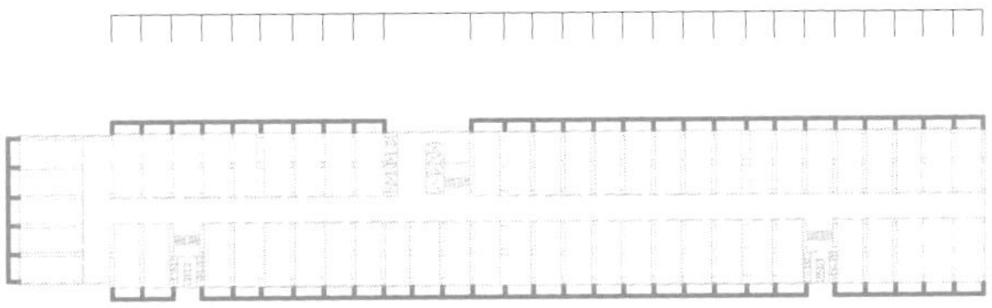

MATERIAL MODULE

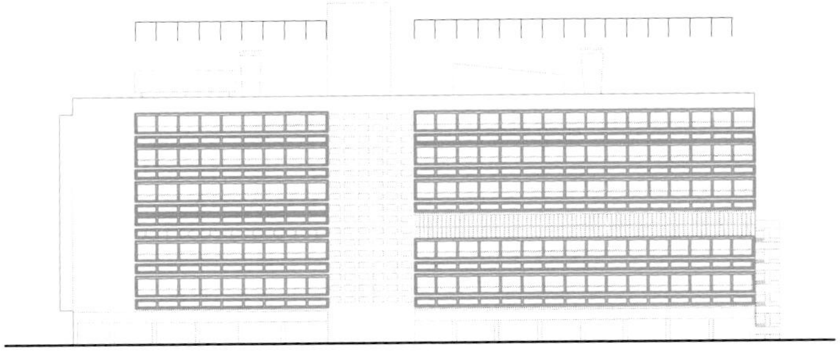

MATERIAL MODULE

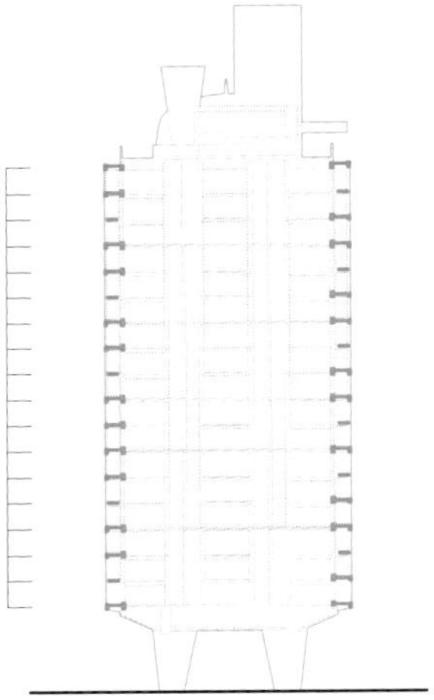

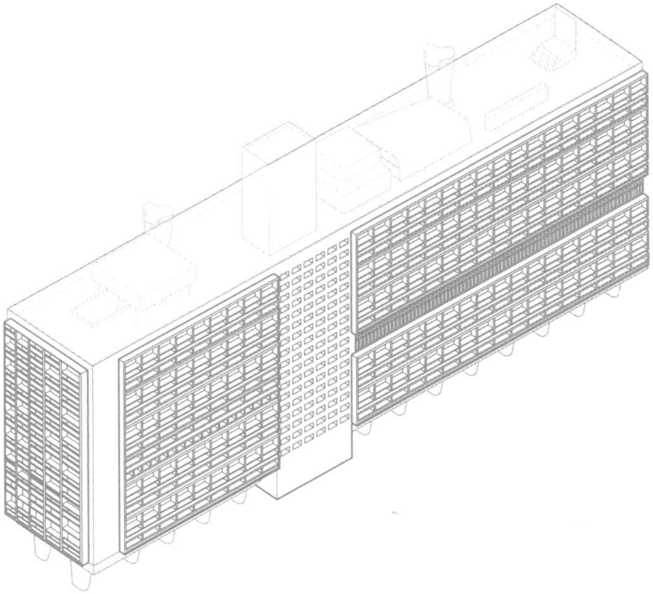

MATERIAL MODULE

MATERIAL GEOMETRY

CAST-IN-PLACE CONCRETE

UNITE D'HABITATION
LE CORBUSIER
MARSEILLE, FRANCE

1952

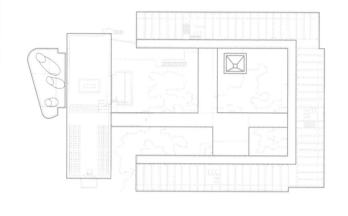

MATERIAL FUNCTION

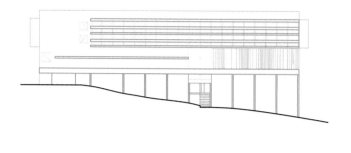

MATERIAL ORDER

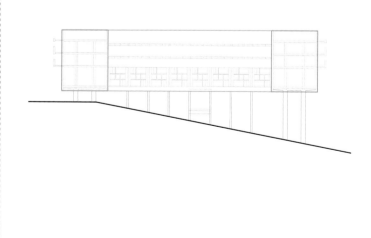

MATERIAL GEOMETRY

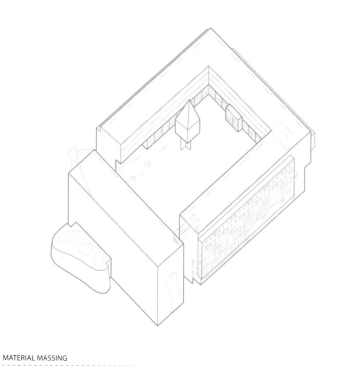

MATERIAL MASSING

CAST-IN-PLACE CONCRETE

CONVENT DE LA TOURETTE
LE CORBUSIER
EVEUX-SUR-ARBRESLE, FRANCE

1960

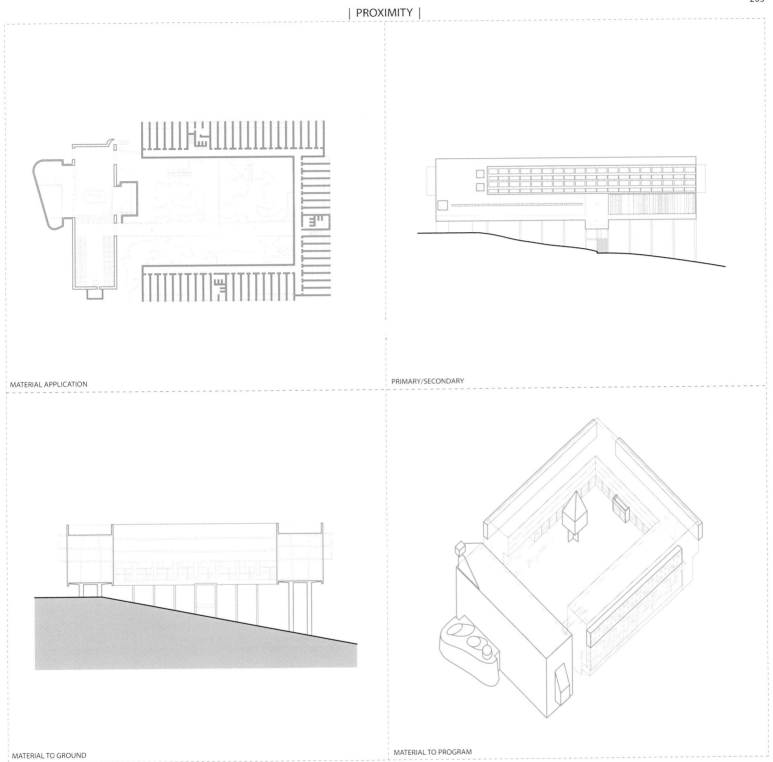

MATERIAL APPLICATION

PRIMARY/SECONDARY

MATERIAL TO GROUND

MATERIAL TO PROGRAM

CAST-IN-PLACE CONCRETE

CONVENT DE LA TOURETTE
LE CORBUSIER
EVEUX-SUR-ARBRESLE, FRANCE

1960

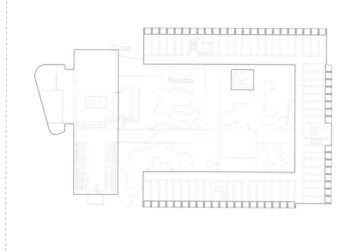

MATERIAL ENCLOSURE [PERIMETER]

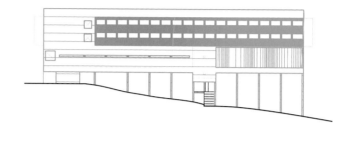

MATERIAL ORDER

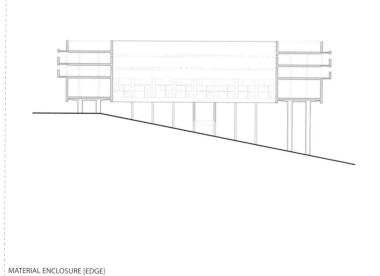

MATERIAL ENCLOSURE [EDGE]

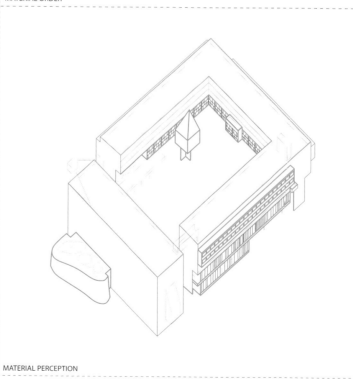

MATERIAL PERCEPTION

CAST-IN-PLACE CONCRETE

CONVENT DE LA TOURETTE
LE CORBUSIER
EVEUX-SUR-ARBRESLE, FRANCE

1960

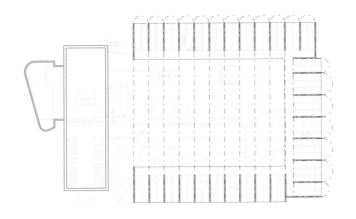

STRUCTURAL MATERIAL [BAY/MODULE]

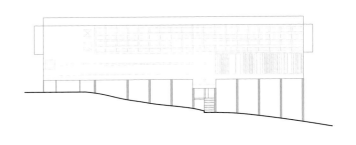

STRUCTURAL MATERIAL LEGIBILITY

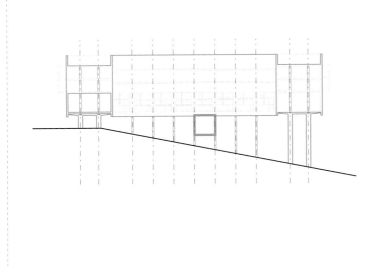

STRUCTURAL MATERIAL SYSTEM

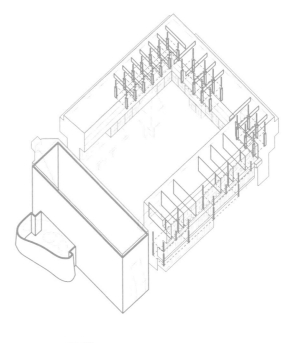

STRUCTURAL MATERIAL [LINE/POINT]

CAST-IN-PLACE CONCRETE

CONVENT DE LA TOURETTE
LE CORBUSIER
EVEUX-SUR-ARBRESLE, FRANCE

1960

| MODULE |

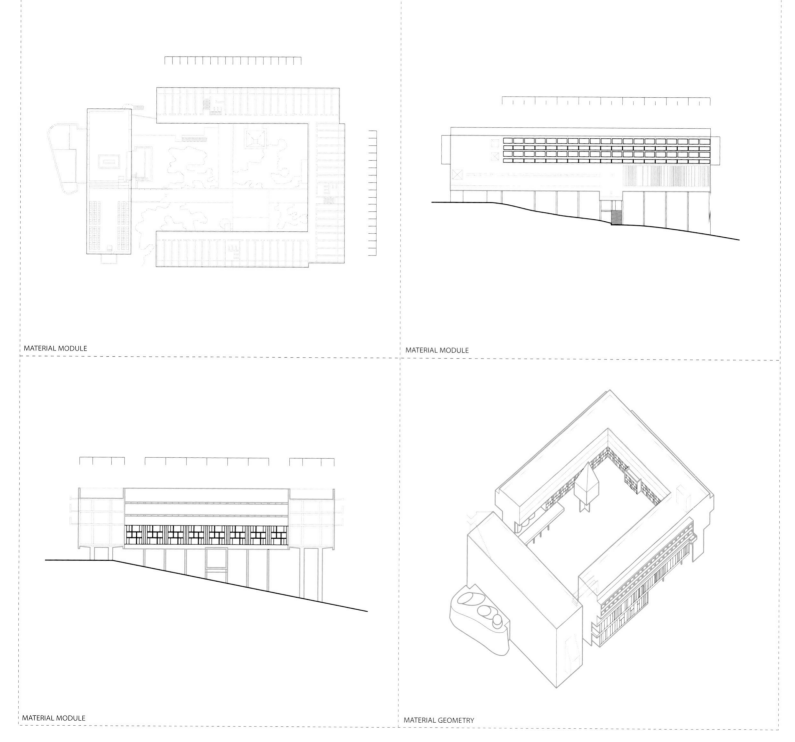

MATERIAL MODULE

MATERIAL MODULE

MATERIAL MODULE

MATERIAL GEOMETRY

CAST-IN-PLACE CONCRETE

CONVENT DE LA TOURETTE
LE CORBUSIER
EVEUX-SUR-ARBRESLE, FRANCE

1960

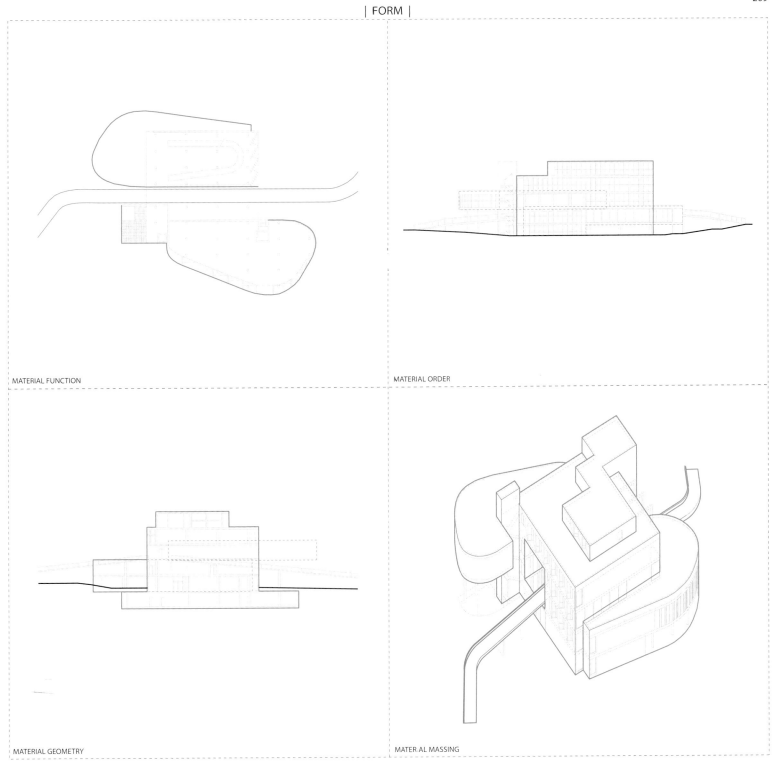

MATERIAL FUNCTION

MATERIAL ORDER

MATERIAL GEOMETRY

MATER AL MASSING

CAST-IN-PLACE CONCRETE

CARPENTER CENTER
LE CORBUSIER
CAMBRIDGE, MASSACHUSETTS

1964

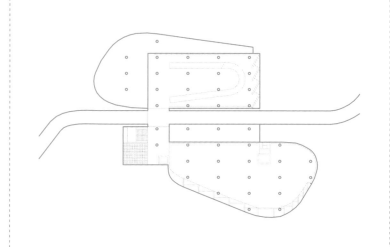

MATERIAL APPLICATION

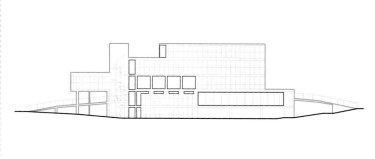

PRIMARY/SECONDARY

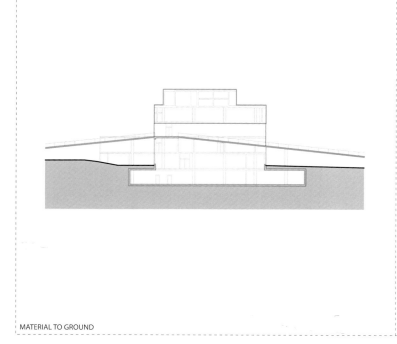

MATERIAL TO GROUND

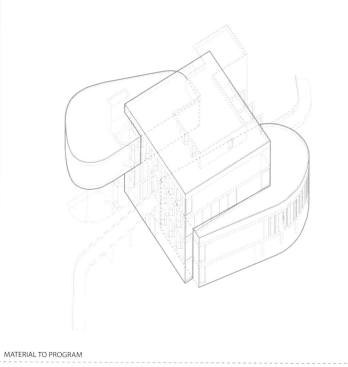

MATERIAL TO PROGRAM

CAST-IN-PLACE CONCRETE

CARPENTER CENTER
LE CORBUSIER
CAMBRIDGE, MASSACHUSETTS

1964

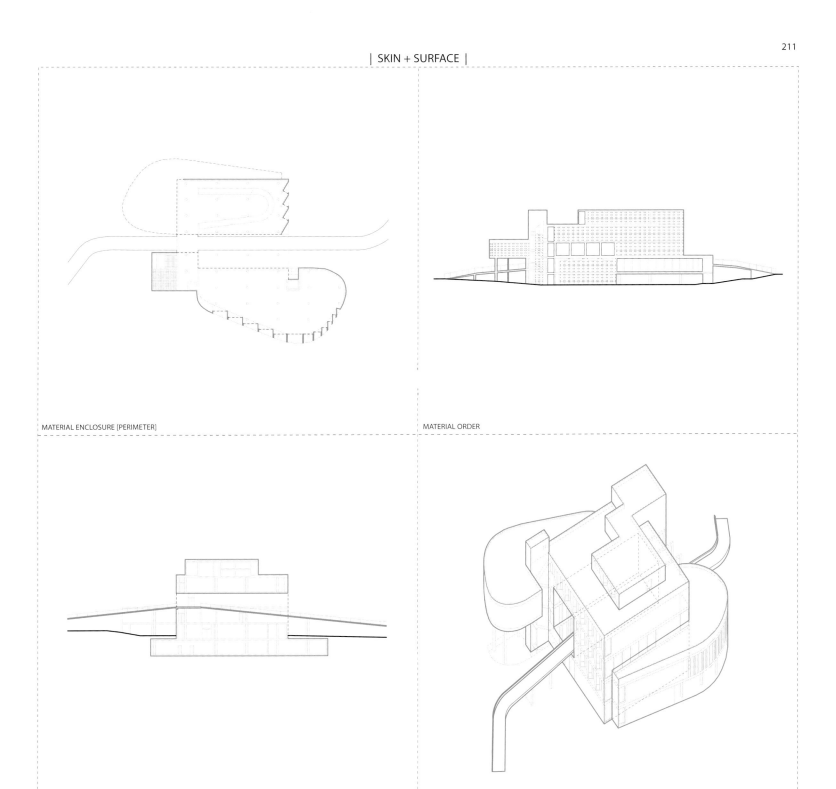

MATERIAL ENCLOSURE [PERIMETER]

MATERIAL ORDER

MATERIAL ENCLOSURE [EDGE]

MATERIAL PERCEPTION

CAST-IN-PLACE CONCRETE

CARPENTER CENTER
LE CORBUSIER
CAMBRIDGE, MASSACHUSETTS

1964

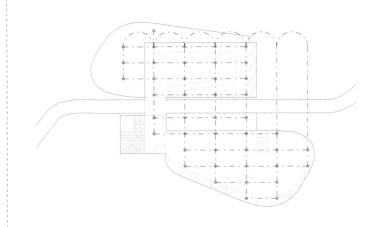

STRUCTURAL MATERIAL [BAY/MODULE]

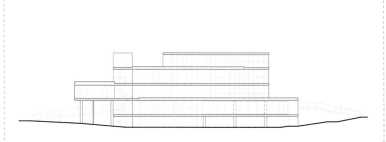

STRUCTURAL MATERIAL LEGIBILITY

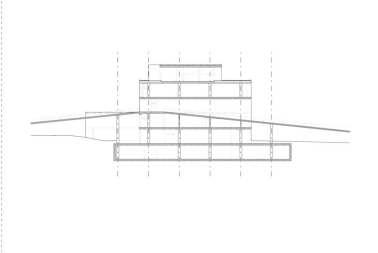

STRUCTURAL MATERIAL SYSTEM

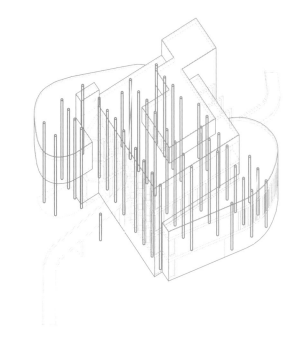

STRUCTURAL MATERIAL [LINE/POINT]

CAST-IN-PLACE CONCRETE

CARPENTER CENTER
LE CORBUSIER
CAMBRIDGE, MASSACHUSETTS

1964

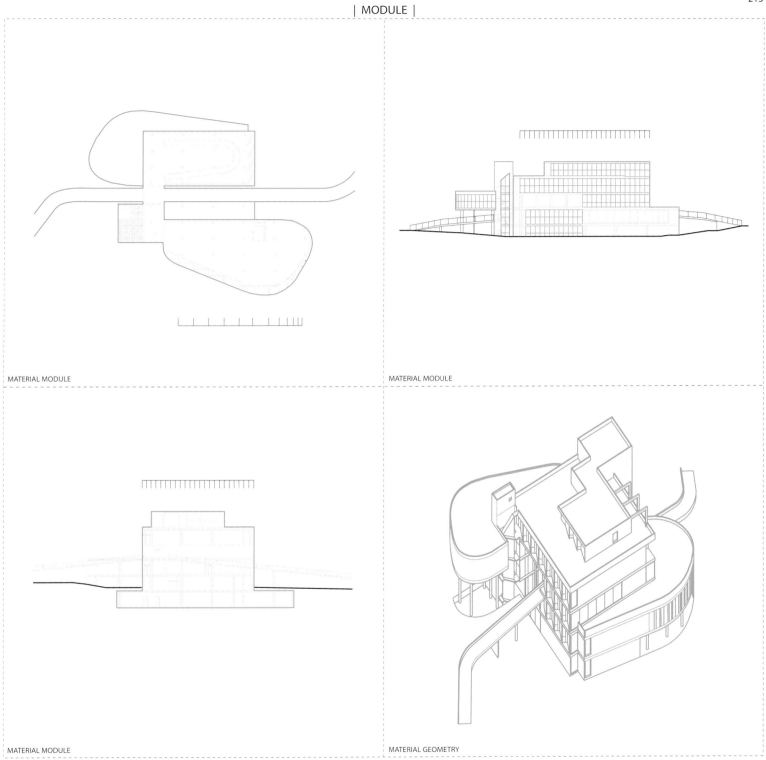

MATERIAL MODULE

MATERIAL MODULE

MATERIAL MODULE

MATERIAL GEOMETRY

CAST-IN-PLACE CONCRETE

CARPENTER CENTER
LE CORBUSIER
CAMBRIDGE, MASSACHUSETTS

1964

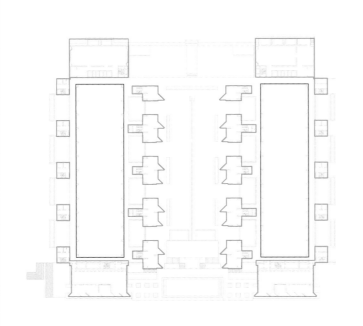

MATERIAL FUNCTION

MATERIAL ORDER

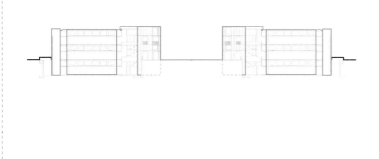

MATERIAL GEOMETRY

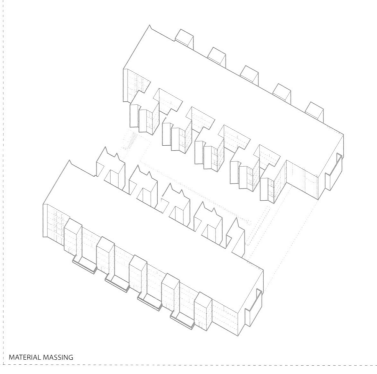

MATERIAL MASSING

CAST-IN-PLACE CONCRETE

SALK INSTITUTE OF BIOLOGICAL SCIENCES
LOUIS I. KAHN
LA JOLLA, CALIFORNIA

1966

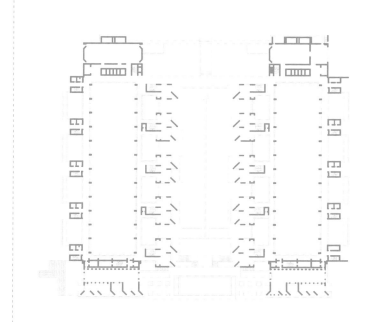

MATERIAL APPLICATION

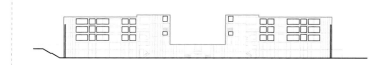

PRIMARY/SECONDARY

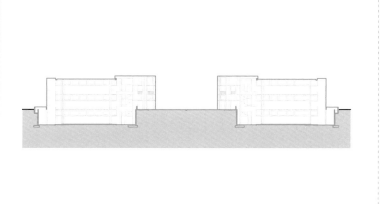

MATERIAL TO GROUND

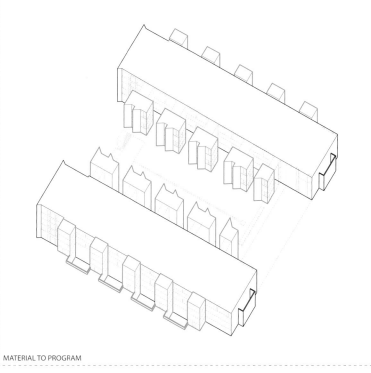

MATERIAL TO PROGRAM

CAST-IN-PLACE CONCRETE

SALK INSTITUTE OF BIOLOGICAL SCIENCES
LOUIS I. KAHN
LA JOLLA, CALIFORNIA

1966

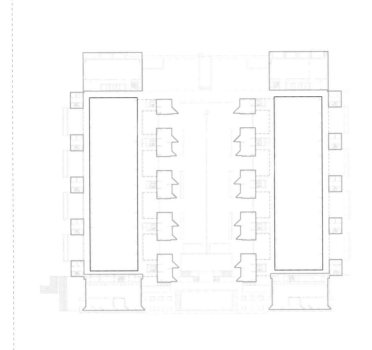

MATERIAL ENCLOSURE [PERIMETER]

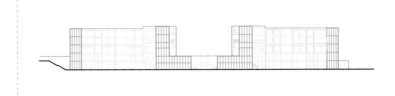

MATERIAL ORDER

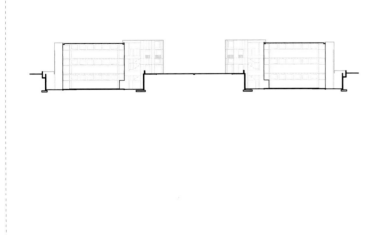

MATERIAL ENCLOSURE [EDGE]

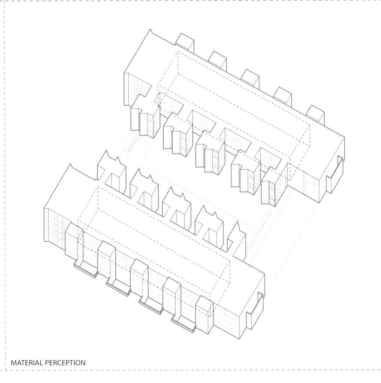

MATERIAL PERCEPTION

CAST-IN-PLACE CONCRETE

SALK INSTITUTE OF BIOLOGICAL SCIENCES
LOUIS I. KAHN
LA JOLLA, CALIFORNIA

1966

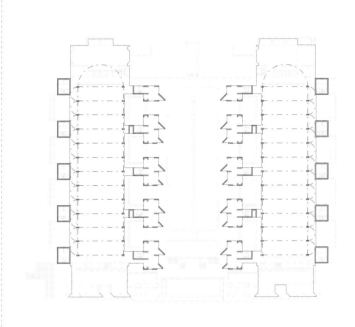

STRUCTURAL MATERIAL [BAY/MODULE]

STRUCTURAL MATERIAL LEGIBILITY

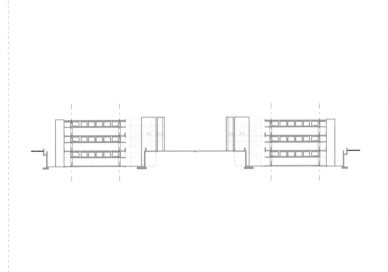

STRUCTURAL MATERIAL SYSTEM

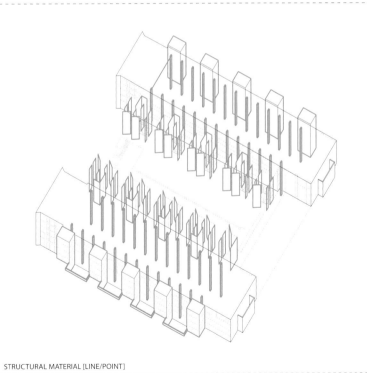

STRUCTURAL MATERIAL [LINE/POINT]

CAST-IN-PLACE CONCRETE

SALK INSTITUTE OF BIOLOGICAL SCIENCES
LOUIS I. KAHN
LA JOLLA, CALIFORNIA

1966

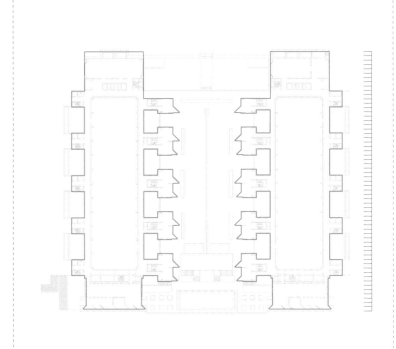

MATERIAL MODULE

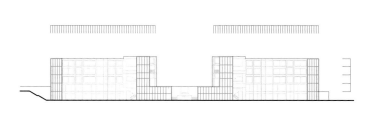

MATERIAL MODULE

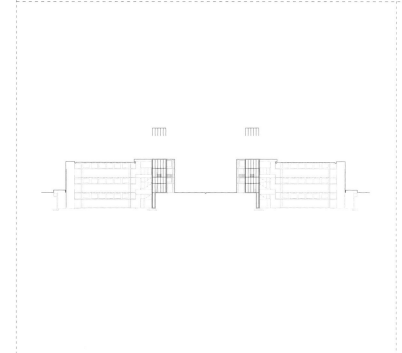

MATERIAL MODULE

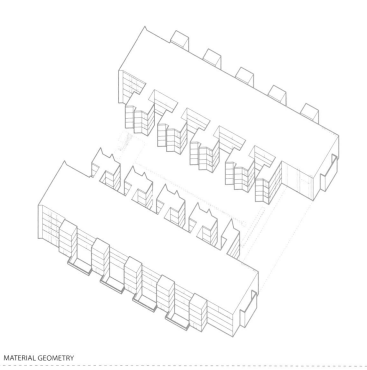

MATERIAL GEOMETRY

CAST-IN-PLACE CONCRETE

SALK INSTITUTE OF BIOLOGICAL SCIENCES
LOUIS I. KAHN
LA JOLLA, CALIFORNIA

1966

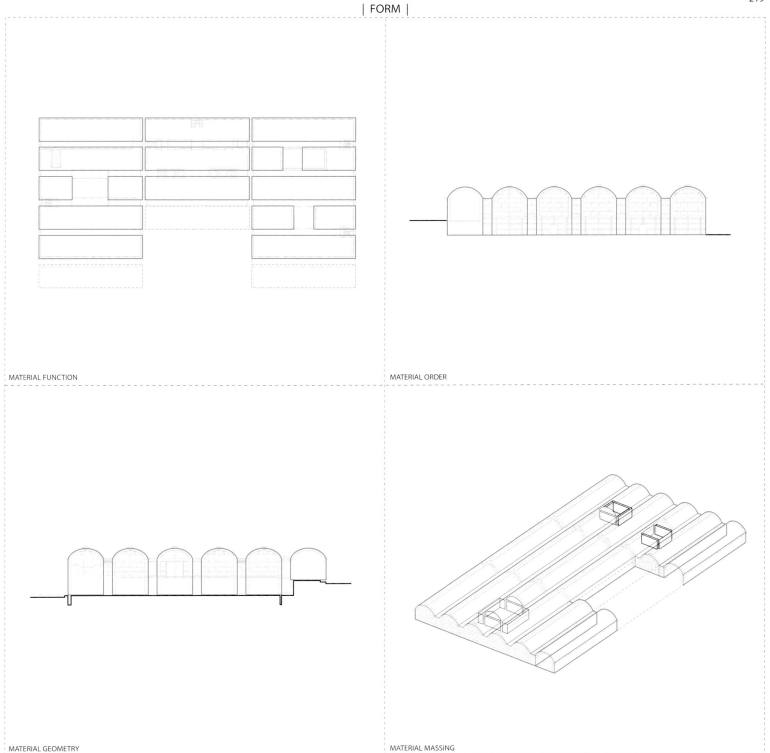

MATERIAL FUNCTION

MATERIAL ORDER

MATERIAL GEOMETRY

MATERIAL MASSING

CAST-IN-PLACE CONCRETE

KIMBELL ART MUSEUM
LOUIS I. KAHN
FORT WORTH, TEXAS

1972

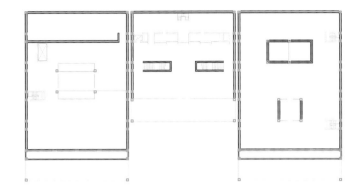

MATERIAL APPLICATION

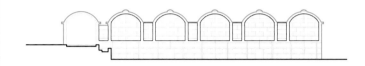

PRIMARY/SECONDARY

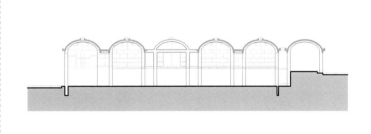

MATERIAL TO GROUND

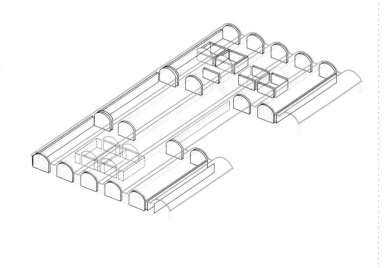

MATERIAL TO PROGRAM

CAST-IN-PLACE CONCRETE

KIMBELL ART MUSEUM
LOUIS I. KAHN
FORT WORTH, TEXAS

1972

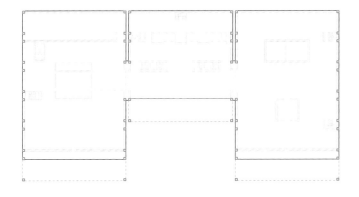

MATERIAL ENCLOSURE [PERIMETER]

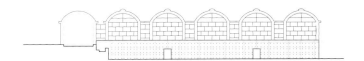

MATERIAL ORDER

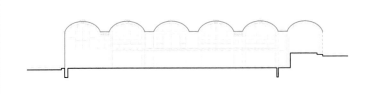

MATERIAL ENCLOSURE [EDGE]

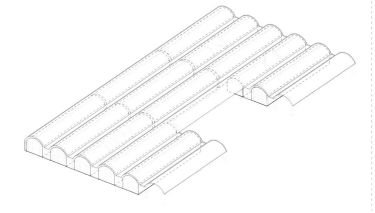

MATERIAL PERCEPTION

CAST-IN-PLACE CONCRETE

KIMBELL ART MUSEUM
LOUIS I. KAHN
FORT WORTH, TEXAS

1972

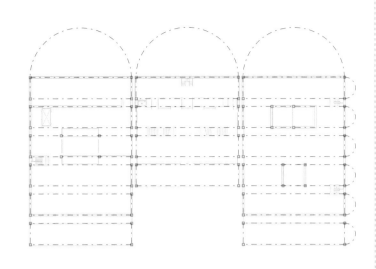

STRUCTURAL MATERIAL [BAY/MODULE]

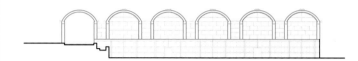

STRUCTURAL MATERIAL LEGIBILITY

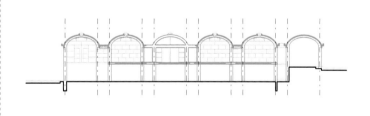

STRUCTURAL MATERIAL SYSTEM

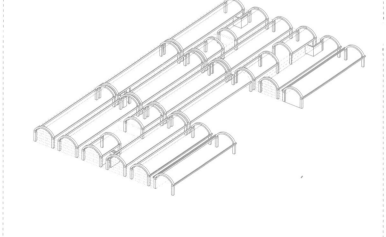

STRUCTURAL MATERIAL [LINE/POINT]

CAST-IN-PLACE CONCRETE

KIMBELL ART MUSEUM
LOUIS I. KAHN
FORT WORTH, TEXAS

1972

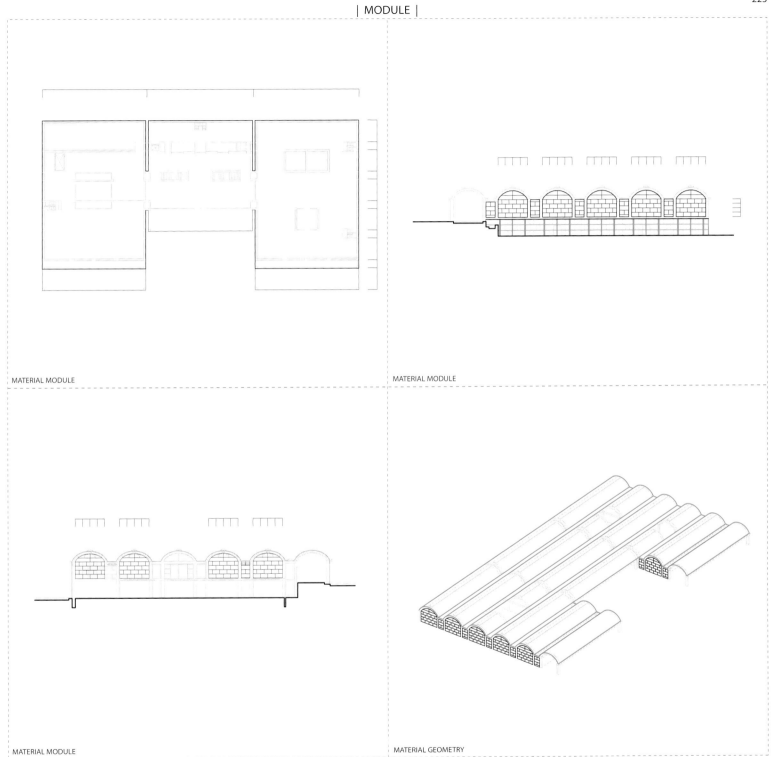

MATERIAL MODULE

MATERIAL MODULE

MATERIAL MODULE

MATERIAL GEOMETRY

CAST-IN-PLACE CONCRETE

KIMBELL ART MUSEUM
LOUIS I. KAHN
FORT WORTH, TEXAS

1972

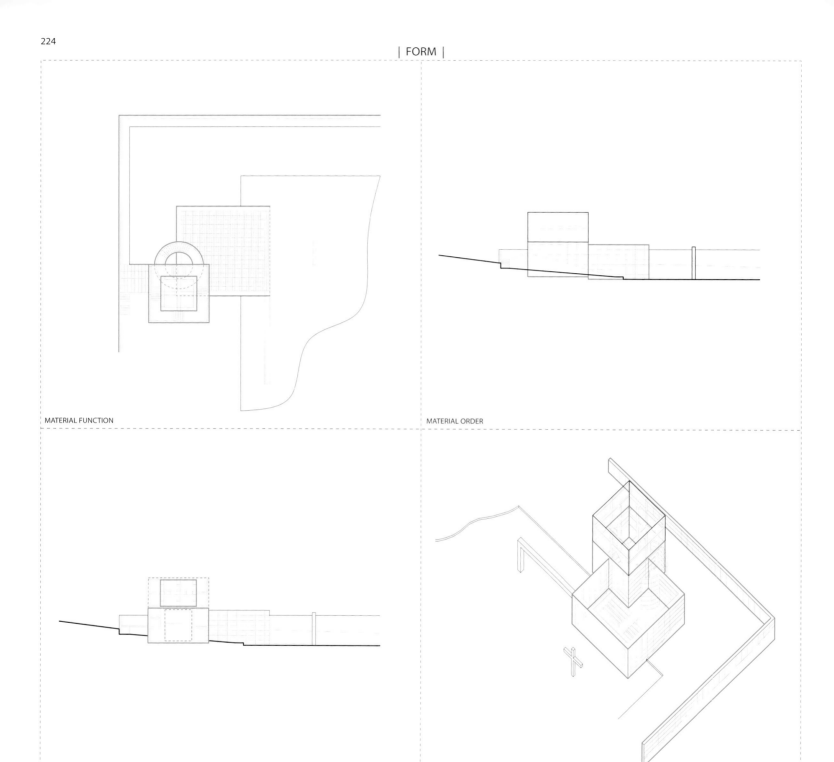

MATERIAL FUNCTION

MATERIAL ORDER

MATERIAL GEOMETRY

MATERIAL MASSING

CAST-IN-PLACE CONCRETE

CHURCH ON THE WATER
TADAO ANDO
HOKKAIDO, JAPAN

1988

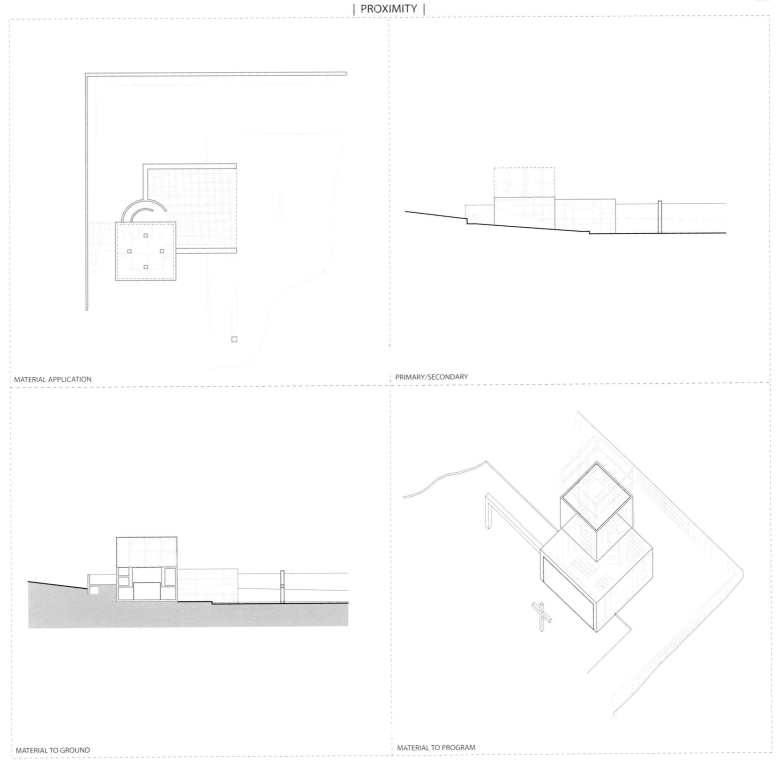

MATERIAL APPLICATION

PRIMARY/SECONDARY

MATERIAL TO GROUND

MATERIAL TO PROGRAM

CAST-IN-PLACE CONCRETE

CHURCH ON THE WATER
TADAO ANDO
HOKKAIDO, JAPAN

1988

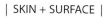

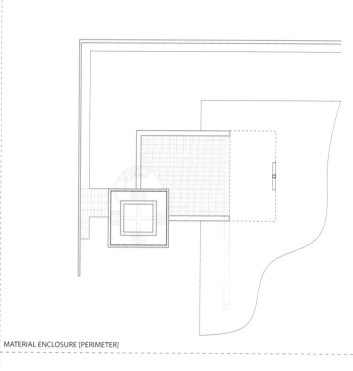

MATERIAL ENCLOSURE [PERIMETER]

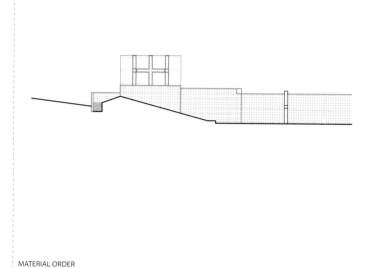

MATERIAL ORDER

MATERIAL ENCLOSURE [EDGE]

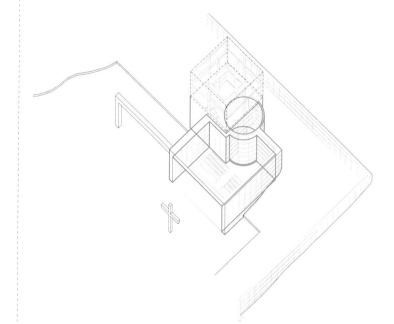

MATERIAL PERCEPTION

CAST-IN-PLACE CONCRETE

CHURCH ON THE WATER
TADAO ANDO
HOKKAIDO, JAPAN

1988

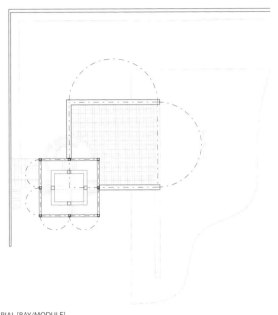

STRUCTURAL MATERIAL [BAY/MODULE]

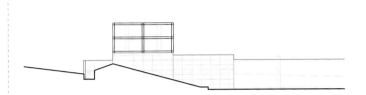

STRUCTURAL MATERIAL LEGIBILITY

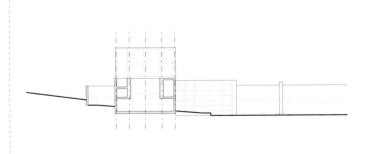

STRUCTURAL MATERIAL SYSTEM

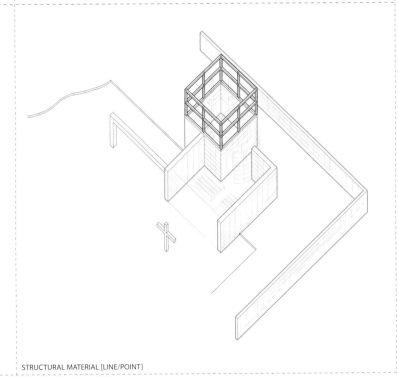

STRUCTURAL MATERIAL [LINE/POINT]

CAST-IN-PLACE CONCRETE

CHURCH ON THE WATER
TADAO ANDO
HOKKAIDO, JAPAN

1988

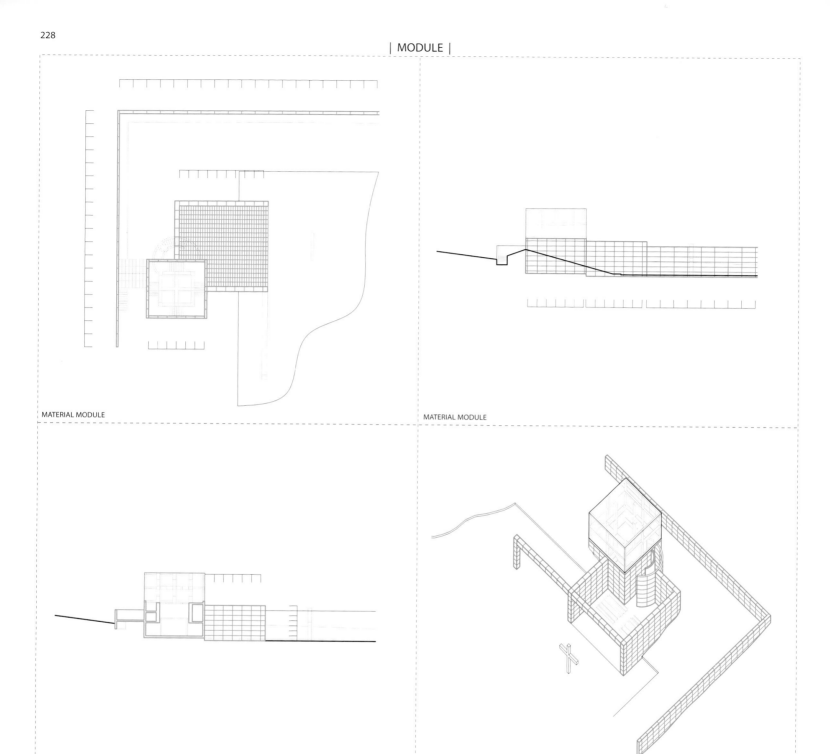

MATERIAL MODULE

MATERIAL MODULE

MATERIAL MODULE

MATERIAL GEOMETRY

CAST-IN-PLACE CONCRETE

CHURCH ON THE WATER
TADAO ANDO
HOKKAIDO, JAPAN

1988

| FORM |

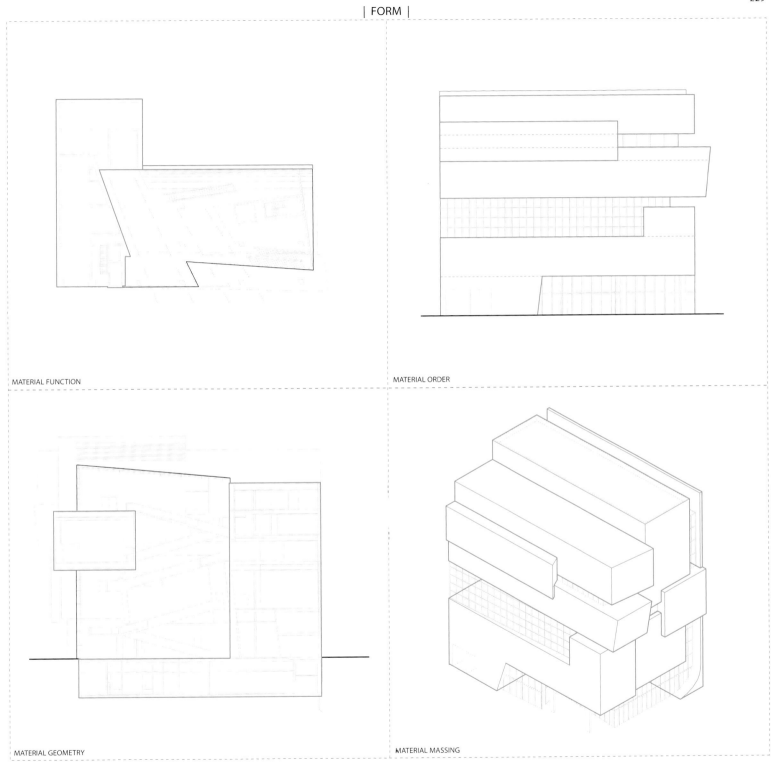

MATERIAL FUNCTION

MATERIAL ORDER

MATERIAL GEOMETRY

MATERIAL MASSING

CAST-IN-PLACE CONCRETE

ROSENTHAL CENTER FOR CONTEMPORARY ART
ZAHA HADID
CINCINNATI, OHIO

2003

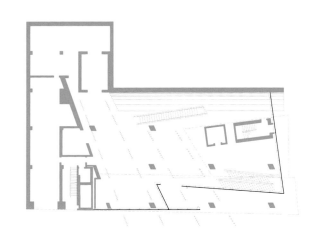

MATERIAL APPLICATION

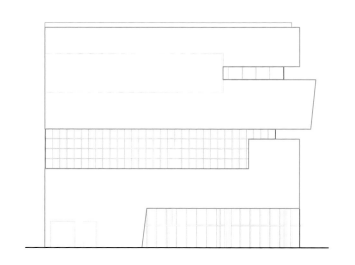

PRIMARY/SECONDARY

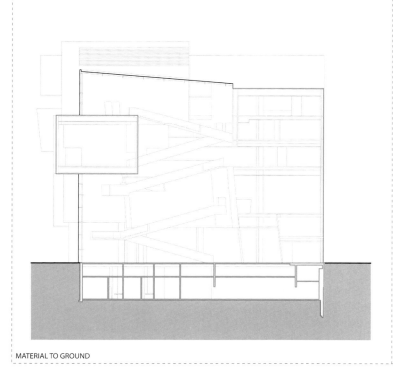

MATERIAL TO GROUND

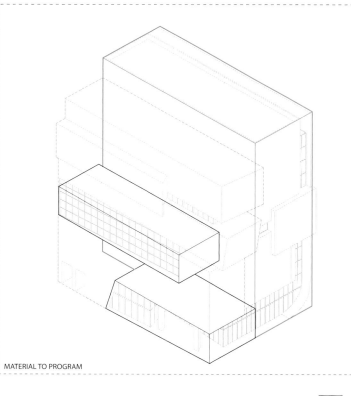

MATERIAL TO PROGRAM

CAST-IN-PLACE CONCRETE

ROSENTHAL CENTER FOR CONTEMPORARY ART
ZAHA HADID
CINCINNATI, OHIO

2003

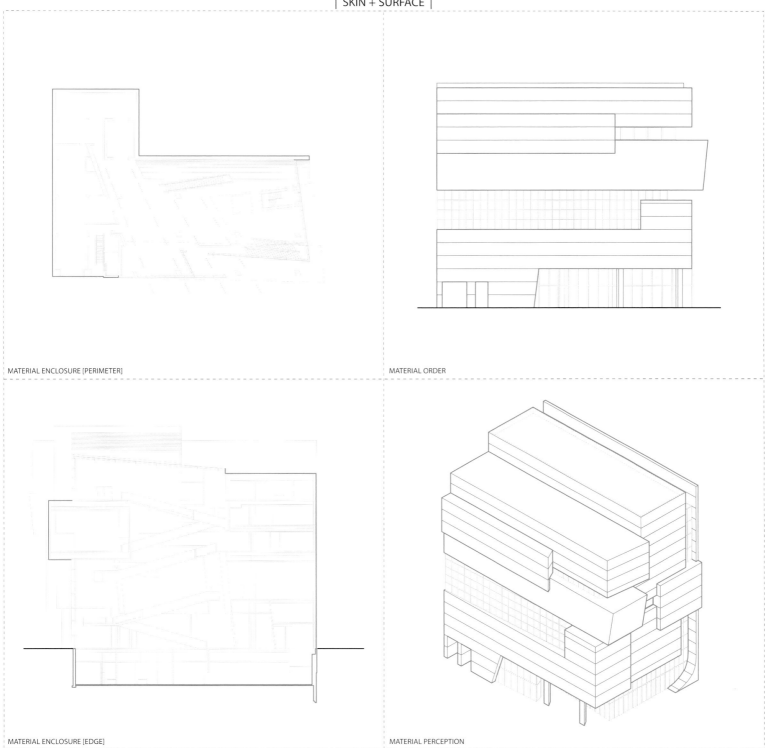

MATERIAL ENCLOSURE [PERIMETER]

MATERIAL ORDER

MATERIAL ENCLOSURE [EDGE]

MATERIAL PERCEPTION

CAST-IN-PLACE CONCRETE

ROSENTHAL CENTER FOR CONTEMPORARY ART
ZAHA HADID
CINCINNATI, OHIO

2003

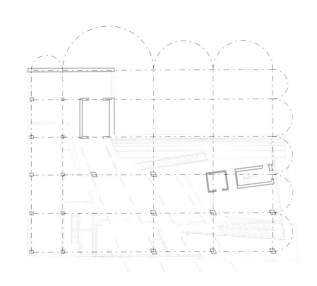

STRUCTURAL MATERIAL [BAY/MODULE]

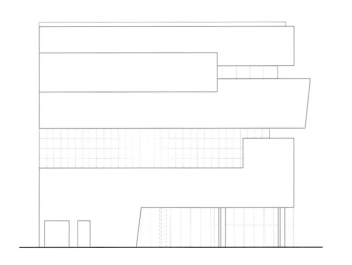

STRUCTURAL MATERIAL LEGIBILITY

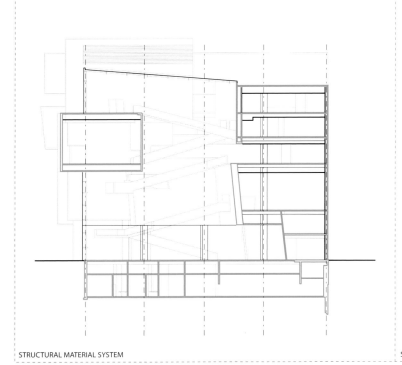

STRUCTURAL MATERIAL SYSTEM

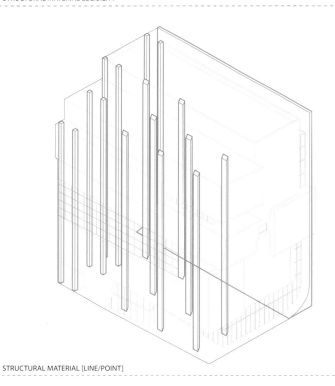

STRUCTURAL MATERIAL [LINE/POINT]

CAST-IN-PLACE CONCRETE

ROSENTHAL CENTER FOR CONTEMPORARY ART
ZAHA HADID
CINCINNATI, OHIO

2003

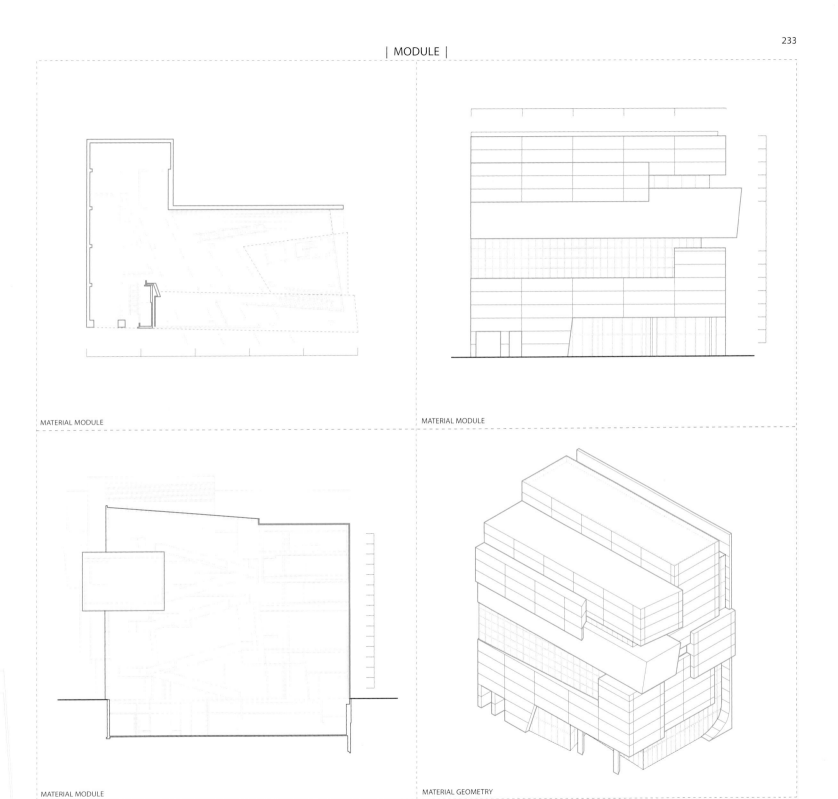

MATERIAL MODULE

MATERIAL MODULE

MATERIAL MODULE

MATERIAL GEOMETRY

CAST-IN-PLACE CONCRETE

ROSENTHAL CENTER FOR CONTEMPORARY ART
ZAHA HADID
CINCINNATI, OHIO

2003

| FORM |

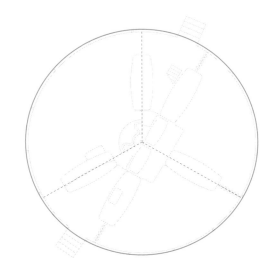

MATERIAL FUNCTION

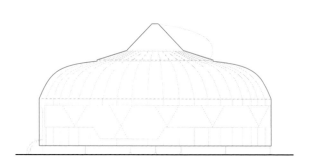

MATERIAL ORDER

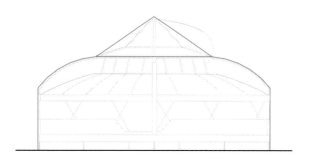

MATERIAL GEOMETRY

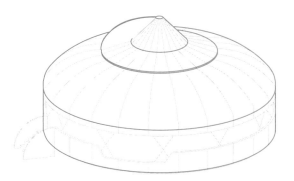

MATERIAL MASSING

ALUMINUM METAL

WICHITA HOUSE
BUCKMINSTER FULLER
DEARBORN, MICHIGAN

1946

MATERIAL APPLICATION

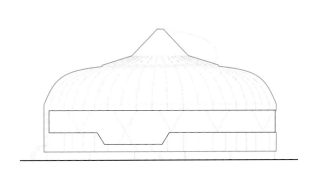

PRIMARY/SECONDARY

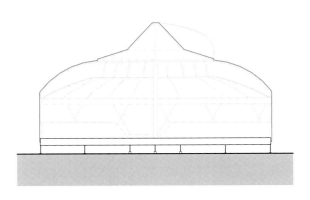

MATERIAL TO GROUND

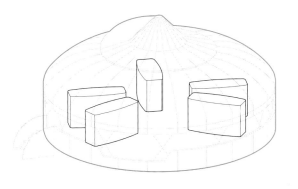

MATERIAL TO PROGRAM

ALUMINUM METAL

WICHITA HOUSE
BUCKMINSTER FULLER
DEARBORN, MICHIGAN

1946

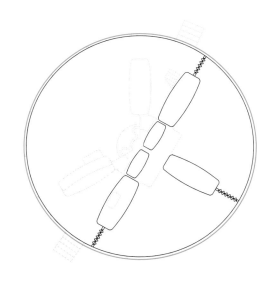

MATERIAL ENCLOSURE [PERIMETER]

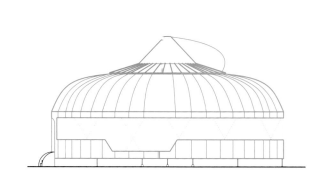

MATERIAL ORDER

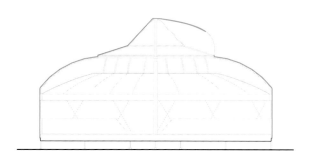

MATERIAL ENCLOSURE [EDGE]

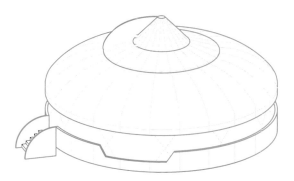

MATERIAL PERCEPTION

ALUMINUM METAL

WICHITA HOUSE
BUCKMINSTER FULLER
DEARBORN, MICHIGAN

1946

STRUCTURAL MATERIAL [BAY/MODULE]

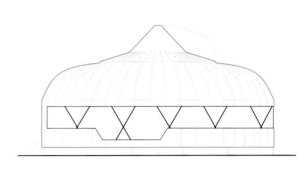

STRUCTURAL MATERIAL LEGIBILITY

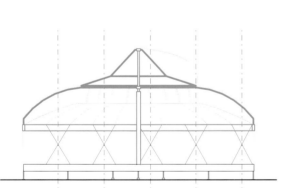

STRUCTURAL MATERIAL SYSTEM

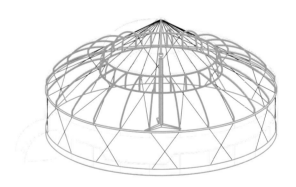

STRUCTURAL MATERIAL [LINE/POINT]

ALUMINUM METAL

WICHITA HOUSE
BUCKMINSTER FULLER
DEARBORN, MICHIGAN

1946

MATERIAL MODULE

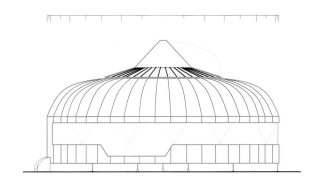

MATERIAL MODULE

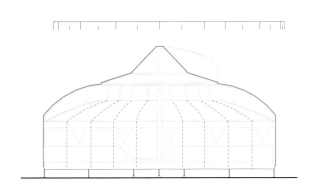

MATERIAL MODULE

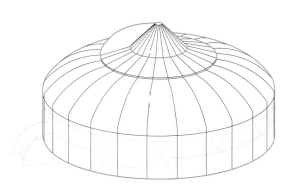

MATERIAL GEOMETRY

ALUMINUM METAL

WICHITA HOUSE
BUCKMINSTER FULLER
DEARBORN, MICHIGAN

1946

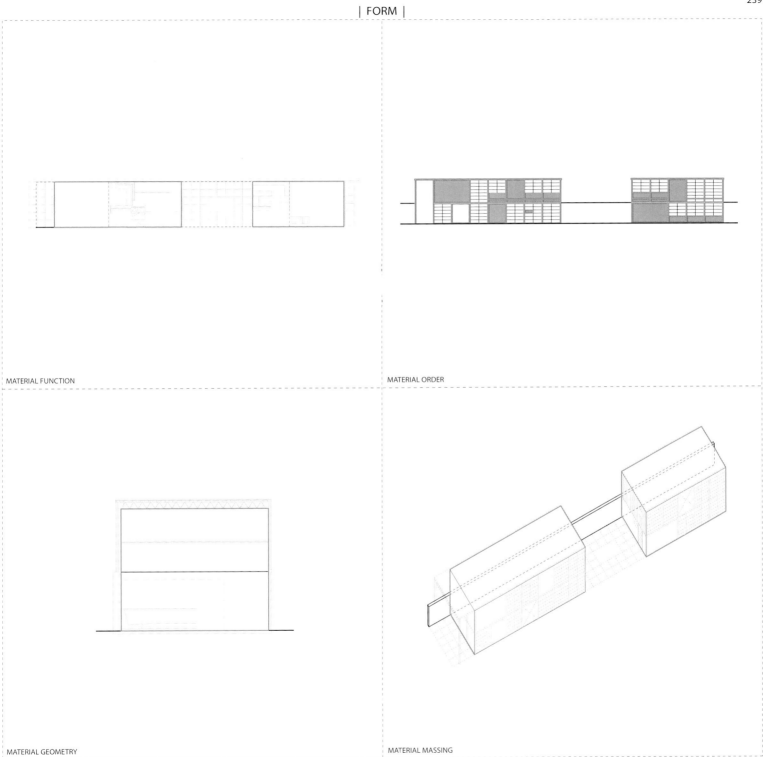

MATERIAL FUNCTION

MATERIAL ORDER

MATERIAL GEOMETRY

MATERIAL MASSING

PAINTED STEEL METAL

EAMES HOUSE
CHARLES AND RAY EAMES
PACIFIC PALISADES, CALIFORNIA

1949

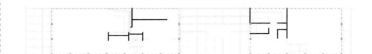

MATERIAL APPLICATION

PRIMARY/SECONDARY

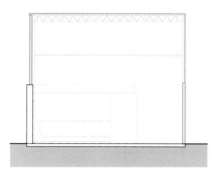

MATERIAL TO GROUND

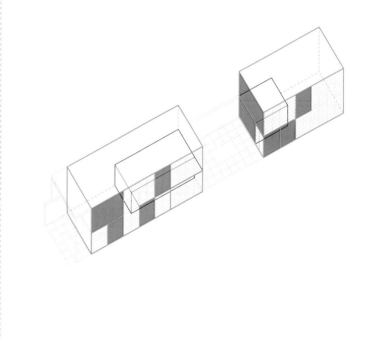

MATERIAL TO PROGRAM

PAINTED STEEL METAL

EAMES HOUSE
CHARLES AND RAY EAMES
PACIFIC PALISADES, CALIFORNIA

1949

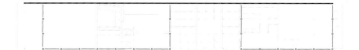

MATERIAL ENCLOSURE [PERIMETER]

MATERIAL ORDER

MATERIAL ENCLOSURE [EDGE]

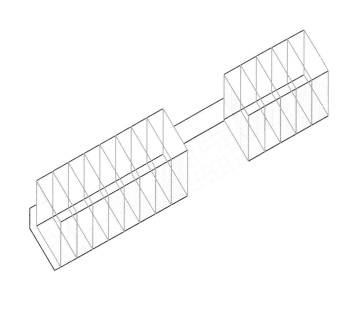

MATERIAL PERCEPTION

PAINTED STEEL METAL

EAMES HOUSE
CHARLES AND RAY EAMES
PACIFIC PALISADES, CALIFORNIA

1949

STRUCTURAL MATERIAL [BAY/MODULE]

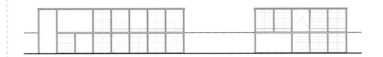

STRUCTURAL MATERIAL LEGIBILITY

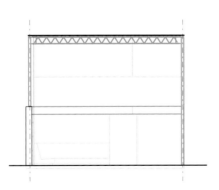

STRUCTURAL MATERIAL SYSTEM

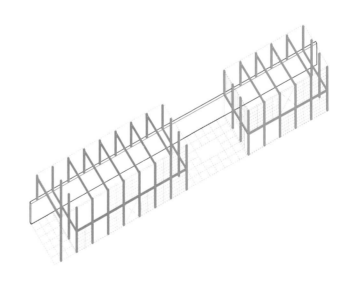

STRUCTURAL MATERIAL [LINE/POINT]

PAINTED STEEL METAL

EAMES HOUSE
CHARLES AND RAY EAMES
PACIFIC PALISADES, CALIFORNIA

1949

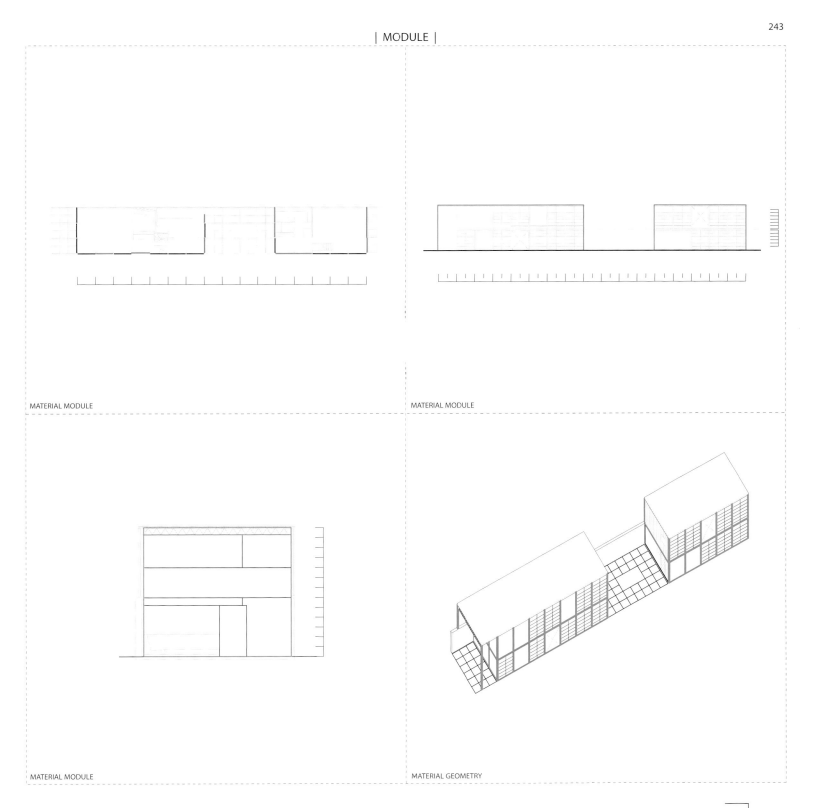

MATERIAL MODULE

MATERIAL MODULE

MATERIAL MODULE

MATERIAL GEOMETRY

PAINTED STEEL METAL

EAMES HOUSE
CHARLES AND RAY EAMES
PACIFIC PALISADES, CALIFORNIA

1949

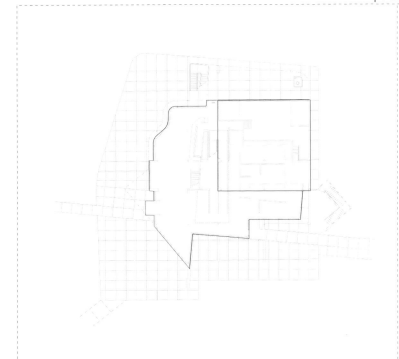

MATERIAL FUNCTION

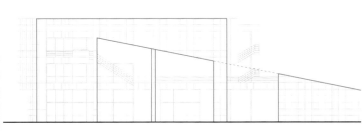

MATERIAL ORDER

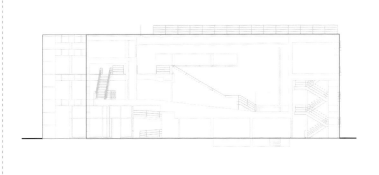

MATERIAL GEOMETRY

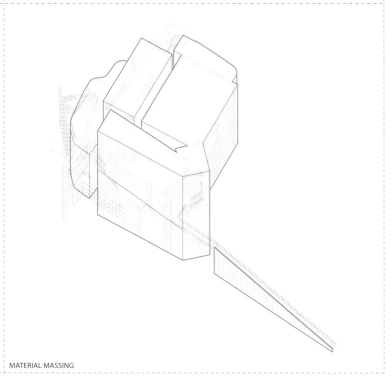

MATERIAL MASSING

PORCELAIN-ENAMELED METAL CLADDING

THE ATHENEUM
RICHARD MEIER
NEW HARMONY, INDIANA

1979

MATERIAL APPLICATION

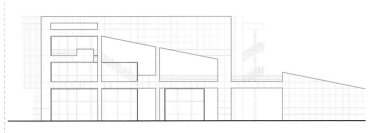

PRIMARY/SECONDARY

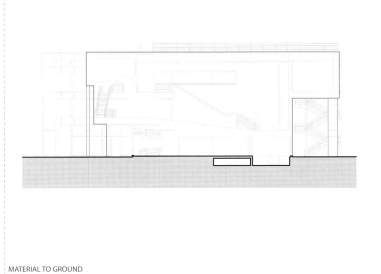

MATERIAL TO GROUND

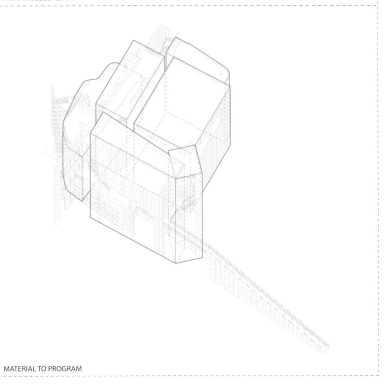

MATERIAL TO PROGRAM

PORCELAIN-ENAMELED METAL CLADDING

THE ATHENEUM
RICHARD MEIER
NEW HARMONY, INDIANA

1979

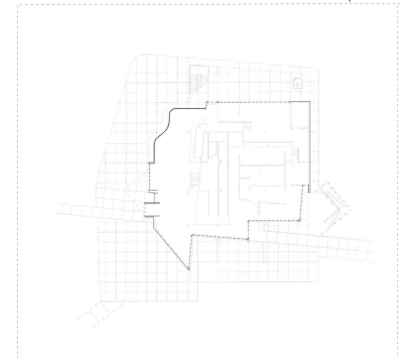

MATERIAL ENCLOSURE [PERIMETER]

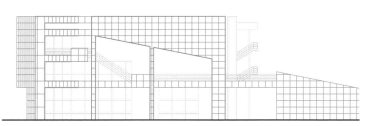

MATERIAL ORDER

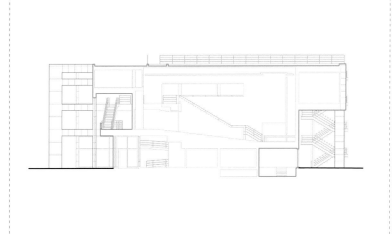

MATERIAL ENCLOSURE [EDGE]

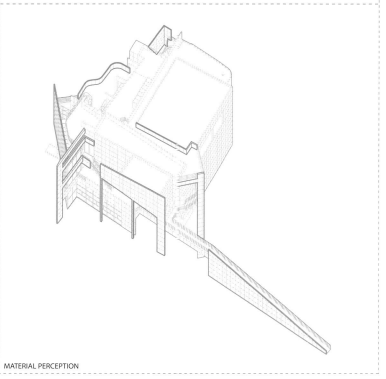

MATERIAL PERCEPTION

PORCELAIN-ENAMELED METAL CLADDING

THE ATHENEUM
RICHARD MEIER
NEW HARMONY, INDIANA

1979

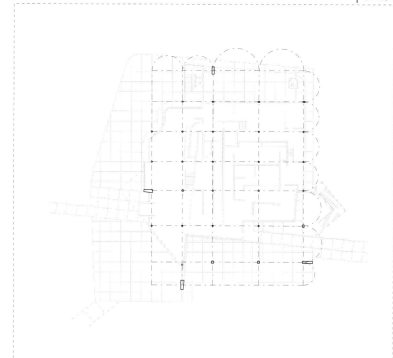

STRUCTURAL MATERIAL [BAY/MODULE]

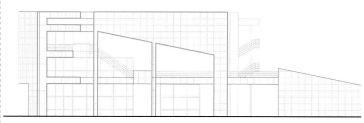

STRUCTURAL MATERIAL LEGIBILITY

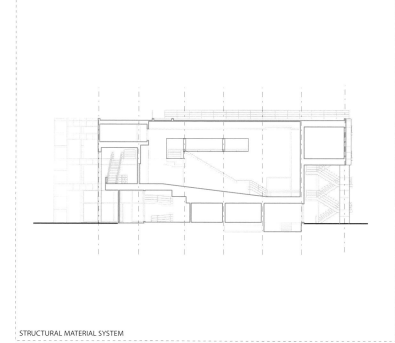

STRUCTURAL MATERIAL SYSTEM

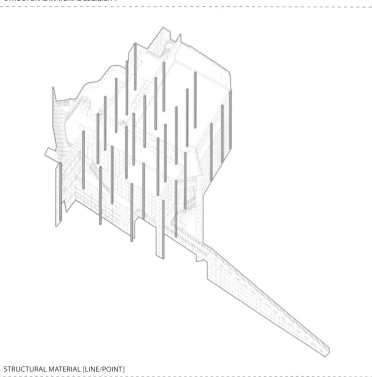

STRUCTURAL MATERIAL [LINE/POINT]

PORCELAIN-ENAMELED METAL CLADDING

THE ATHENEUM
RICHARD MEIER
NEW HARMONY, INDIANA

1979

MATERIAL MODULE

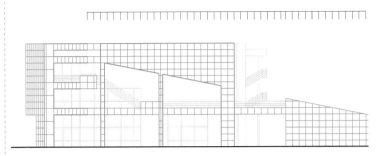

MATERIAL MODULE

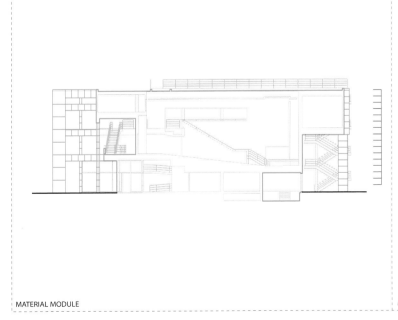

MATERIAL MODULE

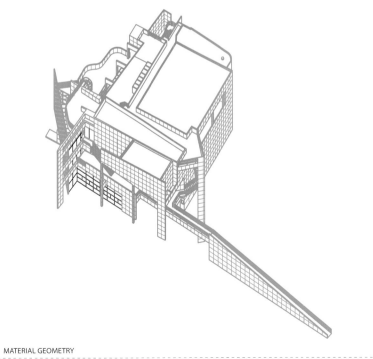

MATERIAL GEOMETRY

PORCELAIN-ENAMELED METAL CLADDING

THE ATHENEUM
RICHARD MEIER
NEW HARMONY, INDIANA

1979

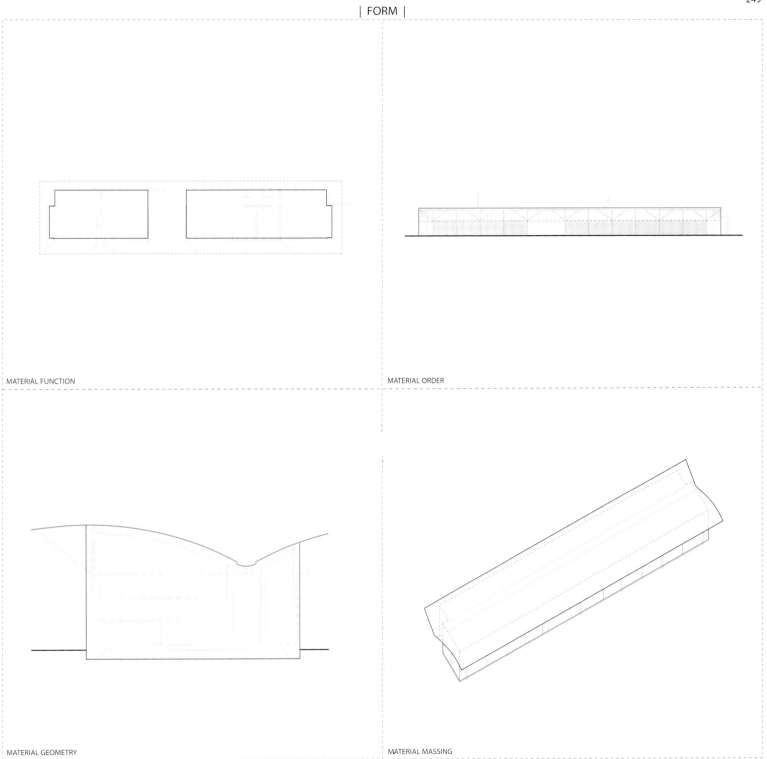

MATERIAL FUNCTION

MATERIAL ORDER

MATERIAL GEOMETRY

MATERIAL MASSING

CORRUGATED METAL SHEATHING

MAGNEY HOUSE
GLENN MURCUTT
BINGIE POINT, MORUYA, AUSTRALIA

1984

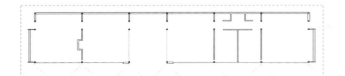

MATERIAL APPLICATION

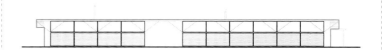

PRIMARY/SECONDARY

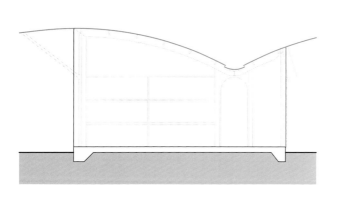

MATERIAL TO GROUND

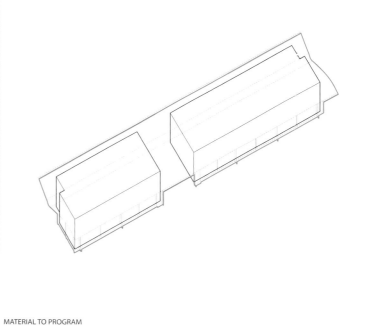

MATERIAL TO PROGRAM

CORRUGATED METAL SHEATHING

MAGNEY HOUSE
GLENN MURCUTT
BINGIE POINT, MORUYA, AUSTRALIA

1984

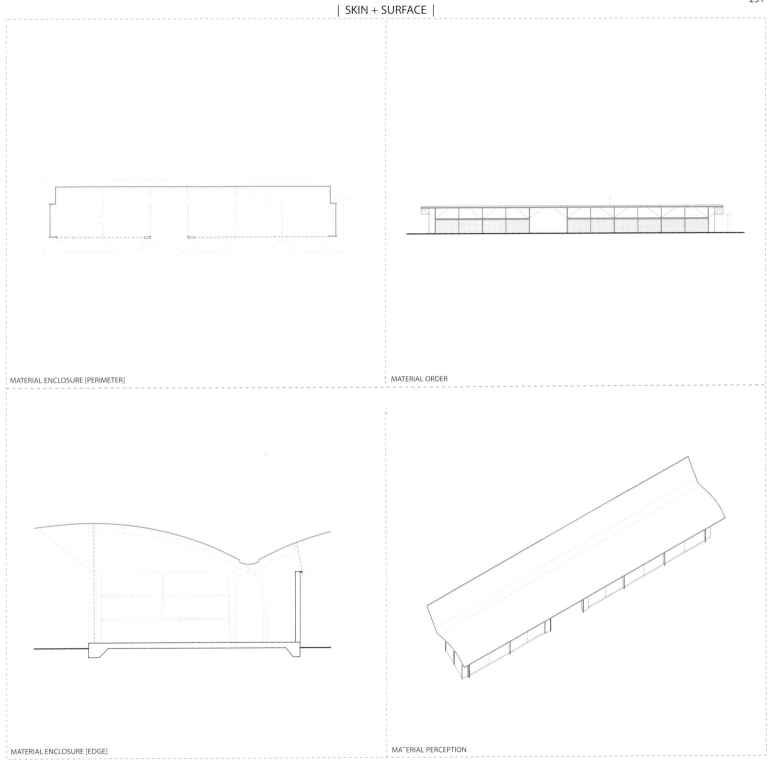

MATERIAL ENCLOSURE [PERIMETER]

MATERIAL ORDER

MATERIAL ENCLOSURE [EDGE]

MATERIAL PERCEPTION

CORRUGATED METAL SHEATHING

MAGNEY HOUSE
GLENN MURCUTT
BINGIE POINT, MORUYA, AUSTRALIA

1984

STRUCTURAL MATERIAL [BAY/MODULE]

STRUCTURAL MATERIAL LEGIBILITY

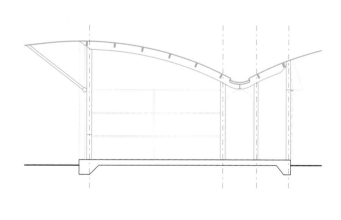

STRUCTURAL MATERIAL SYSTEM

STRUCTURAL MATERIAL [LINE/POINT]

CORRUGATED METAL SHEATHING

MAGNEY HOUSE
GLENN MURCUTT
BINGIE POINT, MORUYA, AUSTRALIA

1984

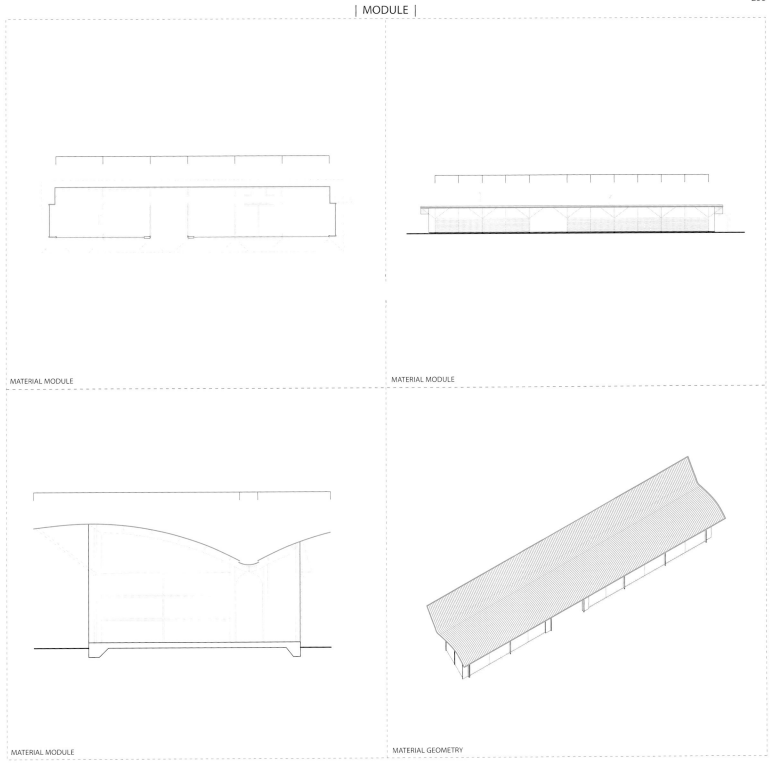

MATERIAL MODULE

MATERIAL MODULE

MATERIAL MODULE

MATERIAL GEOMETRY

CORRUGATED METAL SHEATHING

MAGNEY HOUSE
GLENN MURCUTT
BINGIE POINT, MORUYA, AUSTRALIA

1984

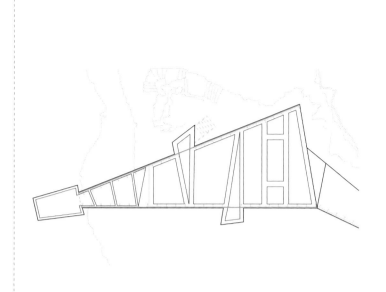

MATERIAL FUNCTION

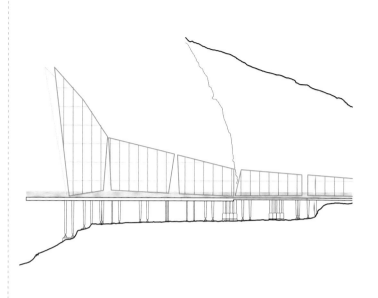

MATERIAL ORDER

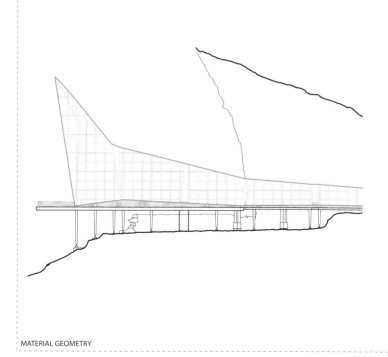

MATERIAL GEOMETRY

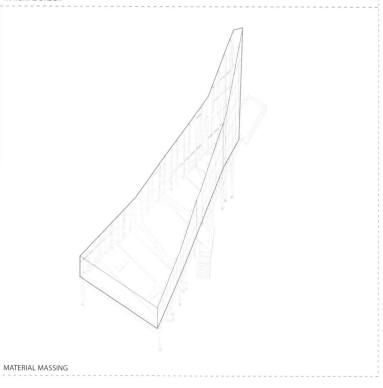

MATERIAL MASSING

CORTEN STEEL METAL

NIAUX CAVE
MASSIMILIANO FUKSAS
ARIEGE, FRANCE

1993

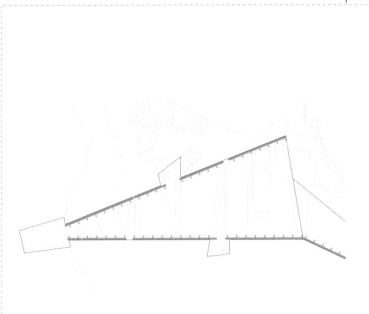

MATERIAL APPLICATION

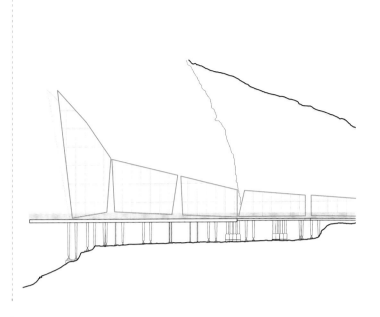

PRIMARY/SECONDARY

MATERIAL TO GROUND

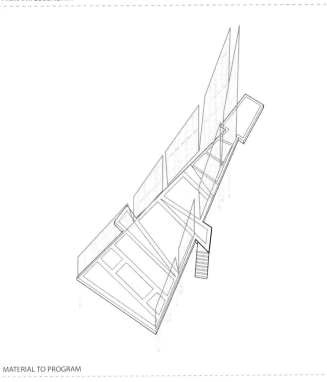

MATERIAL TO PROGRAM

CORTEN STEEL METAL

NIAUX CAVE
MASSIMILIANO FUKSAS
ARIEGE, FRANCE

1993

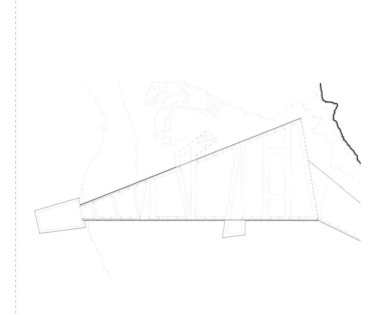

MATERIAL ENCLOSURE [PERIMETER]

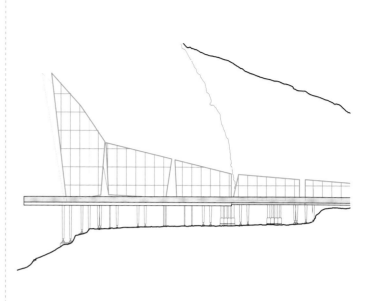

MATERIAL ORDER

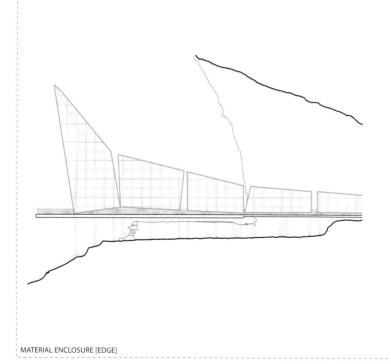

MATERIAL ENCLOSURE [EDGE]

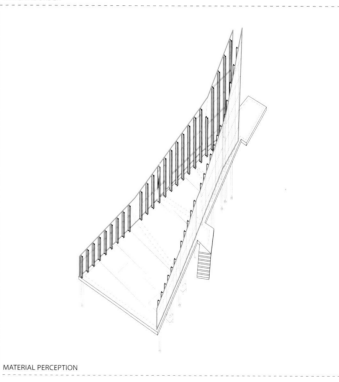

MATERIAL PERCEPTION

CORTEN STEEL METAL

NIAUX CAVE
MASSIMILIANO FUKSAS
ARIEGE, FRANCE

1993

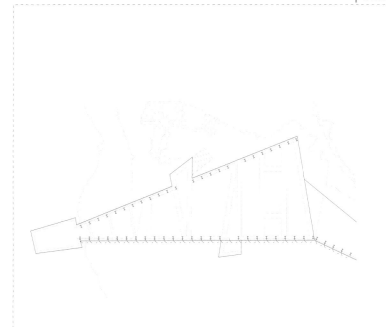

STRUCTURAL MATERIAL [BAY/MODULE]

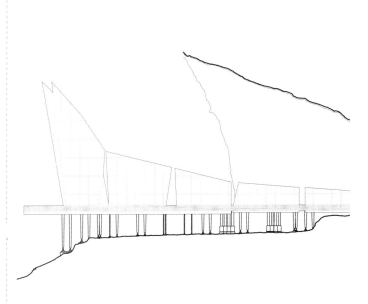

STRUCTURAL MATERIAL LEGIBILITY

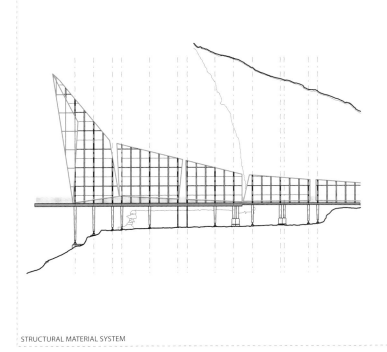

STRUCTURAL MATERIAL SYSTEM

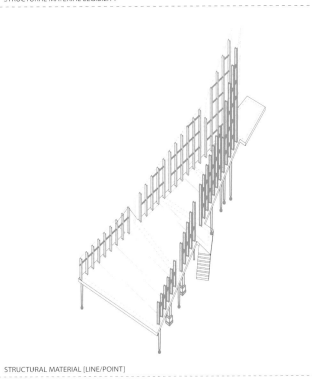

STRUCTURAL MATERIAL [LINE/POINT]

CORTEN STEEL METAL

NIAUX CAVE
MASSIMILIANO FUKSAS
ARIEGE, FRANCE

1993

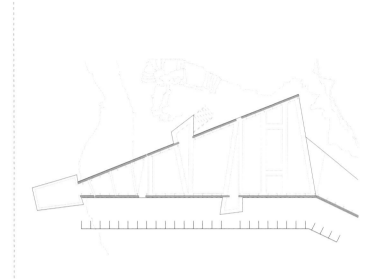

MATERIAL MODULE

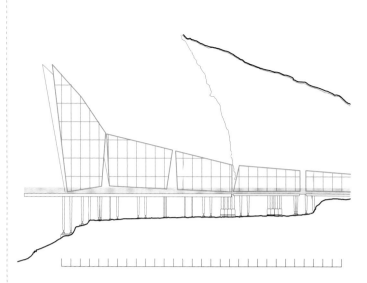

MATERIAL MODULE

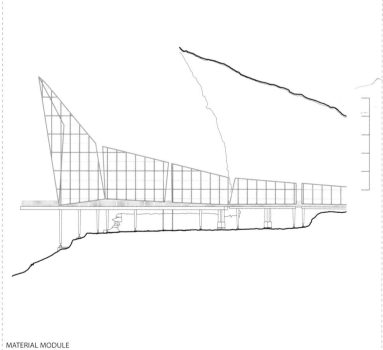

MATERIAL MODULE

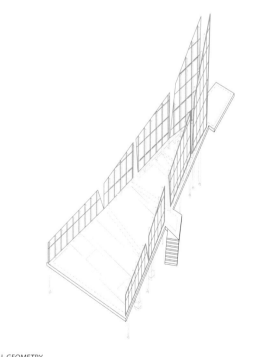

MATERIAL GEOMETRY

CORTEN STEEL METAL

NIAUX CAVE
MASSIMILIANO FUKSAS
ARIEGE, FRANCE

1993

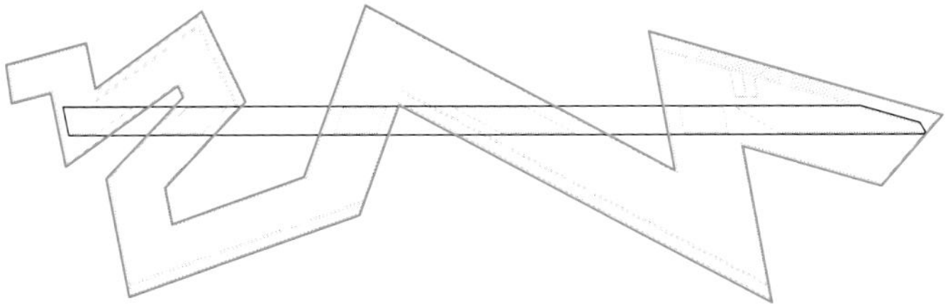

MATERIAL FUNCTION

MATERIAL ORDER

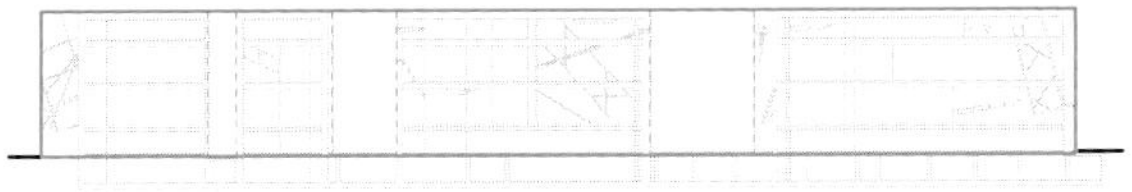

MATERIAL GEOMETRY

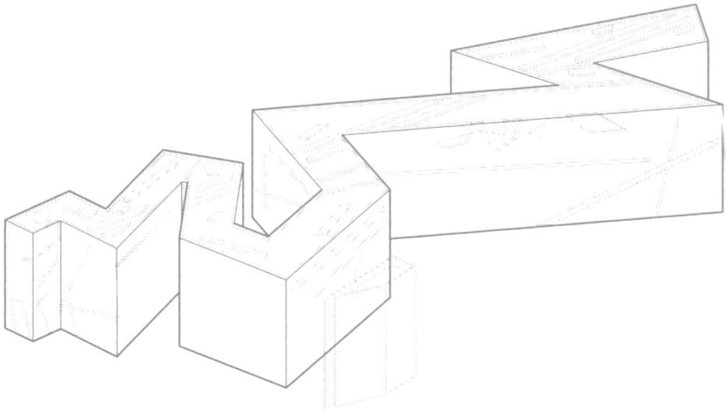

MATERIAL MASSING

ZINC METAL

JEWISH MUSEUM
DANIEL LIBESKIND
BERLIN, GERMANY

1999

MATERIAL APPLICATION

PRIMARY/SECONDARY

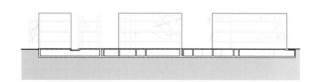

MATERIAL TO GROUND

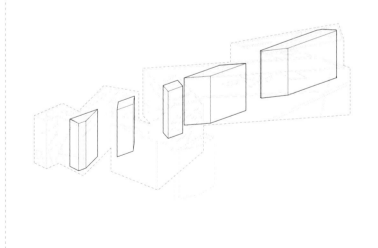

MATERIAL TO PROGRAM

ZINC METAL

JEWISH MUSEUM
DANIEL LIBESKIND
BERLIN, GERMANY

1999

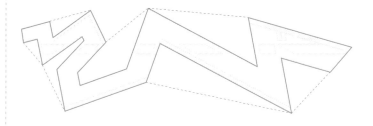

MATERIAL ENCLOSURE [PERIMETER]

MATERIAL ORDER

MATERIAL ENCLOSURE [EDGE]

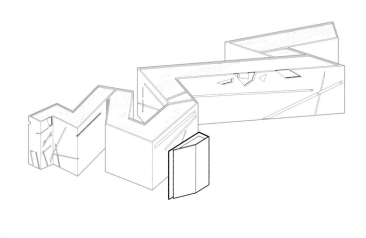

MATERIAL PERCEPTION

ZINC METAL

JEWISH MUSEUM
DANIEL LIBESKIND
BERLIN, GERMANY

1999

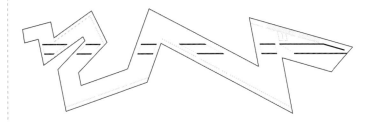

STRUCTURAL MATERIAL [BAY/MODULE]

STRUCTURAL MATERIAL LEGIBILITY

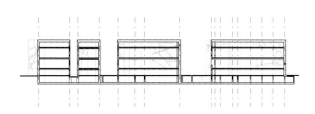

STRUCTURAL MATERIAL SYSTEM

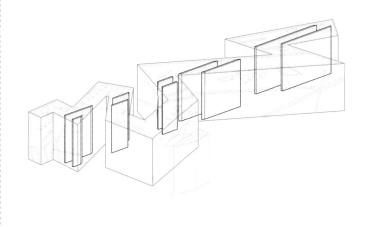

STRUCTURAL MATERIAL [LINE/POINT]

ZINC METAL

JEWISH MUSEUM
DANIEL LIBESKIND
BERLIN, GERMANY

1999

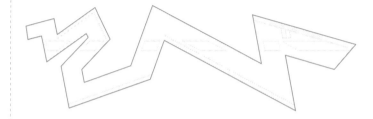

MATERIAL MODULE

MATERIAL MODULE

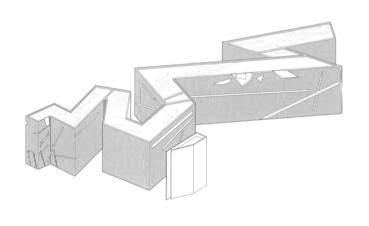

MATERIAL MODULE

MATERIAL GEOMETRY

ZINC METAL

JEWISH MUSEUM
DANIEL LIBESKIND
BERLIN, GERMANY

1999

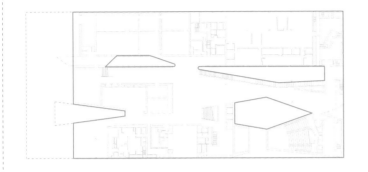

MATERIAL FUNCTION

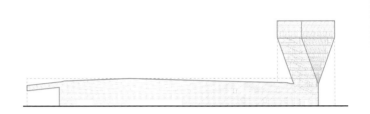

MATERIAL ORDER

MATERIAL GEOMETRY

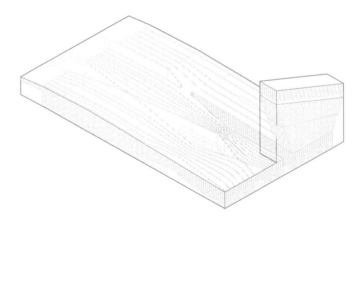

MATERIAL MASSING

PERFORATED COPPER METAL

DE YOUNG MUSEUM
HERZOG & DE MEURON
SAN FRANCISCO, CALIFORNIA

2005

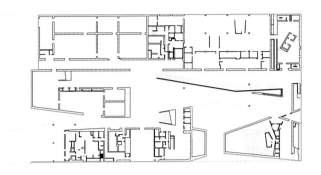

MATERIAL APPLICATION

PRIMARY/SECONDARY

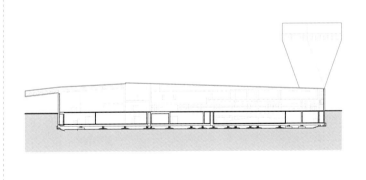

MATERIAL TO GROUND

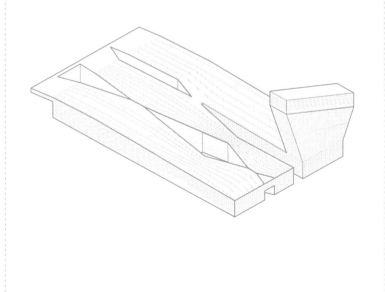

MATERIAL TO PROGRAM

PERFORATED COPPER METAL

DE YOUNG MUSEUM
HERZOG & DE MEURON
SAN FRANCISCO, CALIFORNIA

2005

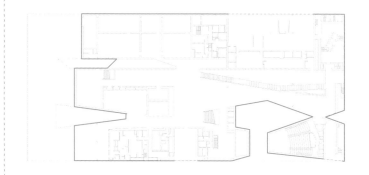

MATERIAL ENCLOSURE [PERIMETER]

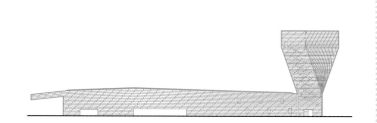

MATERIAL ORDER

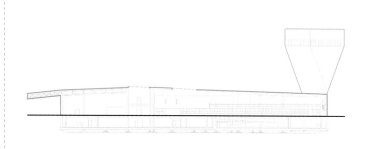

MATERIAL ENCLOSURE [EDGE]

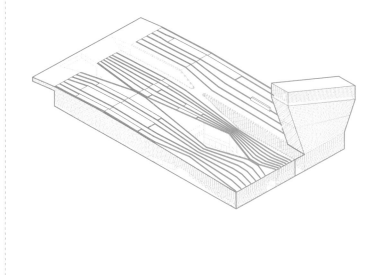

MATERIAL PERCEPTION

PERFORATED COPPER METAL

DE YOUNG MUSEUM
HERZOG & DE MEURON
SAN FRANCISCO, CALIFORNIA

2005

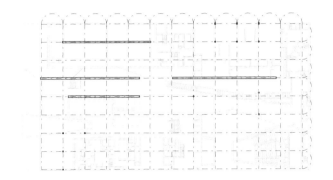

STRUCTURAL MATERIAL [BAY/MODULE]

STRUCTURAL MATERIAL LEGIBILITY

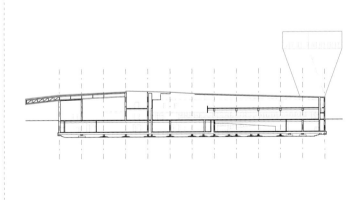

STRUCTURAL MATERIAL SYSTEM

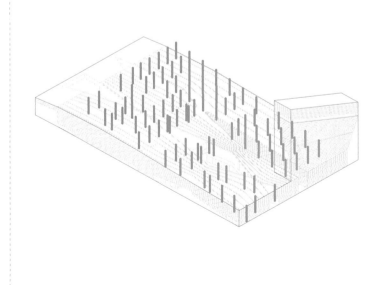

STRUCTURAL MATERIAL [LINE/POINT]

PERFORATED COPPER METAL

DE YOUNG MUSEUM
HERZOG & DE MEURON
SAN FRANCISCO, CALIFORNIA

2005

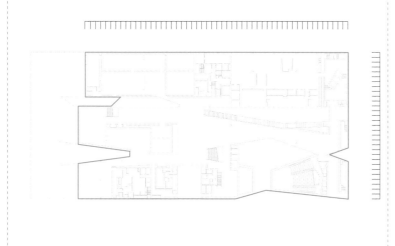

MATERIAL MODULE

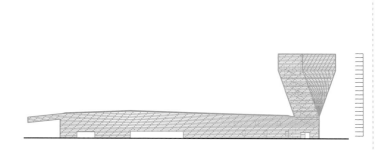

MATERIAL MODULE

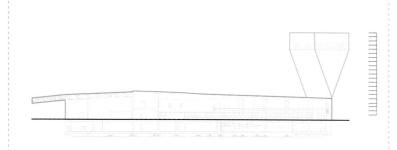

MATERIAL MODULE

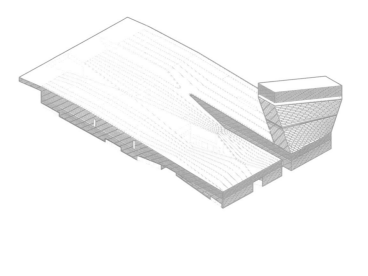

MATERIAL GEOMETRY

PERFORATED COPPER METAL

DE YOUNG MUSEUM
HERZOG & DE MEURON
SAN FRANCISCO, CALIFORNIA

2005

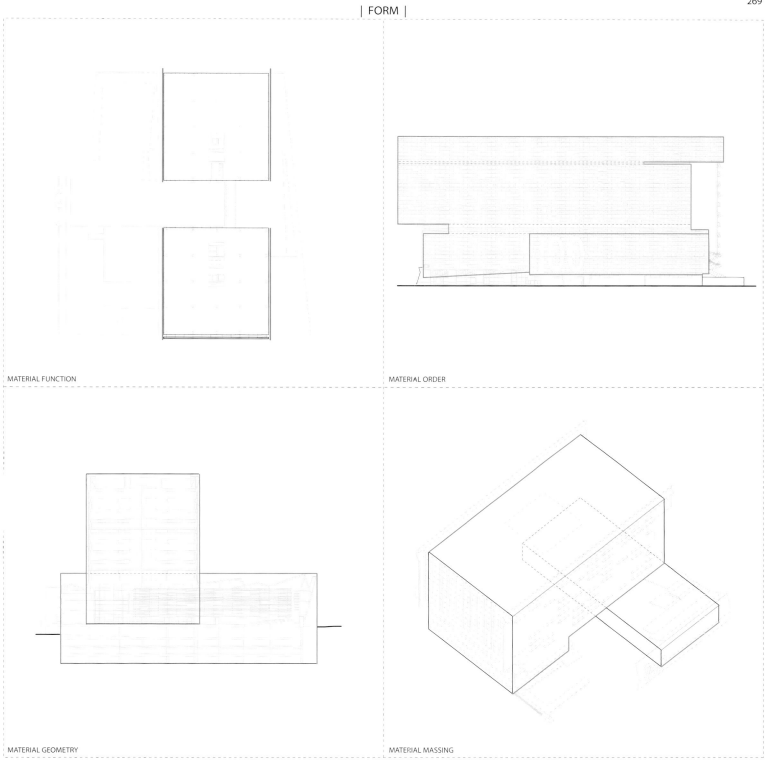

MATERIAL FUNCTION

MATERIAL ORDER

MATERIAL GEOMETRY

MATERIAL MASSING

PERFORATED METAL PANEL

CALTRANS DISTRICT 7 HQ
MORPHOSIS
LOS ANGELES, CALIFORNIA

2005

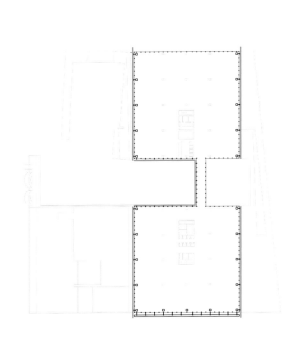

MATERIAL APPLICATION

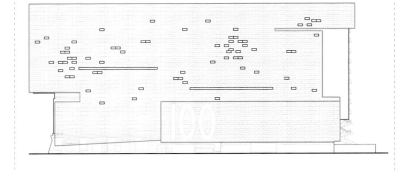

PRIMARY/SECONDARY

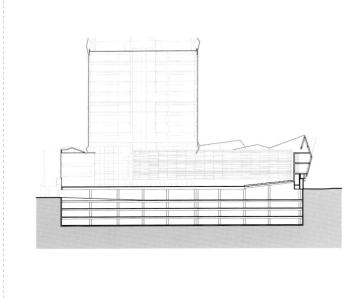

MATERIAL TO GROUND

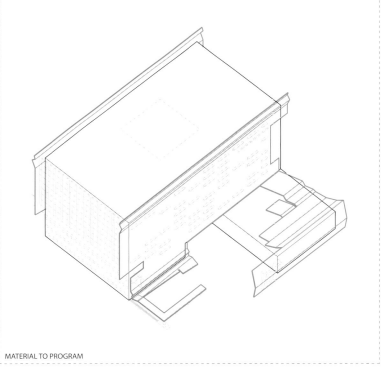

MATERIAL TO PROGRAM

PERFORATED METAL PANEL

CALTRANS DISTRICT 7 HQ
MORPHOSIS
LOS ANGELES, CALIFORNIA

2005

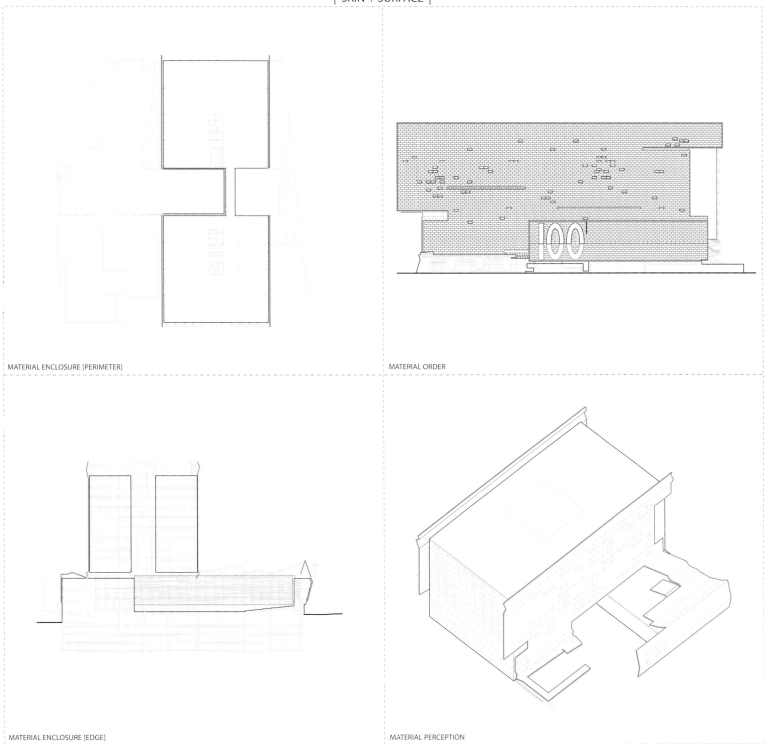

MATERIAL ENCLOSURE [PERIMETER]

MATERIAL ORDER

MATERIAL ENCLOSURE [EDGE]

MATERIAL PERCEPTION

PERFORATED METAL PANEL

CALTRANS DISTRICT 7 HQ
MORPHOSIS
LOS ANGELES, CALIFORNIA

2005

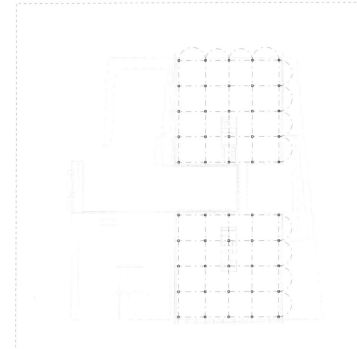

STRUCTURAL MATERIAL [BAY/MODULE]

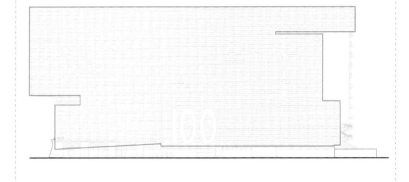

STRUCTURAL MATERIAL LEGIBILITY

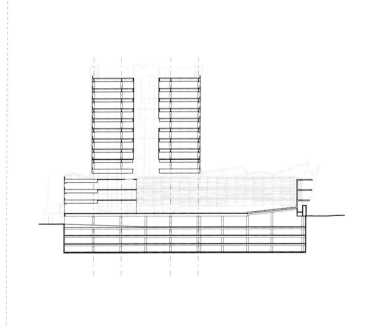

STRUCTURAL MATERIAL SYSTEM

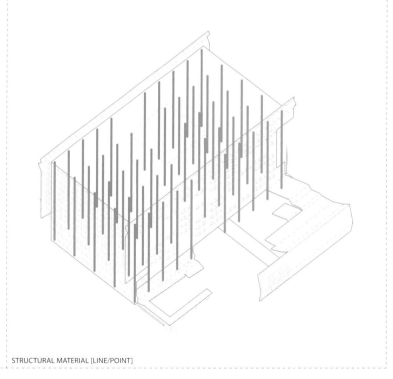

STRUCTURAL MATERIAL [LINE/POINT]

PERFORATED METAL PANEL

CALTRANS DISTRICT 7 HQ
MORPHOSIS
LOS ANGELES, CALIFORNIA

2005

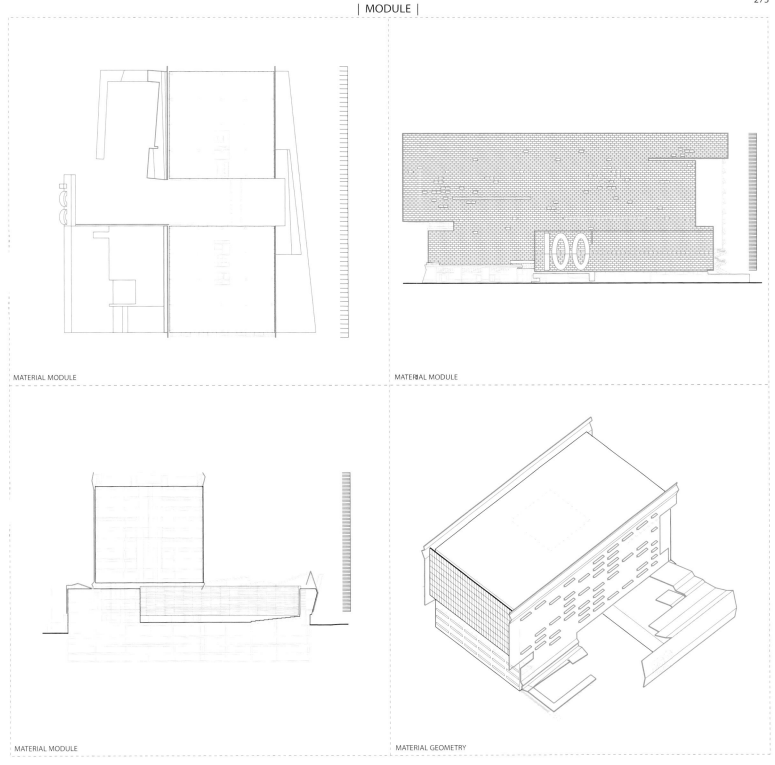

MATERIAL MODULE

MATERIAL MODULE

MATERIAL MODULE

MATERIAL GEOMETRY

PERFORATED METAL PANEL

CALTRANS DISTRICT 7 HQ
MORPHOSIS
LOS ANGELES, CALIFORNIA

2005

274

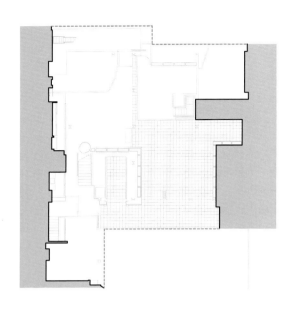

MATERIAL FUNCTION

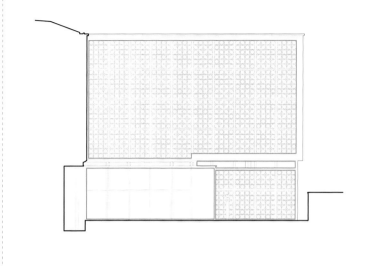

MATERIAL ORDER

MATERIAL GEOMETRY

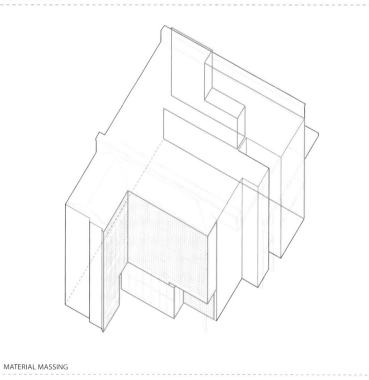

MATERIAL MASSING

GLASS BLOCK

MAISON DE VERRE
PIERRE CHAREAU
PARIS, FRANCE

1932

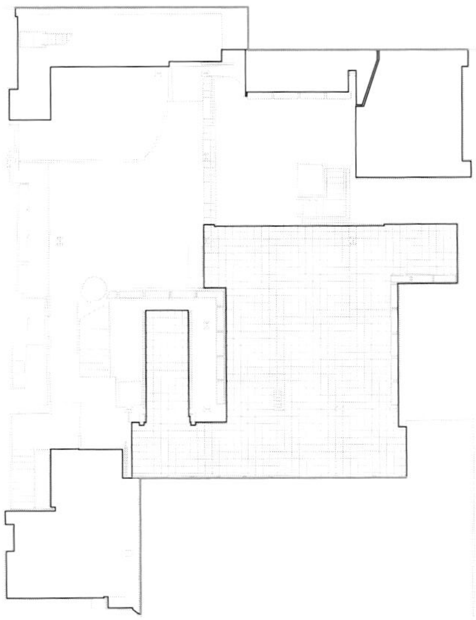

MATERIAL APPLICATION

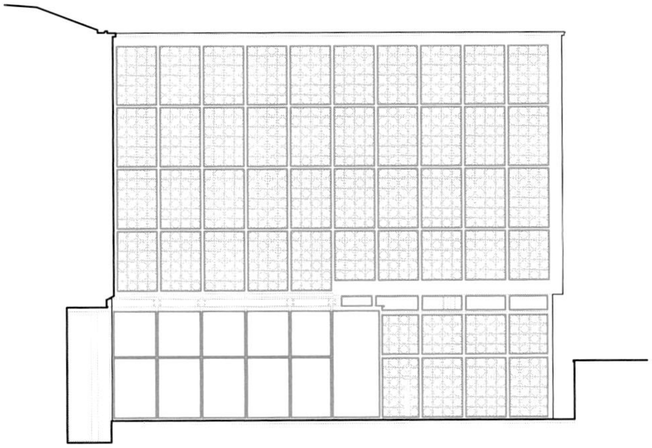

PRIMARY/SECONDARY

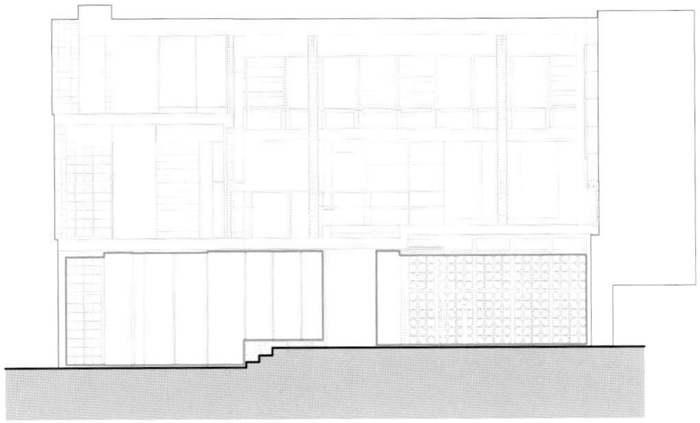

MATERIAL TO GROUND

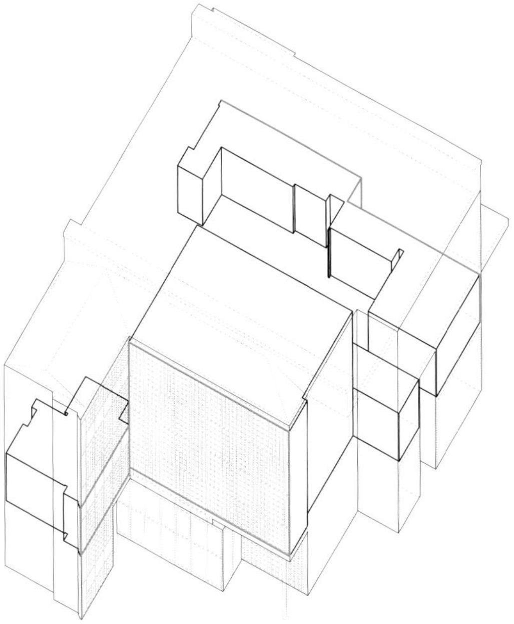

MATERIAL TO PROGRAM

GLASS BLOCK

MAISON DE VERRE
PIERRE CHAREAU
PARIS, FRANCE

1932

MATERIAL ENCLOSURE [PERIMETER]

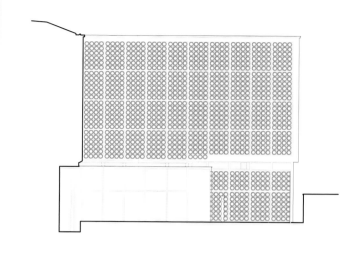

MATERIAL ORDER

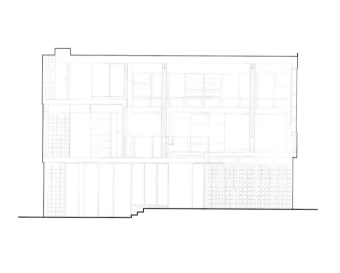

MATERIAL ENCLOSURE [EDGE]

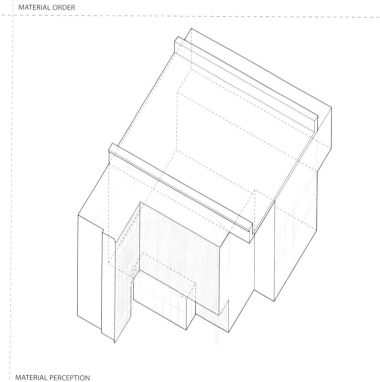

MATERIAL PERCEPTION

GLASS BLOCK

MAISON DE VERRE
PIERRE CHAREAU
PARIS, FRANCE

1932

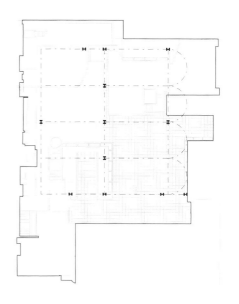

STRUCTURAL MATERIAL [BAY/MODULE]

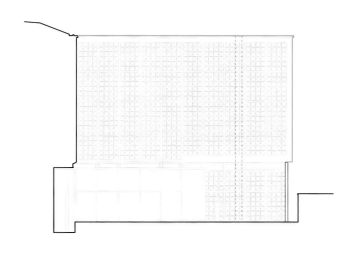

STRUCTURAL MATERIAL LEGIBILITY

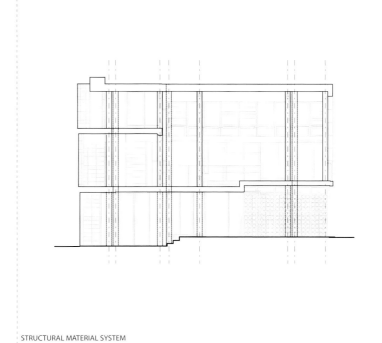

STRUCTURAL MATERIAL SYSTEM

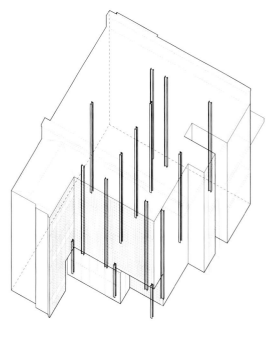

STRUCTURAL MATERIAL [LINE/POINT]

GLASS BLOCK

MAISON DE VERRE
PIERRE CHAREAU
PARIS, FRANCE

1932

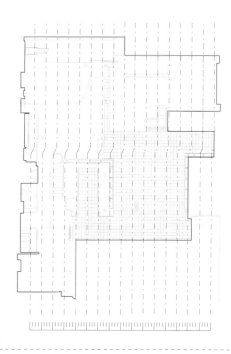

MATERIAL MODULE

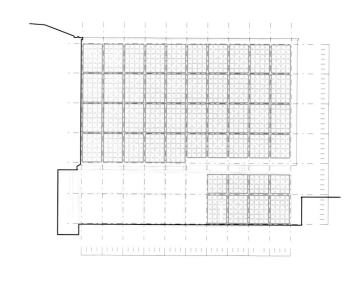

MATERIAL MODULE

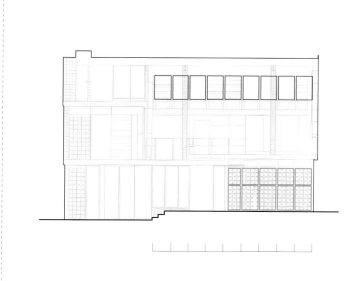

MATERIAL MODULE

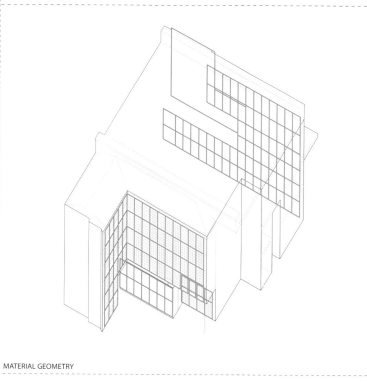

MATERIAL GEOMETRY

GLASS BLOCK

MAISON DE VERRE
PIERRE CHAREAU
PARIS, FRANCE

1932

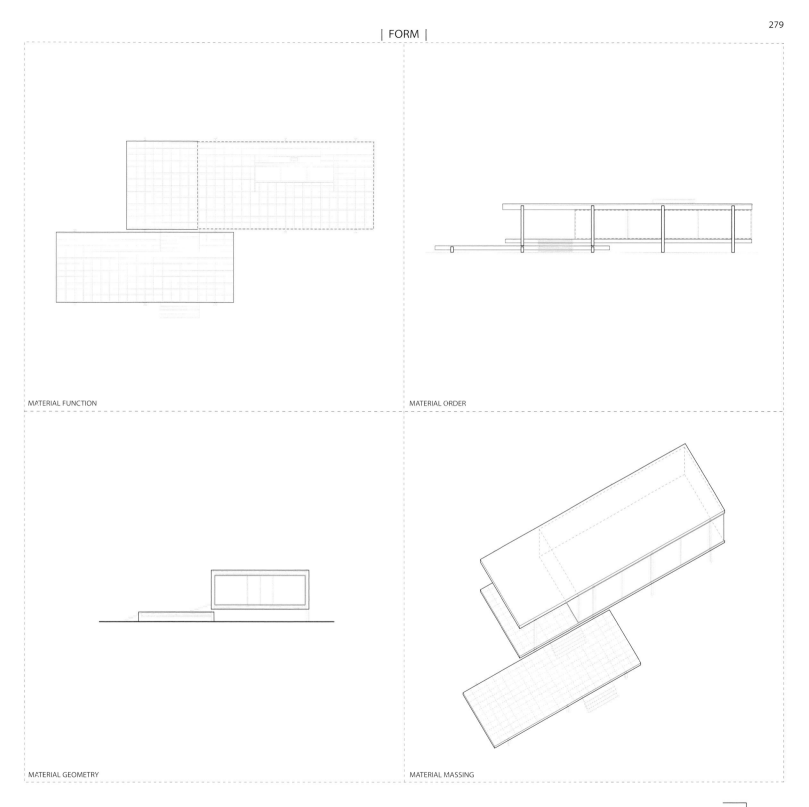

MATERIAL FUNCTION

MATERIAL ORDER

MATERIAL GEOMETRY

MATERIAL MASSING

GLASS

FARNSWORTH HOUSE
MIES VAN DER ROHE
PLANO, ILLINOIS

1950

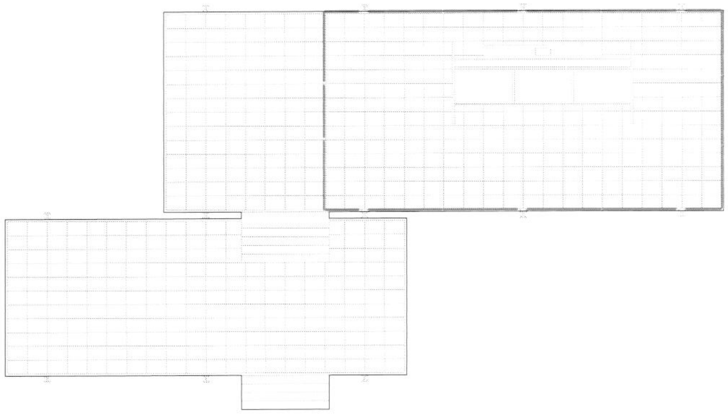

MATERIAL APPLICATION

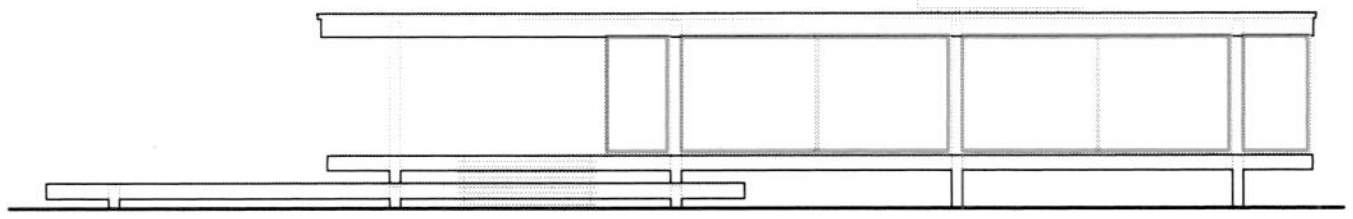

PRIMARY/SECONDARY

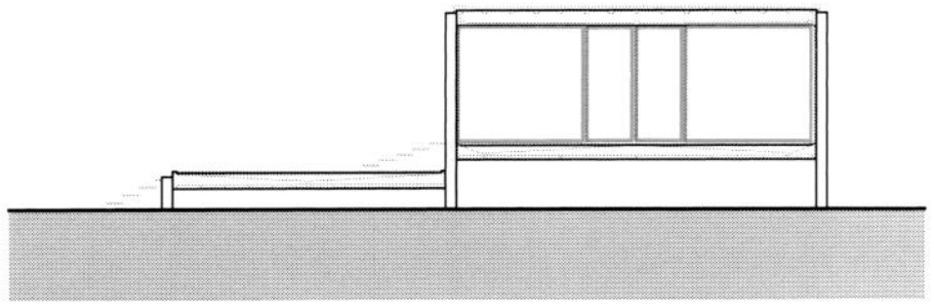

MATERIAL TO GROUND

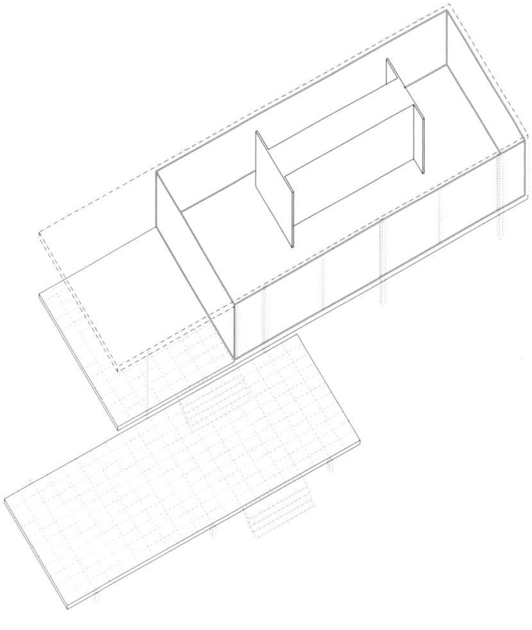

MATERIAL TO PROGRAM

GLASS

FARNSWORTH HOUSE
MIES VAN DER ROHE
PLANO, ILLINOIS

1950

MATERIAL ENCLOSURE [PERIMETER]

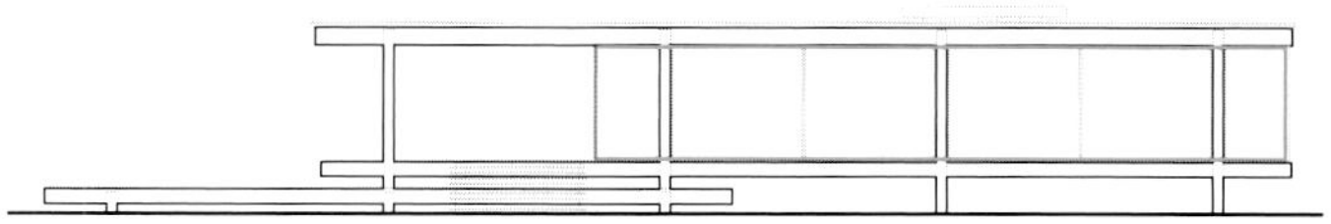

MATERIAL ORDER

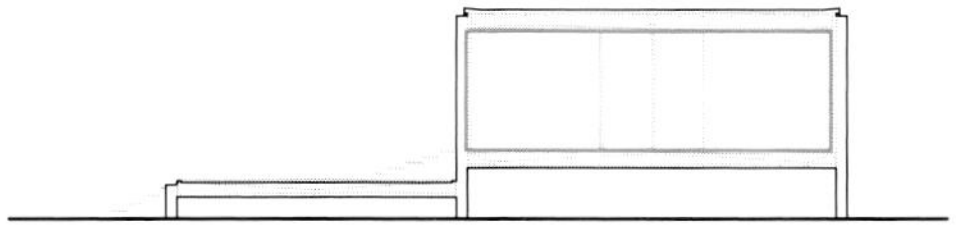

MATERIAL ENCLOSURE [EDGE]

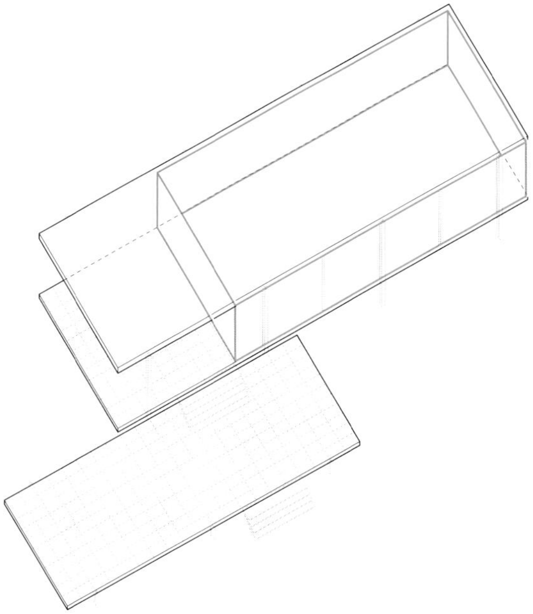

MATERIAL PERCEPTION

GLASS

FARNSWORTH HOUSE
MIES VAN DER ROHE
PLANO, ILLINOIS

1950

| STRUCTURE |

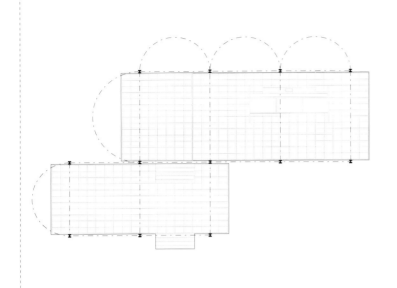

STRUCTURAL MATERIAL [BAY/MODULE]

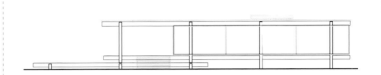

STRUCTURAL MATERIAL LEGIBILITY

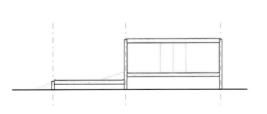

STRUCTURAL MATERIAL SYSTEM

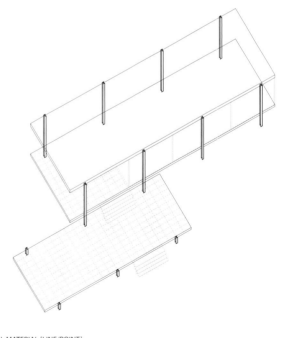

STRUCTURAL MATERIAL [LINE/POINT]

GLASS

FARNSWORTH HOUSE
MIES VAN DER ROHE
PLANO, ILLINOIS

1950

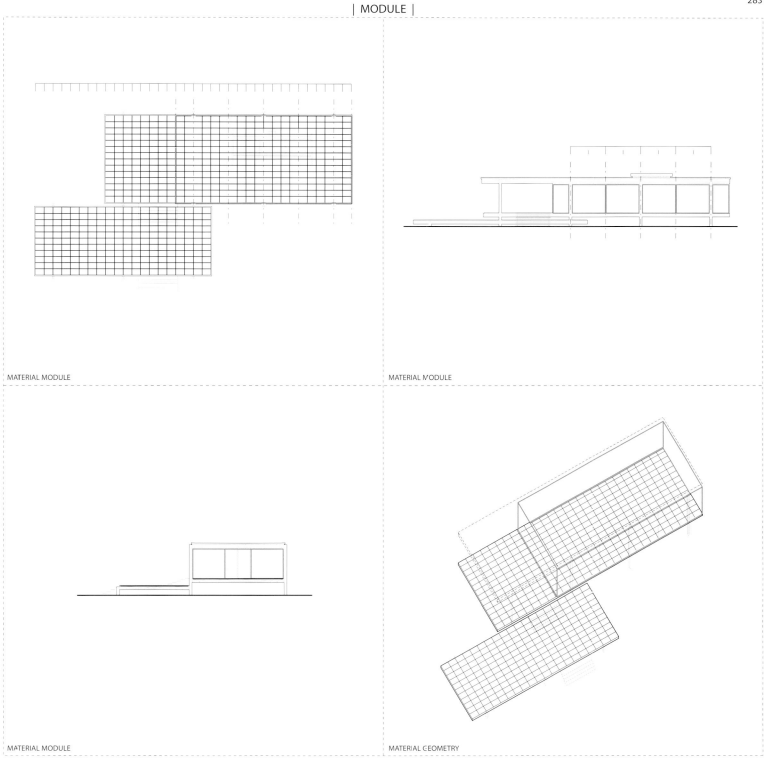

MATERIAL MODULE

MATERIAL MODULE

MATERIAL MODULE

MATERIAL GEOMETRY

GLASS

FARNSWORTH HOUSE
MIES VAN DER ROHE
PLANO, ILLINOIS

1950

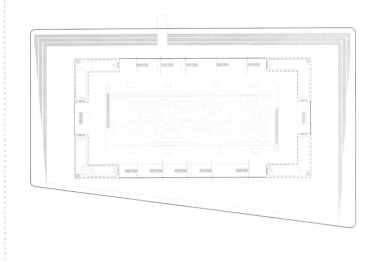

MATERIAL FUNCTION

MATERIAL ORDER

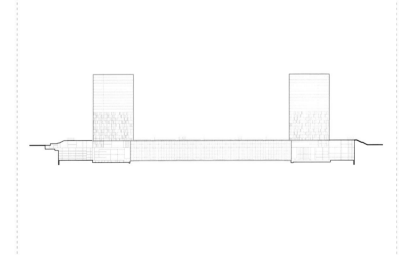

MATERIAL GEOMETRY

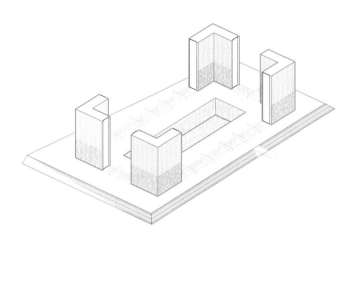

MATERIAL MASSING

GLASS

FRENCH NATIONAL LIBRARY
DOMINIQUE PERRAULT
PARIS, FRANCE

1995

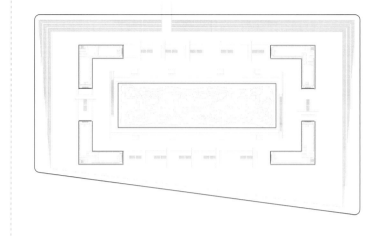

MATERIAL APPLICATION

PRIMARY/SECONDARY

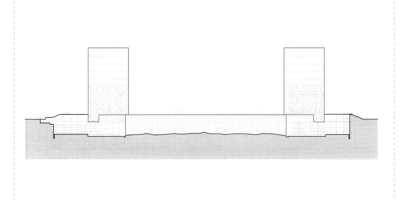

MATERIAL TO GROUND

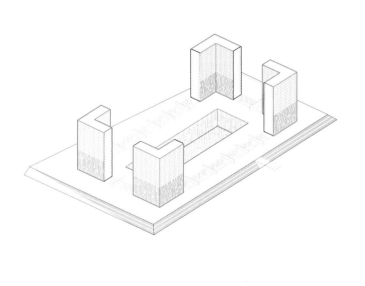

MATERIAL TO PROGRAM

GLASS

FRENCH NATIONAL LIBRARY
DOMINIQUE PERRAULT
PARIS, FRANCE

1995

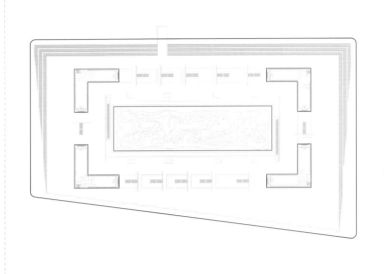

MATERIAL ENCLOSURE [PERIMETER]

MATERIAL ORDER

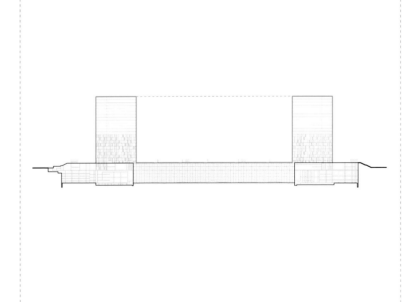

MATERIAL ENCLOSURE [EDGE]

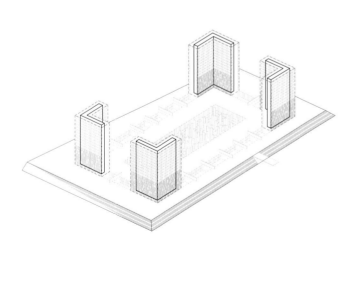

MATERIAL PERCEPTION

GLASS

FRENCH NATIONAL LIBRARY
DOMINIQUE PERRAULT
PARIS, FRANCE

1995

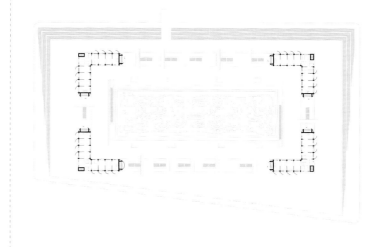

STRUCTURAL MATERIAL [BAY/MODULE]

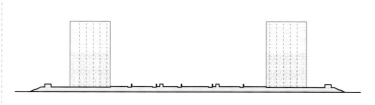

STRUCTURAL MATERIAL LEGIBILITY

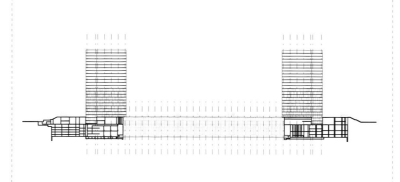

STRUCTURAL MATERIAL SYSTEM

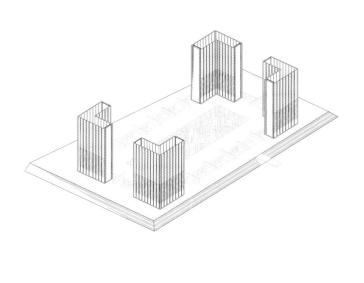

STRUCTURAL MATERIAL [LINE/POINT]

GLASS

FRENCH NATIONAL LIBRARY
DOMINIQUE PERRAULT
PARIS, FRANCE

1995

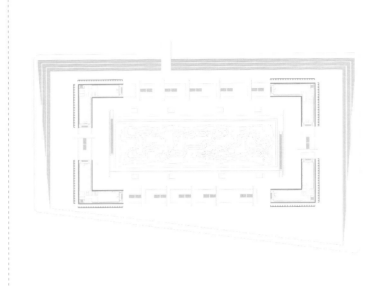

MATERIAL MODULE

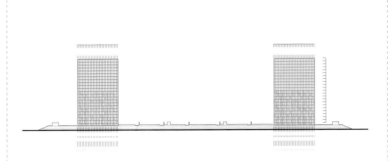

MATERIAL MODULE

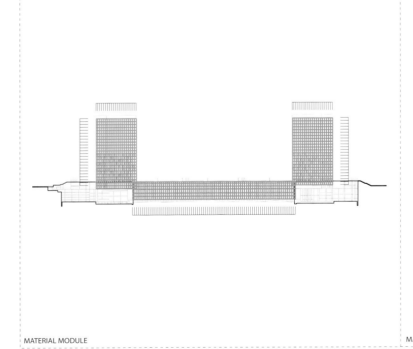

MATERIAL MODULE

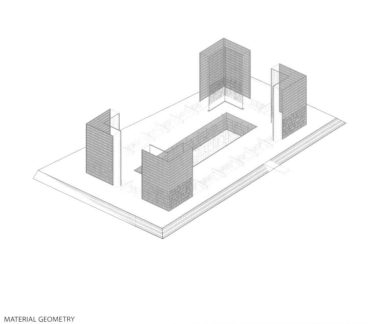

MATERIAL GEOMETRY

GLASS

FRENCH NATIONAL LIBRARY
DOMINIQUE PERRAULT
PARIS, FRANCE

1995

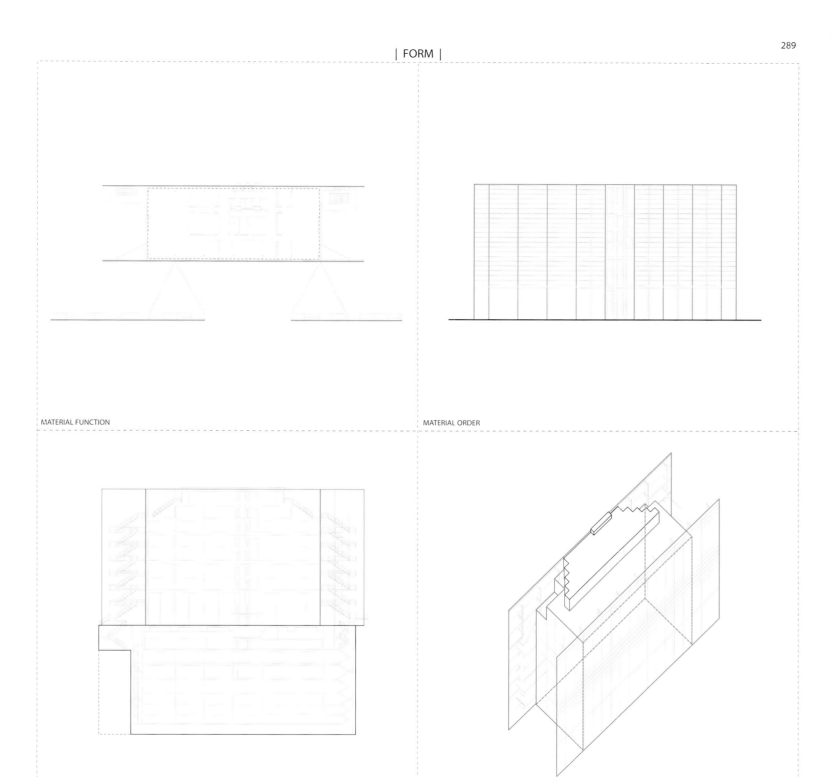

MATERIAL FUNCTION

MATERIAL ORDER

MATERIAL GEOMETRY

MATERIAL MASSING

GLASS

CARTIER FOUNDATION
JEAN NOUVEL
PARIS, FRANCE

1995

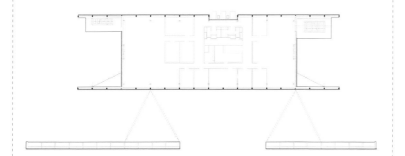

MATERIAL APPLICATION

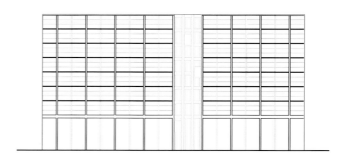

PRIMARY/SECONDARY

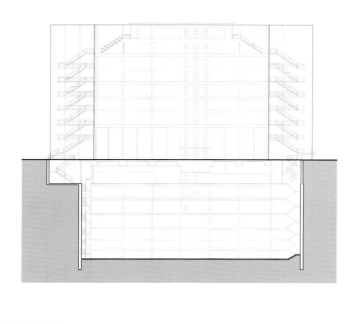

MATERIAL TO GROUND

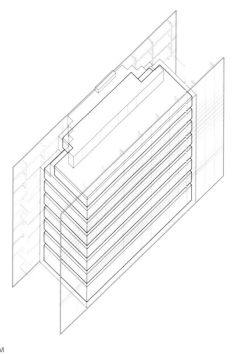

MATERIAL TO PROGRAM

GLASS

CARTIER FOUNDATION
JEAN NOUVEL
PARIS, FRANCE

1995

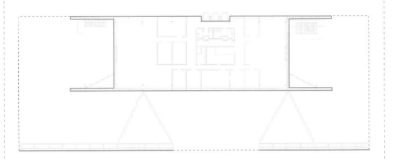

MATERIAL ENCLOSURE [PERIMETER]

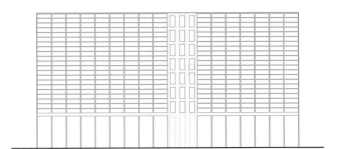

MATERIAL ORDER

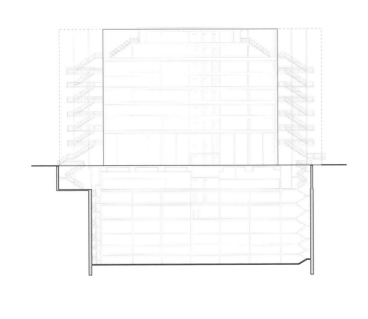

MATERIAL ENCLOSURE [EDGE]

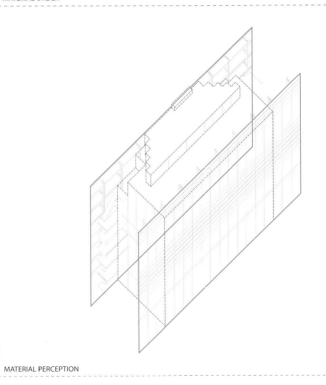

MATERIAL PERCEPTION

GLASS

CARTIER FOUNDATION
JEAN NOUVEL
PARIS, FRANCE

1995

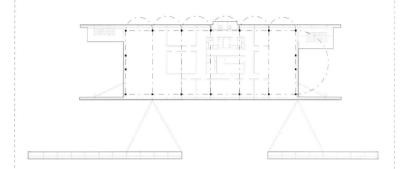

STRUCTURAL MATERIAL [BAY/MODULE]

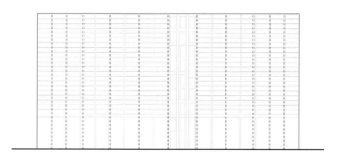

STRUCTURAL MATERIAL LEGIBILITY

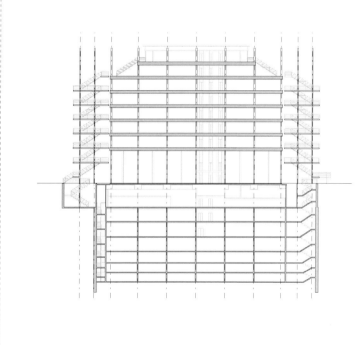

STRUCTURAL MATERIAL SYSTEM

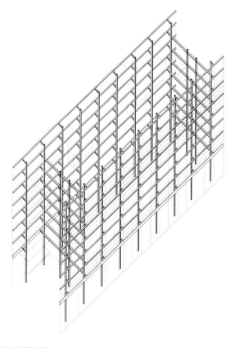

STRUCTURAL MATERIAL [LINE/POINT]

GLASS

CARTIER FOUNDATION
JEAN NOUVEL
PARIS, FRANCE

1995

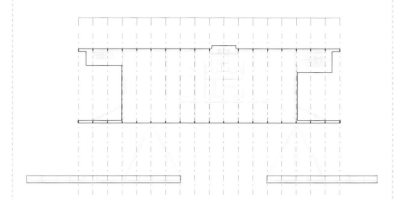

MATERIAL MODULE

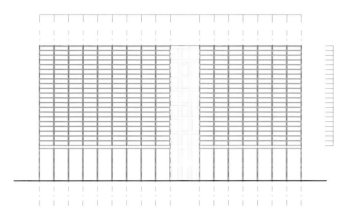

MATERIAL MODULE

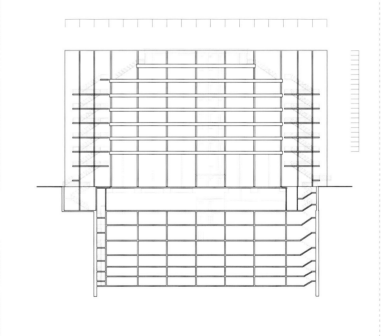

MATERIAL MODULE

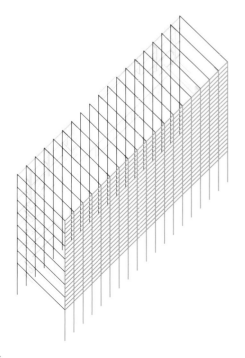

MATERIAL GEOMETRY

GLASS

CARTIER FOUNDATION
JEAN NOUVEL
PARIS, FRANCE

1995

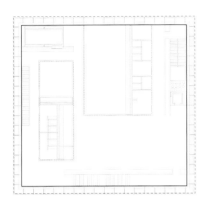

MATERIAL FUNCTION

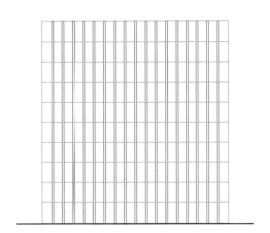

MATERIAL ORDER

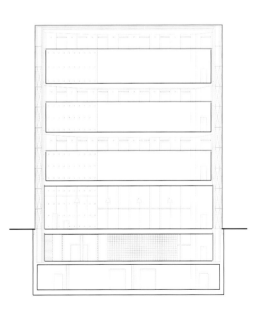

MATERIAL GEOMETRY

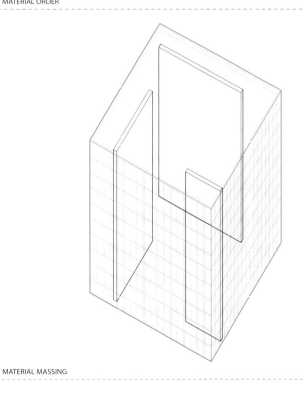

MATERIAL MASSING

ETCHED GLASS SHINGLES

KUNSTHAUS BREGENZ
PETER ZUMTHOR
BREGENZ, AUSTRIA

1997

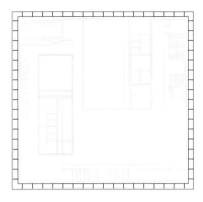

MATERIAL APPLICATION

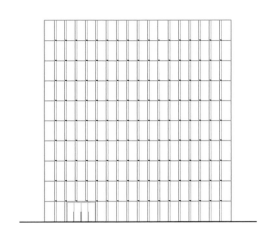

PRIMARY/SECONDARY

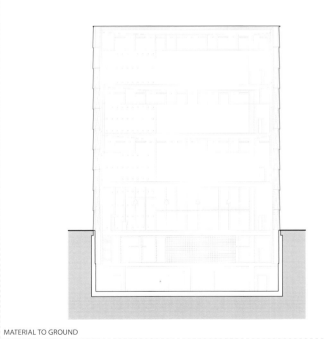

MATERIAL TO GROUND

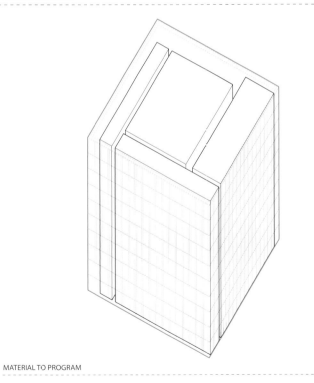

MATERIAL TO PROGRAM

ETCHED GLASS SHINGLES

KUNSTHAUS BREGENZ
PETER ZUMTHOR
BREGENZ, AUSTRIA

1997

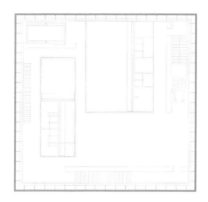

MATERIAL ENCLOSURE [PERIMETER]

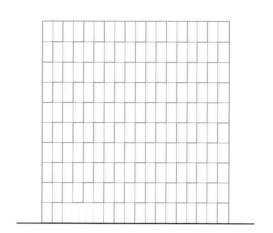

MATERIAL ORDER

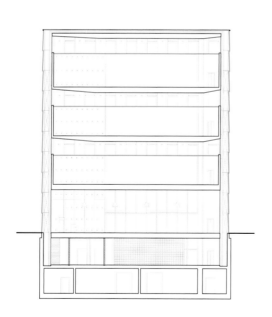

MATERIAL ENCLOSURE [EDGE]

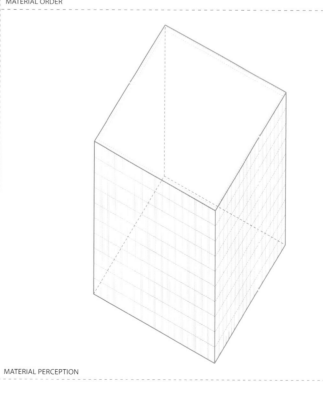

MATERIAL PERCEPTION

ETCHED GLASS SHINGLES

KUNSTHAUS BREGENZ
PETER ZUMTHOR
BREGENZ, AUSTRIA

1997

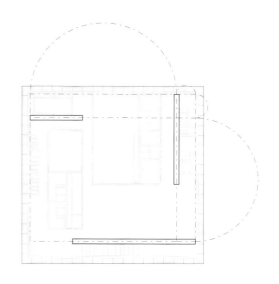

STRUCTURAL MATERIAL [BAY/MODULE]

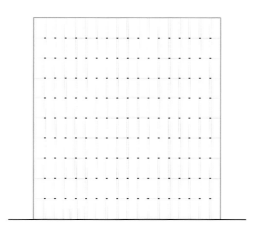

STRUCTURAL MATERIAL LEGIBILITY

STRUCTURAL MATERIAL SYSTEM

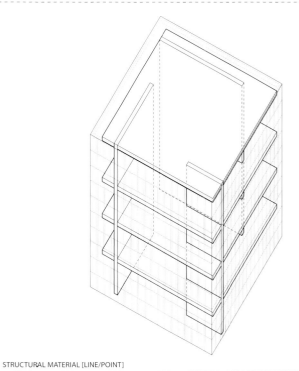

STRUCTURAL MATERIAL [LINE/POINT]

ETCHED GLASS SHINGLES

KUNSTHAUS BREGENZ
PETER ZUMTHOR
BREGENZ, AUSTRIA

1997

| MODULE |

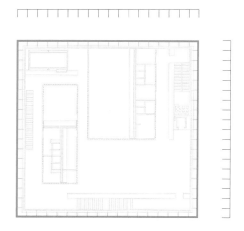

MATERIAL MODULE

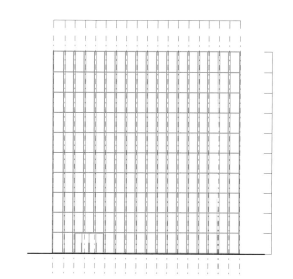

MATERIAL MODULE

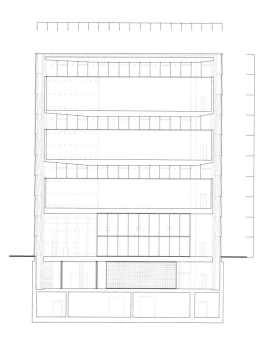

MATERIAL MODULE

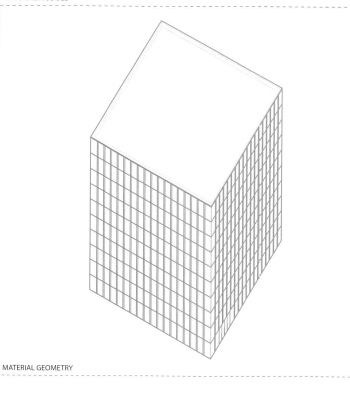

MATERIAL GEOMETRY

ETCHED GLASS SHINGLES

KUNSTHAUS BREGENZ
PETER ZUMTHOR
BREGENZ, AUSTRIA

1997

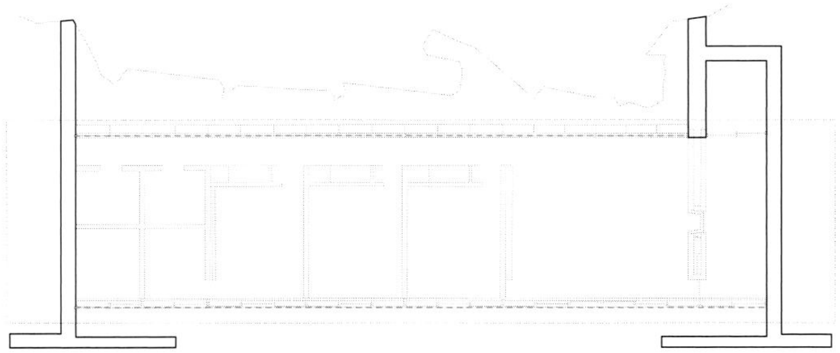

MATERIAL FUNCTION

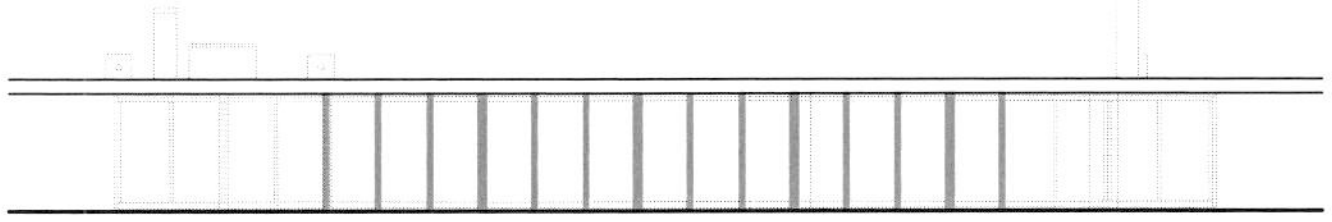

MATERIAL ORDER

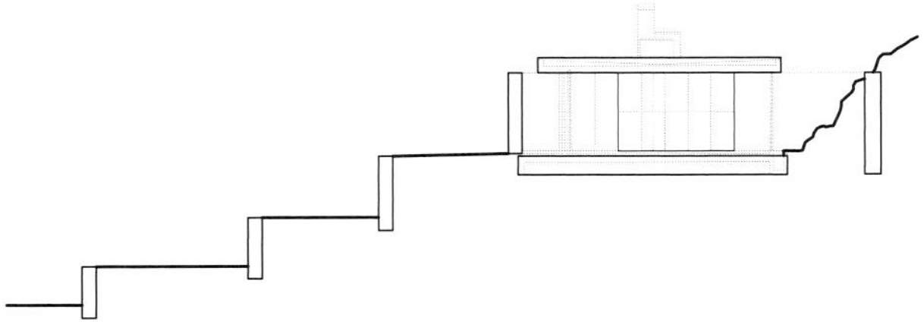

MATERIAL GEOMETRY

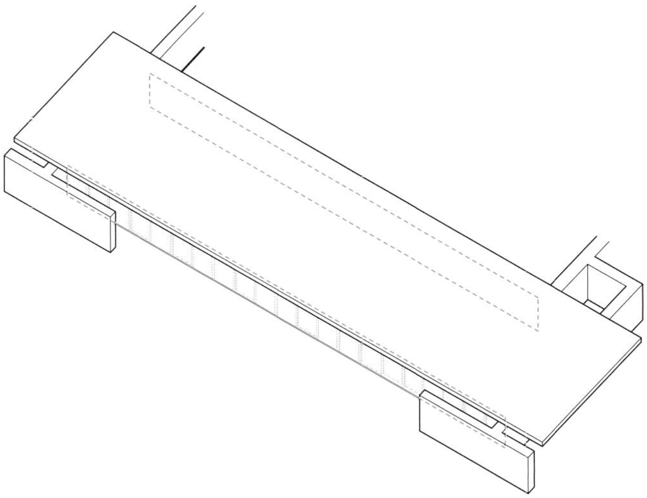

MATERIAL MASSING

GLASS

HOUSE AT MOLEDO
EDUARDO SOUTO DE MOURA
CAMINHA, PORTUGAL

1998

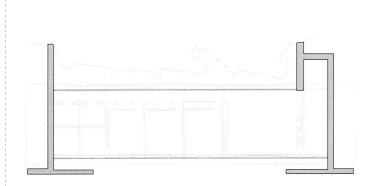

MATERIAL APPLICATION

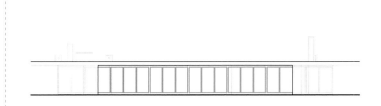

PRIMARY/SECONDARY

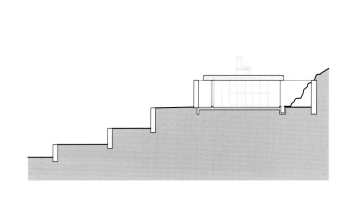

MATERIAL TO GROUND

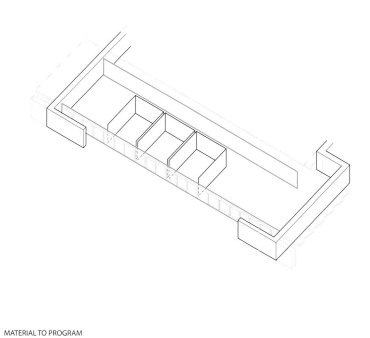

MATERIAL TO PROGRAM

GLASS

HOUSE AT MOLEDO
EDUARDO SOUTO DE MOURA
CAMINHA, PORTUGAL

1998

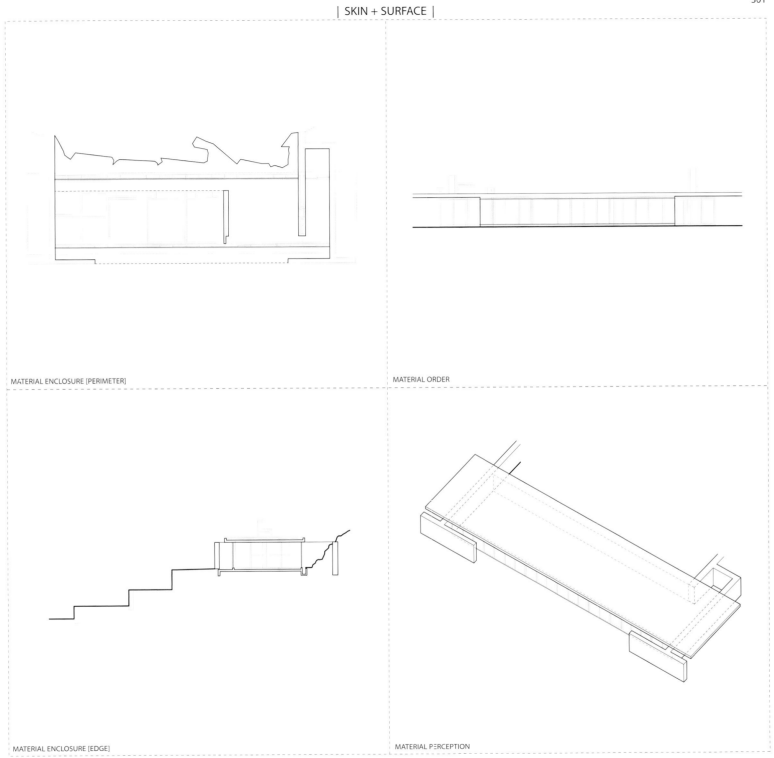

MATERIAL ENCLOSURE [PERIMETER]

MATERIAL ORDER

MATERIAL ENCLOSURE [EDGE]

MATERIAL PERCEPTION

GLASS

HOUSE AT MOLEDO
EDUARDO SOUTO DE MOURA
CAMINHA, PORTUGAL

1998

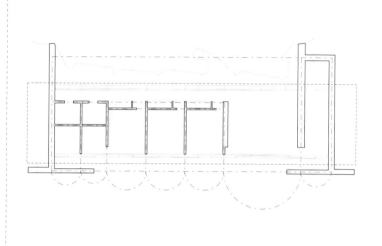

STRUCTURAL MATERIAL [BAY/MODULE]

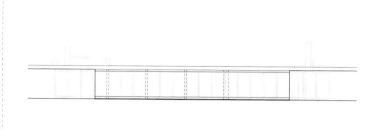

STRUCTURAL MATERIAL LEGIBILITY

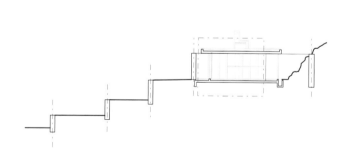

STRUCTURAL MATERIAL SYSTEM

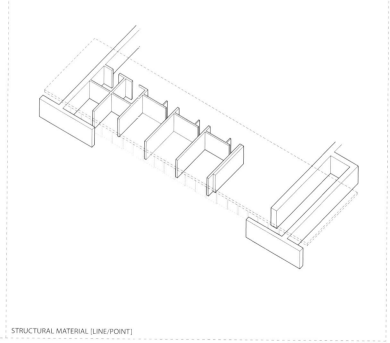

STRUCTURAL MATERIAL [LINE/POINT]

GLASS

HOUSE AT MOLEDO
EDUARDO SOUTO DE MOURA
CAMINHA, PORTUGAL

1998

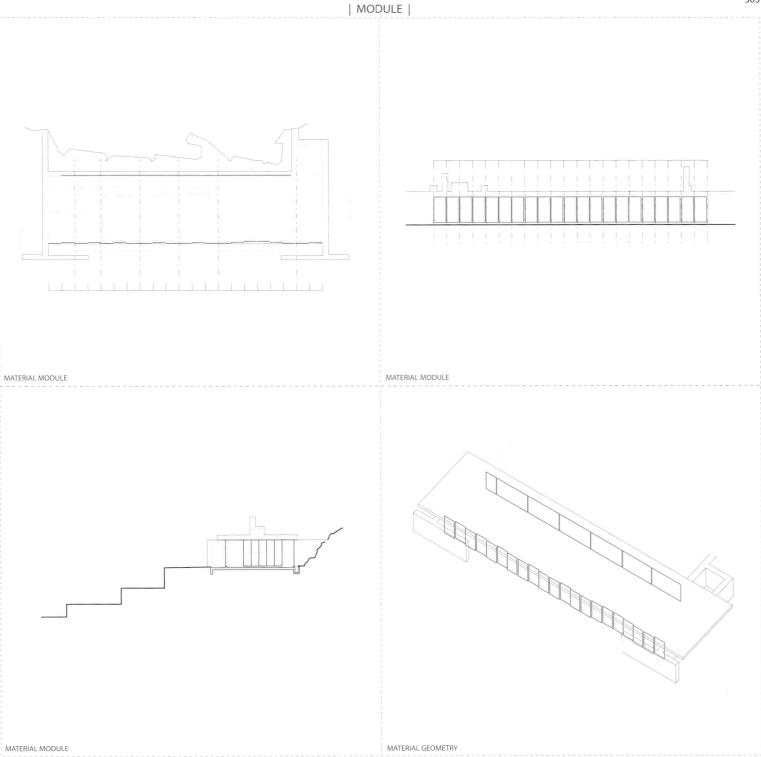

MATERIAL MODULE

MATERIAL MODULE

MATERIAL MODULE

MATERIAL GEOMETRY

GLASS

HOUSE AT MOLEDO
EDUARDO SOUTO DE MOURA
CAMINHA, PORTUGAL

1998

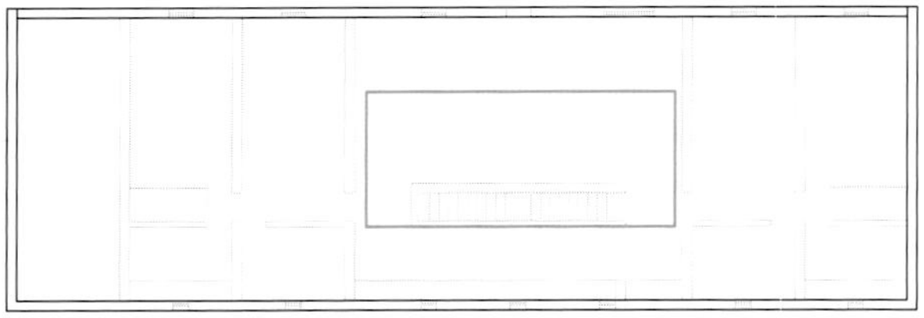

MATERIAL FUNCTION

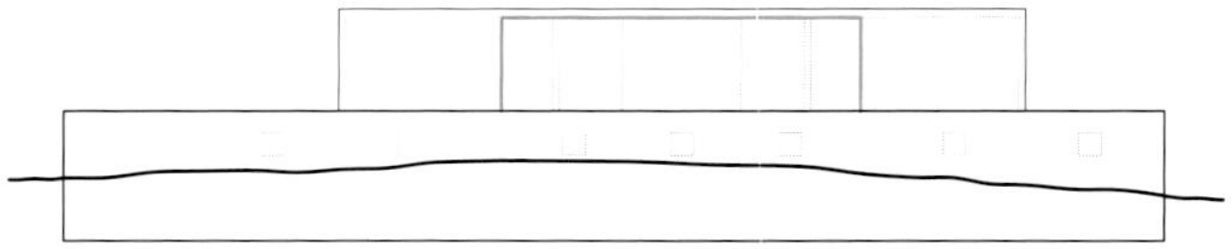

MATERIAL ORDER

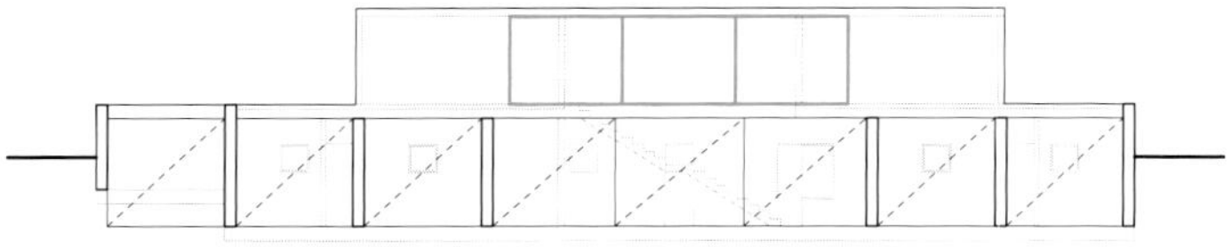

MATERIAL GEOMETRY

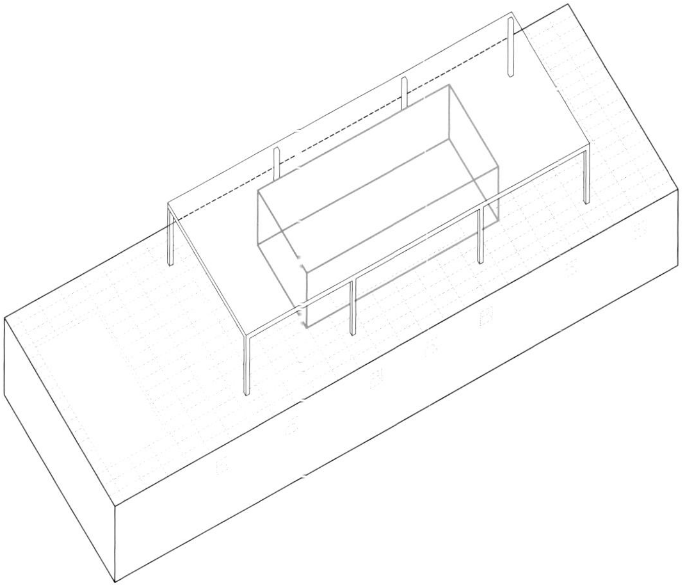

MATERIAL MASSING

GLASS

DE BLAS HOUSE
ALBERTO CAMPO BAEZA
MADRID, SPAIN

2001

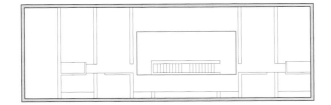

MATERIAL APPLICATION

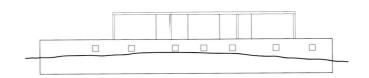

PRIMARY/SECONDARY

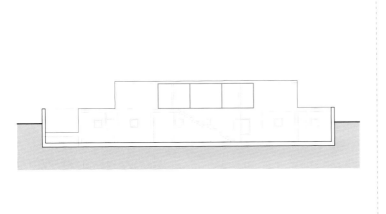

MATERIAL TO GROUND

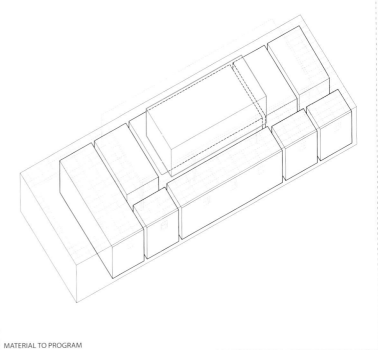

MATERIAL TO PROGRAM

GLASS

DE BLAS HOUSE
ALBERTO CAMPO BAEZA
MADRID, SPAIN

2001

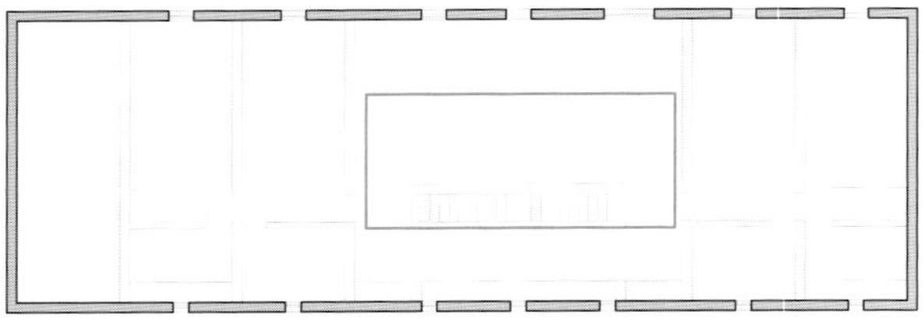

MATERIAL ENCLOSURE [PERIMETER]

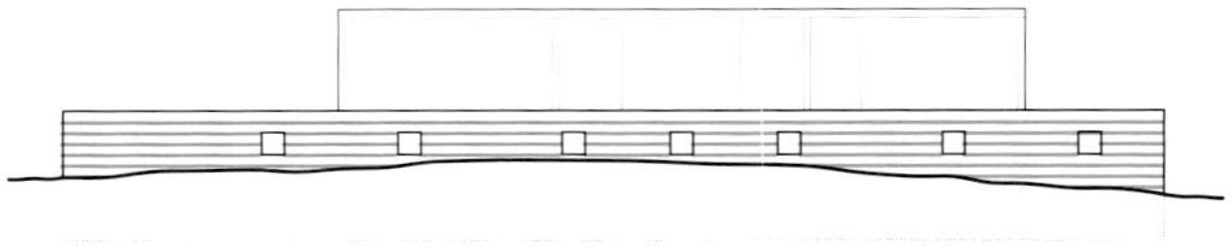

MATERIAL ORDER

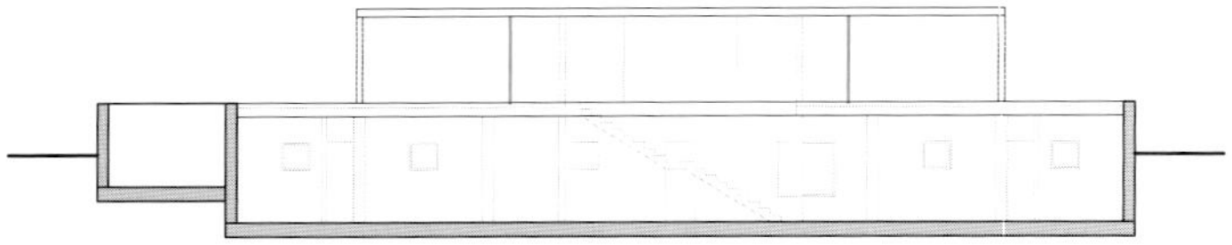

MATERIAL ENCLOSURE [EDGE]

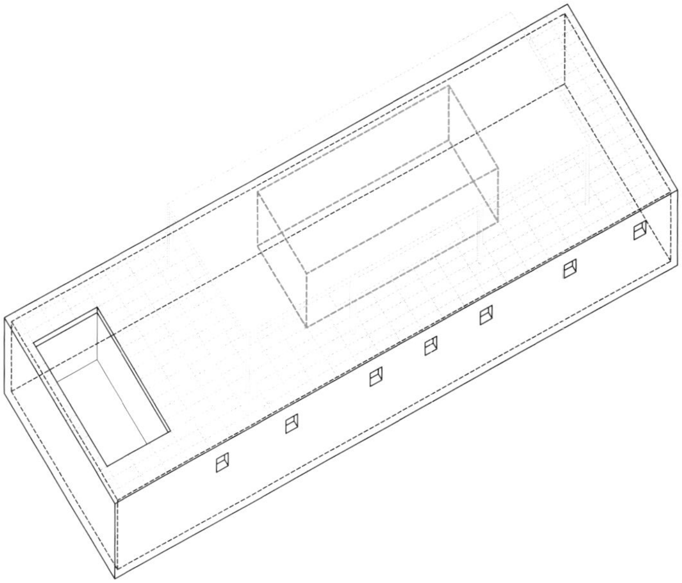

MATERIAL PERCEPTION

GLASS

DE BLAS HOUSE
ALBERTO CAMPO BAEZA
MADRID, SPAIN

2001

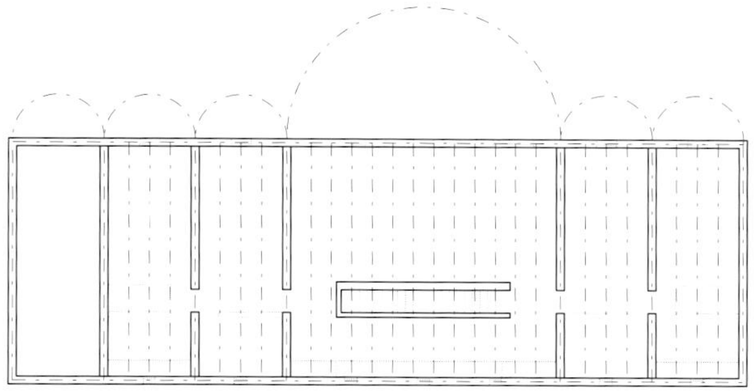

STRUCTURAL MATERIAL [BAY/MODULE]

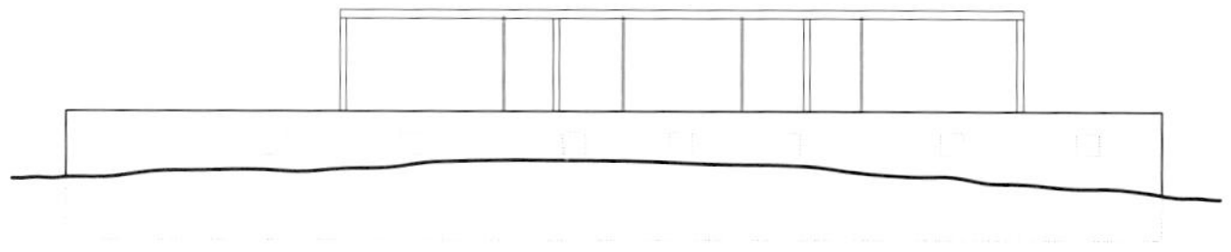

STRUCTURAL MATERIAL LEGIBILITY

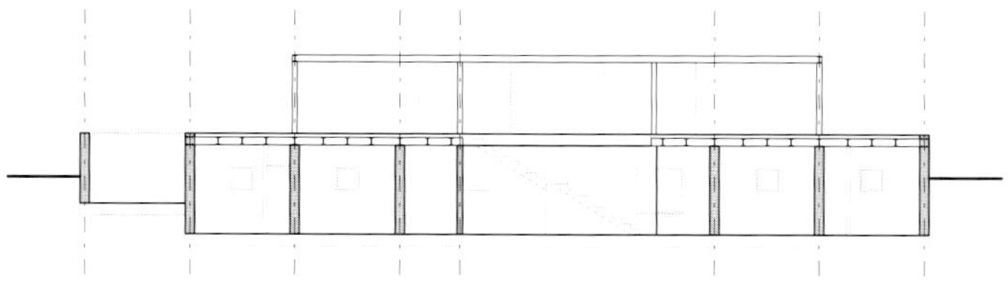

STRUCTURAL MATERIAL SYSTEM

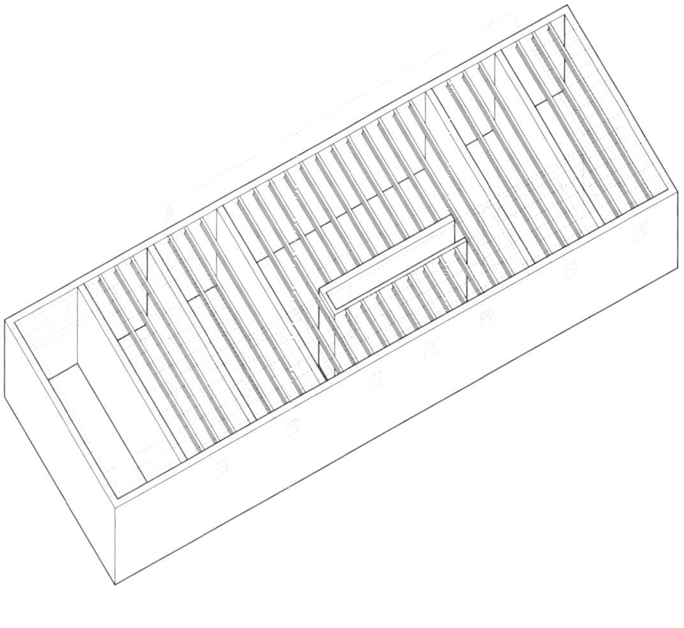

STRUCTURAL MATERIAL [LINE/POINT]

GLASS

DE BLAS HOUSE
ALBERTO CAMPO BAEZA
MADRID, SPAIN

2001

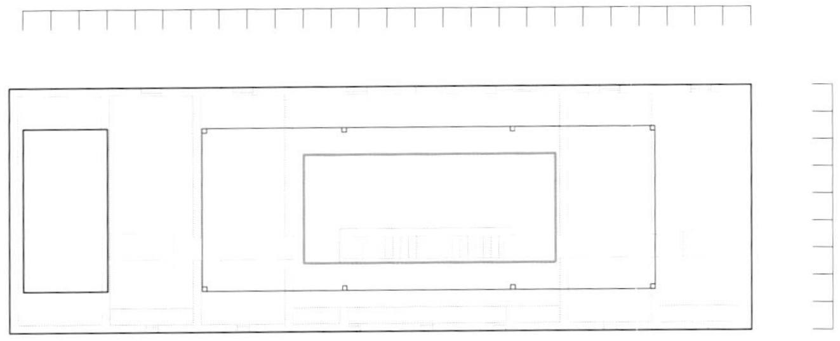

MATERIAL MODULE

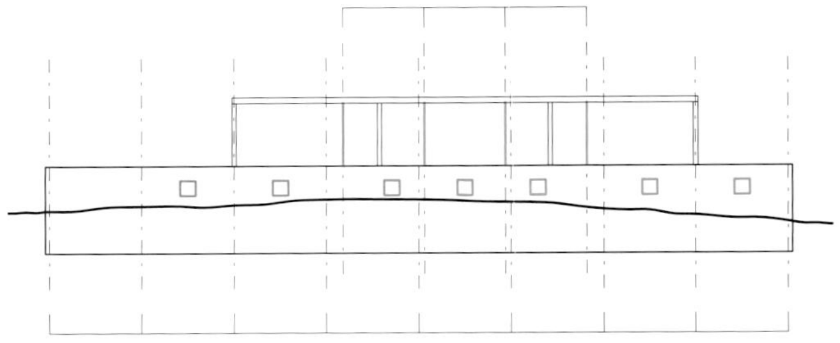

MATERIAL MODULE

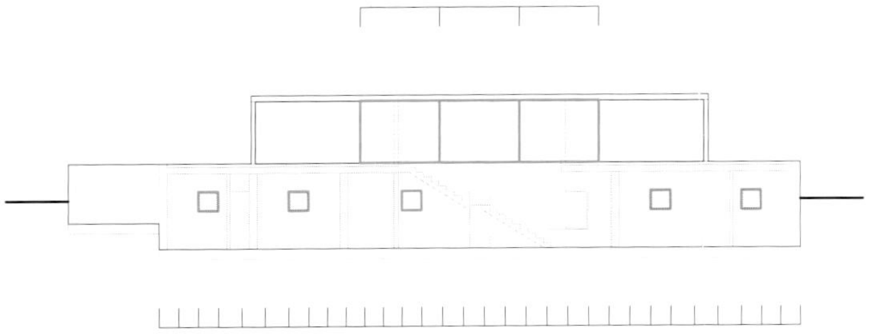

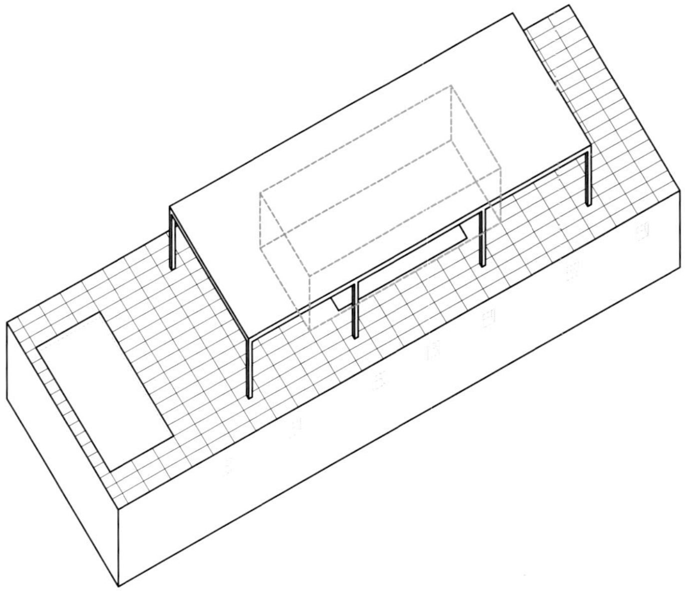

MATERIAL MODULE

MATERIAL GEOMETRY

GLASS

DE BLAS HOUSE
ALBERTO CAMPO BAEZA
MADRID, SPAIN

2001

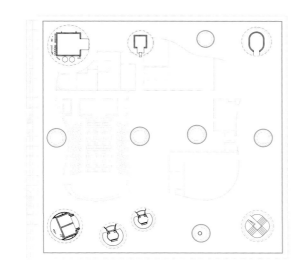

MATERIAL FUNCTION

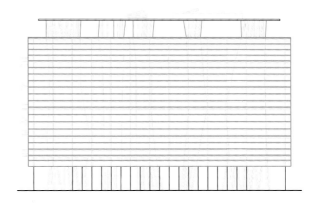

MATERIAL ORDER

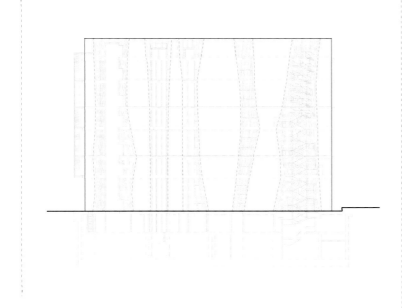

MATERIAL GEOMETRY

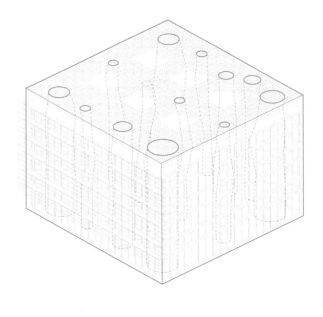

MATERIAL MASSING

GLASS

SENDAI MEDIATHEQUE
TOYO ITO
SENDAI-SHI, JAPAN

2001

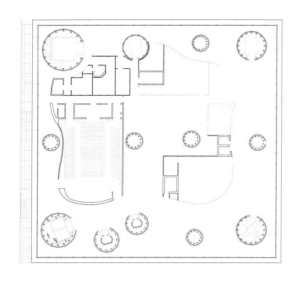

MATERIAL APPLICATION

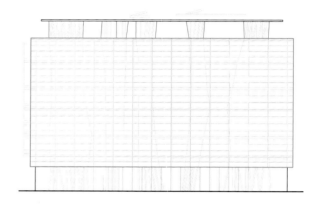

PRIMARY/SECONDARY

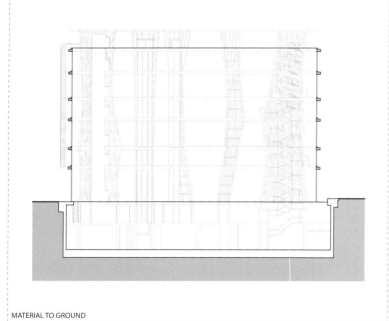

MATERIAL TO GROUND

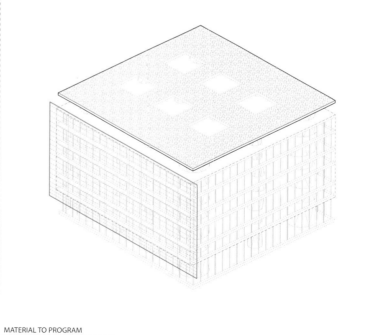

MATERIAL TO PROGRAM

GLASS

SENDAI MEDIATHEQUE
TOYO ITO
SENDAI-SHI, JAPAN

2001

MATERIAL ENCLOSURE [PERIMETER]

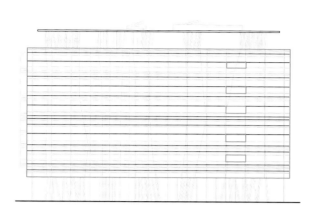

MATERIAL ORDER

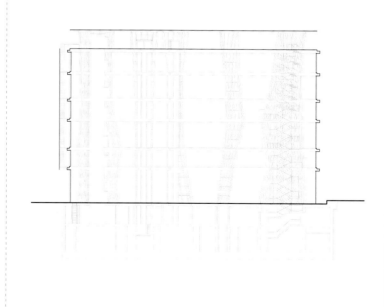

MATERIAL ENCLOSURE [EDGE]

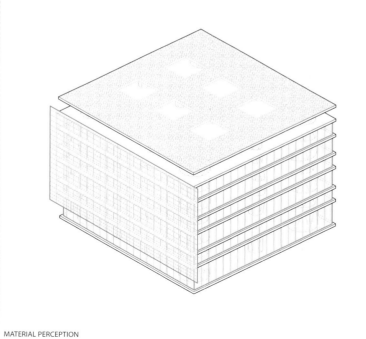

MATERIAL PERCEPTION

GLASS

SENDAI MEDIATHEQUE
TOYO ITO
SENDAI-SHI, JAPAN

2001

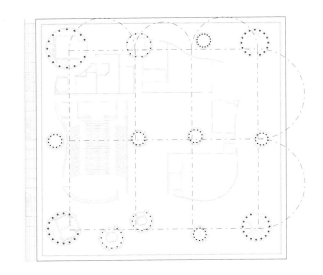

STRUCTURAL MATERIAL [BAY/MODULE]

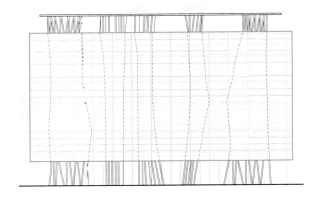

STRUCTURAL MATERIAL LEGIBILITY

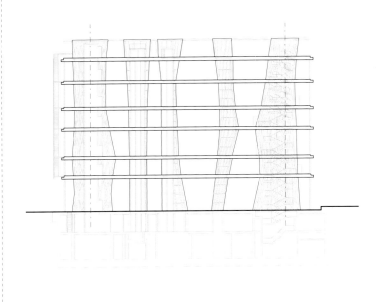

STRUCTURAL MATERIAL SYSTEM

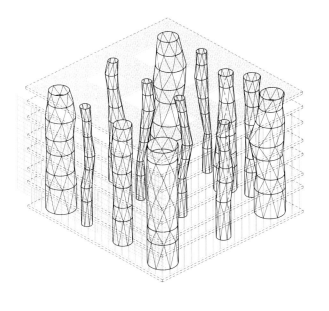

STRUCTURAL MATERIAL [LINE/POINT]

GLASS

SENDAI MEDIATHEQUE
TOYO ITO
SENDAI-SHI, JAPAN

2001

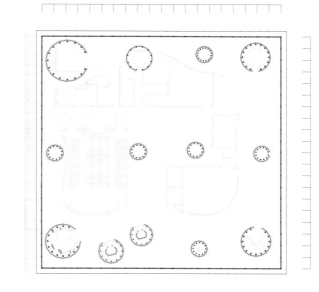

MATERIAL MODULE

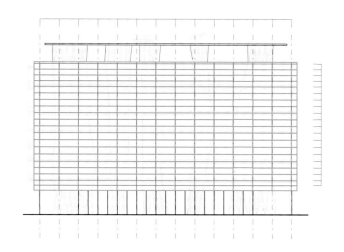

MATERIAL MODULE

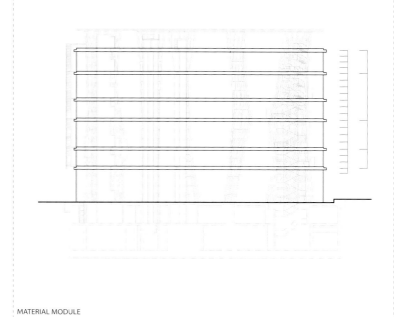

MATERIAL MODULE

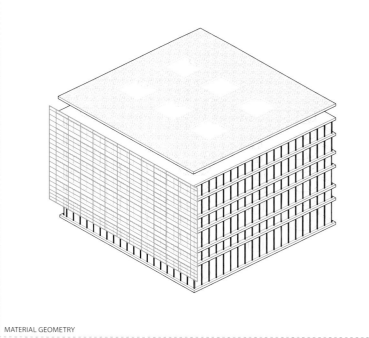

MATERIAL GEOMETRY

GLASS

SENDAI MEDIATHEQUE
TOYO ITO
SENDAI-SHI, JAPAN

2001

MATERIAL FUNCTION

MATERIAL ORDER

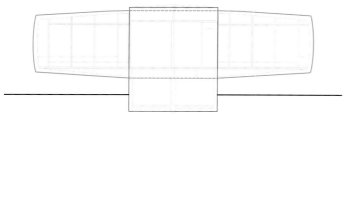

MATERIAL GEOMETRY

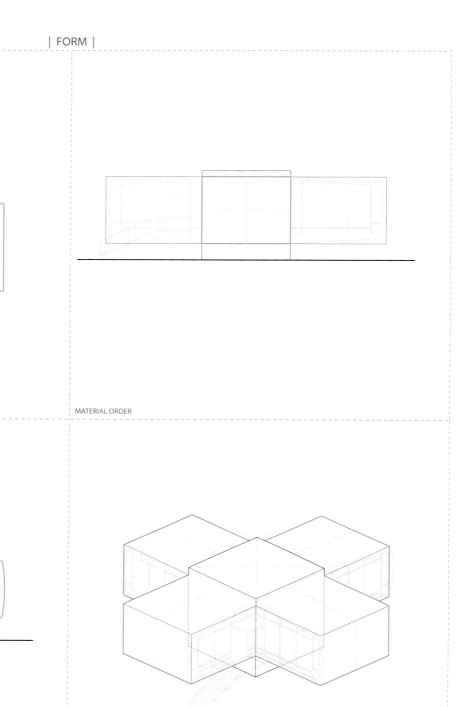

MATERIAL MASSING

PLASTIC

MONSANTO HOUSE OF THE FUTURE
GOODY AND HAMILTON
ANAHEIM, CALIFORNIA

1957

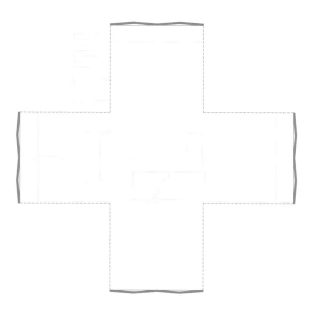

MATERIAL APPLICATION

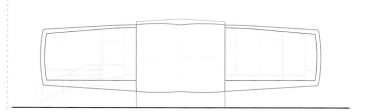

PRIMARY/SECONDARY

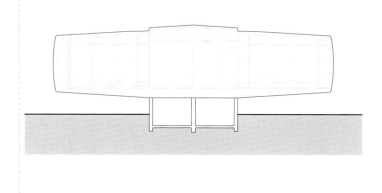

MATERIAL TO GROUND

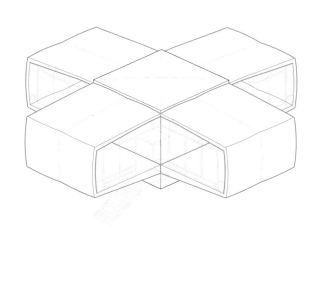

MATERIAL TO PROGRAM

PLASTIC

MONSANTO HOUSE OF THE FUTURE
GOODY AND HAMILTON
ANAHEIM, CALIFORNIA

1957

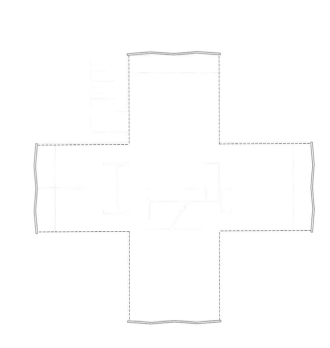

MATERIAL ENCLOSURE [PERIMETER]

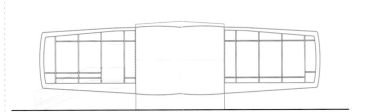

MATERIAL ORDER

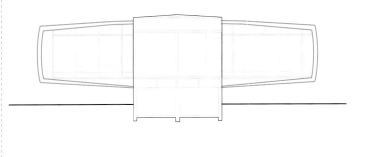

MATERIAL ENCLOSURE [EDGE]

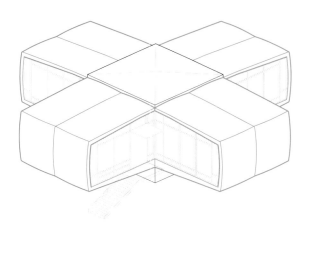

MATERIAL PERCEPTION

PLASTIC

MONSANTO HOUSE OF THE FUTURE
GOODY AND HAMILTON
ANAHEIM, CALIFORNIA

1957

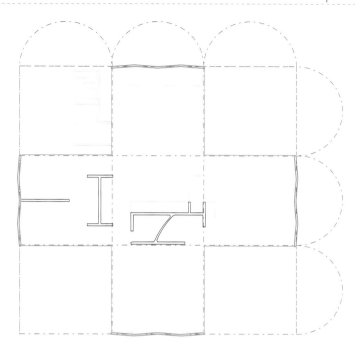

STRUCTURAL MATERIAL [BAY/MODULE]

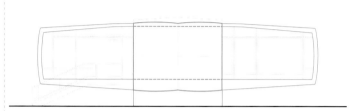

STRUCTURAL MATERIAL LEGIBILITY

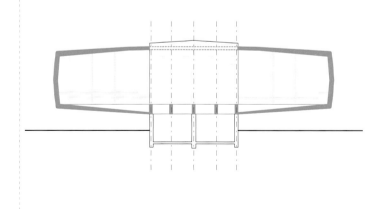

STRUCTURAL MATERIAL SYSTEM

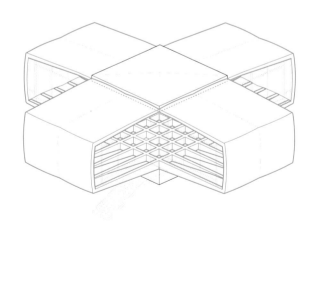

STRUCTURAL MATERIAL [LINE/POINT]

PLASTIC

MONSANTO HOUSE OF THE FUTURE
GOODY AND HAMILTON
ANAHEIM, CALIFORNIA

1957

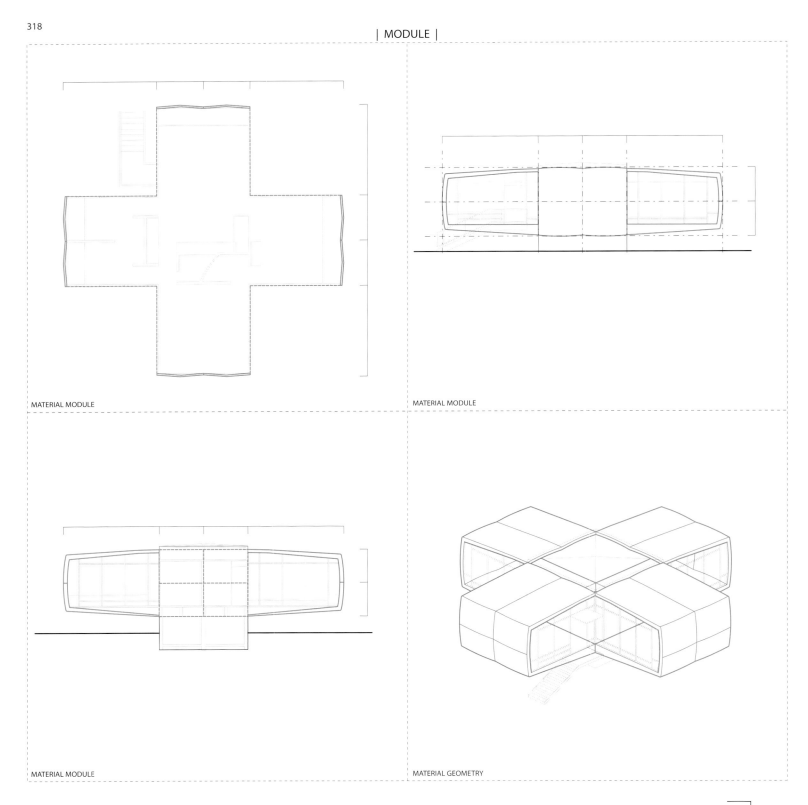

MATERIAL MODULE

MATERIAL MODULE

MATERIAL MODULE

MATERIAL GEOMETRY

PLASTIC

MONSANTO HOUSE OF THE FUTURE
GOODY AND HAMILTON
ANAHEIM, CALIFORNIA

1957

| FORM |

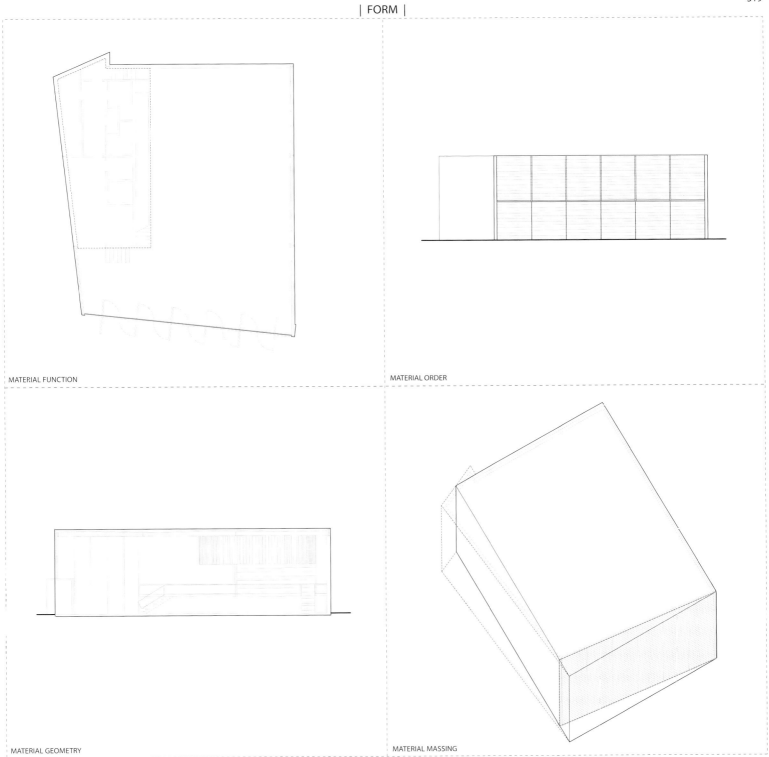

MATERIAL FUNCTION

MATERIAL ORDER

MATERIAL GEOMETRY

MATERIAL MASSING

CORRUGATED PLASTIC POLYCARBONATE

COLMENAREJO MUNICIPAL HALL
ABALOS & HERREROS
COLMENAREJO, SPAIN

1999

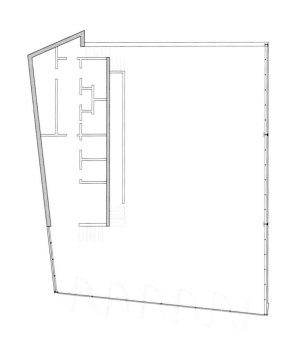

MATERIAL APPLICATION

PRIMARY/SECONDARY

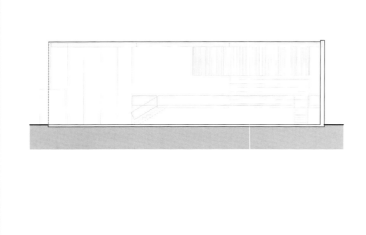

MATERIAL TO GROUND

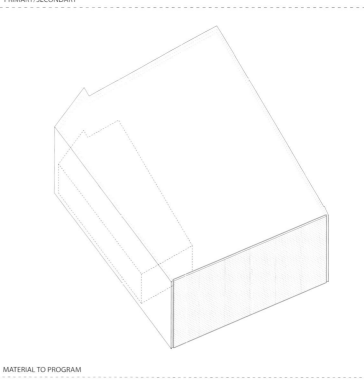

MATERIAL TO PROGRAM

CORRUGATED PLASTIC POLYCARBONATE

COLMENAREJO MUNICIPAL HALL
ABALOS & HERREROS
COLMENAREJO, SPAIN

1999

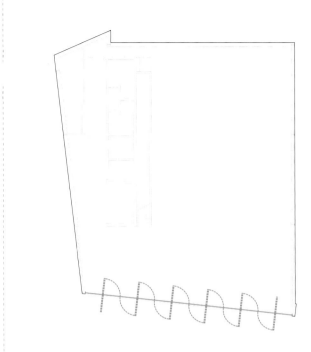

MATERIAL ENCLOSURE [PERIMETER]

MATERIAL ORDER

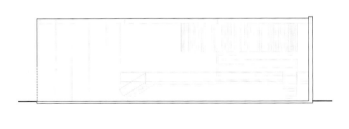

MATERIAL ENCLOSURE [EDGE]

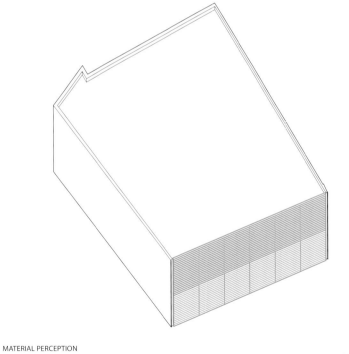

MATERIAL PERCEPTION

CORRUGATED PLASTIC POLYCARBONATE

COLMENAREJO MUNICIPAL HALL
ABALOS & HERREROS
COLMENAREJO, SPAIN

1999

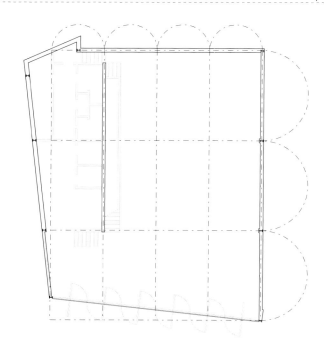

STRUCTURAL MATERIAL [BAY/MODULE]

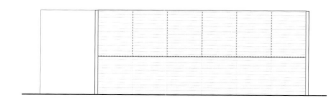

STRUCTURAL MATERIAL LEGIBILITY

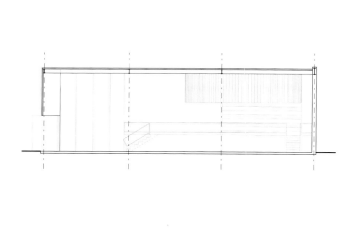

STRUCTURAL MATERIAL SYSTEM

STRUCTURAL MATERIAL [LINE/POINT]

CORRUGATED PLASTIC POLYCARBONATE

COLMENAREJO MUNICIPAL HALL
ABALOS & HERREROS
COLMENAREJO, SPAIN

1999

| MODULE |

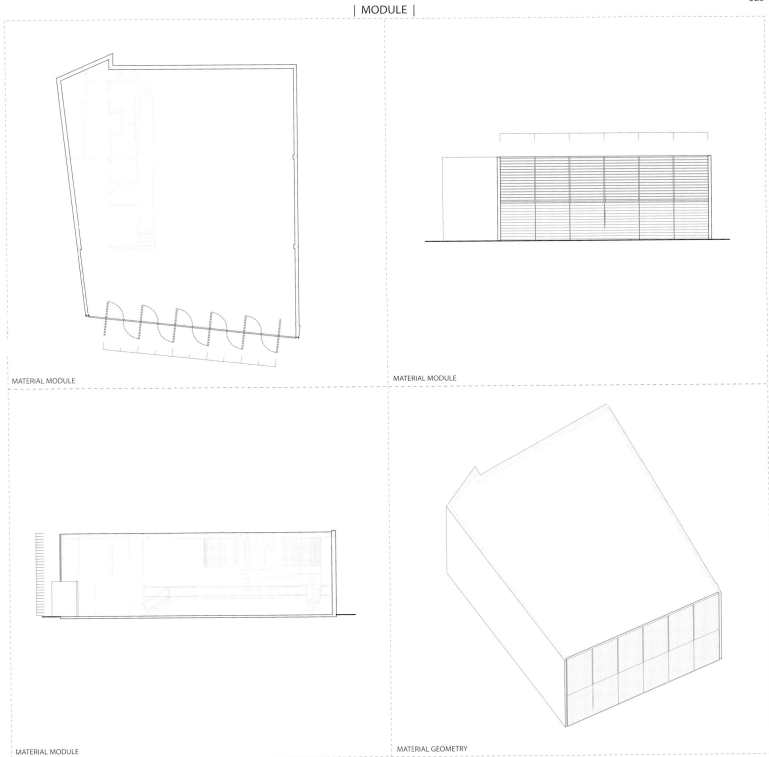

MATERIAL MODULE

MATERIAL MODULE

MATERIAL MODULE

MATERIAL GEOMETRY

CORRUGATED PLASTIC POLYCARBONATE

COLMENAREJO MUNICIPAL HALL
ABALOS & HERREROS
COLMENAREJO, SPAIN

1999

MATERIAL FUNCTION

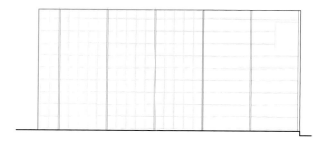

MATERIAL ORDER

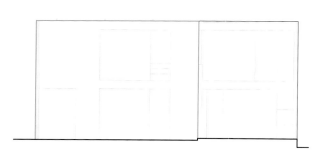

MATERIAL GEOMETRY

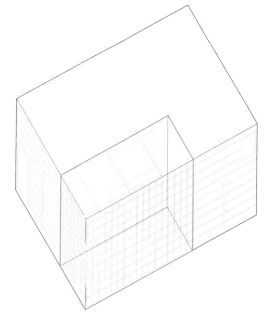

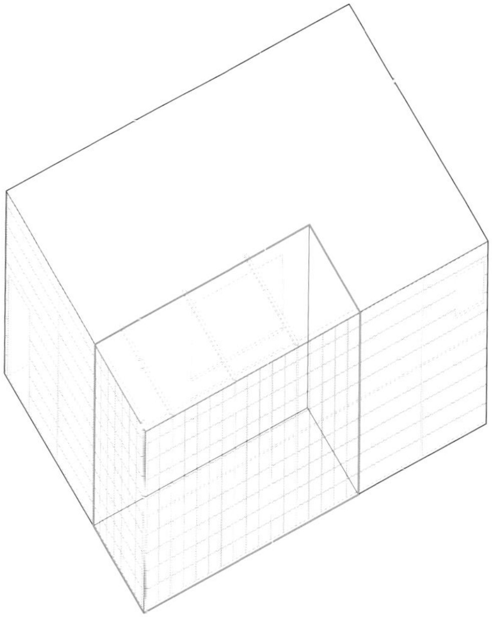

MATERIAL MASSING

CORRUGATED PLASTIC POLYCARBONATE

HOUSE IN IMAZATO
KATSUYASU KISHIGAMI
IMAZATO, JAPAN

1999

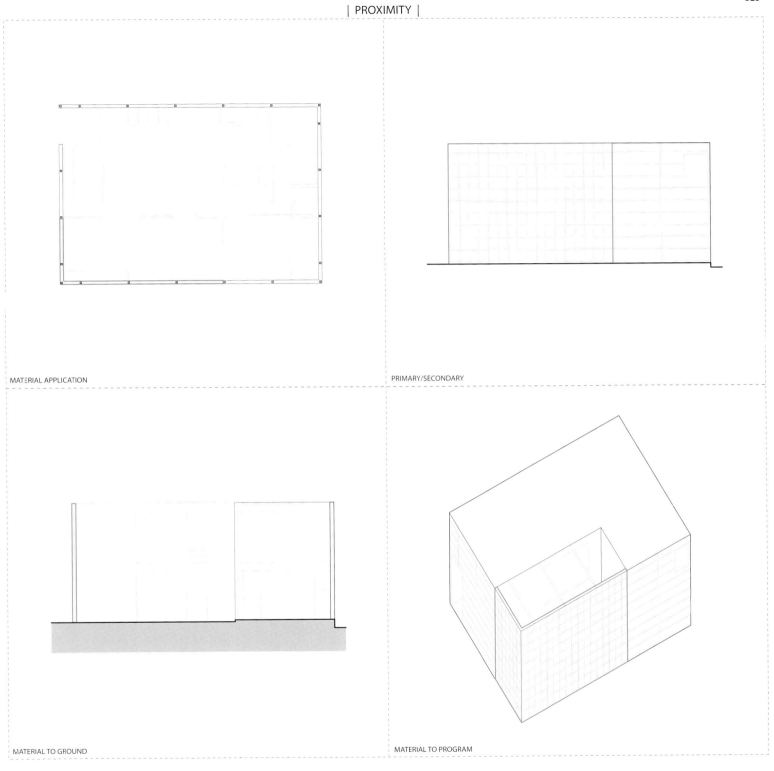

MATERIAL APPLICATION

PRIMARY/SECONDARY

MATERIAL TO GROUND

MATERIAL TO PROGRAM

CORRUGATED PLASTIC POLYCARBONATE

HOUSE IN IMAZATO
KATSUYASU KISHIGAMI
IMAZATO, JAPAN

1999

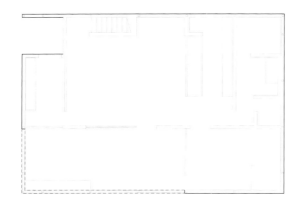

MATERIAL ENCLOSURE [PERIMETER]

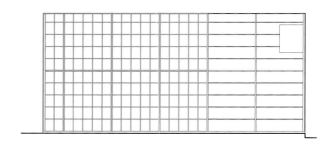

MATERIAL ORDER

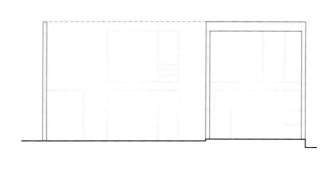

MATERIAL ENCLOSURE [EDGE]

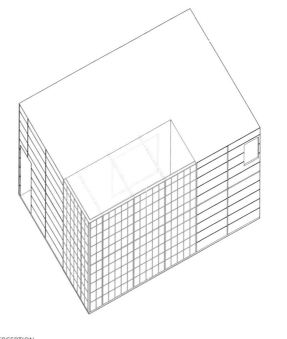

MATERIAL PERCEPTION

CORRUGATED PLASTIC POLYCARBONATE

HOUSE IN IMAZATO
KATSUYASU KISHIGAMI
IMAZATO, JAPAN

1999

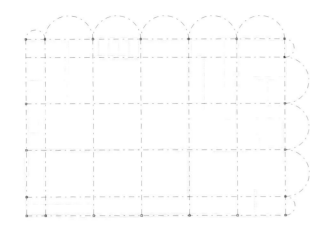

STRUCTURAL MATERIAL [BAY/MODULE]

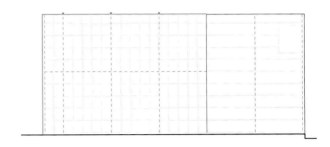

STRUCTURAL MATERIAL LEGIBILITY

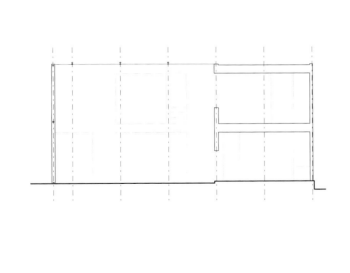

STRUCTURAL MATERIAL SYSTEM

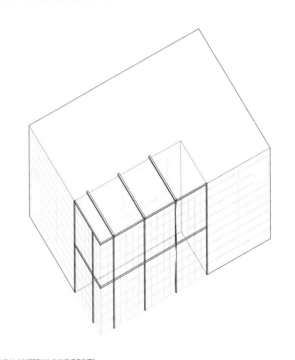

STRUCTURAL MATERIAL [LINE/POINT]

CORRUGATED PLASTIC POLYCARBONATE

HOUSE IN IMAZATO
KATSUYASU KISHIGAMI
IMAZATO, JAPAN

1999

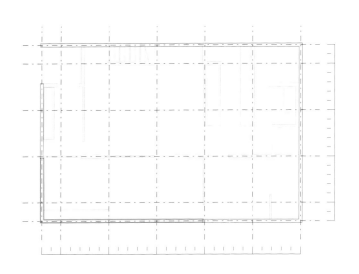

MATERIAL MODULE

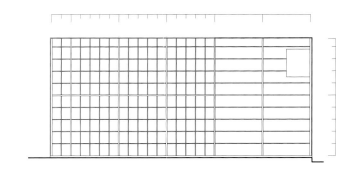

MATERIAL MODULE

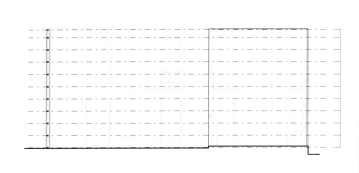

MATERIAL MODULE

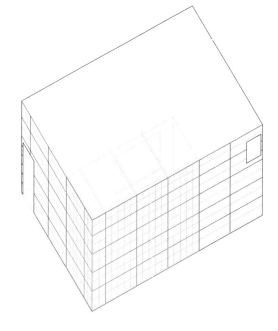

MATERIAL GEOMETRY

CORRUGATED PLASTIC POLYCARBONATE

HOUSE IN IMAZATO
KATSUYASU KISHIGAMI
IMAZATO, JAPAN

1999

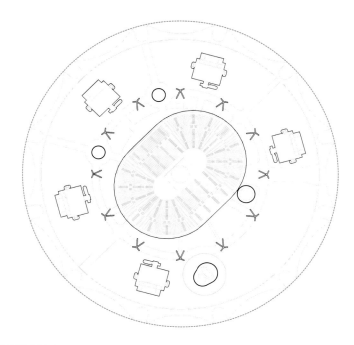

MATERIAL FUNCTION

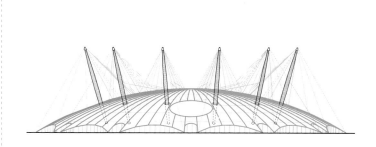

MATERIAL ORDER

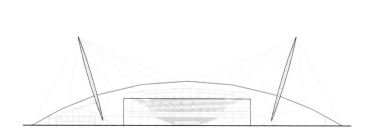

MATERIAL GEOMETRY

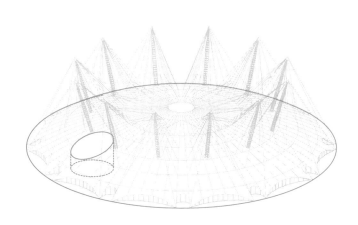

MATERIAL MASSING

PTFE-COATED GLASS FIBER FABRIC PLASTIC

MILLENNIUM DOME
RICHARD ROGERS
LONDON, UNITED KINGDOM

1999

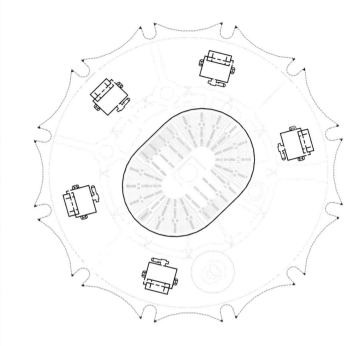

MATERIAL APPLICATION

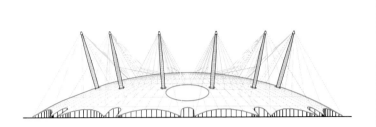

PRIMARY/SECONDARY

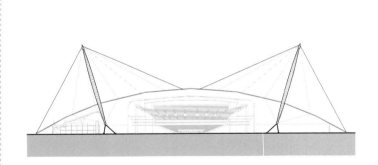

MATERIAL TO GROUND

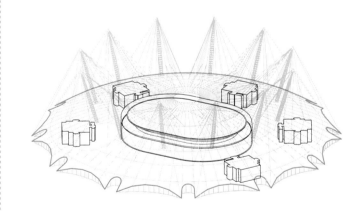

MATERIAL TO PROGRAM

PTFE-COATED GLASS FIBER FABRIC PLASTIC

MILLENNIUM DOME
RICHARD ROGERS
LONDON, UNITED KINGDOM

1999

MATERIAL ENCLOSURE [PERIMETER]

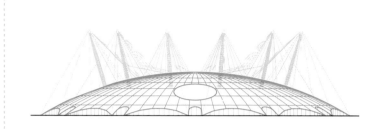

MATERIAL ORDER

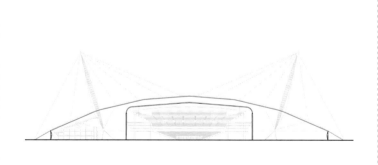

MATERIAL ENCLOSURE [EDGE]

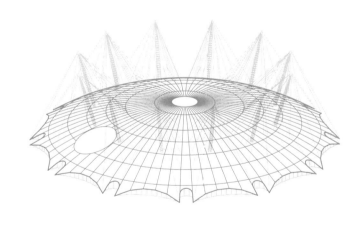

MATERIAL PERCEPTION

PTFE-COATED GLASS FIBER FABRIC PLASTIC

MILLENNIUM DOME
RICHARD ROGERS
LONDON, UNITED KINGDOM

1999

STRUCTURAL MATERIAL [BAY/MODULE]

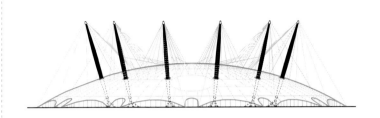

STRUCTURAL MATERIAL LEGIBILITY

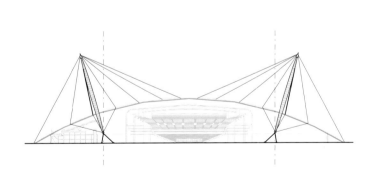

STRUCTURAL MATERIAL SYSTEM

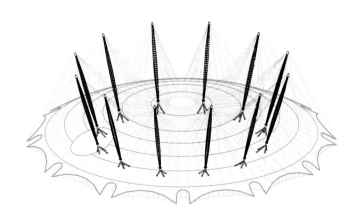

STRUCTURAL MATERIAL [LINE/POINT]

PTFE-COATED GLASS FIBER FABRIC PLASTIC

MILLENNIUM DOME
RICHARD ROGERS
LONDON, UNITED KINGDOM

1999

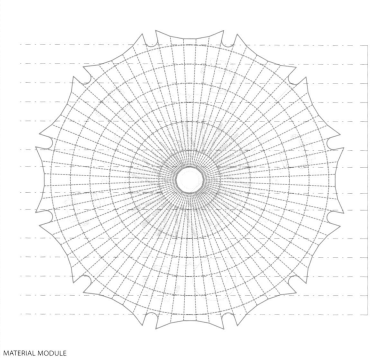

MATERIAL MODULE

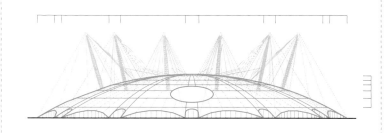

MATERIAL MODULE

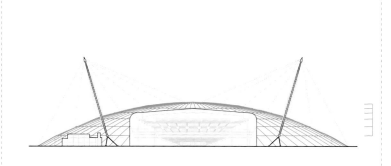

MATERIAL MODULE

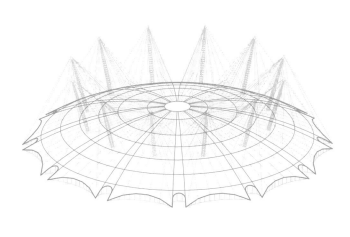

MATERIAL GEOMETRY

PTFE-COATED GLASS FIBER FABRIC PLASTIC

MILLENNIUM DOME
RICHARD ROGERS
LONDON, UNITED KINGDOM

1999

MATERIAL FUNCTION

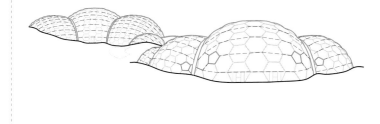

MATERIAL ORDER

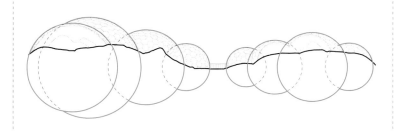

MATERIAL GEOMETRY

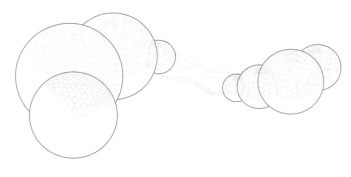

MATERIAL MASSING

ETHYLENE TETRAFLUOROETHYLENE PLASTIC (ETFE)

EDEN PROJECT
NICHOLAS GRIMSHAW
CORNWALL, UNITED KINGDOM

2001

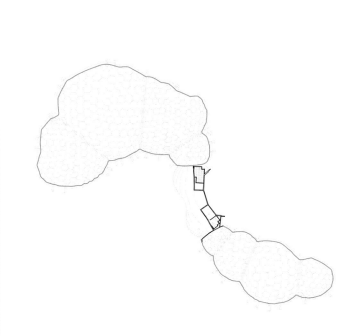

MATERIAL APPLICATION

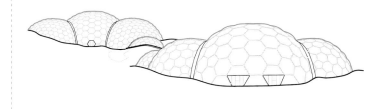

PRIMARY/SECONDARY

MATERIAL TO GROUND

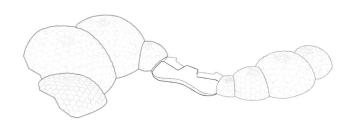

MATERIAL TO PROGRAM

ETHYLENE TETRAFLUOROETHYLENE PLASTIC (ETFE)

EDEN PROJECT
NICHOLAS GRIMSHAW
CORNWALL, UNITED KINGDOM

2001

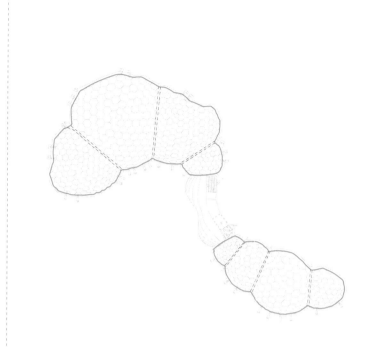

MATERIAL ENCLOSURE [PERIMETER]

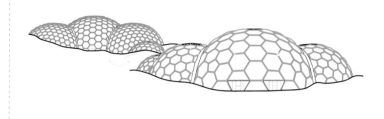

MATERIAL ORDER

MATERIAL ENCLOSURE [EDGE]

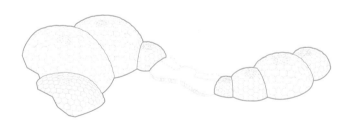

MATERIAL PERCEPTION

ETHYLENE TETRAFLUOROETHYLENE PLASTIC (ETFE)

EDEN PROJECT
NICHOLAS GRIMSHAW
CORNWALL, UNITED KINGDOM

2001

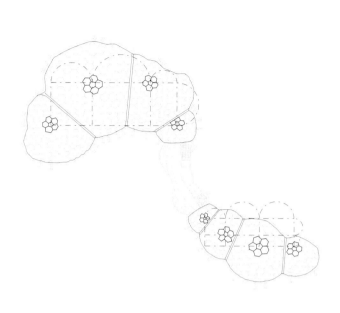

STRUCTURAL MATERIAL [BAY/MODULE]

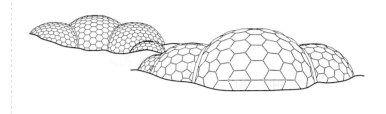

STRUCTURAL MATERIAL LEGIBILITY

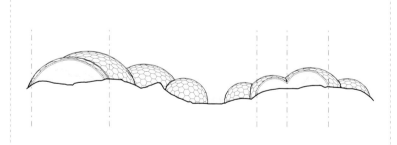

STRUCTURAL MATERIAL SYSTEM

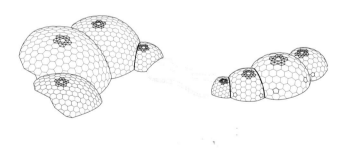

STRUCTURAL MATERIAL [LINE/POINT]

ETHYLENE TETRAFLUOROETHYLENE PLASTIC (ETFE)

EDEN PROJECT
NICHOLAS GRIMSHAW
CORNWALL, UNITED KINGDOM

2001

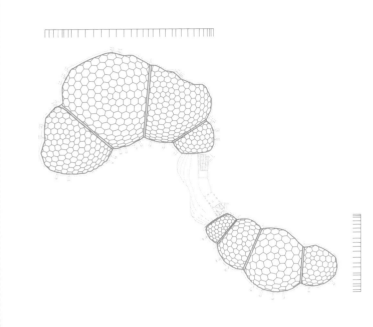

MATERIAL MODULE

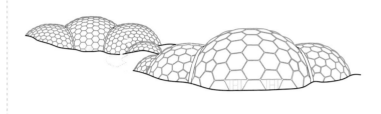

MATERIAL MODULE

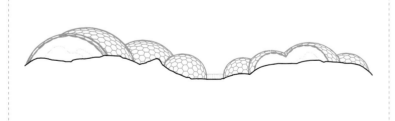

MATERIAL MODULE

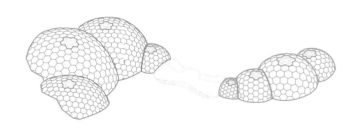

MATERIAL GEOMETRY

ETHYLENE TETRAFLUOROETHYLENE PLASTIC (ETFE)

EDEN PROJECT
NICHOLAS GRIMSHAW
CORNWALL, UNITED KINGDOM

2001

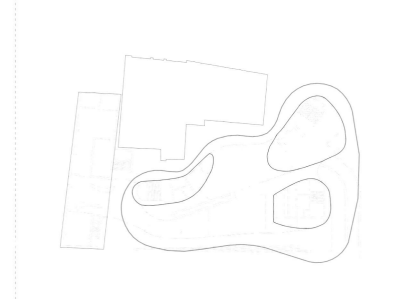

MATERIAL FUNCTION

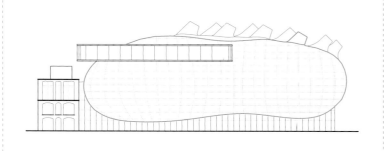

MATERIAL ORDER

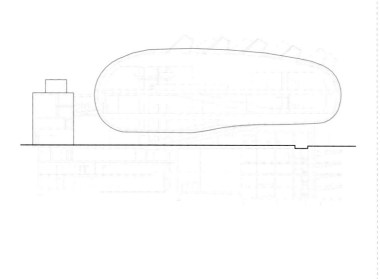

MATERIAL GEOMETRY

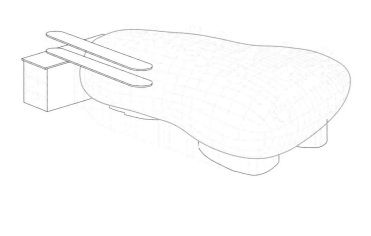

MATERIAL MASSING

TRANSLUCENT WARM BLUE ACRYLIC PLASTIC

KUNSTHAUS GRAZ
COOK AND FOURNIER
GRAZ, AUSTRIA

2003

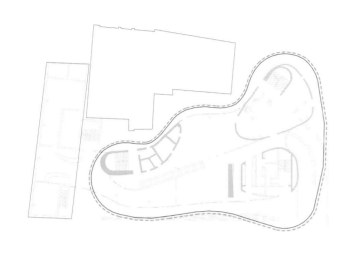

MATERIAL APPLICATION

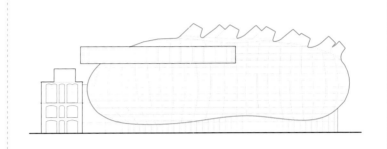

PRIMARY/SECONDARY

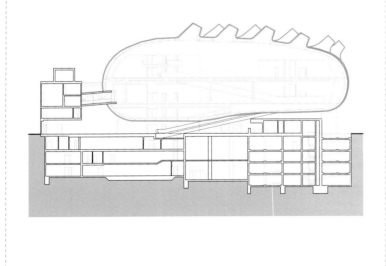

MATERIAL TO GROUND

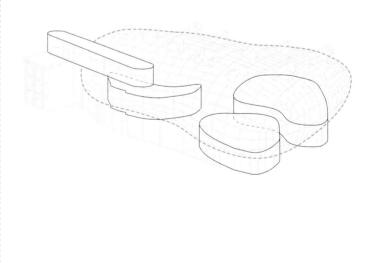

MATERIAL TO PROGRAM

TRANSLUCENT WARM BLUE ACRYLIC PLASTIC

KUNSTHAUS GRAZ
COOK AND FOURNIER
GRAZ, AUSTRIA

2003

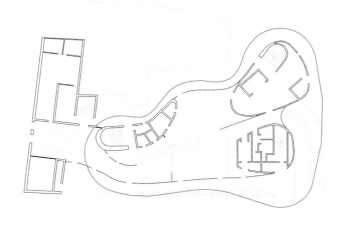

MATERIAL ENCLOSURE [PERIMETER]

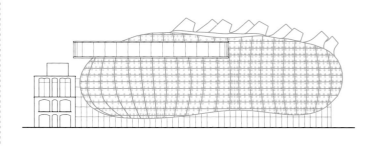

MATERIAL ORDER

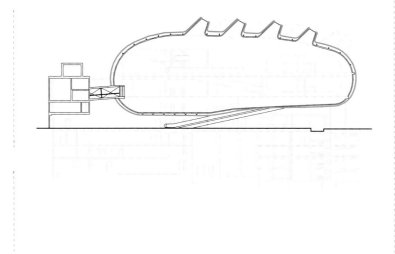

MATERIAL ENCLOSURE [EDGE]

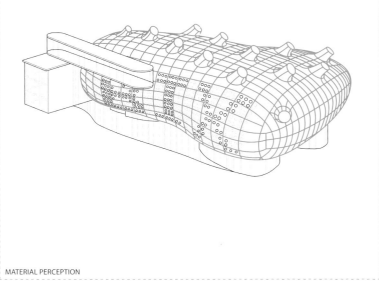

MATERIAL PERCEPTION

TRANSLUCENT WARM BLUE ACRYLIC PLASTIC

KUNSTHAUS GRAZ
COOK AND FOURNIER
GRAZ, AUSTRIA

2003

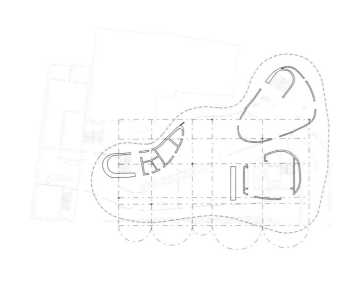

STRUCTURAL MATERIAL [BAY/MODULE]

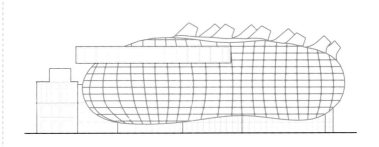

STRUCTURAL MATERIAL LEGIBILITY

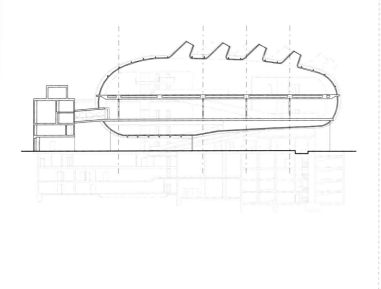

STRUCTURAL MATERIAL SYSTEM

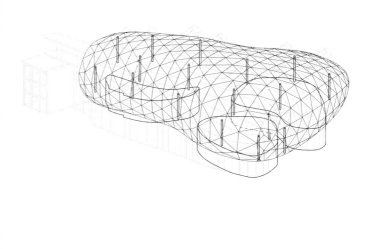

STRUCTURAL MATERIAL [LINE/POINT]

TRANSLUCENT WARM BLUE ACRYLIC PLASTIC

KUNSTHAUS GRAZ
COOK AND FOURNIER
GRAZ, AUSTRIA

2003

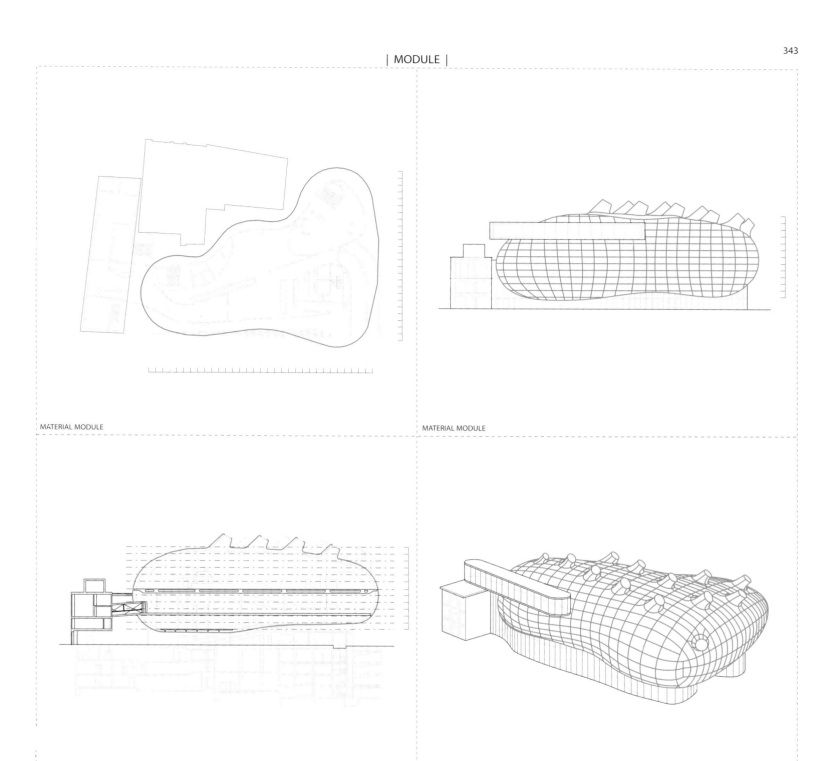

MATERIAL MODULE

MATERIAL MODULE

MATERIAL MODULE

MATERIAL GEOMETRY

TRANSLUCENT WARM BLUE ACRYLIC PLASTIC

KUNSTHAUS GRAZ
COOK AND FOURNIER
GRAZ, AUSTRIA

2003

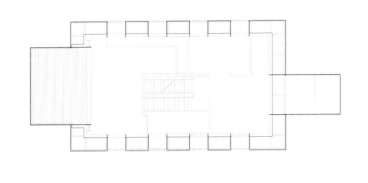

MATERIAL FUNCTION

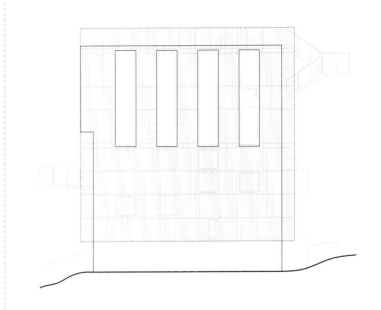

MATERIAL ORDER

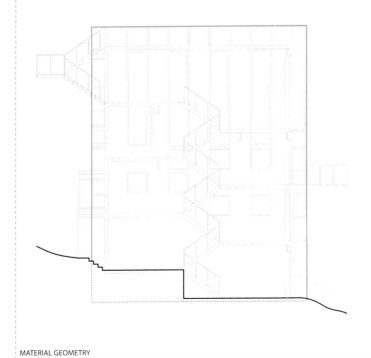

MATERIAL GEOMETRY

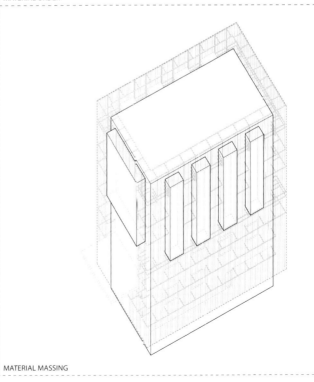

MATERIAL MASSING

CORRUGATED ACRYLIC PLASTIC

CHAMELEON HOUSE
ANDERSON & ANDERSON
NORTHPORT, MICHIGAN

2006

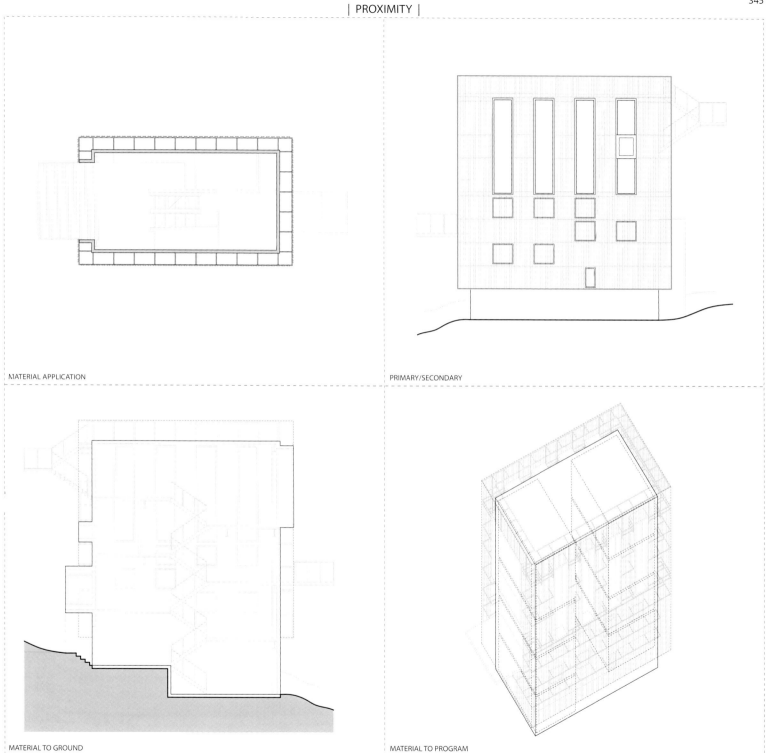

MATERIAL APPLICATION

PRIMARY/SECONDARY

MATERIAL TO GROUND

MATERIAL TO PROGRAM

CORRUGATED ACRYLIC PLASTIC

CHAMELEON HOUSE
ANDERSON & ANDERSON
NORTHPORT, MICHIGAN

2006

MATERIAL ENCLOSURE [PERIMETER]

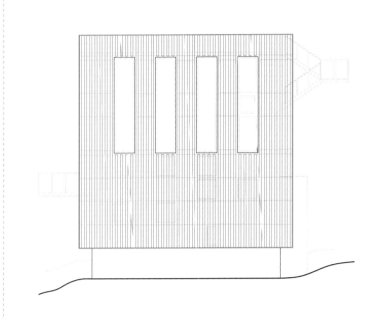

MATERIAL ORDER

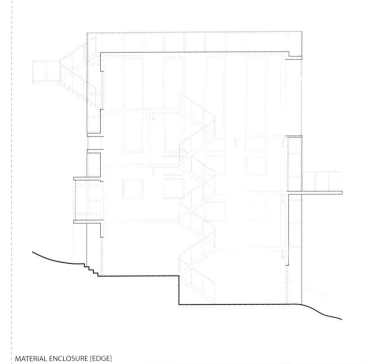

MATERIAL ENCLOSURE [EDGE]

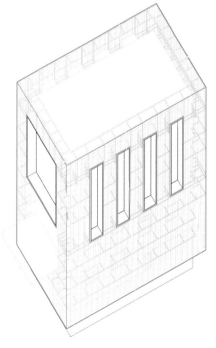

MATERIAL PERCEPTION

CORRUGATED ACRYLIC PLASTIC

CHAMELEON HOUSE
ANDERSON & ANDERSON
NORTHPORT, MICHIGAN

2006

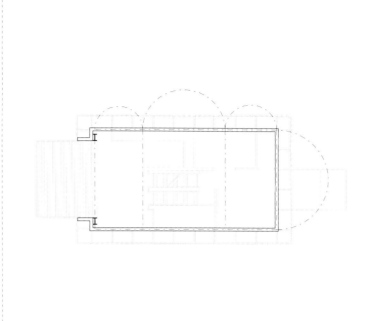

STRUCTURAL MATERIAL [BAY/MODULE]

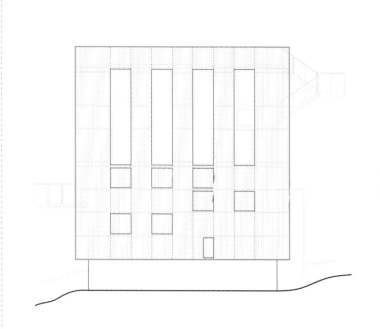

STRUCTURAL MATERIAL LEGIBILITY

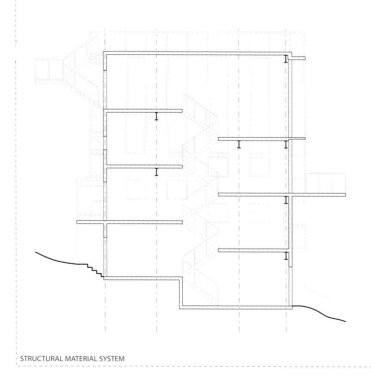

STRUCTURAL MATERIAL SYSTEM

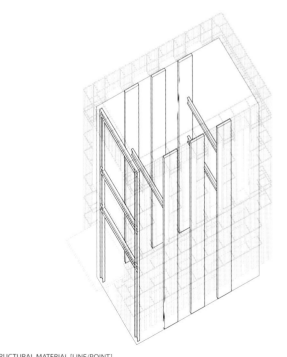

STRUCTURAL MATERIAL [LINE/POINT]

CORRUGATED ACRYLIC PLASTIC

CHAMELEON HOUSE
ANDERSON & ANDERSON
NORTHPORT, MICHIGAN

2006

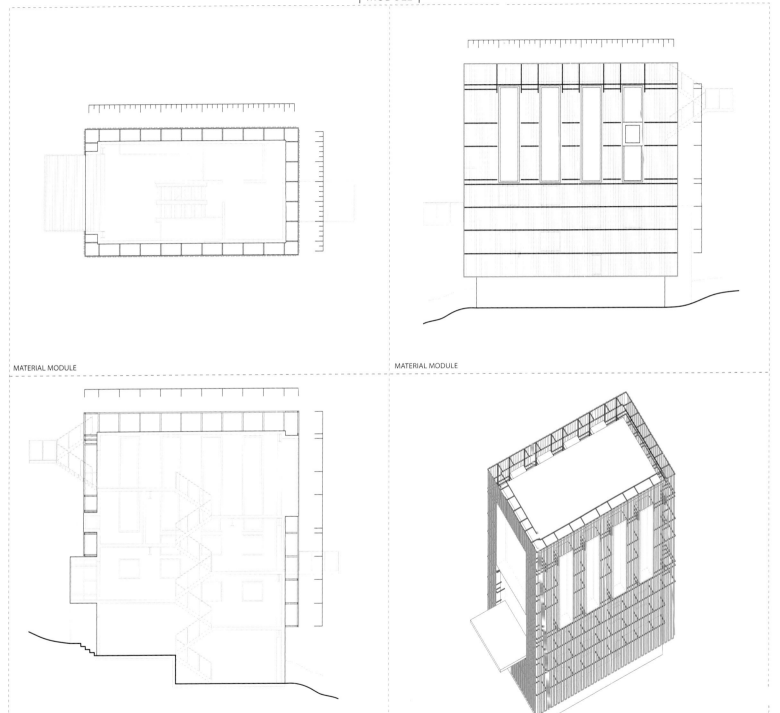

MATERIAL MODULE

MATERIAL MODULE

MATERIAL MODULE

MATERIAL GEOMETRY

CORRUGATED ACRYLIC PLASTIC

CHAMELEON HOUSE
ANDERSON & ANDERSON
NORTHPORT, MICHIGAN

2006

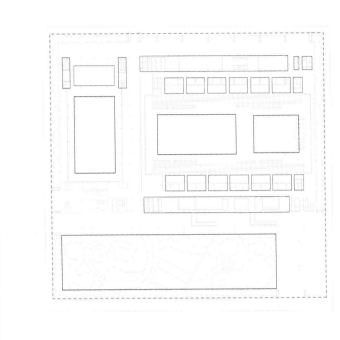

MATERIAL FUNCTION

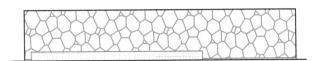

MATERIAL ORDER

MATERIAL GEOMETRY

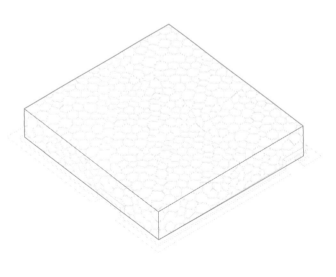

MATERIAL MASSING

ETHYLENE TETRAFLUOROETHYLENE PLASTIC (ETFE)

WATER CUBE
PTW ARCHITECTS
BEIJING, CHINA

2007

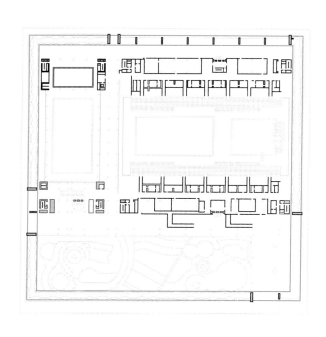

MATERIAL APPLICATION

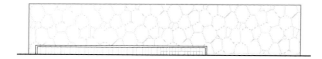

PRIMARY/SECONDARY

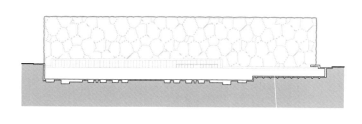

MATERIAL TO GROUND

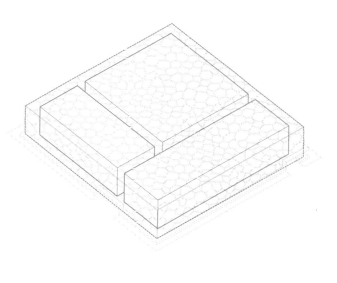

MATERIAL TO PROGRAM

ETHYLENE TETRAFLUOROETHYLENE PLASTIC (ETFE)

WATER CUBE
PTW ARCHITECTS
BEIJING, CHINA

2007

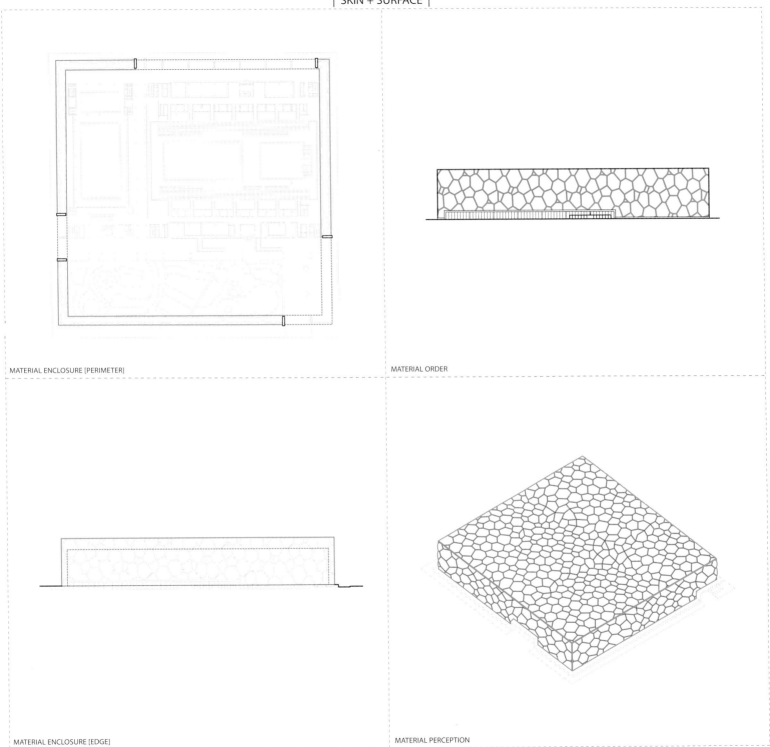

MATERIAL ENCLOSURE [PERIMETER]

MATERIAL ORDER

MATERIAL ENCLOSURE [EDGE]

MATERIAL PERCEPTION

ETHYLENE TETRAFLUOROETHYLENE PLASTIC (ETFE)

WATER CUBE
PTW ARCHITECTS
BEIJING, CHINA

2007

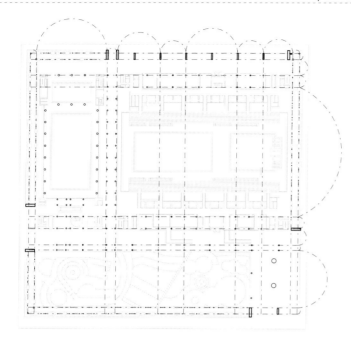

STRUCTURAL MATERIAL [BAY/MODULE]

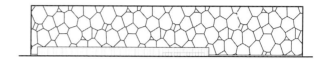

STRUCTURAL MATERIAL LEGIBILITY

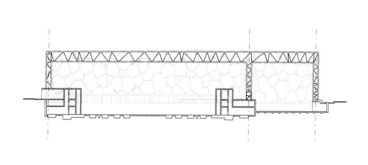

STRUCTURAL MATERIAL SYSTEM

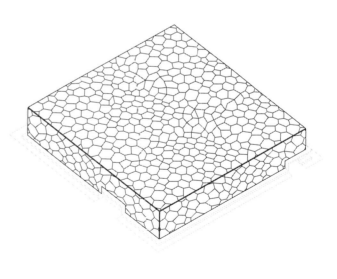

STRUCTURAL MATERIAL [LINE/POINT]

ETHYLENE TETRAFLUOROETHYLENE PLASTIC (ETFE)

WATER CUBE
PTW ARCHITECTS
BEIJING, CHINA

2007

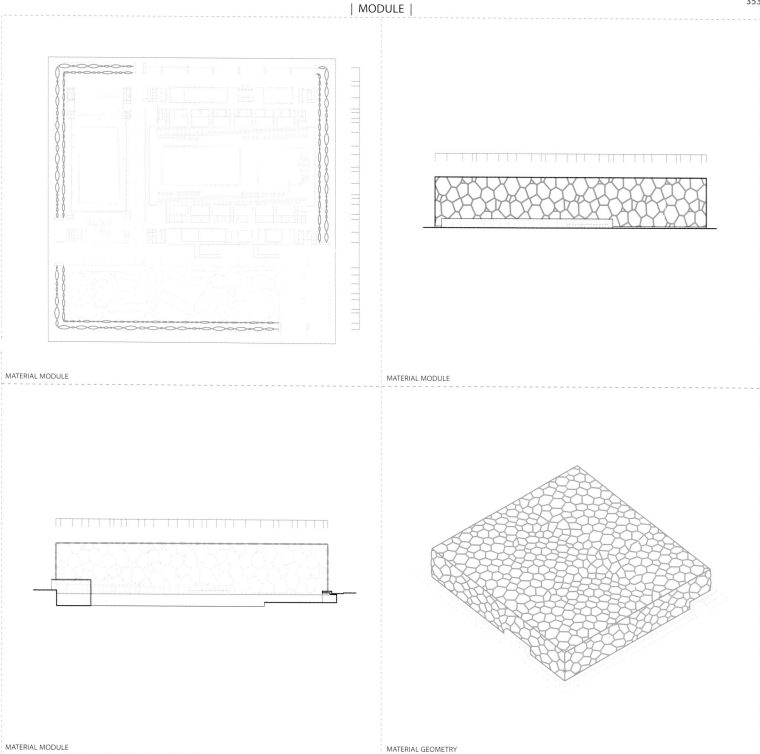

MATERIAL MODULE

MATERIAL MODULE

MATERIAL MODULE

MATERIAL GEOMETRY

ETHYLENE TETRAFLUOROETHYLENE PLASTIC (ETFE)

WATER CUBE
PTW ARCHITECTS
BEIJING, CHINA

2007

COMPARATIVE APPLICATIONS

A cross-sectional comparison of precedents across type, time, geography and architect yet consistent in material allows for a focused look at a specific aspect of materiality. The simultaneity of the presentation of these diagrams permits a trending of use and a description of architectural methodologies. The relative trends suggest the diverse methods of applications and the consistencies, similarities, and variables in material approach. Each diagram type is examined using a cross-sectional comparative method. With the chronological arrangement of the diagram types (left to right and top to bottom) the implications of history and technology relative to a singular conceptual consideration become graphically overt.

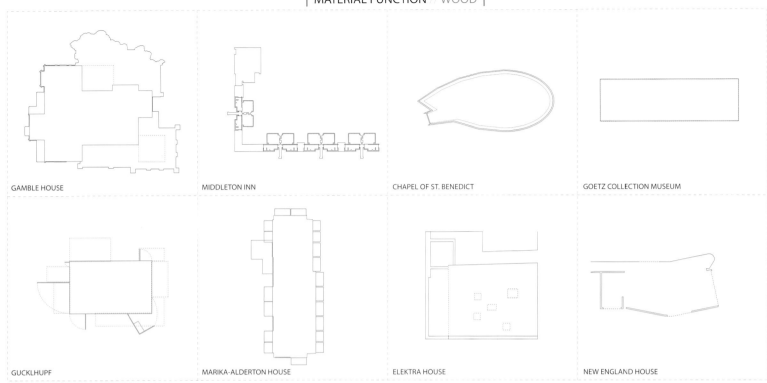

GAMBLE HOUSE

MIDDLETON INN

CHAPEL OF ST. BENEDICT

GOETZ COLLECTION MUSEUM

GUCKLHUPF

MARIKA-ALDERTON HOUSE

ELEKTRA HOUSE

NEW ENGLAND HOUSE

[WOOD] MATERIAL FUNCTION diagrams in plan the relationship between material use and the formal and technical associations required by its functional application. These diagrams examine the role of a material's specific performance properties and its employment relative to the functional and practical necessities of the program and building performance. Each material expresses of the conditions and requirements of its deployment.

Defining the premise of skin in each application, material serves as the iconic designation of form in each project. The associated material tectonic employed extends its influence to express itself through the spatial concepts of the architecture. Steel defines vertical lines [Eames House and Niaux Cave], concrete defines planes and frames with variable openings [Lovell Beach House, La Tourette, Church on the Water] and masonry creates modulated solid edges [Casa Barragan and Murcia Town Hall]. Glass establishes transparent veils: flat, ambiguous surfaces that exist but slip into a nonpresence allowing the dissolve of the enclosure and a perceived spatial connection between inside and outside. This is most prevalent in the De Blas Haus and the Cartier Foundation, though it exists even when the glass is frosted and figured, as in the glass block façade of the Maison de Verre. Each material relative to its function determines form.

In each case study, regardless of the material, the cloak of the primary material is the defining figure of the primary form. The Gamble House is a highly considered and tectonically articulated wood building sitting on a brick plinth. Consisting of diverse overlapping and interlocking rectangular figures, the house is an aggregation of its rooms; the Middleton Inn is defined by the wood of the façade establishing the stacks of individual rooms huddled around the fireplaces, repeating itself in symmetrical tower elements along the masonry connecting wall; the Chapel of St. Benedict is a singular figure of wood with articulated layers to the skin separating structure from cladding to reveal each system tectonically; the Goetz Collection is characterized by the wood panels producing a levitating belt; the Gucklhupf is a double wood box with a highly operable perimeter panel; the Marika-Alderton House is defined by the lightness of variable wood infill between the steel frame; the Electra House is an infill volume clad in the blank opacity of its dark wood siding; and Office dA's New England House is a repetitive segmental wood skin system responding to the internal functions and their relative orientation to the surrounding context.

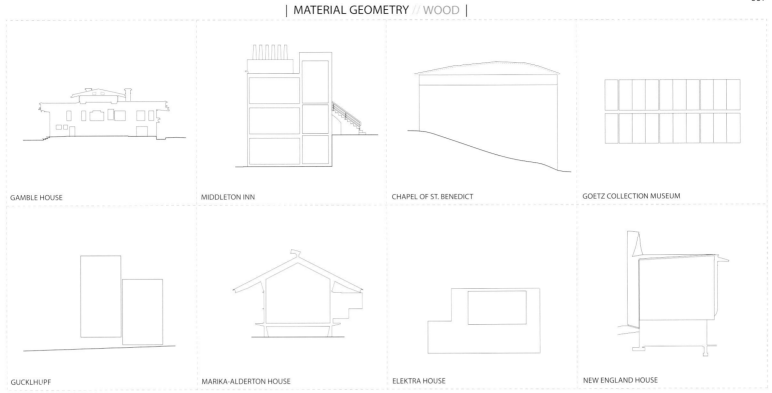

GAMBLE HOUSE

MIDDLETON INN

CHAPEL OF ST. BENEDICT

GOETZ COLLECTION MUSEUM

GUCKLHUPF

MARIKA-ALDERTON HOUSE

ELEKTRA HOUSE

NEW ENGLAND HOUSE

[WOOD] MATERIAL GEOMETRY diagrams the sectional geometric implications of material on form. By introducing the potential structural implications of a material and of the relationship of "skin to bones" or surface to structure becomes relative to the intrinsic qualities of a material. Establishing the dimensional module [both of performance, fabrication and installation limitations, the capabilities of a material express themselves beyond the figure of the form to address the geometry of the space.

The module of a material can be established by three potential scales. The first scale is the module of the unit: a single brick, a sheet of plywood [as direct application of sheathing or as indirect application of formwork], a glass pane with either concealed or revealed frame systems, or a steel member. In each of these conditions the unit is defined by a structural need, a material property, or a manufacturing module. The second scale is the bay of the module produced through the assemblies or structure. For example, the Eames House window wall module is an aggregate of the individual panes, the double high bay module, and the superstructural steel frame. The final scale is the designed geometry of the building's mass expressed through material, i.e., the formal figure of the object as a whole. Each of these three levels can coexist or be independently exploited. The material in each case is, however, the beginning, the dimensional collaborator based on the intrinsic properties and performance of the base material.

The Gamble House is an essay in the performance, form, and capability of wood: as exposed stick structure, complicated interlocking joints for structural rigidity, siding and roofing for cladding and shedding water, and interior details for windows, ornament, stairs, flooring, paneling, and furniture, virtually every aspect of the house is a celebrated articulation of wood; the Middleton Inn deploys wood [as structural framing, cladding, and interior finish] for the bedrooms with concrete block for the wet bathroom conditions; the Chapel of St. Benedict is cloaked in a wood skin of shingled siding over an expressed frame of wood columns and beams; the Goetz Collection panels the wood and glass bands to produce a sectional condition that has a hidden ambiguity relative to the legibility on the façade; the Gucklhupf is a double plywood box with the same surface expressed on the inside as on the outside; the Marika-Alderton House uses repetitive modular bays of wood panels that are easily crafted to accommodate diverse functional and performance-based configurations set between the repetitive metal ribs; the Elektra House loses the connection of the wood exterior for a minimal white interior, allowing the clerestory window frames to be the only moment of expression of the wood lattice frame below; and Office dA's New England House varies, (in section and plan alike), the form as a response to the movement and perception of the building's skin.

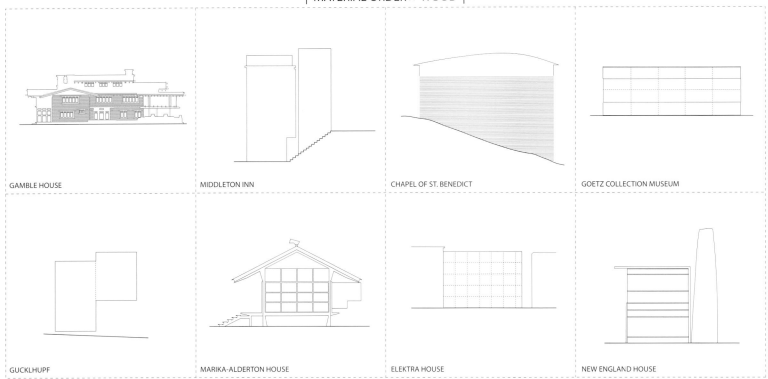

GAMBLE HOUSE

MIDDLETON INN

CHAPEL OF ST. BENEDICT

GOETZ COLLECTION MUSEUM

GUCKLHUPF

MARIKA-ALDERTON HOUSE

ELEKTRA HOUSE

NEW ENGLAND HOUSE

[WOOD] MATERIAL ORDER diagrams in elevation the hierarchy, sequence, and organizational methods of material's influence on the architectural form. As in the examination in section, the implication here is more spatial than formal. Looking at the organizational geometries and governing patterns of material relative to the form, the implications and legibility of volume and mass are articulated through the aggregation of the material pieces.

The extension of the material module into the overarching order of the formal expression is the ultimate collaboration of material with design. The definition of the overall form relative to the piece, the manner in which an aperture is made as a removal [in terms of both module and structural implications], and the relation of these compositional pieces to the formal whole are the defining characteristics of a material's influence on form.

The Gamble House reveals the primary force lines of the structural cage in the elevation of the build ng, reading both the line of the frame and the plane of the framed and clad wall; the Middleton Inn sets the lightness of the wood frame against the weigh of the planar mass of masonry through a contrasting scale of aperture [large floor-to-ceiling windows wrapping the wood hotel rooms, while the apertures in the bathroom remain smaller and even then deploy glass block [a masonry unit] to continue the surface of the façade]; the Chapel of St. Benedict sits anonymously, with only the clerestory band separating the figure of the building from the roof. The scale and articulation come from the patterned layering of the shingle siding; the Goetz Collection sets the center of weight as a levitating belt bracketed mysteriously by glass; the Gucklhupf plays the rigidity and simplicity of the closed figure against the dynamism and mutability of the unfolded composition; the Marika-Alderton House sets a rectangular grid into the metal structural ribbed frame to produce an anthropomorphic scale and an infill system relative to the dimensional characteristics of wood; the Electra House uniformly patterns the street façade with a staggered and anonymous panel pattern; and Office dA's New England House bands, forms, and articulates its façade to respond to the choreography of the body's engagement with the skin and the perception of the building's space as one moves through it.

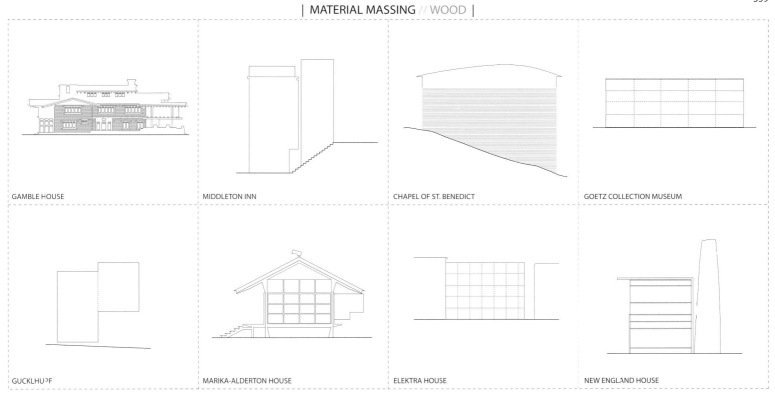

GAMBLE HOUSE

MIDDLETON INN

CHAPEL OF ST. BENEDICT

GOETZ COLLECTION MUSEUM

GUCKLHUPF

MARIKA-ALDERTON HOUSE

ELEKTRA HOUSE

NEW ENGLAND HOUSE

[WOOD] MATERIAL MASSING diagrams in axonometric the overall legibility of the primary material to the superstructural form, presence, and mass of the architectural form. Focusing primarily on the mass and volume of form as defined by the material application to the exterior, the legibility of compositional intention and the geometric hierarchy are mapped.

The significance of mass [as defined by material in particular] concerns the clarity of formal intention in relation to the actual legibility and reading in the building. The conceptual ideas that govern the design of a building become legible through their tectonic manifestations in the form. The hierarchy of the primary massing determines the figuration to which all else must respond. The material relationship with this massing and the deployment of the tectonic expression of the assembly determine whether a material is read as segmented, disassociated, panelized, repetitive, or monolithic.

The Gamble House uses diverse extending roofs that reiterate the volumes of the rooms below; the Middleton Inn uses a repetitive tower symmetrically flanking a fireplace core repeating along the bent surface of the service wall set into the topography of the site; the Chapel of St. Benedict uses a single teardrop form possible through the segmentation and flexibility of wood; the Goetz Collection eliminates verticality by emphasizing the horizontal bands of glass, wood, glass to produce an enigmatic, horizontally symmetrical composition; the Gucklhupf reiterates the machined geometry of the plywood panels in a strict orthogonal volume, and the movement of the skin establishes the foil to this figuration; the Marika-Alderton House is an extruded "house" bar huddling beneath an oversized pitched metal roof; the Electra House has a primary volume established by the site conditions and reiterated by the blank street wall; and Office dA's New England House has a bending form made possible by the flexibility of the aggregated wood surface.

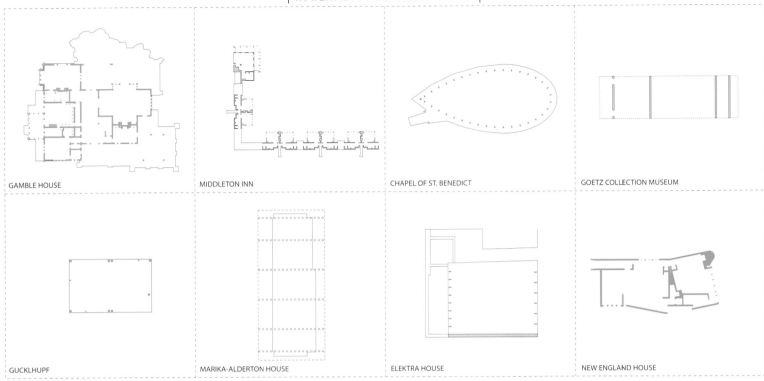

GAMBLE HOUSE

MIDDLETON INN

CHAPEL OF ST. BENEDICT

GOETZ COLLECTION MUSEUM

GUCKLHUPF

MARIKA-ALDERTON HOUSE

ELEKTRA HOUSE

NEW ENGLAND HOUSE

[WOOD] MATERIAL APPLICATION diagrams in plan the deployment of material and the associated perceptual, formal, and functional readings. Engaging the relationship between material and function, the formal expression becomes the primary mediating element. The expression of the material's use and the tectonic deployment determine the functional programmatic legibility of the building. This begins with the formal expression intrinsic to the material, followed by issues of practical performance, including durability, porosity, and visual effect.

A material can be selected for various reasons: availability, cost, durability, module, structural capability, or simply the functional applicability [metal to combat combustion, concrete for construction in corrosive environments, or masonry as a low-maintenance, durable skin]. In each scenario the fundamental physical properties of the material are the baseline of design consideration. These properties, mediated by the method of manufacturing and limited by the method of working [wood is easy to cut, metal can be welded, masonry is heavy and modular], develop the second tier of consideration. Finally, and perhaps with the most variability, is the assembly and application. The systemization of the manufactured pieces and their formal and technical articulation comprise material design application.

The Gamble House uses the same techniques of joinery and materiality across diverse functions, varying the scale and level of exposure to reveal the discrete nature of each component; the Middleton Inn uses wood siding [painted black] to produce a seemingly monolithic figure of the hotel rooms referencing a historical color palette indigenous to its context; the Chapel of St. Benedict separates the structural layer of the columnar frame from the planar nature of the skin of enclosure; the Goetz Collection employs enigmatic wood paneling as a looping belt to gather the diverse programs of office, circulation, and gallery into one prismatic form; the Gucklhupf has a structural frame system clad with modular plywood panels; the Marika-Alderton House uses wood to mediate between the regimented metal of the structure and roof through a diaphanous skin that modulates light and serves as a porous furniture perimeter; the Electra House wraps the primary volume with the blank material figure of the black wood; and Office dA's New England House breaks and modulates the form to generate an architectural sequence and experience of the skin, building, and site simultaneously.

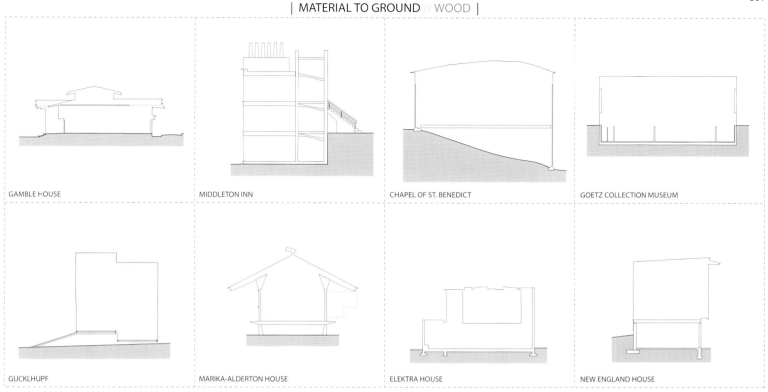

GAMBLE HOUSE

MIDDLETON INN

CHAPEL OF ST. BENEDICT

GOETZ COLLECTION MUSEUM

GUCKLHUPF

MARIKA-ALDERTON HOUSE

ELEKTRA HOUSE

NEW ENGLAND HOUSE

[WOOD] Proximity – MATERIAL TO GROUND diagrams the sectional relationship in which a building meets the ground, engages landscape, and addresses the material point of connection with the site. The point of contact between a building and the earth is determined by the material approach to the architecture. Factors that determine and affect this condition include soil characteristics, climate, context, structural system, and building weight [both actual and perceived].

The history of structural and material technology is the history of how a building meets the ground. The selection of material cladding and structural framing results in a specific formal articulation of this condition that is intrinsic to the material and tectonic. Technologically determined, this joint [between building and ground] is created by the system of both the structure and the cladding. Historically, load-bearing wall systems of wood or masonry required continuous contact of the building with the ground and limited the scale and frequency of openings. Materials such as steel and concrete allowed for a formal disengagement from the ground plane, turning structural planes into points and shifting from a wall system to a cage.

The Gamble House sets the wood structure atop a clay masonry plinth to create both a platform that blurs the boundary between inside and outside and material protection from water and insects; the Middleton Inn sets the block bath wall into the hillside and then stacks the units three levels high [the one in the middle at grade, and one up and one down in section]; the Chapel of St. Benedict holds a horizontal plane at the datum of the entry height but allows the building to fall and ascend in height with the natural topography to create a heroic figure from the exterior; the Goetz Collection, though seemingly horizontally symmetrical, in fact sets into the ground to reveal two stacked double-height spaces that are at differential heights to the ground plane; the Gucklhupf floats off the ground on legs providing a gangplank entryway and clear announcement of the separation of the building from the site; the Marika-Alderton House touches only on the twelve points of the metal frame to allow minimal impact on the site and permit the natural breezes and groundwater to flow beneath the building; the Electra House sits plainly on the ground, relying upon the solemn uniformity of the façade to create the minimal yet enigmatic relationship with its surroundings; and Office dA's New England House floats above and on the site, set partially into the hill both laterally and longitudinally, allowing the movement of the form to be further emphasized by the varied relationship with the topography.

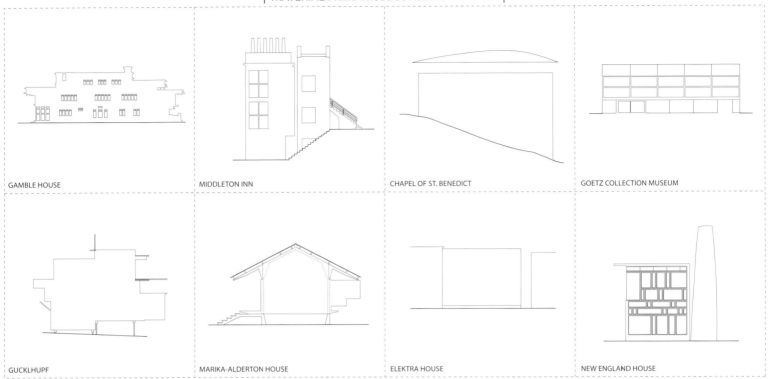

GAMBLE HOUSE

MIDDLETON INN

CHAPEL OF ST. BENEDICT

GOETZ COLLECTION MUSEUM

GUCKLHUPF

MARIKA-ALDERTON HOUSE

ELEKTRA HOUSE

NEW ENGLAND HOUSE

[WOOD] Proximity – PRIMARY / SECONDARY diagrams in elevation the relationship of the primary building material, to the secondary building material, focusing on the formal, functional, and practical interrelationships of their material application. The hierarchy between these two levels is both formally and materially evident, establishing the organizing geometries of the diverse layers.

The proximity of a primary figure to a secondary figure builds on the formal reading of material application diagrams but engages the interrelationship with the secondary systemization. The interaction of the two can occur through superimposition, contrasting figures, interpenetration, banding, layering, or any other adverbial relationship. The result is a primary figuration and the secondary subsystemization that, through its geometry, breaks down the material into fabricateable and installable pieces and reveals the tectonic intention of their aggregation.

The Gamble House employs wood for almost every aspect of its construction, relying only upon [1] glass for the decorative quality of the ornamental composition and light and [2] masonry for the protective plinth of the surrounding skirt; the Middleton Inn sets the wood volumes as articulated sanctuary towers of hotel rooms against the linear horizontal, homogeneous stucco bath wall; the Chapel of St. Benedict uniformly blankets the surface with the shingled siding, instead juxtaposing the roof as a segmented and ribbed metal figure despite the ability of wood to assume such responsibilities; the Goetz Collection equally divides the façade between the opaque central band of the wood and the frosted glass bands at grade and at the clerestory; the Gucklhupf foils the plywood panels with a series of secondary metal armatures that serve as the scaffolding for the operable components. As a result, even when closed, the figure reveals the potential movements of its skin; the Marika-Alderton House balances the wood panels with high articulation and variety [due to the ease of working with wood] against the regularity and standardization of the sheet metal roof and the metal structural ribs; the Electra House uses the context of traditional masonry construction as the foil to the blank wood façade; and Office dA's New England House uses the large expanses of glass and the metal-clad figure of the twisting chimney.

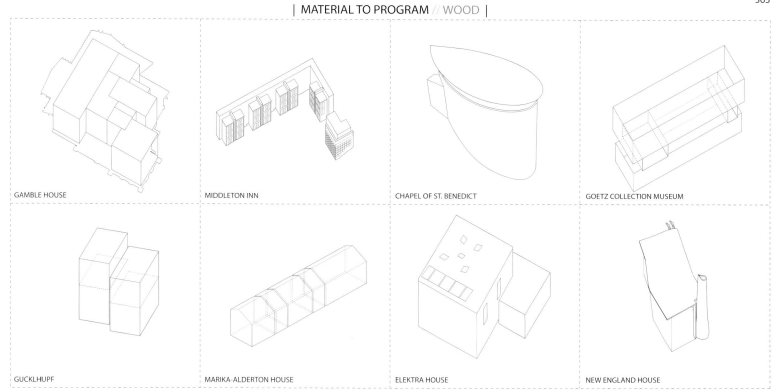

GAMBLE HOUSE

MIDDLETON INN

CHAPEL OF ST. BENEDICT

GOETZ COLLECTION MUSEUM

GUCKLHUPF

MARIKA-ALDERTON HOUSE

ELEKTRA HOUSE

NEW ENGLAND HOUSE

[WOOD] Proximity – MATERIAL TO PROGRAM diagrams in axonometric the overall relationship of material usage to the primary programmatic and functional usages. By focusing on the three-dimensional volumetric associations of material to programmatic usage [and the associated functional requirements of a particular program], the articulation of "form following function" can be examined through material association.

The relationship of the programmatic usage to the material selected depicts the narrative of the association, creating the opportunity and potential for material to be an expressive sign system. The legibility of a material comes from a technical knowledge that engages an understanding of raw material, manufacturing processes, construction traditions and techniques, weathering and biological attack, and cultural associations. These innate properties of matter translate into forms that collaborate with materials to reveal their process.

The Gamble House uses the same material across the diverse programs, employing a transition in scale and ornament to define the legible variation from public to private; the Middleton Inn uses repetitive masses lining the superstructural L of the masonry wall; the Chapel of St. Benedict illustrates the singular and practical shape of the sanctuary; the Goetz Collection has two floors separated by double-height spaces that bridge the grade level, with the exception of an office and a circulation space that read as ghosted masses behind the translucent frosted glass perimeter; the Gucklhupf shows the two equally rendered volumes associated with the domestic program of public and private; the Marika-Alderton House segments the tubular form of the house in layered functional bays along a gradient from public to private, all cohered through the continuity of the overhanging roof and the regularity of the structural ribs; the Electra House, with a blankness to the perimeter, relies upon an articulated roof to choreograph the interior spaces and volumes; and Office dA's New England House uses a transitional scale in its skin to illustrate the lower public space, the frontal double-height figure of the living spaces, and the compressed privatized spaces of the upper bedrooms.

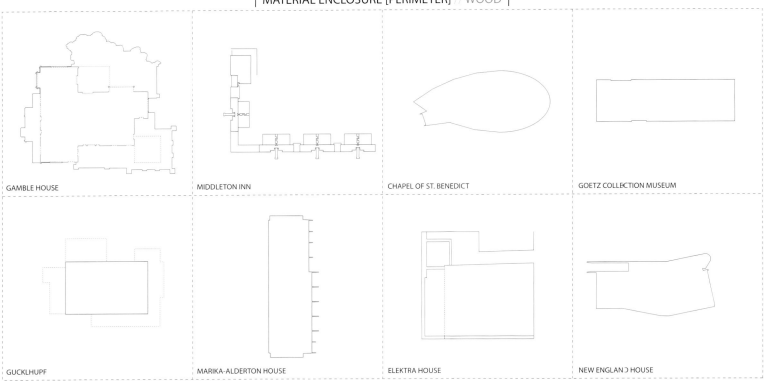

GAMBLE HOUSE

MIDDLETON INN

CHAPEL OF ST. BENEDICT

GOETZ COLLECTION MUSEUM

GUCKLHUPF

MARIKA-ALDERTON HOUSE

ELEKTRA HOUSE

NEW ENGLAND HOUSE

[WOOD] Skin + Surface – MATERIAL ENCLOSURE [PERIMETER] diagrams in plan the relationship of the outer plane of enclosure [skin] to the spatial, formal, and structural organization. Expressing the process by which materials assemble into systems, the figuration of the perimeter is dependent not simply upon the piece but also upon the joint. The collaboration of these two generates specific forms intrinsic to a material and expressively identifiable.

The use of skin to define the perimeter over the structure and the programmatic innards establishes the legibility of architectural idea's purity through the articulation of edge and boundary. The continuity and complexity of this envelope widely explicate the material articulation and the tectonic intricacy. The relationship of craft to figure is found in the method of material manipulation.

The Gamble House diffuses the skin with as much porosity as possible for the era and complements this with a second layer of exterior spaces [both downstairs and upstairs] that integrate the interior spaces with the exterior [possible in the Southern California climate]; the Middleton Inn forms an L shape lined with locally symmetrical double square towers; the Chapel of St. Benedict uses an axially symmetrical figure slightly morphed to allow the entry to asymmetrically penetrate the figure; the Goetz Collection is a simple rectilinear figure with enigmatic reversals of heavy and light; the Gucklhupf has simple figured skin that derives its complexity from the operability of the variable composed apertures in the panels' perimeter; the Marika-Alderton House has a rectilinear base form with a highly choreographed and articulated perimeter responding to the environmental conditions the Electra House hugs the wood L against the existing surroundings to cloak and create a new uniform perimeter; and Office dA's New England House bends with the program and site to activate the boundary between outside and inside both formally and tectonically.

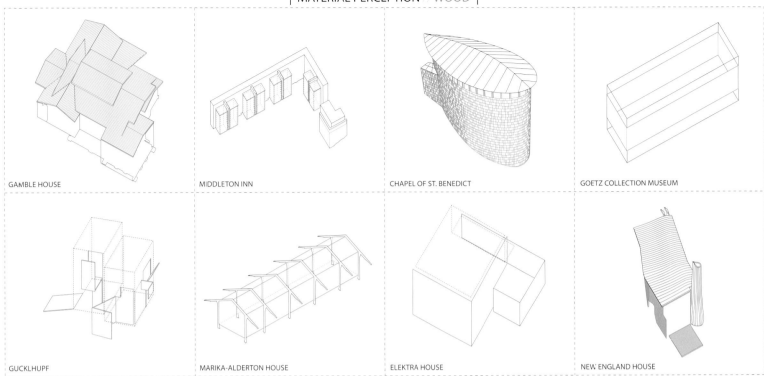

GAMBLE HOUSE

MIDDLETON INN

CHAPEL OF ST. BENEDICT

GOETZ COLLECTION MUSEUM

GUCKLHUPF

MARIKA-ALDERTON HOUSE

ELEKTRA HOUSE

NEW ENGLAND HOUSE

[WOOD] Skin + Surface – MATERIAL PERCEPTION diagrams in axonometric the primary reading of material experience. By transitioning from the sectional reading that focuses on the two-dimensional interior spatial conditions or the material application, the reading in elevation speaks to the composition of the façade but again within the shallow space of a two-dimensional reading, while the axonometric examination illustrates the compositional legibility of the building as a total object.

By engaging all three dimensions, the figuration of the architecture and the legibility of a material's perception relative to the total object lend a volumetric legibility to a material's perception. A truly monolithic architecture is nearly impossible; thus the connection and change from one piece to the next define the moment of intervention and design decision. The perception of the whole after the resolution of these local "events" is the perception of the architecture. Focusing specifically on the material impact upon these decisions allows the design intention to be revealed by the tectonic view of the whole through the piece.

The Gamble House reveals its material and tectonic at every level, from overarching figure to structural legibility to expression of frame and joint to the details and tactile moments of flooring and railing; the Middleton Inn masses repetitive bodies along the wall culminating in a larger "head" piece that contains the communal spaces of the hotel; the Chapel of St. Benedict plays the reading of skin and surface of the exterior against the frame and component of the interior, masterfully employing the two methods of expressing the same material; the Goetz Collection overtly simplifies the form and then subtly inverts the conceptions of the composition's legibility; the Gucklhupf perceptually generates the serially produced simplicity of the panelized box while introducing the whimsy and contextual and programmatic response through the irregular figured operability of this same surface; the Marika-Alderton House regularly ribs an extruded wood space; the Electra House blankets existing and new structures and spaces to provide a solemn homogeneity; and Office dA's New England House creates a dynamic figure as a result of localized experiential and tectonic decisions.

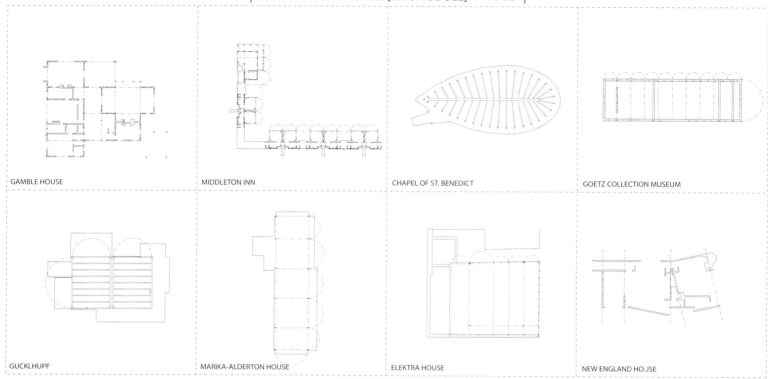

GAMBLE HOUSE

MIDDLETON INN

CHAPEL OF ST. BENEDICT

GOETZ COLLECTION MUSEUM

GUCKLHUPF

MARIKA-ALDERTON HOUSE

ELEKTRA HOUSE

NEW ENGLAND HOUSE

[WOOD] STRUCTURAL MATERIAL [BAY/MODULE] diagrams in plan the structural module of the building. Focusing on the influence of the structural material, it illustrates the engineered structural response of material relative to performative need. Dependent upon the dimension of span relative to the spatial capabilities of the material, an organizing geometry is established that sets the scale and legibility of a space.

The role of structure in plan is of particular formal importance relative to material as the premise of line [load-bearing walls] versus point [columns]. Each system establishes a certain way of making space. Load-bearing materials versus cladding materials are revealed, and their variation and interdependence are highlighted.

The Gamble House has a primary superstructure of expressed columns and beams that similarly establish the spatial and programmatic delineation; the Middleton Inn has a repetitive wood structure that spans the entire volume of each room-dimensioned tower; the Chapel of St. Benedict pulls from the perimeter columns a radial rib structure gathering at a central beam, simply yet exquisitely expressing the structural forces; the Goetz Collection has a lateral bay frame that spans from edge to edge to remove the legibility of the structural points by embedding them in the walls; the Gucklhupf uses a regimented regularized structure to support the thin exterior panels; the Marika-Alderton House has six identical frames positioned with four major center bays and two reduced end bays allowing the formal variability to come through the method of infill; the Electra House integrates an existing masonry wall with a new steel frame to engage line as a separate system from the plane of enclosure; and Office dA's New England House relies upon the perimeter walls as bearing planes only, disrupting the interior with the primary core between the single-height and double-height spaces.

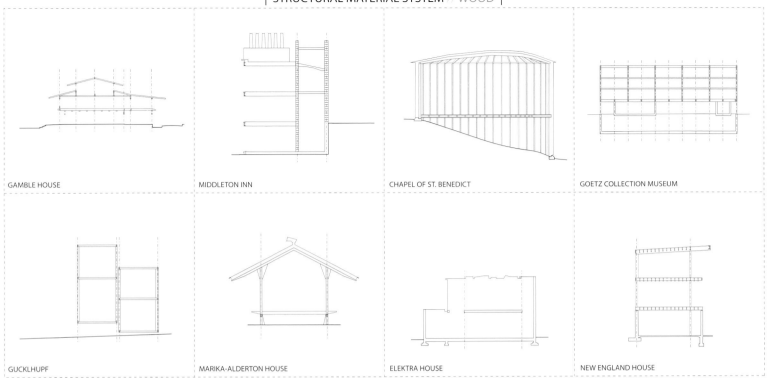

GAMBLE HOUSE

MIDDLETON INN

CHAPEL OF ST. BENEDICT

GOETZ COLLECTION MUSEUM

GUCKLHUPF

MARIKA-ALDERTON HOUSE

ELEKTRA HOUSE

NEW ENGLAND HOUSE

[WOOD] STRUCTURAL MATERIAL [BAY/MODULE] diagrams the sectional implications of the structural module. Focusing on the influence of the structural material, it illustrates the engineered structural response of material relative to performative need. In this diagram set, the structure is materially examined in its vertical figuration of the sectional articulation.

Building on the bay system of the plan, the section depicts the shape and configuration of the repetitive unit and the effectual relationship to the space of the building. Perceived or concealed, primary [as figuration] or coincidental in presence, the role of the sectional structural bay engages the verticality of the building.

The Gamble House uses a superstructural module that establishes the full span of spaces and is expressed through the heavy timber construction of its exposed frame; the Middleton Inn sets the flat surface of the wood section against the arching and parged surfaces of the masonry walled baths; the Chapel of St. Benedict pulls the columnar system out of the wall plane to express the frame as a discrete element from the surface of enclosure; the Goetz Collection uses concrete walls for the lower levels and wood frames for the upper lattice concealed within the walls; the Gucklhupf uses a superstructural frame to hold the thin panels; the Marika-Alderton House has a frame on pier foundation system to set lightly on the ground and establish primary ribs that determine the base of the spatial envelope to be manipulated by the variable wood skin; the Electra House suspends a second floor between the front and back planes of enclosure, allowing light and space to occupy the separation; and Office dA's New England House doubles the longitudinal walls to allow for a flexibility of structure to span variably across the surface and create a flexibly thickened structural edge allowing for the formal and tectonic playfulness in this zone.

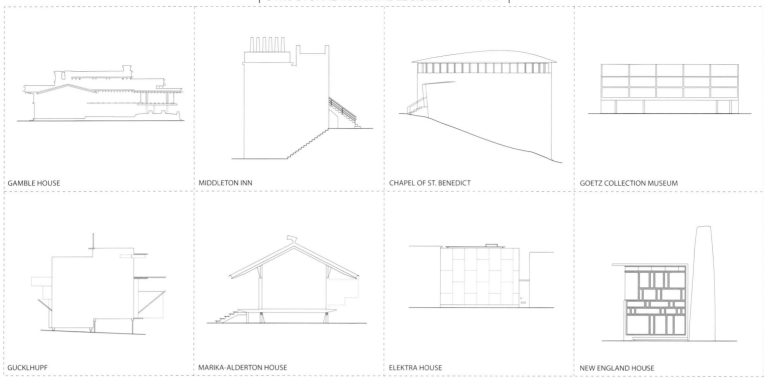

GAMBLE HOUSE

MIDDLETON INN

CHAPEL OF ST. BENEDICT

GOETZ COLLECTION MUSEUM

GUCKLHUPF

MARIKA-ALDERTON HOUSE

ELEKTRA HOUSE

NEW ENGLAND HOUSE

[WOOD] STRUCTURAL MATERIAL LEGIBILITY diagrams in elevation the reading of the structural material. Focusing on the influence of the structural material, it illustrates the interrelation of the engineered structural response of material and performative need to the form and composition. Questioning how the system reads from the exterior and whether the structural material is ever seen, the legibility diagrams examine the relationship of the forces of gravity to the formal expression.

The integration of structure to skin and ultimately to form is about the engagement of the physical requirements of a building to perform structurally with the formal intentions and the legibility of these two systems. The idea of [1] reading a person's bones literally through the skin, [2] versus the broader legibility of a leg as column to transfer vertical loads, [3] versus a denial of all understanding of how the figure works structurally are the three basic stages of structural depiction: [1] literal, [2] figural, or [3] denied.

The Gamble House reveals at all scales the tectonics of the structure from the exposed joinery to the articulated pieces defining the composition; the Middleton Inn bays the wood on the surface to imply a structural skeleton organization within the wall; the Chapel of St. Benedict masks the lower reading of the structural skeleton, allowing it to reveal itself only through the clerestory band; the Goetz Collection picks up the bay of the structure in the skin but reconstructs it as a surface drawing of an abstract geometric system; the Gucklhupf covers the frame with panel cladding, only revealing the extension lines through the feet extending beneath; in the Marika-Alderton House the skin is legible both outside and inside through the depressions of the performative outcroppings and the extension of the structure to create legs that elevate the building to the site; the Electra House masks the façade uniformly, hiding the eclectic composite structure of masonry, steel, and wood behind; and Office dA's New England House celebrates the wrapper but enigmatically disguises the practical responsibilities of this surface in favor of their experiential and formal opportunity.

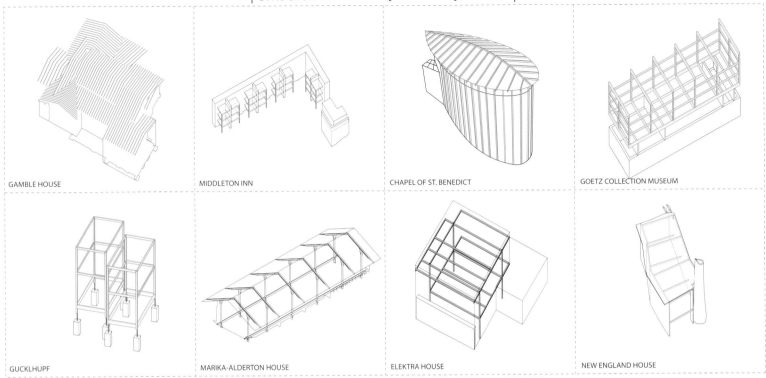

GAMBLE HOUSE

MIDDLETON INN

CHAPEL OF ST. BENEDICT

GOETZ COLLECTION MUSEUM

GUCKLHUPF

MARIKA-ALDERTON HOUSE

ELEKTRA HOUSE

NEW ENGLAND HOUSE

[WOOD] STRUCTURAL MATERIAL [LINE/POINT] diagrams in axonometric the primary geometric and formal response of the structural material/system. "Line" refers to the registration of a wall surface as a structural bearing wall in plan, while "point" refers to the columnar system. Materials subscribe intrinsically to one or the other [typically]; metal is point, while masonry is line. Certain materials, like concrete and wood, have the potential to be either.

The axonometric diagramming of the structural system and the material expression of this system suggest the three-dimensional resolution of the underlying structure superimposed on the form. The relationship of the structural material to the primary material parallels the discussion of revelation and concealment and homogeneity verses cladding.

The Gamble House holds equally the segmented and aggregated componential assembly of the piece with the superstructural form of the whole; the Middleton Inn uses a planar system for the masonry walls juxtaposed with a lighter framed method for the hotel rooms to allow for a dissolution of the wall and optimize transparency; the Chapel of St. Benedict reveals the simple and rational extension of the linear wall structure into the roof ribs; the Goetz Collection uses a planar system below grade that reaches up through the first story to transition to a frame system for the upper levels, allowing the enigmatic hovering of the façade; the Gucklhupf establishes a regimented steel frame beneath the paneled boxes; the Marika-Alderton House uses a repetitive frame system at variable intervals with an elevated floor plate to minimize the footprint in twelve minimal points; the Electra House uses an existing masonry street wall and a new steel frame to allow for the dynamic spatial configuration of the interior, all cloaked by the anonymity of the blank exterior skin; and Office dA's New England House uses the two longitudinal walls as bearing planes to support the connecting beams of the roof.

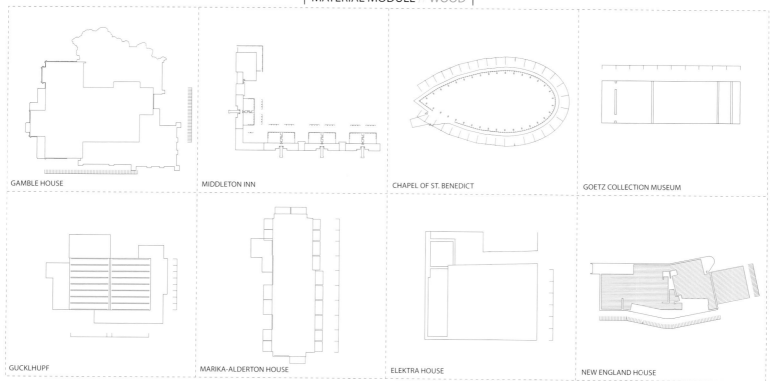

GAMBLE HOUSE

MIDDLETON INN

CHAPEL OF ST. BENEDICT

GOETZ COLLECTION MUSEUM

GUCKLHUPF

MARIKA-ALDERTON HOUSE

ELEKTRA HOUSE

NEW ENGLAND HOUSE

[WOOD] Module – MATERIAL MODULE diagrams in plan the relationships of the manufacturing module intrinsic to a material to the space, form, and dimensions. Mapping the inherited dimensional constraints determined by the production and movement of a material, the patterning of these scale elements and the articulation of their joinery to establish larger architectural forms address the relationship of piece to whole and unit to system.

The module of materials is an intrinsic fact that must be addressed. Certain materials default to a secondary system [such as concrete with formwork] to generate a dimensional constraint, but every material has a "natural" form and dimension. The negotiation of these constraints and the collaboration with these numeric proportions determine the dimensions of the whole and the integration of the modular unit into the consistency of the superstructural organization.

The Gamble House uses the workability of wood to produce localized solutions expressive of need but celebrated in expression to serve as ornament; the Middleton Inn uses a simple span in the window module capable with relatively small wood members; the Chapel of St. Benedict uses the module of the shingle on the exterior and the module of the structural stick on the interior; the Goetz Collection uses a regular bay system that accommodates both the upper wood frame and the lower concrete walls; the Gucklhupf uses the module of the plywood panel to determine its dimension, allowing the flexibility to emerge through the composition of the aperture; the Marika-Alderton House uses a common middle bay and then varies the bay slightly for the ends, relying upon a halving subdivision of the structural metal rib to establish the wood module for the infill elements; the Electra House uses the standard bay of the plywood panel to establish the module of the street façade; and Office dA's New England House uses the segmented repetition of the siding unit to allow for figural flexibility.

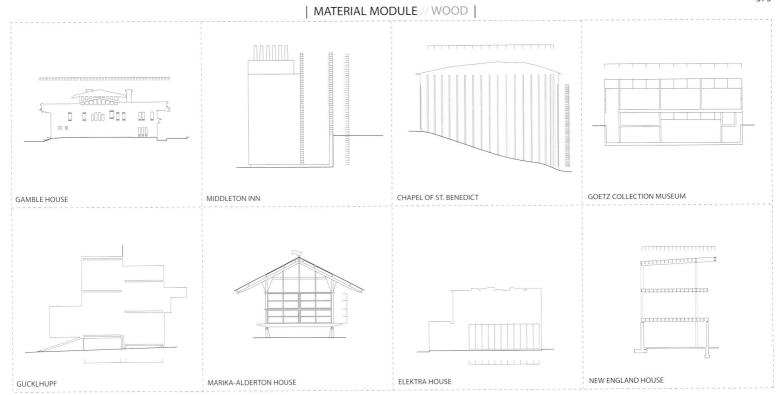

GAMBLE HOUSE

MIDDLETON INN

CHAPEL OF ST. BENEDICT

GOETZ COLLECTION MUSEUM

GUCKLHUPF

MARIKA-ALDERTON HOUSE

ELEKTRA HOUSE

NEW ENGLAND HOUSE

[WOOD] Module – MATERIAL MODULE diagrams in section the relationships of the manufacturing module intrinsic to a material to the space, form, and dimensions. Mapping the inherited dimensional constraints determined by the production and movement of a material to the sectional implications, the patterning of these scale elements and the articulation of their joinery establish larger architectural spaces derived from addressing the relationship of piece to whole and unit to system.

The module of material is an intrinsic fact that must be addressed. Certain materials default to a secondary system [such as concrete with formwork] to generate a dimensional constraint, but every material has a "natural" form and dimension. The negotiation of these constraints and the collaboration with these numeric proportions determine the dimensions of the whole and the integration of the modular unit into the consistency of the superstructural organization. In section, the implications of the human hand of construction relative to the material coursing relative to the body's perception develop the scale and legibility of this module to the spatial presence as a whole.

The Gamble House is a building responsively designed on site by a master craftsman creating a locally adjusted structure that evolves within itself; the Middleton Inn works with the concrete block coursing but then eliminates its legibility with a slave coat topping, while the wood reveals itself through the horizontal siding and banded shutter fields behind the glass windows of the hotel rooms; the Chapel of St. Benedict uses the module of the shingle on the exterior and the module of the structural stick on the interior; the Goetz Collection sets a submodule of wood panels that is geometrically organizing but ambiguous and indiscernible on the interior due the white erasure of detail and expression; the Gucklhupf staggers the interior floor plates despite the standardized exterior panels; the Marika-Alderton House uses the frame as the base geometry and then subdivides the wooden infill with a repetitive four by three square grid module of variable infill; the Electra House reveals the material module on the interior through the exposed wood columns within the windows; and Office dA's New England House masks the material figuration of the exterior, providing a varied yet complementary experience within.

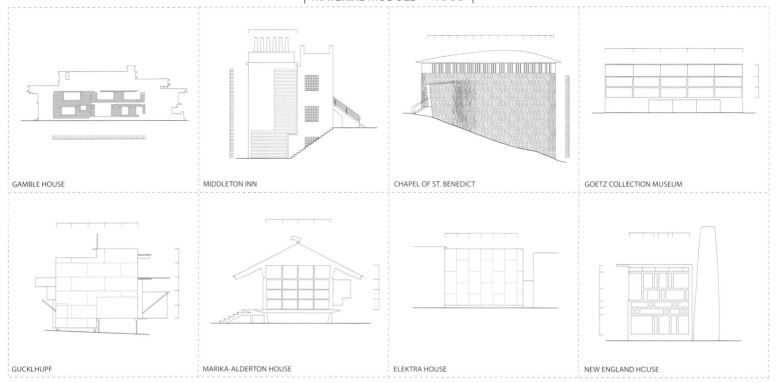

GAMBLE HOUSE

MIDDLETON INN

CHAPEL OF ST. BENEDICT

GOETZ COLLECTION MUSEUM

GUCKLHUPF

MARIKA-ALDERTON HOUSE

ELEKTRA HOUSE

NEW ENGLAND HOUSE

[WOOD] Module – MATERIAL MODULE diagrams in elevation the implications of the relationships of the manufacturing module intrinsic to a material to the space, form, and dimensions. Mapping the inherited dimensional constraints determined by the production and movement of a material to the façade, the formal legibility and implications of an architectural patterning of these scale elements rely upon the articulation of their joinery to establish larger architectural spaces.

The surface reading is derived from addressing the relationship of piece to whole and unit to system through the intrinsic module of a material. Certain materials default to a secondary system [such as concrete with formwork] to generate a dimensional constraint, but every material has a "natural" form and dimension. The negotiation of these constraints and the collaboration with these numeric proportions determine the dimensions of the whole and the integration of the modular unit into the consistency of the superstructural organization. In elevation, the implications of the human hand of construction relative to the material assemblies relative to the body's perception develop the scale and legibility of this module and its spatial presence as a whole.

The Gamble House is a building responsively designed on site by a master craftsman creating a locally adjusted structure that evolves within itself; the Middleton Inn works with the concrete block coursing but then eliminates its legibility with a slave coat topping, while the wood reveals itself through the horizontal siding [graphically illustrating the floor plates on the façade] and banded shutter fields behind the glass of the hotel rooms; the Chapel of St. Benedict uses the module of the repetitive shingle to create a delicate grain to the exterior skin; the Goetz Collection sets a submodule of wood panels that carry through the glass bands to produce a repetitive modular geometry across materials providing a simultaneous ambiguity to the material and scale alike; the Gucklhupf uses the panelized skin to establish the pattern against which the variable operability occurs; the Marika-Alderton House uses the frame as the base geometry and then subdivides the wooden infill with a repetitive four by three square module grid of variable infill; the Electra House uniformly blankets the façade with a quiet scaled pattern derivative of the wood panel; and Office dA's New England House segments the façade to produce a composed but effectual experience of the skin and material.

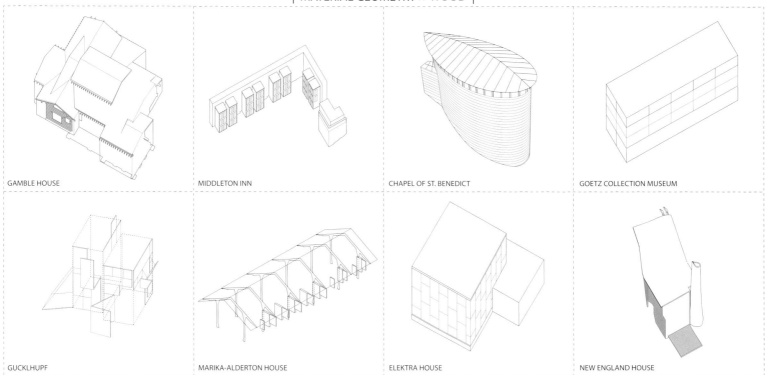

GAMBLE HOUSE

MIDDLETON INN

CHAPEL OF ST. BENEDICT

GOETZ COLLECTION MUSEUM

GUCKLHUPF

MARIKA-ALDERTON HOUSE

ELEKTRA HOUSE

NEW ENGLAND HOUSE

[WOOD] Module – MATERIAL GEOMETRY diagrams in axonometric the three-dimensional relationships of the manufacturing module intrinsic to a material to the space, form, and dimensions. Mapping the inherited dimensional constraints determined by the production and movement of a material into the three-dimensional ramifications of the total form, the legibility of an architectural patterning of scale elements relies upon the articulation of their joinery to establish larger architectural spaces.

The surface reading is derived from addressing the relationship of piece to whole and unit to system through the intrinsic module of a material. Certain materials default to a secondary system [such as concrete with formwork] to generate a dimensional constraint, but every material has a "natural" form and dimension. The negotiation of these constraints and the collaboration with these numeric proportions determine the dimensions of the whole and the integration of the modular unit into the consistency of the superstructural organization. In axonometric, the module governs the formal legibility of the three-dimensional building component and ultimately the formal reading of the building as a whole.

The Gamble House responds to the flexibility of hand-worked wood, reacting in detail and configuration to the localized expression and necessity of its use; the Middleton Inn masses the banded, black-painted wood against the smooth gray slave coat of the stucco-surfaced masonry to create contrasting juxtaposition of form; the Chapel of St. Benedict creates a unique form through the small-scale segmentation and then emphasizes the figure through the removal of variability in favor of the repetitive expression of serial pieces; the Goetz Collection sets a submodule of wood panels that carries through the glass bands to produce a repetitive modular geometry across materials, providing simultaneous ambiguity to the material and scale alike; the Gucklhupf wraps its surfaces in the standardized figure of the plywood panels juxtaposed with the composed and divergently operable apertures; the Marika-Alderton House uses the frame as the base geometry and then subdivides the wooden infill with a repetitive, quartered module for variable infill; the Electra House establishes a quiet hierarchy to the interior through the solemn blankness of the exterior; and Office dA's New England House emphasizes the localized experience through the deformed and responsive form of the whole.

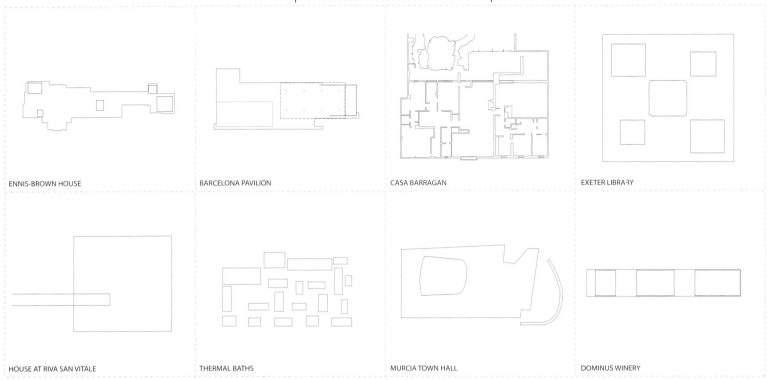

ENNIS-BROWN HOUSE

BARCELONA PAVILION

CASA BARRAGAN

EXETER LIBRARY

HOUSE AT RIVA SAN VITALE

THERMAL BATHS

MURCIA TOWN HALL

DOMINUS WINERY

[MASONRY] MATERIAL FUNCTION diagrams in plan the relationship between material use and the formal and technical associations required by its functional application. These diagrams examine the role of a material's specific performance properties and its employment relative to the functional and practical necessities of the program and building performance. Each material expresses the conditions and requirements of its deployment.

Defining the premise of skin in each application, material serves as the iconic designation of form in each project. The associated material tectonic employed extends its influence to express itself through the spatial concepts of the architecture. Steel defines vertical lines [Eames House and Niaux Cave], concrete defines planes and frames with variable openings [Lovell Beach House, La Tourette, Church on the Water], and masonry creates modulated solid edges [Casa Barragan and Murcia Town Hall]. Glass establishes transparent veils: flat, ambiguous surfaces that exist but slip into a nonpresence allowing the dissolve of the enclosure and a perceived spatial connection between inside and outside. This is most prevalent in the De Blas Haus and the Cartier Foundation, though it exists even when the glass is frosted and figured, as in the glass block façade of the Maison de Verre. Each material relative to its function determines form.

In each case study, regardless of material, the cloak of the primary material is the defining figure of the primary form: in Frank Lloyd Wright's Ennis-Brown House, by the repetitive aggregation of the textile blocks; in the Barcelona Pavilion by the travertine plinth and the sliding marble walls; in the Casa Barragan by the mass of the walls and the weight of its form; in the Exeter Library by the dimension of the clay masonry brick and its slow removal as the structural need tapers in elevation; in the House at Riva San Vitale by Botta's relentless respect of the module of the masonry unit founding his proportional system and form on its intrinsic qualities; in the Thermal Baths at Vals with the horizontal thinness of the layered stone; in the Murcia Town Hall by the modular pattern of the masonry emerging from a reinterpretation of context; and in the Dominus Winery by the stacked gabions that hold the variably dimensioned rock.

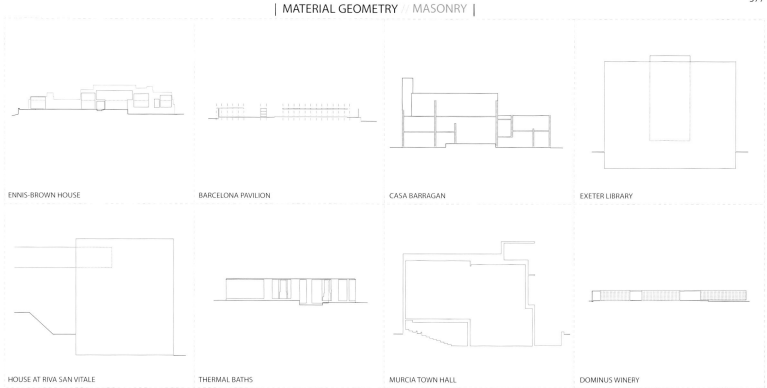

ENNIS-BROWN HOUSE

BARCELONA PAVILION

CASA BARRAGAN

EXETER LIBRARY

HOUSE AT RIVA SAN VITALE

THERMAL BATHS

MURCIA TOWN HALL

DOMINUS WINERY

[MASONRY] MATERIAL GEOMETRY diagrams the sectional geometric implications of material for form. By introducing the potential structural implications of a material, the relationship of "skin to bones" or surface to structure becomes relative to the intrinsic qualities of a material. Establishing the dimensional module [both of performance and of fabrication and installation limitations], the capabilities of a material express themselves beyond the figure of the form to address the geometry of the space.

The module of a material can be established by three potential scales. The first scale is the module of the unit: a single brick, a sheet of plywood [as direct application of sheathing or as indirect application of formwork], a glass pane with either concealed or revealed frame systems, or a steel member. In each of these conditions, the unit is defined by a structural need, a material property, or a manufacturing module. The second scale is the bay of the module produced through the assemblies or structure. For example, the Eames House window wall module is an aggregate of the individual panes, the double high bay module, and the superstructural steel frame. The final scale is the designed geometry of the building's mass expressed through material, i.e., the formal figure of the object as a whole. Each of these three levels can coexist or be independently exploited. The material in each case is, however, the beginning, the dimensional collaborator based on the intrinsic properties and performance of the base material.

The Ennis-Brown House uses the massiveness of the concrete masonry textile blocks to emerge out of the steep hillside topography and establish both the base and the eruptions of the primary figures of the building; the Barcelona Pavilion uses the travertine tile of the base to establish a repetitive grid field and spatial mat across which elements slide and shift, while the wall panels use the ornamental veining of the natural marble and pattern it through book-matched panels to create a centrally symmetrical composition; the Casa Barragan uses the structural limits of masonry as a vertical planar system to resolve gravity loads; the Exeter Library establishes the dense perimeter of the masonry exterior, with reading carrels and book stacks around the inner void of the concrete atrium; the House at Riva San Vitale uses the module of a brick to establish the skin, cutting away to reveal the frame and its relationship to the surface; the Thermal Baths at Vals use the stone-clad concrete masts as umbrella structures that hover to embrace and define the pools below; the Murcia Town Hall extends the horizontal coursing of the exterior masonry through the building to establish the geometry of the floor plates; and the Dominus Winery establishes an open-closed rhythm between the solid exterior plane shielding the internalized spaces and the open transfer points for functional and compositional access.

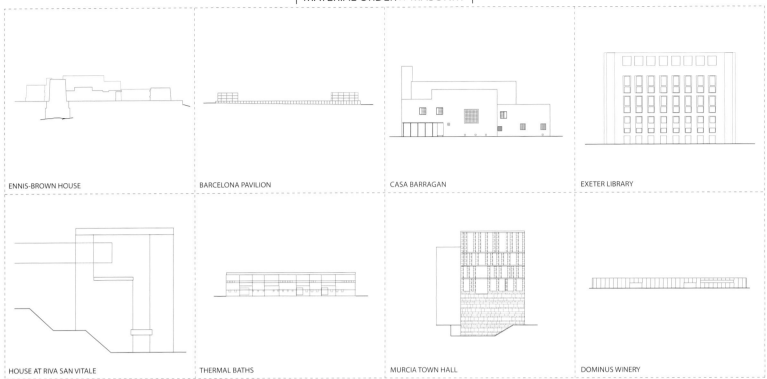

ENNIS-BROWN HOUSE

BARCELONA PAVILION

CASA BARRAGAN

EXETER LIBRARY

HOUSE AT RIVA SAN VITALE

THERMAL BATHS

MURCIA TOWN HALL

DOMINUS WINERY

[MASONRY] MATERIAL ORDER diagrams in elevation the hierarchy, sequence, and organizational methods of material's influence on the architectural form. As in the examination in section, the implication here is more spatial than formal. Looking at the organizational geometries and governing patterns of material relative to the form, the implications and legibility of volume and mass are articulated through the aggregation of the material pieces.

The extension of the material module into the overarching order of the formal expression is the ultimate collaboration of material with design. The definition of the overall form relative to the piece, the manner in which an aperture is made as a removal [in terms of both module and structural implications], and the relation of these compositional pieces to the formal whole are the defining characteristics of a material's influence on form.

The Ennis-Brown House has tapering pylon forms that step in height to establish scale and hierarchy; the Barcelona Pavilion brackets the elevated plinth with perimeter U walls; the Casa Barragan has repetitive orthogonal openings that correspond with the coursing of the modularity intrinsic to masonry; the Exeter Library has increasingly dimensioned openings and decreasing wall as the building's elevation ascends; the House at Riva San Vitale breaks the façade with horizontal lines expressing the floor plates as lintels and revealing the figure of the cross section pulled through the façade; the Thermal Baths at Vals have a repetitive open-closed façade delicately striated by the material scale; the Murcia Town Hall uses the horizontals of the floor plates to establish the primary sectional rhythm and then deploys variable verticals to compose the remaining infill transitioning from an opaque base to the dissolved columnar frames of the upper levels; and the Dominus Winery has two segmental dimensions: one based upon the repetitive bay of the gabion wall, the other upon the superstructural openings for functional purposes.

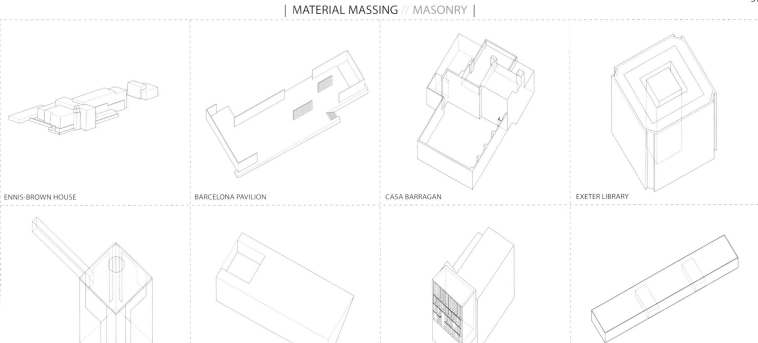

ENNIS-BROWN HOUSE

BARCELONA PAVILION

CASA BARRAGAN

EXETER LIBRARY

HOUSE AT RIVA SAN VITALE

THERMAL BATHS

MURCIA TOWN HALL

DOMINUS WINERY

[MASONRY] MATERIAL MASSING diagrams in axonometric the overall legibility of the primary material to the superstructural form, presence, and mass of the architectural form. Focusing primarily on the mass and volume of form as defined by the material application to the exterior, the legibility of compositional intention and the geometric hierarchy are mapped.

The significance of mass [as defined by material in particular] concerns the clarity of formal intention in relation to the actual legibility and reading in the building. The conceptual ideas that govern the design of a building become legible through their tectonic manifestations in the form. The hierarchy of the primary massing determines the figuration to which all else must respond. The material relationship with this massing and the deployment of the tectonic expression of the assembly determine whether a material is read as segmented, disassociated, panelized, repetitive, or monolithic.

The Ennis-Brown House expresses the weight of the material and the massive connection to the Los Angeles hillside site; the Barcelona Pavilion uses bracket walls of travertine to produce a framed space that allows the jeweled sliding and free-floating figure walls of marble to read as objects disrupting the field of space to form the specifics of the composition and sequence; the Casa Barragan deploys the masonry to define the mass and weight of the building, creating composed courtyards [at various levels] that extend into the landscape despite being within the dense fabric of Mexico City; the Exeter Library expresses the mass of the building while simultaneously accentuating the planar skin of the four masonry perimeter walls; the House at Riva San Vitale emphasizes the square of its plan as an extruded surface cut away to reveal the interior; the Thermal Baths at Vals set the massive concrete and stone form building into and under the hillside. The material and form express the massive weight of both the surrounding earth it buttresses against and the water that it holds inside; the Murcia Town Hall, clad in masonry, extends the fabric of the city with the back volume and adjusts the front piece in both form and orientation to address the adjacent buildings of the town square; and the Dominus Winery sits as a simple volume in its natural surroundings, deriving its articulation from the variable patterns of the gabion cages, rock dimensions, and irregular fragments of the stone itself.

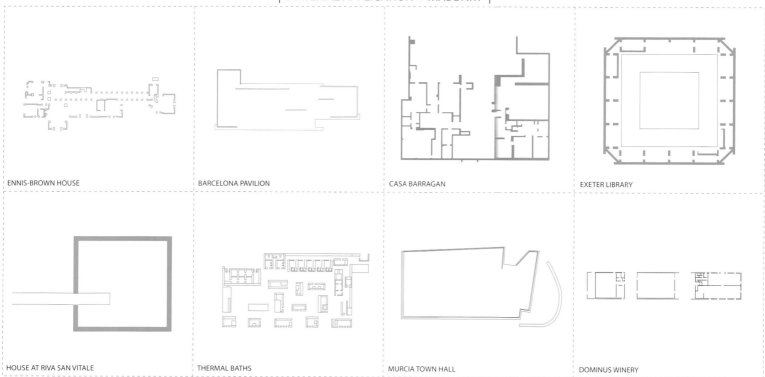

ENNIS-BROWN HOUSE   BARCELONA PAVILION   CASA BARRAGAN   EXETER LIBRARY

HOUSE AT RIVA SAN VITALE   THERMAL BATHS   MURCIA TOWN HALL   DOMINUS WINERY

[MASONRY] MATERIAL APPLICATION diagrams in plan the deployment of material and the associated perceptual, formal, and functional readings. Engaging the relationship between material and function, the formal expression becomes the primary mediating element. The expression of the material's use and the tectonic deployment determine the functional programmatic legibility of the building. This begins with the formal expression intrinsic to the material followed by issues of practical performance, including durability, porosity, and visual effect.

A material can be selected for various reasons: availability, cost, durability, module, structural capability, or simply functional applicability [metal to combat combustion, concrete for construction in corrosive environments, or masonry as a low-maintenance, durable skin]. In each scenario the fundamental physical properties of the material are the baseline of design consideration. These properties, mediated by the method of manufacturing and limited by the method of working [wood is easy to cut, metal can be welded, masonry is heavy and modular], develop the second tier of consideration. Finally, and perhaps with the most variability, is the assembly and application. The systemization of the manufactured pieces and their formal and technical articulation comprise material design application.

The Ennis-Brown House uses the concrete textile block for nearly everything: as flooring, interior wall finish, exterior finish, ornament, and enclosure alike, the system was deployed to [and perhaps beyond] its capabilities; the Barcelona Pavilion selects jewel-like masonry of the travertine base and marble walls to illustrate a regality through the natural ornamentation despite the reductive forms; the Casa Barragan deploys massive masonry walls [expressing the weight and solidity of the material for privacy and security] indigenous to the city as the typical vernacular construction, using the thickness of the opaque walls to contrast with the transparency of the glass walls; the Exeter Library rings the building with the planar exterior walls of masonry set against the perpendicular repetitive fin walls. These two systems establish the outer identity, while concrete is deployed for the inner volume of the central atrium; the House at Riva San Vitale deploys masonry as the modular skin establishing the form and the geometric purity of the perimeter enclosure as the defining module of the entire house; the Thermal Baths at Vals deploy stone as a liner for the concrete piers that define the field of interiors and the tower segments that define the pools and segment the volume of the building; the Murcia Town Hall wraps the perimeter of the concrete structural frame in masonry to give a load-bearing wall an appearance typical of the adjacent city fabric while deploying the coursing to create the articulation and systemization of the formal identity; and the Dominus Winery applies the stone gabions as a perimeter veil, unifying the diversely segmented program behind it.

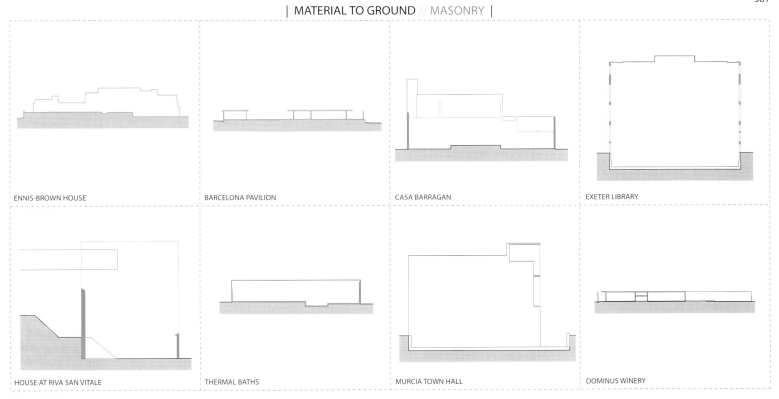

ENNIS-BROWN HOUSE

BARCELONA PAVILION

CASA BARRAGAN

EXETER LIBRARY

HOUSE AT RIVA SAN VITALE

THERMAL BATHS

MURCIA TOWN HALL

DOMINUS WINERY

[MASONRY] Proximity – MATERIAL TO GROUND diagrams the sectional relationship in which a building meets the ground, engages landscape, and addresses the material point of connection with the site. The point of contact between a building and the earth is determined by the material approach to the architecture. Factors that determine and affect this condition include soil characteristics, climate, context, structural system, and building weight [both actual and perceived].

The history of structural and material technology is the history of how a building meets the ground. The selection of material cladding and structural framing results in a specific formal articulation of this condition that is intrinsic to the material and tectonic. Technologically determined, this joint [between building and ground] is created by the system of both the structure and the cladding. Historically, load-bearing wall systems of wood or masonry required continuous contact of the building with the ground and limited the scale and frequency of openings. Materials such as steel and concrete allowed for a formal disengagement from the ground plane, turning structural planes into points and shifting from a wall system to a cage.

The Ennis-Brown House steps into the landscape by both engaging and emerging from it; the Barcelona Pavilion establishes a massive plinth of travertine as a podium for the abstract composition of the pavilion itself to operate on, the tacit disengagement from the natural ground plane and the expressive ascension to this geometrically pure ground plane establishing a new framework for the understanding of and engagement with the building; the Casa Barragan connects the weight of the masonry walls to the earth with authority, allowing for lateral connections to blur the boundary between outside and inside; the Exeter Library sets on the ground, allowing the openings in the wall to form a colonnade, as well as imply the submersion of the punctured aperture plane of the façade below grade; the House at Riva San Vitale sets the weight of the masonry at the base of the hill, disengaging from the sloping hillside and bridging as a formal expression between the hill and the masonry tower with a delicate steel truss bridge [the primary entry]; the Thermal Baths at Vals use the stone to engage the ground plane and emphasize the articulation and significance of the ground plane's relationship to the pools. The varied terracing and depths establish the physical and spatial qualities of the aquatic chambers; the Murcia Town Hall folds the perimeter of the masonry into the plaza façade to create a perceived exaggerated slippage of the front masonry surface into the ground, drawing the entry into an antechamber of a sunken exterior courtyard before actually penetrating the front façade; and the Dominus Winery sets on the ground plane, expressing the sacred quality of the vegetative landscape.

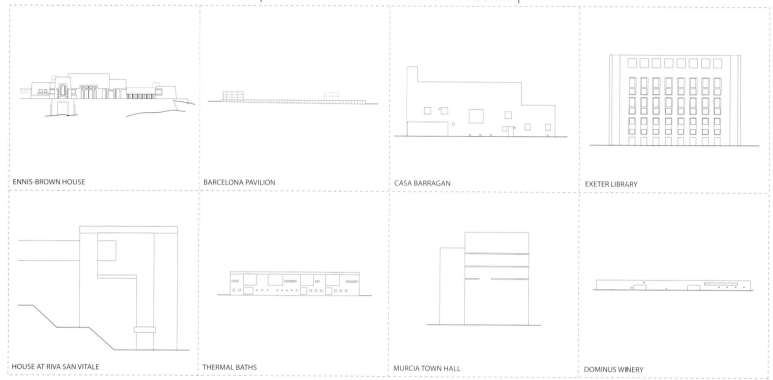

ENNIS-BROWN HOUSE

BARCELONA PAVILION

CASA BARRAGAN

EXETER LIBRARY

HOUSE AT RIVA SAN VITALE

THERMAL BATHS

MURCIA TOWN HALL

DOMINUS WINERY

[MASONRY] Proximity – PRIMARY / SECONDARY diagrams in elevation the relationship of the primary building material to the secondary building material, focusing on the formal, functional, and practical interrelationships of their material application. The hierarchy between these two levels is both formally and materially evident, establishing the organizing geometries of the diverse layers.

The proximity of a primary figure to a secondary figure builds on the formal reading of material application diagrams but engages the interrelationship with the secondary systemization. The interaction of the two can occur through superimposition, contrasting figures, interpenetration, banding, layering, or any other adverbial relationship. The result is a primary figuration and the secondary subsystemization that, through its geometry, breaks down the material into fabricateable and installable pieces and reveals the tectonic intention of their aggregation.

The Ennis-Brown House deploys its devotion to the concrete textile block relentlessly, allowing wood and glass only as an absolute necessity to complement. The transparency of the voids as subtractions in the masonry form allow the massiveness of the wall to break down and allow for the connection between the interior and exterior; the Barcelona Pavilion has primary figuration in the masonry of the plinth and bracket walls against the secondary "jewel" marble walls. Within each of these materially variable systems, the subdivisions [the repetitive modules of the stone panels] establish variable geometries: a grid for the neutral ground and framing walls and a biaxial symmetry for the marble walls that objectifies them with a central axis viewpoint that transitions them from mere partitions into objectified compositions, almost as paintings or sculptures set into the space; the Casa Barragan, with its stucco-clad masonry, denies the unit of the material to emphasize the monolithic nature of its overarching form, engaging the secondary system as the removal of the wall, the apertures that are read through the homogeneity of material expression as pure composed geometry; the Exeter Library uses the wood and glass insets of the study carrels threaded into the regimented openings of the masonry façades to allow for the individuation of light and ventilation and introduce a human scale to the abstracted massiveness of the overall architectural figure; the House at Riva San Vitale sets the field of the masonry as a perimeter surface that is cut and removed to reveal the horizontal bands of the lintel/caps of the horizontal floor plates and the piercing trussed metal entry bridge; the Thermal Baths at Vals set the delicacy of the horizontal stone figure against the datum of a concrete cap that reestablishes the datum of the ground plane and holds the planted roofscape; the Murcia Town Hall has two primary masses, each clad in masonry subdividing the primary plaza faced with the horizontal banding of the concrete floor plates; and the Dominus Winery uses glass to compose the transparent voids in the façade.

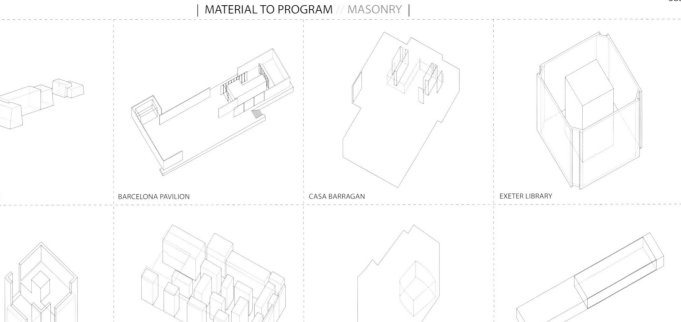

ENNIS-BROWN HOUSE

BARCELONA PAVILION

CASA BARRAGAN

EXETER LIBRARY

HOUSE AT RIVA SAN VITALE

THERMAL BATHS

MURCIA TOWN HALL

DOMINUS WINERY

[MASONRY] Proximity – MATERIAL TO PROGRAM diagrams in axonometric the overall relationship of material usage to the primary programmatic and functional usages. By focusing on the three-dimensional volumetric associations of material to programmatic usage [and the associated functional requirements of a particular program], the articulation of "form following function" can be examined through material association.

The relationship of the programmatic usage to the material selected depicts the narrative of the association, creating the opportunity and potential for material to be an expressive sign system. The legibility of a material comes from a technical knowledge that engages an understanding of raw material, manufacturing processes, construction traditions and techniques, weathering and biological attack, and cultural associations. These innate properties of matter translate into forms that collaborate with materials to reveal their process.

The Ennis-Brown House sets up the primary pavilion volumes of the form as the primary programmatic components; the Barcelona Pavilion separates the two spaces of service and served, adorning them with a hierarchy through the quality of masonry privileging the main pavilion with marble, while the secondary pavilion brings the travertine of the horizontal surface to the vertical walls; the Casa Barragan uses subtractive courtyards to break down the mass and homogeneity of the masonry; the Exeter Library establishes a planar perimeter with a void as a volumetric center allowing the stacks to exist between the two figures; the House at Riva San Vitale has subvolumes pinwheeling around a central core but carefully contained within the purity of the outer form; the Thermal Baths at Vals generate a series of pavilion-like volumes that define the intimately scaled and service-related programs; the Murcia Town Hall has a masonry envelope over a concrete substructure with a wooden theater lodged in the belly; and the Dominus Winery establishes a single box within a box diagram juxtaposing the office components against the processing functions.

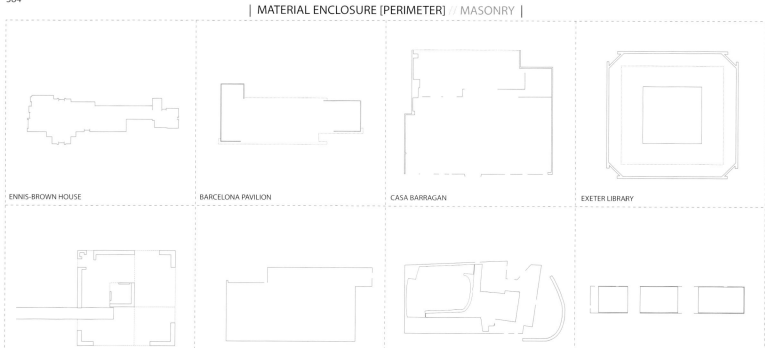

ENNIS-BROWN HOUSE

BARCELONA PAVILION

CASA BARRAGAN

EXETER LIBRARY

HOUSE AT RIVA SAN VITALE

THERMAL BATHS

MURCIA TOWN HALL

DOMINUS WINERY

[MASONRY] Skin + Surface – MATERIAL ENCLOSURE [PERIMETER] diagrams in plan the relationship of the outer plane of enclosure [skin] to the spatial, formal, and structural organization. Expressing the process by which materials assemble into systems, the figuration of the perimeter is dependent not simply upon the piece but also upon the joint. The collaboration of these two generates specific forms intrinsic to a material and expressively identifiable.

The use of skin to define the perimeter of the structure and the programmatic innards establishes the legibility of architectural idea's purity through the articulation of edge and boundary. The continuity and complexity of this envelope widely explicate the material articulation and the tectonic intricacy. The relationship of craft to figure is found in the method of material manipulation.

The Ennis-Brown House uses the double-wythe concrete textile block system to create the perimeter. It is made porous through the formal disintegration of the colonnade and the framed openings central to the façade of each volumetric piece; the Barcelona Pavilion uses two travertine-clad U-shaped bracketing walls to crop and frame the pavilion; the Casa Barragan defines a perimeter carved out of the city fabric; the Exeter Library uses a planar reading to the clay masonry at the skin while reestablishing a different vocabulary for the interior circulation cores and central atrium; the House at Riva San Vitale establishes a rigid figure with the square masonry footprint pierced by the metal entry bridge; the Thermal Baths at Vals create a series of interior perimeters that allow the boundary of interior and exterior to become vague and thread the spatial continuity from inside to outside; the Murcia Town Hall has a masonry figure defined as an extension of the city fabric and adjacent monuments juxtaposed against a wood-lined figure of the primary public spaces; and the Dominus Winery deploys the gabions as a skin perimeter with a secondary series of glass skins inside that locally produce the climatic separation.

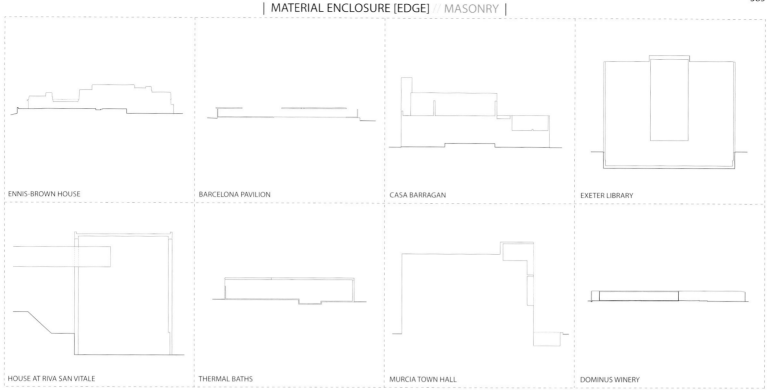

ENNIS-BROWN HOUSE

BARCELONA PAVILION

CASA BARRAGAN

EXETER LIBRARY

HOUSE AT RIVA SAN VITALE

THERMAL BATHS

MURCIA TOWN HALL

DOMINUS WINERY

[MASONRY] Skin + Surface – MATERIAL ENCLOSURE [EDGE] diagrams in section the relationship of the outer plane of enclosure [skin] to the spatial, formal, and structural organization. Expressing the process by which materials assemble into systems, the figuration of the perimeter as expressed through section extends the moves of plan in the Y axis [still dependent not simply upon the piece but also upon the joint].

The collaboration of piece with joint determines the sectional spatial forms intrinsic to a material, resulting in expressive and identifiable associations. The role of skin in section similarly works to define the perimeter over the structure and the interior functions. The figure establishes the legibility of an architectural idea's purity through the articulation of edge and boundary as extended into the vertical and thus the now spatial dimension. The continuity and complexity of this line widely explicate the material articulation and the tectonic intricacy. The relationship of exterior material through the surface of the building to impact and define interior space is moderated by the material manipulation of this edge.

The Ennis-Brown House uses the massiveness of the wall construction system to define simultaneously the interior and exterior finished wall systems. The overall massing of the weighty volumes of the individual pieces is amplified by their tapered wall section buttressing against the interior spaces; the Barcelona Pavilion uses the end walls to bracket, crop, and frame the pavilion, allowing a floating yet extended canopy to slide across the top, producing movement through a dynamic, visually framing plane; the Casa Barragan defines a perimeter carved out of the city fabric with courtyards in back and on the roof; the Exeter Library layers the space, from the thin perimeter of the load-bearing masonry exterior wall through the sequential layers of programmatic and material spaces behind; the House at Riva San Vitale establishes a rigid figure with the masonry pierced by the metal entry bridge; the Thermal Baths at Vals invert the typical relationship of building from wall to roof and develop the ground plane to wall connection with the roof suspended as delicate plates in a distinctly different material; the Murcia Town Hall has a masonry enveloping figure defined by the city fabric and adjacent monuments juxtaposed against the regimented pancake floor slabs that negotiate at their edge with the primary public façade; and the Dominus Winery uses the skin as a material veil that modulates light and establishes the exterior figuration, but it is independent of the plane of enclosure and the interior methods of spatial subdivision.

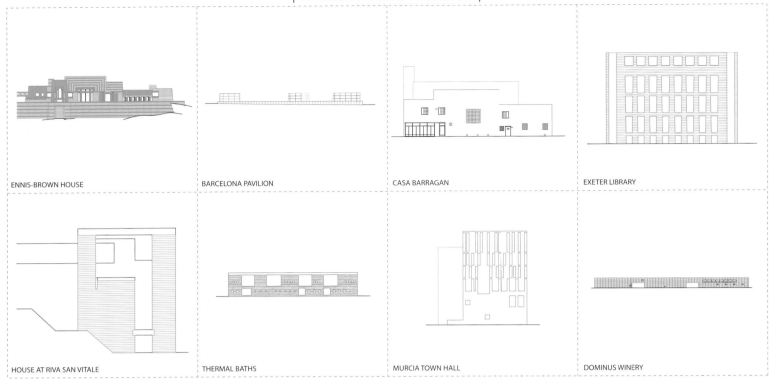

ENNIS-BROWN HOUSE

BARCELONA PAVILION

CASA BARRAGAN

EXETER LIBRARY

HOUSE AT RIVA SAN VITALE

THERMAL BATHS

MURCIA TOWN HALL

DOMINUS WINERY

[MASONRY] Skin + Surface – MATERIAL TEXTURE diagrams in elevation the legibility of the material texture, color, and surface. Defining the compositional aesthetics of the elevation, the collagist sensibility of pattern, texture, color, and depth of plane are all legible against light. Like a composed painting, this image is dissected from the visual perceptual stance of the material on the architectural composition.

The textural reading refers to the actual color and composition of the material. Wood, for example, can be classified as a generic type, but the performance qualities, colors, hardness, resistance to rot, durability, and workability are vastly different from species to species. This same textural legibility comes through the assembly and expression of the unit and the joint. The scale and articulation of these connections define the legibility of the collective material reading and the overall compositional reading of the architecture.

The Ennis-Brown House uses the unit of the concrete textile block masonry to develop the grid patterning of the façade. Within this system, there is further variation within the block type to provide ornamental figuration that highlights, accentuates, and prioritizes the surface; the Barcelona Pavilion relies upon the texture of the material and the grid of the panel systems [and, in particular, the extension of the walls ending on a nongrid line to emphasize movement]; the Casa Barragan has composed window punches positioned like canvases hung on the monolithic blank walls to compositionally engage the exterior, but more importantly, to light and define the interior; the Exeter Library is rationally unitized, employing full clay masonry units as a horizontal texture and shallow jack arches over the opening to illustrate the wall as a load-bearing structural component; the House at Riva San Vitale establishes the regularity and purity of the outer skin based on the module of the masonry unit, and then composes a removal that emphasizes the corner and the cap; the Thermal Baths at Vals create a monolithic reading of the material despite its highly striated and unitized construction through the thinness of the coursing and the emphasis of the horizontal joints; the Murcia Town Hall creates variable header courses to emphasize the consistency of the bed joints and produce a horizontal banding to the façade that is emphasized further by the expression of the concrete floor plates; and the Dominus Winery juxtaposes the irregular geometry of the loose rock with the regimented geometry of the metal cages. The further patterning, by varying the aggregate size from gabion to gabion, allows for a manipulation of visual densities.

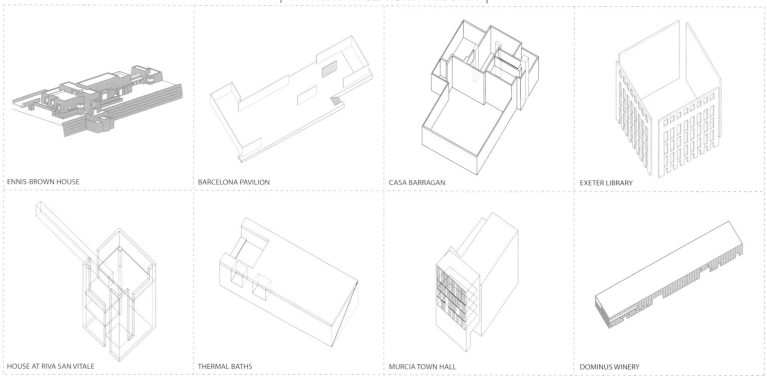

ENNIS-BROWN HOUSE

BARCELONA PAVILION

CASA BARRAGAN

EXETER LIBRARY

HOUSE AT RIVA SAN VITALE

THERMAL BATHS

MURCIA TOWN HALL

DOMINUS WINERY

[MASONRY] Skin + Surface – MATERIAL PERCEPTION diagrams in axonometric the primary reading of material experience. By transitioning from the sectional reading that focuses on the two-dimensional interior spatial conditions or the material application, the reading in elevation speaks to the composition of the façade but, again, within the shallow space of a two-dimensional reading, while the axonometric examination illustrates the compositional legibility of the building as a total object.

By engaging all three dimensions, the figuration of the architecture and the legibility of a material's perception relative to the total object lend a volumetric legibility to a material's perception. A truly monolithic architecture is nearly impossible; thus, the connection and change from one piece to the next define the moment of intervention and design decision. The perception of the whole after the resolution of these local "events" is the perception of the architecture. Focusing specifically on the material impact upon these decisions allows the design intention to be revealed by the tectonic view of the whole through the piece.

The Ennis-Brown House uses the primary massing to articulate the programmatic components and develop a sequence and hierarchy among the pieces, while the secondary concrete textile block detail provides a level of ornamentation and further accentuates the programmatic use and hierarchy; the Barcelona Pavilion establishes a hierarchy of the primary base and frame of travertine [white and recessive] against the object-like marble walls, with all else disappearing [highly reflective chromed columns, thin mullioned glass walls, light floating roof canopies, reflective pools drawing the sky down, etc.]; the Casa Barragan has the mass of the masonry to define the body, allowing the intricacies of the additions and subtractions to produce the quietness of the space; the Exeter Library accentuates the planar nature of the masonry skin and the simultaneous formal and structural capabilities of the clay masonry unit; the House at Riva San Vitale uses masonry to establish the purity of the form and then subdivide the space functionally and compositionally to produce variable floor plates within the homogeneous geometry; the Thermal Baths at Vals emphasize the mass and solidity of the whole from the exterior while providing a distinctly segmented and aerosolized interior; the Murcia Town Hall extends and caps the city fabric with a timelessly simple yet sophisticated banding; and the Dominus Winery uses the wrapper of the skin to create a unity of form that corrals the diverse functional programs and scales within.

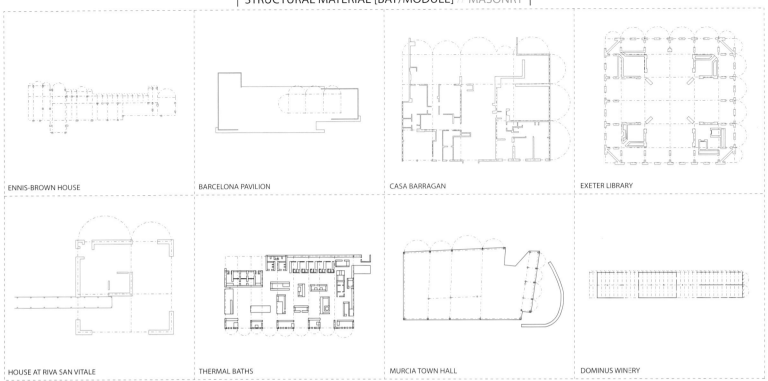

ENNIS-BROWN HOUSE   BARCELONA PAVILION   CASA BARRAGAN   EXETER LIBRARY

HOUSE AT RIVA SAN VITALE   THERMAL BATHS   MURCIA TOWN HALL   DOMINUS WINERY

[MASONRY] STRUCTURAL MATERIAL [BAY/MODULE] diagrams in plan the structural module of the building. Focusing on the influence of the structural material, it illustrates the engineered structural response of material relative to performative need. Dependent upon the dimension of span relative to the spatial capabilities of the material, an organizing geometry is established that sets the scale and legibility of a space.

The role of structure in plan is of particular formal importance relative to material as the premise of line [load-bearing walls] versus point [columns]. Each system establishes a certain way of making space. Load-bearing materials verse cladding materials are revealed, and their variation and interdependence are highlighted.

The Ennis-Brown House uses a repetitive horizontal module along the contour lines of the hillside. Its variable dimension responds to the scale and hierarchy of the programmatic and volumetric components; the Barcelona Pavilion establishes a regular grid with the columns [which shift off the grid of the paving], interior walls, and planes of enclosure; the Casa Barragan sets up regular lines for the load-bearing masonry walls with relatively close spacing to allow for short horizontal spans in wood; the Exeter Library uses a 16-square module with a two-thirds perimeter volume that corresponds between the brick outer layer and the concrete inner layer; the House at Riva San Vitale establishes a load-bearing masonry perimeter with select voids that allow the lateral transfer of forces through the connecting floor plates; the Thermal Baths at Vals use a minor-major oscillating open-closed patterning to create a locally tailored dimension within a rigorously composed rhythm; the Murcia Town Hall has a cast-in-place substructure that is primarily regulated to the walls to parallel and emphasize the depiction of the masonry as a structural system; and the Dominus Winery uses a blanket equal bay that corresponds to a multiple of the gabion dimension. The regulated field allows the diversity of composition to defer to the material and skin.

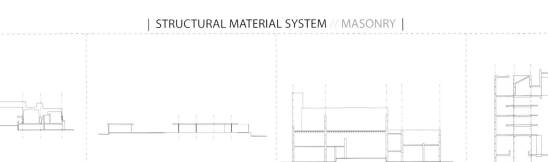

ENNIS-BROWN HOUSE   BARCELONA PAVILION   CASA BARRAGAN   EXETER LIBRARY

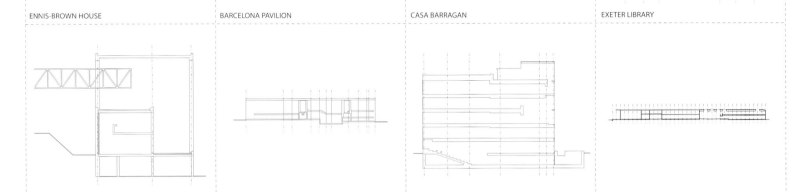

HOUSE AT RIVA SAN VITALE   THERMAL BATHS   MURCIA TOWN HALL   DOMINUS WINERY

[MASONRY] STRUCTURAL MATERIAL [BAY/MODULE] diagrams the sectional implications of the structural module. Focusing on the influence of the structural material, it illustrates the engineered structural response of material relative to performative need. In this diagram set, the structure is materially examined in its vertical figuration of the sectional articulation.

Building on the bay system of the plan, the section depicts the shape and configuration of the repetitive unit and the effectual relationship to the space of the building. Perceived or concealed, primary [as figuration] or coincidental in presence, the role of the sectional structural bay engages the verticality of the building.

The Ennis-Brown House uses the primary walls of the house to establish the vertical structural planes. They flank the primary spaces (interior and exterior) as regimented bookends; the Barcelona Pavilion illustrates its thin, clearly vertical elements of wall spanning from base to roof but never connecting at an edge; the Casa Barragan establishes primary walls, but they remain nonhierarchical to the space, simply serving as figured masses that orchestrate and define variable spaces; the Exeter Library uses the plane of the exterior layers of masonry structure as a foil to the frame of the concrete inner structure; the House at Riva San Vitale uses the perimeter as the primary bearing points, with the center as a bridge between edges to support the floor plates that do not span the entire space; the Thermal Baths at Vals use the field of pavilions as structural masts holding the branch roof plates that huddle together to form the enclosure; the Murcia Town Hall has regular concrete floor plates with a columnar support system that hugs the perimeter and subdivides the interior into bays as minimally as is practically necessary to emphasize the opacity of the outer surface and the structural integrity concealed within it; and the Dominus Winery uses a regimented and standardized steel frame to create a functional and economical bay in the building.

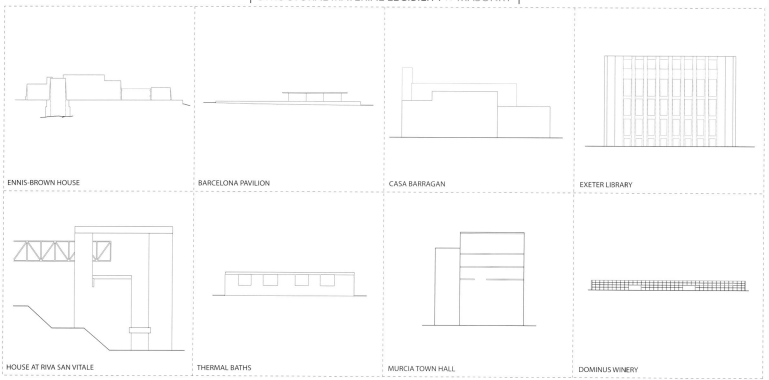

ENNIS-BROWN HOUSE

BARCELONA PAVILION

CASA BARRAGAN

EXETER LIBRARY

HOUSE AT RIVA SAN VITALE

THERMAL BATHS

MURCIA TOWN HALL

DOMINUS WINERY

[MASONRY] STRUCTURAL MATERIAL LEGIBILITY diagrams in elevation the reading of the structural material. Focusing on the influence of the structural material, it illustrates the interrelation of the engineered structural response of material and performative need to the form and composition. Questioning how the system reads from the exterior and whether the structural material is ever seen, the legibility diagrams examine the relationship of the forces of gravity to the formal expression.

The integration of structure to skin and ultimately to form is about the engagement of the physical requirements of a building to perform structurally with the formal intentions and the legibility of these two systems. The idea of [1] reading a person's bones literally through the skin, [2] versus the broader legibility of a leg as column to transfer vertical loads, [3] versus a denial of all understanding of how the figure works structurally are the three basic stages of structural depiction: [1] literal, [2] figural, or [3] denied.

The Ennis-Brown House has great structural legibility through the monolithic nature of the building's form and relentless deployment of the concrete textile block; the Barcelona Pavilion reveals the structural lines of the columns but simultaneously tries to deny their presence through their chromed finish reflecting the world around them as opposed to expressing themselves; the Casa Barragan masses the building in the form of the masonry units but does not specify any structural articulation or systemization; the Exeter Library is marked by its clarity and systemization; vertically, the wall dematerializes as the structural mass is not needed by removing one brick per floor. In a reciprocal reaction, the fenestration increases in dimension to amplify the light and porosity of the surface; the House at Riva San Vitale illustrates the load-bearing walls and then exaggerates the lintel required for the floor plates to negotiate the removals; the Thermal Baths at Vals stitch the structural components together with the ground plinth through the stone veneer to provide a singular solidity to the formal reading of the building; the Murcia Town Hall exposes the concrete only when it is pulled through the façade at the upper levels on the primary façade to create horizontal banding to the formal organization; and the Dominus Winery aligns the steel structure with the perimeter skin module, but holds it off the gabion wall on the interior to distinctly express the structure as a separate but related system to the skin.

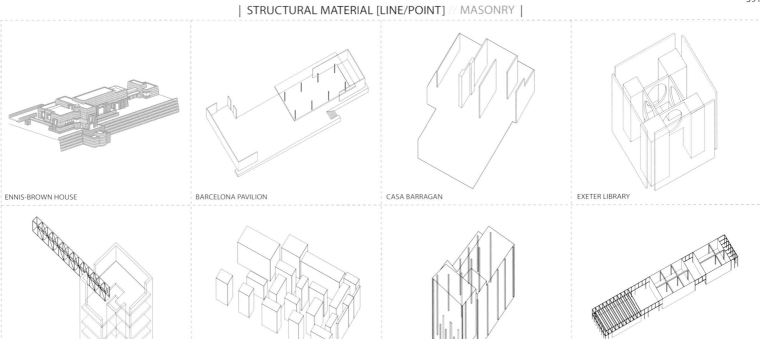

ENNIS-BROWN HOUSE

BARCELONA PAVILION

CASA BARRAGAN

EXETER LIBRARY

HOUSE AT RIVA SAN VITALE

THERMAL BATHS

MURCIA TOWN HALL

DOMINUS WINERY

[MASONRY] STRUCTURAL MATERIAL [LINE/POINT] diagrams in axonometric the primary geometric and formal response of the structural material/system. "Line" refers to the registration of a wall surface as a structural bearing wall in plan, while "point" refers to the columnar system. Materials subscribe intrinsically to one or the other [typically]; metal is point, while masonry is line. Certain materials, like concrete and wood, have the potential to be either.

The axonometric diagramming of the structural system and the material expression of this system suggest the three-dimensional resolution of the underlying structure superimposed on the form. The relationship of the structural material to the primary material parallels the discussions of revelation versus concealment and homogeneity versus cladding.

The Ennis-Brown House establishes the weight of the concrete textile block planes and aggregates them to create the figure and presence of the components as a whole. The massing of the building emerges out of a direct relationship with the solidity and form of the material; the Barcelona Pavilion uses both line and point, with the point being the primary structural component and the line subdividing space and adding additional shear strength; the Casa Barragan use masonry walls with a variable bay system of continuous walls; the Exeter Library has a planar configuration in the four faces of the clay masonry exterior, while the internal concrete corner masts support the circular frame that connects them; the House at Riva San Vitale has a planar perimeter that allows the floor plates to span variably across the masonry tube; the Thermal Baths at Vals express the solidity of the concrete masts that support the floating roof; the Murcia Town Hall uses a concrete columnar system that hugs the masonry skin to emphasize the planar nature of the vernacular construction despite a more modern structural system; and the Dominus Winery uses the frame and wall as exposed interior tectonic systems, both veiled by the gabion exterior.

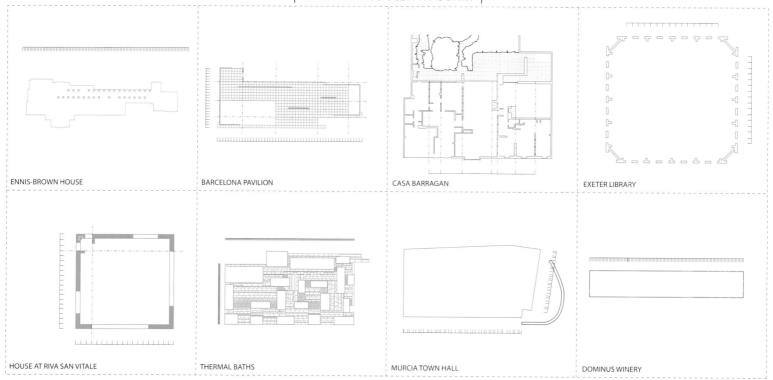

ENNIS-BROWN HOUSE

BARCELONA PAVILION

CASA BARRAGAN

EXETER LIBRARY

HOUSE AT RIVA SAN VITALE

THERMAL BATHS

MURCIA TOWN HALL

DOMINUS WINERY

[MASONRY] Module – MATERIAL MODULE diagrams in plan the relationships of the manufacturing module intrinsic to a material to the space, form, and dimensions. Mapping the inherited dimensional constraints determined by the production and movement of a material, the patterning of these scale elements and the articulation of their joinery to establish larger architectural forms address the relationship of piece to whole and unit to system.

The module of materials is an intrinsic fact that must be addressed. Certain materials default to a secondary system [such as concrete with formwork] to generate a dimensional constraint, but every material has a "natural" form and dimension. The negotiation of these constraints and the collaboration with these numeric proportions determine the dimensions of the whole and the integration of the modular unit into the consistency of the superstructural organization.

The Ennis-Brown House is regimented by the square module of the textile block establishing a spatial and graphic grid across the surface of the building; the Barcelona Pavilion uses variable modules for the ground, the frame walls, and the marble icon walls to produce variable geometric effects relative to their hierarchy and sense of motion; the Casa Barragan develops primary walls with a spacing relative to the spanning characteristics of the wood floor joists irrelevant to the mud brick masonry, as the plaster coating masks any legibility; the Exeter Library creates a plan based completely on the unit dimension of the clay masonry module; the House at Riva San Vitale defines its dimensions from the module of the masonry unit, never requiring a cut; the Thermal Bath at Vals deploy a quilted pattern to the horizontal surface to define a boundary to the space and volume of each chamber while allowing for continuity of space; the Murcia Town Hall uses three geometries for the three primary components of [1] the body, [2] the main façade, and [3] the theater; and the Dominus Winery uses the gabion cages that hold the rock to establish a highly geometric module for an otherwise incredibly organic material.

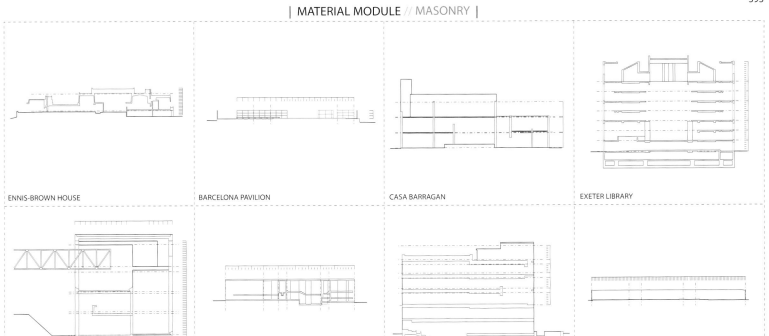

ENNIS-BROWN HOUSE

BARCELONA PAVILION

CASA BARRAGAN

EXETER LIBRARY

HOUSE AT RIVA SAN VITALE

THERMAL BATHS

MURCIA TOWN HALL

DOMINUS WINERY

[MASONRY] Module – MATERIAL MODULE diagrams in section the relationships of the manufacturing module intrinsic to a material to the space, form, and dimensions. Mapping the inherited dimensional constraints determined by the production and movement of a material to the sectional implications, the patterning of these scale elements and the articulation of their joinery establish larger architectural spaces derived from addressing the relationship of piece to whole and unit to system.

The module of material is an intrinsic fact that must be addressed. Certain materials default to a secondary system [such as concrete with formwork] to generate a dimensional constraint, but every material has a "natural" form and dimension. The negotiation of these constraints and the collaboration with these numeric proportions determine the dimensions of the whole and the integration of the modular unit into the consistency of the superstructural organization. In section, the implications of the human hand of construction relative to the material coursing relative to the body's perception develop the scale and legibility of this module to the spatial presence as a whole.

The Ennis-Brown House uses the textile block and its module as both a vertical and horizontal surface and thus as a spatial module mandating the parameters for prescriptive geometries; the Barcelona Pavilion modulates three distinct systems for the base, the bracket walls, and the jewel walls, each determined by the practical weight and availability of stone but choreographed to produce a spatial implication to the joint and a figural composition in the jewel walls; the Casa Barragan bands a constant floor-to-floor height across the variable load-bearing walls to find a consistent cross-sectional dimension despite a desire to erase the sectional modularity of the material through the monolithic nature of the stucco-coated surfaces; the Exeter Library uses the sectional increment of the masonry unit to govern the floor-to-floor heights requiring the more dimensionally flexible concrete to adhere in kind; the House at Riva San Vitale courses the horizontal bed joints to align with the floor plates, allowing the rhythmic horizontal bands to integrate and collaborate with the perimeter wall; the Thermal Baths at Vals use simplicity of form and continuity of material as a foil against the variable dimensionality, position, and spatial effect of the discrete chambers; the Murcia Town Hall uses the floor-to-floor module, subdivided, to engage the coursing of the masonry and allow the registration of the floor plates through the front elevation; and the Dominus Winery uses the geometry of the cage against the irregular rock to create a skin system that is systematically varied.

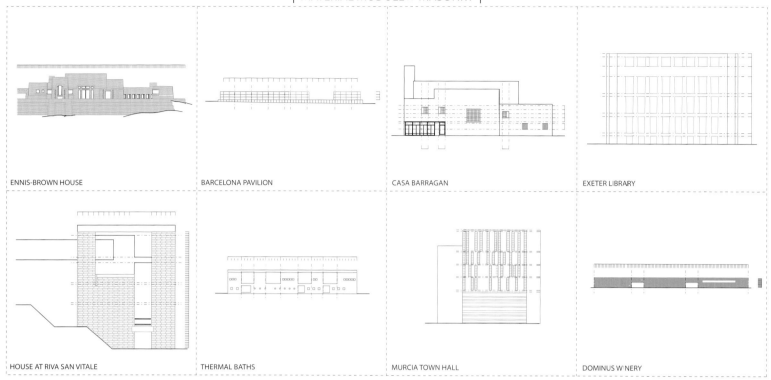

ENNIS-BROWN HOUSE

BARCELONA PAVILION

CASA BARRAGAN

EXETER LIBRARY

HOUSE AT RIVA SAN VITALE

THERMAL BATHS

MURCIA TOWN HALL

DOMINUS WINERY

[MASONRY] Module – MATERIAL MODULE diagrams in elevation the implications of the relationships of the manufacturing module intrinsic to a material to the space, form, and dimensions. Mapping the inherited dimensional constraints determined by the production and movement of a material to the façade, the formal legibility and implications of an architectural patterning of these scale elements rely upon the articulation of their joinery to establish larger architectural spaces.

The surface reading is derived from addressing the relationship of piece to whole and unit to system through the intrinsic module of a material. Certain materials default to a secondary system [such as concrete with formwork] to generate a dimensional constraint, but every material has a "natural" form and dimension. The negotiation of these constraints and the collaboration with these numeric proportions determine the dimensions of the whole and the integration of the modular unit into the consistency of the superstructural organization. In elevation, the implications of the human hand of construction relative to the material assemblies relative to the body's perception develop the scale and legibility of this module and its spatial presence as a whole.

The Ennis-Brown House is regimented by the square module of the textile block establishing a spatial and graphic grid across the surface of the building; the Barcelona Pavilion modulates three distinct systems for the base, the bracket walls, and the jewel walls, each determined by the practical weight and availability of the stone but choreographed to produce a spatial implication to the joint and a figural composition in the jewel walls; the Casa Barragan courses the windows in variable superimposed bands, each maintaining the mass of the wall with the continuity of the glass block windows as an extension of a transparent masonry within an opaque masonry wall; the Exeter Library completely collaborates with the material module to conceptually, formally, and structurally embrace the dimensional capability and aesthetic of clay masonry brick; the House at Riva San Vitale courses the horizontal bed joints to align with the floor plates and read as the rhythmic horizontal bands integrated and collaborating with the perimeter wall; the Thermal Baths at Vals produce a material module at such a fine scale that the pattern of joinery disappears to establish a monolithic figure that then uses open and closed masses and voids to define its geometry; the Murcia Town Hall uses variable coursing on the lower portion with regimented coursing for the upper portion to allow for the variable vertical voids; and the Dominus Winery uses the gabion cages that hold the rock to establish a repetitive grid field that composes the encased organic fill.

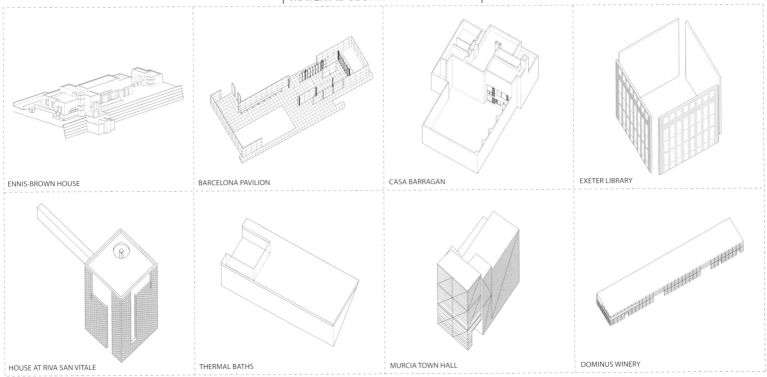

ENNIS-BROWN HOUSE

BARCELONA PAVILION

CASA BARRAGAN

EXETER LIBRARY

HOUSE AT RIVA SAN VITALE

THERMAL BATHS

MURCIA TOWN HALL

DOMINUS WINERY

[MASONRY] Module – MATERIAL GEOMETRY diagrams in axonometric the three-dimensional relationships of the manufacturing module intrinsic to a material to the space, form, and dimensions. Mapping the inherited dimensional constraints determined by the production and movement of a material into the three-dimensional ramifications of the total form, the legibility of an architectural patterning of scale elements relies upon the articulation of their joinery to establish larger architectural spaces.

The surface reading is derived from addressing the relationship of piece to whole and unit to system through the intrinsic module of a material. Certain materials default to a secondary system [such as concrete with formwork] to generate a dimensional constraint, but every material has a "natural" form and dimension. The negotiation of these constraints and the collaboration with these numeric proportions determine the dimensions of the whole and the integration of the modular unit into the consistency of the superstructural organization. In axonometric, the module governs the formal legibility of the three-dimensional building component and ultimately the formal reading of the building as a whole.

The Ennis-Brown House uses the innovate textile block system to deploy a self-created technique that generates a very specific formalism; the Barcelona Pavilion modulates three distinct systems for the base, the bracket walls, and the jewel walls, each determined by the practical weight and availability of scale of the stone but also choreographed to produce a spatial implication to the joint and figural composition; the Casa Barragan deploys the monolithic nature of the stucco-coated masonry to produce a singular articulated form with choreographed openings and framed exterior open-on-one-face rooms; the Exeter Library uses the module of the brick to relentlessly define its dimensions; the House at Riva San Vitale courses the horizontal bed joints to align with the floor plates to read as the rhythmic horizontal bands integrated and collaborating with the perimeter wall; the Thermal Baths at Vals use the scale and coursing of the stone to create a uniformity to the surface and a continuity of form; the Murcia Town Hall uses variable coursing on the lower portion of the front tower with regimented coursing for the upper portion and "back building"; and the Dominus Winery uses a geometric module to establish the organizational matrix for the gravitationally placed rock infill.

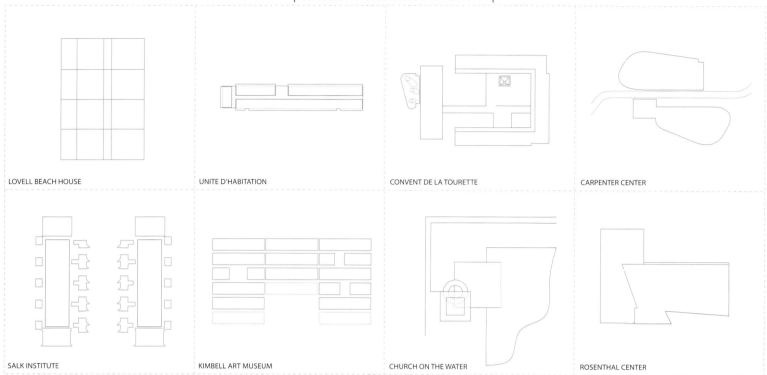

LOVELL BEACH HOUSE

UNITE D'HABITATION

CONVENT DE LA TOURETTE

CARPENTER CENTER

SALK INSTITUTE

KIMBELL ART MUSEUM

CHURCH ON THE WATER

ROSENTHAL CENTER

[CONCRETE] MATERIAL FUNCTION diagrams in plan the relationship between material use and the formal and technical associations required by its functional application. These diagrams examine the role of a material's specific performance properties and its employment relative to the functional and practical necessities of the program and building performance. Each material expresses of the conditions and requirements of its deployment.

Defining the premise of skin in each application, material serves as the iconic designation of form in each project. The associated material tectonic employed extends its influence to express itself through the spatial concepts of the architecture. Steel defines vertical lines [Eames House and Niaux Cave], concrete defines planes and frames with variable openings [Lovell Beach House, La Tourette, Church on the Water], and masonry creates modulated solid edges [Casa Barragan and Murcia Town Hall]. Glass establishes transparent veils: flat, ambiguous surfaces that exist but slip into a nonpresence allowing the dissolve of the enclosure and a perceived spatial connection between inside and outside. This is most prevalent in the De Blas Haus and the Cartier Foundation, though it exists even when the glass is frosted and figured, as in the glass block façade of the Maison de Verre. Each material relative to its function determines form.

In each case study, regardless of material, the cloak of the primary material is the defining figure of the primary form. The Lovell Beach House is defined by the primary lateral planes of the concrete frame; Le Corbusier's Unite d'Habitation in Marseille uses concrete for every aspect of the building, from structure to finish, consistently illustrating the method of construction and revealing the functional durability; La Tourette uses the monolithic plasticity of concrete that assumes responsibility for structure, enclosure, and ornament as both interior and exterior finished surface; the Carpenter Center maps the internal spatial module on the exterior through the formwork and surface patterning; the Salk Institute uses concrete to establish the primary planes of the building [both horizontal and vertical], carefully integrating their force lines and fabrication patterns into the overall figure and composition; Kahn's Kimbell Art Museum similarly uses concrete to illustrate the hierarchy of the form, using concrete to express the column and beam structure capped in a barrel vault; the Church on the Water uses modular formwork to establish the spatial patterning and minimal geometry of the spaces; and the Rosenthal Center for Contemporary Art uses concrete to define the composition of its figural form.

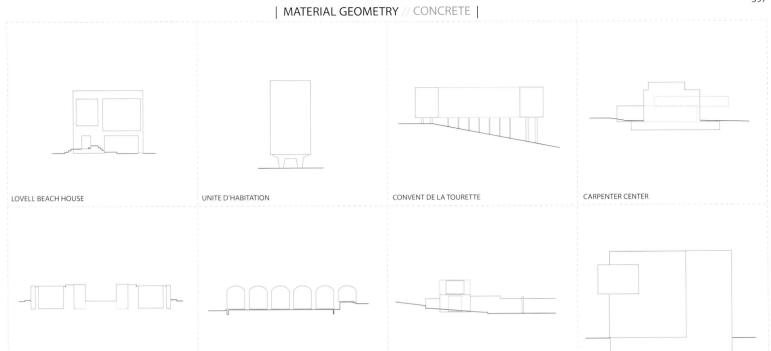

LOVELL BEACH HOUSE

UNITE D'HABITATION

CONVENT DE LA TOURETTE

CARPENTER CENTER

SALK INSTITUTE

KIMBELL ART MUSEUM

CHURCH ON THE WATER

ROSENTHAL CENTER

[CONCRETE] MATERIAL GEOMETRY diagrams the sectional geometric implications of material for form. By introducing the potential structural implications of a material, the relationship of "skin to bones" or surface to structure becomes relative to the intrinsic qualities of a material. Establishing the dimensional module [both of performance and of fabrication and installation limitations], the capabilities of a material express themselves beyond the figure of the form to address the geometry of the space.

The module of a material can be established by three potential scales. The first scale is the module of the unit: a single brick, a sheet of plywood [as direct application of sheathing or as indirect application of formwork], a glass pane with either concealed or revealed frame systems, or a steel member. In each of these conditions the unit is defined by a structural need, a material property, or a manufacturing module. The second scale is the bay of the module produced through the assemblies or structure. For example, the Eames House window wall module is an aggregate of the individual panes, the double high bay module, and the superstructural steel frame. The final scale is the designed geometry of the building's mass expressed through material, i.e., the formal figure of the object as a whole. Each of these three levels can coexist or be independently exploited. The material in each case is, however, the beginning, the dimensional collaborator based on the intrinsic properties and performance of the base material.

The Lovell Beach House extends the interior floor levels established by the concrete frame through the house to define the programmatic arrangement; Le Corbusier's Unite d'Habitation in Marseille uses the classic interlocking L-shaped units for the space of ownership, but their aggregation makes for a monolithic bar mass; La Tourette uses the typological form of the monastery and overlays the subdivisions of the fenestration patterning systems and the texture and module of the various methods of formwork to produce localized formal articulation; the Carpenter Center lodges a series of volumes into a central figure punctured by the outdoor ramp penetrating the heart of the building; the Salk Institute emphasizes the frame of the slab floor and wall system with a wood and glass infill; Kahn's Kimbell Art Museum uses a repetitive bay three wide and six deep; the Church on the Water defines the primary geometric figures with the pure mass of the material and then subdivides their surfaces through the imprinted formwork module and tectonics; and the Rosenthal Center for Contemporary Art loads the opaque galleries against the street edge, leaving a massive volume between these figures and the adjacent building.

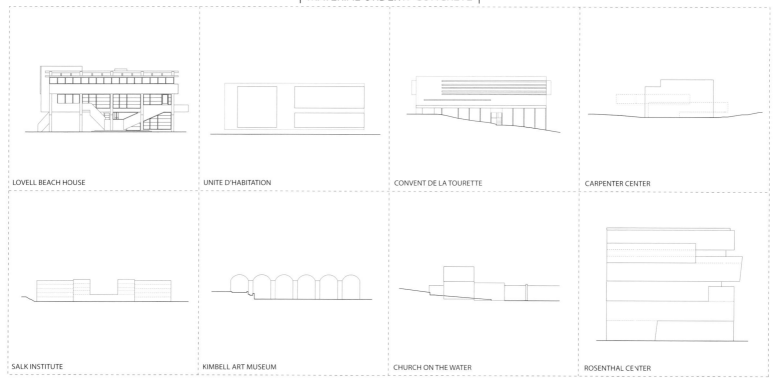

LOVELL BEACH HOUSE

UNITE D'HABITATION

CONVENT DE LA TOURETTE

CARPENTER CENTER

SALK INSTITUTE

KIMBELL ART MUSEUM

CHURCH ON THE WATER

ROSENTHAL CENTER

[CONCRETE] MATERIAL ORDER diagrams in elevation the hierarchy, sequence, and organizational methods of material's influence on the architectural form. As in the examination in section, the implication here is more spatial than formal. Looking at the organizational geometries and governing patterns of material relative to the form, the implications and legibility of volume and mass are articulated through the aggregation of the material pieces.

The extension of the material module into the overarching order of the formal expression is the ultimate collaboration of material with design. The definition of the overall form relative to the piece, the manner in which an aperture is made as a removal [in terms of both module and structural implications], and the relation of these compositional pieces to the formal whole are the defining characteristics of a material's influence on form.

The Lovell Beach House reveals the concrete frames as rhythmic verticals on its primary broad façade, while the solid infill panels are horizontal extensions of the removed frame voids; Le Corbusier's Unite d'Habitation in Marseille breaks down the massive façade through a patterned segmentation fracturing the residential unit with the vertical core and the horizontal shopping level; La Tourette subdivides the façade through the assignment of varied fenestration systems that express the programmatic function of the spaces behind while maintaining a synthesized continuity through the consistency of the material applied across the various forms; the Carpenter Center allows free-form figured spaces to float and lodge in the cubic central body of the building; the Salk Institute breaks down the mass of the laboratories with layers of courtyards and office or service towers to move the building's reading from solid to void; Kahn's Kimbell Art Museum establishes the rhythm of the structural concrete frame and the panelized travertine infill; the Church on the Water has a tripartite material order with concrete [1] defining the entry and sanctuary that set into the ground, glass [2] expressing the lightness of the elevated lantern volume, and steel [3] creating the iconic cruciform of the cross set in the reflecting pool and ringing the lantern walls; and the Rosenthal Center for Contemporary Art uses composed interlocking figures of varied scales, colors, and patterns to compose an otherwise opaque façade.

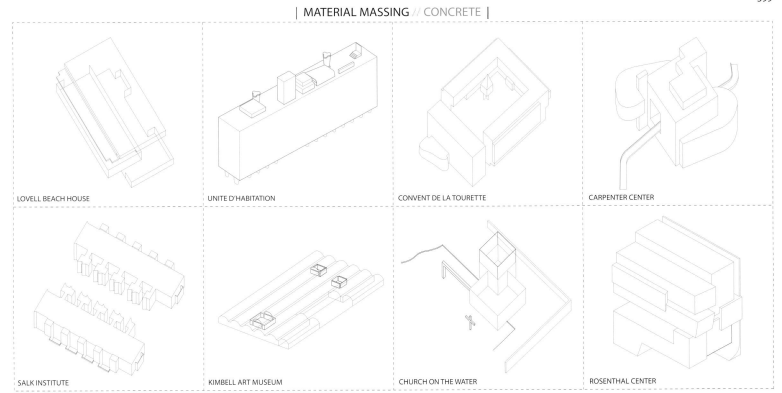

LOVELL BEACH HOUSE

UNITE D'HABITATION

CONVENT DE LA TOURETTE

CARPENTER CENTER

SALK INSTITUTE

KIMBELL ART MUSEUM

CHURCH ON THE WATER

ROSENTHAL CENTER

[CONCRETE] MATERIAL MASSING diagrams in axonometric the overall legibility of the primary material to the superstructural form, presence, and mass of the architectural form. Focusing primarily on the mass and volume of form as defined by the material application to the exterior, the legibility of compositional intention and the geometric hierarchy are mapped.

The significance of mass [as defined by material in particular] concerns the clarity of formal intention in relation to the actual legibility and reading in the building. The conceptual ideas that govern the design of a building become legible through their tectonic manifestations in the form. The hierarchy of the primary massing determines the figuration to which all else must respond. The material relationship with this massing and the deployment of the tectonic expression of the assembly determine whether a material is read as segmented, disassociated, panelized, repetitive, or monolithic.

The Lovell Beach House extends the primary horizontal volumes as tubes sliding through the voids of the repetitive frames employing the monolithic nature of concrete to provide continuity to the variable formal pieces; Le Corbusier's Unite d'Habitation in Marseille has a massive figure cloaked in a hyperarticulated brise-soleil skin diffused on the bottom with pilotis and on the top with a series of communal pavilions; La Tourette reinterprets the monastic courtyard to create a dissolving yet monolithic ambulatory perimeter; the Carpenter Center has fluid forms engulfing and penetrating the central orthogonal figure of the building; the Salk Institute has two parallel massive central blocks with flanking rows of towers creating a powerful void between them; Kahn's Kimbell Art Museum is a series of parallel vaults with dissolves and voids defining a sequence through the field; the Church on the Water has two grounded, overlapping, rectilinear concrete figures with a circle set at the respective corner/center of each with an independent and variably oriented axis; and the Rosenthal Center for Contemporary Art uses formally composed overlapping volumes to bring dynamism to the otherwise blank façade.

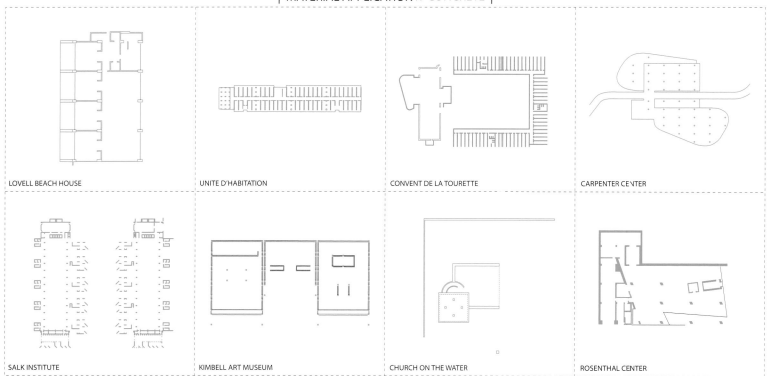

LOVELL BEACH HOUSE

UNITE D'HABITATION

CONVENT DE LA TOURETTE

CARPENTER CENTER

SALK INSTITUTE

KIMBELL ART MUSEUM

CHURCH ON THE WATER

ROSENTHAL CENTER

[CONCRETE] MATERIAL APPLICATION diagrams in plan the deployment of material and the associated perceptual, formal, and functional readings. Engaging the relationship between material and function, the formal expression becomes the primary mediating element. The expression of the material's use and the tectonic deployment determine the functional programmatic legibility of the building. This begins with the formal expression intrinsic to the material followed by issues of practical performance, including durability, porosity, and visual effect.

A material can be selected for various reasons: availability, cost, durability, module, structural capability, or simply the functional applicability [metal to combat combustion, concrete for construction in corrosive environments, or masonry as a low-maintenance, durable skin]. In each scenario the fundamental physical properties of the material are the baseline of design consideration. These properties, mediated by the method of manufacturing and limited by the method of working [wood is easy to cut, metal can be welded, masonry is heavy and modular], develop the second tier of consideration. Finally, and perhaps with the most variability, is the assembly and application. The systemization of the manufactured pieces and their formal and technical articulation comprise material design application.

The Lovell Beach House selects concrete frames [whose structural openings determine the subdivision of space between public and private] to combat the salt air of its seaside setting; Le Corbusier's Unite d'Habitation in Marseille uses concrete almost exclusively because of the availability of the material and the lack of a skilled work force; La Tourette deploys concrete [a highly durable and flexible material that can assume the form of the vessel it is cast into] to be interior surface, exterior surface, wall, floor, window, furniture, and so on simultaneously; the Carpenter Center uses concrete as structure and as interior and exterior finish due to the flexibility of its formal figure and the legibility of process intrinsic to its nature; the Salk Institute cloaks the laboratories in glass to reduce the presence of their mass and then diffuses the building to either side to reduce the scale and emphasize the "in-between" as a figure; Kahn's Kimbell Art Museum applies concrete to the frame and roof, allowing an emphasis to edge; the Church on the Water uses Ando's refined concrete with a highly ordered formwork module and form tie system to establish the rigorous geometry of the spaces; and the Rosenthal Center for Contemporary Art uses the raw texture of concrete to complement the form and aid in the composition and articulation of an otherwise opaque façade. The inner structure is similarly concrete for both column grid and party wall.

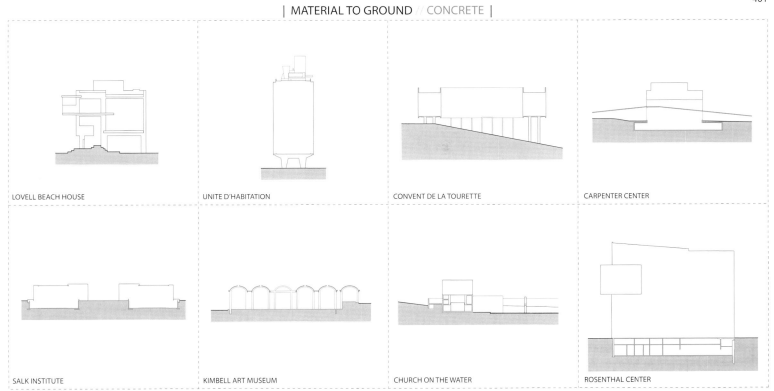

LOVELL BEACH HOUSE · UNITE D'HABITATION · CONVENT DE LA TOURETTE · CARPENTER CENTER

SALK INSTITUTE · KIMBELL ART MUSEUM · CHURCH ON THE WATER · ROSENTHAL CENTER

[CONCRETE] Proximity – MATERIAL TO GROUND diagrams the sectional relationship in which a building meets the ground, engages landscape, and addresses the material point of connection with the site. The point of contact between a building and the earth is determined by the material approach to the architecture. Factors that determine and affect this condition include soil characteristics, climate, context, structural system, and building weight [both actual and perceived].

The history of structural and material technology is the history of how a building meets the ground. The selection of material cladding and structural framing results in a specific formal articulation of this condition that is intrinsic to the material and tectonic. Technologically determined, this joint [between building and ground] is created by the system of both the structure and the cladding. Historically, load-bearing wall systems of wood or masonry required continuous contact of the building with the ground and limited the scale and frequency of openings. Materials such as steel and concrete allowed for a formal disengagement from the ground plane, turning structural planes into points and shifting from a wall system to a cage.

The Lovell Beach House articulates the open ground plane to create a series of levels that begin the spatial sequence of the house before one actually enters the formal threshold of the front door; Le Corbusier's Unite d'Habitation in Marseille, characteristically of his five points, floats off the ground to allow for continuity of the ground plane and the natural park-like landscape; La Tourette touches the upper hillside, levitating as the topography drops away, revealing a columnar field below; the Carpenter Center similarly levitates on a structure of pilotis, folding the ground plane up and through the building with the ramp that bridges through the block from sidewalk to sidewalk; the Salk Institute embeds itself into the hillside to carve a void space between the buildings, allowing for a layering, both horizontal and sectional, of courtyards and spaces; Kahn's Kimbell Art Museum similarly sets into the sectional landscape, allowing for a vehicular entrance on the lower level and a pedestrian entry on the main level; the Church on the Water uses the concrete to carve rooms out of the landscape: the large perimeter wall, the pool, and the two enclosed spaces that set directly into the earth, with glass and steel emerging from their primary monolithic forms; and the Rosenthal Center for Contemporary Art, though embedded in the ground, dissolves the ground floor with glass to imply a hovering figuration to the massive concrete figures above.

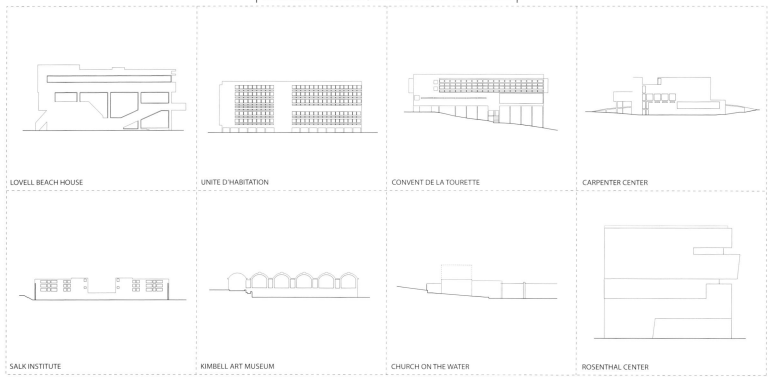

LOVELL BEACH HOUSE

UNITE D'HABITATION

CONVENT DE LA TOURETTE

CARPENTER CENTER

SALK INSTITUTE

KIMBELL ART MUSEUM

CHURCH ON THE WATER

ROSENTHAL CENTER

[CONCRETE] Proximity – PRIMARY / SECONDARY diagrams in elevation the relationship of the primary building material to the secondary building material, focusing on the formal, functional, and practical interrelationships of their material application. The hierarchy between these two levels is both formally and materially evident, establishing the organizing geometries of the diverse layers.

The proximity of a primary figure to a secondary figure builds on the formal reading of material application diagrams but engages the interrelationship with the secondary systemization. The interaction of the two can occur through superimposition, contrasting figures, interpenetration, banding, layering, or any other adverbial relationship. The result is a primary figuration and the secondary subsystemization that, through its geometry, breaks down the material into fabricateable and installable pieces and reveals the tectonic intention of their aggregation.

The Lovell Beach House contrasts in elevation the opacity of the primary masses against the recessive void of the negative spaces and the intricacy of the ornament and articulation of the windows. The monolithic formal nature facilitated by the concrete engages the positive figure of the frame with the negative space of the wood infill as the primary and secondary elements; Le Corbusier's Unite d'Habitation in Marseille uses concrete almost exclusively, relying upon glass for the transparency of the unit end walls; La Tourette figures the mass of the whole with areas of articulated concrete employed for fenestration; the Carpenter Center juxtaposes the massiveness of the concrete with the transparency of the large glass panels; the Salk Institute juxtaposes wood with the concrete as an infill system that brings a tactility to the severity of the concrete and mimics the formwork in both dimension and figuration; Kahn's Kimbell Art Museum pairs the concrete frame and vault with infill and flooring panels of travertine to elevate the formality of the building and dictate the legibility of skin to frame; the Church on the Water uses two concrete forms set in the landscape, each with a separate axis of orientation that determines the visual focus on its secondary elements: the entry looks upward to the expressive steel crossed perimeter frame and the glazed glass volume, while the sanctuary has an operable fourth wall that can be retracted to visually connect to the steel cross in the reflecting pool; and the Rosenthal Center for Contemporary Art uses concrete in diverse formwork configurations, scales, and finishes to create a dynamism to the opaque façade.

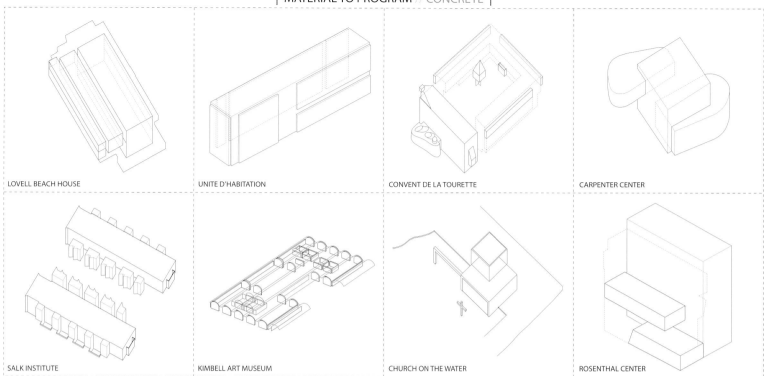

LOVELL BEACH HOUSE

UNITE D'HABITATION

CONVENT DE LA TOURETTE

CARPENTER CENTER

SALK INSTITUTE

KIMBELL ART MUSEUM

CHURCH ON THE WATER

ROSENTHAL CENTER

[CONCRETE] Proximity – MATERIAL TO PROGRAM diagrams in axonometric the overall relationship of material usage to the primary programmatic and functional usages. By focusing on the three-dimensional volumetric associations of material to programmatic usage [and the associated functional requirements of a particular program], the articulation of "form following function" can be examined through material association.

The relationship of the programmatic usage to the material selected depicts the narrative of the association, creating the opportunity and potential for material to be an expressive sign system. The legibility of a material comes from a technical knowledge that engages an understanding of raw material, manufacturing processes, construction traditions and techniques, weathering and biological attack, and cultural associations. These innate properties of matter translate into forms that collaborate with materials to reveal their process.

The Lovell Beach House uses the same material across the various domestic programs, relying upon scale to differentiate the diverse functions; Le Corbusier's Unite d'Habitation in Marseille varies the field [defined by function] to break down the scale and provide diversified articulation to the façade; La Tourette uses concrete for every element in the diverse composition but deploys a secondary scale of elements that collaborate with the primary masses to produce a diverse system of articulation and formal expression; the Carpenter Center pulls the gallery and studio functions out of the form to give them identifiable organic figures; the Salk Institute layers the concrete as solid walls for the outer service towers, a concrete Vierendeel frame for the middle layer of laboratories, and slab wall and floor plate frames for the inner layer of offices; Kahn's Kimbell Art Museum uses the concrete as a frame anonymously bracketing the internal functions, regardless of program; the Church on the Water has two primary figures, each rotated in orientation to address its secondary pieces: a glass view toward the "heavens" and the horizontal view across the reflecting pool toward a composed "earth"; and the Rosenthal Center for Contemporary Art inverts the blank figure of the exterior with the void space of the interior.

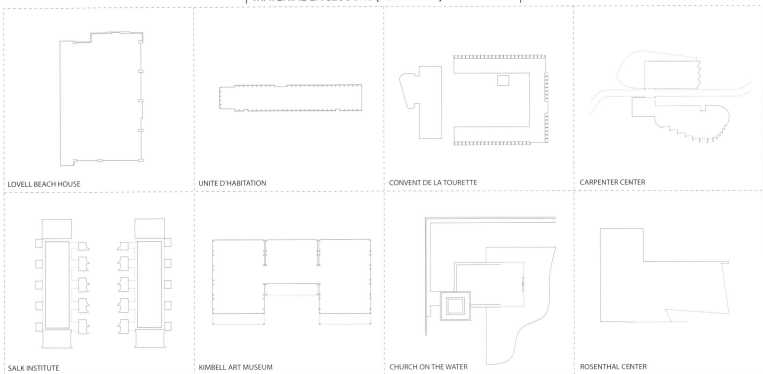

LOVELL BEACH HOUSE

UNITE D'HABITATION

CONVENT DE LA TOURETTE

CARPENTER CENTER

SALK INSTITUTE

KIMBELL ART MUSEUM

CHURCH ON THE WATER

ROSENTHAL CENTER

[CONCRETE] Skin + Surface – MATERIAL ENCLOSURE [PERIMETER] diagrams in plan the relationship of the outer plane of enclosure [skin] to the spatial, formal, and structural organization. Expressing the process by which materials assemble into systems, the figuration of the perimeter is dependent not simply upon the piece but also upon the joint. The collaboration of these two generates specific forms intrinsic to a material and expressively identifiable.

The use of skin to define the perimeter over the structure and the programmatic innards establishes the legibility of architectural idea's purity through the articulation of edge and boundary. The continuity and complexity of this envelope widely explicate the material articulation and the tectonic intricacy. The relationship of craft to figure is found in the method of material manipulation.

The Lovell Beach House has a perimeter that extends variably beyond the frame to create a figured body; Le Corbusier's Unite d'Habitation in Marseille crenellates the façade thickening the depth of the wall and the reading of boundary with the brise-soleil; La Tourette circumscribes a courtyard with an articulated exterior surface scaled to the anthropomorphic sequence of perception; the Carpenter Center interweaves outside and inside by bringing the exterior ramp [undulating in both plan and section] through the heart of the building; the Salk Institute layers the building both in mass and in detail to provide depth to the form and openness to the connection of layers; Kahn's Kimbell Art Museum diffuses the front façade by translating the barrel vault from enclosure to open frame porch in massing, while in detail the open joint separates the concrete skeletal system from the travertine infill wall; the Church on the Water sets frame within frame within frame, all inscribed with relentless modularity derived from the formwork; and the Rosenthal Center for Contemporary Art defines its two adjacent edges with the formal engagement of the context, while the street corner diffuses with a minimal glass presence to levitate the concrete figures above.

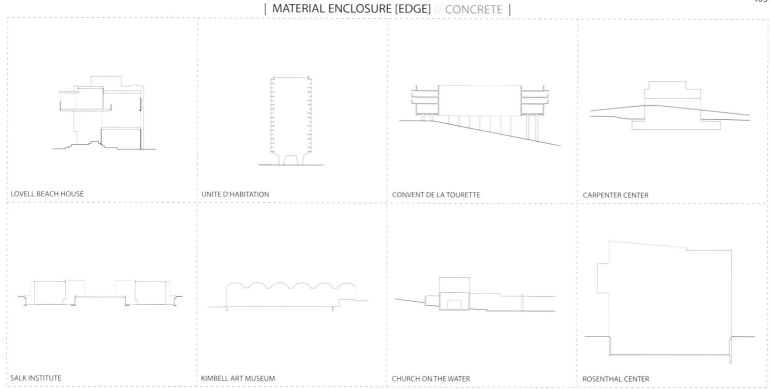

LOVELL BEACH HOUSE

UNITE D'HABITATION

CONVENT DE LA TOURETTE

CARPENTER CENTER

SALK INSTITUTE

KIMBELL ART MUSEUM

CHURCH ON THE WATER

ROSENTHAL CENTER

[CONCRETE] Skin + Surface – MATERIAL ENCLOSURE [EDGE] diagrams in section the relationship of the outer plane of enclosure [skin] to the spatial, formal, and structural organization. Expressing the process by which materials assemble into systems, the figuration of the perimeter as expressed through section extends the moves of plan in the Y axis [still dependent not simply upon the piece but also upon the joint].

The collaboration of piece with joint determines the sectional spatial forms intrinsic to a material, resulting in expressive and identifiable associations. The role of skin in section similarly works to define the perimeter over the structure and the interior functions. The figure establishes the legibility of an architectural idea's purity through the articulation of edge and boundary as extended to the vertical and thus the now spatial dimension. The continuity and complexity of this line widely explicate the material articulation and the tectonic intricacy. The relationship of exterior material through the surface of the building to impact and define interior space is moderated by the material manipulation of this edge.

The Lovell Beach House has a perimeter that extends variably beyond the frame to create a figured body; Le Corbusier's Unite d'Habitation in Marseille similarly crenellates [in section, as it does in plan] the façade, thickening the depth of the wall and the reading of boundary with the brise-soleil; La Tourette circumscribes a courtyard with an articulated exterior surface scaled to the anthropomorphic sequence of perception associated with programmatic sectional layering; the Carpenter Center opens the building off the ground, through the ramp and with a thickened edge of brise-soleil; the Salk Institute layers the building with rows of programmatic pieces leaving voids as positive spaces embedded within; Kahn's Kimbell Art Museum, through a repetitive bay system and a primal architectural form, bounds a simple figure articulated by the gradient of light; the Church on the Water sets frame within frame within frame, all inscribed with relentless modularity derived from the formwork and alternating of X, Y, and Z axes; and the Rosenthal Center for Contemporary Art oscillates between open and closed, from the fully transparent to the fully opaque, to juxtapose the weight and presence of mass and figure with the delicate immateriality of surface and skin.

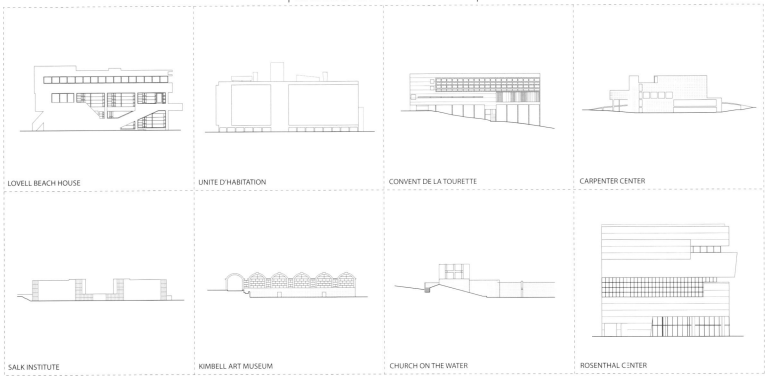

LOVELL BEACH HOUSE   UNITE D'HABITATION   CONVENT DE LA TOURETTE   CARPENTER CENTER

SALK INSTITUTE   KIMBELL ART MUSEUM   CHURCH ON THE WATER   ROSENTHAL CENTER

[CONCRETE] Skin + Surface – MATERIAL TEXTURE diagrams in elevation the legibility of the material texture, color, and surface. Defining the compositional aesthetics of the elevation, the collagist sensibility of pattern, texture, color, and depth of plane are all legible against light. Like a composed painting, this image is dissected from the visual perceptual stance of the material on the architectural composition.

The textural reading refers to the actual color and composition of the material. Wood, for example, can be classified as a generic type, but the performance qualities, colors, hardness, resistance to rot, durability, and workability are vastly different from species to species. This same textural legibility comes through the assembly and expression of the unit and the joint. The scale and articulation of these connections define the legibility of the collective material reading and the overall compositional reading of the architecture.

The Lovell Beach House contrasts the monolithic and homogeneous nature of the solid walls with a highly articulated and ornamental wooden lattice window system [derivative of Frank Lloyd Wright's style of ornamentation]; Le Corbusier's Unite d'Habitation in Marseille develops its pattern through the articulation of the brise-soleil; La Tourette maintains material homogeneity while variably producing a series of brise-soleil techniques that protrude to form balconies for the monks' cells, striate the dining hall, and linearly stripe the ambulatory corridors; the Carpenter Center gets its visual texture from the formwork patterning that reiterates the legibility of the interior floor plates; the Salk Institute relentlessly considers the formwork in both dimension and craft to allow for increased legibility of seams that pattern, scale, and rationalize the surfaces; Kahn's Kimbell Art Museum sets the concrete frame against the paneled travertine infill to provide a simultaneous superstructural grain against the anthropomorphic scale; the Church on the Water develops a material texture through the rectilinear modules of the formwork and then further subdivides this with the circular points marking the location of the form ties, allowing each system to produce a scale and detail to the material and space that provides order and expression of the history and sequence of assembly; and the Rosenthal Center for Contemporary Art juxtaposes surface patterning in the concrete, as determined by the formwork, against the patterned segmentation of the mullions in the glass curtain wall to produce a collaged effect.

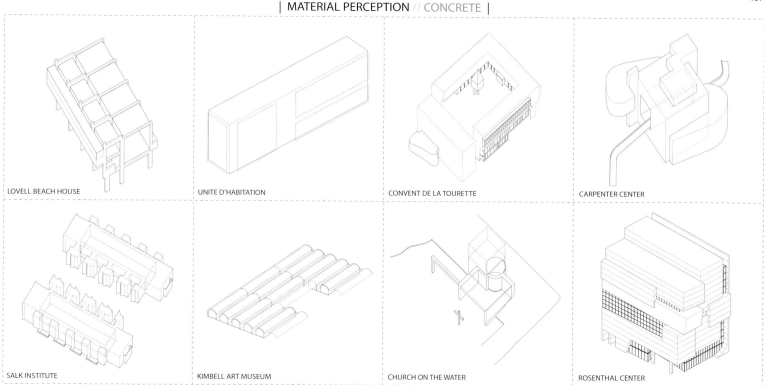

LOVELL BEACH HOUSE

UNITE D'HABITATION

CONVENT DE LA TOURETTE

CARPENTER CENTER

SALK INSTITUTE

KIMBELL ART MUSEUM

CHURCH ON THE WATER

ROSENTHAL CENTER

[CONCRETE] Skin + Surface – MATERIAL PERCEPTION diagrams in axonometric the primary reading of material experience. By transitioning from the sectional reading that focuses on the two-dimensional interior spatial conditions or the material application, the reading in elevation speaks to the composition of the façade, but again within the shallow space of a two-dimensional reading, while the axonometric examination illustrates for the compositional legibility of the building as a total object.

By engaging all three dimensions, the figuration of the architecture and the legibility of a material's perception relative to the total object lend a volumetric legibility to a material's perception. A truly monolithic architecture is nearly impossible; thus, the connection and change from one piece to the next define the moment of intervention and design decision. The perception of the whole after the resolution of these local "events" is the perception of the architecture. Focusing specifically on the material impact upon these decisions allows the design intention to be revealed by the tectonic view of the whole through the piece.

The Lovell Beach House consistently allows for a legibility of the frame against the volumetric infill despite the variety of materials employed; Le Corbusier's Unite d'Habitation in Marseille uses concrete everywhere, with varied scales of application to transition scales reading the whole figure, the secondary subdivisions of individual residential units juxtaposed against the communal infrastructures, and the tertiary scale of the formwork and sun modulation elements; La Tourette allows the material to become ubiquitous to emphasize form [the figure of the building provides a reference to the heritage of the monastic courtyard typology]; the Carpenter Center allows the figured forms of the saddlebag galleries to emerge from the orthogonal core; the Salk Institute sets two bars lined with diffusing towers to edge the central court; Kahn's Kimbell Art Museum uses the repetitive frame supporting the extruded barrel vaults to provide a consistency of formal directional grain and light to the spaces; the Church on the Water uses purity of material application and form to collaborate in a highly ordered and decisively legible formal perception; and the Rosenthal Center for Contemporary Art collages a variety of mass figures with interspersed transparent voids to create a gravitationally irreverent composition.

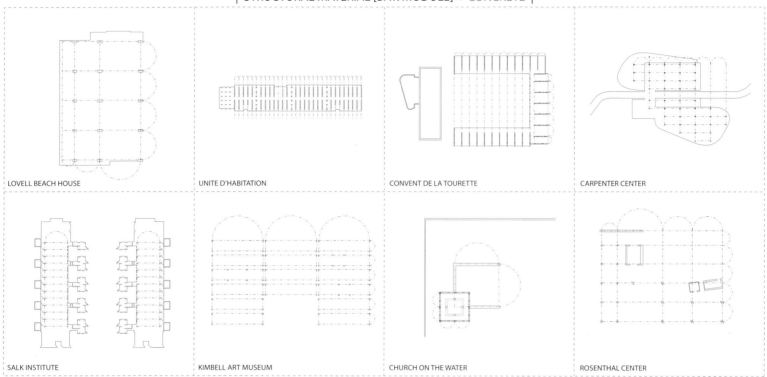

[CONCRETE] STRUCTURAL MATERIAL [BAY/MODULE] diagrams in plan the structural module of the building. Focusing on the influence of the structural material, it illustrates the engineered structural response of material relative to performative need. Dependent upon the dimension of span relative to the spatial capabilities of the material, an organizing geometry is established that sets the scale and legibility of a space.

The role of structure in plan is of particular formal importance relative to material as the premise of line [load-bearing walls] versus point [columns]. Each system establishes a certain way of making space. Load-bearing materials versus cladding materials are revealed, and their variation and interdependence are highlighted.

The Lovell Beach House uses the same structural spacing of the exposed cast-in-place concrete frames with a lateral major then minor void then double minor cantilever for the volumes of the extruded floor plates; Le Corbusier's Unite d'Habitation in Marseille establishes the module based upon the dimension of the housing unit, using bearing walls to separate the modular pieces; La Tourette finds its bay based on the variable programs [and associated fenestration systems] lodged within the overall organizing form; the Carpenter Center uses a dynamic form independent of the regularized structural column grid; the Salk Institute uses a regularized bay to the laboratory wings with a Vierendeel structure to allow for flexibility to the structurally unbroken floor space; Kahn's Kimbell Art Museum uses a single structural and formal bay celebrating its legibility and repetition; the Church on the Water employs cast-in-place walls that geometrically emerge from modular subdivisions of the pure geometry of the formwork expressed in its surface; and the Rosenthal Center for Contemporary Art, despite its irregular figural geometry, uses a standardized structural geometry.

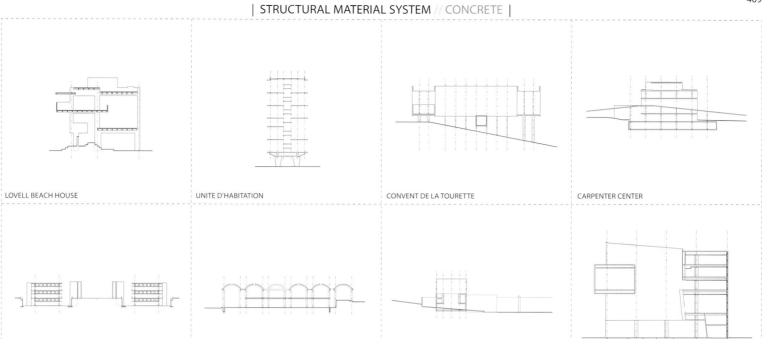

LOVELL BEACH HOUSE

UNITE D'HABITATION

CONVENT DE LA TOURETTE

CARPENTER CENTER

SALK INSTITUTE

KIMBELL ART MUSEUM

CHURCH ON THE WATER

ROSENTHAL CENTER

[CONCRETE] STRUCTURAL MATERIAL [BAY/MODULE] diagrams the sectional implications of the structural module. Focusing on the influence of the structural material, it illustrates the engineered structural response of material relative to performative need. In this diagram set, the structure is materially examined in its vertical figuration of the sectional articulation.

Building on the bay system of the plan, the section depicts the shape and configuration of the repetitive unit and the effectual relationship to the space of the building. Perceived or concealed, primary [as figuration] or coincidental in presence, the role of the sectional structural bay engages the verticality of the building.

The Lovell Beach House clearly depicts the concrete frames and the figured subtractions unique to each rib as the defining forms organizing the position of the floor plates; Le Corbusier's Unite d'Habitation in Marseille is segmented in section, with an L-shaped configuration of the interlocking units that both bridges the entire width of the structure and provides for a two-level unit with a double-height space; La Tourette, despite the seemingly figured and collagist sensibility of the façade, has a very regular structural bay established by the columnar system on the lowest level extending through the section to establish the subdivision of spaces; the Carpenter Center has a free-form figure skewered by a structural skeleton; the Salk Institute layers systems of wall structures in the flanking towers on either face of the central laboratory frame structure; Kahn's Kimbell Art Museum uses a repetitive bay held apart with an interstitial minor zone, allowing for discrete legibility to each of the framed bays; the Church on the Water uses the purity of the geometry established by the formwork to determine the dimensions of the load-bearing concrete perimeters; and the Rosenthal Center for Contemporary Art skewers the diverse forms of the galleries with a standardized columnar system.

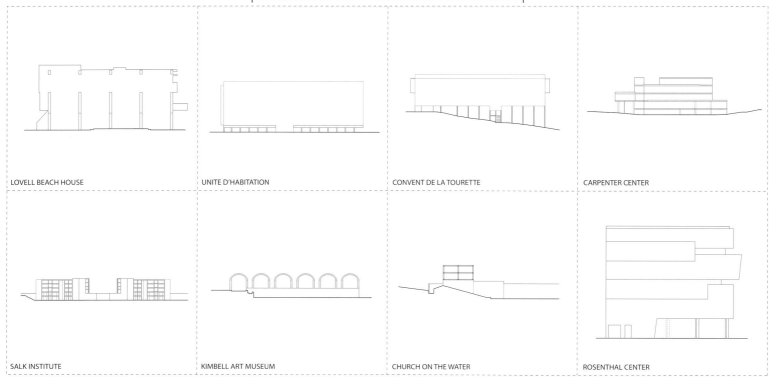

LOVELL BEACH HOUSE   UNITE D'HABITATION   CONVENT DE LA TOURETTE   CARPENTER CENTER

SALK INSTITUTE   KIMBELL ART MUSEUM   CHURCH ON THE WATER   ROSENTHAL CENTER

[CONCRETE] STRUCTURAL MATERIAL LEGIBILITY diagrams in elevation the reading of the structural material. Focusing on the influence of the structural material, it illustrates the interrelation of the engineered structural response of material and performative need to the form and composition. Questioning how the system reads from the exterior and whether the structural material is ever seen, the legibility diagrams examine the relationship of the forces of gravity to the formal expression.

The integration of structure to skin and ultimately to form is about the engagement of the physical requirements of a building to perform structurally with the formal intentions and the legibility of these two systems. The idea of [1] reading a person's bones literally through the skin, [2] versus the broader legibility of a leg as column to transfer vertical loads, [3] versus a denial of all understanding of how the figure works structurally are the three basic stages of structural depiction: [1] literal, [2] figural, or [3] denied.

The Lovell Beach House is a literal system relying upon an exoskeleton that slides through the house to be continuously visible and serve as the meter for the space; Le Corbusier's Unite d'Habitation in Marseille holds the mass of the building off the ground, revealing the structural weight through the massive figural forms of the pilotis; La Tourette starts the buildings' base with a clear structural line but then embeds it in the hovering form above to deny the full continuity and reading of the system; the Carpenter Center pulls the legibility of the striated floor plates through the formwork patterning on the façade; the Salk Institute layers the wall systems of the towers read through their surface against the evaporative nature of the laboratory clad in glass and lightened by a columnar truss system; Kahn's Kimbell Art Museum reveals the concrete frame in the skin articulating the difference between skin and structure; the Church on the Water modulates the surface of the concrete with the formwork and prevents any apertures to emphasize the monolithic and continuous nature of the structural wall; and the Rosenthal Center for Contemporary Art from the exterior appears to have a structural mass to its walls yet masks the internal columnar system.

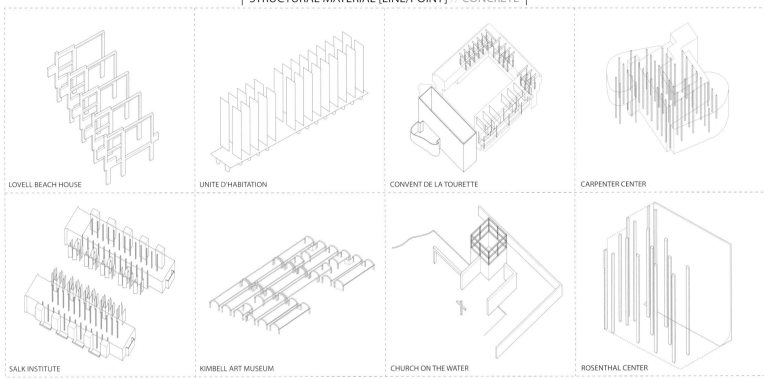

LOVELL BEACH HOUSE

UNITE D'HABITATION

CONVENT DE LA TOURETTE

CARPENTER CENTER

SALK INSTITUTE

KIMBELL ART MUSEUM

CHURCH ON THE WATER

ROSENTHAL CENTER

[CONCRETE] STRUCTURAL MATERIAL [LINE/POINT] diagrams in axonometric the primary geometric and formal response of the structural material/system. "Line" refers to the registration of a wall surface as a structural bearing wall in plan, while "point" refers to the columnar system. Materials subscribe intrinsically to one or the other [typically]; metal is point, while masonry is line. Certain materials, like concrete and wood, have the potential to be either.

The axonometric diagramming of the structural system and the material expression of this system suggest the three-dimensional resolution of the underlying structure superimposed on the form. The relationship of the structural material to the primary material parallels the discussion of revelation versus concealment and homogeneity versus cladding.

The Lovell Beach House uses concrete frames as lines that erode to generate points synthesizing the two forms possible in concrete; Le Corbusier's Unite d'Habitation in Marseille uses load-bearing party walls to separate the units and transfer the vertical loads; La Tourette uses a columnar system at the ground level that transitions to a planar wall system in the upper levels, allowing a synthesis of structural subdivisions with the spatial subdivisions; the Carpenter Center relies upon the columnar field to support the formal figuration; the Salk Institute reveals the wall in the edge towers while providing transparent walls to the central laboratory buildings to illustrate their frame system; Kahn's Kimbell Art Museum sets the layered vaults on an exposed concrete column-and-beam system; the Church on the Water uses continuous cast-in-place concrete walls as site markers and enclosure with no breaks or openings to interfere with their solidity and structural consistency; and the Rosenthal Center for Contemporary Art uses a party wall to address its neighbor, otherwise relying upon a regimented columnar system.

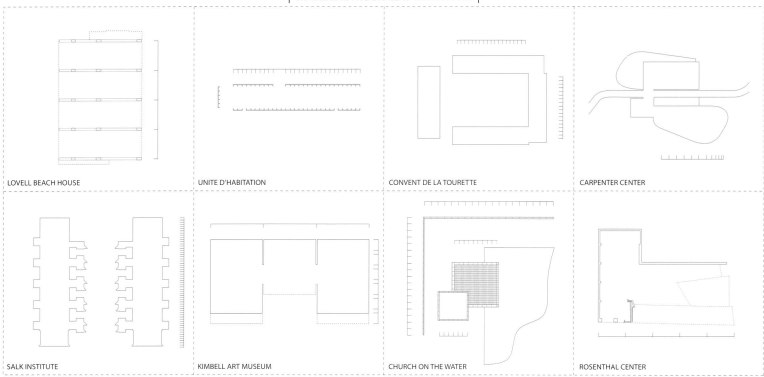

LOVELL BEACH HOUSE

UNITE D'HABITATION

CONVENT DE LA TOURETTE

CARPENTER CENTER

SALK INSTITUTE

KIMBELL ART MUSEUM

CHURCH ON THE WATER

ROSENTHAL CENTER

[CONCRETE] Module – MATERIAL MODULE diagrams in plan the relationships of the manufacturing module intrinsic to a material to the space, form, and dimensions. Mapping the inherited dimensional constraints determined by the production and movement of a material, the patterning of these scale elements and the articulation of their joinery to establish larger architectural forms address the relationship of piece to whole and unit to system.

The module of materials is an intrinsic fact that must be addressed. Certain materials default to a secondary system [such as concrete with formwork] to generate a dimensional constraint, but every material has a "natural" form and dimension. The negotiation of these constraints and the collaboration with these numeric proportions determine the dimensions of the whole and the integration of the modular unit into the consistency of the superstructural organization.

The Lovell Beach House relies upon the module of the window to produce a submodule of the concrete board-formed cast-in-place concrete frames; Le Corbusier's Unite d'Habitation in Marseille uses the module of formwork as the expressive surface bridging between the anthropomorphic dimension and the massive scale of the building. The interstitial scale of the module is determined by the width of the residential unit, establishing a simultaneous spatial and structural module; La Tourette uses the monk's cell dimension [based on the modular] to establish a bay that doubles to produce the structural rhythm [overlaying order on the most flexible material: concrete]; the Carpenter Center maps the module of the formwork against the spatial module to coordinate the experience with the making; the Salk Institute coordinates the concrete material module with the wood formwork module and the final wood infill module, delicately separating their connection while celebrating the craft and techniques of their construction; Kahn's Kimbell Art Museum separates the concrete frame from the travertine infill, establishing a structural module of concrete alongside the segmented module of the travertine cladding; the Church on the Water uses concrete but defers to a highly ordered formwork system to establish the module imprinted on its surfaces; and the Rosenthal Center for Contemporary Art emphasizes the formwork to provide a dimension to the otherwise massive figural forms.

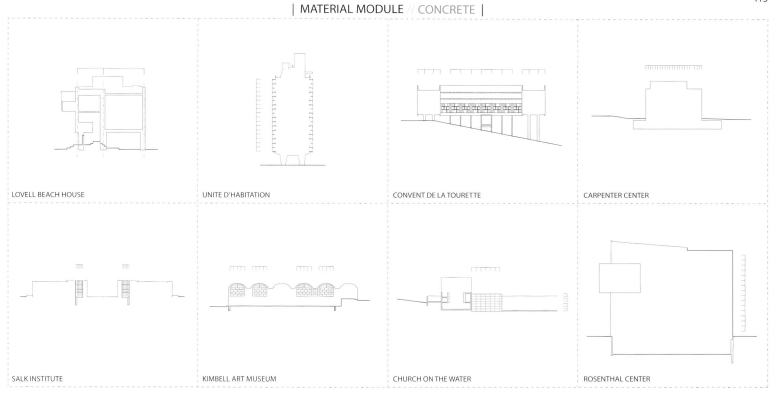

LOVELL BEACH HOUSE

UNITE D'HABITATION

CONVENT DE LA TOURETTE

CARPENTER CENTER

SALK INSTITUTE

KIMBELL ART MUSEUM

CHURCH ON THE WATER

ROSENTHAL CENTER

[CONCRETE] Module – MATERIAL MODULE diagrams in section the relationships of the manufacturing module intrinsic to a material to the space, form, and dimensions. Mapping the inherited dimensional constraints determined by the production and movement of a material to the sectional implications, the patterning of these scale elements and the articulation of their joinery establish larger architectural spaces derived from addressing the relationship of piece to whole and unit to system.

The module of material is an intrinsic fact that must be addressed. Certain materials default to a secondary system [such as concrete with formwork] to generate a dimensional constraint, but every material has a "natural" form and dimension. The negotiation of these constraints and the collaboration with these numeric proportions determine the dimensions of the whole and the integration of the modular unit into the consistency of the superstructural organization. In section, the implications of the human hand of construction relative to the material coursing relative to the body's perception develop the scale and legibility of this module to the spatial presence as a whole.

The Lovell Beach House uses the autonomy of the board-formed cast-in-place frame to register the horizontal banding of the form while deploying a more "designed module" of the double-height public living spaces and the more compact single-height sleeping spaces; Le Corbusier's Unite d'Habitation in Marseille uses a single-level floor-to-ceiling height to establish the vertical casting module; La Tourette uses a module of the fenestration derived from a geometric overlay to produce the patterning of the materials' surface despite its homogeneous nature; the Carpenter Center reveals the patterning of the cast surface on the interior to dimension the scale of construction against the scale of the body; the Salk Institute uses an expressed dimension of the formwork to establish the grain and scale of the spaces; Kahn's Kimbell Art Museum uses the constant expression of the concrete frame to establish a relative scale of space to building; the Church on the Water uses extended geometries from the formwork mapped into the surface as repetitive modules that carry into the steel framing and glass panels with a high level of precision and consistency; and the Rosenthal Center for Contemporary Art uses a faint pattern of surface to reveal the scale of construction in the surface of the figure while emphasizing overall form over the expression of the part.

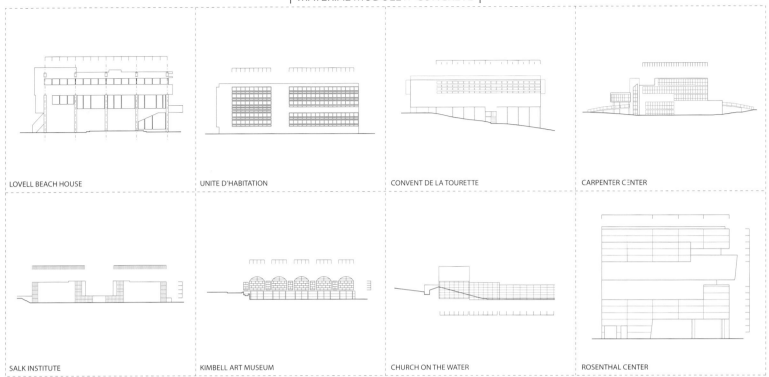

LOVELL BEACH HOUSE

UNITE D'HABITATION

CONVENT DE LA TOURETTE

CARPENTER CENTER

SALK INSTITUTE

KIMBELL ART MUSEUM

CHURCH ON THE WATER

ROSENTHAL CENTER

[CONCRETE] Module – MATERIAL MODULE diagrams in elevation the implications of the relationships of the manufacturing module intrinsic to a material to the space, form, and dimensions. Mapping the inherited dimensional constraints determined by the production and movement of a material to the façade, the formal legibility and implications of an architectural patterning of these scale elements rely upon the articulation of their joinery to establish larger architectural spaces.

The surface reading is derived from addressing the relationship of piece to whole and unit to system through the intrinsic module of a material. Certain materials default to a secondary system [such as concrete with formwork] to generate a dimensional constraint, but every material has a "natural" form and dimension. The negotiation of these constraints and the collaboration with these numeric proportions determine the dimensions of the whole and the integration of the modular unit into the consistency of the superstructural organization. In elevation, the implications of the human hand of construction relative to the material assemblies relative to the body's perception develop the scale and legibility of this module and its spatial presence as a whole.

The Lovell Beach House with board-formed cast-in-place concrete establishes a anthropomorphic texture that is increased through the custom-made wood windows scaled to the torso; Le Corbusier's Unite d'Habitation in Marseille carries the module through the elevation in the subdivisions of the brise-soleil; La Tourette uses a module of the fenestration derived from the monk's cells to produce a patterned geometric overlay despite the homogeneous nature of the material; the Carpenter Center maps the module of the formwork against the spatial module to coordinate the experience with the making; the Salk Institute articulates the surface relentlessly with the hierarchy sequence and method of construction, relying upon the open joint to celebrate each material system independently, and their articulated and coordinated assembly; Kahn's Kimbell Art Museum similarly holds the exposed frame and skin apart, allowing for the localized celebration of a singular material as well as the combined celebration of their integration; the Church on the Water uses extended geometries from the formwork mapped into the surface as repetitive modules that carry into the steel framing and glass panels with a high level of precision and consistency; and the Rosenthal Center for Contemporary Art similarly reveals the subtle patterning of the fabrication formwork on the exterior figure to reveal the scale of construction in the surface.

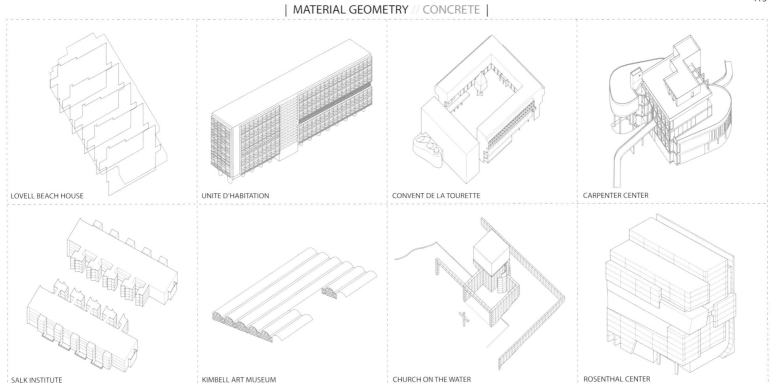

LOVELL BEACH HOUSE

UNITE D'HABITATION

CONVENT DE LA TOURETTE

CARPENTER CENTER

SALK INSTITUTE

KIMBELL ART MUSEUM

CHURCH ON THE WATER

ROSENTHAL CENTER

[CONCRETE] Module – MATERIAL GEOMETRY diagrams in axonometric the three-dimensional relationships of the manufacturing module intrinsic to a material to the space, form, and dimensions. Mapping the inherited dimensional constraints determined by the production and movement of a material into the three-dimensional ramifications of the total form, the legibility of an architectural patterning of scale elements relies upon the articulation of their joinery to establish larger architectural spaces.

The surface reading is derived from addressing the relationship of piece to whole and unit to system through the intrinsic module of a material. Certain materials default to a secondary system [such as concrete with formwork] to generate a dimensional constraint, but every material has a "natural" form and dimension. The negotiation of these constraints and the collaboration with these numeric proportions determine the dimensions of the whole and the integration of the modular unit into the consistency of the superstructural organization. In axonometric, the module governs the formal legibility of the three-dimensional building component and ultimately the formal reading of the building as a whole.

The Lovell Beach House with board-formed cast-in-place concrete planar frames establishes an anthropomorphic texture and dimensional void creating a rhythm and hierarchy to the house; Le Corbusier's Unite d'Habitation in Marseille diversely composes the formwork to celebrate the functional, dimensional, structural, and even ornamental capabilities of surface; La Tourette uses a module of the fenestration derived from the monk's cell to produce a patterned geometric overlay and then adds additional formal elements to the composition to create dramatic compositional variety despite the homogeneous nature of the material; the Carpenter Center uses diverse fenestration techniques [ribs, frames, brise-soleil, etc.] to reinforce the formal geometries; the Salk Institute quilts the surface with the module and method of construction, allowing the shift from the large central figure to the smaller-scaled edge figures; Kahn's Kimbell Art Museum uses a repetitive bay system that establishes a classical overarching scale; the Church on the Water uses extended geometries from the formwork mapped into the surface as repetitive modules that carry into the steel framing and glass panels with a high level of precision and consistency; and the Rosenthal Center for Contemporary Art figures the overall composition and then subdivides these forms into equal segments to allow for the construction.

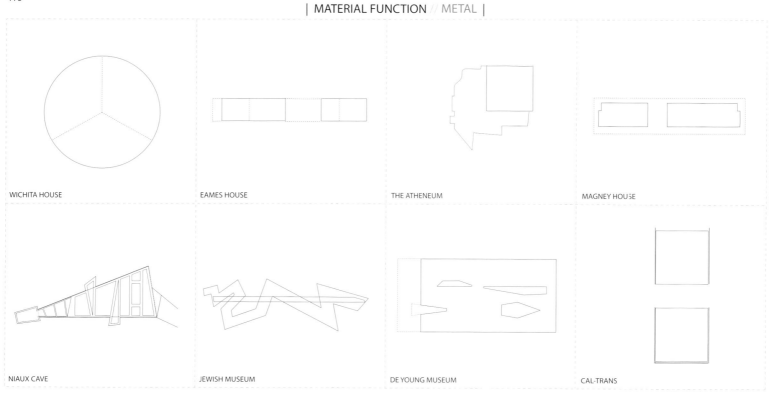

WICHITA HOUSE

EAMES HOUSE

THE ATHENEUM

MAGNEY HOUSE

NIAUX CAVE

JEWISH MUSEUM

DE YOUNG MUSEUM

CAL-TRANS

[METAL] MATERIAL FUNCTION diagrams in plan the relationship between material use and the formal and technical associations required by its functional application. These diagrams examine the role of a material's specific performance properties and its employment relative to the functional and practical necessities of the program and building performance. Each material expresses of the conditions and requirements of its deployment.

Defining the premise of skin in each application, material serves as the iconic designation of form in each project. The associated material tectonic employed extends its influence to express itself through the spatial concepts of the architecture. Steel defines vertical lines [Eames House and Niaux Cave], concrete defines planes and frames with variable openings [Lovell Beach House, La Tourette, Church on the Water], and masonry creates modulated solid edges [Casa Barragan and Murcia Town Hall]. Glass establishes transparent veils: flat, ambiguous surfaces that exist but slip into a nonpresence allowing the dissolve of the enclosure and a perceived spatial connection between inside and outside. This is most prevalent in the De Blas Haus and the Cartier Foundation, though it exists even when the glass is frosted and figured, as in the glass block façade of the Maison de Verre. Each material relative to its function determines form.

Fuller's Wichita House is obsessed with the manufacturing and weight of the metal cladding. Machined, modulated, and efficient, the house takes the circle in plan to maximize the area of enclosure while minimizing surface, material, and weight; the Eames House is defined by the light steel frame that creates a structural skeleton; Meier's Atheneum uses the material across the diverse forms to generate a homogeneity to the surface and emphasizes form over tectonic; the Magney House extrudes a constant section along the bar of the house separating the figure in plan into two distinct zones, public and private; the Niaux Cave relies upon the funneling line of frame and the plane of surface to define a choreographed entry; Libeskind's Jewish Museum juxtaposes the simple datum of the concrete central core against the dynamic figure of the metal galleries; the De Young Museum blankets a mat building with cracked courtyards that allow slivers of exterior space to penetrate the large figure of the building's footprint; and the Cal-Trans Building by Morphosis employs a simple box figure clad in a performative skin that modulates the environment and produces the formal figuration of the project.

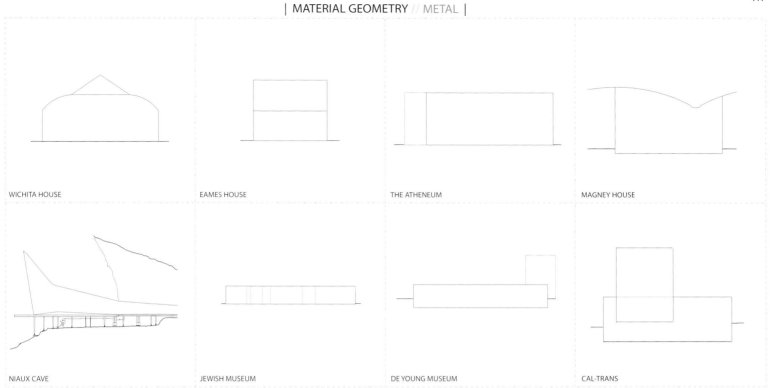

WICHITA HOUSE

EAMES HOUSE

THE ATHENEUM

MAGNEY HOUSE

NIAUX CAVE

JEWISH MUSEUM

DE YOUNG MUSEUM

CAL-TRANS

[METAL] MATERIAL GEOMETRY diagrams the sectional geometric implications of material for form. By introducing the potential structural implications of a material, the relationship of "skin to bones" or surface to structure becomes relative to the intrinsic qualities of a material. Establishing the dimensional module [both of performance and of fabrication and installation limitations], the capabilities of a material express themselves beyond the figure of the form to address the geometry of the space.

The module of a material can be established by three potential scales. The first scale is the module of the unit: a single brick, a sheet of plywood [as direct application of sheathing or as indirect application of formwork], a glass pane with either concealed or revealed frame systems, or a steel member. In each of these conditions the unit is defined by a structural need, a material property, or a manufacturing module. The second scale is the bay of the module produced through the assemblies or structure. For example, the Eames House window wall module is an aggregate of the individual panes, the double high bay module, and the superstructural steel frame. The final scale is the designed geometry of the building's mass expressed through material, i.e., the formal figure of the object as a whole. Each of these three levels can coexist or be independently exploited. The material in each case is, however, the beginning, the dimensional collaborator based on the intrinsic properties and performance of the base material.

Fuller's Wichita House uses repetitive segments to produce the radial figure of ribs and skin; the Eames House has a stacked double module within the structural frame to create an anthropomorphic scale; Meier's Atheneum cloaks the interior in sheet rock whiteness, removing the reference to material to emphasize light and form; the Magney House uses the figural shape of the corrugated metal roof to define the sectional layering of spaces; the Niaux Cave has a sculpted geometry of skin superimposed on a rational grid subgeometry of structural framing; Libeskind's Jewish Museum uses figured cuts to reveal the regularly banded pattern of the exterior surface; the De Young Museum cloaks the interior with a requisite white wall for the gallery, revealing the perforated skin through the courtyards and apertures; and the Cal-Trans Building by Morphosis interlocks a horizontal figure with a vertical figure, both clad in the perforated metal skin that folds and figures to respond to the functional necessities and environmental requirements.

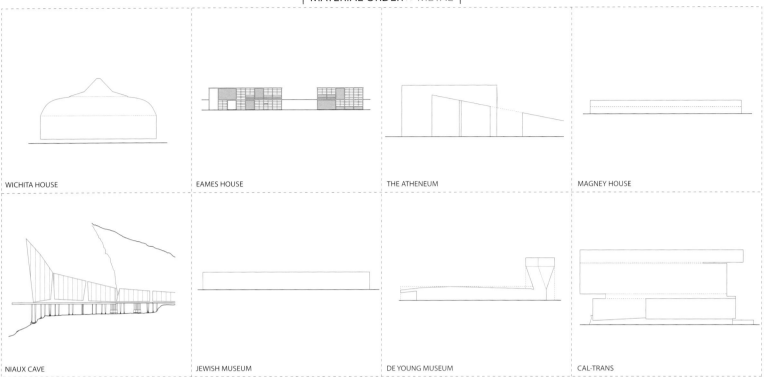

WICHITA HOUSE EAMES HOUSE THE ATHENEUM MAGNEY HOUSE

NIAUX CAVE JEWISH MUSEUM DE YOUNG MUSEUM CAL-TRANS

[METAL] MATERIAL ORDER diagrams in elevation the hierarchy, sequence, and organizational methods of material's influence on the architectural form. As in the examination in section, the implication here is more spatial than formal. Looking at the organizational geometries and governing patterns of material relative to the form, the implications and legibility of volume and mass are articulated through the aggregation of the material pieces.

The extension of the material module into the overarching order of the formal expression is the ultimate collaboration of material with design. The definition of the overall form relative to the piece, the manner in which an aperture is made as a removal [in terms of both module and structural implications], and the relation of these compositional pieces to the formal whole are the defining characteristics of a material's influence on form.

Fuller's Wichita House segments the building into a tripartite configuration of equal rib pieces; the Eames House deploys the repetitive bay of the structural metal infilling this system with a series of repetitive opaque and transparent subdivisions; Meier's Atheneum blankets the diverse forms in a square multivalent grid of white porcelain enameled panels; the Magney House is a repetitive extruded section that is choreographed to respond to the local environmental conditions; the Niaux Cave vertically striates the panels to deny the segmentation and emphasize the figuration over any surface articulation; Libeskind's Jewish Museum regularly panelizes the surface, creating both horizontal and vertical pin striping that allows for a greater contrast to the dynamic and violent apertures; the De Young Museum variably perforates the façade to pixilated, abstracted imagery of context and produces a dynamically responsive pattern to the skin that reads at variable scales; and the Cal-Trans Building by Morphosis uses variable densities in its perforated skin to create patterned opacity.

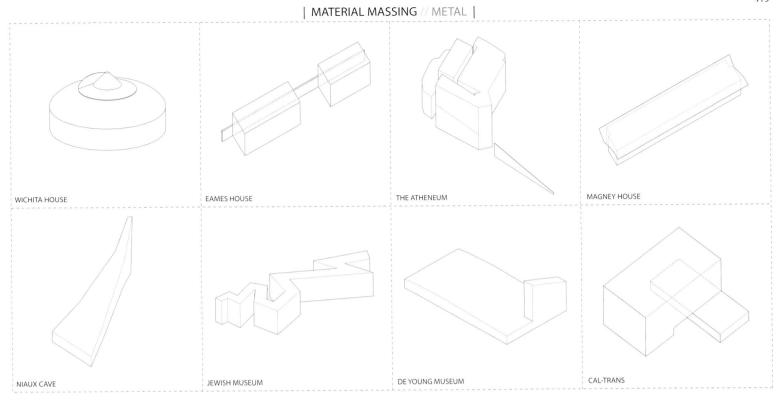

WICHITA HOUSE

EAMES HOUSE

THE ATHENEUM

MAGNEY HOUSE

NIAUX CAVE

JEWISH MUSEUM

DE YOUNG MUSEUM

CAL-TRANS

[METAL] MATERIAL MASSING diagrams in axonometric the overall legibility of the primary material to the superstructural form, presence, and mass of the architectural form. Focusing primarily on the mass and volume of form as defined by the material application to the exterior, the legibility of compositional intention and the geometric hierarchy are mapped.

The significance of mass [as defined by material in particular] concerns the clarity of formal intention in relation to the actual legibility and reading in the building. The conceptual ideas that govern the design of a building become legible through their tectonic manifestations in the form. The hierarchy of the primary massing determines the figuration to which all else must respond. The material relationship with this massing and the deployment of the tectonic expression of the assembly determine whether a material is read as segmented, disassociated, panelized, repetitive, or monolithic.

Fuller's Wichita House uses a circular plan that arches to create a uniformity to its centralized plan; the Eames House removes bays of the repetitive system to produce a courtyard void between the two figures that pit work and living spaces as fluid and interconnected yet discrete elements; Meier's Atheneum uses a series of rotated interlocking geometries to produce the composed dynamism of its form; the Magney House develops an articulated, environmentally responsive section that it then extrudes longitudinally along the length of the house ; the Niaux Cave uses two funneling planes segmented into vertical panels at the structural interval to draw the visitor into the caves; Libeskind's Jewish Museum uses a central concrete line juxtaposed against the dynamic folded form that relates to historical, contextual, experiential, and compositional axes within the project and the city; the De Young Museum slices open the rectangular mat figure of the horizontal element and slowly rotates the vertical figure to transition from local to distant site conditions; and the Cal-Trans Building by Morphosis floats a conventional bar building across a lower-level bar, cladding the two volumes [through the two longitudinal faces] in layered skins of figured perforations.

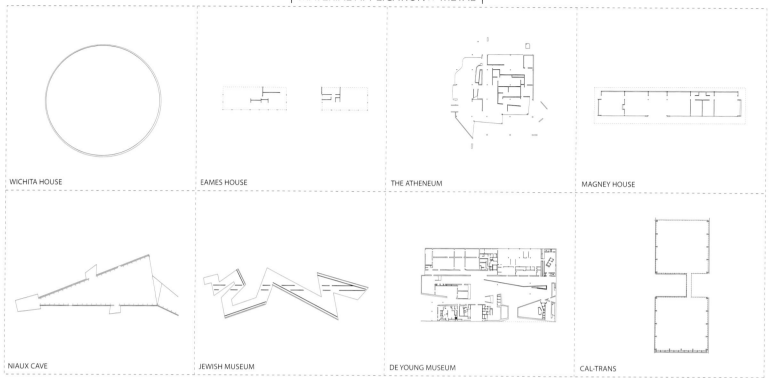

WICHITA HOUSE

EAMES HOUSE

THE ATHENEUM

MAGNEY HOUSE

NIAUX CAVE

JEWISH MUSEUM

DE YOUNG MUSEUM

CAL-TRANS

[METAL] MATERIAL APPLICATION diagrams in plan the deployment of material and the associated perceptual, formal, and functional readings. Engaging the relationship between material and function, the formal expression becomes the primary mediating element. The expression of the material's use and the tectonic deployment determine the functional programmatic legibility of the building. This begins with the formal expression intrinsic to the material followed by issues of practical performance including durability, porosity, and visual effect.

A material can be selected for various reasons: availability, cost, durability, module, structural capability, or simply the functional applicability [metal to combat combustion, concrete for construction in corrosive environments, or masonry as a low-maintenance, durable skin]. In each scenario the fundamental physical properties of the material are the baseline of design consideration. These properties, mediated by the method of manufacturing and limited by the method of working [wood is easy to cut, metal can be welded, masonry is heavy and modular], develop the second tier of consideration. Finally, and perhaps with the most variability, is the assembly and application. The systemization of the manufactured pieces and their formal and technical articulation comprise material design application.

Fuller's Wichita House uses aluminum to optimize the structure and engage fabrication processes developed during World War II. The combination of the materiality with the inventive and expressive assembly system establishes the machined iconography of the house; the Eames House uses metal to create a frame that is as slender as possible to allow the walls to be choreographed at will [the house allows for variability through the method of aggregation and the composition of the assembly], yet standardized to express of an embrace of new premanufactured assembly-line systems; Meier's Atheneum uses both the ubiquitous square grid and the white porcelain panels to abstract the building and defer the legibility to the form; the Magney House uses durable yet simple corrugated metal to create a delicate yet thin enclosure. The composed section allows for the customization of the pieces, but the extruded length allows for the serial efficiency; the Niaux Cave emphasizes the triangular plan to create a funnel that expands and contracts the threshold into the caves; Libeskind's Jewish Museum uses the stark and shiny metal skin to produce a drama and presence to the building as a contrasting figure in the Berlin cityscape. The regularized panels establish a datum field against which the drama of the dynamically composed iconographic window system is juxtaposed to heighten their presence; the De Young Museum uses the skin as the responsive iconography for the building. Here, unlike most prior Herzog and DeMeuron buildings, the form is more whimsically engaged at the same time, giving the reading of the rectangular mat building as a series of bent, aggregated tubes with sliver courtyards between them; and the Cal-Trans Building by Morphosis deploys a very simple and cost-effective bar building, producing the dynamism and effect through the layered, perforated metal cladding.

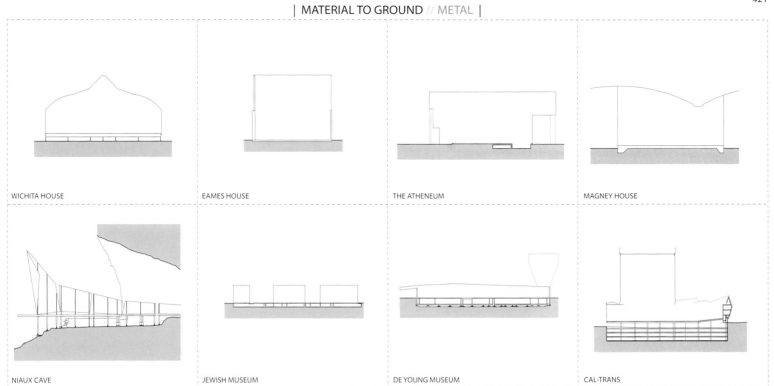

WICHITA HOUSE

EAMES HOUSE

THE ATHENEUM

MAGNEY HOUSE

NIAUX CAVE

JEWISH MUSEUM

DE YOUNG MUSEUM

CAL-TRANS

[METAL] Proximity – MATERIAL TO GROUND diagrams the sectional relationship in which a building meets the ground, engages landscape, and addresses the material point of connection with the site. The point of contact between a building and the earth is determined by the material approach to the architecture. Factors that determine and affect this condition include soil characteristics, climate, context, structural system, and building weight [both actual and perceived].

The history of structural and material technology is the history of how a building meets the ground. The selection of material cladding and structural framing results in a specific formal articulation of this condition that is intrinsic to the material and tectonic. Technologically determined, this joint [between building and ground] is created by the system of both the structure and the cladding. Historically, load-bearing wall systems of wood or masonry required continuous contact of the building with the ground and limited the scale and frequency of openings. Materials such as steel and concrete allowed for a formal disengagement from the ground plane, turning structural planes into points and shifting from a wall system to a cage.

Fuller's Wichita House floats off the ground to emphasize the centralized structure; the Eames House relates asymmetrically to the two sides of the house: the hillside sets the frame on top of a concrete retaining wall, while the frame side remains an open skeleton; Meier's Atheneum pulls out of the landscape, dramatically emphasized by the long linear ascent of the exterior ramp and the dissolving figures of the building as it transitions from frame to volume to mass; the Magney House sets simply on the ground, reserving its dynamism for the roof plane; the Niaux Cave pulls the datum of the ground plane of the cave through the entry pavilion as an elevated platform supported by a series of columns that establish the structural grid for the platform and skin simultaneously; Libeskind's Jewish Museum has a significant experiential and metaphorical relationship with the ground, requiring the visitor to move below grade and then ascend up through the building for both experiential and metaphorical purposes; the De Young Museum sets simply on the ground, dissolving the surface through the perforation and the formal figuration; and the Cal-Trans Building by Morphosis separates the skin from the ground [while the building proper engages the ground plane in a traditional and matter-of-fact manner], allowing the dynamic wrapper to transition from street edge to canopy to sunscreen.

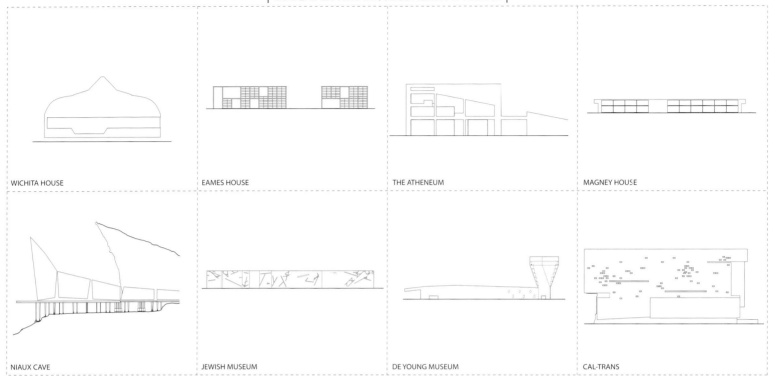

WICHITA HOUSE

EAMES HOUSE

THE ATHENEUM

MAGNEY HOUSE

NIAUX CAVE

JEWISH MUSEUM

DE YOUNG MUSEUM

CAL-TRANS

[METAL] Proximity – PRIMARY / SECONDARY diagrams in elevation the relationship of the primary building material to the secondary building material, focusing on the formal, functional, and practical interrelationships of their material application. The hierarchy between these two levels is both formally and materially evident, establishing the organizing geometries of the diverse layers.

The proximity of a primary figure to a secondary figure builds on the formal reading of material application diagrams but engages the interrelationship with the secondary systemization. The interaction of the two can occur through superimposition, contrasting figures, interpenetration, banding, layering, or any other adverbial relationship. The result is a primary figuration and the secondary subsystemization that, through its geometry, breaks down the material into fabricateable and installable pieces and reveals the tectonic intention of their aggregation.

Fuller's Wichita House sets the exterior shell of aluminum against the ribbon window of glass; the Eames House sets against the primary geometry of the two building pieces and the rhythmic consistency of their repetitive structural bay, the two vertical layers of panels that are systematized but diverse in their dispensation; Meier's Atheneum juxtaposes the opaque yet abstract metal panels against the transparency of the glass to play compositionally with the relationship between solid and void; the Magney House uses the figured opacity of the roof extending into the simple blankness of the back metal wall against the entirely glass wall of the opposing face to create directionality and hierarchy; the Niaux Cave segments its external revelation and concealment of the substructure with the occupied plane: below this surface the primary members of the structural lattice are exposed, while above this level the corten sheets define the sculpted planar surfaces; Libeskind's Jewish Museum uses the exposed lines of windows to create the signified composition of the façade; the De Young Museum veils the entire building in the copper perforated cladding, eliminating almost all reference to the secondary surface materials that are withheld until entry; and the Cal-Trans Building by Morphosis uses the relentless perforated metal skin to variably and responsively clad the glass box beneath.

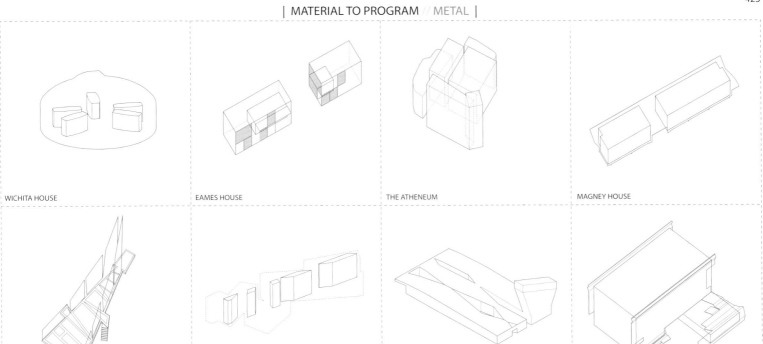

WICHITA HOUSE

EAMES HOUSE

THE ATHENEUM

MAGNEY HOUSE

NIAUX CAVE

JEWISH MUSEUM

DE YOUNG MUSEUM

CAL-TRANS

[METAL] Proximity – MATERIAL TO PROGRAM diagrams in axonometric the overall relationship of material usage to the primary programmatic and functional usages. By focusing on the three-dimensional volumetric associations of material to programmatic usage [and the associated functional requirements of a particular program], the articulation of "form following function" can be examined through material association.

The relationship of the programmatic usage to the material selected depicts the narrative of the association, creating the opportunity and potential for material to be an expressive sign system. The legibility of a material comes from a technical knowledge that engages an understanding of raw material, manufacturing processes, construction traditions and techniques, weathering and biological attack, and cultural associations. These innate properties of matter translate into forms that collaborate with materials to reveal their process.

Fuller's Wichita House as a centralized scheme segments the house into wedge-shaped programs that, despite their various functionalities, have relatively standardized radial spaces; the Eames House separates the primary form into two pieces of office and living, then further subdivides these spaces into service and served zones with interior wood walls; Meier's Atheneum uses the programmatic zones to establish the primary figuration of the composition geometry and spatial hierarchy; the Magney House uses a standardized section and then modularly subdivides the spaces linearly to gradate privacy and function through layered adjacencies; the Niaux Cave has a secondary presence of the wood horizontal surface that provides a lateral patterning to the strong metal vertical systems; Libeskind's Jewish Museum emphasizes the composition and spatial effect of the gallery so much that, upon completion, there was debate as to whether the collection should actually be installed; the De Young Museum uses the same material relentlessly across the building, but allows for variability to the perforations and indentations to produce variable compositions and opacities as a local response; and the Cal-Trans Building by Morphosis similarly relies upon the dynamism and responsiveness of the skin [both formally and in terms of porosity] to locally produce functional responses while maintaining a connectivity and consistency to the surface and the composition as a whole.

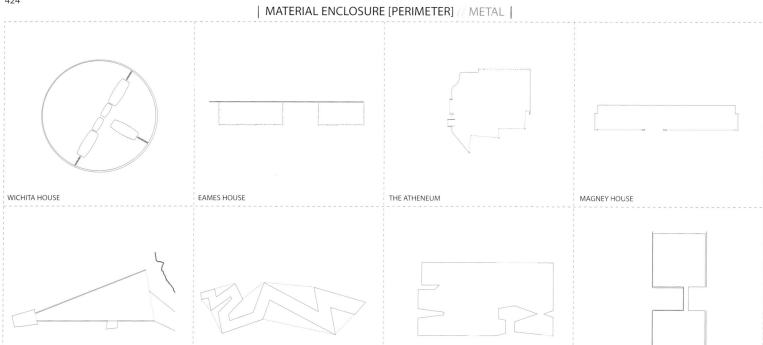

WICHITA HOUSE

EAMES HOUSE

THE ATHENEUM

MAGNEY HOUSE

NIAUX CAVE

JEWISH MUSEUM

DE YOUNG MUSEUM

CAL-TRANS

[METAL] Skin + Surface – MATERIAL ENCLOSURE [PERIMETER] diagrams in plan the relationship of the outer plane of enclosure [skin] to the spatial, formal, and structural organization. Expressing the process by which materials assemble into systems, the figuration of the perimeter is dependent not simply upon the piece but also upon the joint. The collaboration of these two generates specific forms intrinsic to a material and expressively identifiable.

The use of skin to define the perimeter over the structure and the programmatic innards establishes the legibility of architectural idea's purity through the articulation of edge and boundary. The continuity and complexity of this envelope widely explicate the material articulation and the tectonic intricacy. The relationship of craft to figure is found in the method of material manipulation.

Fuller's Wichita House uses a simple shell to create a singular dynamic space. The thinness of the edge is complemented by the requisite strut system that pulls the surface through the space; the Eames House defines two volumes through the thinness of the steel and glass enclosure; Meier's Atheneum, through its exposed circulation system and variable geometries, produces a dynamic formal perimeter that is tectonically blanketed in a standardized surface; the Magney House parallels a largely opaque back wall against the largely transparent front wall, allowing localized adjacencies to establish the longitudinal layering; the Niaux Cave has a funneled primary figure with a secondary surface that leaks out for view platforms as it funnels the visitor into the caves; Libeskind's Jewish Museum has the characteristically identifiable jagged geometry formed by the extension lines of contextual axis and generating a violent and figured spatial experience appropriate to the building's contents; the De Young Museum uses the veil of perforated and dented copper to make the otherwise largely opaque box ephemeral, supple, and dynamic; and the Cal-Trans Building by Morphosis holds the outer perforated skin off the wall of the building, allowing it a formal and figurative freedom.

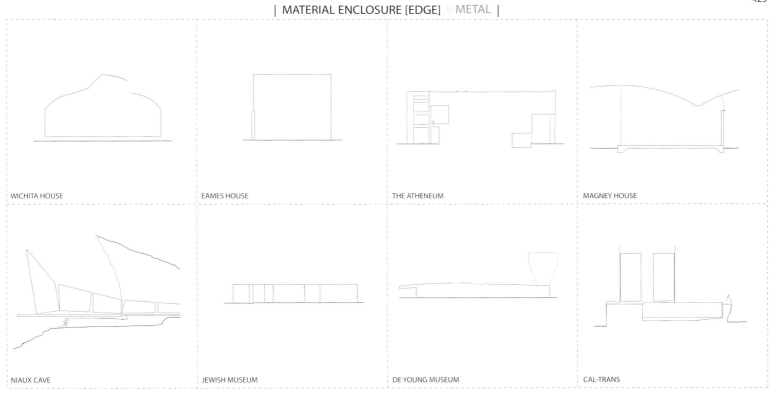

WICHITA HOUSE

EAMES HOUSE

THE ATHENEUM

MAGNEY HOUSE

NIAUX CAVE

JEWISH MUSEUM

DE YOUNG MUSEUM

CAL-TRANS

[METAL] Skin + Surface – MATERIAL ENCLOSURE [EDGE] diagrams in section the relationship of the outer plane of enclosure [skin] to the spatial, formal, and structural organization. Expressing the process by which materials assemble into systems, the figuration of the perimeter as expressed through section extends the moves of plan in the Y axis [still dependent not simply upon the piece but also upon the joint].

The collaboration of piece with joint determines the sectional spatial forms intrinsic to a material, resulting in expressive and identifiable associations. The role of skin in section similarly works to define the perimeter over the structure and the interior functions. The figure establishes the legibility of an architectural idea's purity through the articulation of edge and boundary as extended to the vertical and thus the now spatial dimension. The continuity and complexity of this line widely explicate the material articulation and the tectonic intricacy. The relationship of exterior material through the surface of the building to impact and define interior space is moderated by the material manipulation of this edge.

Fuller's Wichita House uses the shell of the building to create a single volumetric enclosure then subdivided by interior service cores; the Eames House defines its volume through the thinness of the steel and glass enclosure; Meier's Atheneum diffuses the legibility of a single wall plane through the expanded depth of its composition and the relentless desire to make it visually consistent, focusing the eye instead on the compositional effects of its thickness, position, and scale; the Magney House emphasizes the thinness possible through the rigidity of the metal cladding, reducing the scale of the opaque elements to express their edge, and juxtaposes this with the transparency of large glass surfaces; the Niaux Cave has a funneled sectional figure with secondary breaks that leak lateral views as it funnels the visitor into the caves; Libeskind's Jewish Museum defaults to the concrete core as the material expressed on the interior, using the thickness and material layers of the wall [metal skin, structural skeleton, interior surface and the expressed tectonic connections] to allow the apertures to reveal the archaeology of the systems and their palimpsest history and compositional diversity; the De Young Museum masks the material largely on the interior, revealing it only at apertures and courts; and the Cal-Trans Building by Morphosis further subdivides the secondary skin panels through the wire meshes and perforations to transition the composition across scales, allowing for a figured continuity of part to whole.

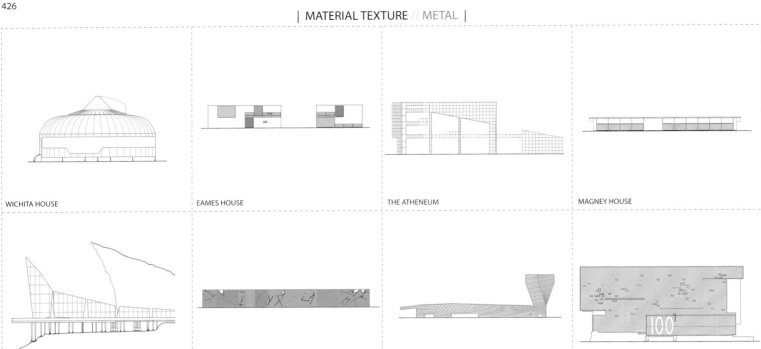

WICHITA HOUSE   EAMES HOUSE   THE ATHENEUM   MAGNEY HOUSE

NIAUX CAVE   JEWISH MUSEUM   DE YOUNG MUSEUM   CAL-TRANS

[METAL] Skin + Surface – MATERIAL TEXTURE diagrams in elevation the legibility of the material texture, color, and surface. Defining the compositional aesthetics of the elevation, the collagist sensibility of pattern, texture, color, and depth of plane are all legible against light. Like a composed painting, this image is dissected from the visual perceptual stance of the material on the architectural composition.

The textural reading refers to the actual color and composition of the material. Wood, for example, can be classified as a generic type, but the performance qualities, colors, hardness, resistance to rot, durability, and workability are vastly different from species to species. This same textural legibility comes through the assembly and expression of the unit and the joint. The scale and articulation of these connections define the legibility of the collective material reading and the overall compositional reading of the architecture.

Fuller's Wichita House derives its texture from the segmented skin and the articulation of its joinery; the uniformity of the ribbon window compositionally reassembles the discontinuous surface; the Eames House creates a collagist infill of the hyperrational and regular modular bay system producing compositions varying from opaque, to diagonal ties, to colored metal infill panels, all within the large glass wall; Meier's Atheneum relies upon the field of the grid to establish a consistent pattern for recession of field and the legibility of the form as it cuts it; the Magney House uses the corrugation of the opaque metal surfaces to generate the pattern detail, carrying the effect through the metal screens shading the longitudinal window wall; the Niaux Cave uses large metal panels to produce a drama of scale but employs corten steel for the organic nature of its surface to associate and produce a dialogue with the natural conditions of the site; Libeskind's Jewish Museum uses the thickness and material layers of the wall [metal skin, structural skeleton, interior surface and the expressed tectonic connections] to allow the apertures to reveal the archaeology of the systems and their palimpsest history and compositional diversity; the De Young Museum denies the joint to emphasize the pattern of the surface; and the Cal-Trans Building by Morphosis further subdivides the secondary skin panels through the wire meshes and perforations to transition the composition across scales, allowing for a figured continuity of part to whole.

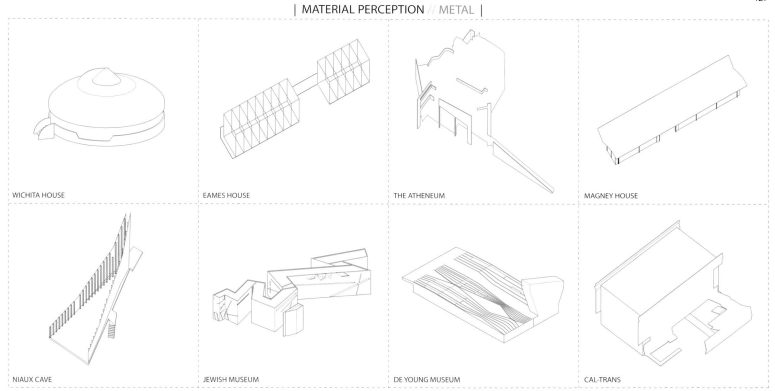

WICHITA HOUSE

EAMES HOUSE

THE ATHENEUM

MAGNEY HOUSE

NIAUX CAVE

JEWISH MUSEUM

DE YOUNG MUSEUM

CAL-TRANS

[METAL] Skin + Surface – MATERIAL PERCEPTION diagrams in axonometric the primary reading of material experience. By transitioning from the sectional reading that focuses on the two-dimensional interior spatial conditions or the material application, the reading in elevation speaks to the composition of the façade but again within the shallow space of a two-dimensional reading, while the axonometric examination illustrates the compositional legibility of the building as a total object.

By engaging all three dimensions, the figuration of the architecture and the legibility of a material's perception relative to the total object lend a volumetric legibility to a material's perception. A truly monolithic architecture is nearly impossible; thus, the connection and change from one piece to the next define the moment of intervention and design decision. The perception of the whole after the resolution of these local "events" is the perception of the architecture. Focusing specifically on the material impact upon these decisions allows the design intention to be revealed through the tectonic view of the whole through the piece.

Fuller's Wichita House celebrates the radial form in its cornerless, frontless figure; the Eames House simply articulates itself with the regimented ribs and the consistent cross section of the house; Meier's Atheneum creates a layered volumetric central figure with perimeter frames, planes, and circulation systems to diffuse the figure of the building; the Magney House celebrates the simplicity of a line distinctly calibrated in section; the Niaux Cave funnels and figures the entryway; Libeskind's Jewish Museum allows the broken geometries to generate the complexity of its figurative form; the De Young Museum reestablishes the form-making process through the ribbing of its roof showing the bunching of the spatial strands; and the Cal-Trans Building by Morphosis emphasizes the secondary surface of the porous perforated metal veils that powerfully mediate between the boundary of the site and the enclosure of the building.

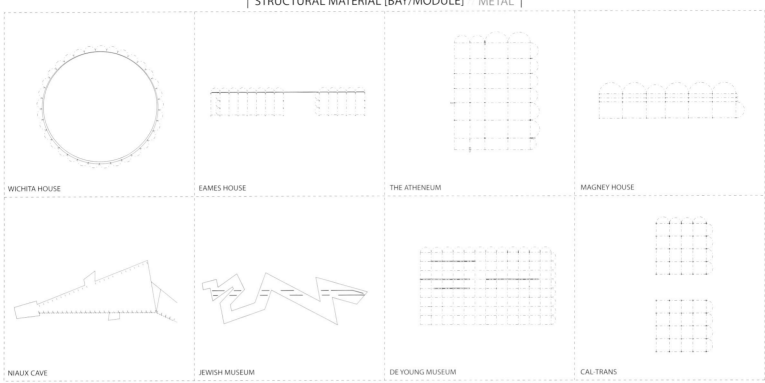

WICHITA HOUSE

EAMES HOUSE

THE ATHENEUM

MAGNEY HOUSE

NIAUX CAVE

JEWISH MUSEUM

DE YOUNG MUSEUM

CAL-TRANS

[METAL] STRUCTURAL MATERIAL [BAY/MODULE] diagrams in plan the structural module of the building. Focusing on the influence of the structural material, it illustrates the engineered structural response of material relative to performative need. Dependent upon the dimension of span relative to the spatial capabilities of the material, an organizing geometry is established that sets the scale and legibility of a space.

The role of structure in plan is of particular formal importance relative to material as the premise of line [load-bearing walls] versus point [columns]. Each system establishes a certain way of making space. Load-bearing materials versus cladding materials are revealed, and their variation and interdependence are highlighted.

Fuller's Wichita House uses a standardized radial geometry that creates wedge-shaped sections; the Eames House has a repetitive bay system with a perimeter steel frame that bridges from inside to outside; Meier's Atheneum uses a standardized grid in a Corbusian manner to establish structural regularity to the free-formed walls; the Magney House establishes a simple repetitive linear structure that serves as the spatial and programmatic subdivisions of the bar; the Niaux Cave has a standard plan module for the lattice backing to the metal walls that aggregate in variable numbers to produce the figured pieces of each panel; Libeskind's Jewish Museum juxtaposes the interior system of the concrete central line against the exterior internally regularized but superstructurally formally driven metal wall; the De Young Museum establishes a repetitive columnar bay system allowing the skin to move dynamically independent of structure; and the Cal-Trans Building by Morphosis uses a cost-effective, simple grid to the traditional bar building, allowing the skin to be expressively dynamic and independent.

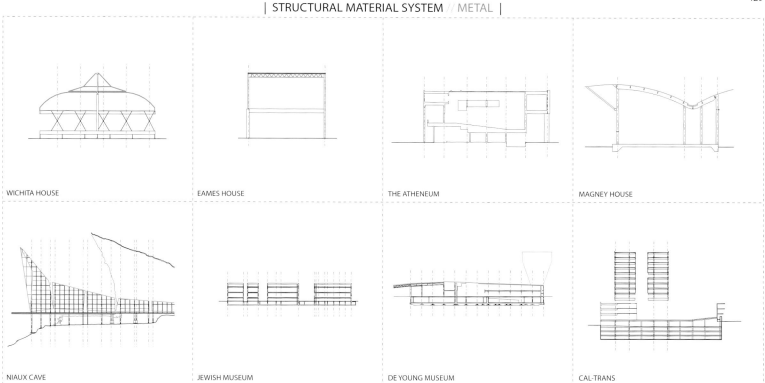

WICHITA HOUSE

EAMES HOUSE

THE ATHENEUM

MAGNEY HOUSE

NIAUX CAVE

JEWISH MUSEUM

DE YOUNG MUSEUM

CAL-TRANS

[METAL] STRUCTURAL MATERIAL [BAY/MODULE] diagrams the sectional implications of the structural module. Focusing on the influence of the structural material, it illustrates the engineered structural response of material relative to performative need. In this diagram set, the structure is materially examined in its vertical figuration of the sectional articulation.

Building on the bay system of the plan, the section depicts the shape and configuration of the repetitive unit and the effectual relationship to the space of the building. Perceived or concealed, primary [as figuration] or coincidental in presence, the role of the sectional structural bay engages the verticality of the building.

Fuller's Wichita House uses a suspended system of struts, ribs, and panels to lightly hover over the aluminum perimeter; the Eames House has a perimeter structure with the insert of an episodic second floor to bridge across the space operating within variables of the standardized system; Meier's Atheneum uses the standardized grid to skewer the spaces and juxtapose the ordering system of the structure with the compositional system of the skin; the Magney House supports the roof at four main points in section: two to establish the outer edge while providing a solar overhang and two to establish an inner core that laterally divides the space and provides a guide for interior circulation and service systems; the Niaux Cave creates a figured skin over a standardized lattice backing that shows a doppelganger effect to the two faces with an outer that is about surface [plane] and an inner that is about frame [line]; Libeskind's Jewish Museum masks the structure in the wall to emphasize the concrete core chamber and the dynamism of the surface cuts on the spatial perception; the De Young Museum uses a standardized grid that is largely and anonymously concealed within the walls to emphasize the artworks collected within the galleries; and the Cal-Trans Building by Morphosis pulls the structural grid back from the façade to allow for compositional flexibility while maintaining structural efficiency.

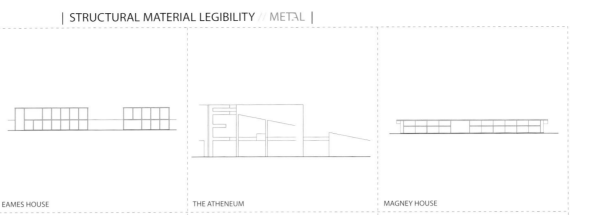

WICHITA HOUSE

EAMES HOUSE

THE ATHENEUM

MAGNEY HOUSE

NIAUX CAVE

JEWISH MUSEUM

DE YOUNG MUSEUM

CAL-TRANS

[METAL] STRUCTURAL MATERIAL LEGIBILITY diagrams in elevation the reading of the structural material. Focusing on the influence of the structural material, it illustrates the interrelation of the engineered structural response of material and performative need to the form and composition. Questioning how the system reads from the exterior and whether the structural material is ever seen, the legibility diagrams examine the relationship of the forces of gravity to the formal expression.

The integration of structure to skin and ultimately to form is about the engagement of the physical requirements of a building to perform structurally with the formal intentions and the legibility of these two systems. The idea of [1] reading a person's bones literally through the skin, [2] versus the broader legibility of a leg as column to transfer vertical loads, [3] versus a denial of all understanding of how the figure works structurally are the three basic stages of structural depiction: [1] literal, [2] figural, or [3] denied.

Fuller's Wichita House reveals the struts through the window and the segments of the panels on its ribbed surface; the Eames House lets the structure ride the edge between outside and inside as an ever-present frame and meter of the programs and spaces; Meier's Atheneum emphasizes the structural systems of the diverse pieces, cutting away the wall to leave the functional bones as compositional elements; the Magney House uses the structural bay to establish the material, spatial, and compositional bay of the entire building; the Niaux Cave conceals to emphasize the surface above the platform level and reveals its legs below; Libeskind's Jewish Museum composes the skin independently of the structure, allowing its revelation and concealment at will; the De Young Museum has a surface blanketed in dimpled and perforated metal that masks the forces lines and emphasizes the skin over the structure; and the Cal-Trans Building by Morphosis cloaks the building in a skin that hides the building and prevents its substructure from being read.

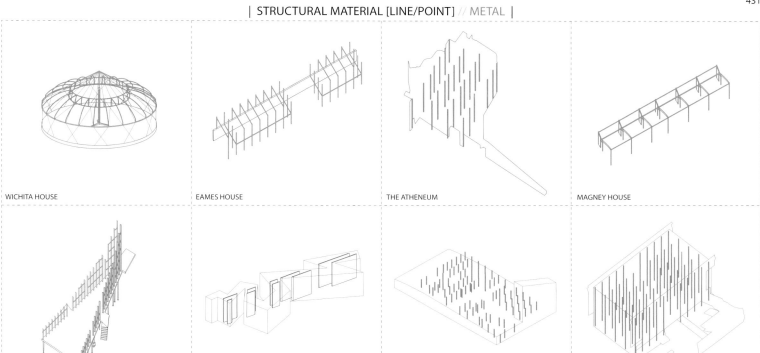

WICHITA HOUSE

EAMES HOUSE

THE ATHENEUM

MAGNEY HOUSE

NIAUX CAVE

JEWISH MUSEUM

DE YOUNG MUSEUM

CAL-TRANS

[METAL] STRUCTURAL MATERIAL [LINE/POINT] diagrams in axonometric the primary geometric and formal response of the structural material/system. "Line" refers to the registration of a wall surface as a structural bearing wall in plan, while "point" refers to the columnar system. Materials subscribe intrinsically to one or the other [typically]; metal is point, while masonry is line. Certain materials, like concrete and wood, have the potential to be either.

The axonometric diagramming of the structural system and the material expression of this system suggest the three-dimensional resolution of the underlying structure superimposed on the form. The relationship of the structural material to the primary material parallels the discussion of revelation versus concealment and homogeneity versus cladding.

Fuller's Wichita House uses a complex web of compressive and tensile elements to create an intricate, but delicately efficient, structural system; the Eames House uses lines of looping U frames that bracket the building, transforming it into a planar system when the transition on the hillside wall requires a concrete retaining wall; Meier's Atheneum skewers the figured volumes of space with the structural column grid; the Magney House creates a standard frame on regularized increments; the Niaux Cave develops the two edges with a frame system that holds the panels on the upper portion and reveals itself to support the pedestrian deck on the lower portion; Libeskind's Jewish Museum contrasts the line of the concrete central hall with the irregular figure of the metal wall lattice frame; the De Young Museum deploys a field of columns across the rectangular mat building to emphasize the interior chambered spaces of the galleries; and the Cal-Trans Building by Morphosis uses an efficiently standardized column grid to structure the bar.

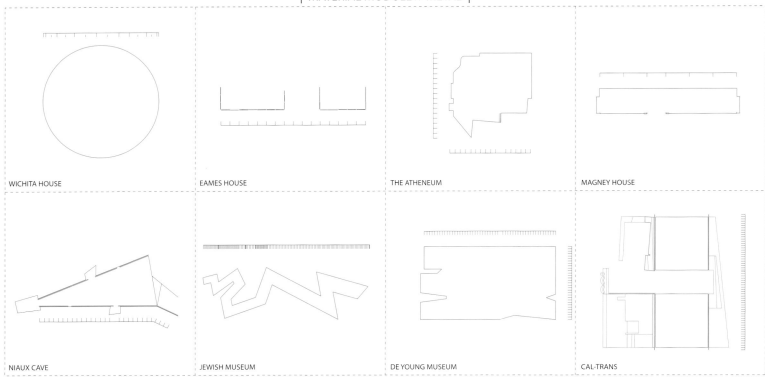

WICHITA HOUSE

EAMES HOUSE

THE ATHENEUM

MAGNEY HOUSE

NIAUX CAVE

JEWISH MUSEUM

DE YOUNG MUSEUM

CAL-TRANS

[METAL] Module – MATERIAL MODULE diagrams in plan the relationships of the manufacturing module intrinsic to a material to the space, form, and dimensions. Mapping the inherited dimensional constraints determined by the production and movement of a material, the patterning of these scale elements and the articulation of their joinery to establish larger architectural forms address the relationship of piece to whole and unit to system.

The module of materials is an intrinsic fact that must be addressed. Certain materials default to a secondary system [such as concrete with formwork] to generate a dimensional constraint, but every material has a "natural" form and dimension. The negotiation of these constraints and the collaboration with these numeric proportions determine the dimensions of the whole and the integration of the modular unit into the consistency of the superstructural organization.

Fuller's Wichita House uses a standardized radial bay; the Eames House uses a regimented bay system filling and leaving void as necessary; Meier's Atheneum uses a square grid panel in both plan and elevation; the Magney House establishes a coincident material and structural bay; the Niaux Cave uses a regular increment varying the number included in the plan-based length to produce a seemingly variable skin system; Libeskind's Jewish Museum uses a standard panelized surface to read the divergent form and apertures; the De Young Museum uses repetitive panels that are subdued by the perforated and dimpled patterns on their surfaces; and the Cal-Trans Building by Morphosis uses the panel dimension of the perforated metal to provide an anthropomorphic scale to the massive façades of the building.

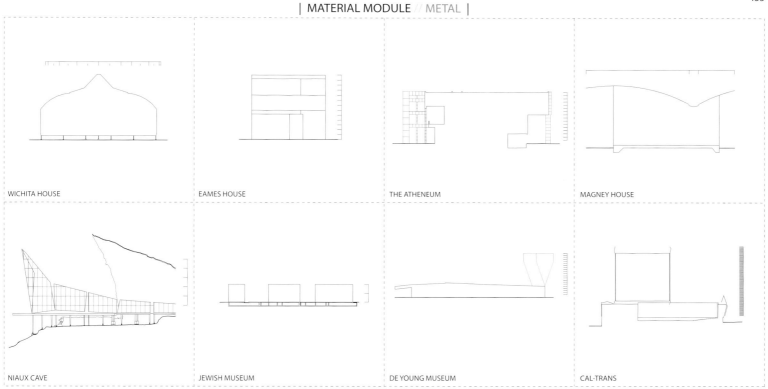

WICHITA HOUSE

EAMES HOUSE

THE ATHENEUM

MAGNEY HOUSE

NIAUX CAVE

JEWISH MUSEUM

DE YOUNG MUSEUM

CAL-TRANS

[METAL] Module – MATERIAL MODULE diagrams in section the relationships of the manufacturing module intrinsic to a material to the space, form, and dimensions. Mapping the inherited dimensional constraints determined by the production and movement of a material to the sectional implications, the patterning of these scale elements and the articulation of their joinery establish larger architectural spaces derived from addressing the relationship of piece to whole and unit to system.

The module of material is an intrinsic fact that must be addressed. Certain materials default to a secondary system [such as concrete with formwork] to generate a dimensional constraint, but every material has a "natural" form and dimension. The negotiation of these constraints and the collaboration with these numeric proportions determine the dimensions of the whole and the integration of the modular unit into the consistency of the superstructural organization. In section, the implications of the human hand of construction relative to the material coursing relative to the body's perception develop the scale and legibility of this module to the spatial presence as a whole.

Fuller's Wichita House standardized plan panel creates a recession of field that is legible in section; the Eames House uses the big bay cut in half by the floor plate and then further bayed into seven equal bands [including the floor plate transom band]; Meier's Atheneum stops the panels of the exterior on the interior to simplify the surface and create a homogeneous reading; the Magney House uses the section to emphasize the spatial impact of the functionally formed skin; the Niaux Cave sets a regular horizontal and vertical banding to the columns and perlins determined by the thickness of the skin and the structural rigidity necessary for wind loads on the frame; Libeskind's Jewish Museum simplifies the interior, emphasizing the apertures to allow for a sectional legibility to the systematized layers of the exterior walls; the De Young Museum denies the material module on the interior; and the Cal-Trans Building by Morphosis uses the transparency of the enclosure wall to allow the module of the perforated metal second skin to carry inside.

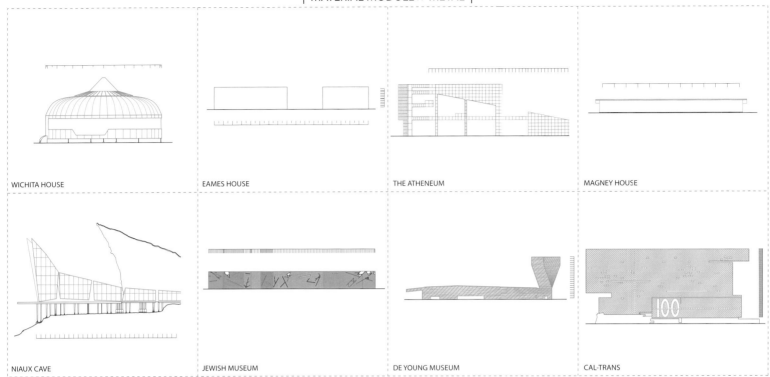

WICHITA HOUSE

EAMES HOUSE

THE ATHENEUM

MAGNEY HOUSE

NIAUX CAVE

JEWISH MUSEUM

DE YOUNG MUSEUM

CAL-TRANS

[METAL] Module – MATERIAL MODULE diagrams in elevation the implications of the relationships of the manufacturing module intrinsic to a material to the space, form, and dimensions. Mapping the inherited dimensional constraints determined by the production and movement of a material to the façade, the formal legibility and implications of an architectural patterning of these scale elements rely upon the articulation of their joinery to establish larger architectural spaces.

The surface reading is derived from addressing the relationship of piece to whole and unit to system through the intrinsic module of a material. Certain materials default to a secondary system [such as concrete with formwork] to generate a dimensional constraint, but every material has a "natural" form and dimension. The negotiation of these constraints and the collaboration with these numeric proportions determine the dimensions of the whole and the integration of the modular unit into the consistency of the superstructural organization. In elevation the implications of the human hand of construction relative to the material assemblies relative to the body's perception develop the scale and legibility of this module and its spatial presence as a whole.

Fuller's Wichita House is defined by its systems of fabrication and construction; the Eames House uses the big bay cut in half by the floor plate and then further bayed into equal bands to produce a rational grid field that then compositionally changes the infill material; Meier's Atheneum uses a ubiquitous module to blanket its figured form; the Magney House uses the lightness, scale, and flexibility of the corrugated metal to collaborate with its structural bay; the Niaux Cave masks the upper level of horizontal and vertical banding of the columns and pelins, revealing them below the level of the platform; Libeskind's Jewish Museum bands the façade with the standardized metal panels; the De Young Museum uses a compositional material module to diffuse the legibility of the panel edge in favor of the graphic surface treatment; and the Cal-Trans Building by Morphosis embraces the scale and detail of the variable metal panels to create a hyperarticulated surface of enclosure.

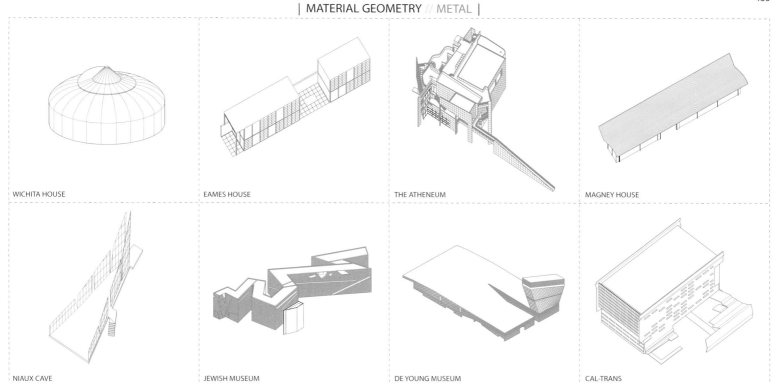

WICHITA HOUSE

EAMES HOUSE

THE ATHENEUM

MAGNEY HOUSE

NIAUX CAVE

JEWISH MUSEUM

DE YOUNG MUSEUM

CAL-TRANS

[METAL] Module – MATERIAL GEOMETRY diagrams in axonometric the three-dimensional relationships of the manufacturing module intrinsic to a material to the space, form, and dimensions. Mapping the inherited dimensional constraints determined by the production and movement of a material into the three-dimensional ramifications of the total form, the legibility of an architectural patterning of scale elements relies upon the articulation of their joinery to establish larger architectural spaces.

The surface reading is derived from addressing the relationship of piece to whole and unit to system through the intrinsic module of a material. Certain materials default to a secondary system [such as concrete with formwork] to generate a dimensional constraint, but every material has a "natural" form and dimension. The negotiation of these constraints and the collaboration with these numeric proportions determine the dimensions of the whole and the integration of the modular unit into the consistency of the superstructural organization. In axonometric, the module governs the formal legibility of the three-dimensional building component and ultimately the formal reading of the building as a whole.

In Fuller's Wichita House the simplicity of the figure is articulated through the expression of the componental assembly system; the Eames House uses the big bay cut in half by the floor plate and then further bayed into equal bands to produce a rational grid field that then compositionally changes the infill material; the Atheneum uses the relentless square grid to map the formal and figural compositional decisions; the Magney House choreographs the roof figure to provide a visual, spatial, and performative effect to the simple plan; the Niaux Cave applies sheet cladding to the upper level of horizontal and vertical banding of the columns and perlins while revealing them below the level of the platform; Libeskind's Jewish Museum uses a localized pattern to produce a standardized field against which the superstructural form of the building and the localized façade compositions play; the De Young Museum emphasizes the massive horizontal of its mat base against the twisting figure of its tower; and the Cal-Trans Building by Morphosis uses the dynamic second skin of the metal surface to compose and transition the skin from vertical to horizontal and back.

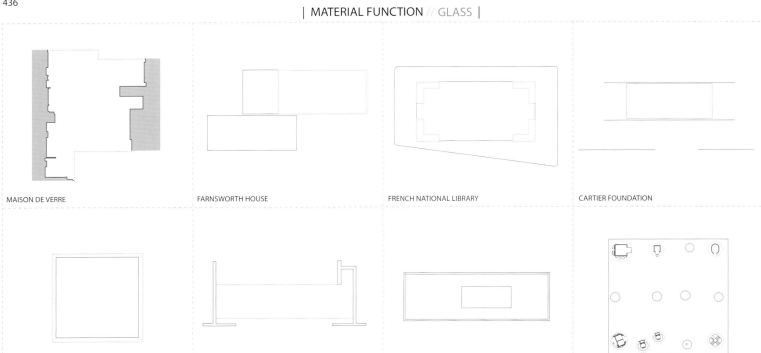

MAISON DE VERRE

FARNSWORTH HOUSE

FRENCH NATIONAL LIBRARY

CARTIER FOUNDATION

KUNSTHAUS BREGENZ

HOUSE AT MOLEDO

DE BLAS HOUSE

SENDAI MEDIATHEQUE

[GLASS] MATERIAL FUNCTION diagrams in plan the relationship between material use and the formal and technical associations required by its functional application. These diagrams examine the role of a material's specific performance properties and its employment relative to the functional and practical necessities of the program and building performance. Each material expresses the conditions and requirements of its deployment.

Defining the premise of skin in each application, material serves as the iconic designation of form in each project. The associated material tectonic employed extends its influence to express itself through the spatial concepts of the architecture. Steel defines vertical lines [Eames House and Niaux Cave], concrete defines planes and frames with variable openings [Lovell Beach House, La Tourette, Church on the Water], and masonry creates modulated solid edges [Casa Barragan and Murcia Town Hall]. Glass establishes transparent veils: flat, ambiguous surfaces that exist but slip into a nonpresence allowing the dissolve of the enclosure and a perceived spatial connection between inside and outside. This is most prevalent in the De Blas Haus and the Cartier Foundation, though it exists even when the glass is frosted and figured, as in the glass block façade of the Maison de Verre. Each material relative to its function determines form.

In each case study, regardless of material, the cloak of the primary material is the defining figure of the primary form: the Maison de Verre by its uniform glass block façade; the Farnsworth House by the delicacy of its evaporative glass skin; the French National Library by the homogeneity of the glass wall panels and the repetitive bracketing corner towers; the Cartier Foundation by the parallel glass planes dissolving the edges; the Kunsthaus Bregenz by the vacant anonymity of the perimeter glass; the House at Moledo through the positive negative play of refined and delicate glass wall juxtaposed against the natural rough rock landscape walls; the De Blas House by the glass that allows the upper level to disappear; and the Sendai Mediatheque by using glass to create continuity from outside to inside allowing the external perception of the dramatic structural tube cores.

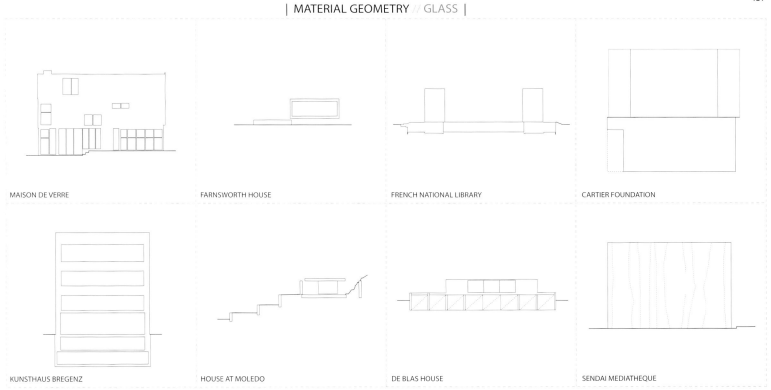

MAISON DE VERRE

FARNSWORTH HOUSE

FRENCH NATIONAL LIBRARY

CARTIER FOUNDATION

KUNSTHAUS BREGENZ

HOUSE AT MOLEDO

DE BLAS HOUSE

SENDAI MEDIATHEQUE

[GLASS] MATERIAL GEOMETRY diagrams the sectional geometric implications of material for form. By introducing the potential structural implications of a material, the relationship of "skin to bones" or surface to structure becomes relative to the intrinsic qualities of a material. Establishing the dimensional module [both of performance and of fabrication and installation limitations], the capabilities of a material express themselves beyond the figure of the form to address the geometry of the space.

The module of a material can be established by three potential scales. The first scale is the module of the unit: a single brick, a sheet of plywood [as direct application of sheathing or as indirect application of formwork], a glass pane with either concealed or revealed frame systems, or a steel member. In each of these conditions the unit is defined by a structural need, a material property, or a manufacturing module. The second scale is the bay of the module produced through the assemblies or structure. For example, the Eames House window wall module is an aggregate of the individual panes, the double high bay module, and the superstructural steel frame. The final scale is the designed geometry of the building's mass expressed through material, i.e., the formal figure of the object as a whole. Each of these three levels can coexist or be independently exploited. The material in each case is, however, the beginning, the dimensional collaborator based on the intrinsic properties and performance of the base material.

The Maison de Verre uses the module of the glass block within the metal frame as a geometric infill field; the Farnsworth House sets the glass against the white steel of the floating floor and roof plates to barely delineate a skin of enclosure; the French National Library uses the glass to diffuse the buildings' presence above the wood plinth; the Cartier Foundation layers the glass enclosure of the building behind the larger glass site wall hugging the urban boundary and holding the line of the street; the Kunsthaus Bregenz uses the segments of the skin to engrain an anthropomorphic dimension into the otherwise scaleless yet enigmatic blankness of the façade; the House at Moledo plays the regimented machined rhythm of the façade against the organic meter of the adjacent stone landscape walls; the De Blas Haus minimizes tectonic expression to rely on a reductive purity of geometrically determined spaces; and the Sendai Mediatheque bands a second middle performative skin to create a traditional tripartite façade organization.

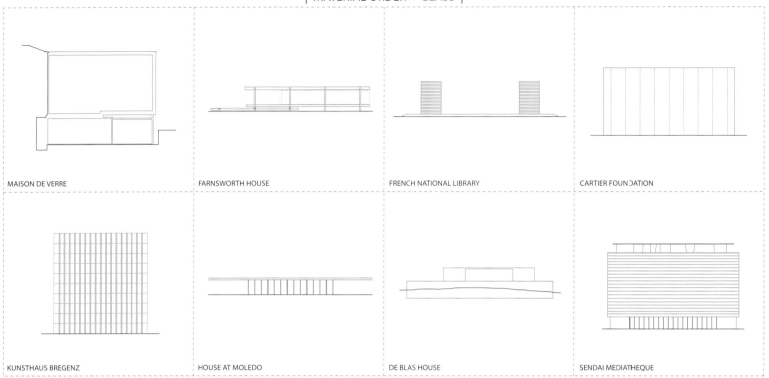

MAISON DE VERRE

FARNSWORTH HOUSE

FRENCH NATIONAL LIBRARY

CARTIER FOUNDATION

KUNSTHAUS BREGENZ

HOUSE AT MOLEDO

DE BLAS HOUSE

SENDAI MEDIATHEQUE

[GLASS] MATERIAL ORDER diagrams in elevation the hierarchy, sequence, and organizational methods of material's influence on the architectural form. As in the examination in section, the implication here is more spatial than formal. Looking at the organizational geometries and governing patterns of material relative to the form, the implications and legibility of volume and mass are articulated through the aggregation of the material pieces.

The extension of the material module into the overarching order of the formal expression is the ultimate collaboration of material with design. The definition of the overall form relative to the piece, the manner in which an aperture is made as a removal [in terms of both module and structural implications], and the relation of these compositional pieces to the formal whole are the defining characteristics of a material's influence on form.

The Maison de Verre establishes a primary double-height volume for the living spaces with a massive glass block wall while recessing the transparent lower level for the entry and dental office; the Farnsworth House sleeves the externalized structural steel frame with a glass liner to dematerialize the traditional reading of window and wall; the French National Library lines the inaccessible sunken courtyard with glazing to produce a window into the forested central court, and also deploys the relentless repetition of panel to plane, plane to tower, and tower to plinth to illustrate the scale and scope of the encased book stacks; the Cartier Foundation attempts to eliminate the subdivisions required by the practicalities of glass to emphasize the planar reflective and transparent surface; the Kunsthaus Bregenz layers both the exterior skin and the interior ceilings with veils of translucent glass to alter the perception of dimension and sanitize the physical expression of detail; the House at Moledo sets the transparent walls against the thickened masonry walls to produce a thickened spatial perception of edge; the De Blas Haus has an opaque concrete base with repetitive punched square openings, while the upper level evaporates with a mullionless glass enclosure; and the Sendai Mediatheque dissolves the perimeter to emphasize the removal of surface [both perceptually and structurally], emphasizing the hierarchy and figuration of the thirteen inner cores.

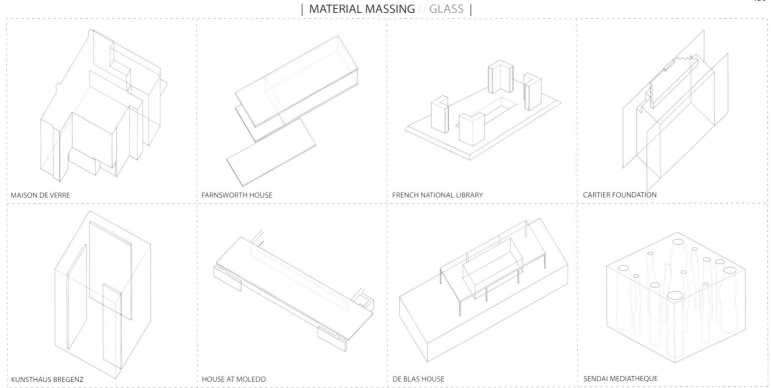

MAISON DE VERRE

FARNSWORTH HOUSE

FRENCH NATIONAL LIBRARY

CARTIER FOUNDATION

KUNSTHAUS BREGENZ

HOUSE AT MOLEDO

DE BLAS HOUSE

SENDAI MEDIATHEQUE

[GLASS] MATERIAL MASSING diagrams in axonometric the overall legibility of the primary material to the superstructural form, presence, and mass of the architectural form. Focusing primarily on the mass and volume of form as defined by the material application to the exterior, the legibility of compositional intention and the geometric hierarchy are mapped.

The significance of mass [as defined by material in particular] concerns the clarity of formal intention in relation to the actual legibility and reading in the building. The conceptual ideas that govern the design of a building become legible through their tectonic manifestations in the form. The hierarchy of the primary massing determines the figuration to which all else must respond. The material relationship with this massing and the deployment of the tectonic expression of the assembly determine whether a material is read as segmented, disassociated, panelized, repetitive, or monolithic.

The Maison de Verre layers the skin with the translucency of glass to provide as much light as possible on the two exposed faces of the site [buried within the fabric of its Parisian block] while maintaining privacy; the Farnsworth House emphasizes the horizontal, evaporating the vertical planes and extending the horizontal plates; the French National Library uses the L corner form to create a spatial bracket on the openness of the plinth to emphasize the courtyard and announce the world below; the Cartier Foundation fills between two extended glass planes that negotiate the scale of the park-like site and the compact nature of the transparent building; the Kunsthaus Bregenz stops the eye at the figure of the building but allows the luminous and translucent surface to exist enigmatically between solid and transparent; the House at Moledo floats the pieces of roof, landscape wall, and enclosure off of one another to create spatial and perceptual layers of boundary; the De Blas Haus stacks an evaporative glass box shielded by a protective canopy atop a massive concrete box set into the hillside; and the Sendai Mediatheque holds the rectilinear edge of the urban contextual form but dissolves its presence through the material to allow the organic figuration of the inner cores to be fully legible.

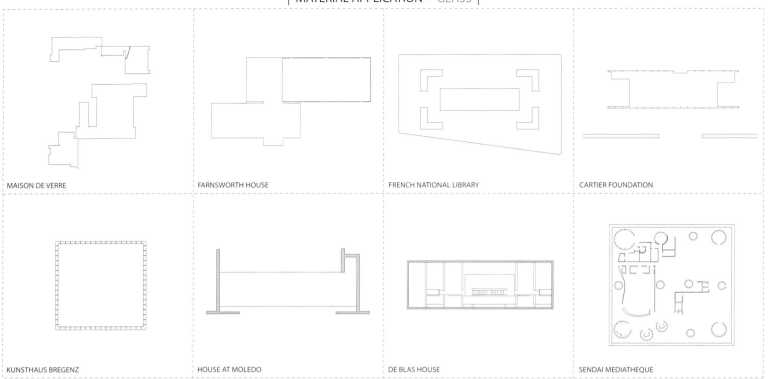

MAISON DE VERRE

FARNSWORTH HOUSE

FRENCH NATIONAL LIBRARY

CARTIER FOUNDATION

KUNSTHAUS BREGENZ

HOUSE AT MOLEDO

DE BLAS HOUSE

SENDAI MEDIATHEQUE

[GLASS] MATERIAL APPLICATION diagrams in plan the deployment of material and the associated perceptual, formal, and functional readings. Engaging the relationship between material and function, the formal expression becomes the primary mediating element. The expression of the material's use and the tectonic deployment determine the functional programmatic legibility of the building. This begins with the formal expression intrinsic to the material followed by issues of practical performance including: durability, porosity, and visual effect.

A material can be selected for various reasons: availability, cost, durability, module, structural capability, or simply the functional applicability [metal to combat combustion, concrete for construction in corrosive environments, or masonry as a low-maintenance, durable skin]. In each scenario the fundamental physical properties of the material are the baseline of design consideration. These properties, mediated by the method of manufacturing and limited by the method of working [wood is easy to cut, metal can be welded, masonry is heavy and modular], develop the second tier of consideration. Finally, and perhaps with the most variability, is the assembly and application. The systemization of the manufactured pieces and their formal and technical articulation comprise material design application.

The Maison de Verre selects the new material of glass block to allow for a maximum amount of light while maintaining privacy in the circumscribed courtyard site; the Farnsworth House lines the perimeter with massive glass planes to reduce the boundary between outside and inside; the French National Library edges the brackets tower to play with the massiveness of the internal collection and the delicacy of the external reading; the Cartier Foundation uses glass to create a visual void in the dense urban fabric of Paris and lend an evaporative and ambiguous quality to the building by blurring the boundary between outside and inside; the Kunsthaus Bregenz uses an unbroken perimeter of translucent glass to create an enigmatic veil that masks the detail and anonymously articulates the building; the House at Moledo dissolves the longitudinal walls with glass, while the lateral walls engage the mass and materiality of the stone retaining landscape walls; the De Blas Haus has an internal bay system in the concrete plinth [primarily sleeping spaces], with the glass second level evaporating the perimeter for the living room; and the Sendai Mediatheque uses a glass skin on both the perimeter and select inner cores expose of the detail and articulation of the pieces, allowing the structural and service functions to become the ornament and figuration of the building.

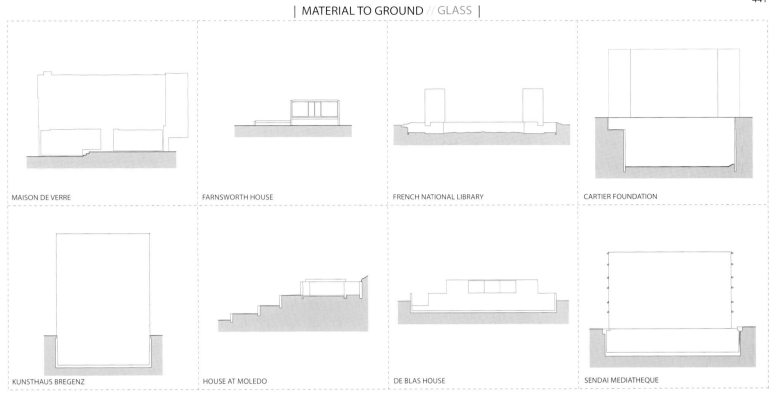

MAISON DE VERRE

FARNSWORTH HOUSE

FRENCH NATIONAL LIBRARY

CARTIER FOUNDATION

KUNSTHAUS BREGENZ

HOUSE AT MOLEDO

DE BLAS HOUSE

SENDAI MEDIATHEQUE

[GLASS] Proximity – MATERIAL TO GROUND diagrams the sectional relationship in which a building meets the ground, engages landscape, and addresses the material point of connection with the site. The point of contact between a building and the earth is determined by the material approach to the architecture. Factors that determine and affect this condition include soil characteristics, climate, context, structural system, and building weight [both actual and perceived].

The history of structural and material technology is the history of how a building meets the ground. The selection of material cladding and structural framing results in a specific formal articulation of this condition that is intrinsic to the material and tectonic. Technologically determined, this joint [between building and ground] is created by the system of both the structure and the cladding. Historically, load-bearing wall systems of wood or masonry required continuous contact of the building with the ground and limited the scale and frequency of openings. Materials such as steel and concrete allowed for a formal disengagement from the ground plane, turning structural planes into points and shifting from a wall system to a cage.

The Maison de Verre slots itself below an existing third floor producing a ground plane both below and above the house with layered levels of transparency and translucency between; the Farnsworth House floats the building off the landscape for practical and effectual reasons; the French National Library creates an open plinth embedding the public functions in the ground, while the private closed stacks and offices inhabit the towers; the Cartier Foundation has almost an equal number of levels below grade to deal with the large parking requirement while leaving the upper levels programmatically liberated to permit smaller floor plates and greater transparency; the Kunsthaus Bregenz sets into the earth but masks the actual size through its material composition and abrupt relationship to the ground; the House at Moledo layers the landscape walls with the transparent walls setting the house into the section and producing a secondary plane of enclosure; the De Blas Haus sets the massive concrete lower level as a plinth into the hillside, establishing a base for the delicate upper frame and glass perimeter; and the Sendai Mediatheque sets the transparent perimeter directly on the ground to provide a simplicity of enclosure and a singularity to the space inside in order to emphasize the figural structural cores.

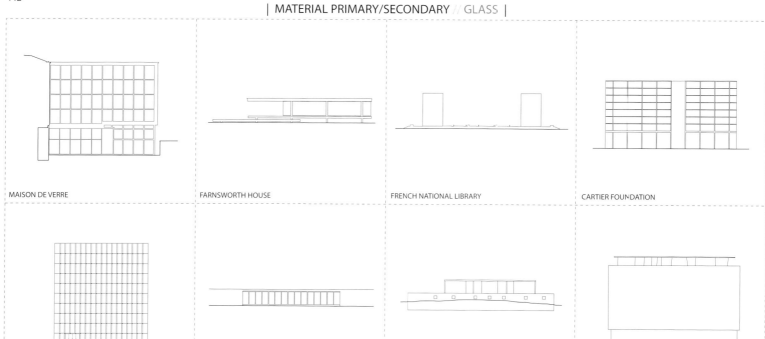

MAISON DE VERRE

FARNSWORTH HOUSE

FRENCH NATIONAL LIBRARY

CARTIER FOUNDATION

KUNSTHAUS BREGENZ

HOUSE AT MOLEDO

DE BLAS HOUSE

SENDAI MEDIATHEQUE

[GLASS] Proximity – PRIMARY / SECONDARY diagrams in elevation the relationship of the primary building material, to the secondary building material, focusing on the formal, functional, and practical interrelationships of their material application. The hierarchy between these two levels is both formally and materially evident, establishing the organizing geometries of the diverse layers.

The proximity of a primary figure to a secondary figure builds on the formal reading of material application diagrams but engages the interrelationship with the secondary systemization. The interaction of the two can occur through superimposition, contrasting figures, interpenetration, banding, layering, or any other adverbial relationship. The result is a primary figuration and the secondary subsystemization that, through its geometry, breaks down the material into fabricateable and installable pieces and reveals the tectonic intention of their aggregation.

The Maison de Verre sets a secondary metal frame into the glass walls that establishes a superstructural grid geometry; the Farnsworth House juxtaposes the evaporative glass against the boldly figured white steel; the French National Library sets the glass against the wood of the plinth and the operable panels of the tower's second skin; the Cartier Foundation segments the massive glass plane with vertical steel elements that are minimized in size but required to structurally segment the large surface; the Kunsthaus Bregenz uses the subtlety of the clip system to articulate the panels; the House at Moledo contrasts the lightness of the glass with the weight of the rock wall; the De Blas Haus sets the most opaque and defensive materials of the concrete base against the most ephemeral detailing of the evaporative glass living room atop; and the Sendai Mediatheque establishes a primary elevation with the main glass body and a secondary base and top.

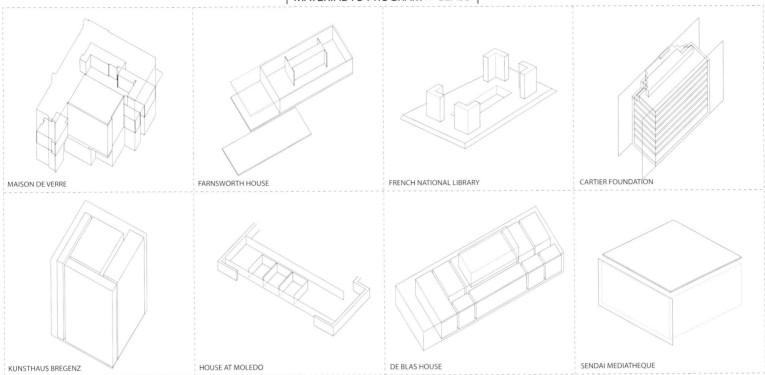

MAISON DE VERRE

FARNSWORTH HOUSE

FRENCH NATIONAL LIBRARY

CARTIER FOUNDATION

KUNSTHAUS BREGENZ

HOUSE AT MOLEDO

DE BLAS HOUSE

SENDAI MEDIATHEQUE

[GLASS] Proximity – MATERIAL TO PROGRAM diagrams in axonometric the overall relationship of material usage to the primary programmatic and functional usages. By focusing on the three-dimensional volumetric associations of material to programmatic usage [and the associated functional requirements of a particular program], the articulation of "form following function" can be examined through material association.

The relationship of the programmatic usage to the material selected depicts the narrative of the association, creating the opportunity and potential for material to be an expressive sign system. The legibility of a material comes from a technical knowledge that engages an understanding of raw material, manufacturing processes, construction traditions and techniques, weathering and biological attack, and cultural associations. These innate properties of matter translate into forms that collaborate with materials to reveal their process.

The Maison de Verre dispenses the glass block for the primary living space, while the service spaces are carved into the adjacent mass of the side buildings to be considered as subtractive volumes from the fabric; the Farnsworth House uses the glass to incorporate the house as a single volume, using the core to segment into specified spaces; the French National Library places the stacks in the glass towers with the public functions located below the plinth; the Cartier Foundation uses tightly spaced layered floors to deemphasize the vertical and spatially compact the inner spaces to emphasize the explosive expansion of the transparent perimeter; the Kunsthaus Bregenz cloaks the entire figure in a singular glass volume, using three cores to subdivide the interior spaces; the House at Moledo brackets a room with landscape stone walls and then encloses the space with two parallel glass planes; rooms sit inside as furniture boxes; the De Blas Haus has repetitive bays and subunits within the bays on the lower level, with the transparent jewel sitting in the center as an iconic figure; and the Sendai Mediatheque floats a frontal skin and a roof skin off the volume of the body to create a functional skin.

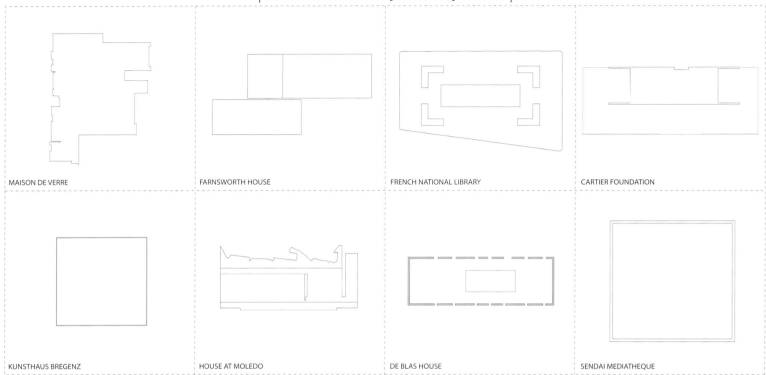

MAISON DE VERRE

FARNSWORTH HOUSE

FRENCH NATIONAL LIBRARY

CARTIER FOUNDATION

KUNSTHAUS BREGENZ

HOUSE AT MOLEDO

DE BLAS HOUSE

SENDAI MEDIATHEQUE

[GLASS] Skin + Surface – MATERIAL ENCLOSURE [PERIMETER] diagrams in plan the relationship of the outer plane of enclosure [skin] to the spatial, formal, and structural organization. Expressing the process by which materials assemble into systems, the figuration of the perimeter is dependent not simply upon the piece but also upon the joint. The collaboration of these two generates specific forms intrinsic to a material and expressively identifiable.

The use of skin to define the perimeter over the structure and the programmatic innards establishes the legibility of architectural idea's purity through the articulation of edge and boundary. The continuity and complexity of this envelope widely explicate the material articulation and the tectonic intricacy. The relationship of craft to figure is found in the method of material manipulation.

The Maison de Verre carves on the transverse faces while holding a pure face on the lateral glass façades; the Farnsworth House bounds a portion of the space sandwiched between the roof and floor planes; the French National Library creates L-shaped bracket towers to define a concentric room around the central courtyard; the Cartier Foundation has three primary walls: one disengaged for the urban scale and two for the longitudinal sides of the building, each emphasizing a slippage that dissolves the corner; the Kunsthaus Bregenz creates a uniform perimeter façade; the House at Moledo juxtaposes the machined line of the glass enclosure against the organic and natural figuration of the rock walls; the De Blas Haus uses three concentric rectangles to define the concrete plinth, the canopy, and the glass enclosure in respective scales; and the Sendai Mediatheque uses the glass to define the purity of the perimeter, layered by a variable floor-to-floor height and glass enclosure type, yet understated to allow the internal world to be functionally figurative.

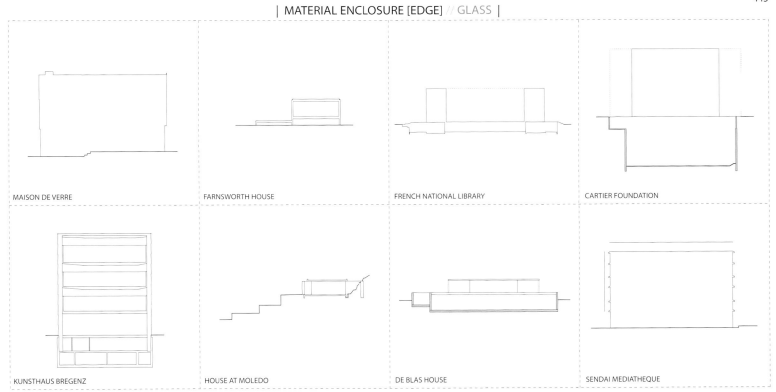

MAISON DE VERRE
FARNSWORTH HOUSE
FRENCH NATIONAL LIBRARY
CARTIER FOUNDATION
KUNSTHAUS BREGENZ
HOUSE AT MOLEDO
DE BLAS HOUSE
SENDAI MEDIATHEQUE

[GLASS] Skin + Surface – MATERIAL ENCLOSURE [EDGE] diagrams in section the relationship of the outer plane of enclosure [skin] to the spatial, formal, and structural organization. Expressing the process by which materials assemble into systems, the figuration of the perimeter as expressed through section extends the moves of plan in the Y axis [still dependent not simply upon the piece but also upon the joint].

The collaboration of piece with joint determines the sectional spatial forms intrinsic to a material, resulting in expressive and identifiable associations. The role of skin in section similarly works to define the perimeter over the structure and the interior functions. The figure establishes the legibility of an architectural idea's purity through the articulation of edge and boundary as extended to the vertical and thus the now spatial dimension. The continuity and complexity of this line widely explicate the material articulation and the tectonic intricacy. The relationship of the exterior material through the surface of the building to impact and define interior space is moderated by the material manipulation of this edge.

The Maison de Verre dissolves the façades through the transparency of the glass despite engulfing the maximum volume allowable on the site; the Farnsworth House bounds between the two primary horizontal planes; the French National Library bounds two chambers vertically and horizontally: one filled by forest, the other by the void of sky; the Cartier Foundation sits as a transparent figure atop a subterranean infrastructural base; the Kunsthaus Bregenz wraps the exterior figure and recurs in each interior space to provide a sense of release and continuity; the House at Moledo bounds a room with the landscape wall, then further segments between outside and inside through the delicate glass planes; the De Blas Haus uses three rectangles of the concrete plinth, the canopy, and the glass enclosure in respective scales; and the Sendai Mediatheque encloses with one banded figure and then buffers with a secondary performative roof and façade veil.

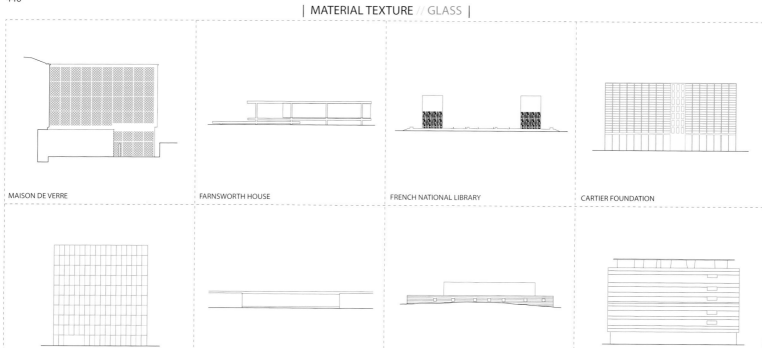

MAISON DE VERRE   FARNSWORTH HOUSE   FRENCH NATIONAL LIBRARY   CARTIER FOUNDATION

KUNSTHAUS BREGENZ   HOUSE AT MOLEDO   DE BLAS HOUSE   SENDAI MEDIATHEQUE

[GLASS] Skin + Surface – MATERIAL TEXTURE diagrams in elevation the legibility of the material texture, color, and surface. Defining the compositional aesthetics of the elevation, the collagist sensibility of pattern, texture, color, and depth of plane are all legible against light. Like a composed painting, this image is dissected from the visual perceptual stance of the material on the architectural composition.

The textural reading refers to the actual color and composition of the material. Wood, for example, can be classified as a generic type, but the performance qualities, colors, hardness, resistance to rot, durability, and workability are vastly different from species to species. This same textural legibility comes through the assembly and expression of the unit and the joint. The scale and articulation of these connections define the legibility of the collective material reading and the overall compositional reading of the architecture.

The Maison de Verre establishes the grid of the units and the superstructural grid of the framing bay system to create a uniform and semianonymous field; the Farnsworth House removes the articulation of the glass, minimizing mullions and emphasizing the simplicity of the geometry to the form; the French National Library sets a relentless rhythm with the glass panel allowing for variability and the human touch to come through the operable inner wood panel wall; the Cartier Foundation bands the glass but denies the joint to emphasize the surface; the Kunsthaus Bregenz shingles the façade with identical glass panels allowing uniformity and abstraction to the field; the House at Moledo poses the simplicity of the glass against the natural roughness of the adjacent stone walls; the De Blas Haus expresses the board forming of the concrete as a rough base to contrast with the hyper-clean, crystalline walls of the glass living room; and the Sendai Mediatheque bands the façade as a functional veil with the inner façade determined by layer.

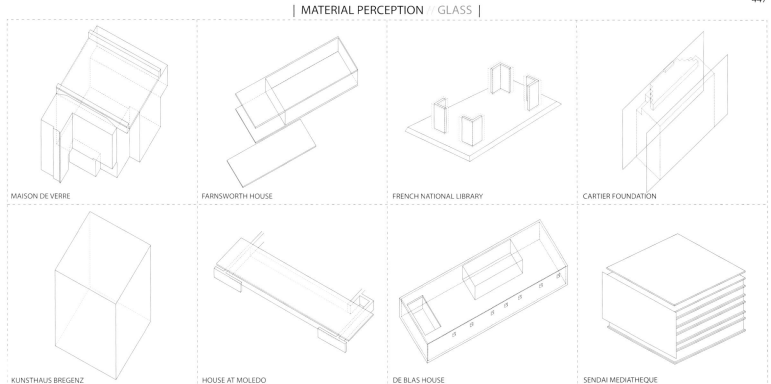

MAISON DE VERRE

FARNSWORTH HOUSE

FRENCH NATIONAL LIBRARY

CARTIER FOUNDATION

KUNSTHAUS BREGENZ

HOUSE AT MOLEDO

DE BLAS HOUSE

SENDAI MEDIATHEQUE

[GLASS] Skin + Surface – MATERIAL PERCEPTION diagrams in axonometric the primary reading of material experience. By transitioning from the sectional reading that focuses on the two-dimensional interior spatial conditions or the material application, the reading in elevation speaks to the composition of the façade but again within the shallow space of a two-dimensional reading, while the axonometric examination illustrates the compositional legibility of the building as a total object.

By engaging all three dimensions, the figuration of the architecture and the legibility of a material's perception relative to the total object lend a volumetric legibility to a material's perception. A truly monolithic architecture is nearly impossible; thus, the connection and change from one piece to the next define the moment of intervention and design decision. The perception of the whole after the resolution of these local "events" is the perception of the architecture. Focusing specifically on the material impact upon these decisions allows the design intention to be revealed by the tectonic view of the whole through the piece.

The Maison de Verre, due to its site nestled in the fabric of the courtyard and the adjacencies of the dense urban block, relies upon the façade as the figure, and the monolithic and relentless nature of the glass block to permit a translucent material to accomplish this task; the Farnsworth House attempts to minimize the perception of the material proper and instead to optimize its capabilities to provide a boundless connection between inside and outside; the French National Library cloaks the building in glass to make the figure more delicate, providing a depth and an enigmatic quality to the façade through the second skin; the Cartier Foundation dramatically dissolves the outer planes to produce a series of transparent overextended layers that blur the boundary and definition of the wall; the Kunsthaus Bregenz emphasizes the figure, minimizing the material articulation and privileging the overarching figure of the building; the House at Moledo allows the galls to recede behind the site walls and the dominant horizontal roof minimizing its presence; the De Blas Haus engages the base with the landscape, allowing the delicacy and transparency of the second-story glass room to be optimized in contrast; and the Sendai Mediatheque bands the floor levels behind the perimeter glass enclosure, figuring the cores and privileging their formal perception over the material of enclosure.

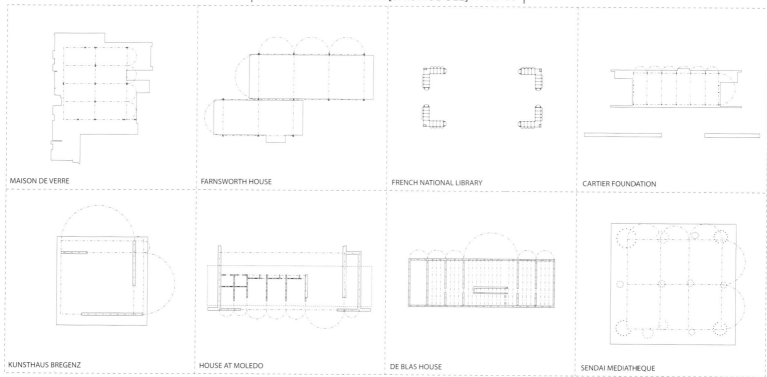

MAISON DE VERRE

FARNSWORTH HOUSE

FRENCH NATIONAL LIBRARY

CARTIER FOUNDATION

KUNSTHAUS BREGENZ

HOUSE AT MOLEDO

DE BLAS HOUSE

SENDAI MEDIATHEQUE

[GLASS] STRUCTURAL MATERIAL [BAY/MODULE] diagrams in plan the structural module of the building. Focusing on the influence of the structural material, it illustrates the engineered structural response of material relative to performative need. Dependent upon the dimension of span relative to the spatial capabilities of the material, an organizing geometry is established that sets the scale and legibility of a space.

The role of structure in plan is of particular formal importance relative to material as the premise of line [load-bearing walls] versus point [columns]. Each system establishes a certain way of making space. Load-bearing materials versus cladding materials are revealed, and their variation and interdependence are highlighted.

The Maison de Verre has an inner columnar frame that holds up the structure as well as the upper floor of the neighbor's apartment that the house was built beneath; the Farnsworth House is defined by the three bays of the main building with the glass enclosure receding within; the French National Library bays the structure in accordance with an accumulated bay of the glass paneling; the Cartier Foundation has a metal frame pulled in from the façade to emphasize the surface of the exterior while graphically revealing the tectonic on the interior; the Kunsthaus Bregenz shingles the exterior with a module of the glass cladding, cloaking the opaque interior and masking the structure entirely; the House at Moledo uses the end walls as the primary structural system, allowing the glazing and interior partitions to read as simple infill; the De Blas Haus has a cast-in-place base that regularly spans to match the repetitive spatial module of the subdivision of the rooms; and the Sendai Mediatheque establishes three lines of cores [each varied in dimension and use] that are emphatically choreographed to be viewed through and against the regulated geometry of the transparent façade.

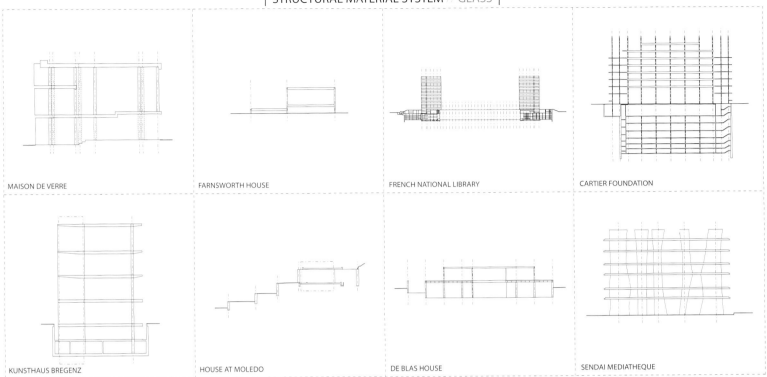

MAISON DE VERRE

FARNSWORTH HOUSE

FRENCH NATIONAL LIBRARY

CARTIER FOUNDATION

KUNSTHAUS BREGENZ

HOUSE AT MOLEDO

DE BLAS HOUSE

SENDAI MEDIATHEQUE

[GLASS] STRUCTURAL MATERIAL [BAY/MODULE] diagrams the sectional implications of the structural module. Focusing on the influence of the structural material, it illustrates the engineered structural response of material relative to performative need. In this diagram set, the structure is materially examined in its vertical figuration of the sectional articulation.

Building on the bay system of the plan, the section depicts the shape and configuration of the repetitive unit and the effectual relationship to the space of the building. Perceived or concealed, primary [as figuration] or coincidental in presence, the role of the sectional structural bay engages the verticality of the building.

The Maison de Verre uses the vertical lines of the primary metal columns as skewers through the entire building that the floor plates variably meet to create diverse sectional heights; the Farnsworth House runs the glass from floor to ceiling to eliminate the reading of the surface itself in favor of its transparent qualities; the French National Library runs the bayed structural system through the towers and plinth as a module of the glass bays; the Cartier Foundation has a regular steel columnar system at a half frequency to the glass mullion system that produces a delicate structural cage; the Kunsthaus Bregenz pulls the structure off the façade to deemphasize the wall in favor of an internalized system; the House at Moledo uses lateral end walls for support, allowing the interstitial space to be left unbroken; the De Blas Haus sets a concrete base that corresponds to the upper canopy, allowing the glass enclosure to float unadorned between the two systems; and the Sendai Mediatheque internalizes the structure to the tubular cores, allowing for the removal of the structure from the skin.

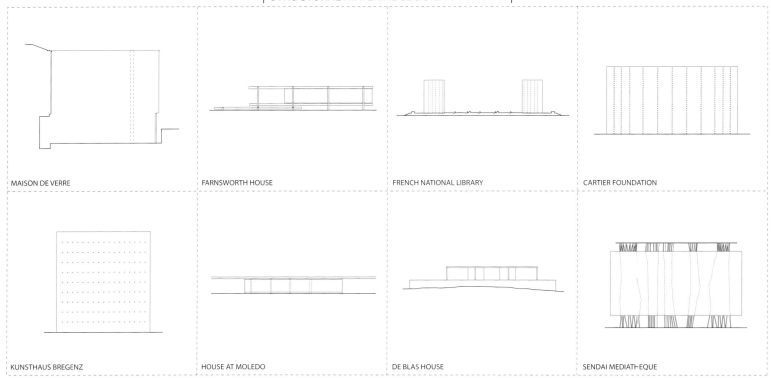

MAISON DE VERRE

FARNSWORTH HOUSE

FRENCH NATIONAL LIBRARY

CARTIER FOUNDATION

KUNSTHAUS BREGENZ

HOUSE AT MOLEDO

DE BLAS HOUSE

SENDAI MEDIATHEQUE

[GLASS] STRUCTURAL MATERIAL LEGIBILITY diagrams in elevation the reading of the structural material. Focusing on the influence of the structural material, it illustrates the interrelation of the engineered structural response of material and performative need to the form and composition. Questioning how the system reads from the exterior and whether the structural material is ever seen, the legibility diagrams examine the relationship of the forces of gravity to the formal expression.

The integration of structure to skin and ultimately to form is about the engagement of the physical requirements of a building to perform structurally with the formal intentions and the legibility of these two systems. The idea of [1] reading a person's bones literally through the skin, [2] versus the broader legibility of a leg as column to transfer vertical loads, [3] versus a denial of all understanding of how the figure works structurally are the three basic stages of structural depiction: [1] literal, [2] figural, or [3] denied.

The Maison de Verre establishes the rhythm of the columns through the superstructural bays of the glass block front façade but does not directly reveal them in the surface of the skin; the Farnsworth House externalizes the structure, making the figure of the steel dominant on the façade; the French National Library internalizes the columnar structure, so, despite geometric congruency, the direct legibility is masked; the Cartier Foundation, through the transparency of the skin, reveals the vertical lines of the structure as an x-ray showing skin and bones simultaneously; the Kunsthaus Bregenz veils the entire façade in the blanket cladding system, disguising the structural system; the House at Moledo uses massive edge walls to allow for spatial continuity, material flexibility, and compositional freedom to the inner configuration; the De Blas Haus sets one system atop another with careful plan resolution and coordination but dramatic juxtaposition and transition from one system to the next in elevation; and the Sendai Mediatheque makes the perimeter simple in form and transparent in perception to allow the complication and figuration of the inner cores to dominate the composition.

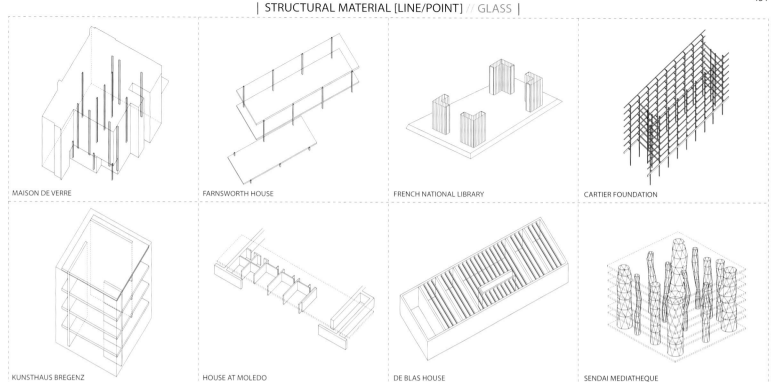

MAISON DE VERRE

FARNSWORTH HOUSE

FRENCH NATIONAL LIBRARY

CARTIER FOUNDATION

KUNSTHAUS BREGENZ

HOUSE AT MOLEDO

DE BLAS HOUSE

SENDAI MEDIATHEQUE

[GLASS] STRUCTURAL MATERIAL [LINE/POINT] diagrams in axonometric the primary geometric and formal response of the structural material/system. "Line" refers to the registration of a wall surface as a structural bearing wall in plan, while "point" refers to the columnar system. Materials subscribe intrinsically to one or the other [typically]; metal is point, while masonry is line. Certain materials, like concrete and wood, have the potential to be either.

The axonometric diagramming of the structural system and the material expression of this system suggest the three-dimensional resolution of the underlying structure superimposed on the form. The relationship of the structural material to the primary material parallels the discussion of revelation versus concealment and homogeneity versus cladding.

The Maison de Verre uses a metal columnar system connected with horizontal concrete plates; the Farnsworth House uses the steel moment frame with the glass as the minimal enclosure; the French National Library uses a concrete column and plate system with glass and wood as infill elements; the Cartier Foundation uses a frame system expressed and revealed through the transparent skin extending the visual lightness of the building; the Kunsthaus Bregenz relies upon the concrete shear walls of the cores to establish the vertical elements, allowing the skin to be freed from structural responsibilities; the House at Moledo uses exterior load-bearing masonry walls to provide interior flexibility; the De Blas Haus uses concrete bearing walls that allow for a transverse span for the glass box to sit atop; and the Sendai Mediatheque uses a tubular steel structure at the perimeter of the cores to serve as massive columns supporting the variably spaced horizontal concrete plates.

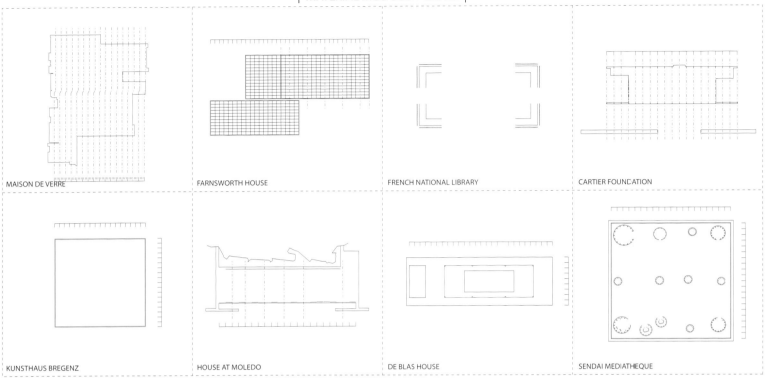

MAISON DE VERRE

FARNSWORTH HOUSE

FRENCH NATIONAL LIBRARY

CARTIER FOUNDATION

KUNSTHAUS BREGENZ

HOUSE AT MOLEDO

DE BLAS HOUSE

SENDAI MEDIATHEQUE

[GLASS] Module – MATERIAL MODULE diagrams in plan the relationships of the manufacturing module intrinsic to a material to the space, form, and dimensions. Mapping the inherited dimensional constraints determined by the production and movement of a material, the patterning of these scale elements and the articulation of their joinery to establish larger architectural forms address the relationship of piece to whole and unit to system.

The module of materials is an intrinsic fact that must be addressed. Certain materials default to a secondary system [such as concrete with formwork] to generate a dimensional constraint, but every material has a "natural" form and dimension. The negotiation of these constraints and the collaboration with these numeric proportions determine the dimensions of the whole and the integration of the modular unit into the consistency of the superstructural organization.

The Maison de Verre carries the submodule of the frame system for the glass block through the house, with a slight shift in the middle due to preexisting site constraints; the Farnsworth House bifurcates the structural module with the glass module; the French National Library uses a standard glass panel optimized for weight and scale and repeats it relentlessly; the Cartier Foundation uses the regular increment of the columns to establish a mullion system for the glass to produce panels of a reasonable scale for fabrication, transport, and installation; the Kunsthaus Bregenz uses a repetitive module to create an enigmatically scaled and blank pattern field to the façade; the House at Moledo uses a vertical anthropomorphic repetitive bay to frame the body against the landscape; the De Blas Haus uses a tight spatial module to determine the organization of the lower level despite great material freedom in the board-formed, cast-in-place concrete structure, while the glass gets as large as practically possible on the upper level to deny the edge; and the Sendai Mediatheque uses a floor-to-floor module to create a simple glass perimeter, standard yet tailored.

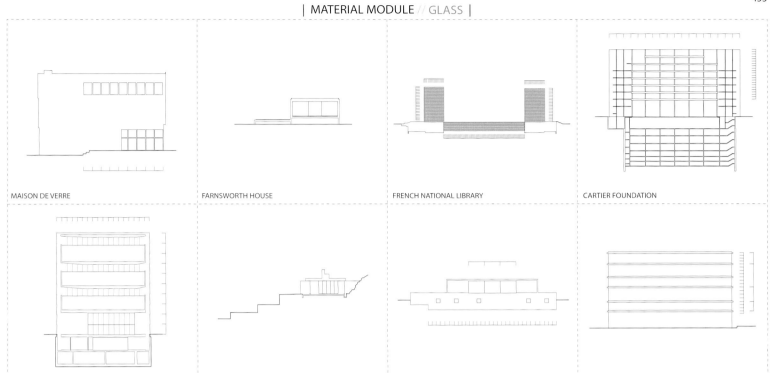

MAISON DE VERRE

FARNSWORTH HOUSE

FRENCH NATIONAL LIBRARY

CARTIER FOUNDATION

KUNSTHAUS BREGENZ

HOUSE AT MOLEDO

DE BLAS HOUSE

SENDAI MEDIATHEQUE

[GLASS] Module – MATERIAL MODULE diagrams in section the relationships of the manufacturing module intrinsic to a material to the space, form, and dimensions. Mapping the inherited dimensional constraints determined by the production and movement of a material to the sectional implications, the patterning of these scale elements and the articulation of their joinery establish larger architectural spaces derived from addressing the relationship of piece to whole and unit to system.

The module of material is an intrinsic fact that must be addressed. Certain materials default to a secondary system [such as concrete with formwork] to generate a dimensional constraint, but every material has a "natural" form and dimension. The negotiation of these constraints and the collaboration with these numeric proportions determine the dimensions of the whole and the integration of the modular unit into the consistency of the superstructural organization. In section, the implications of the human hand of construction relative to the material coursing relative to the body's perception develop the scale and legibility of this module to the spatial presence as a whole.

The Maison de Verre bays the section as an extension of the plan and elevation relative to the aggregate frames embedded in the glass block walls; the Farnsworth House segments into a tripartite configuration to allow for operable window panels; the French National Library extends the module from section through elevation in a floor-to-floor bay; the Cartier Foundation uses a tight floor-to-floor height to maximize floors and minimize building height, deploying the flexibility of steel to span at any dimension; the Kunsthaus Bregenz segments the exterior independently of the interior, adding to a further disassociation between surface and space; the House at Moledo pulls the glass wall back to create layers of exterior space; the De Blas Haus has a banding to the board-formed monolith of the concrete base, while the glass wall panels [limited by weight and cost] segment into a tripartite configuration; and the Sendai Mediatheque establishes a standardized horizontal module, with the vertical module determined by the variable floor-to-floor height and infill type responsive to each level's functional and effectual needs.

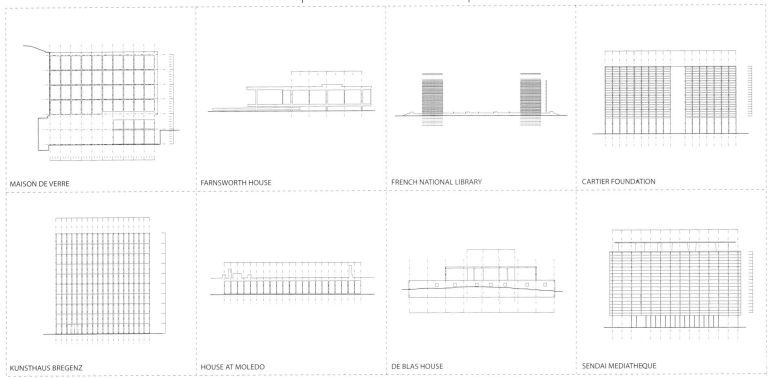

MAISON DE VERRE   FARNSWORTH HOUSE   FRENCH NATIONAL LIBRARY   CARTIER FOUNDATION

KUNSTHAUS BREGENZ   HOUSE AT MOLEDO   DE BLAS HOUSE   SENDAI MEDIATHEQUE

[GLASS] Module – MATERIAL MODULE diagrams in elevation the implications of the relationships of the manufacturing module intrinsic to a material to the space, form, and dimensions. Mapping the inherited dimensional constraints determined by the production and movement of a material to the façade, the formal legibility and implications of an architectural patterning of these scale elements rely upon the articulation of their joinery to establish larger architectural spaces.

The surface reading is derived from addressing the relationship of piece to whole and unit to system through the intrinsic module of a material. Certain materials default to a secondary system [such as concrete with formwork] to generate a dimensional constraint, but every material has a "natural" form and dimension. The negotiation of these constraints and the collaboration with these numeric proportions determine the dimensions of the whole and the integration of the modular unit into the consistency of the superstructural organization. In elevation, the implications of the human hand of construction relative to the material assemblies relative to the body's perception develop the scale and legibility of this module and its spatial presence as a whole.

The Maison de Verre has a regimented module to the metal frame in the block wall that mediates between the module of the individual blocks and the superstructural scale of the massive columns; the Farnsworth House create four half-column bay panels flanked by two quarter bays; the French National Library repeats the floor-to-floor sectional configuration in the elevation; the Cartier Foundation uses a tight grid module to the glass panels to reduce their weight and cost; the Kunsthaus Bregenz is clad with relentless consistency and anonymity; the House at Moledo uses a anthropomorphic dimension to the façade to allow for flexible operability and consistent cinematic framing; the De Blas Haus has a banding to the board-formed monolith of the concrete base, while the glass wall panels [limited by weight and cost] segment into a tripartite configuration with axial symmetry to the entire composition; and the Sendai Mediatheque blankets the façade with standardized horizontal panels, while the vertical module responds to the interior spatial module of floor-to-floor heights.

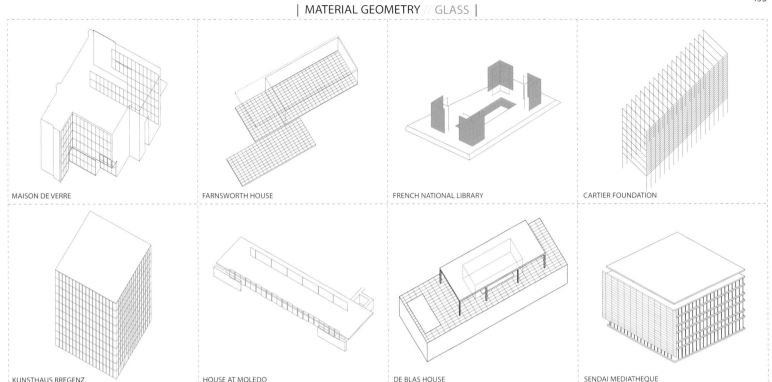

MAISON DE VERRE

FARNSWORTH HOUSE

FRENCH NATIONAL LIBRARY

CARTIER FOUNDATION

KUNSTHAUS BREGENZ

HOUSE AT MOLEDO

DE BLAS HOUSE

SENDAI MEDIATHEQUE

[GLASS] Module – MATERIAL GEOMETRY diagrams in axonometric the three-dimensional relationships of the manufacturing module intrinsic to a material to the space, form, and dimensions. Mapping the inherited dimensional constraints determined by the production and movement of a material into the three-dimensional ramifications of the total form, the legibility of an architectural patterning of scale elements relies upon the articulation of their joinery to establish larger architectural spaces.

The surface reading is derived from addressing the relationship of piece to whole and unit to system through the intrinsic module of a material. Certain materials default to a secondary system [such as concrete with formwork] to generate a dimensional constraint, but every material has a "natural" form and dimension. The negotiation of these constraints and the collaboration with these numeric proportions determine the dimensions of the whole and the integration of the modular unit into the consistency of the superstructural organization. In axonometric, the module governs the formal legibility of the three-dimensional building component and ultimately the formal reading of the building as a whole.

The Maison de Verre has a regimented module to the metal frame in the glass block wall that mediates between the module of the individual glass blocks and the superstructural scale of the massive columns; the Farnsworth House sleeves the glass between the horizontal extended planes; the French National Library concentrically layers the outer and inner walls of the towers with glass; the Cartier Foundation uses a tight grid module to the glass panels to reduce their weight and cost while producing a regularized field that, through its relentlessness, downplays the joint for the surface; the Kunsthaus Bregenz cloaks itself with a repetitive field on all four sides; the House at Moledo glazes the two longitudinal walls, one horizontal and one vertical in emphasis; the De Blas Haus has a monolithic concrete base, scored with a grid on the surface, that establishes the module for the glass enclosure and the offset canopy boundary; and the Sendai Mediatheque glazes the entire volume in bands and then reglazes the primary façade and roof with secondary performative skins.

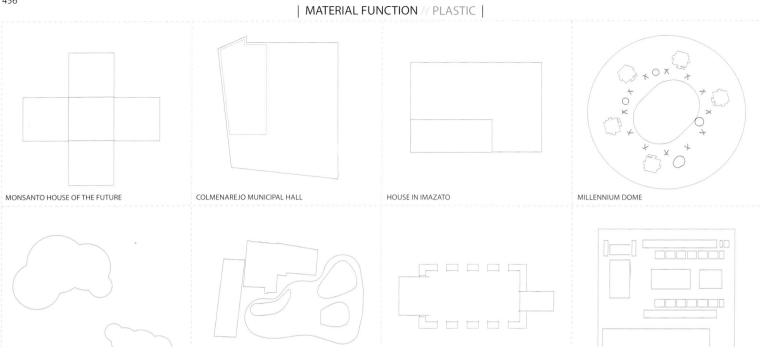

MONSANTO HOUSE OF THE FUTURE

COLMENAREJO MUNICIPAL HALL

HOUSE IN IMAZATO

MILLENNIUM DOME

EDEN PROJECT

KUNSTHAUS GRAZ

CHAMELEON HOUSE

WATER CUBE

[PLASTIC] MATERIAL FUNCTION diagrams in plan the relationship between material use and the formal and technical associations required by its functional application. These diagrams examine the role of a material's specific performance properties and its employment relative to the functional and practical necessities of the program and the building's performance. Each material expresses the conditions and requirements of its deployment.

Defining the premise of skin in each application, material serves as the iconic designation of form in each project. The associated material tectonic employed extends its influence to express itself through the spatial concepts of the architecture. Steel defines vertical lines [Eames House and Niaux Cave], concrete defines planes and frames with variable openings [Lovell Beach House, La Tourette, Church on the Water], and masonry creates modulated solid edges [Casa Barragan and Murcia Town Hall]. Glass establishes transparent veils: flat, ambiguous surfaces that exist but slip into a nonpresence allowing the dissolve of the enclosure and a perceived spatial connection between inside and outside. This is most prevalent in the De Blas Haus and the Cartier Foundation, though it exists even when the glass is frosted and figured, as in the glass block façade of the Maison de Verre. Each material relative to its function determines form.

The Monsanto House of the Future uses the plastic loops of the four external wings to cantilever off the central core and determine the cruciform figure; the Colmenarejo Municipal Hall defines the front wall of the infill figure with the translucent polycarbonate of its flexible skin; the House in Imazato completes the figure of its footprint with the translucent wall enclosing the garden courtyard; the Millennium Dome establishes the primary perimeter figure with the plastic tensile skin; the Eden Project uses intersecting spherical forms that create layered overlapping circles in plan that simultaneously define the plan and the figure of enclosure; the Kunsthaus Graz permits an amorphous multivalent form by the formal flexibility of the plastic façade; the Chameleon House wraps the central body of the house with a second skin of plastic; and the Water Cube bounds the various interior forms with a patterned plastic perimeter enclosure.

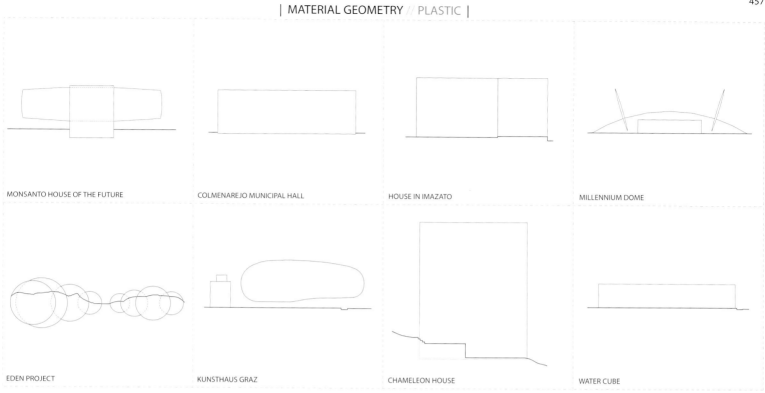

MONSANTO HOUSE OF THE FUTURE

COLMENAREJO MUNICIPAL HALL

HOUSE IN IMAZATO

MILLENNIUM DOME

EDEN PROJECT

KUNSTHAUS GRAZ

CHAMELEON HOUSE

WATER CUBE

[PLASTIC] MATERIAL GEOMETRY diagrams the sectional geometric implications of material for form. By introducing the potential structural implications of a material, the relationship of "skin to bones" or surface to structure becomes relative to the intrinsic qualities of a material. Establishing the dimensional module [both of performance and of fabrication and installation limitations], the capabilities of a material express themselves beyond the figure of the form to address the geometry of the space.

The module of a material can be established by three potential scales. The first scale is the module of the unit: a single brick, a sheet of plywood [as direct application of sheathing or as indirect application of formwork], a glass pane with either concealed or revealed frame systems, or a steel member. In each of these conditions the unit is defined by a structural need, a material property, or a manufacturing module. The second scale is the bay of the module produced through the assemblies or structure. For example, the Eames House window wall module is an aggregate of the individual panes, the double high bay module, and the superstructural steel frame. The final scale is the designed geometry of the building's mass expressed through material, i.e., the formal figure of the object as a whole. Each of these three levels can coexist or be independently exploited. The material in each case is, however, the beginning, the dimensional collaborator based on the intrinsic properties and performance of the base material.

The Monsanto House of the Future cantilevers symmetrical loops of the central concrete core; the Colmenarejo Municipal Hall is a simple rectilinear form, with the main plaza face being the translucent wall of pivoting panels; the House in Imazato has a rectangular figure with a transparent corner to the otherwise opaque figure; the Millennium Dome has a parabolic form defined by the tensile structure; the Eden Project deploys overlapping spheres to create an arched sectional enclosure; the Kunsthaus Graz uses a flexible material in the X, Y, and Z axes to produce a formally expressive morphology; the Chameleon House cloaks the main body of the house to produce an enigmatic effect on the simple form; and the Water Cube gathers the various pools under the single figure of a varied pattern enclosure.

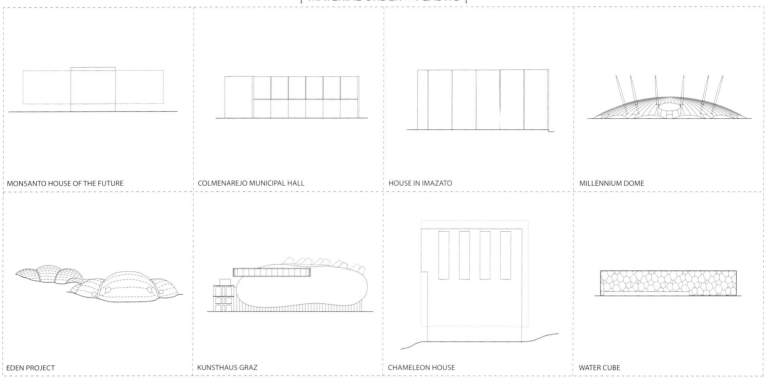

MONSANTO HOUSE OF THE FUTURE COLMENAREJO MUNICIPAL HALL HOUSE IN IMAZATO MILLENNIUM DOME

EDEN PROJECT KUNSTHAUS GRAZ CHAMELEON HOUSE WATER CUBE

[PLASTIC] MATERIAL ORDER diagrams in elevation the hierarchy, sequence, and organizational methods of material's influence on the architectural form. As in the examination in section, the implication here is more spatial than formal. Looking at the organizational geometries and governing patterns of material relative to the form, the implications and legibility of volume and mass are articulated through the aggregation of the material pieces.

The extension of the material module into the overarching order of the formal expression is the ultimate collaboration of material with design. The definition of the overall form relative to the piece, the manner in which an aperture is made as a removal [in terms both of module and structural implications], and the relation of these compositional pieces to the formal whole are the defining characteristics of a material's influence on form.

The Monsanto House of the Future has a consistency of section to elevation with the four identical radiating plastic shells of the cruciform wings; the Colmenarejo Municipal Hall has a panelized polycarbonate façade with an operable lower course; the House in Imazato transitions the consistent bays of the house through the variable of material; the Millennium Dome has a shallow segmented dome; the Eden Project has transparent spherical bubble forms that are consistent from inside to outside; the Kunsthaus Graz uses the transparency of glass to detach the primary amorphous form of the illuminated plastic skin pierced by an elevated datum of the view platform to provide a compositional edge; the Chameleon House veils the house in a simple rectangle of polycarbonate; and the Water Cube has a rectangular figure with an internal structural and figural pattern.

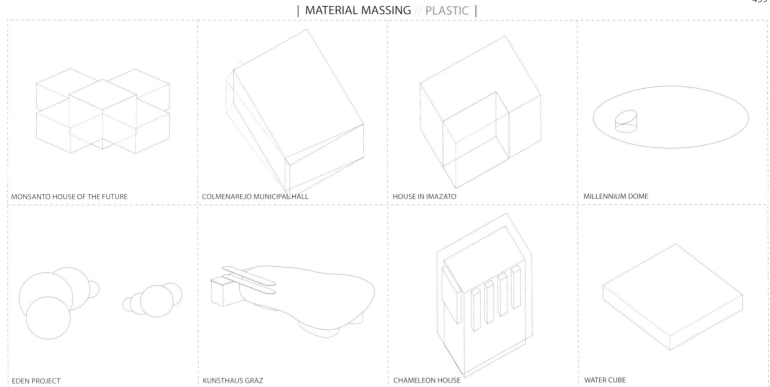

MONSANTO HOUSE OF THE FUTURE

COLMENAREJO MUNICIPAL HALL

HOUSE IN IMAZATO

MILLENNIUM DOME

EDEN PROJECT

KUNSTHAUS GRAZ

CHAMELEON HOUSE

WATER CUBE

[PLASTIC] MATERIAL MASSING diagrams in axonometric the overall legibility of the primary material to the superstructural form, presence, and mass of the architectural form. Focusing primarily on the mass and volume of form as defined by the material application to the exterior, the legibility of compositional intention and the geometric hierarchy are mapped.

The significance of mass [as defined by material in particular] concerns to the clarity of formal intention in relation to the actual legibility and reading in the building. The conceptual ideas that govern the design of a building become legible through their tectonic manifestations in the form. The hierarchy of the primary massing determines the figuration to which all else must respond. The material relationship with this massing and the deployment of the tectonic expression of the assembly determine whether a material is read as segmented, disassociated, panelized, repetitive, or monolithic.

The Monsanto House of the Future has clearly distinct cantilevered structural loops; the Colmenarejo Municipal Hall has a slightly shifted geometry with a primary operable and translucent wall to respond to the urban context; the House in Imazato has a simple rectangular form with one corner removed to create an exterior courtyard cloaked in translucent plastic; the Millennium Dome has a shallow dome figure; the Eden Project has a series of intersecting spherical volumes that aggregate to define the figure of the enclosure; the Kunsthaus Graz builds off an existing building to float a formal figure in the city center; the Chameleon House has a simple vertical building cloaked in a secondary skin of translucent plastic; and the Water Cube has a simple rectangular figure.

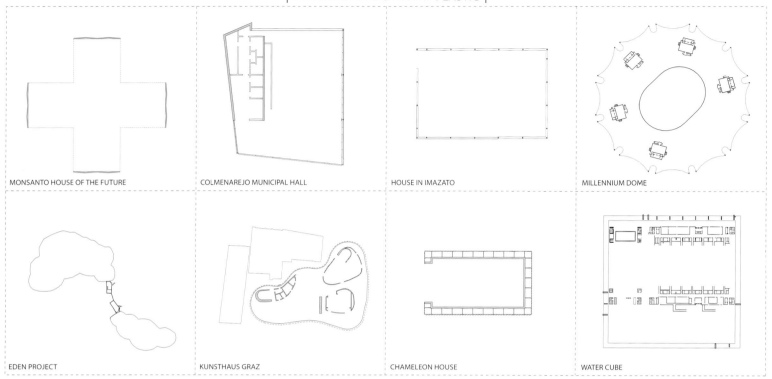

MONSANTO HOUSE OF THE FUTURE

COLMENAREJO MUNICIPAL HALL

HOUSE IN IMAZATO

MILLENNIUM DOME

EDEN PROJECT

KUNSTHAUS GRAZ

CHAMELEON HOUSE

WATER CUBE

[PLASTIC] MATERIAL APPLICATION diagrams in plan the deployment of material and the associated perceptual, formal, and functional readings. Engaging the relationship between material and function, the formal expression becomes the primary mediating element. The expression of the material's use and the tectonic deployment determine the functional programmatic legibility of the building. This begins with the formal expression intrinsic to the material followed by issues of practical performance including durability, porosity, and visual effect.

A material can be selected for various reasons: availability, cost, durability, module, structural capability, or simply the functional applicability [metal to combat combustion, concrete for construction in corrosive environments, or masonry as a low-maintenance, durable skin]. In each scenario the fundamental physical properties of the material are the baseline of design consideration. These properties, mediated by the method of manufacturing and limited by the method of working [wood is easy to cut, metal can be welded, masonry is heavy and modular], develop the second tier of consideration. Finally, and perhaps with the most variability, is the assembly and application. The systemization of the manufactured pieces and their formal and technical articulation are material design application.

The Monsanto House of the Future deploys plastic as skin and structure to define the looping shell form; the Colmenarejo Municipal Hall has an infill figure with a segmented front wall; the House in Imazato has a consistent boundary that changes in materiality from inside to outside; the Millennium Dome has an elliptical figure in plan that is locally scalloped by the segmented tensile cable structuring; the Eden Project has a bubbled perimeter that defines the structural segregation; the Kunsthaus Graz has three cores with compartmentalized plan subdivisions, leaving the dynamic formalism of the plastic figure to be a free plan for the gallery spaces; the Chameleon House wraps the main figure of the building with a simple orthogonally segmented skin; and the Water Cube has a double-walled perimeter engulfing the compartmentalized interior.

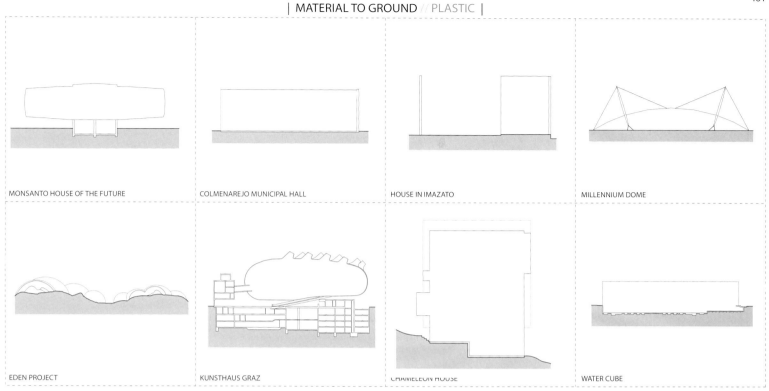

[PLASTIC] Proximity – MATERIAL TO GROUND diagrams the sectional relationship by which a building meets the ground, engages landscape, and addresses the material point of connection with the site. The point of contact between a building and the earth is determined by the material approach to the architecture. Factors that determine and affect this condition include soil characteristics, climate, context, structural system, and building weight [both actual and perceived].

The history of structural and material technology is the history of how a building meets the ground. The selection of material cladding and structural framing results in a specific formal articulation of this condition that is intrinsic to the material and tectonic. Technologically determined, this joint [between building and ground] is created by the system of both the structure and the cladding. Historically, load-bearing wall systems of wood or masonry required continuous contact of the building with the ground and limited the scale and frequency of openings. Materials such as steel and concrete allowed for a formal disengagement from the ground plane, turning structural planes into points and shifting from a wall system to a cage.

The Monsanto House of the Future hovers off the ground through a structural cantilever from the central concrete mast; the Colmenarejo Municipal Hall sets on the ground and into the dense urban fabric, emerging through the distinctly contrasting surface material; the House in Imazato holds the polycarbonate off the house as a plane bounding a space between itself and the mass of the body of the house; the Millennium Dome anchors to the ground, hugging it to create its enclosure; the Eden Project floats over, yet engages, the ground plane with a form that seems to continue below grade, engaging the surface for its greenhouse function; the Kunsthaus Graz disengages the primary form of the building from the ground to allow for a six-sided continuity to its figure, relying upon a transparent perimeter to define the enclosure and the connection to occur through three recessed interior pavilions; the Chameleon House sets into the slope of the hill, allowing the plastic to hover above as a pure geometric figure; and the Water Cube sets into the earth, with the skin set upon the engaged plinth of the pool surface.

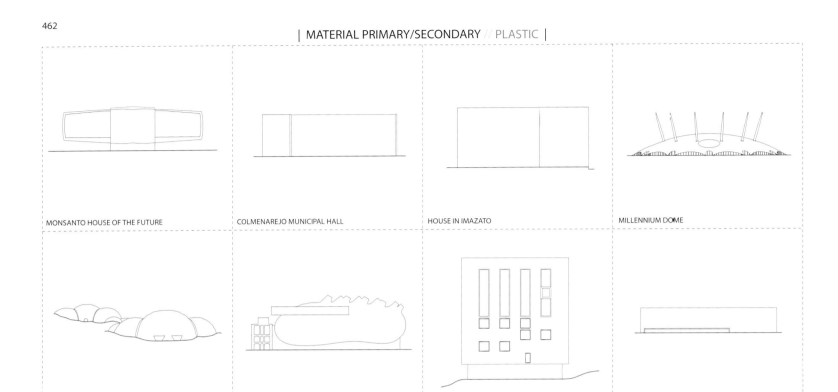

[PLASTIC] Proximity – PRIMARY / SECONDARY diagrams in elevation the relationship of the primary building material to the secondary building material, focusing on the formal, functional, and practical interrelationships of their material application. The hierarchy between these two levels is both formally and materially evident, establishing the organizing geometries of the diverse layers.

The proximity of a primary figure to a secondary figure builds on the formal reading of material application diagrams but engages the interrelationship with the secondary systemization. The interaction of the two can occur through superimposition, contrasting figures, interpenetration, banding, layering, or any other adverbial relationship. The result is a primary figuration and the secondary subsystemization that, through its geometry, breaks down the material into fabricateable and installable pieces and reveals the tectonic intention of their aggregation.

The Monsanto House of the Future uses the primary figure of the plastic with the secondary infill of glass to emphasize the presence and material of the shell; the Colmenarejo Municipal Hall juxtaposes the modern plastic façade material with the masonry and steel structure of the building's body; the House in Imazato maintains a consistent bay dimension in both the polycarbonate wall and the corrugated galvarium metal wall of the house; the Millennium Dome uses the structural steel mast and cable system to support the plastic skin; the Eden Project relies upon the secondary metal web to provide structure and maintain the pressurization system for the ethylene tetrafluoroethylene (ETFE) pillows; the Kunsthaus Graz contrasts the newness of form and material against the historical and orthogonal figure of the existing building; the Chameleon House cloaks the wood of the house with a plastic second skin; and the Water Cube uses a facet patterned steel skeletal system to hold the plastic infill pillows.

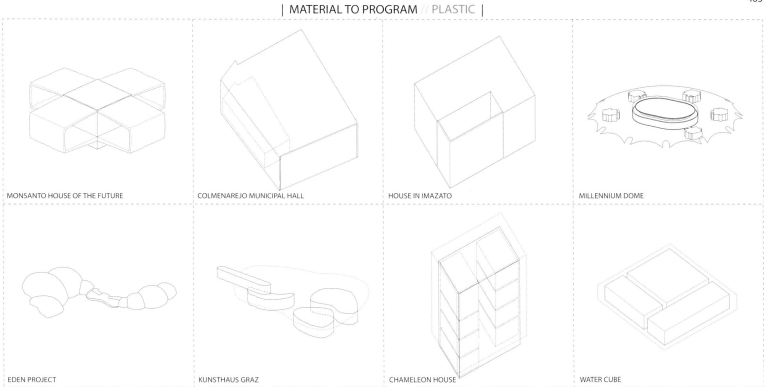

MONSANTO HOUSE OF THE FUTURE

COLMENAREJO MUNICIPAL HALL

HOUSE IN IMAZATO

MILLENNIUM DOME

EDEN PROJECT

KUNSTHAUS GRAZ

CHAMELEON HOUSE

WATER CUBE

[PLASTIC] Proximity – MATERIAL TO PROGRAM diagrams in axonometric the overall relationship of material usage to the primary programmatic and functional usages. By focusing on the three-dimensional volumetric associations of material to programmatic usage [and the associated functional requirements of a particular program], the articulation of "form following function" can be examined through material association.

The relationship of the programmatic usage to the material selected depicts the narrative of the association, creating the opportunity and potential for material to be an expressive sign system. The legibility of a material comes from a technical knowledge that engages an understanding of raw material, manufacturing processes, construction traditions and techniques, weathering and biological attack, and cultural associations. These innate properties of matter translate into forms that collaborate with materials to reveal their process.

The Monsanto House of the Future has a centralized scheme of four looping plastic figures; the Colmenarejo Municipal Hall has a frontal plastic public wall; the House in Imazato wraps the courtyard with the plastic, while the house proper is wrapped in metal; the Millennium Dome shells the arena with the plastic figure; the Eden Project encloses the garden with the ETFE bubbles; the Kunsthaus Graz engages three plan-based curvilinear figures that support the main figure, which is three-dimensionally curvilinear, topped by a datum bar that pierces the shape and establishes a rectilinear urban edge; the Chameleon House drapes the house with a plastic second skin; and the Water Cube uniformly cloaks the diverse pools.

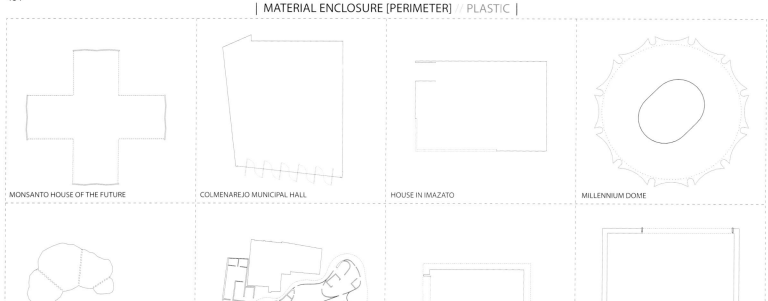

MONSANTO HOUSE OF THE FUTURE

COLMENAREJO MUNICIPAL HALL

HOUSE IN IMAZATO

MILLENNIUM DOME

EDEN PROJECT

KUNSTHAUS GRAZ

CHAMELEON HOUSE

WATER CUBE

[PLASTIC] Skin + Surface – MATERIAL ENCLOSURE [PERIMETER] diagrams in plan the relationship of the outer plane of enclosure [skin] to the spatial, formal, and structural organization. Expressing the process by which materials assemble into systems, the figuration of the perimeter is dependent not simply upon the piece but also upon the joint. The collaboration of these two generates specific forms intrinsic to a material and expressively identifiable.

The use of skin to define the perimeter over the structure and the programmatic innards establishes the legibility of architectural idea's purity through the articulation of edge and boundary. The continuity and complexity of this envelope widely explicate the material articulation and the tectonic intricacy. The relationship of craft to figure is found in the method of material manipulation.

The Monsanto House of the Future reveals the plastic shell in plan through the four opaque end walls; the Colmenarejo Municipal Hall is clad with the polycarbonate only on the frontal plaza wall; the House in Imazato cloaks the plastic corner of the courtyard; the Millennium Dome encircles the perimeter yet touches only at points of structural connection; the Eden Project uses the plastic ETFE pillows as the skin of enclosure; the Kunsthaus Graz bridges the rectilinear existing fabric into the plan-based curvilinear geometry, ultimately arriving at a full three-dimensional amorphous figuration; the Chameleon House wraps the perimeter of the house; and the Water Cube wraps the perimeter with concrete-framed openings for pedestrian access.

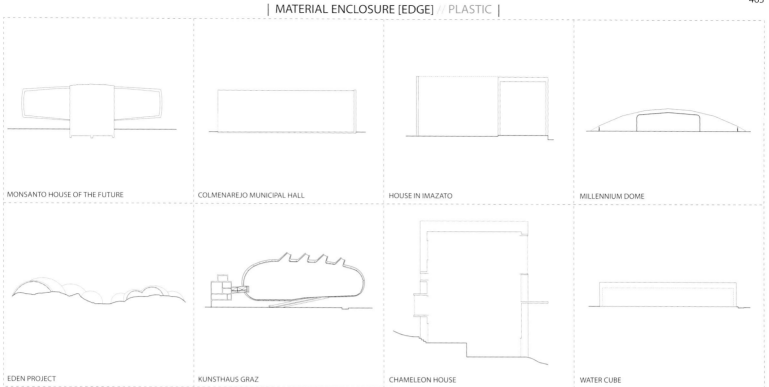

MONSANTO HOUSE OF THE FUTURE

COLMENAREJO MUNICIPAL HALL

HOUSE IN IMAZATO

MILLENNIUM DOME

EDEN PROJECT

KUNSTHAUS GRAZ

CHAMELEON HOUSE

WATER CUBE

[PLASTIC] Skin + Surface – MATERIAL ENCLOSURE [EDGE] diagrams in section the relationship of the outer plane of enclosure [skin] to the spatial, formal, and structural organization. Expressing the process by which materials assemble into systems, the figuration of the perimeter as expressed through section extends the moves of plan in the Y axis [still dependent not simply upon the piece but also upon the joint].

The collaboration of piece with joint determines the sectional spatial forms intrinsic to a material, resulting in expressive and identifiable associations. The role of skin in section similarly works to define the perimeter over the structure and the interior functions. The figure establishes the legibility of an architectural idea's purity through the articulation of edge and boundary as extended to the vertical and thus the now spatial dimension. The continuity and complexity of this line widely explicate the material articulation and the tectonic intricacy. The relationship of exterior material through the surface of the building to impact and define interior space is moderated by the material manipulation of this edge.

The Monsanto House of the Future uses the shell figure of the plastic loop to define the skin, surface, structure, and enclosure; the Colmenarejo Municipal Hall clads the front façade with a polycarbonate skin over a frame that creates the surface as an enigmatically translucent and flexibly operable surface; the House in Imazato uses the corrugated polycarbonate as a fence-like extension of the buildings' figure, maintaining a consistency of surface but varying the materiality and translucency of the skin; the Millennium Dome is the skin and surface of the tensile canopy; the Eden Project creates a surface of steel structure with an infill ETFE pillow as simultaneous structure and skin; the Kunsthaus Graz bridges the rectilinear existing fabric into the three-dimensional amorphous figuration; the Chameleon House uses the plastic as a second skin, an ephemeral ghost over the first, with the inner volume touching and even protruding at times; and the Water Cube uses a double skin of polygonal patterned ETFE pillows to define structure and surface.

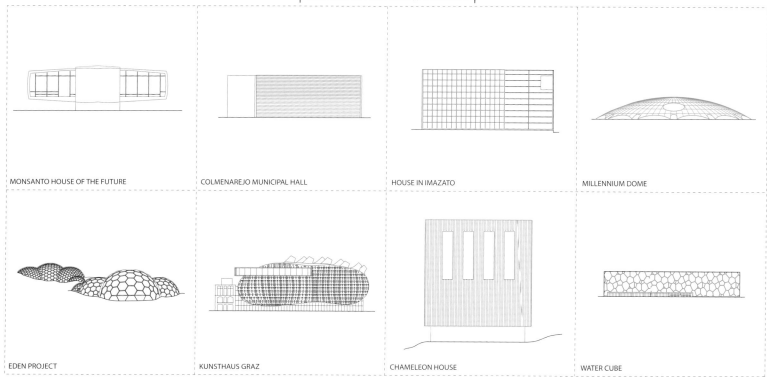

MONSANTO HOUSE OF THE FUTURE   COLMENAREJO MUNICIPAL HALL   HOUSE IN IMAZATO   MILLENNIUM DOME

EDEN PROJECT   KUNSTHAUS GRAZ   CHAMELEON HOUSE   WATER CUBE

[PLASTIC] Skin + Surface – MATERIAL TEXTURE diagrams in elevation the legibility of the material's texture, color, and surface. Defining the compositional aesthetics of the elevation, the collagist sensibility of pattern, texture, color, and depth of plane are all legible against light. Like a composed painting, this image is dissected from the visual perceptual stance of the material on the architectural composition.

The textural reading refers to the actual color and composition of the material. Wood, for example, can be classified as a generic type, but the performance qualities, colors, hardness, resistance to rot, durability, and workability are vastly different from species to species. This same textural legibility comes through the assembly and expression of the unit and the joint. The scale and articulation of these connections define the legibility of the collective material reading and the overall compositional reading of the architecture.

The Monsanto House of the Future deploys the smoothness of the plastic shell contrasted by the subdivided mullions of the lateral glass walls to give scale and detail to form; the Colmenarejo Municipal Hall uses the striation of the corrugated polycarbonate to provide a scaleless uniformity to the façade to mask the mutable flexibility of the façade; the House in Imazato uses the subframe to the translucent polycarbonate to produce a ghosted grid with the mullions; the Millennium Dome uses a segmented skin for material and structural purposes that produces a subdivision to the heroic scale of the stadium enclosure; the Eden Project uses hexagonal shapes to generate the geometry of the structure and skin, and subdivides the even larger formal presence into legible components through its pattern despite their massive scale; the Kunsthaus Graz sets a light array below the plastic skin to produce a variable embedded sign system that allows the skin to serve simultaneously as figure, enclosure, sign, and animation; the Chameleon House uses an almost transparent polycarbonate, so the connections and substrata skin are evident but striated by the plastic surface; and the Water Cube uses a variable steel frame to segment the façade with a dynamic pattern, allowing for an enigmatic scale while providing for the functional and practical limitations of the ETFE pillows.

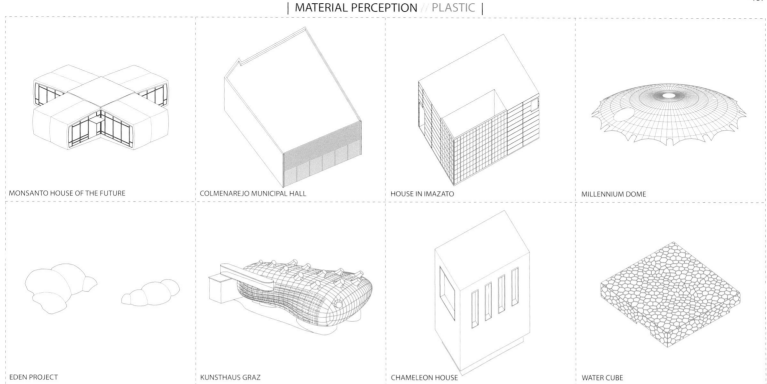

MONSANTO HOUSE OF THE FUTURE

COLMENAREJO MUNICIPAL HALL

HOUSE IN IMAZATO

MILLENNIUM DOME

EDEN PROJECT

KUNSTHAUS GRAZ

CHAMELEON HOUSE

WATER CUBE

[PLASTIC] Skin + Surface – MATERIAL PERCEPTION diagrams in axonometric the primary reading of material experience. By transitioning from the sectional reading that focuses on the two-dimensional interior spatial conditions or the material application, the reading in elevation speaks to the composition of the façade but again within the shallow space of a two-dimensional reading, while the axonometric examination illustrates the compositional legibility of the building as a total object.

By engaging all three dimensions, the figuration of the architecture and the legibility of a material's perception relative to the total object lend a volumetric legibility to a material's perception. A truly monolithic architecture is nearly impossible; thus, the connection and change from one piece to the next define the moment of intervention and design decision. The perception of the whole after the resolution of these local "events" is the perception of the architecture. Focusing specifically on the material impact upon these decisions allows the design intention to be revealed by the tectonic view of the whole through the piece.

The Monsanto House of the Future is dominated by the four identical cantilevered wings, each separated into four bays (two wide and then symmetrical about the horizontal axis); the Colmenarejo Municipal Hall bands the front façade horizontally, with the lower half segmented by the fully operable pivot walls and the upper half similarly segmented but with a fixed position; the House in Imazato pulls the skin of the building fully around the purity of the geometry despite the removal of spaces behind, denoting the change from outside to inside only through the variation in the surface material; the Millennium Dome uses a regular radial geometry to segment the shallow dome and create the open scalloped edge for pedestrian access beneath; the Eden Project has multiple components for the different microclimates it is required to provide for plant life, yet each of these uses a similar methodology of intersecting spheres nestled into the undulating landscape to generate the geometry of the figure and the hexagonal subdivision that defines the pattern and structure of the surface; the Kunsthaus Graz produces a figuration and then negotiates the connections and practicalities through parallel systems; the Chameleon House cloaks the building with a transparent second veil, allowing pieces to emerge through or be shielded by the veil; and the Water Cube carries the irregular pattern of the surface across the five sizes of the building, with localized variability but overarching homogeneity to the pattern of the surface.

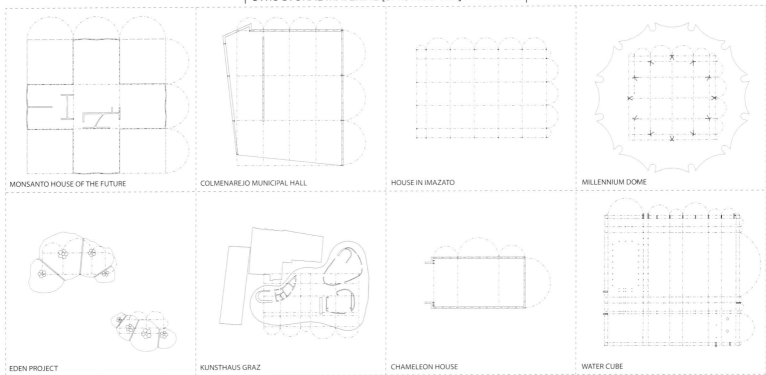

MONSANTO HOUSE OF THE FUTURE

COLMENAREJO MUNICIPAL HALL

HOUSE IN IMAZATO

MILLENNIUM DOME

EDEN PROJECT

KUNSTHAUS GRAZ

CHAMELEON HOUSE

WATER CUBE

[PLASTIC] STRUCTURAL MATERIAL [BAY/MODULE] diagrams in plan the structural module of the building. Focusing on the influence of the structural material, it illustrates the engineered structural response of material relative to performative need. Dependent upon the dimension of span relative to the spatial capabilities of the material, an organizing geometry is established that sets the scale and legibility of a space.

The role of structure in plan is of particular formal importance relative to material as the premise of line [load-bearing walls] versus point [columns]. Each system establishes a certain way of making space. Load-bearing materials versus cladding materials are revealed, and their variation and interdependence are highlighted.

The Monsanto House of the Future uses a nine square geometry with a central mast, allowing the four cruciform cantilevers and the corners to dissolve to openness; the Colmenarejo Municipal Hall has a regularized three by four structural bay despite the irregular footprint established by the context; the House in Imazato is a hyperregulated square module with a half-bay perimeter on three sides; the Millennium Dome uses a radial geometry for the upper canopy with an orthogonal geometry for the service plinth below; the Eden Project uses proportional modules to establish the center points of the spheres that generate the overarching geometry; the Kunsthaus Graz has a series of columns exposed and concealed in the ground floor pavilions that regularly walk across the ground floor and support the irregular form above; the Chameleon House flanks a central primary module with two side half-modules; and the Water Cube establishes the primary bays based upon the entry portals and the programmatic components foiled against the continuity of the regularized skin.

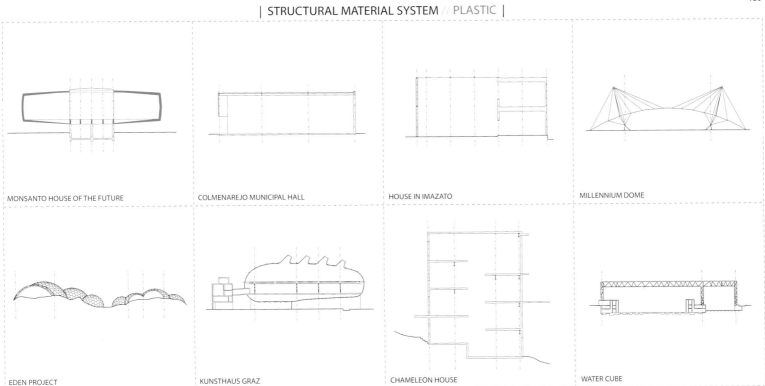

MONSANTO HOUSE OF THE FUTURE

COLMENAREJO MUNICIPAL HALL

HOUSE IN IMAZATO

MILLENNIUM DOME

EDEN PROJECT

KUNSTHAUS GRAZ

CHAMELEON HOUSE

WATER CUBE

[PLASTIC] STRUCTURAL MATERIAL [BAY/MODULE] diagrams the sectional implications of the structural module. Focusing on the influence of the structural material, it illustrates the engineered structural response of material relative to performative need. In this diagram set, the structure is materially examined in its vertical figuration of the sectional articulation.

Building on the bay system of the plan, the section depicts the shape and configuration of the repetitive unit and the effectual relationship to the space of the building. Perceived or concealed, primary [as figuration] or coincidental in presence, the role of the sectional structural bay engages the verticality of the building.

The Monsanto House of the Future uses the identical bay of the wing piece to allow for repetitive mold manufacturing of the rigid shell; the Colmenarejo Municipal Hall creates a classically bayed front façade divided vertically into two bays: operable and fixed; the House in Imazato has a standardized bay that is read through the skin but largely unaffecting to the space; the Millennium Dome shows the shallow dome of the enclosure balanced by the dominant structural mast system; the Eden Project establishes a regularized hexagonal geometry that has an infill of ETFE air pillows; the Kunsthaus Graz has a central truss system held by columns that emerge from the open ground floor plan and carry through the shaped space to hold up the dynamic outer shell; the Chameleon House reestablishes the bay of the structurally insulated panels (SIPs) in the connections to the polycarbonate veil, allowing the windows to recognize the bay by oscillating an open-closed-open-closed pattern; and the Water Cube uses the double-skinned enclosure to create a space frame to span the long open space of the swimming hall.

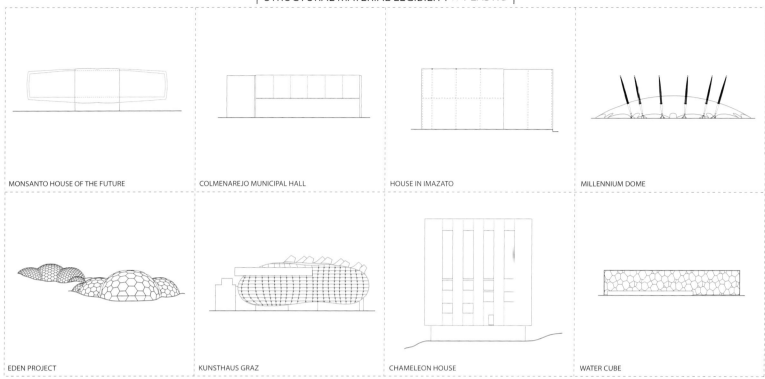

MONSANTO HOUSE OF THE FUTURE

COLMENAREJO MUNICIPAL HALL

HOUSE IN IMAZATO

MILLENNIUM DOME

EDEN PROJECT

KUNSTHAUS GRAZ

CHAMELEON HOUSE

WATER CUBE

[PLASTIC] STRUCTURAL MATERIAL LEGIBILITY diagrams in elevation the reading of the structural material. Focusing on the influence of the structural material, it illustrates the interrelation of the engineered structural response of material and performative need to the form and composition. Questioning how the system reads from the exterior and whether the structural material is ever seen, the legibility diagrams examine the relationship of the forces of gravity to the formal expression.

The integration of structure to skin and ultimately to form is about the engagement of the physical requirements of a building to perform structurally with the formal intentions and the legibility of these two systems. The idea of [1] reading a person's bones literally through the skin, [2] versus the broader legibility of a leg as column to transfer vertical loads, [3] versus a denial of all understanding of how the figure works structurally are the three basic stages of structural depiction: [1] literal, [2] figural, or [3] denied.

The Monsanto House of the Future reveals the structural shell of the building through its form and dramatic cantilever; the Colmenarejo Municipal Hall, through the translucency of the material, allows an x-ray view of the skeletal structural system; the House in Imazato uses the translucency of the material to reveal the inner frame skeleton of the structural system in the plastic panels, implying a similar system running beneath the opaque metal panels; the Millennium Dome is pierced by the mast system that allows a fully celebrated expression of the tensile structural system; the Eden Project makes the building fully transparent, allowing both an interior and an exterior simultaneity to the reading of structure and skin; the Kunsthaus Graz uses three diverse methods for the base, top, and intruding viewing platform, each with an internal and unexpressed structural system; the Chameleon House allows the transparency of the outer skin to be stopped by the inner skin of the SIPs allowing a partial depth to the wall; and the Water Cube reveals the pattern of the structure through the mullion system of the ETFE pillows.

| STRUCTURAL MATERIAL [LINE/POINT] // PLASTIC |

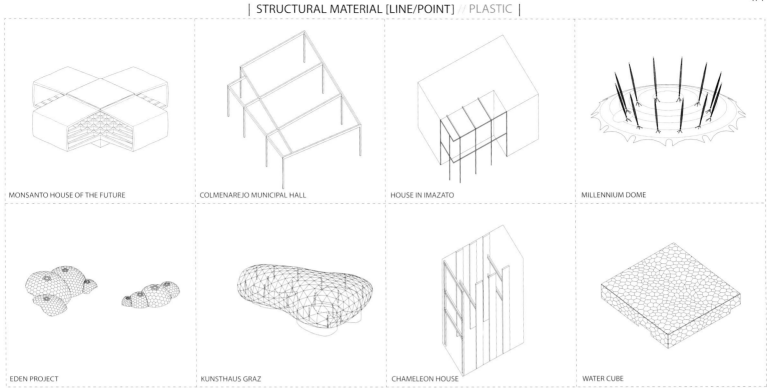

MONSANTO HOUSE OF THE FUTURE

COLMENAREJO MUNICIPAL HALL

HOUSE IN IMAZATO

MILLENNIUM DOME

EDEN PROJECT

KUNSTHAUS GRAZ

CHAMELEON HOUSE

WATER CUBE

[PLASTIC] STRUCTURAL MATERIAL [LINE/POINT] diagrams in axonometric the primary geometric and formal response of the structural material/system. "Line" refers to the registration of a wall surface as a structural bearing wall in plan, while "point" refers to the columnar system. Materials subscribe intrinsically to one or the other [typically]; metal is point, while masonry is line. Certain materials, like concrete and wood, have the potential to be either.

The axonometric diagramming of the structural system and the material expression of this system suggest the three-dimensional resolution of the underlying structure superimposed on the form. The relationship of the structural material to the primary material parallels the discussion of revelation versus concealment and homogeneity versus cladding.

The Monsanto House of the Future has a ribbed shell structure providing the necessary depth to the cantilever while maintaining an exterior smoothness of the monolithic shell; the Colmenarejo Municipal Hall has an internal steel frame that runs parallel to the façade and thus is legible only from the interior of the space; the House in Imazato has an internal structural frame that is masked in the opaque surfaces but revealed in the translucency of the courtyard walls; the Millennium Dome uses the columnar line system to suspend the fabric canopy with tension cables; the Eden Project uses a hexagonal system that is evident in its elevation with operable panels at the pinnacle of each dome to allow for air release; the Kunsthaus Graz sits on a field of columns that hold the skin and then resolve the structural loads through its surface; the Chameleon House uses a combination of a steel frame system and the SIPs all cloaked in the plastic veil. Despite the exterior transparency, the legibility of these systems is felt majorily from the interior; and the Water Cube uses a localized frame system to establish the overall structure, as well as the perimeter frame for each ETFE pillow.

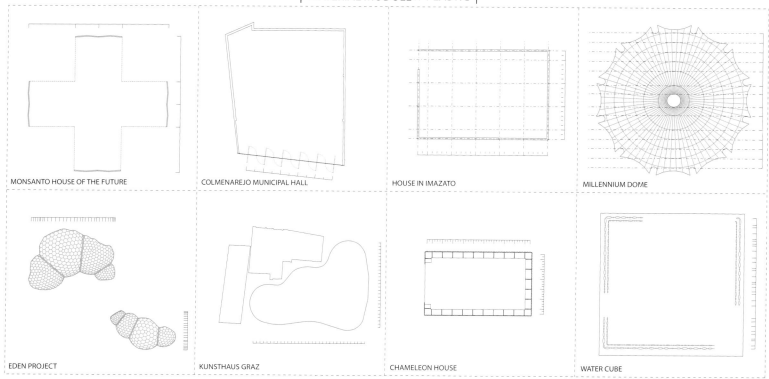

MONSANTO HOUSE OF THE FUTURE

COLMENAREJO MUNICIPAL HALL

HOUSE IN IMAZATO

MILLENNIUM DOME

EDEN PROJECT

KUNSTHAUS GRAZ

CHAMELEON HOUSE

WATER CUBE

[PLASTIC] Module – MATERIAL MODULE diagrams in plan the relationships of the manufacturing module intrinsic to a material to the space, form, and dimensions. Mapping the inherited dimensional constraints determined by the production and movement of a material, the patterning of these scale elements and the articulation of their joinery to establish larger architectural forms address the relationship of piece to whole and unit to system.

The module of materials is an intrinsic fact that must be addressed. Certain materials default to a secondary system [such as concrete with formwork] to generate a dimensional constraint, but every material has a "natural" form and dimension. The negotiation of these constraints and the collaboration with these numeric proportions determine the dimensions of the whole and the integration of the modular unit into the consistency of the superstructural organization.

The Monsanto House of the Future uses an identical double module for each wing, repeating the form around a center structural mast [a repetition resulting from the required similarity of mold use]; the Colmenarejo Municipal Hall uses a two-bay subdivision of the larger structural bay of the front wall; the House in Imazato uses a five-bay subdivision of the structural bay to coordinate the material module with the larger structural system; the Millennium Dome uses radial bays in the fabric skin to allow for the dome figure; the Eden Project uses a repetitive hexagonal geometry that allows for the curvature of each segment and frames the individual skin system panels; the Kunsthaus Graz uses a regular grid for the columns to establish a datum field for the various amorphous figures and highly flexible materials deployed in the project; the Chameleon House uses a segmented bay to the larger connection system that is a result of the SIPs backer wall coordinating the outer and inner skins skillfully; and the Water Cube, on a local scale, creates individual forms for each cell of the structural frame to produce the frame for the infill of the ETFE material.

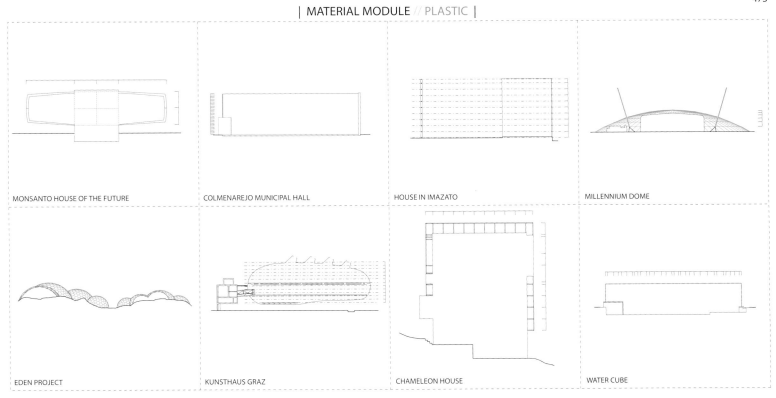

MONSANTO HOUSE OF THE FUTURE

COLMENAREJO MUNICIPAL HALL

HOUSE IN IMAZATO

MILLENNIUM DOME

EDEN PROJECT

KUNSTHAUS GRAZ

CHAMELEON HOUSE

WATER CUBE

[PLASTIC] Module – MATERIAL MODULE diagrams in section the relationships of the manufacturing module intrinsic to a material to the space, form, and dimensions. Mapping the inherited dimensional constraints determined by the production and movement of a material to the sectional implications, the patterning of these scale elements and the articulation of their joinery establish larger architectural spaces derived from addressing the relationship of piece to whole and unit to system.

The module of material is an intrinsic fact that must be addressed. Certain materials default to a secondary system [such as concrete with formwork] to generate a dimensional constraint, but every material has a "natural" form and dimension. The negotiation of these constraints and the collaboration with these numeric proportions determine the dimensions of the whole and the integration of the modular unit into the consistency of the superstructural organization. In section, the implications of the human hand of construction relative to the material coursing relative to the body's perception develop the scale and legibility of this module to the spatial presence as a whole.

The Monsanto House of the Future has a single large-scale module of premanufacturing that allowed the superscaled components to be craned on site and joined with minimal seams to emphasize the continuity of the whole over the articulation of the part; the Colmenarejo Municipal Hall in section uses the striations of the polycarbonate skin to create a uniformity despite the variable flexibility; the House in Imazato continues the corrugation of the metal cladding through the identical corrugation of the plastic cladding; the Millennium Dome segments the large fabric shell into slices for the scale of manufacturing, structural scale, and fabrication practicalities; the Eden Project segments the façade into hexagonal pieces, each individually inflated and pressurized to allow the scale of both the material and the pressure chamber to be easily manageable; the Kunsthaus Graz has a regular horizontal bay system to the floor plates that corresponds to the panels even though the segmentation of the plastic skin is not legible from the interior of the space; the Chameleon House bands the material through both internal corrugations and the panel bays to create an ephemeral yet patterned skin; and the Water Cube segments the façade with the metal frames that support each of the air pillows.

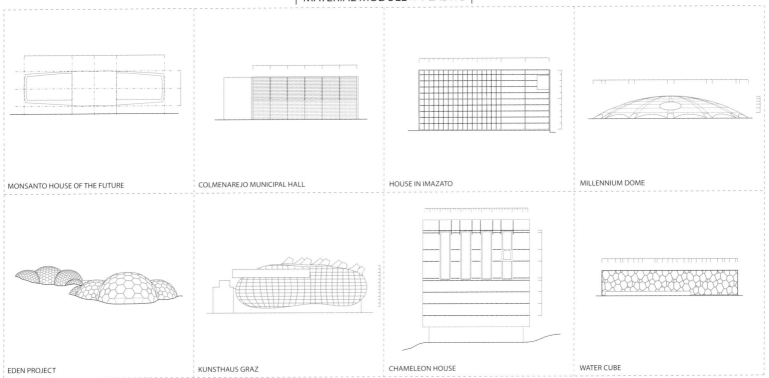

MONSANTO HOUSE OF THE FUTURE

COLMENAREJO MUNICIPAL HALL

HOUSE IN IMAZATO

MILLENNIUM DOME

EDEN PROJECT

KUNSTHAUS GRAZ

CHAMELEON HOUSE

WATER CUBE

[PLASTIC] Module – MATERIAL MODULE diagrams in elevation the implications of the relationships of the manufacturing module intrinsic to a material to the space, form, and dimensions. Mapping the inherited dimensional constraints determined by the production and movement of a material to the façade, the formal legibility and implications of an architectural patterning of these scale elements rely upon the articulation of their joinery to establish larger architectural spaces.

The surface reading is derived from addressing the relationship of piece to whole and unit to system through the intrinsic module of a material. Certain materials default to a secondary system [such as concrete with formwork] to generate a dimensional constraint, but every material has a "natural" form and dimension. The negotiation of these constraints and the collaboration with these numeric proportions determine the dimensions of the whole and the integration of the modular unit into the consistency of the superstructural organization. In elevation, the implications of the human hand of construction relative to the material assemblies relative to the body's perception develop the scale and legibility of this module and its spatial presence as a whole.

The Monsanto House of the Future shows the biaxial symmetry of the plastic wings in elevation; the Colmenarejo Municipal Hall, when appropriately lit, reveals the material bay in elevation as corresponding to the substrata of the structural bay beneath; the House in Imazato, when backlit, reveals the interior skeletal structure; the Millennium Dome, as a tensile structure, reveals all aspects of its construction, dependent upon the material segmentation to provide a transition of scale; the Eden Project reveals through its transparency all systems, finding its primary local identity in the material and the structural module; the Kunsthaus Graz has a regular horizontal bay system in the floor plates and panels that allows the deformation and flexibility of the skin to occur independently of the joint; the Chameleon House, with a transparent façade, allows a full revelation of the wall and system beneath; and the Water Cube, as a redundant system revealed on both the inside and outside, allows for the legibility of the material piece to the patterned whole.

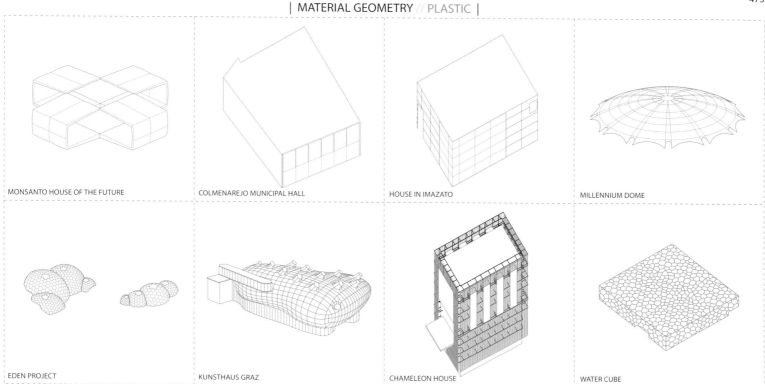

MONSANTO HOUSE OF THE FUTURE

COLMENAREJO MUNICIPAL HALL

HOUSE IN IMAZATO

MILLENNIUM DOME

EDEN PROJECT

KUNSTHAUS GRAZ

CHAMELEON HOUSE

WATER CUBE

[PLASTIC] Module – MATERIAL GEOMETRY diagrams in axonometric the three-dimensional relationships of the manufacturing module intrinsic to a material to the space, form, and dimensions. Mapping the inherited dimensional constraints determined by the production and movement of a material into the three-dimensional ramifications of the total form, the legibility of an architectural patterning of scale elements relies upon the articulation of their joinery to establish larger architectural spaces.

The surface reading is derived from addressing the relationship of piece to whole and unit to system through the intrinsic module of a material. Certain materials default to a secondary system [such as concrete with formwork] to generate a dimensional constraint, but every material has a "natural" form and dimension. The negotiation of these constraints and the collaboration with these numeric proportions determine the dimensions of the whole and the integration of the modular unit into the consistency of the superstructural organization. In axonometric, the module governs the formal legibility of the three-dimensional building component and ultimately the formal reading of the building as a whole.

The Monsanto House of the Future uses the loops of the structural shell to define the space and figure of the buildings and the rooms; the Colmenarejo Municipal Hall develops the front wall with the uniformity of exterior surface while embedding layers and operability within; the House in Imazato focuses on the continuity of the overall form, allowing the material, but not the structure or geometry, to change in response to the exterior space behind; the Millennium Dome suspends a delicate fabric shell over the massive scale of the structure; the Eden Project uses the geometry of the figure and the surface to allow for a purity of expression of material to form; the Kunsthaus Graz has a regular horizontal and vertical bay system to emphasize the joints and form of the main figure, with simple vertical banding for the street level and elevated view platform; the Chameleon House cloaks the building with a second skin to create a dematerialized legibility of surface and skin; and the Water Cube uniformly blankets the surface with segmented ETFE pillows, allowing for a continuous interior and exterior reading to the building's shell.

Postscript

Practice and pedagogy have shifted dramatically over the past century to engage emerging technologies, newly accessible materials, new materials, and a changing workforce and method of project delivery and construction. With an interest in engaging a new literalism of architectural production, through the actual material construction and experimentation focused on performance and material expression, this book attempts to unpack iconic figures of architectural history and catalog their methodology relative to material.

Material is the matter-of-fact of architecture. It is the means of execution, a major force of resistance, and a means of expression. In contrast to paper or cardboard architecture, which was interested in removing the variable and agency of material (and where representation trumped construction), the architectural discipline today has begun to radically reorient itself toward a renewed relationship with materiality. Materials as a topic is the big question of our generation. How do we engage architectural thought through making? Issues of craft and shifting methods of production transfer the way in which things are made while, perhaps even more importantly, shifting the practice and the methodology by which things are designed. The previous opposition that existed between theory and materiality is now gone and the simplicity of the modernist legacy or the material-to-idea disjunction of postmodernism thought is gone ushering in a new era.

An understanding of fundamental issues of structures and construction materials is necessary for the pursuit of architecture. Proficiency with these technical principles will stimulate their design possibilities and increase their practical and technical value. This book relates the theories of architecture to the technologies of construction and materials so that their interaction can be better understood historically and in their current practice.

Comparative diagramming allows the exposure of trends: historical, tectonic, and cultural variations. Illuminating these iconic buildings from the specific vantage point of materiality and a common method of diagrammatic representation to illustrate the trends and relativisms of each project provides for an architectural lineage and historical mapping of materials and their deployment. The analytical and comparative nature of the text attempts to map associations of materiality with the diverse considerations influencing a project: budget, climate, availability of materials, dimensional characteristics, joinery, methods of fabrication and assembly, workability, sustainability, time of construction, durability, structural capability and legibility, and, of course, formal intention [to name a few]. The collective implications of these decisions and the resolution of these practical requirements in support of the architectural intention are essential to the execution of architecture. Serving as precedents, these case studies illustrate how some of the best designers over the past century have addressed the issues of materiality and, as a collective, have produced a handbook of modern tectonics.

Material

Architect

Building